JAVA RESERVED WORDS

Java reserves and gives predefined meanings to the following reserved words. You may not redefine these words or use them for other purposes. The reserved words *const* and *goto* are reserved by Java, even though they are not currently used in Java. This may allow a Java compiler to produce better error messages if these C++ keywords incorrectly appear in Java programs.

abstract	default	goto	null	synchronized
boolean	do	if	package	this
break	double	implements	private	throw
byte	else	import	protected	throws
case	extends	instanceof	public	transient
catch	false	int	return	try
char	final	interface	short	void
class	finally	long	static	volatile
const	float	native	super	while
continue	for	new	switch	

DATA ABSTRACTION AND PROBLEM SOLVING WITH JAVA™

WALLS AND MIRRORS

First Edition

Frank M. Carrano
University of Rhode Island

Janet J. Prichard
Bryant College

Boston San Francisco New York
London Toronto Sydney Tokyo Singapore Madrid
Mexico City Munich Paris Cape Town Hong Kong Montreal

Senior Acquisitions Editor: *Susan Hartman*
Project Manager: *Katherine Harutunian*
Production Supervision: *Diane Freed Publishing Services*
Design Editor: *Regina Hagen*
Text Design: *The Book Company*
Composition: *Argosy, Inc.*
Copyeditor: *Rebecca Pepper*
Proofreader: *Trillium Project Management*
Manufacturing Coordinator: *Caroline Fell*

Cover Photo: ©Herb Schmitz/Tony Stone Worldwide

Access the latest information about Addison-Wesley titles from our World
Wide Web Site: http://www.awl.com/cs

Library of Congress Cataloging-in-Publication Data

Carrano, Frank M.
  Data abstraction and problem solving with Java: walls and mirrors /
Frank M. Carrano, Janet J. Prichard.
    p. cm.
  ISBN 0-201-70220-7
    1. Java (Computer program language)   2. Data structures
  (Computer science)   I. Prichard, Janet.   II. Title.

  QA76.73.J38.C37 2001
  005.13'3—dc21   00-029315

Preface

Welcome to the first edition of *Data Abstraction and Problem Solving with Java: Walls and Mirrors*. Java has become popular in beginning computer science courses. It is particularly suitable to teaching data abstraction in an object-oriented way, and this edition reflects our experience in doing so.

This book is based on the original *Intermediate Problem Solving and Data Structures: Walls and Mirrors* by Paul Helman and Robert Veroff (© 1986 by The Benjamin/Cummings Publishing Company, Inc.). This work builds on their organizational framework and overall perspective and includes technical and textual content, examples, figures, and exercises derived from the original work. Professors Helman and Veroff introduced two powerful analogies, walls and mirrors, that have made it easier for us to teach—and to learn—computer science.

With its focus on data abstraction and other problem-solving tools, this book is designed for a second course in computer science. In recognition of the dynamic nature of the discipline and the great diversity in undergraduate computer science curricula, this book includes comprehensive coverage of enough topics to make it appropriate for other courses as well. For example, you can use this book in courses such as introductory data structures or advanced programming and problem solving. The goal remains to give students a superior foundation in data abstraction, object-oriented programming, and other modern problem-solving techniques.

TO THE STUDENT

Thousands of students before you have read and learned from *Walls and Mirrors*. The walls and mirrors in the title represent two fundamental problem-solving techniques that appear throughout the presentation. Data abstraction isolates and hides the implementation details of a module from the rest of the program, much as a wall can isolate and hide you from your neighbor. Recursion is a repetitive technique that solves a problem by solving smaller problems of exactly the same type, much as mirror images grow smaller with each reflection.

This book was written with you in mind. As former college students, and as educators who are constantly learning, we appreciate the importance of a clear presentation. Our goal is to make this book as understandable as possible. To help you learn and to review for exams, we have

included such learning aids as margin notes, chapter summaries, self-test exercises with answers, and a glossary. As a help during programming, you will find Java reference material in the appendixes and inside the covers. You should review the list of this book's features given later in this preface in the section "Pedagogical Features."

The presentation makes some basic assumptions about your knowledge of Java. Some of you may need to review this language or learn it for the first time by consulting Appendix A of this book. You will need to know about the selection statements *if* and *switch*; the iteration statements *for*, *while*, and *do*; classes, methods, and arguments; arrays; strings; and files. In addition to the material in Appendix A, this book discusses Java classes in Chapters 3 and 8. We assume no experience with recursive methods, which are included in Chapters 2 and 5.

All of the Java source code that appears in this book is available for your use. Later in this preface, the description of supplementary materials tells you how to obtain these files. Note, however, that your instructor may already have obtained them for you.

APPROACH

This edition of *Walls and Mirrors* uses Java to enhance its emphasis on data abstraction and data structures. The book carefully accounts for the strengths and weaknesses of the Java language and remains committed to a pedagogical approach that makes the material accessible to students at the introductory level.

Prerequisites

We assume that readers either know the fundamentals of Java or know another language and have an instructor who will help them make the transition to Java by using Appendix A. In addition to this appendix, the book formally discusses Java classes. Included are the basic concepts of a class, inheritance, polymorphism, interfaces, and packages. Although the book provides an introduction to these topics in connection with the implementations of abstract data types (ADTs) as classes, the emphasis remains on the ADTs, not on Java. The material is presented in the context of object-based programming, but it assumes that future courses will cover object-oriented design and software engineering in detail, so that the focus can remain on data abstraction.

Flexibility

The extensive coverage of this book should provide you with the material that you want for your course. You can select the topics you desire and present them in an order that fits your schedule. The chapter dependency chart shows which chapters should be covered before a given chapter can be taught.

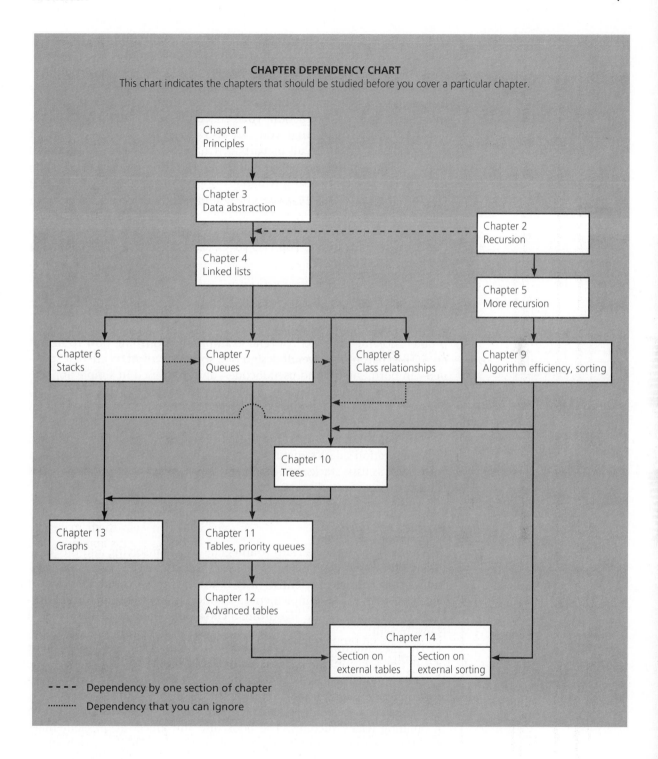

CHAPTER DEPENDENCY CHART
This chart indicates the chapters that should be studied before you cover a particular chapter.

Chapter 1
Principles

Chapter 3
Data abstraction

Chapter 2
Recursion

Chapter 4
Linked lists

Chapter 5
More recursion

Chapter 6
Stacks

Chapter 7
Queues

Chapter 8
Class relationships

Chapter 9
Algorithm efficiency, sorting

Chapter 10
Trees

Chapter 13
Graphs

Chapter 11
Tables, priority queues

Chapter 12
Advanced tables

Chapter 14

Section on external tables

Section on external sorting

- - - - Dependency by one section of chapter

.... Dependency that you can ignore

In Part I, you can choose among topics according to your students' background. Three of the chapters in this part provide an extensive introduction to data abstraction and recursion. Both topics are important, and there are various opinions about which should be taught first. Although in this book a chapter on recursion both precedes and follows the chapter on data abstraction, you can simply rearrange this order.

Part II treats topics that you can also cover in a flexible order. For example, you can cover all or parts of Chapter 8 on class relationships either before or after you cover stacks (Chapter 6). You can cover algorithm efficiency and sorting (Chapter 9) any time after Chapter 5. You can introduce trees before queues or graphs before tables, or cover hashing, balanced search trees, or priority queues any time after tables and in any order. You also can cover external methods (Chapter 14) earlier in the course. For example, you can cover external sorting after you cover mergesort in Chapter 9.

Data Abstraction

The design and use of abstract data types (ADTs) permeate this book's problem-solving approach. Several examples demonstrate how to design an ADT as part of the overall design of a solution. All ADTs are first specified—in both English and pseudocode—and then used in simple applications before implementation issues are considered. The distinction between an ADT and the data structure that implements it remains in the forefront throughout the discussion. The book explains both encapsulation and Java classes early. Students see how Java classes hide an implementation's data structure from the client of the ADT. Abstract data types such as lists, stacks, queues, trees, tables, heaps, and priority queues form the basis of our discussions.

Problem Solving

This book helps students learn to integrate problem-solving and programming abilities by emphasizing both the thought processes and the techniques that computer scientists use. Learning how a computer scientist develops, analyzes, and implements a solution is just as important as learning the mechanics of the algorithm; a cookbook approach to the material is insufficient.

The presentation includes analytical techniques for the development of solutions within the context of example problems. Abstraction, the successive refinement of both algorithms and data structures, and recursion are used to design solutions to problems throughout the book.

Java references and linked list processing are introduced early and used in building data structures. The book also introduces at an elementary level the order-of-magnitude analysis of algorithms. This approach allows the consideration—first at an informal level, and then more quantitatively—of the advantages and disadvantages of array-based and reference-based data structures. An emphasis on the trade-offs among potential solutions and implementations is a central problem-solving theme.

Finally, programming style, documentation including preconditions and postconditions, debugging aids, and loop invariants are important parts of the problem-solving methodology used to implement and verify solutions. These topics are covered throughout the book.

Applications

Classic application areas arise in the context of the major topics of this book. For example, the binary search, quicksort, and mergesort algorithms provide important applications of recursion and introduce order-of-magnitude analysis. Such topics as balanced search trees, hashing, and file indexing continue the discussion of searching. Searching and sorting are considered again in the context of external files.

Algorithms for recognizing and evaluating algebraic expressions are first introduced in the context of recursion and are considered again later as an application of stacks. Other applications include, for example, the Eight Queens problem as an example of backtracking, event-driven simulation as an application of queues, and graph searching and traversals as other important applications of stacks and queues.

NEW AND REVISED MATERIAL

This edition retains the underlying approach and philosophy of the C++ edition. We present data abstraction and programming both as general concepts and in the context of Java. No sentence, example, margin note, or figure escaped scrutiny during the preparation of this edition. Many changes, additions, and deletions to the text, figures, and margin notes were made to update and clarify the presentation.

The pseudocode for all algorithms was revised to reflect Java's object-oriented approach, and all programming examples are in Java. Although we revised all chapters and appendixes, here is a list of the major changes to the book.

- Chapter 1 bases its discussion of implementation and style issues on common Java practices.

- Chapter 3 reviews Java classes and briefly introduces inheritance. Also covered are Java interfaces, the class *Object*, exceptions, garbage collection, and object equality. These topics are then integrated into the discussion of ADT specifications. Java interfaces in particular are used to separate specification from implementation. The ADTs in this chapter and throughout the text store objects instead of primitives and use exceptions to flag error conditions.

- Chapter 4 reviews Java references as the basis for the revised treatment of linked lists. Nodes in the linked list are instances of a *Node* class. A new section now highlights tail references for a linked list. The solution to the inventory problem has been improved and introduces object serialization.

- Chapter 8 provides a deeper discussion of inheritance than was given earlier in Chapter 3. Also covered are Java packages, field modifiers, abstract classes, method overloading, interfaces, and iterators.

- Chapter 10 redesigns the tree class hierarchy and uses a tree iterator for traversal operations. Both Chapter 10 and Chapter 12 use a class to define tree nodes.

- Appendix A is a review of Java.

- Appendix B contains a UNICODE table.

- Appendix C provides an overview of the Java API and gives links to additional Java resources.

- **New exercises and programming problems.** Many exercises and programming problems were revised or replaced.

- **Java code.** The Java implementations are not simply translations from C++, but rather reflect the advantages that Java provides.

OVERVIEW

The pedagogical features and organization of this book were carefully designed to facilitate learning and to allow instructors to tailor the material easily to a particular course.

Pedagogical Features

This book contains the following features that help students not only during their first reading of the material, but also during subsequent review:

- Chapter outlines and previews.

- Boxes listing key concepts in the material.

- Margin notes.

- Chapter summaries.

- Cautionary warnings about common errors and misconceptions.

- Self-test exercises with answers.

- Chapter exercises and programming problems. The most challenging exercises are labeled with asterisks. Answers to the exercises appear in the *Instructor's Resource Manual.*

- Specifications for all major ADTs in both English and pseudocode.

- Java class definitions for all major ADTs.
- Examples that illustrate the role of ADTs in the problem-solving process.
- Appendixes, including a review of Java.
- Glossary of terms.

Organization

The chapters in this book are organized into two parts. In most cases, Chapters 1 through 11 will form the core of a one-semester course. Chapters 1 or 2 might be review material for your students. The coverage given to Chapters 11 through 14 will depend on the role the course plays in your curriculum. More detailed suggestions for using this book with different courses appear in the *Instructor's Resource Manual*.

Part I: Problem-Solving Techniques. The first chapter in Part I resembles an extension of an introductory course in that its emphasis is on major issues in programming and software engineering. The next chapter introduces recursion for those students who have had little exposure to this important topic. The ability to think recursively is one of the most useful skills that a computer scientist can possess and is often of great value in helping one to understand better the nature of a problem. Recursion is discussed extensively in this chapter and again in Chapter 5 and is used throughout the book. Included examples range from simple recursive definitions to recursive algorithms for language recognition, searching, and sorting.

Chapter 3 discusses data abstraction and abstract data types (ADTs) in detail. After a discussion of the specification and use of an ADT, the chapter discusses Java classes, interfaces, and exceptions, and uses them to implement ADTs. Chapter 4 presents additional implementation tools in its discussion of Java reference variables and linked lists.

You can choose among the topics in Part I according to the background of your students and cover these topics in several orders.

Part II: Problem Solving with Abstract Data Types. Part II continues the use of data abstraction as a problem-solving technique. Basic abstract data types such as the stack, queue, binary tree, binary search tree, table, heap, and priority queue are first specified and then implemented as classes. The ADTs are used in examples and their implementations are compared.

Chapter 8 extends the treatment of Java classes by covering inheritance, packages, the relationships among classes, and iterators. Chapter 9 formalizes the earlier discussions of an algorithm's efficiency by introducing order-of-magnitude analysis and Big O notation. The chapter examines the efficiency of several searching and sorting algorithms, including the recursive mergesort and quicksort.

Part II also includes advanced topics—such as balanced search trees (2-3, 2-3-4, red-black, and AVL trees) and hashing—that are examined as table implementations. These implementations are analyzed to determine the table operations that each supports best.

Finally, data storage in external direct access files is considered. Mergesort is modified to sort such data, and external hashing and B-tree indexes are used to search it. These searching algorithms are generalizations of the internal hashing schemes and 2-3 trees already developed.

ONLINE SUPPLEMENTARY MATERIALS

The following supplementary materials are available online to assist instructors and students.

- *Source code.* All of the Java classes, methods, and programs that appear in the book are available to readers.

- *Errata.* We have tried not to make mistakes, but mistakes are inevitable. A list of detected errors is available and updated as necessary. You are invited to contribute your finds.

    The source code and errata list are available from the ftp site

    ```
    ftp.aw.com
    ```

    in the directory

    ```
    /cseng/authors/carrano/java
    ```

- *Instructor's Resource Manual.* Solutions to the exercises at the end of the chapters as well as teaching notes and suggestions are available only to instructors through your Addison Wesley Longman sales representative.

TALK TO US

Walls and Mirrors continues to evolve. Your comments, suggestions, and corrections will be greatly appreciated. You can contact us directly by e-mail at

```
prichard@bryant.edu
```

or

```
carrano@acm.org
```

or through the publisher:

Computer Science Editorial Office
Addison Wesley Longman, Inc.
One Jacob Way
Reading, MA 01867

ACKNOWLEDGMENTS

The suggestions from outstanding reviewers contributed greatly to this book's present form. In alphabetical order, they are

> Ronald Alferez—*University of California at Santa Barbara*
>
> Claude W. Anderson—*Rose-Hulman Institute of Technology*
>
> Don Bailey—*Carleton University*
>
> N. Dwight Barnette—*Virginia Tech*
>
> Jack Beidler—*University of Scranton*
>
> Susan Gauch—*University of Kansas*
>
> Lily Hou—*SUN Microsystems, Inc.*
>
> Rameen Mohammadi—*SUNY, Oswego*
>
> Narayan Murthy—*Pace University*
>
> Thaddeus F. Pawlicki—*University of Rochester*

We especially thank the people who produced this book. Our editors at Addison Wesley Longman, Susan Hartman and Katherine Harutunian, provided invaluable guidance and assistance. Also, Diane Freed, Pat Mahtani, Joe Vetere, Gina Hagen, Jared Gibbons, Michelle Renda, and Michael Hirsch contributed their expertise and care during the final production of the book. Many thanks to our copyeditor, Rebecca Pepper, for her patience and attention to detail.

Many other wonderful people have contributed in various ways. They are Doug McCreadie, Michael Hayden, Sarah Hayden, Andrew Hayden, Albert Prichard, Maybeth Conway, Ted Emmott, Lorraine Berube, Marge White, James Kowalski, Ed Lamagna, Gerard Baudet, Joan Peckham, Victor Fay-Wolfe, Bala Ravikumar, Karl Abrahamson, Ronnie Smith, James Wirth, Randy Hale, John Cardin, Gail Armstrong, Tom Manning, Jim Abreu, and Bill Harding.

Numerous other people provided input for the previous editions of *Walls and Mirrors* at various stages of its development. All of their comments were useful and greatly appreciated. In alphabetical order, they are: Stephen Alberg, Vicki Allan, Jihad Almahayni, James Ames, Andrew Azzinaro, Tony Baiching, Don Bailey, Wolfgang W. Bein, Sto Bell, David Berard, John Black, Richard Botting, Wolfin Brumley, Philip Carrigan, Stephen Clamage, Michael Clancy, David Clayton, Michael Cleron, Chris Constantino, Shaun Cooper, Charles Denault, Vincent J. DiPippo, Suzanne Dorney, Colleen Dunn, Carl Eckberg, Karla Steinbrugge Fant, Jean Foltz, Marguerite Hafen, George Hamer, Judy Hankins, Lisa Hellerstein, Mary Lou Hines, Jack Hodges, Stephanie Horoschak, John Hubbard, Kris Jensen, Thomas Judson, Laura Kenney, Roger King, Ladislav Kohout, Jim LaBonte, Jean Lake, Janusz Laski, Cathie LeBlanc, Urban LeJeune, John M. Linebarger, Ken Lord, Paul Luker, Manisha Mande, Pierre-Arnoul de Marneffe, John Marsaglia, Jane Wallace Mayo, Mark McCormick, Dan McCracken, Vivian McDougal, Shirley McGuire, Sue Medeiros, Jim Miller,

Guy Mills, Cleve Moler, Paul Nagin, Rayno Niemi, John O'Donnell, Andrew Oldroyd, Larry Olsen, Raymond L. Paden, Roy Pargas, Brenda C. Parker, Keith Pierce, Lucasz Pruski, George B. Purdy, David Radford, Steve Ratering, Stuart Regis, J. D. Robertson, John Rowe, Michael E. Rupp, Sharon Salveter, Charles Saxon, Chandra Sekharan, Linda Shapiro, Yujian Sheng, Mary Shields, Carl Spicola, Richard Snodgrass, Neil Snyder, Chris Spannabel, Paul Spirakis, Clinton Staley, Matt Stallman, Mark Stehlick, Harriet Taylor, David Teague, David Tetreault, John Turner, Susan Wallace, James E. Warren, Jerry Weltman, Nancy Wiegand, Howard Williams, Brad Wilson, Salih Yurttas, and Alan Zaring.

Finally, we thank Robert A. Rossi and Benjamin T. Schomp of the University of Rhode Island for writing the answers to the exercises for the *Instructor's Resource Manual*.

Thank you all.

                                                         F. M. C.
                                                         J. J. P.

Brief Contents

Contents

Appendices

PART I

Problem-Solving Techniques

The primary concern of the five chapters in Part I of this book is to develop a repertoire of problem-solving techniques that form the basis of the rest of the book. Chapter 1 begins by describing the characteristics of a good solution and the ways to achieve one. These techniques emphasize abstraction, modularity, and information hiding. The remainder of Part I discusses data abstraction for solution design, Java classes and references for use in implementations, and recursion as a problem-solving strategy.

1

Principles of Programming and Software Engineering

Problem Solving and Software Engineering

What Is Problem Solving?
The Life Cycle of Software
What Is a Good Solution?

Achieving a Modular Design

Abstraction and Information Hiding
Object-Oriented Design
Top-Down Design
General Design Guidelines

A Summary of Key Issues in Programming

Modularity
Modifiability
Ease of Use
Fail-Safe Programming
Style
Debugging

Summary

Cautions

Self-Test Exercises

Exercises

Programming Problems

PREVIEW This chapter summarizes several fundamental principles that serve as the basis for dealing with the complexities of large programs. The discussion both reinforces the basic principles of programming and demonstrates that writing well-designed and well-documented programs is cost-effective. The chapter also presents a brief discussion of algorithms and data abstraction and indicates how these topics relate to the book's main theme of developing problem-solving and programming skills. In subsequent chapters, the focus will shift from programming principles to ways of organizing and using data. Even when the focus of discussion is on these new techniques, you should note how all solutions adhere to the basic principles discussed in this chapter.

PROBLEM SOLVING AND SOFTWARE ENGINEERING

Where did you begin when you wrote your last program? After reading the problem specifications and procrastinating for a certain amount of time, most novice programmers simply begin to write code. Obviously, their goal is to get their programs to execute, preferably with correct results. There-fore, they run their programs, examine error messages, insert semicolons, change the logic, delete semicolons, pray, and otherwise torture their pro-grams until they work. Most of their time is probably spent checking both syntax and program logic. Certainly, your programming skills are better now than when you wrote your first program, but will you be able to write a really large program by using the approach just described? Maybe, but there are better ways.

Coding without a solution design increases debugging time

Realize that an extremely large software development project gen-erally requires a team of programmers rather than a single individual. Teamwork requires an overall plan, organization, and communication. A haphazard approach to programming will not serve a team programmer well and will not be cost-effective. Fortunately, an emerging engineering field related to a branch of computer science—**software engineering**—provides techniques to facilitate the development of computer programs.

Software engineering facilitates development of programs

Whereas a first course in computer science typically emphasizes pro-gramming issues, the focus in this book will be on the broader issues of problem solving. This chapter begins with an overview of the problem-solving process and the various ways of approaching a problem.

What Is Problem Solving?

Here the term **problem solving** refers to the entire process of taking the statement of a problem and developing a computer program that solves that problem. This process requires you to pass through many phases, from gaining an understanding of the problem to be solved, through designing a conceptual solution, to implementing the solution with a computer program.

A solution specifies algorithms and ways to store data

Exactly what is a solution? Typically, a **solution** consists of two com-ponents: algorithms and ways to store data. An **algorithm** is a step-by-step specification of a method to solve a problem within a finite amount of time. One action that an algorithm often performs is to operate on a collection of data. For example, an algorithm may have to put new data into a collection, remove data from a collection, or ask questions about a collection of data.

Perhaps this description of a solution leaves the false impression that all the cleverness in problem solving goes into developing the algorithm and that how you store your data plays only a supporting role. This impression is far from the truth. You need to do much more than simply store your data. When constructing a solution, you must organize your data collection so that you can operate on the data easily in the manner that the algorithm requires. In fact, most of this book describes ways of organizing data.

When you design a solution to a given problem, you can use several techniques that will make your task easier. This chapter introduces those techniques, and subsequent chapters will provide more detail.

The Life Cycle of Software

The development of good software involves a lengthy and continuing process known as the software's **life cycle.** This process begins with an initial idea, includes the writing and debugging of programs, and continues for years to involve corrections and enhancements to the original software. Figure 1-1 pictures the nine phases of the software life cycle as

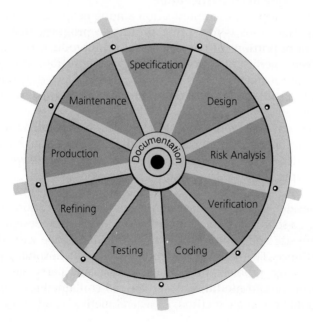

Figure 1-1

The life cycle of software as a water wheel that can rotate from one phase to any other phase segments on a water wheel.[1] This arrangement suggests that the phases are part of a cycle and are not simply a linear list. Although you start by specifying a problem, typically you move from any phase to any other phase. For example, testing a program can suggest changes to either the problem specifications or the solution design. Also notice that the nine phases surround a documentation core in the figure. Documentation is not a separate phase, as you might expect. Rather, it is integrated into all phases of the software life cycle.

Here, then, are the phases in the life cycle of typical software. Although all phases are important, only those that are most relevant to this book are discussed in detail.

Phase 1: Specification.   Given an initial statement of the software's purpose, you must specify clearly all aspects of the problem. Often the people who describe the problem are not programmers, so the initial problem statement might be imprecise. The specification phase, then, requires that you bring precision and detail to the original problem statement and that you communicate with both programmers and nonprogrammers.

Make the problem statement precise and detailed

Here are some questions that you must answer as you write the specifications for the software: What is the input data? What data is valid and what data is invalid? Who will use the software, and what user interface should be used? What error detection and error messages are desirable? What assumptions are possible? Are there special cases? What is the form of the output? What documentation is necessary? What enhancements to the program are likely in the future?

Prototype programs can clarify the problem

One way to improve communication among people and to clarify the software specifications is to write a **prototype program** that simulates the behavior of portions of the desired software product. For example, a simple—even inefficient—program could demonstrate the proposed user interface for analysis. It is better to discover any difficulties or to change your mind now than to do so after programming is underway or even complete.

Your previous programming assignments probably stated the program specifications for you. Perhaps aspects of these specifications were unclear and you had to seek clarification, but most likely you have had little practice in writing your own program specifications.

Phase 2: Design.   Once you have completed the specification phase, you must design a solution to the problem. Most people who design solutions of moderate size and complexity find it difficult to cope with the entire program at once. The best way to simplify the problem-solving process is to divide a large problem into small, manageable parts. The resulting program will contain **modules**, which are self-contained units of code. A module could be a single method, or several methods and other blocks of

---

[1]Thanks to Raymond L. Paden for suggesting that "wheel" be "water wheel."

code. You should design modules that are as independent, or **loosely coupled**, as possible, except, of course, for their **interfaces**, which are the communication mechanisms among modules. You can develop such modules in virtual isolation from the other modules. Each module should perform one well-defined task; that is, it should be **highly cohesive**. Thus, **modularity** describes a program that is organized into loosely coupled, highly cohesive modules.

Loosely coupled modules are independent

Highly cohesive modules each perform one well-defined task

During the design phase, it is also important that you clearly specify not only the purpose of each module but also the **data flow** among modules. For example, you should provide answers to these questions for each module: What data is available to the module before its execution? What does the module assume? What actions have taken place, and what does the data look like after the module executes? Thus, you should specify in detail the assumptions, input, and output for each module.

Specify each module's purpose, assumptions, input, and output

For example, if you as program designer needed to provide a method for a shape object that moves it to a new location on the screen, you might write the following specification:

The method will receive an (x, y) coordinate.

The method will move the shape to the new location on the screen.

You can view these specifications as the terms of a **contract** between your method and the module that calls it.

Specifications as a contract

If you alone write the entire program, this contract helps you systematically decompose the problem into smaller tasks. If the program is a team project, the contract helps delineate responsibilities. Whoever writes the move method must live up to this contract. After the move method has been written and tested, the contract tells the rest of the program how to call the move method properly and lets it know the result of doing so.

It is important to notice, however, that a module's contract does not commit the module to a particular way of performing its task. If another part of the program assumes anything about the method, it does so at its own risk. Thus, for example, if at some later date you rewrite your method to use a different algorithm for moving the shape on the screen, you should not need to change the rest of the program at all. As long as the new method honors the terms of the original contract, the rest of the program should be oblivious to the change.

A module's specification should not describe a method of solution

This discussion should not be news to you. Although you might not have explicitly used the term "contract" before, the concept should be familiar. You write a contract when you write a method's **precondition**, which is a statement of the conditions that must exist at the beginning of a method, as well as when you write its **postcondition**, which is a statement of the conditions at the end of a method. For example, the move method that adheres to the previous contract could appear in pseudocode[2] as

Method specifications include precise preconditions and postconditions

---

[2]Pseudocode in this book appears in italics.

First-draft specifications

```
move(x, y)
// Moves a shape to a new location on the screen.
// Precondition: The calling program provides an
// (x, y) pair, both integers.
// Postcondition: The shape is moved to the new
// location.
```

These particular pre- and postconditions are actually deficient, as may be the case in a first-draft contract. For example, does "moved" mean that the shape is moved relative to its previous location by *(x, y)* or that the shape is moved to the new coordinate location *(x, y)*? What is the range of values for *x* and *y*? While implementing this method, you might assume that "moved" means the shape is moved to a new coordinate location *(x, y)* and that the range for *x* and *y* is 0 through 100. Imagine the difficulties that can arise when another person tries to use *move* to move a shape relative to its previous location using *(-5, -5)*. This user does not know your assumptions unless you document them by revising the pre- and postconditions, as follows:

Revised specifications

```
move(x, y)
// Moves a shape to coordinate (x, y) on the screen.
// Precondition: The calling program provides an
// (x, y) pair, both integers, where
// 0 <= x <= MAX_XCOOR, 0 <= y <= MAX_YCOOR, where
// MAX_XCOOR and MAX_YCOOR are class constants that
// specify the maximum coordinate values.
// Postcondition: The shape is moved to coordinate
// (x, y).
```

When you write a precondition, begin by describing the method's formal parameters, mention any class named constants that the method uses, and finally list any assumptions that the method makes. Similarly, when you write a postcondition, begin by describing the method's effect on its parameters—or in the case of a valued method, the value it returns—and then describe any other action that has occurred. (Although people tend to use the words parameter and argument interchangeably, we will use parameter to mean formal parameter and argument to mean actual argument.)

Precise documentation is essential

Novice programmers tend to dismiss the importance of precise documentation, particularly when they are simultaneously designer, programmer, and user of a small program. If you design *move* but do not write down the terms of the contract, will you remember them when you later implement the method? Will you remember how to use *move* weeks after you have written it? To refresh your memory, would you rather examine your Java code or read a simple set of pre- and postconditions? As the size of a program increases, good documentation becomes even more important, regardless of whether you are the sole author or part of a team.

You should not ignore the possibility that you or someone else has already implemented some of the required modules or methods. Java

facilitates the reuse of software components, which are typically organized into class libraries that group classes into packages containing
compiled code. That is, you will not always have access to a method's
Java code. The Java **Application Programming Interface** (API) is an
example of one such collection of preexisting software. For example, you
know how to use the static method *sqrt* contained in the Java API
package *java.lang.Math*, yet you do not have access to its source statements, because it is precompiled. You know, however, that if you pass *sqrt*
an expression of type *double*, it will return the square root of the value of
that expression as a *double*. You can use *java.lang.Math.sqrt* even
though you do not know its implementation. Furthermore, it may be that
java.lang.Math.sqrt was written in a language other than Java! There is
so much about *java.lang.Math.sqrt* that you do not know, yet you can
use it in your program without concern, *as long as you know its specifications*.

Incorporate existing software components into your design

If, in the past, you have spent little or no time in the design phase for
your programs, you must change this habit! The end result of the design
phase should be a solution that is easy to translate into the constructs of a
particular programming language. By spending adequate time in the design
phase, you will spend less time when you write and debug your program.

We will resume our discussion of design later.

Phase 3: Risk analysis.   Building software entails risks. Some risks are the
same for all software projects and some are peculiar to a particular
project. You can predict some risks, while others are unknown. Risks can
affect a project's timetable or cost, the success of a business, or the health
and lives of people. You can eliminate or reduce some risks but not
others. Techniques exist to identify, assess, and manage the risks of creating a software product. You will learn these techniques if you study software engineering in a subsequent course. The outcome of risk analysis
will affect the other phases of the life cycle.

You can predict and manage some, but not all, risks

Phase 4: Verification.   Formal, theoretical methods are available for proving that an algorithm is correct. Although research in this area is incomplete, it is useful to mention some aspects of the verification process.

An **assertion** is a statement about a particular condition at a certain
point in an algorithm. Preconditions and postconditions are simply
assertions about conditions at the beginning and end of methods. An
invariant is a condition that is always true at a particular point in an
algorithm. A **loop invariant** is a condition that is true before and after
each execution of an algorithm's loop. As you will see, loop invariants
can help you to write correct loops. By using invariants, you can detect
errors before you begin coding and thereby reduce your debugging and
testing time. Overall, invariants can save you time.

Proving that an algorithm is correct is like proving a theorem in
geometry. For example, to prove that a method is correct, you would start
with its preconditions—which are analogous to the axioms and assumptions in geometry—and demonstrate that the steps of the algorithm lead
to the postconditions. To do so, you would consider each step in the

You can prove the correctness of some algorithms

algorithm and show that an assertion before the step leads to a particular assertion after the step.

By proving the validity of individual statements, you can prove that sequences of statements, and then methods, and finally the program itself are correct. For example, suppose you show that if assertion A_1 is true and statement S_1 executes, assertion A_2 is true. Also, suppose you have shown that assertion A_2 and statement S_2 lead to assertion A_3. You can then conclude that if assertion A_1 is true, executing the sequence of statements S_1 and S_2 will lead to assertion A_3. By continuing in this manner, you eventually will be able to show that the program is correct.

Clearly, if you discovered an error during the verification process, you would correct your algorithm and possibly modify the problem specifications. Thus, by using invariants, it is likely that your algorithm will contain fewer errors *before* you begin coding. As a result, you will spend less time debugging your program.

You can formally prove that particular constructs such as *if* statements, loops, and assignments are correct. An important technique uses loop invariants to demonstrate the correctness of iterative algorithms. For example, we will prove that the following simple loop computes the sum of the first *n* elements in the array *item*:

```
// computes the sum of item[0], item[1], . . .,
// item[n-1] for any n >= 1
int sum = 0;
int j = 0;
while (j < n) {
   sum += item[j];
   ++j;
}  // end while
```

Before this loop begins execution, *sum* is 0 and *j* is 0. After the loop executes once, *sum* is *item[0]* and *j* is 1. In general,

Loop invariant   *sum is the sum of the elements item[0] through item[j-1]*

This statement is the invariant for this loop.

The invariant for a correct loop is true at the following points:

- Initially, after any initialization steps, but before the loop begins execution
- Before every iteration of the loop
- After every iteration of the loop
- After the loop terminates

For the previous loop example, these points are as follows:

```
int sum = 0;
int j = 0;
                          ←the invariant is true here
while (j < n) {
                          ←the invariant is true here
```

```
        sum += item[j];
        ++j;
```
                          ←*the invariant is true here*
```
    }  // end while
```
                          ←*the invariant is true here*

You can use these observations to prove the correctness of an iterative algorithm. For the previous example, you must show that each of the following four points is true:

Steps to establish the correctness of an algorithm

1. **The invariant must be true initially,** before the loop begins execution for the first time. In the previous example, `sum` is 0 and `j` is 0 initially. In this case, the invariant states that `sum` contains the sum of the elements `item[0]` through `item[-1]`; the invariant is true because there are no elements in this range.

2. **An execution of the loop must preserve the invariant.** That is, if the invariant is true before any given iteration of the loop, you must show that it is true after the iteration. In the example, the loop adds `item[j]` to `sum` and then increments `j` by 1. Thus, after an execution of the loop, the most recent element added to `sum` is `item[j-1]`; that is, the invariant is true after the iteration.

3. **The invariant must capture the correctness of the algorithm.** That is, you must show that if the invariant is true when the loop terminates, the algorithm is correct. When the loop in the previous example terminates, `j` contains `n`, and the invariant is true: `sum` contains the sum of the elements `item[0]` through `item[n-1]`, which is the sum that you intended to compute.

4. **The loop must terminate.** That is, you must show that the loop will terminate after a finite number of iterations. In the example, `j` begins at 0 and then increases by 1 at each execution of the loop. Thus, `j` eventually will equal `n` for any $n \geq 1$. This fact and the nature of the `while` statement guarantee that the loop will terminate.

Not only can you use invariants to show that your loop is correct, but you can also use them to show that your loop is wrong. For example, suppose that the expression in the previous `while` statement was `j <= n` instead of `j < n`. Steps 1 and 2 of the previous demonstration would be the same, but Step 3 would differ: When the loop terminated, `j` would contain $n + 1$ and, because the invariant would be true, `sum` would contain the sum of the elements `item[0]` through `item[n]`. Since this is not the desired sum, you know that something is wrong with your loop.

Notice the clear connection between Steps 1 through 4 and **mathematical induction.**[3] Showing the invariant to be true initially, which establishes the **base case,** is analogous to establishing that a property of

---

[3]A review of mathematical induction appears in Appendix D.

the natural numbers is true for zero. Showing that each iteration of the loop preserves the invariant is the **inductive step**. This step is analogous to showing that if a property is true for an arbitrary natural number k, then the property is true for the natural number $k + 1$. After proving the four points just described, you can conclude that the invariant is true after every iteration of the loop—just as mathematical induction allows you to conclude that a property is true for every natural number.

Identifying loop invariants will help you to write correct loops. You should state the invariant as a comment that either precedes or begins each loop, as appropriate. For example, in the previous example, you might write the following:

State loop invariants in your programs

```
// Invariant: 0 <= j <= n and
// sum = item[0] +...+ item[j-1]
while (j < n)
    . . .
```

Confirm that the invariants for the following unrelated loops are correct. Remember that each invariant must be true both before the loop begins and after each iteration of the loop, including the final one. Also, you might find it easier to understand the invariant for a *for* loop if you temporarily convert it to an equivalent *while* loop.

Examples of loop invariants

```
// Computes an approximation to e^x for a real x
double t = 1.0, s = 1.0;
int     k = 1;
// Invariant: t == x^(k-1)/(k-1)! and
// s == 1+x+x^2/2!+...+x^(k-1)/(k-1)!
while (k <= n) {
   t *= x/k;
   s += t;
   ++k;
}   // end while


// Computes n! for an integer n >= 0
int f = 1;
// Invariant: f == (j-1)!
for (int j = 1; j <= n; ++j) {
   f *= j;
}   // end for
```

Coding is a relatively minor phase in the software life cycle

Phase 5: Coding. The coding phase involves translating the design into a particular programming language and removing the syntax errors. Although this phase is probably your concept of what programming is all about, it is important to realize that the coding phase is not the major part of the life cycle for most software—actually, it is a relatively minor part.

Phase 6: Testing.   During the testing phase, you need to remove as many logical errors as you can. One approach is to test the individual methods of the objects first, using valid input data that leads to a known result. If certain data must lie within a range, include values at the endpoints of the range. For example, if the input value for *n* can range from 1 to 10, be sure to include test cases in which *n* is 1 and 10. Also, include invalid data to test the error-detection capability of the program. Try some random data, and finally try some actual data. Testing is both a science and an art. You will learn more about testing in subsequent courses.

Design a set of test data to test your program

Phase 7: Refining the solution.   The result of Phases 1 through 6 of the solution process is a working program, which you have tested extensively and debugged as necessary. If you have a program that solves your original problem, you might wonder about the significance of this phase of the solution process.

Develop a working program under simplifying assumptions; then add refining sophistication

Often the best approach to solving a problem is first to make some simplifying assumptions during the design of the solution—for example, you could assume that the input will be in a certain format and will be correct—and next to develop a complete working program under these assumptions. You can then add more sophisticated input and output routines, additional features, and more error checks to the working program.

Thus, the approach of simplifying the problem initially makes a refinement step necessary in the solution process. Of course, you must take care to ensure that the final refinements do not require a complete redesign of the solution. You can usually make these additions cleanly, however, particularly when you have used a modular design. In fact, the ability to proceed in this manner is one of the key advantages of having a modular design! Also, realize that any time you modify a program—no matter how trivial the changes might seem—you must thoroughly test it again.

Changes to a program require that you test it again

This discussion illustrates that the phases within the life cycle of software are not completely isolated from one another and are not linear. To make realistic simplifying assumptions early in the design process, you should have some idea of how you will account for those assumptions later on. Testing a program can suggest changes to its design, but changes to a program require that you test the program again.

Phase 8: Production.   When the software product is complete, it is distributed to its intended users, installed on their computers, and used.

Phase 9: Maintenance.   Maintaining a program is not like maintaining a car. Software does not wear out if you neglect it. However, users of your software invariably will detect errors that you did not discover during the testing phase. Correcting these errors is part of maintaining the software. Another aspect of the maintenance phase involves enhancing the software by adding more features or by modifying existing portions to suit the users better. Rarely will the people who design and implement the original

Correcting user-detected errors and adding features are aspects of software maintenance

program perform this maintenance step. Good documentation then becomes even more important.

Is a program's life cycle relevant to your life? It definitely should be! You should view Phases 1 through 7 as the steps in a problem-solving process. Using this strategy, you first design and implement a solution (Phases 1 through 6) based on some initial simplifying assumptions. The outcome is a well-structured program that solves a somewhat simplified problem. The last step of the solution process (Phase 7) refines your work into a sophisticated program that meets the original problem specifications.

What Is a Good Solution?

Before you devote your time and energy to the study of problem-solving techniques, it seems only fair that you see at the outset why mastery of these techniques will help to make you a good problem solver. An obvious statement is that the use of these techniques will produce good solutions. This statement, however, leads to the more fundamental question, what *is* a good solution? A brief attempt at answering this question concludes this section.

Because a computer program is the final form your solutions will take, consider what constitutes a good computer program. Presumably, you write a program to perform some task. In the course of performing that task, there is a real and tangible **cost**. This cost includes such factors as the computer resources (computing time and memory) that the program consumes, any difficulties encountered by those who use the program, and the consequences of a program that does not behave correctly.

However, the costs just mentioned do not give the whole picture. They pertain to only one phase of the life cycle of a solution—the phase in which it is an operational program. In assessing whether or not a solution is good, you also must consider the phases during which you developed the solution and the phases after you wrote the initial program that implemented the solution. Each of these phases incurs costs, too. The total cost of a solution must take into account the value of the time of the people who developed, refined, coded, debugged, and tested it. A solution's cost must also include the cost of maintaining, modifying, and expanding it.

Thus, when calculating the overall cost of a solution, you must include a diverse set of factors. If you adopt such a multidimensional view of cost, it is reasonable to evaluate a solution against the following criterion:

A multidimensional view of a solution's cost

> *A solution is good if the total cost it incurs over all phases of its life cycle is minimal.*

It is interesting to consider how the relative importance of the various components of this cost has changed since the early days of computing. In the beginning, the cost of computer time relative to human time was extremely high. In addition, people tended to write programs to perform very specific, narrowly defined tasks. If the task changed somewhat, a new program was written. Program maintenance was probably not much of an issue, so there was little concern if a program was hard to read. A program typically had only one user, its author. As a consequence, programmers tended not to worry about misuse or ease of use of their programs; a program's interface generally was not considered important.

In this type of environment, one cost clearly overshadowed all others: computer resources. If two programs performed the same task, the one that required less time and memory was better. How things have changed! Since the early days of computers, computing costs have dropped dramatically, thus making the value of the problem solver's and programmer's time a much more significant factor in the cost of a solution. Another consequence of the drop in computing costs is that computers now are used to perform tasks in a wide variety of areas, many of them nonscientific. People who interact with computers often have no technical expertise and no knowledge of the workings of programs. People want their software to be easy to use.

Today, programs are larger and more complex than ever before. They are often so large that many people are involved in their design, use, and maintenance. Good structure and documentation are thus of the utmost importance. As programs perform more highly critical tasks, the prices for malfunctions will soar. Thus, society needs both well-structured programs and techniques for formally verifying their correctness. People will not and should not entrust their livelihoods—or their lives—to a program that only its authors can understand and maintain.

Programs must be well structured and documented

These developments have made obsolete the notion that the most efficient solution is always the best. If two programs perform the same task, it is no longer true that the faster one is necessarily better. Programmers who use every trick in the book to save a few microseconds of computing time at the expense of clarity are not in tune with the cost structure of today's world. You must write programs with people as well as computers in mind.

At the same time, do not get the false impression that the efficiency of a solution is no longer important. To the contrary, in many situations efficiency is the prime determinant of whether a solution is even usable. The point is that a solution's efficiency is only one of many factors that you must consider. If two solutions have approximately the same efficiency, other factors should dominate the comparison. However, when the efficiencies of solutions differ *significantly,* this difference can be the overriding concern. The stages of the problem-solving process at which you should be most concerned about efficiency are those during which you develop the underlying methods of solution. The choice of a solution's components—the algorithms and ways to store data—rather than the code you write, leads to significant differences in efficiency.

Efficiency is only one aspect of a solution's cost

This book advocates a problem-solving philosophy that views the cost of a solution as multidimensional. This philosophy is reasonable in today's world, and it likely will be reasonable in the years to come.

ACHIEVING A MODULAR DESIGN

You have seen the importance of specifying each module during the design of a solution by writing precise pre- and postconditions, but how do you determine the modules in the first place? The techniques that help you to choose modules for a particular solution are the subject of entire texts and future courses; these techniques quickly go beyond this book's scope. This section will simply provide an overview of two important design techniques. Both techniques use abstraction, so we begin with this essential concept.

Abstraction and Information Hiding

Specify what to do, not how to do it

When you design a modular solution to a problem, each module begins as a box that states what it does but not how it does it. No one box may "know" how any other box performs its task—it may know only what that task is. For example, if one part of a solution is to sort some data, one of the boxes will be a sorting algorithm, as Figure 1-2 illustrates. The other boxes will know that the sorting box sorts, but they will not know how it sorts. In this way, the various components of a solution are kept isolated from one another.

Write specifications for each module before implementing it

Abstraction separates the purpose of a module from its implementation. Modularity and abstraction complement each other. Modularity breaks a solution into modules; abstraction specifies each module clearly *before* you implement it in a programming language. For example, what does the module assume and what action does it take? Such specifications will clarify the design of your solution because you will be able to focus on its high-level functionality without the distraction of imple-

Specifications do not indicate how to implement a module

mentation details. In addition, these principles allow you to modify one

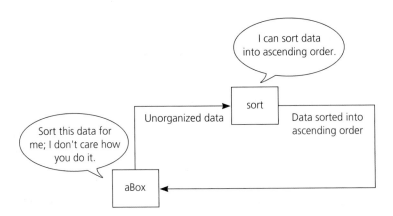

Figure 1-2

The details of the sorting algorithm are hidden from other parts of the solution

part of a solution without significantly affecting the other parts. For example, you should be able to change the sorting algorithm in the previous example without affecting the rest of the solution.

As the problem-solving process proceeds, you gradually refine the boxes until eventually you implement their actions by writing Java code—typically, methods. You should separate the purpose of a method from its implementation. This process is known as **procedural abstraction.** Once a method is written, you can use it without knowing the particulars of its algorithm as long as you have a statement of its purpose and a description of its parameters. Assuming that the method is documented properly, you will be able to use it knowing only its declaration and its initial descriptive comments; you will not need to look at its implementation.

Specify what a method does, not how to do it

Procedural abstraction is essential to team projects. After all, in a team situation, you will have to use methods written by others, frequently without knowledge of their algorithms. Will you actually be able to use such a method without studying its code? In fact, you do so each time you use a method from the Java API, such as `Math.sqrt`, as was noted earlier.

Consider now a collection of data and a set of operations on the data. The operations might include ones that add new data to the collection, remove data from the collection, or search for some data. **Data abstraction** focuses on what the operations do instead of on how you will implement them. The other modules of the solution will "know" *what* operations they can perform, but they will not know *how* the data is stored or *how* the operations are performed.

Specify what you will do to data, not how to do it

For example, you have used an array, but have you ever stopped to think about what an array actually is? You will see many pictures of arrays throughout this book. This artist's conception of an array might resemble the way a Java array is implemented on a computer, and then again it might not. The point is that you are able to use an array without knowing what it "looks like"—that is, how it is implemented. Although different systems may implement arrays in different ways, the differences are transparent to the programmer. For instance, regardless of how the array *years* is implemented, you can always store the value 1492 in location *index* of the array by using the statement

```
years[index] = 1492;
```

and later write out that value by using the statement

```
System.out.println(years[index]);
```

Thus, you can use an array without knowing the details of its implementation, just as you can use the method `Math.sqrt` without knowing the details of its implementation.

Most of this book is about data abstraction. To enable you to think abstractly about data—that is, to focus on what operations you will perform on the data instead of how you will perform them—you should define an **abstract data type,** or **ADT.** An ADT is a collection of data *and* a set of operations on the data. You can use an ADT's operations, if you know their specifications, without knowing how the operations are implemented or how the data is stored.

An ADT is not a fancy name for a data structure

Ultimately, someone—perhaps you—will implement the ADT by using a **data structure**, which is a construct that you can define within a programming language to store a collection of data. For example, you might store some data in a Java array of integers or in an array of objects or in an array of arrays.

Develop algorithms and ADTs in tandem

Within problem solving, abstract data types support algorithms, and algorithms are part of what constitutes an abstract data type. As you design a solution, you should develop algorithms and ADTs in tandem. The global algorithm that solves a problem suggests operations that you need to perform on the data, which in turn suggest ADTs and algorithms for performing the operations on the data. However, the development of the solution may proceed in the opposite direction as well. The kinds of ADTs that you are able to design can influence the strategy of your global algorithm for solving a problem. That is, your knowledge of which data operations are easy to perform and which are difficult can have a large effect on how you approach a problem.

As you probably have surmised from this discussion, you often cannot sharply distinguish between an "algorithms problem" and a "data structures problem." Frequently, you can look at a program from one perspective and feel that the data structures support a clever algorithm and then look at the same program from another perspective and feel that the algorithms support a clever data structure.

Information hiding.   As you have seen, abstraction tells you to write specifications for each module that describe its outside, or **public**, view. However, abstraction also helps you to identify details that you should hide from public view—details that should not be in the specifications but should be **private.** The principle of **information hiding** tells you not only to hide such details within a module, but also ensures that no other module can tamper with these hidden details.

All modules and ADTs should hide something

Information hiding limits the ways in which you need to deal with methods and data. As a user of a module, you do not worry about the details of its implementation. As an implementer of a module, you do not worry about its uses.

Object-Oriented Design

One way to achieve a modular solution is by identifying components—called **objects**—within a problem that combine data and operations on the data. Such an **object-oriented** approach to modularity produces a collection of objects that have behaviors.

Objects encapsulate data and operations

Although you may have been unaware of them, you have seen objects before. The alarm clock that awoke you this morning **encapsulates** both time and operations such as "set the alarm." To *encapsulate* means to encase or enclose; thus, encapsulation is a technique that hides inner details. Whereas methods encapsulate actions, objects encapsulate

Encapsulation hides inner details

data as well as actions. Even though you request the clock to perform certain operations, you cannot see how it works. You see only the results of those operations.

Suppose that you want to write a program to display a clock on your computer screen. To simplify the example, consider a digital clock without an alarm, as Figure 1-3 illustrates. You would begin the task of designing a modular solution by identifying the objects in the problem.

Several techniques are available for identifying objects, but no single one is always the best approach. One simple technique[4] considers the nouns and verbs in the problem specifications. The nouns will suggest objects whose actions are indicated by the verbs. For example, you could specify the clock problem as follows:

> The program will maintain a digital clock that displays the time in hours and minutes. The hour indicator and minute indicator are both digital devices that display values from 1 to 12 and 0 to 59, respectively. You should be able to set the time by setting the hour and minute indicators, and the clock should maintain the time by updating these indicators.

Specifications for a program that displays a digital clock

Even without a detailed problem specification, you know that one of the objects is the clock itself. The clock performs operations such as

```
Set the time
Advance the time
Display the time
```

The hour indicator and minute indicator are also objects and are quite similar to each other. Each indicator performs operations such as

```
Set its value
Advance its value
Display its value
```

In fact, both indicators can be the same type of object. A set of objects that have the same type is called a **class.** Thus, what you need to

Figure 1-3
A digital clock

---

[4] This technique is not foolproof. The problem specification must use nouns and verbs consistently. If, for example, "display" is sometimes a verb and sometimes a noun, identifying objects and their operations can be unclear.

An object is an instance of a class

specify is not a particular object, but a class of objects. In fact, you need a class of clocks and a class of indicators. A clock object, which is an **instance** of the clock class, will then contain two indicator objects, which are instances of the indicator class.

Chapter 3 discusses encapsulation further and, in particular, introduces Java classes. In subsequent chapters, you will study various ADTs and their implementations as Java classes. The focus will be on data abstraction and encapsulation. This approach to programming is **object based.**

Object-oriented programming, or OOP, adds two more principles to encapsulation:

KEY CONCEPTS

Three Principles of Object-Oriented Programming

1. Encapsulation: Objects combine data and operations.
2. Inheritance: Classes can inherit properties from other classes.
3. Polymorphism: Objects can determine appropriate operations at execution time.

Classes can **inherit** properties from other classes. For example, once you have defined a class of clocks, you can design a class of alarm clocks that inherits the properties of a clock but adds operations to provide an alarm. You will be able to produce an alarm clock quickly because the clock portion is done. Thus, **inheritance** allows you to reuse classes that you defined earlier—perhaps for different but related purposes—with appropriate modification.

Inheritance may make it impossible for the compiler to determine which operation you require in a particular situation. However, **polymorphism**—which literally means *many forms*—enables this determination to be made at execution time. That is, the outcome of a particular operation depends upon the objects on which the operation acts. For example, if you use the + operator with numeric operands in Java, addition occurs, but if you use it with string operands, concatenation occurs. Although in this simple example, the compiler can determine the correct meaning of +, polymorphism allows situations in which the meaning of an operation is unknown until execution time.

The + operator has multiple meanings

Chapter 8 discusses inheritance and polymorphism further.

Top-Down Design

Generally, an object-oriented approach produces modular solutions for problems that primarily involve data. When you need to design an algorithm for a particular method, or sometimes when the emphasis of your problem is on algorithms and not data, a **top-down design** will lead to a modular solution. Whereas object-oriented design identifies objects by

focusing on the nouns in the problem statement, top-down design identifies actions by focusing on the verbs.

The philosophy of a top-down design is that you should address a task
at successively lower levels of detail. Consider a simple example. Suppose
that you wanted to find the median among a collection of test scores.
Figure 1-4 uses a **structure chart** to illustrate the hierarchy of, and interaction among, the modules that solve this problem. At first, each module
is little more than a statement of *what* it needs to solve and is devoid of
detail. You refine each module by partitioning it into additional smaller
modules. The result is a hierarchy of modules; each module is refined by
its successors, which solve smaller problems and contain more detail
about *how* to solve the problem than their predecessors. The refinement
process continues until the modules at the bottom of the hierarchy are
simple enough for you to translate directly into Java methods and isolated blocks of code that solve very small, independent problems.

*A structure chart shows
the relationship among modules*

Notice in Figure 1-4 that you can break the solution down into three
independent tasks:

```
Read the test scores
Sort the scores
Get the "middle" score
```

*A solution consisting of
independent tasks*

If the three modules in this example perform their tasks, then by calling
them in order you will correctly find the median, regardless of *how* each
module performs its task.

You begin to develop each module by dividing it into subtasks. For
example, you can refine the task of reading the test scores by dividing it
into the following two modules:

```
Prompt the user for a score
Place the score into an array
```

Subtasks

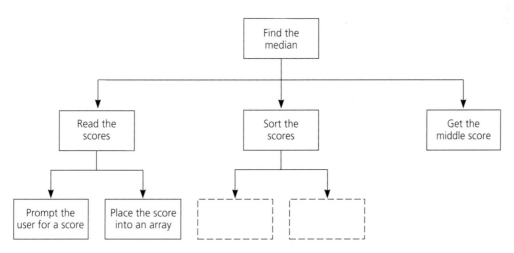

Figure 1-4

A structure chart showing the hierarchy of modules

You continue the solution process by developing, in a similar manner, modules for each of these two tasks. Finally, you can use pseudocode to specify the details of the algorithms.

General Design Guidelines

Typically, you use object-oriented design (OOD), top-down design (TDD), abstraction, and information hiding when you design a solution to a problem. The following design guidelines summarize an approach that leads to modular solutions.

KEY CONCEPTS

Design Guidelines

1. Use OOD and TDD together to produce modular solutions. That is, develop abstract data types and algorithms in tandem.
2. Use OOD for problems that primarily involve data.
3. Use TDD to design algorithms for an object's operations.
4. Consider TDD to design solutions to problems that emphasize algorithms over data.
5. Focus on *what*, not *how*, when designing both ADTs and algorithms.
6. Consider incorporating previously written software components into your design.

A SUMMARY OF KEY ISSUES IN PROGRAMMING

Given that a good solution is one that, in the course of its life cycle, incurs a small cost, the next questions to ask are, what are the specific characteristics of good solutions, and how can you construct good solutions? This section summarizes the answers to these very difficult questions.

The programming issues that this section discusses should be familiar to you. However, it is usually the case that the novice programmer does not truly appreciate their importance. After the first course in programming, many students still simply want to "get the thing to run." The discussion that follows should help you realize just how important these issues really are.

One of the most widespread misconceptions held by novice programmers is that a computer program is "read" only by a computer. As a consequence, they tend to consider only whether the computer will be able to "understand" the program—that is, will the program compile, execute, and produce the correct output? The truth is, of course, that other people often must read and modify programs. In a typical programming environment, many individuals share a program. One person may write a program, which other people use in conjunction with other programs written

People read programs, too

by other people, and a year later, a different person may modify the program. It is therefore essential that you take great care to design a program that is easy to read and understand.

You should always keep in mind the following six issues of program structure and design:

Six Key Programming Issues

1. Modularity
2. Modifiability
3. Ease of use
4. Fail-safe programming
5. Style
6. Debugging

Modularity

As this book will continually emphasize, you should strive for modularity in all phases of the problem-solving process, beginning with the initial design of a solution. You know from the earlier discussion of modular design that many programming tasks become more difficult as the size and complexity of a program grows. Modularity slows the rate at which the level of difficulty grows. More specifically, modularity has a favorable impact on the following aspects of programming:

- **Constructing the program.** The primary difference between a small modular program and a large modular program is simply the number of modules each contains. Because the modules are independent, writing one large modular program is not very different from writing many small, independent programs. On the other hand, working on a large nonmodular program is more like working on many interrelated programs simultaneously. Modularity also permits team programming, where several programmers work independently on their own modules before combining them into one program.

Modularity facilitates programming

- **Debugging the program.** Debugging a large program can be a monstrous task. Imagine that you type a 10,000-line program and eventually get it to compile. Neither of these tasks would be much fun. Now imagine that you execute your program and, after a few hundred lines of output, you notice an incorrect number. You should anticipate spending the next day or so tracing through the intricacies of your program before discovering a problem such as an erroneous arithmetic expression.

   A great advantage of modularity is that the task of debugging a large program is reduced to one of debugging many small

Modularity isolates errors

programs. When you begin to code a module, you should be almost certain that all other modules coded so far are correct. That is, before you consider a module finished, you should test it extensively, both separately and in context with the other modules, by calling it with actual arguments carefully chosen to induce all possible behaviors of the modules. If this testing is done thoroughly, you can feel fairly sure that any problem is a result of an error in the last module added. *Modularity isolates errors.*

More theoretically, as was mentioned before, you can use formal methods to establish the correctness of a program. Modular programs are amenable to this verification process.

Modular programs are easy to read

- **Reading the program.** A person reading a large program may have trouble seeing the forest for the trees. Just as a modular design helps the programmer cope with the complexities of solving a problem, so too will a modular program help its reader understand how the program works. A modular program is easy to follow because the reader can get a good idea of what is going on without reading any of the code. A well-written method can be understood fairly well from only its name, initial comments, and the names of the other methods that it calls. Readers of a program need to study actual code only if they require a detailed understanding of how the program operates. Program readability is discussed further in the section on style later in this chapter.

Modularity isolates modifications

- **Modifying the program.** Modifiability is the topic of the next section, but as the modularity of a program has a direct bearing on its modifiability, a brief mention is appropriate here. A small change in the requirements of a program should require only a small change in the code. If this is not the case, it is likely that the program is poorly written and, in particular, that it is not modular. To accommodate a small change in the requirements, a modular program usually requires a change in only a few of its modules, particularly when the modules are independent (that is, loosely coupled) and each module performs a single well-defined task (that is, is highly cohesive).

    When making changes to a program, it is best to make a few at a time. By maintaining a modular design, you can reduce a fairly large modification to a set of small and relatively simple modifications to isolated parts of the program. *Modularity isolates modifications.*

Modularity eliminates redundancies

- **Eliminating redundant code.** Another advantage of modular design is that you can identify a computation that occurs in many different parts of the program and implement it as a method. Thus, the code for the computation will appear only once, resulting in an increase in both readability and modifiability. The example in the next section demonstrates this point.

Modifiability

Imagine that the specification for a program changes after some period of time. Frequently, people require that a program do something differently than they specified originally, or they ask that it do more than they requested originally. This section offers two examples of how you can make a program easy to modify: through the use of methods and named constants.

Methods. Suppose that a library has a large program to catalog its books. At several points, the program displays the information about a requested book. At each of these points, the program could include a `System.out.println` statement to display the book's call number, author, and title. You could also replace each occurrence of this statement with a call to a method `displayBook` that displays the same information about the book. Alternatively, you could provide an implementation of the method `toString` in the book class that contains the information you want to display about a book. The method `toString` is invoked when a book object appears in a `System.out.println` statement. Appendix A discusses printing objects using the `toString` method.

Not only does the use of a method such as `displayBook` have the obvious advantage of eliminating redundant code, it also makes the resulting program easier to modify. For example, to change the format of the output, you need to change only the implementation of `displayBook` instead of numerous occurrences of the `System.out.println` statement. If you had not used a method, the modification would have required you to make changes at each point where the program displays the information. Merely finding each of these points could be difficult, and you probably would overlook a few. In this simple example, the advantages of using methods should be clear.

Methods make a program easier to modify

For another illustration, recall the earlier example of a solution that, as one of its tasks, sorted some data. Developing the sorting algorithm as an independent module and eventually implementing it as a method would make the program easier to modify. For instance, if you found that the sorting algorithm was too slow, you could replace the sort method without even looking at the rest of the program. You could simply "cut out" the old method and "paste in" the new one. If instead the sort was integrated into the program, the required surgery might be quite intricate.

In general, be concerned if you need to rewrite a program to accommodate small modifications. Usually, it is easy to modify a well-structured program slightly: Because each module solves only a small part of the overall problem, a small change in problem specifications usually affects only a few of the modules.

Named constants. The use of named constants is another way to enhance the modifiability of a program. For example, the restriction that an array must be of a predefined, fixed size causes a bit of difficulty.

Named constants make a program easier to modify

Suppose that a program uses an array to process the SAT scores of the computer science majors at your university. When the program was written, there were 202 computer science majors, so the array was declared by

```
int [] scores = new int[202];
```

The program processes the array in several ways. For example, it reads the scores, writes the scores, and averages the scores. The pseudocode for each of these tasks contains a construct such as

```
for (index = 0 through 201)
    Process the score
```

If the number of majors changes, not only must you revise the declaration of *scores*, but you must also change each loop that processes the array to reflect the new array size. In addition, other statements in the program might depend on the size of the array. A 202 here, a 201 there—which to change?

On the other hand, if you use a named constant such as

```
final int NUMBER_OF_MAJORS = 202;
```

you can declare the array by using

```
int [] scores = new int[NUMBER_OF_MAJORS];
```

and write the pseudocode for the processing loops in this form:

```
for (index = 0 through NUMBER_OF_MAJORS - 1)
    Process the score
```

If you write expressions that depend on the size of the array in terms of the constant *NUMBER_OF_MAJORS* (such as *NUMBER_OF_MAJORS - 1*), you can change the array size simply by changing the definition of the constant and compiling the program again.

Ease of Use

Another area in which you need to keep people in mind is the design of the user interface. Humans often process a program's input and output. Here are a few obvious points:

Prompt the user for input

- In an interactive environment, the program should always prompt the user for input in a manner that makes it quite clear what it expects. For example, the prompt "?" is not nearly as enlightening as the prompt "Please enter account number for deposit." You should never assume that the users of your program will know what response the program requires.

Echo the input

- A program should always echo its input. Whenever a program reads data, either from a user or from a file, the program should include the values it reads in its output. This inclusion serves two purposes: First, it gives the user a check on the data entered—a guard against typos and errors in data transmission. This check is particularly useful in the case of interactive input. Second, the output is more meaningful and self-explanatory when it contains a record of what input generated the output.

- The output should be well labeled and easy to read. An output of

Label the output

```
1800   6   1
Jones, Q.   223 2234.00 1088.19  N, J  Smith, T. 111
110.23 I,  Harris, V.  44  44000.00 22222.22
```

is more prone to misinterpretation than

```
CUSTOMER ACCOUNTS AS OF 1800 HOURS ON JUNE 1

Account status codes: N=new, J=joint, I=inactive

NAME          ACC#   CHECKING    SAVINGS      STATUS

Jones, Q.     223    $ 2234.00   $ 1088.19    N, J
Smith, T.     111    $  110.23   ---------    I
Harris, V.     44    $44000.00   $22222.22    ------
```

These characteristics of a good user interface are only the basics. Several more subtle points separate a program that is merely usable from one that is user friendly. Students tend to ignore a good user interface, but by investing a little extra time here, you can make a big difference: the difference between a good program and one that only solves the problem. For example, consider a program that requires a user to enter a line of data in some fixed format, with exactly one blank between the items. A free-form input that allows any number of blanks between the items would be much more convenient for the user. It takes so little time to write code that skips blanks, so why require the user to follow an exact format? Once you have made this small additional effort, it is a permanent part of both your program and your library of techniques. The user of your program never has to think about input format.

A good user interface is important

Fail-Safe Programming

A fail-safe program is one that will perform reasonably no matter how anyone uses it. Unfortunately, this goal is usually unattainable. A more realistic goal is to anticipate the ways that people might misuse the program and to guard carefully against these abuses.

This discussion considers two types of errors. The first type is an *error in input data*. For example, suppose that a program expects a nonnegative integer but reads –12. When a program encounters this type of problem, it should not produce incorrect results or abort with a vague error message. Instead, a fail-safe program provides a message such as

Check for errors in input

```
-12 is not a valid number of children.
Please enter this number again.
```

The second type of error is an *error in the program logic*. Although a discussion of this type of error belongs in the debugging section at the end of this chapter, detecting errors in program logic is also an issue of fail-safe programming. A program that appears to have been running correctly may, at some point, behave unexpectedly, even if the data that it reads is valid. For example, the program may not have accounted for the particular data that elicited the surprise behavior, even though you tried your best to test the program's logic. Or perhaps you modified the program and that modification invalidated an assumption that you made in some other part of the program. Whatever the difficulty, a program should have built-in safeguards against these kinds of errors. It should monitor itself and be able to indicate that something is wrong and you should not trust the results.

Check for errors in logic

Guarding against errors in input data.   Suppose that you are computing statistics about the people in income brackets between $10,000 and $100,000. The brackets are rounded to the nearest thousand dollars: $10,000, $11,000, and so on to $100,000. The raw data is a file of one or more lines of the form

> G   N

where N is the number of people with an income that falls into the G-thousand-dollar group. If several people have compiled the data, several entries for the same value of G might occur. As the user enters data, the program must add up and record the number of people for each value of G. From the problem's context, it is clear that G is an integer in the range 10 to 100 inclusive, and N is a nonnegative integer.

As an example of how to guard against errors in input, consider an input method for this problem. The first attempt at writing this method will illustrate several common ways in which a program can fall short of the fail-safe ideal. Eventually you will see an input method that is much closer to the fail-safe ideal than the original solution.

A first attempt at the class and methods might be

```
public class IncomeStatistics {
   final static int LOW_END = 10;      // low end of incomes
   final static int HIGH_END = 100;    // high end of incomes
   final static int TABLE_SIZE = HIGH_END - LOW_END + 1;

   int[] incomeData;      // used to store the income data,
         // incomeData[G] stores the total number of
         // people that fall into the G-thousand-dollar group

   public IncomeStatistics() {
      incomeData = new int[TABLE_SIZE];
   }  // end constructor
```

```
public void readData() throws IOException {          This method is not fail-safe
// -----------------------------------------------------
// Reads and organizes income statistics.
// Precondition: The calling module gives directions and
// prompts the user. Input data is error-free, and each
// input line is in the form G N, where N is the number of
// people with an income in the G-thousand-dollar group
// and LOW_END <= G <= HIGH_END. An input line with values
// of zero for both G and N terminates the input.
// Postcondition: incomeData[G-LOW_END] = total number of
// people with an income in the G-thousand-dollar group
// for each G read. The values read are displayed.
// -----------------------------------------------------
  int group, number;                        // input values
  BufferedReader stdin = new BufferedReader(
                      new InputStreamReader(System.in));
  StringTokenizer inputLine;

  for (group = LOW_END; group <= HIGH_END; ++group)  {
    // clear array
    incomeData[index(group)] = 0;
  }  // end for
  inputLine = new StringTokenizer(stdin.readLine());
  group = Integer.parseInt(inputLine.nextToken());
  number = Integer.parseInt(inputLine.nextToken());
  while ((group != 0) || (number != 0)) {
    System.out.println("Income group "+group+" contains " +
                      number + " people.");
    incomeData[index(group)] += number;

    inputLine = new StringTokenizer(stdin.readLine());
    group = Integer.parseInt(inputLine.nextToken());
    number = Integer.parseInt(inputLine.nextToken());
  }  // end while
}  // end readData

private int index(int group) {
// Returns the array index corresponding to group number.
  return group - LOW_END;
}  // end index

// other methods for class IncomeStatistics would follow

} // end IncomeStatistics
```

The *readData* method has some problems. If an input line contains unexpected data, the program will not behave reasonably. Consider two specific possibilities:

- The first integer on the input line, which the method assigns to *group*, is not in the range *LOW_END* to *HIGH_END*. The reference *incomeData[index(group)]* will then throw the exception *IndexOutOfBoundsException*.

- The second number on the input line, which the method assigns to *number*, is negative. Although a negative value for *number* is invalid because you cannot have a negative number of people in an income group, the method will add *number* to the group's array entry. Thus, the array *incomeData* will be incorrect.

Test for invalid input data

After the method reads values for *group* and *number*, it must check to see whether *group* is in the range *LOW_END* to *HIGH_END* and whether *number* is positive. If either value is not in range, you must handle the input error.

Instead of checking *number*, you might think to check the value of *incomeData[index(group)]*, after adding *number*, to see whether it is positive. This approach is insufficient. First, notice that it is possible to add a negative value to an entry of *incomeData* without that entry becoming negative. For example, if *number* is −4,000 and the corresponding entry in *incomeData* is 10,000, the sum is 6,000. Thus, a negative value for *number* could remain undetected and invalidate the results of the rest of the program.

One possible course of action for the method to take when it detects invalid data is to set an error flag and terminate. Another possibility is for it to set an error flag, ignore the bad input line, and continue. Which action is correct really depends on how the program uses the data once it is read.

The following *readData* method attempts to be as universally applicable as possible and to make the program that uses it as modifiable as possible. When the method encounters an error in input, it sets a flag, ignores the data line, and continues. By setting a flag and later returning its value, the method leaves it to the calling module to determine the appropriate action—such as abort or continue—when an input error occurs. Thus, you can use the same input method in many contexts and can easily modify the action taken upon encountering an error.

A method that includes fail-safe programming

```
public boolean readData() throws IOException {
   // -------------------------------------------------------
   // Reads and organizes income statistics.
   // Precondition: The calling program gives directions and
   // prompts the user. Each input line contains exactly two
   // integers in the form G N, where N is the number of people
   // with an income in the G-thousand-dollar group and
   // LOW_END <= G <= HIGH_END. An input line with values of zero
   // for both G and N terminates the input.
```

```
// Postcondition: incomeData[G-LOW_END] = total number of
// people with an income in the G-thousand-dollar group. The
// values read are displayed. If either G or N is erroneous (G
// and N are not both 0, and either G < LOW_END, G > HIGH_END,
// or N < 0), the method ignores the data line, sets the
// return value to false, and continues. In this case,
// the calling program should take action.
// The return value is true if the data is error free.
// --------------------------------------------------------
  int group, number;            // input values
  boolean dataCorrect = true;   // no data error found as yet
  BufferedReader stdin = new BufferedReader(
                       new InputStreamReader(System.in));
  StringTokenizer inputLine;

  for (group = low; group <= high; ++group) { // clear array
    incomeData[index(group)] = 0;
  }  // end for
  inputLine = new StringTokenizer(stdin.readLine());
  group = Integer.parseInt(inputLine.nextToken());
  number = Integer.parseInt(inputLine.nextToken());
  while ((group != 0) || (number != 0)) {
    // Invariant: group and number are not both 0
    System.out.println("Income group " + group +
                       " contains " + number + " people.");
    if ((group >= LOW_END) && (group <= HIGH_END) &&
        (number >= 0)) {
      // input data is valid -- add it to tally
      incomeData[index(group)] += number;
    }
    else {
      // error in input data: set error flag and ignore line
      dataCorrect = false;
    }  // end if
    inputLine = new StringTokenizer(stdin.readLine());
    group = Integer.parseInt(inputLine.nextToken());
    number = Integer.parseInt(inputLine.nextToken());
  }  // end while
  return dataCorrect;
}  // end readData
```

Although this input method will behave gracefully in the face of most common input errors, it is not completely fail-safe. What happens if an input line contains only one integer? What happens if an input line contains a noninteger? The method would be more fail-safe if it read its input character by character, converted the characters to an integer, and checked for an end-of-line character. In most contexts, this processing would be a bit extreme. However, if the people who enter the data frequently err by typing nonintegers, you could alter the input method easily because the method is an isolated module. In any case, the method's initial comments should include any assumptions it makes about the data and an indication of what might make the program abort abnormally.

Guarding against errors in program logic. Now consider the second type of error that a program should guard against: errors in its own logic. These are errors that you may not have caught when you debugged the program or that you may have introduced through program modification.

Unfortunately, a program cannot reliably let you know when something is wrong with it. (Could you rely on a program to tell you that something is wrong with its mechanism for telling you that something is wrong?) You can, however, build into a program checks that ensure that certain conditions always hold when the program is correctly implementing its algorithm. As was mentioned earlier, such conditions are called invariants.

Methods should check their invariants

As a simple example of an invariant, consider again the previous example. *All integers in the array incomeData must be greater than or equal to zero.* Although the previous discussion argued that the method *read-Data* should not check the validity of the entries of *incomeData* instead of checking *number*, it could do so *in addition to* checking *number*. For example, if the method finds that an element in the array *incomeData* is outside some range of believability, it can signal a potential problem to its users.

Methods should enforce their preconditions

Another general way in which you should make a program fail-safe is to make each method check its precondition. For example, consider the following method, *factorial*, which returns the factorial of an integer:

```
public static int factorial(int n) {
// ----------------------------------------------------
// Computes the factorial of an integer.
// Precondition: n >= 0.
// Postcondition: Returns n * (n-1)*...*1, if n > 0;
// returns 1 if n = 0.
// ----------------------------------------------------
   int result = 1;

   for (int i = n; i > 1; --i) {
     result *= i;
   }  // end for
   return result;
} // end factorial
```

The initial comments in this method contain a precondition—information about what assumptions are made—as should always be the case. The value that this method returns is valid only if the precondition is met. If *n* is less than zero, the method will return the incorrect value of 1.

In the context of the program for which this method was written, it may be reasonable to make the assumption that *n* will never be negative.

That is, if the rest of the program is working correctly, it will call *facto-rial* only with correct values of *n*. Ironically, this last observation gives you a good reason for *factorial* to check the value of *n*: If *n* is less than zero, the warning that results from the check indicates that something may be wrong elsewhere in the program.

Another reason the method *factorial* should check whether *n* is less than zero is that the method should be correct outside the context of its program. That is, if you borrow the method for use in another program, the method should warn you if you use it incorrectly by passing it an *n* that is negative. A stronger check than simply the statement of the pre-condition in a comment is desirable. Thus, *a method should state its assumptions and, when possible, check that its arguments conform to these assumptions.*

In this example, *factorial* could check the value of *n* and, if it is negative, return zero, since factorials are never zero. The program that uses *factorial* could then check for this unusual value.

Alternatively, *factorial* could abort execution if its argument was negative. Many programming languages, such as Java, support a mecha-nism for error handling called an **exception**. A module indicates that an error has occurred by **throwing** an exception. A module reacts to an exception that another module throws by **catching** the exception and executing code to deal with the error condition. You may already have seen exceptions when you used some of the methods from the Java API. For example, when an array subscript goes out of range, the exception *java.lang.IndexOutOfBoundsException* is thrown. If the exception is not caught, the program will terminate with a message indicating that the *java.lang.IndexOutOfBoundsException* occurred. Chapter 3 pro-vides more information about exceptions. Error handling is discussed further in the next section about programming style.

Methods should check the values of their arguments

Style

This section considers the following five issues of personal style in programming:

KEY CONCEPTS

Five Issues of Style

1. Extensive use of methods
2. Use of private data fields
3. Error handling
4. Readability
5. Documentation

Admittedly, much of the following discussion reflects the personal taste of the authors; certainly other good programming styles are possible.

It is difficult to overuse methods

Extensive use of methods.   It is difficult to overuse methods. If a set of statements performs an identifiable, recurring task, it should be a method. However, a task need not be recurrent to justify the use of a method.

Although a program with all its code in-line runs faster than one that calls methods, programs without methods are not cheaper to use. The use of methods is cost-effective if you consider human time as a significant component of the program's cost. You have already seen the advantages of a modular program.

Use of private data fields.   Each object has a set of methods that represents the operations that can be performed on the object. The object also contains data fields to store information within the object. You should hide the exact representation of these data fields from modules that use the object by making all of the data fields private. Doing so supports the principle of information hiding. The details of the object's implementation are hidden from view, with methods providing the only mechanism to get information to and from the object. Even in a situation where the only operations involved with a particular data field are read and write, the object should provide a simple method—called an **accessor**—that returns the data field's value and another method—called a **mutator**—that sets the data field's value. For example, a `Person` object could provide access to the data field `theName` through the methods `getname()` to return the person's name and `setName()` to change the person's name.

Error handling.   A fail-safe program checks for errors in both its input and its logic and attempts to behave gracefully when it encounters them. A method should check for certain types of errors, such as invalid input or argument values. What action should a method take when it encounters an error? Depending on context, the appropriate action in the face of an error can range from ignoring erroneous data and continuing execution to terminating the program. The method `readData` in the income statistics program earlier in this chapter returned a boolean value to the calling module to indicate that it had encountered an invalid line of data. Thus, the method left it to the calling module to decide on the appropriate action. In general, methods should return a value or throw an exception instead of displaying a message when an error occurs.

In case of an error, methods should return a value or throw an exception, but not display a message

In some situations, it is more appropriate for the method itself to take the action in case of an error. In the case of a fatal error that calls for termination of the program, Java provides a class `java.lang.Error`. The program will throw an object of type `java.lang.Error` when the error encountered in the program is too severe to warrant continued execution of the program. Dividing an integer by zero is a simple example of a situation that will cause the program to terminate abnormally in this manner. Chapter 3 discusses Java exceptions and errors.

Readability.   For a program to be easy to follow, it should have a good structure and design, a good choice of identifiers, good indentation and use of blank lines, and good documentation. Avoid clever programming tricks that save a little computer time at the expense of much human time. You will see examples of these points in programs throughout the book.

Choose identifiers that describe their purpose, that is, are self-documenting. Distinguish between keywords, such as *int*, and user-defined identifiers. This book uses the following conventions:

- Keywords are lowercase and appear in boldface.

- User-defined identifiers use both upper- and lowercase letters, as follows: *Identifier style*
  - Class names are nouns, with each word in the identifier capitalized.
  - Method names are verbs, with the first letter lowercase and subsequent internal words capitalized. Variables begin with a lowercase letter. Remaining words in multiple-word identifiers each begin with an uppercase letter.
  - Named constants are entirely uppercase and use underscores to separate words.

Use a good indentation style to enhance the readability of a program. The layout of a program should make it easy for a reader to identify the program's modules. Use blank lines to offset each method. Also, within methods, you should indent individual blocks of code visibly and offset them with blank lines. These blocks are generally—but are not limited to—the actions performed within a control structure, such as a *while* loop or an *if* statement.

You can choose from among several good indentation styles. The five most important general requirements of an indentation style are as follows:

- Blocks should be indented sufficiently so that they stand out clearly. *Guidelines for indentation style*

- Indentation should be consistent: Always indent the same type of construct in the same manner.

- The indentation style should provide a reasonable way to handle the problem of **rightward drift**, the problem of nested blocks bumping against the right-hand margin of the page.

- In a compound statement, the opening brace should be at the end of the line that begins the compound statement; the closing brace should line up with the beginning of the line that begins the compound statement:

```
while (i > 0) {
   statement(s)
}   // end while
```

- Braces are used around all statements, even single statements, when they are part of a control structure, such as an *if-else* or *for* statement. This makes it easier to add statements without accidentally introducing bugs due to forgetting to add braces.

Within these guidelines there is room for personal taste. Here is a summary of the style you will see in this book.

Indentation style in this book

- A *for* or *while* statement is written for a simple or compound action as

```
while (expression) {
    statement(s)
}  // end while
```

- A *do* statement is written for a simple or compound action as

```
do {
    statement(s)
}  while (expression);
```

- An *if* statement is written for simple or compound actions as

```
if (expression) {
    statement(s)
}
else {
    statement(s)
}  // end if
```

Nested *if* statements that choose among three or more different courses of action are written as

```
if (condition₁) {
    action₁
}
else if (condition₂) {
    action₂
}
else if (condition₃) {
    action₃
}  // end if
```

This indentation style better reflects the nature of the construct, which is like a generalized *switch* statement:

```
switch (expression) {
    case constant₁ : action₁; break;
    case constant₂ : action₂; break;
    case constant₃ : action₃; break;

}  // end switch
```

Documentation. A program should be well documented so that others can read, use, and modify it easily. Many acceptable styles for documentation are in use today, and exactly what you should include often depends on the particular program or your individual circumstances. The following are the essential features of any program's documentation:

Essential Features of Program Documentation

1. An initial comment for the program that includes

    a. Statement of purpose

    b. Author and date

    c. Description of the program's input and output

    d. Description of how to use the program

    e. Assumptions such as the type of data expected

    f. Statement of exceptions, that is, what could go wrong

    g. Brief description of the major classes

2. Initial comments in each class that state its purpose and describe the data contained in the class (constants and variables)

3. Initial comments in each method that state its purpose, preconditions, postconditions, and methods called

4. Comments in the body of each method to explain important features or subtle logic

Beginning programmers tend to downplay the importance of documentation because the computer does not read comments. By now, you should realize that people also read programs. Your comments must be clear enough for someone else to either use your method in a program or modify it. Thus, some of your comments are for people who want to use your method, while others are for people who will revise its implementation. You should distinguish between different kinds of comments.

Consider who will read your comments when you write them

Beginners have a tendency to document programs as a last step. You should, however, write documentation as you develop the program. Since the task of writing a large program might extend over a period of several weeks, you may find that the method that seemed so obvious when you wrote it seems confusing when you try to revise it a week later. Why not benefit from your own documentation by writing it now, while it's fresh in your mind?

You benefit from your own documentation by writing it now instead of later

Debugging

No matter how much care you take in writing a program, it will contain errors that you need to track down. Fortunately, programs that are modular, clear, and well documented are generally amenable to debugging. Fail-safe techniques, which guard against certain errors and report them when they are encountered, are also a great aid in debugging.

Many students seem to be totally baffled by errors in their programs and have no idea how to proceed. These students simply have not learned to track down errors systematically. Without a systematic approach, finding a small mistake in a large program can indeed be a difficult task.

The difficulty that many people have in debugging a program is perhaps due in part to a desire to believe that their program is really doing what it is supposed to do. For example, on receiving an execution-time error message at line 1098, a student might say, "That's impossible. The statement at line 1098 was not even executed, because it is in the *else* clause, and I am positive that it was not executed." This student must do more than simply protest. The proper approach is either to trace the program's execution by using available debugging facilities or to add *System.out.println* statements that show which part of the *if* statement was executed. By doing so, you verify the value of the expression in the *if* statement. If the expression is 0 when you expect it to be 1, the next step is to determine how it became 0.

How can you find the point in a program where something becomes other than what it should be? Typically, a programming environment allows you to trace a program's execution either by single-stepping through the statements in the program or by setting **breakpoints** at which execution will halt. You also can examine the contents of particular variables by either establishing **watches** or inserting temporary *System.out.println* statements. The key to debugging is simply to use these techniques to tell you what is going on. This may sound pretty mundane, but the real trick is to use these debugging aids in an effective manner. After all, you do not simply put breakpoints, watches, and *System.out.println* statements at random points in the program and have them report random information.

Use either watches or temporary System.out.println statements to find logic errors

The main idea is systematically to locate the points of the program that cause the problem. A program's logic implies that certain conditions should be true at various points in the program. (Recall that these conditions are called invariants.) If the program's results differ from your expectations as stated in the invariants (you *did* write invariants, didn't you?), an error occurs. To correct the error, you must find the first point in the program at which this difference is evident. By inserting either breakpoints and watches or *System.out.println* statements at strategic locations of a program—such as at the entry and departure points of loops and methods—you can systematically isolate the error.

Systematically check a program's logic to determine where an error occurs

These diagnostic techniques should inform you whether things start going wrong before or after a given point in the program. Thus, after you run the program with an initial set of diagnostics, you should be able to trap the error between two points. For example, suppose that things are fine before you call method M_1, but something is wrong by the time you call M_2. This kind of information allows you to focus your attention between these two points. You continue the process until eventually the search is limited to only a few statements. There is really no place in a program for an error to hide.

The ability to place breakpoints, watches, and *System.out.println* statements in appropriate locations and to have them report appropriate information comes in part from thinking logically about the problem and in part from experience. Here are a few general guidelines.

Debugging methods. You should examine the values of a method's arguments at its beginning and end by using either watches or *Sys-*

tem.out.println statements. Ideally, you should debug each major method separately before using it in your program.

Debugging loops. You should examine the values of key variables at the beginnings and ends of loops, as the comments in this example indicate:

```
// check values of start and stop before entering loop
for (index = start; index <= stop; ++index) {
  // check values of index and key variables
  // at beginning of iteration
      .
      .
      .


  // check values of index and key variables
  // at end of iteration
}  // end for
// check values of start and stop after exiting loop
```

Debugging *if* statements. Just before an *if* statement, you should examine the values of the variables within its expression. You can use either breakpoints or *System.out.println* statements to determine which branch the *if* statement takes, as this example indicates:

```
// check variables within expression before executing if
if (expression) {
  System.out.println("Value of expression is true");
  . . .
}
else {
  System.out.println("Value of expression is false");
  . . .
}  // end if
```

Using *System.out.println* statements.   *System.out.println* statements can sometimes be more convenient than watches. Such statements should report both the values of key variables and the location in the program at which the variables have those values. You can use a comment to label the location, as follows:

```
// This is point A
System.out.println("At point A method compute:\n" +
                   "x = " + x + ", y = " + y );
```

Remember to either comment out or remove these statements when your program finally works.

Using special dump methods. Often the variables whose values you wish to examine are arrays or other, more complex data structures. If so, you should write dump methods to display the data structures in a highly read-able manner. You can easily move the single statement that calls each dump method from one point in the program to another as you track down an error. The time that you spend on these methods often proves to be worthwhile, as you can call them repeatedly while debugging different parts of the program.

Hopefully, this discussion has conveyed the importance of the *effective use of diagnostic aids in debugging*. Even the best programmers have to spend some time debugging. Thus, to be a truly good programmer, you must be a good debugger.

SUMMARY

1. Software engineering is a branch of computer science that studies ways to facilitate the development of computer programs.

2. The life cycle of software consists of several phases: specifying the problem, designing the algorithm, analyzing the risks, verifying the algorithm, coding the programs, testing the programs, refining the solution, using the software, and maintaining the software.

3. A loop invariant is a property of an algorithm that is true before and after each iteration of a loop. Loop invariants are useful in developing iterative algorithms and establishing their correctness.

4. When evaluating the quality of a solution, you must consider a diverse set of factors: the solution's correctness, its efficiency, the time that went into its development, its ease of use, and the cost of modifying and expanding it.

5. A combination of object-oriented and top-down design tech-niques will lead to a modular solution. For problems that prima-rily involve data management, encapsulate data with operations on that data by designing classes. The nouns in the problem statement can help you to identify appropriate classes. Break algorithmic tasks into independent subtasks that you gradually refine. In all cases, practice abstraction; that is, focus on what a module does instead of how it does it.

6. Take great care to ensure that your final solution is as easy to modify as possible. Generally, a modular program is easy to mod-ify because changes in the problem's requirements frequently affect only a handful of the modules. Programs should not depend on the particular implementations of its modules.

7. A method should be as independent as possible and perform one well-defined task.

8. A method should always include an initial comment that states its purpose, its precondition—that is, the conditions that must exist at the beginning of a module—and its postcondition—the conditions at the end of a module.

9. A program should be as fail-safe as possible. For example, a program should guard against errors in input and errors in its own logic. By checking invariants—which are conditions that are true at certain points in a program—you can monitor correct program execution.

10. The effective use of available diagnostic aids is one of the keys to debugging. You should use watches or *System.out.println* statements to report the values of key variables at key locations. These locations include the beginnings and ends of methods and loops, and the branches of selection statements.

11. To make it easier to examine the contents of arrays and other, more complex data structures while debugging, you should write dump methods that display the contents of the data structures. You can easily move calls to such methods as you track down an error.

CAUTIONS

1. Your programs should guard against errors. A fail-safe program checks that an input value is within some acceptable range and reports if it is not. An error in input should not cause a program to terminate before it clearly reports what the error was. A fail-safe program also attempts to detect errors in its own logic. For example, in many situations, methods should check that their arguments have valid values.

2. You can write better, correct programs in less time if you pay attention to the following guidelines: Write precise specifications for the program. Use a modular design. Write pre- and postconditions for each method before you implement it. Use meaningful identifiers and consistent indentation. Write comments, including assertions and invariants.

SELF-TEST EXERCISES

The answers to all Self-Test Exercises are at the back of this book.

1. What is the loop invariant for the following?

   ```
   int index = 0;
   int sum = item[0];

   while (index < n) {
     ++index;
     sum += item[index];
   }  // end while
   ```

2. Write specifications for a method that computes the sum of the first five positive integers in an array of N arbitrary integers.

EXERCISES

1. The price of an item that you want to buy is given in dollars and cents. You pay for it in cash by giving the clerk d dollars and c cents. Write specifications for a method that computes the change, if any, that you should receive. Include a statement of purpose, the pre- and postconditions, and a description of the parameters.

2. A date consists of a month, day, and year. Frequently, we represent each of these items as integers. For example, July 4, 1776, is month 7, day 4, and year 1776.

   a. Write specifications for a method that advances any given date by one day. Include a statement of purpose, the pre- and postconditions, and a description of the parameters.

   b. Write a Java implementation of this method. Design and specify any other methods that you need. Include comments that will be helpful to someone who will maintain your implementation in the future.

3. Consider the following method, which interactively reads and writes the identification number, age, salary (in thousands of dollars), and name of each individual in a group of employees. How can you improve the program? Some of the issues are obvious, while others are more subtle. Try to keep in mind all the topics discussed in this chapter.

```java
public static void main(String args[])
                                  throws IOException {
  int x1, x2, x3, i;
  String name;
  BufferedReader stdin = new BufferedReader(
          new InputStreamReader(System.in));
  StringTokenizer inputLine;

  inputLine = new StringTokenizer(stdin.readLine());
  x1 = Integer.parseInt(inputLine.nextToken());
  x2 = Integer.parseInt(inputLine.nextToken());
  x3 = Integer.parseInt(inputLine.nextToken());

  while (x1 != 0) {
    name = new String(inputLine.nextToken());
    System.out.println(x1 + " " + x2 + " " + x3 + name);
    inputLine = new StringTokenizer(stdin.readLine());
    x1 = Integer.parseInt(inputLine.nextToken());
    x2 = Integer.parseInt(inputLine.nextToken());
    x3 = Integer.parseInt(inputLine.nextToken());
  }  // end while

}  // end main
```

4. This chapter stressed the importance of adding fail-safe checks to a program wherever possible. What can go wrong with the following method? How can you protect yourself?

```
public static double computation(double x) {
    return java.lang.Math.sqrt(x)/java.lang.Math.cos(x);
}  // end computation
```

5. Write the loop invariants for the method *factorial*, which appears in the section "Fail-Safe Programming."

6. Write the method that Self-Test Exercise 2 describes, and state the loop invariants.

7. By using loop invariants, demonstrate that the algorithm in Self-Test Exercise 1 correctly computes *item[0]* + *item[1]* + · · · + *item[n]*.

8. The following code is supposed to compute the **floor** of the square root of its input value x. (The floor of a number n is the largest integer less than or equal to n.)

```
// Computes and writes floor(sqrt(x)) for
// an input value x >= 0.
public static void main(String args[])
                                  throws IOException {
    int x;   // input value
    BufferedReader stdin = new BufferedReader(
            new InputStreamReader(System.in));
    StringTokenizer inputLine;
    // initialize
    int result = 0;   // will equal floor of sqrt(x)
    int temp1 = 1;
    int temp2 = 1;

    // read input
    inputLine = new StringTokenizer(stdin.readLine());
    x = Integer.parseInt(inputLine.nextToken());

    // compute floor
    while (temp1 < x) {
        ++result;
        temp2 += 2;
        temp1 += temp2;
    }  // end while

    System.out.println("The floor of the square root of "
                    + x + " is " + result);
}  // end main
```

This program contains an error.

   a. What output does the program produce when $x = 64$?
   b. Run the program and remove the error. Describe the steps that you took to find the error.
   c. How can you make the program more user friendly and fail-safe?

9. Suppose that, due to some severe error, you must abort a program from a location deep inside nested method calls, *while* loops, and *if* statements. Write a diagnostic method that you can call from anywhere in a program. This method should take an error code as an argument, display an appropriate error message, and terminate program execution.

PROGRAMMING PROBLEMS

1. Consider a program that will read employee information into an array of objects, sort the array by employee identification number, write out the sorted array, and compute various statistics on the data, such as the average age of an employee. Write complete specifications for this problem and design a modular solution. What classes and methods did you identify during the design of your solution? Write specifications, including preconditions and postconditions, for each method.

2. Write a program that sorts and evaluates bridge hands.

    The input is a stream of character pairs that represent playing cards. For example,

        2C   QD   TC   AD   6C   3D   TD   3H   5H   7H   AS   JH   KH

    represents the 2 of clubs, queen of diamonds, 10 of clubs, ace of diamonds, and so on. Each pair consists of a rank followed by a suit, where rank is A, 2, . . . , 9, T, J, Q, or K, and suit is C, D, H, or S. You can assume that each input line represents exactly 13 cards and is error-free. Input is terminated by an end-of-file.

    For each line of input, form a hand of 13 cards. Display each hand in a readable form arranged both by suits and by rank within suit (aces are high). Then evaluate the hand by using the following standard bridge values:

    Aces count 4

    Kings count 3

    Queens count 2

    Jacks count 1

    Voids (no cards in a suit) count 3

    Singletons (one card in a suit) count 2

    Doubletons (two cards in a suit) count 1

    Long suits with more than 5 cards in the suit
    count 1 for each card over 5 in number

    For example, for the previous sample input line, the program should produce the output

```
CLUBS          10    6    2
DIAMONDS       A     Q    10    3
HEARTS         K     J    7     5    3
SPADES         A
Points = 16
```

because there are 2 aces, 1 king, 1 queen, 1 jack, 1 singleton, no dou-
bletons, and no long suits. (The singleton ace of spades counts as
both an ace and a singleton.)

   Optional: See how much more flexible and fail-safe you can make
your program. That is, try to remove as many of the previous
assumptions in input as you can.

3. Java provides a class *java.lang.BigInteger* that can be used to handle very large integers. Implement a similar class, called *BigInt*, that
can be used to do simple calculations with very large nonnegative
integers. Design this class carefully. You will need the following:

- A data structure to represent large numbers: for example, a string
  or an array of digits in a number.

- **public** BigInt(String val)

  A constructor that uses a string representation of the integer for
  initialization. The string may contain leading zeros. Do not forget
  that zero is a valid number.

- **public void** display()

  A method to write numbers. Do not write leading zeros, but if the
  number consists of all zeros, write a single zero.

- **public** BigInt add(BigInt val)

  A method that returns the sum of *val* and the instance of *BigInt*
  that invokes *add*.

- **public** BigInt multiply(BigInt val)

  A method that returns the product of *val* and the instance of
  BigInt that invokes *multiply*.

   Optional: Allow signed integers (negative as well as positive integers), and write a method for subtraction.
   Write a program that acts as an interactive calculator capable of
handling very large nonnegative integers that uses the *BigInt* class.
This calculator need perform only the operations of addition and
multiplication.
   In this program each input line is of the form

num_1 *op* num_2

and should produce output such as

```
     num₁
op   num₂
--------
     num₃
```

where num_1 and num_2 are (possibly very large) nonnegative integers,
op is the single character + or *, and num_3 is the integer that results
from the desired calculation. Be sure your interface is user friendly.

2

Recursion: The Mirrors

PREVIEW The goal of this chapter is to ensure that you have a basic under-standing of recursion, which is one of the most powerful techniques of solu-tion available to the computer scientist. This chapter assumes that you have had little or no previous introduction to recursion. If, however, you already have studied recursion, you can review this chapter as necessary.

By presenting several relatively simple problems, the chapter demon-strates the thought processes that lead to recursive solutions. These problems are diverse and include examples of counting, searching, and organizing data. In addition to presenting recursion from a conceptual viewpoint, this chapter discusses techniques that will help you to understand the mechanics of recursion. These techniques are particularly useful for tracing and debug-ging recursive methods.

Some recursive solutions are far more elegant and concise than the best of their nonrecursive counterparts. For example, the classic Towers of Hanoi problem appears to be quite difficult, yet it has an extremely simple recursive solution. On the other hand, some recursive solutions are terribly inefficient, as you will see, and should not be used.

Chapter 5 continues the formal discussion of recursion by examining more-difficult problems. Recursion will play a major role in many of the solu-tions that appear throughout the remainder of this book.

RECURSIVE SOLUTIONS

Recursion is an extremely powerful problem-solving technique. Prob-lems that at first appear to be quite difficult often have simple recursive solutions. Like top-down design, recursion breaks a problem into several smaller problems. What is striking about recursion is that these smaller problems are of *exactly the same type* as the original problem—mirror images, so to speak.

Recursion breaks a problem into smaller identical problems

Did you ever hold a mirror in front of another mirror so that the two mirrors face each other? You will see many images of yourself, each behind and slightly smaller than the other. Recursion is like these mirror images. That is, a recursive solution solves a problem by solving a smaller instance of the same problem! It solves this new problem by solving an even smaller instance of the same problem. Eventually, the new problem will be so small that its solution will be either obvious or known. This solution will lead to the solution of the original problem.

For example, suppose that you could solve problem P_1 if you had the solution to problem P_2, which is a smaller instance of P_1. Suppose further that you could solve problem P_2 if you had the solution to problem P_3, which is a smaller instance of P_2. If you knew the solution to P_3 because it was small enough to be trivial, you would be able to solve P_2. You could then use the solution to P_2 to solve the original problem P_1.

Some recursion solutions are inefficient and impractical

Recursion can seem like magic, especially at first, but as you will see, it is a very real and important problem-solving approach that is an alter-native to **iteration**. An iterative solution involves loops. You should know at the outset that not all recursive solutions are better than itera-tive solutions. In fact, some recursive solutions are impractical because they are so inefficient. Recursion, however, can provide elegantly simple solutions to problems of great complexity.

Complex problems can have simple recursive solutions

As an illustration of the elements in a recursive solution, consider the problem of looking up a word in a dictionary. Suppose you wanted to look up the word "vademecum." Imagine starting at the beginning of the dictionary and looking at every word in order until you found "vade-mecum." That is precisely what a **sequential search** does, and, for obvious reasons, you want a faster way to perform the search.

One such method is the **binary search**, which in spirit is similar to the way in which you actually use a dictionary. You open the dictionary—probably to a point near its middle—and by glancing at the page, determine which "half" of the dictionary contains the desired word. The following pseudocode is a first attempt to formalize this process:

```
// Search a dictionary for a word by using a recursive
// binary search

  if (the dictionary contains only one page) {
    Scan the page for the word
  }
  else {
    Open the dictionary to a point near the middle
    Determine which half of the dictionary contains the
      word
    if (the word is in the first half of the dictionary) {
      Search the first half of the dictionary for the word
    }
    else {
      Search the second half of the dictionary for the word
    }  // end if
  }  // end if
```

A binary search of a dictionary

Parts of this solution are intentionally vague: How do you scan a single page? How do you find the middle of the dictionary? Once the middle is found, how do you determine which half contains the word? The answers to these questions are not difficult, but they will only obscure the solution strategy right now.

The previous search strategy reduces the problem of searching the dic-tionary for a word to a problem of searching half of the dictionary for the word, as Figure 2-1 illustrates. Notice two important points. First, once you have divided the dictionary in half, you already know how to search the appropriate half: You can use exactly the same strategy that you employed to search the original dictionary. Second, note that there is a special case that is different from all the other cases: After you have divided the dictionary so many times that you are left with only a single page, the halving ceases. At this point, the problem is sufficiently small that you can solve it directly by scanning the single page that remains for

Figure 2-1

A recursive solution

A base case is a special case whose solution you know

A binary search uses a divide-and-conquer strategy

the word. This special case is called the **base case** (or **basis** or **degenerate case**).

This strategy is one of **divide and conquer.** You solve the dictionary search problem by first *dividing* the dictionary into two halves and then *conquering* the appropriate half. You solve the smaller problem by using the same divide-and-conquer strategy. The dividing continues until you reach the base case. As you will see, this strategy is inherent in many recursive solutions.

To further explore the nature of the solution to the dictionary problem, consider a slightly more rigorous formulation.

```
search(theDictionary, aWord)

   if (theDictionary is one page in size) {
     Scan the page for aWord
   }
   else {
     Open theDictionary to a point near the middle
     Determine which half of theDictionary contains aWord

     if (aWord is in the first half of theDictionary) {
       search(first half of theDictionary, aWord)
     }
     else {
       search(second half of theDictionary, aWord)
     }  // end if
   }  // end if
```

Writing the solution as a method allows several important observations:

A recursive method calls itself

1. One of the actions of the method is to call itself; that is, the method `search` calls the method `search`. This action is what makes the solution recursive. The solution strategy is to split `theDictionary` in half, determine which half contains `aWord`, and apply the same strategy to the appropriate half.

Each recursive call solves an identical, but smaller, problem

2. Each call to the method `search` made from within the method `search` passes a dictionary that is one-half the size of the

previous dictionary. That is, at each successive call to `search` (`theDictionary`, `aWord`), the size of `theDictionary` is cut in half. The method solves the search problem by solving another search problem that is identical in nature but smaller in size.

3. There is one search problem that you handle differently from all of the others. When `theDictionary` contains only a single page, you use another technique: You scan the page directly. Searching a one-page dictionary is the base case of the search problem. When you reach the base case, the recursive calls stop and you solve the problem directly.

A test for the base case enables the recursive calls to stop

4. The manner in which the size of the problem diminishes ensures that you will eventually reach the base case.

Eventually, one of the smaller problems must be the base case

These facts describe the general form of a recursive solution. Though not all recursive solutions fit these criteria as nicely as this solution does, the similarities are far greater than the differences. As you attempt to construct a new recursive solution, you should keep in mind the following four questions:

KEY CONCEPTS

Four Questions for Constructing Recursive Solutions

1. How can you define the problem in terms of a smaller problem of the same type?
2. How does each recursive call diminish the size of the problem?
3. What instance of the problem can serve as the base case?
4. As the problem size diminishes, will you reach this base case?

Now consider two relatively simple problems: computing the factorial of a number and writing a string backward. Their recursive solutions further illustrate the points raised by the solution to the dictionary search problem. These examples also illustrate the difference between a recursive valued method and a recursive `void` method.

A Recursive Valued Method: The Factorial of n

Consider a recursive solution to the problem of computing the factorial of an integer n. This problem is a good first example because its recursive solution is easy to understand and neatly fits the mold described earlier. However, because the problem has a simple and efficient iterative solution, you should not use the recursive solution in practice.

Do not use recursion if a problem has a simple, efficient iterative solution

To begin, consider the familiar iterative definition of *factorial*(n) (more commonly written $n!$):

$$factorial(n) = n * (n - 1) * (n - 2) * \cdots * 1 \text{ for any integer } n > 0$$

$$factorial(0) = 1$$

An iterative definition of factorial

The factorial of a negative integer is undefined. You should have no trouble writing an iterative factorial method based on this definition.

To define *factorial(n)* recursively, you first need to define *factorial(n)* in terms of the factorial of a smaller number. To do so, simply observe that the factorial of *n* is equal to the factorial of *(n – 1)* multiplied by *n*; that is,

$$factorial(n) = n * [(n - 1) * (n - 2) * \cdots * 1]$$

A recurrence relation
$$= n * factorial(n - 1)$$

The definition of *factorial(n)* in terms of *factorial(n – 1)*, which is an example of a **recurrence relation**, implies that you can also define *factorial(n – 1)* in terms of *factorial(n – 2)*, and so on. This process is analogous to the dictionary search solution, in which you search a dictionary by searching a smaller dictionary in exactly the same way.

The definition of *factorial(n)* lacks one key element: the base case. As was done in the dictionary search solution, here you must define one case differently from all the others, or else the recursion will never stop. The base case for the factorial method is *factorial(0)*, which you know is 1. Because *n* originally is greater than or equal to zero and each call to *factorial* decrements *n* by 1, you will always reach the base case. With the addition of the base case, the complete recursive definition of the factorial method is

A recursive definition of factorial
$$factorial(n) = \begin{cases} 1 & \text{if } n = 0 \\ n * factorial(n - 1) & \text{if } n > 0 \end{cases}$$

To be sure that you understand this recursive definition, apply it to the computation of *factorial(4)*. Since 4 > 0, the recursive definition states that

$$factorial(4) = 4 * factorial(3)$$

Similarly,

$$factorial(3) = 3 * factorial(2)$$

$$factorial(2) = 2 * factorial(1)$$

$$factorial(1) = 1 * factorial(0)$$

You have reached the base case, and the definition directly states that

$$factorial(0) = 1$$

At this point, the application of the recursive definition stops and you still do not know the answer to the original question: What is *factorial(4)*? However, the information to answer this question is now available:

Since *factorial(0)* = 1, then *factorial(1)* = 1 * 1 = 1
Since *factorial(1)* = 1, then *factorial(2)* = 2 * 1 = 2
Since *factorial(2)* = 2, then *factorial(3)* = 3 * 2 = 6
Since *factorial(3)* = 6, then *factorial(4)* = 4 * 6 = 24

You can think of recursion as a process that divides a problem into a task that you can do and a task that a friend can do for you. For example, if I ask you to compute *factorial*(4), you could first determine whether you know the answer immediately. You know immediately that *factorial*(0) is 1—that is, you know the base case—but you do not know the value of *factorial*(4) immediately. However, if your friend computes *factorial*(3) for you, you could compute *factorial*(4) by multiplying *factorial*(3) by 4. Thus, your task will be to do this multiplication, and your friend's task will be to compute *factorial*(3).

Your friend now uses the same process to compute *factorial*(3) as you are using to compute *factorial*(4). Thus, your friend determines that *factorial*(3) is not the base case, and so asks another friend to compute *factorial*(2). Knowing *factorial*(2) enables your friend to compute *factorial*(3), and when you learn the value of *factorial*(3) from your friend, you can compute *factorial*(4).

Notice that the recursive definition of *factorial*(4) yields the same result as the iterative definition, which gives $4 * 3 * 2 * 1 = 24$. To prove that the two definitions of *factorial* are equivalent for all nonnegative integers, you would use **mathematical induction.** (See Appendix D.) Chapter 5 discusses the close tie between recursion and mathematical induction.

The recursive definition of the factorial method has illustrated two points: (1) *Intuitively*, you can define *factorial*(n) in terms of *factorial*(n – 1), and (2) *mechanically*, you can apply the definition to determine the value of a given factorial. Even in this simple example, applying the recursive definition required quite a bit of work. That, of course, is where the computer comes in.

Once you have a recursive definition of *factorial*(n), it is easy to construct a Java method that implements the definition:

```java
public static int fact(int n) {
// ----------------------------------------------------
// Computes the factorial of a nonnegative integer.
// Precondition: n must be greater than or equal to 0.
// Postcondition: Returns the factorial of n.
// ----------------------------------------------------
   if (n == 0) {
     return 1;
   }
   else {
     return n * fact(n-1);
   } // end if
} // end fact
```

Suppose that you use the statement

```java
System.out.println(fact(3));
```

to call the method. Figure 2-2 depicts the sequence of computations that this call would require.

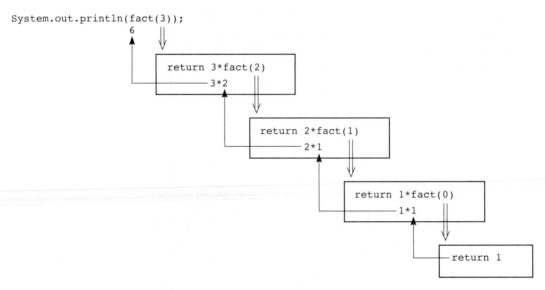

Figure 2-2

fact(3)

Note that the *fact* method is defined as **static**. This means that *fact* is a class method; it is invoked independently of any instance of the class that contains *fact*. Instances of the class share the *fact* method, and if the static method is public, other objects can access it through the class name. For example, *java.lang.Math.sqrt* provides access to the static method *sqrt* contained in the class *java.lang.Math*. Methods that don't need access to instance variables and are self-contained (except for parameter input) are good candidates to be designated as static methods. For this reason, all of the recursive methods in this chapter are declared *static*.

The *fact* method fits the model of a recursive solution given earlier in this chapter as follows:

fact satisfies the four criteria of a recursive solution

1. One action of *fact* is to *call itself*.

2. At each recursive call to *fact*, the integer whose factorial you need to compute is *diminished by 1*.

3. The method handles the factorial of 0 differently from all the other factorials: It does not generate a recursive call. Rather, you know that *fact(0)* is 1. Thus, the *base case* occurs when *n* is 0.

4. Given that *n* is nonnegative, item 2 of this list assures you that you will always *reach the base case*.

At an intuitive level, it should be clear that the method *fact* implements the recursive definition of *factorial*. Now consider the mechanics of executing this recursive method. The logic of *fact* is straightforward except perhaps for the expression in the *else* clause. This expression has the following effect:

1. Each operand of the product *n* * *fact(n-1)* is evaluated.

2. The second operand—*fact(n-1)*—is a call to the method *fact*. Although this is a recursive call (the method *fact* calls the method *fact*), there really is nothing special about it. Imagine substituting a call to another method—the Java API method *java.lang.Math.abs*, for example—for the recursive call to *fact*. The principle is the same: Simply evaluate the method.

In theory, evaluating a recursive method is no more difficult than evaluating a nonrecursive method. In practice, however, the bookkeeping can quickly get out of hand. The **box trace** is a systematic way to trace the actions of a recursive method. You can use the box trace both to help you to understand recursion and to debug recursive methods. However, such a mechanical device is no substitute for an intuitive understanding of recursion. The box trace illustrates how compilers frequently implement recursion. As you read the following description of the method, realize that each box roughly corresponds to an **activation record**, which a compiler typically uses in its implementation of a method call. Chapter 6 will discuss this implementation further.

An activation record is created for each method call

The box trace.   The box trace is illustrated here for the recursive method *fact*. As you will see in the next section, this trace is somewhat simpler for a *void* method, as no value needs to be returned.

1. Label each recursive call in the body of the recursive method. Several recursive calls might occur within a method, and it will be important to distinguish among them. These labels help you to keep track of the correct place to which you must return after a method call completes. For example, mark the expression *fact(n-1)* within the body of the method with the letter A:

```
if (n == 0) {
  return 1;
}
else {
  return n * fact(n-1);
} // end if        Ⓐ
```

Label each recursive call in the method

You return to point A after each recursive call, substitute the computed value for *fact(n-1)*, and continue execution by evaluating the expression *n * fact(n-1)*.

2. Represent each call to the method during the course of execution by a new box in which you note the method's **local environment**. More specifically, each box will contain

Each time a method is called, a new box represents its local environment

   a. The values of the references and primitive types of the method's arguments.

   b. The method's local variables.

   c. A placeholder for the value returned by each recursive call from the current box. Label this placeholder to correspond to the labeling in Step 1.

   d. The value of the method itself.

```
n = 3
A: fact(n-1) = ?
return ?
```

Figure 2-3

A box

When you first create a box, you will know only the values of the input arguments. You fill in the values of the other items as you determine them from the method's execution. For example, you would create the box in Figure 2-3 for the call `fact(3)`. (You will see in later examples that you must handle reference arguments [objects] somewhat differently from value arguments [primitive types] and local variables.)

3. Draw an arrow from the statement that initiates the recursive process to the first box. Then, when you create a new box after a recursive call, as described in Step 2, you draw an arrow from the box that makes the call to the newly created box. Label each arrow to correspond to the label (from Step 1) of the recursive call; this label indicates exactly where to return after the call completes. For example, Figure 2-4 shows the first two boxes generated by the call to `fact` in the statement `System.out.println(fact(3))`.

4. After you create the new box and arrow as described in Steps 2 and 3, start executing the body of the method. Each reference to an item in the method's local environment references the corresponding value in the current box, regardless of how you generated the current box.

5. On exiting the method, cross off the current box and follow its arrow back to the box that called the method. This box now becomes the current box, and the label on the arrow specifies the exact location at which execution of the method should continue. Substitute the value returned by the just-terminated method call into the appropriate item in the current box.

Figure 2-5 is a complete box trace for the call `fact(3)`. In the sequence of diagrams in this figure, the current box is the deepest along the path of arrows and is shaded, whereas crossed-off boxes have a dashed outline.

Invariants.   Writing invariants for recursive methods is as important as writing them for iterative methods, and is often simpler. For example, consider the recursive method *fact*:

```
public static int fact(int n) {
// Precondition: n must be greater than or equal to 0.
// Postcondition: Returns the factorial of n.
  if (n == 0) {
   return 1;
  }
  else { // Invariant: n > 0, so n-1 >= 0.
        // Thus, fact(n-1) returns (n-1)!
     return n * fact(n-1);  // n * (n-1)! is n!
  } // end if
}  // end fact
```

```
System.out.println(fact(3));
```

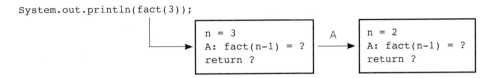

Figure 2-4

The beginning of the box trace

The method requires as its precondition a nonnegative value of *n*. At the time of the recursive call `fact(n-1)`, *n* is positive, so *n* – 1 is nonnegative. Since the recursive call satisfies `fact`'s precondition, you can expect from the postcondition that `fact(n-1)` will return the factorial of *n* – 1. Therefore, `n * fact(n-1)` is the factorial of *n*. Chapter 5 uses mathematical induction to prove formally that `fact(n)` returns the factorial of *n*.

Expect a recursive call's postcondition to be true if the precondition is true

If you ever violated `fact`'s precondition, the method would not behave correctly. That is, if the calling program ever passed a negative value to `fact`, an infinite sequence of recursive calls, terminated only by a system-defined limit, would occur because the method would never reach the base case. For example, `fact(-4)` would call `fact(-5)`, which would call `fact(-6)`, and so on.

Violating `fact`'s precondition causes "infinite" recursion

Figure 2-5

Box trace of `fact(3)`

The initial call is made, and method `fact` begins execution:

```
n = 3
A: fact(n-1)=?
return ?
```

At point A a recursive call is made, and the new invocation of the method `fact` begins execution:

At point A a recursive call is made, and the new invocation of the method `fact` begins execution:

```
n = 3              A    n = 2              A    n = 1
A: fact(n-1)=?   ----->  A: fact(n-1)=?   ----->  A: fact(n-1)=?
return ?                 return ?                 return ?
```

At point A a recursive call is made, and the new invocation of the method `fact` begins execution:

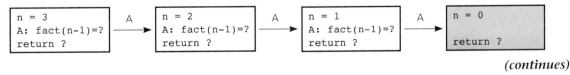

(continues)

Figure 2-5

(continued)

This is the base case, so this invocation of `fact` completes:

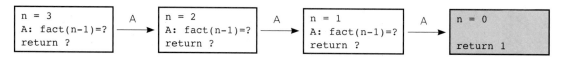

The method value is returned to the calling box, which continues execution:

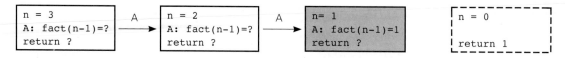

The current invocation of `fact` completes:

```
n = 3          A   n = 2          A   n = 1              n = 0
A: fact(n-1)=?  →  A: fact(n-1)=?  →  A: fact(n-1)=1     A: fact(n-1)=1
return ?           return ?           return 1           return 1
```

The method value is returned to the calling box, which continues execution:

```
n = 3          A   n = 2             n = 1              n = 0
A: fact(n-1)=?  →  A: fact(n-1)=1     A: fact(n-1)=1     A: fact(n-1)=1
return ?           return ?           return 1           return 1
```

The current invocation of `fact` completes:

```
n = 3          A   n = 2             n = 1              n = 0
A: fact(n-1)=?  →  A: fact(n-1)=1     A: fact(n-1)=1     A: fact(n-1)=1
return ?           return 2           return 1           return 1
```

The method value is returned to the calling box, which continues execution:

```
n = 3             n = 2              n = 1              n = 0
A: fact(n-1)=2     A: fact(n-1)=1     A: fact(n-1)=1     A: fact(n-1)=1
return ?           return 2           return 1           return 1
```

The current invocation `fact` completes:

```
n = 3             n = 2              n = 1              n = 0
A: fact(n-1)=2     A: fact(n-1)=1     A: fact(n-1)=1     A: fact(n-1)=1
return 6           return 2           return 1           return 1
```

The value 6 is returned to the initial call.

The method ideally should protect itself by testing for a negative *n*. If *n* < 0, the method could, for example, either return zero to indicate an error or throw an exception. Chapter 1 discussed error checking in the two sections "Fail-Safe Programming" and "Style"; you might want to review that discussion at this time.

A Recursive `void` Method: Writing a String Backward

Now consider a problem that is slightly more difficult: Given a string of characters, write it in reverse order. For example, write the string "cat" as "tac". To construct a recursive solution, you should ask the four questions in the Key Concepts box on page 51.

You can construct a solution to the problem of writing a string of length *n* backward in terms of the problem of writing a string of length *n* – 1 backward. That is, each recursive step of the solution diminishes by 1 the length of the string to be written backward. The fact that the strings get shorter and shorter suggests that the problem of writing some very short strings backward can serve as the base case. One very short string is the empty string, the string of length zero. Thus, you can choose for the base case the problem

> `Write the empty string backward`

The base case

The solution to this problem is to do nothing at all—a very straightforward solution indeed! (Alternatively, you could use the string of length 1 as the base case.)

Exactly how can you use the solution to the problem of writing a string of length *n* – 1 backward to solve the problem of writing a string of length *n* backward? This approach is analogous to the one used to construct the solution to the factorial problem, where you specified how to use *factorial*(*n* – 1) in the computation of *factorial*(*n*). Unlike the factorial problem, however, the string problem does not suggest an immediately clear way to proceed. Obviously, not any string of length *n* – 1 will do. For example, there is no relation between writing "apple" (a string of length 5) backward and writing "pear" (a string of length 4) backward. You must choose the smaller problem carefully so that you can use its solution in the solution to the original problem.

How can you write an n-character string backward, if you can write an (n – 1)-character string backward?

The string of length *n* – 1 that you choose must be a substring (part) of the original string. Suppose that you strip away one character from the original string, leaving a substring of length *n* – 1. For the recursive solution to be valid, the ability to write the substring backward, combined with the ability to perform some minor task, must result in the ability to write the original string backward. Compare this approach with the way you computed *factorial* recursively: The ability to compute *factorial*(*n* – 1), combined with the ability to multiply this value by *n*, resulted in the ability to compute *factorial*(*n*).

You need to decide which character to strip away and which minor task to perform. Consider the minor task first. Since you are writing characters, a likely candidate for the minor task is writing a single character.

As for the character that you should strip away from the string, there are several possible alternatives. Two of the more intuitive alternatives are

> `Strip away the last character`

or

> `Strip away the first character`

Consider the first of these alternatives, stripping away the last character, as Figure 2-6 illustrates.

For the solution to be valid, you must write the last character in the string first. Therefore, you must write the last character before you write the remainder of the string backward. A high-level recursive solution, given the string *s*, is

writeBackward writes a string backward

```
writeBackward(s)

    if (the string s is empty) {
       Do nothing -- this is the base case
    }
    else {
       Write the last character of s
       writeBackward(s minus its last character)
    }  // end if
```

This solution to the problem is conceptual. To obtain a Java method, you must resolve a few implementation issues. Suppose that the method will receive two arguments: a string *s* to be written backward and an integer *size* that specifies the length of the string. To simplify matters, you can assume that the string begins at position 0 and ends at position *size* – 1. That is, all characters, including blanks, in that range are part of the string. The Java method *writeBackward* appears as follows:

```
public static void writeBackward(String s, int size) {
// -----------------------------------------------------
// Writes a character string backward.
// Precondition: The string s contains size
// characters, where size >= 0.
// Postcondition: s is written backward, but remains
// unchanged.
// -----------------------------------------------------
```

Figure 2-6

A recursive solution

```
    if (size > 0) {
      // write the last character
      System.out.println(s.substring(size-1, size));

      // write the rest of the string backward
      writeBackward(s, size-1);  // Point A
    }  // end if
    // size == 0 is the base case - do nothing
  }  // end writeBackward
```

Notice that the recursive calls to *writeBackward* use successively smaller values of *size*. This decrease in *size* has the effect of stripping away the last character of the string and ensures that the base case will be reached.

You can trace the execution of *writeBackward* by using the box trace. As was true for the method *fact*, each box contains the local environment of the recursive call—in this case, the input arguments *s* and *size*. The trace will differ somewhat from the trace of *fact* shown in Figure 2-5 because, as a *void* method, *writeBackward* does not use a *return* statement to return a computed value. Figure 2-7 traces the call to the method *writeBackward* with the string "cat".

writeBackward does not return a computed value

Now consider a slightly different approach to the problem. Recall the two alternatives for the character that you could strip away from the string: the last character or the first character. The solution just given strips away the last character of the string. It will now be interesting to construct a solution based on the second alternative:

```
Strip away the first character
```

To begin, consider a simple modification of the previous pseudocode solution that replaces each occurrence of "last" with "first." Thus, the method writes the first character rather than the last and then recursively writes the remainder of the string backward.

```
writeBackward1(s)

  if (the string s is empty) {
    Do nothing -- this is the base case
  }
  else {
    Write the first character of s
    writeBackward1(s minus its first character)
  }  // end if
```

Does this solution do what you want it to? If you think about this method, you will realize that it writes the string in its normal left-to-right direction instead of backward. After all, the steps in the pseudocode are

```
Write the first character of s
Write the rest of s
```

The initial call is made, and the method begins execution:

```
s = "cat"
size = 3
```

Output line: **t**

Point A (`writeBackward(s, size-1)`) is reached, and the recursive call is made.

The new invocation begins execution:

Output line: **ta**

Point A is reached, and the recursive call is made.

The new invocation begins execution:

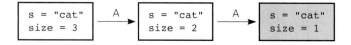

Output line: **tac**

Point A is reached, and the recursive call is made.

The new invocation begins execution:

This is the base case, so this invocation completes.

Control returns to the calling box, which continues execution:

This invocation completes. Control returns to the calling box, which continues execution:

```
s = "cat"     A     s = "cat"        s = "cat"        s = "cat"
size = 3    ----->  size = 2         size = 1         size = 0
```

This invocation completes. Control returns to the calling box, which continues execution:

```
s = "cat"        s = "cat"        s = "cat"        s = "cat"
size = 3         size = 2         size = 1         size = 0
```

This invocation completes. Control returns to the statement following the initial call.

Figure 2-7

Box trace of `writeBackward("cat", 3)`

These steps simply write the string *s*. Naming the method *write-Backward1* does not guarantee that it will actually write the string backward—recursion really is not magic!

You can write *s* backward correctly by using the following recursive formulation:

```
Write string s minus its first character backward
Write the first character of string s
```

In other words, you write the first character of *s* only *after* you have written the rest of *s* backward. This approach leads to the following pseudocode solution:

```
writeBackward2(s)

    if (the string s is empty) {
        Do nothing -- this is the base case
    }
    else {
        writeBackward2(s minus its first character)
        Write the first character of s
    } // end if
```

writeBackward2 writes a string backward

The translation of *writeBackward2* into Java is similar to that of the original *writeBackward* method and is left as an exercise.

It is instructive to carefully trace the actions of the two pseudocode methods *writeBackward* and *writeBackward2*. First, add statements to each method to provide output that is useful to the trace, as follows:

```
writeBackward(s)

  System.out.println("Enter writeBackward, string: " + s );
  if (the string s is empty) {
    Do nothing -- this is the base case
  }
  else {
    System.out.println("About to write last character of " +
                    "string: " + s);
    Write the last character of s
    writeBackward(s minus its last character)  // Point A
  } // end if
  System.out.println("Leave writeBackward, string: " + s);
```

System.out.println statements can help you trace the logic of a recursive method

```
writeBackward2(s)

    System.out.println("Enter writeBackward2, string: " + s);
    if (the string s is empty) {
        Do nothing -- this is the base case
    }
    else {
        writeBackward2(s minus its first character) // Point A
        System.out.println("About to write first character of" +
                           "string: " + s);
        Write the first character of s
    } // end if
    System.out.println("Leave writeBackward2, string: " + s);
```

Figures 2-8 and 2-9 show the output of the revised pseudocode methods *writeBackward* and *writeBackward2*, when initially given the string "cat".

Figure 2-8

Box trace of ***writeBack-ward("cat",3)*** in pseudocode

The initial call is made, and the method begins execution:

Output stream:

```
Enter writeBackward, string: cat
About to write last character of string: cat
t
```

Point A is reached, and the recursive call is made. The new invocation begins execution:

```
s = "cat"    A ───▶    s = "ca"
```

Output stream:

```
Enter writeBackward, string: cat
About to write last character of string: cat
t
Enter writeBackward, string: ca
About to write last character of string: ca
a
```

Point A is reached, and the recursive call is made. The new invocation begins execution:

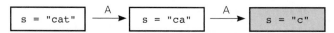

Output stream:

```
Enter writeBackward, string: cat
About to write last character of string: cat
t
Enter writeBackward, string: ca
About to write last character of string: ca
a
Enter writeBackward, string: c
About to write last character of string: c
c
```

Point A is reached, and the recursive call is made. The new invocation begins execution:

Figure 2-8

(continued)

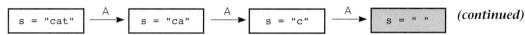

This invocation completes execution, and a return is made.

Output stream:

```
Enter writeBackward, string: cat
About to write last character of string: cat
t
Enter writeBackward, string: ca
About to write last character of string: ca
a
Enter writeBackward, string: c
About to write last character of string: c
c
Enter writeBackward, string:
Leave writeBackward, string:
```

This invocation completes execution, and a return is made.

Output stream:

```
Enter writeBackward, string: cat
About to write last character of string: cat
t
Enter writeBackward, string: ca
About to write last character of string: ca
a
Enter writeBackward, string: c
About to write last character of string: c
c
Enter writeBackward, string:
Leave writeBackward, string:
Leave writeBackward, string: c
```

This invocation completes execution, and a return is made.

Output stream:

```
Enter writeBackward, string: cat
About to write last character of string: cat
t
Enter writeBackward, string: ca
About to write last character of string: ca
a
Enter writeBackward, string: c
About to write last character of string: c
c
Enter writeBackward, string:
Leave writeBackward, string:
Leave writeBackward, string: c
Leave writeBackward, string: ca
```

(continues)

Figure 2-8
(continued)

```
  s = "cat"           s = "ca"           s = "c"           s = " "
```

This invocation completes execution, and a return is made.

Output stream:

```
    Enter writeBackward, string: cat
    About to write last character of string: cat
    t
    Enter writeBackward, string: ca
    About to write last character of string: ca
    a
    Enter writeBackward, string: c
    About to write last character of string: c
    c
    Enter writeBackward, string:
    Leave writeBackward, string:
    Leave writeBackward, string: c
    Leave writeBackward, string: ca
    Leave writeBackward, string: cat
```

Figure 2-9

Box trace of
writeBack-
ward2("cat",3)
in pseudocode

The initial call is made, and the method begins execution:

```
  s = "cat"
```

Output stream:

```
    Enter writeBackward2, string: cat
```

Point A is reached, and the recursive call is made. The new invocation begins execution:

Output stream:

```
    Enter writeBackward2, string: cat
    Enter writeBackward2, string: at
```

Point A is reached, and the recursive call is made. The new invocation begins execution:

```
  s = "cat"   --A-->   s = "at"   --A-->   s = "t"
```

Output stream:

```
    Enter writeBackward2, string: cat
    Enter writeBackward2, string: at
    Enter writeBackward2, string: t
```

Point A is reached, and the recursive call is made. The new invocation begins execution:

This invocation completes execution, and a return is made.

Output stream:

```
Enter writeBackward2, string: cat
Enter writeBackward2, string: at
Enter writeBackward2, string: t
Enter writeBackward2, string:
Leave writeBackward2, string:
```

This invocation completes execution, and a return is made.

Output stream:

```
Enter writeBackward2, string: cat
Enter writeBackward2, string: at
Enter writeBackward2, string: t
Enter writeBackward2, string:
Leave writeBackward2, string:
About to write first character of string: t
t
Leave writeBackward2, string: t
```

This invocation completes execution, and a return is made.

Output stream:

```
Enter writeBackward2, string: cat
Enter writeBackward2, string: at
Enter writeBackward2, string: t
Enter writeBackward2, string:
Leave writeBackward2, string:
About to write first character of string: t
t
Leave writeBackward2, string: t
About to write first character of string: at
a
Leave writeBackward2, string: at
```

This invocation completes execution, and a return is made.

Output stream:

```
Enter writeBackward2, string: cat
Enter writeBackward2, string: at
Enter writeBackward2, string: t
Enter writeBackward2, string:
Leave writeBackward2, string:
About to write first character of string: t
t
```

Figure 2-9
(continued)

(continues)

Figure 2-9
(continued)

```
Leave writeBackward2, string: t
About to write first character of string: at
a
Leave writeBackward2, string: at
About to write first character of string: cat
c
Leave writeBackward2, string: cat
```

You need to be comfortable with the differences between these two methods. The recursive calls that the two methods make generate a different sequence of values for the argument s. Despite this fact, both methods correctly write the string argument backward. They compensate for the difference in the sequence of values for s by writing different characters in the string at different times relative to the recursive calls. In terms of the box traces in Figures 2-8 and 2-9, *writeBackward* writes a character just before generating a new box (just before a new recursive call), whereas *writeBackward2* writes a character just after crossing off a box (just after returning from a recursive call). When these differences are put together, the result is two methods that employ different strategies to accomplish the same task.

This example also illustrates the value of the box trace, combined with well-placed *System.out.println* statements, in debugging recursive methods. The *System.out.println* statements at the beginning, interior, and end of the recursive methods report the value of the argument s. In general, when debugging a recursive method, you should also report both the values of local variables and the point in the method where each recursive call occurred, as in this example:

```
abc(...)

    System.out.println("Calling abc from point A.");
    abc(...)   // this is point A

    System.out.println("Calling abc from point B.");
    abc(... )  // this is point B
```

Well-placed but temporary
System.out.println
statements can help you to
debug a recursive method

Realize that the *System.out.println* statements do not belong in the final version of the method.

Remove System.out.
println statements after you
have debugged the method

COUNTING THINGS

The next three problems require you to count certain events or combinations of events or things. They are good examples of problems with more than one base case. They also provide good examples of tremendously inefficient recursive solutions. Do not let this inefficiency discourage you. Your goal right now is to understand recursion by examining simple problems. Soon you will see useful and efficient recursive solutions.

Multiplying Rabbits (The Fibonacci Sequence)

Rabbits are very prolific breeders. If rabbits did not die, their population would quickly get out of hand. Suppose we assume the following "facts," which were obtained in a recent survey of randomly selected rabbits:

- Rabbits never die.

- A rabbit reaches sexual maturity exactly two months after birth, that is, at the beginning of its third month of life.

- Rabbits are always born in male-female pairs. At the beginning of every month, each sexually mature male-female pair gives birth to exactly one male-female pair.

Suppose you started with a single newborn male-female pair. How many pairs would there be in month 6, counting the births that took place at the beginning of month 6? Since 6 is a relatively small number, you can figure out the solution easily:

Month 1:	1 pair, the original rabbits.
Month 2:	1 pair still, since it is not yet sexually mature.
Month 3:	2 pairs; the original pair has reached sexual maturity and has given birth to a second pair.
Month 4:	3 pairs; the original pair has given birth again, but the pair born at the beginning of month 3 is not yet sexually mature.
Month 5:	5 pairs; all rabbits alive in month 3 (2 pairs) are now sexually mature. Add their offspring to those pairs alive in month 4 (3 pairs) to yield 5 pairs.
Month 6:	8 pairs; 3 newborn pairs from the pairs alive in month 4 plus 5 pairs alive in month 5.

You can now construct a recursive solution for computing *rabbit*(n), the number of pairs alive in month n. You must determine how you can use *rabbit*(n – 1) to compute *rabbit*(n). Observe that *rabbit*(n) is the sum of the number of pairs alive just prior to the start of month n and the number of pairs born at the start of month n. Just prior to the start of month n, there are *rabbit*(n – 1) pairs of rabbits. Not all of these rabbits are sexually mature at the start of month n. Only those who were alive in month n – 2 are ready to reproduce at the start of month n. That is, the number of pairs born at the start of month n is *rabbit*(n – 2). Therefore, you have the recurrence relation

$$rabbit(n) = rabbit(n - 1) + rabbit(n - 2)$$

Figure 2-10 illustrates this relationship.

This recurrence relation introduces a new point. In some cases, you solve a problem by solving more than one smaller problem of the same type. This change does not add much conceptual difficulty, but you must be very careful when selecting the base case. The temptation is simply to

Figure 2-10

**Recursive solution to the
rabbit problem**

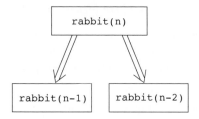

say that *rabbit*(1) should be the base case because its value is 1 according
to the problem's statement. But what about *rabbit*(2)? Applying the
recursive definition to *rabbit*(2) would yield

$$rabbit(2) = rabbit(1) + rabbit(0)$$

Thus, the recursive definition would need to specify the number of pairs
alive in month 0—an undefined quantity.

One possible solution is to define *rabbit*(0) to be 0, but this approach
seems artificial. A slightly more attractive alternative is to treat *rabbit*(2)
itself as a special case with the value of 1. Thus, the recursive definition has
two base cases, *rabbit*(2) and *rabbit*(1). The recursive definition becomes

*Two base cases are necessary
because there are two smaller
problems of the same type*

$$rabbit(n) = \begin{cases} 1 & \text{if } n \text{ is 1 or 2} \\ rabbit(n-1) + rabbit(n-2) & \text{if } n > 2 \end{cases}$$

Incidentally, the series of numbers *rabbit*(1), *rabbit*(2), *rabbit*(3), and so on
is known as the **Fibonacci sequence**, which models many naturally occur-
ring phenomena.

A Java method to compute *rabbit*(n) is easy to write from the previous definition:

*rabbit computes the Fibonacci
sequence but does
so inefficiently*

```
public static int rabbit(int n) {
// ------------------------------------------------------
// Computes a term in the Fibonacci sequence.
// Precondition: n is a positive integer.
// Postcondition: Returns the nth Fibonacci number.
// ------------------------------------------------------
   if (n <= 2) {
      return 1;
   }
   else  { // n > 2, so n-1 > 0 and n-2 > 0
      return rabbit(n-1) + rabbit(n-2);
   } // end if
} // end rabbit
```

Should you actually use this method? Figure 2-11 illustrates the recursive calls that `rabbit(7)` generates. Think about the number of recursive
calls that `rabbit(10)` generates. At best, the method `rabbit` is inefficient. Thus, its use is not feasible for large values of *n*. This problem is
discussed in more detail at the end of this chapter, at which time you
will see some techniques for generating a more efficient solution from
this same recursive relationship.

Figure 2-11

The recursive calls
that *rabbit(7)*
generates

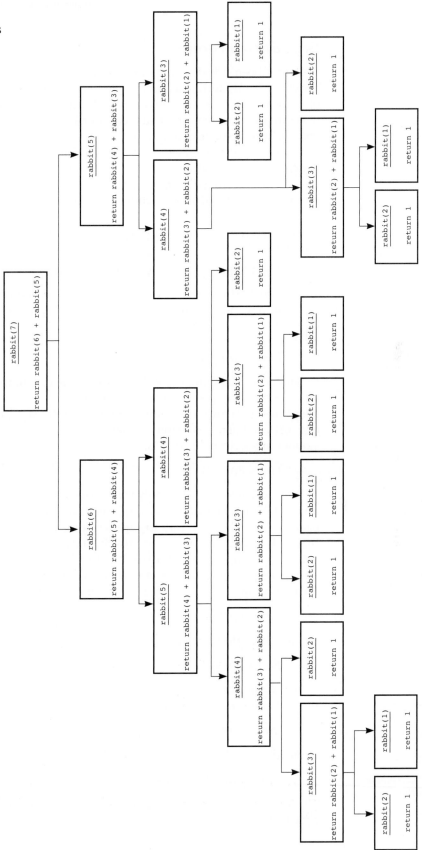

Organizing a Parade

You have been asked to organize the Fourth of July parade, which will consist of bands and floats in a single line. Last year, adjacent bands tried to outplay each other. To avoid this problem, the sponsors have asked you never to place one band immediately after another. In how many ways can you organize a parade of length n?

Assume that you have at least n marching bands and n floats from which to choose. When counting the number of ways to organize the parade, assume that the sequences *band-float* and *float-band*, for example, are different entities and count as two ways.

The parade can end with either a float or a band. The number of ways to organize the parade is simply the sum of the number of parades of each type. That is, let

$P(n)$ be the number of ways to organize a parade of length n

$F(n)$ be the number of parades of length n that end with a float

$B(n)$ be the number of parades of length n that end with a band

Then

$$P(n) = F(n) + B(n)$$

First, consider $F(n)$. You will have a parade of length n that ends with a float simply by placing a float at the end of *any* acceptable parade of length $n - 1$. Hence, the number of acceptable parades of length n that end with a float is precisely equal to the total number of acceptable parades of length $n - 1$; that is,

The number of acceptable parades of length n that end with a float

$$F(n) = P(n - 1)$$

Next, consider $B(n)$. The only way a parade can end with a band is if the unit just before the end is a float. (If it is a band, you will have two adjacent bands.) Thus, the only way to organize an acceptable parade of length n that ends with a band is first to organize a parade of length $n - 1$ that ends with a float and then add a band to the end. Therefore, the number of acceptable parades of length n that end with a band is precisely equal to the number of acceptable parades of length $n - 1$ that end with a float:

The number of acceptable parades of length n that end with a band

$$B(n) = F(n - 1)$$

You use the earlier fact that $F(n) = P(n - 1)$ to obtain

$$B(n) = P(n - 2)$$

Thus, you have solved $F(n)$ and $B(n)$ in terms of the smaller problems $P(n - 1)$ and $P(n - 2)$, respectively. You then use

$$P(n) = F(n) + B(n)$$

to obtain

The number of acceptable parades of length n

$$P(n) = P(n - 1) + P(n - 2)$$

The form of this recurrence relation is identical to the solution for the multiplying rabbits problem.

As you saw in the rabbit problem, two base cases are necessary because the recurrence relation defines a problem in terms of two smaller problems. As you did for the rabbit problem, you can choose $n = 1$ and $n = 2$ for the base cases. Although both problems use the same n's for their base cases, there is no reason to expect that they use the same values for these base cases. That is, there is no reason to expect that *rabbit*(1) is equal to $P(1)$ and that *rabbit*(2) is equal to $P(2)$.

A little thought reveals that for the parade problem,

$P(1) = 2$ (The parades of length 1 are *float* and *band*.)

$P(2) = 3$ (The parades of length 2 are *float-float*, *band-float*, and
      float-band.)

Two base cases are necessary because there are two smaller problems of the same type

In summary, the solution to this problem is

$P(1) = 2$

$P(2) = 3$

$P(n) = P(n - 1) + P(n - 2)$ for $n > 2$

A recursive solution

This example demonstrates the following points about recursion:

- Sometimes you can solve a problem by breaking it up into cases—for example, parades that end with a float and parades that end with a band.

- The values that you use for the base cases are extremely important. Although the recurrence relations for P and *rabbit* are the same, the different values for their base cases ($n = 1$ or 2) cause different values for larger values of n. For example, *rabbit*(20) = 6,765, while $P(20) = 17,711$. The larger the value of n, the larger the discrepancy. You should think about why this is so.

Mr. Spock's Dilemma (Choosing k out of n Things)

The five-year mission of the *U.S.S. Enterprise* is to explore new worlds. The five years are almost up, but the *Enterprise* has just entered an unexplored solar system that contains n planets. Unfortunately, time will allow for visits to only k planets. Mr. Spock begins to ponder how many different choices are possible for exploring k planets out of the n planets in the solar system. Because time is short, he does not care about the order in which he visits the same k planets.

Mr. Spock is especially fascinated by one particular planet, Planet X. He begins to think—in terms of Planet X—about how to pick k planets out of the n. "There are two possibilities: Either we visit Planet X, or we do not visit Planet X. If we do visit Planet X, I will have to choose $k - 1$ other planets to visit from the $n - 1$ remaining planets. On the other hand, if we do not visit Planet X, I will have to choose k planets to visit from the remaining $n - 1$ planets."

Mr. Spock is on his way to a recursive method of counting how many groups of k planets he can possibly choose out of n. Let $c(n, k)$ be the number of groups of k planets chosen from n. Then, in terms of Planet X, Mr. Spock deduces that

$$c(n, k) = \text{(the number of groups of } k \text{ planets that include Planet } X)$$

$$+$$

$$\text{(the number of groups of } k \text{ planets that do not include Planet } X)$$

But Mr. Spock has already reasoned that the number of groups that include Planet X is $c(n - 1, k - 1)$, and the number of groups that do not include Planet X is $c(n - 1, k)$. Mr. Spock has figured out a way to solve his counting problem in terms of two smaller counting problems of the same type:

The number of ways to choose k out of n things is the sum of the number of ways to choose k – 1 out of n – 1 things and the number of ways to choose k out of n – 1 things

$$c(n, k) = c(n - 1, k - 1) + c(n - 1, k)$$

Mr. Spock now has to worry about the base case(s). He also needs to demonstrate that each of the two smaller problems eventually reaches a base case. First, what selection problem does he immediately know the answer to? If the *Enterprise* had time to visit all the planets (that is, if $k = n$), no decision would be necessary; there is only one group of all the planets. Thus, the first base case is

Base case: There is one group of everything

$$c(k, k) = 1$$

If $k < n$, it is easy to see that the second term in the recursive definition, $c(n - 1, k)$, is "closer" to the base case $c(k, k)$ than is $c(n, k)$. However, the first term, $c(n - 1, k - 1)$, is not closer to $c(k, k)$ than is $c(n, k)$—they are the same "distance" apart. *When you solve a problem by solving two (or more) smaller problems, each of the smaller problems must be closer to a base case than the original problem.*

Mr. Spock realizes that the first term does, in fact, approach another trivial selection problem. This problem is the counterpart of his first base case, $c(k, k)$. Just as there is only one group of all the planets ($k = n$), there is also only one group of zero planets ($k = 0$). When there is no time to visit any of the planets, the *Enterprise* must head home without any exploration. Thus, the second base case is

Base case: There is one group of nothing

$$c(n, 0) = 1$$

This base case does indeed have the property that $c(n - 1, k - 1)$ is closer to it than is $c(n, k)$. (Alternatively, you could define the second base case to be $c(n, 1) = n$.)

Mr. Spock adds one final part to his solution:

$$c(n, k) = 0 \quad \text{if } k > n$$

Although k could not be greater than n in the context of this problem, the addition of this case makes the recursive solution more generally applicable.

To summarize, the following recursive solution solves the problem of choosing k out of n things:

The number of groups of k things recursively chosen out of n things

$$c(n, k) = \begin{cases} 1 & \text{if } k = 0 \\ 1 & \text{if } k = n \\ 0 & \text{if } k > n \\ c(n - 1, k - 1) + c(n - 1, k) & \text{if } 0 < k < n \end{cases}$$

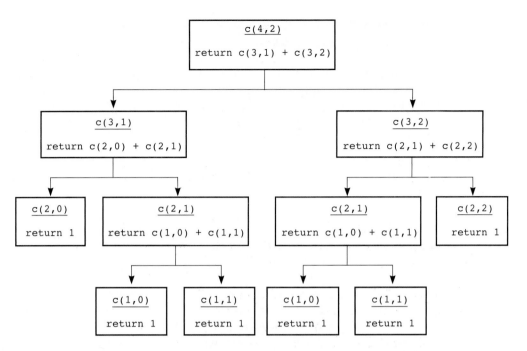

Figure 2-12

The recursive calls that c(4, 2) generates

You can easily derive the following method from this recursive definition:

```java
public static int c(int n, int k) {
// ------------------------------------------------------
// Computes the number of groups of k out of n things.
// Precondition: n and k are nonnegative integers.
// Postcondition: Returns c(n, k).
// ------------------------------------------------------
   if ( (k == 0) || (k == n) ) {
      return 1;
   }
   else if (k > n) {
      return 0;
   }
   else {
      return c(n-1, k-1) + c(n-1, k);
   }  // end if
}  // end c
```

Like the *rabbit* method, this method is inefficient and not practical to use. Figure 2-12 shows the number of recursive calls that the computation of c(4, 2) requires.

SEARCHING AN ARRAY

Searching is an important task that occurs frequently. This chapter began with an intuitive approach to a binary search algorithm. This section develops the binary search and examines other searching problems that have recursive solutions. The goal is to develop further your notion of recursion.

Finding the Largest Item in an Array

Suppose that you have an array *anArray* of integers and you want to find the largest one. You could construct an iterative solution without too much difficulty, but instead consider a recursive formulation:

```
if (anArray has only one item) {
    maxArray(anArray) is the item in anArray
}
else if (anArray has more than one item) {
    maxArray(anArray) is the maximum of
        maxArray(left half of anArray) and
        maxArray(right half of anArray)
}  // end if
```

Notice that this strategy fits the divide-and-conquer model that the binary search algorithm used at the beginning of this chapter. That is, the algorithm proceeds by dividing the problem and conquering the subproblems, as Figure 2-13 illustrates. However, there is a difference between this algorithm and the binary search algorithm. While the binary search algorithm conquers only one of its subproblems at each step, *maxArray* conquers both. In addition, after *maxArray* conquers the subproblems, it must reconcile the two solutions—that is, it must find the maximum of the two maximums. Figure 2-14 illustrates the computations that are necessary to find the largest integer in the array that contains 1, 6, 8, and 3 (denoted here by <1, 6, 8, 3>).

maxArray conquers both of its subproblems at each step

You should develop a recursive solution based on this strategy. In so doing, you may stumble on several subtle programming issues. The

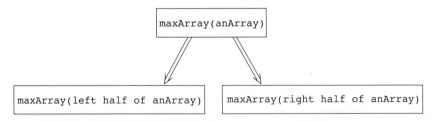

Figure 2-13

Recursive solution to the largest-item problem

binary search problem that follows raises virtually all of these issues, but this is a good opportunity for you to get some practice implementing a recursive solution.

Binary Search

The beginning of this chapter presented—at a high level—a recursive binary search algorithm for finding a word in a dictionary. We now develop this algorithm fully and illustrate some important programming issues.

Recall the earlier solution to the dictionary problem:

```
search(theDictionary, aWord)
  if (theDictionary is one page in size) {
    Scan the page for aWord
  }
  else {
    Open theDictionary to a point near the middle
    Determine which half of theDictionary contains
        aWord
    if (aWord is in first half of theDictionary) {
      search(first half of theDictionary, aWord)
    }
    else {
      search(second half of theDictionary, aWord)
    }  // end if
  }  // end if
```

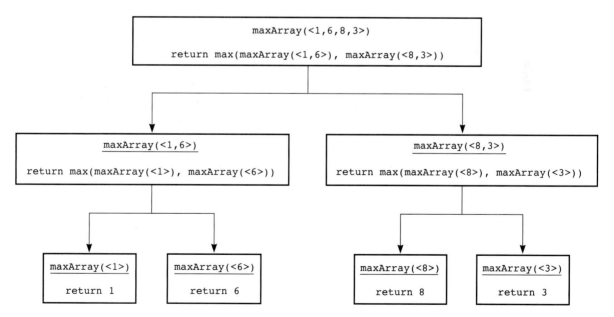

Figure 2-14

The recursive calls that *maxArray(<1,6,8,3>)* generates

Now alter the problem slightly by searching an array *anArray* of integers for a given value. The array, like the dictionary, must be sorted, or else a binary search is not applicable. Hence, assume that

An array must be sorted before you can apply a binary search to it

$$anArray[0] \leq anArray[1] \leq anArray[2] \leq \cdots \leq anArray[size-1]$$

where *size* is the size of the array. A high-level binary search for the array problem is

```
binarySearch(anArray, value)

  if (anArray is of size 1) {
    Determine if anArray's item is equal to value
  }
  else {
    Find the midpoint of anArray
    Determine which half of anArray contains value
    if (value is in the first half of anArray) {
      binarySearch(first half of anArray, value)
    }
    else {
      binarySearch(second half of anArray, value)
    }  // end if
  }  // end if
```

Although the solution is conceptually sound, you must consider several details before you can implement the algorithm:

1. **How will you pass "half of *anArray*" to the recursive calls to *binarySearch*?** You can pass the entire array at each call but have *binarySearch* search only *anArray[first..last]*,[1] that is, the portion *anArray[first]* through *anArray[last]*. Thus, you would also pass the integers *first* and *last* to *binarySearch*:

    binarySearch(anArray, first, last, value)

    With this convention, the new midpoint is given by

    mid = (first + last)/2

The array halves are **anArray [first..mid-1]** *and* **anArray[mid+1..last]**; *neither half contains* **anArray[mid]**

    Then *binarySearch(first half of anArray, value)* becomes

    binarySearch(anArray, first, mid-1, value)

    and *binarySearch(second half of anArray, value)* becomes

    binarySearch(anArray, mid+1, last, value)

---

[1] You will see this notation in the rest of the book to represent a portion of an array.

2. **How do you determine which half of the array contains value?** One possible implementation of

> **if** *(value is in the first half of anArray)*

is

> **if** *(value < anArray[mid])*

However, there is no test for equality between *value* and *anArray[mid]*. This omission can cause the algorithm to miss *value*. After the previous halving algorithm splits *anArray* into halves, *anArray[mid]* is not in either half of the array. (In this case, two halves do not make a whole!) Therefore, you must determine whether *anArray[mid]* is the value you seek *now* because later it will not be in the remaining half of the array. The interaction between the halving criterion and the termination condition (the base case) is subtle and is often a source of error. We need to rethink the base case.

Determine whether anArray[mid] is the value you seek

3. **What should the base case(s) be?** As it is written, *binarySearch* terminates only when an array of size 1 occurs; this is the only base case. By changing the halving process so that *anArray[mid] remains in one of the halves,* it is possible to implement the binary search correctly so that it has only this single base case. However, it can be clearer to have two distinct base cases as follows:

a. *first > last.* You will reach this base case when *value* is not in the original array.

Two base cases

b. *value == anArray[mid].* You will reach this base case when *value* is in the original array.

These base cases are a bit different from any you have encountered previously. In a sense, the algorithm determines the answer to the problem from the base case it reaches. Many search problems have this flavor.

4. **How will binarySearch indicate the result of the search?** If *binarySearch* successfully locates *value* in the array, it could return the index of the array item that is equal to *value*. Since this index would never be negative, *binarySearch* could return a negative value if it does not find *value* in the array.

The Java method *binarySearch* that follows implements these ideas. The two recursive calls to *binarySearch* are labeled as *X* and *Y* for use in a later box trace of this method.

```
public static int binarySearch(int anArray[], int first,
                               int last, int value) {
// Searches the array items anArray[first] through
// anArray[last] for value by using a binary search.
// Precondition: 0 <= first, last <= SIZE-1, where
// SIZE is the maximum size of the array, and
```

```
// anArray[first] <= anArray[first+1] <= ... <=
// anArray[last].
// Postcondition: If value is in the array, the method
// returns the index of the array item that equals value;
// otherwise the method returns -1.
  int index;
  if (first > last) {
    index = -1;          // value not in original array
  }
  else {
    // Invariant: If value is in anArray,
    //              anArray[first] <= value <= anArray[last]
    int mid = (first + last)/2;
    if (value == anArray[mid]) {
      index = mid;   // value found at anArray[mid]
    }

    else if (value < anArray[mid]) {
      // point X
      index = binarySearch(anArray, first, mid-1, value);
    }
    else {
      // point Y
      index = binarySearch(anArray, mid+1, last, value);
    }  // end if
  }  // end if

  return index;
}  // end binarySearch
```

Notice that *binarySearch* has the following invariant: If *value* occurs in the array, then *anArray[first]* $\leq$ *value* $\leq$ *anArray[last]*.

Figure 2-15 shows box traces of *binarySearch* when it searches the array containing 1, 5, 9, 12, 15, 21, 29, and 31. Notice how the labels *X* and *Y* of the two recursive calls to *binarySearch* appear in the diagram. Exercise 13 at the end of this chapter asks you to perform other box traces with this method.

There is another implementation issue—one that deals specifically with Java—to consider. Recall that an array is an object, and when the method *binarySearch* is called, only the reference to the array is copied to the method, not the entire array contents. This aspect of Java is particularly useful in a recursive method such as *binarySearch*. If the array *anArray* is large, many recursive calls to *binarySearch* may be necessary. If each call copied *anArray*, much memory and time would be wasted.

A box trace of a recursive method that has an array argument requires a new consideration. Because only the reference to *anArray* is passed and it is not a local variable, the contents of the array are not a part of the method's local environment and should not appear within each box.

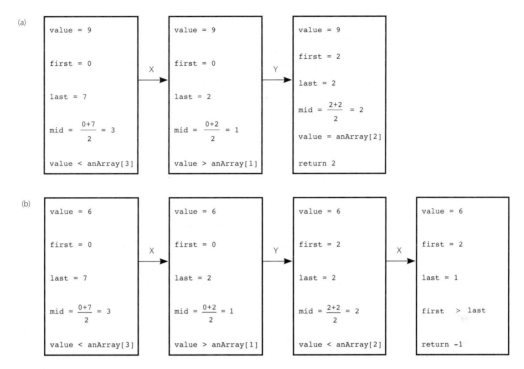

Figure 2-15

Box traces of *binarySearch* with *anArray* = <1,5,9,12,15,21,29,31>:
(a) a successful search for 9; (b) an unsuccessful search for 6

Therefore, as Figure 2-16 shows, you represent *anArray* outside the boxes, and all references to *anArray* affect this single representation.

Finding the kth Smallest Item in an Array

Our discussion of searching concludes with a more difficult problem. Although you could skip this example now, Chapter 9 uses aspects of it in a sorting algorithm.

The previous two examples presented recursive methods for finding the largest item in an arbitrary array and for finding an arbitrary item in a sorted array. This example describes a recursive solution for finding the kth smallest item in an arbitrary array *anArray*. Would you ever be interested in such an item? Statisticians often want the median value in a collection of data. The median value in an ordered collection of data occurs in the middle of the collection. In an unordered collection of data, there are about the same number of values smaller than the median value as there are larger values. Thus, if you have 49 items, the 25th smallest item is the median value.

Obviously, you could solve this problem by sorting the array. Then the kth smallest item would be *anArray[k-1]*. Although this approach is

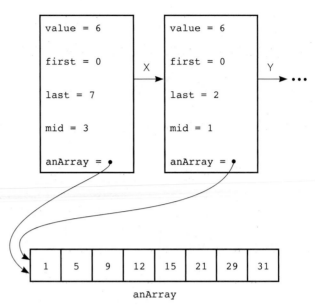

Figure 2-16

Box trace with a reference to an array

a legitimate solution, it does more than the problem requires; a more efficient solution is possible. The solution outlined here finds the kth smallest item without completely sorting the array.

By now, you know that you solve a problem recursively by writing its solution in terms of one or more smaller problems of the same type in such a way that this notion of *smaller* ensures that you will always reach a base case. For all of the earlier recursive solutions, the reduction in problem size between recursive calls is *predictable*. For example, the factorial method always decreases the problem size by 1; the binary search always halves the problem size. In addition, the base cases for all the previous problems except the binary search have a static, predefined size. Thus, by knowing only the size of the original problem, you can determine the number of recursive calls that are necessary before you reach the base case.

For all previous examples, you know the amount of reduction made in the problem size by each recursive call

The solution that you are about to see for finding the kth smallest item departs from these traditions. Although you solve the problem in terms of a smaller problem, just how much smaller this problem is depends on the items in the array and cannot be predicted in advance. Also, the size of the base case depends on the items in the array, as it did for the binary search. (Recall that you reach a base case for a binary search when the middle item is the one sought.)

You cannot predict in advance the size of either the smaller problems or the base case in the recursive solution to the kth smallest item problem

This "unpredictable" type of solution is caused by the nature of the problem: The relationship between the rankings of the items in any predetermined parts of the array and the ranking of the items in the entire array is not strong enough to determine the kth smallest item. For example, suppose that *anArray* contains the items shown in Figure 2-17.

Figure 2-17

A sample array

Notice that 6, which is in *anArray[3]*, is the third smallest item in the first half of *anArray* and that 8, which is in *anArray[4]*, is the third smallest item in the second half of *anArray*. Can you conclude from these observations anything about the location of the third smallest item in all of *anArray*? The answer is no; these facts about parts of the array do not allow you to draw any useful conclusions about the entire array. You should experiment with other fixed splitting schemes as well.

The recursive solution proceeds by

1. Selecting a **pivot item** in the array
2. Cleverly arranging, or **partitioning**, the items in the array about this pivot item
3. Recursively applying the strategy to *one* of the partitions

Consider the details of the recursive solution: You want to find the kth smallest item in the array segment *anArray[first..last]*. Let the pivot p be any item of the array segment. (For now, ignore how to choose p.) You can partition the items of *anArray[first..last]* into three regions: S_1, which contains the items less than p; the pivot p itself; and S_2, which contains the items greater than or equal to p. This partition implies that all the items in S_1 are smaller than all the items in S_2. Figure 2-18 illustrates this partition.

Partition anArray into three parts: items < p, p, and items ≥ p

All items in *anArray[first..pivotIndex-1]*, in terms of array subscripts, are less than p, and all items in *anArray[pivotIndex+1..last]* are greater than or equal to p. Notice that the sizes of the regions S_1 and S_2 depend on both p and the other items of *anArray[first..last]*.

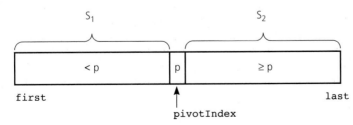

Figure 2-18

A partition about a pivot

This partition induces three "smaller problems," such that the solution to one of the problems will solve the original problem:

1. If S_1 contains k or more items, S_1 contains the k smallest items of the array segment `anArray[first..last]`. In this case, the kth smallest item must be in S_1. Since S_1 is the array segment `anArray[first..pivotIndex–1]`, this case occurs if $k < pivotIndex - first + 1$.

2. If S_1 contains $k - 1$ items, the kth smallest item must be the pivot p. This is the base case; it occurs if $k = pivotIndex - first + 1$.

3. If S_1 contains fewer than $k - 1$ items, the kth smallest item in `anArray[first..last]` must be in S_2. Because S_1 contains $pivotIndex - first$ items, the kth smallest item in `anArray[first..last]` is the $(k - (pivotIndex - first + 1))^{th}$ smallest item in S_2. This case occurs if $k > pivotIndex - first + 1$.

A recursive definition can summarize this discussion. Let

```
kSmall(k, anArray, first, last) =
```
$$k^{th} \text{ smallest item in } \texttt{anArray[first..last]}$$

After you select the pivot item p and partition `anArray[first..last]` into S_1 and S_2, you have that

```
kSmall(k, anArray, first, last)
```

The kth smallest item in
`anArray[first..last]`

$$
= \begin{cases}
\texttt{kSmall(k, anArray, first, pivotIndex-1)} & \\
\qquad\qquad\qquad\qquad\qquad\qquad \text{if } k < pivotIndex - first + 1 \\
p \qquad\qquad\qquad\qquad\qquad\quad \text{if } k = pivotIndex - first + 1 \\
\texttt{kSmall(k-(pivotIndex-first+1), anArray,} \\
\qquad\quad \texttt{pivotIndex+1, last)} \quad \text{if } k > pivotIndex - first + 1
\end{cases}
$$

There is always a pivot, and since it is not part of either S_1 or S_2, the size of the array segment to be searched decreases by at least 1 at each step. Thus, you will eventually reach the base case: The desired item is a pivot. A high-level pseudocode solution is as follows:

```
kSmall(k, anArray, first, last)
// Returns the kth smallest value in anArray[first..last].

   Choose a pivot item p from anArray[first..last]
   Partition the items of anArray[first..last] about p

   if (k < pivotIndex - first + 1) {
      return kSmall(k, anArray, first, pivotIndex-1)
   }
   else if (k == pivotIndex - first + 1) {
      return p
   }
   else {
      return kSmall(k-(pivotIndex-first+1), anArray,
                      pivotIndex+1, last)
   }  // end if
```

This pseudocode is not far from a Java method. The only questions that remain are how to choose the pivot item p and how to partition the array about the chosen p. The choice of p is arbitrary. Any p in the array will work, although the sequence of choices will affect how soon you reach the base case. Chapter 9 gives an algorithm for partitioning the items about p. There you will see how to turn the method *kSmall* into a sorting algorithm.

ORGANIZING DATA

Given some data organized in one way, you might need to organize the data in another way. Thus, you will actually change some aspect of the data and not, for example, simply search it. The problem in this section is called the Towers of Hanoi. Although this classic problem probably has no direct real-world application, we consider it because its solution so well illustrates the use of recursion.

The Towers of Hanoi

Many, many years ago, in a distant part of the Orient—in the Vietnamese city of Hanoi—the Emperor's wiseperson passed on to join his ancestors. The Emperor needed a replacement wiseperson. Being a rather wise person himself, the Emperor devised a puzzle, declaring that its solver could have the job of wiseperson.

The Emperor's puzzle consisted of n disks (he didn't say exactly how many) and three poles: A (the source), B (the destination), and C (the spare). The disks were of different sizes and had holes in the middle so that they could fit on the poles. Because of their great weight, the disks could be placed only on top of disks larger than themselves. Initially, all the disks were on pole A, as shown in Figure 2-19a. The puzzle was to move the disks, one by one, from pole A to pole B. A person could also use pole C in the course of the transfer, but again a disk could be placed only on top of a disk larger than itself.

As the position of wiseperson was generally known to be a soft job, there were many applicants. Scholars and peasants alike brought the Emperor their solutions. Many solutions were thousands of steps long, and many contained *goto*'s. "I can't understand these solutions," bellowed the Emperor. "There must be an easy way to solve this puzzle."

And indeed there was. A great Buddhist monk came out of the mountains to see the Emperor. "My son," he said, "the puzzle is so easy, it almost solves itself." The Emperor's security chief wanted to throw this strange person out, but the Emperor let him continue.

Figure 2-19

(a) The initial state;
(b) move *n* – 1 disks from
A to *C*; (c) move one disk
from *A* to *B*; (d) move
n – 1 disks from *C* to *B*

"If you have only one disk (that is, $n = 1$), move it from pole *A* to pole *B*." So far, so good, but even the village idiot got that part right. "If you have more than one disk (that is, $n > 1$), simply

1.   "Ignore the bottom disk and solve the problem for $n - 1$ disks, with the small modification that pole *C* is the destination and pole *B* is the spare." (See Figure 2-19b.)

2.   "After you have done this, $n - 1$ disks will be on pole *C*, and the largest disk will remain on pole *A*. So solve the problem for $n = 1$ (recall that even the village idiot could do this) by moving the large disk from *A* to *B*." (See Figure 2-19c.)

3.   "Now all you have to do is move the $n - 1$ disks from pole *C* to pole *B*; that is, solve the problem with pole *C* as the source, pole *B* as the destination, and pole *A* as the spare." (See Figure 2-19d.)

There was silence for a few moments, and finally the Emperor said impatiently, "Well, are you going to tell us your solution or not?" The monk simply gave an all-knowing smile and vanished.

The Emperor obviously was not a recursive thinker, but you should realize that the monk's solution is perfectly correct. The key to the solution is the observation that you can solve the Towers problem of *n* disks by solving three smaller—in the sense of number of disks—Towers problems. Let *towers(count, source, destination, spare)* denote the problem of moving *count* disks from pole *source* to pole *destination*, using pole *spare* as a spare. Notice that this definition makes sense even if there are more than *count* disks on pole *source*; in this case, you concern yourself with only the top *count* disks and ignore the others. Similarly, the poles *destination* and *spare* might have disks on them before you begin; you ignore these, too, except that you may place only smaller disks on top of them.

You can restate the Emperor's problem as follows: Beginning with n disks on pole A and 0 disks on poles B and C, solve *towers(n, A, B, C)*. You can state the monk's solution as follows:

The problem statement

The solution

Step 1. Starting in the initial state—with all the disks on pole A—solve the problem

```
towers(n-1, A, C, B)
```

That is, ignore the bottom (largest) disk and move the top $n-1$ disks from pole A to pole C, using pole B as a spare. When you are finished, the largest disk will remain on pole A, and all the other disks will be on pole C.

Step 2. Now, with the largest disk on pole A and all others on pole C, solve the problem

```
towers(1, A, B, C)
```

That is, move the largest disk from pole A to pole B. Because this disk is larger than the disks already on the spare pole C, you really could not use the spare. However, fortunately—and obviously—you do not need to use the spare in this base case. When you are done, the largest disk will be on pole B and all other disks will remain on pole C.

Step 3. Finally, with the largest disk on pole B and all the other disks on pole C, solve the problem

```
towers(n-1, C, B, A)
```

That is, move the $n-1$ disks from pole C to pole B, using A as a spare. Notice that the destination pole B already has the largest disk, which you ignore. When you are done, you will have solved the original problem: All the disks will be on pole B.

The problem *towers(count, source, destination, spare)* has the following pseudocode solution:

```
solveTowers(count, source, destination, spare)

  if (count is 1) {
    Move a disk directly from source to destination
  }
```

```
else {
    solveTowers(count-1, source, spare, destination)
    solveTowers(1, source, destination, spare)
    solveTowers(count-1, spare, destination, source)
}  // end if
```

This recursive solution follows the same basic pattern as the recursive solutions you saw earlier in this chapter:

The solution to the Towers problem satisfies the four criteria of a recursive solution

1.   You solve a Towers problem by solving other Towers problems.

2.   These other Towers problems are smaller than the original problem; they have fewer disks to move. In particular, the number of disks decreases by 1 at each recursive call.

3.   When a problem has only one disk—the base case—the solution is easy to solve directly.

4.   The way that the problems become smaller ensures that you will reach a base case.

Solving the Towers problem requires you to solve many smaller Towers problems recursively. Figure 2-20 illustrates the resulting recursive calls and their order when you solve the problem for three disks.

Now consider a Java implementation of this algorithm. Notice that since most computers do not have arms (at the time of this writing), the method moves a disk by giving directions to a human. Thus, the formal parameters that represent the poles are of type *char*, and the

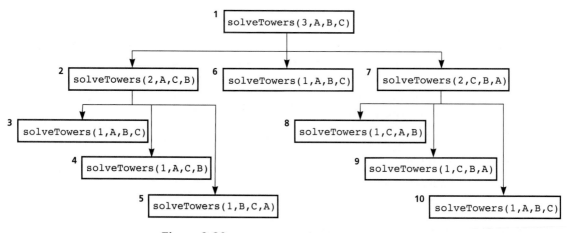

Figure 2-20

The order of recursive calls that results from *solveTowers(3, A, B, C)*

corresponding actual arguments could be `'A'`, `'B'`, and `'C'`. The call
`solveTowers(3, 'A', 'B', 'C')` produces this output:

The solution for three disks

```
Move top disk from pole A to pole B
Move top disk from pole A to pole C
Move top disk from pole B to pole C
Move top disk from pole A to pole B
Move top disk from pole C to pole A
Move top disk from pole C to pole B
Move top disk from pole A to pole B
```

The Java method follows:

```java
public static void solveTowers(int count, char source,
                       char destination, char spare) {
  if (count == 1) {
    System.out.println("Move top disk from pole " + source +
                 " to pole " + destination);
  }
  else {
    solveTowers(count-1, source, spare, destination); // X
    solveTowers(1, source, destination, spare);       // Y
    solveTowers(count-1, spare, destination, source); // Z
  }  // end if
}  // end solveTowers
```

The three recursive calls in the method are labeled *X*, *Y*, and *Z*. These
labels appear in the box trace of `solveTowers(3, 'A', 'B', 'C')` in
Figure 2-21. The recursive calls are also numbered to correspond to the
numbers used in Figure 2-20. (Figure 2-21 abbreviates `destination` as
dest to save space.)

The initial call 1 is made, and `solveTowers` begins execution:

Figure 2-21

Box trace of
`solveTowers(3, 'A', 'B', 'C')`

At point X, recursive call 2 is made, and the new invocation of the method begins execution:

At point X, recursive call 3 is made, and the new invocation of the method begins execution:

Figure 2-21
(continued)

This is the base case, so a disk is moved, the return is made, and the method continues execution.

At point Y, recursive call 4 is made, and the new invocation of the method begins execution:

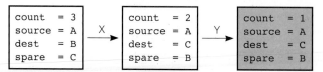

This is the base case, so a disk is moved, the return is made, and the method continues execution.

At point Z, recursive call 5 is made, and the new invocation of the method begins execution:

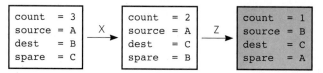

This is the base case, so a disk is moved, the return is made, and the method continues execution.

This invocation completes, the return is made, and the method continues execution.

At point Y, recursive call 6 is made, and the new invocation of the method begins execution:

This is the base case, so a disk is moved, the return is made, and the method continues execution.

At point Z, recursive call 7 is made, and the new invocation of the method begins execution:

```
count  = 3        count  = 2
source = A   Z    source = C
dest   = B        dest   = B
spare  = C        spare  = A
```

At point X, recursive call 8 is made, and the new invocation of the method begins execution:

```
count  = 3        count  = 2        count  = 1
source = A   Z    source = C   X    source = C
dest   = B        dest   = B        dest   = A
spare  = C        spare  = A        spare  = B
```

This is the base case, so a disk is moved, the return is made, and the method continues execution.

```
count  = 3        count  = 2        count  = 1
source = A   Z    source = C        source = C
dest   = B        dest   = B        dest   = A
spare  = C        spare  = A        spare  = B
```

At point Y, recursive call 9 is made, and the new invocation of the method begins execution:

```
count  = 3        count  = 2        count  = 1
source = A   Z    source = C   Y    source = C
dest   = B        dest   = B        dest   = B
spare  = C        spare  = A        spare  = A
```

This is the base case, so a disk is moved, the return is made, and the method continues execution.

```
count  = 3        count  = 2        count  = 1
source = A   Z    source = C        source = C
dest   = B        dest   = B        dest   = B
spare  = C        spare  = A        spare  = A
```

At point Z, recursive call 10 is made, and the new invocation of the method begins execution:

```
count  = 3        count  = 2        count  = 1
source = A   Z    source = C   Z    source = A
dest   = B        dest   = B        dest   = B
spare  = C        spare  = A        spare  = C
```

This is the base case, so a disk is moved, the return is made, and the method continues execution.

```
count  = 3        count  = 2        count  = 1
source = A   Z    source = C        source = A
dest   = B        dest   = B        dest   = B
spare  = C        spare  = A        spare  = C
```

This invocation completes, the return is made, and the method continues execution.

```
count  = 3        spare  = 2        count  = 1
source = A        source = C        source = A
dest   = B        dest   = B        dest   = B
spare  = C        spare  = A        spare  = C
```

Figure 2-21
(continued)

RECURSION AND EFFICIENCY

Recursion is a powerful problem-solving technique that often produces very clean solutions to even the most complex problems. Recursive solutions can be easier to understand and to describe than iterative solutions. By using recursion, you can often write simple, short implementations of your solution.

The overriding concern of this chapter has been to give you a solid understanding of recursion so that you will be able to construct recursive solutions on your own. Most of our examples, therefore, have been simple. Unfortunately, many of the recursive solutions in this chapter are so inefficient that you should not use them. The recursive methods *binarySearch* and *solveTowers* are the notable exceptions, as they are quite efficient.[2]

Two factors contribute to the inefficiency of some recursive solutions:

Factors that contribute to the inefficiency of some recursive solutions

- The overhead associated with method calls
- The inherent inefficiency of some recursive algorithms

The first of these factors does not pertain specifically to recursive methods but is true of methods in general. In most implementations of Java and other high-level programming languages, a method call incurs a bookkeeping overhead. As was mentioned earlier, each method call produces an activation record, which is analogous to a box in the box trace. Recursive methods magnify this overhead because a single initial call to the method can generate a large number of recursive calls. For example, the call *fact(n)* generates *n* recursive calls. On the other hand, the use of recursion, as is true with modularity in general, can greatly clarify complex programs. This clarification frequently more than compensates for the additional overhead. Thus, the use of recursion is often consistent with the multidimensional view of the cost of a computer program, as Chapter 1 describes.

Recursion can clarify complex solutions

However, you should not use recursion just for the sake of using recursion. For example, you probably should not use the recursive factorial method in practice. You easily can write an iterative factorial method given the iterative definition that was stated earlier in this chapter. The iterative method is almost as clear as the recursive one and is more efficient. There is no reason to incur the overhead of recursion when its use does not gain anything. *Recursion is truly valuable when a problem has no simple iterative solutions.*

Do not use a recursive solution if it is inefficient and you have a clear, efficient iterative solution

The second point about recursion and efficiency is that some recursive algorithms are inherently inefficient. This inefficiency is a very different issue than that of overhead. It has nothing to do with how a compiler happens to implement a recursive method but rather is related to the method of solution that the algorithm employs.

---

[2]Chapters 5 and 9 present other practical, efficient applications of recursion.

As an example, recall the recursive solution for the multiplying rabbits problem that you saw earlier in this chapter:

$$rabbit(n) = \begin{cases} 1 & \text{if } n \text{ is 1 or 2} \\ rabbit(n-1) + rabbit(n-2) & \text{if } n > 2 \end{cases}$$

The recursive version of `rabbit` *is inherently inefficient*

The diagram in Figure 2-11 illustrated the computation of *rabbit(7)*. Earlier, you were asked to think about what the diagram would look like for *rabbit(10)*. If you thought about this question, you may have come to the conclusion that such a diagram would fill up most of this chapter. The diagram for *rabbit(100)* would fill up most of this universe!

The fundamental problem with *rabbit* is that it computes the same values over and over again. For example, in the diagram for *rabbit(7)*, you can see that *rabbit(3)* is computed five times. When *n* is moderately large, many of the values are recomputed literally trillions of times. This enormous number of computations makes the solution infeasible, even if each computation required only a trivial amount of work (for example, if you could perform 100 million of these computations per second).

However, do not conclude that the recurrence relation is of no use. One way to solve the rabbit problem is to construct an iterative solution based on this same recurrence relation. The iterative solution goes forward instead of backward and computes each value only once. You can use the following iterative method to compute *rabbit(n)* even for very large values of *n*.

You can use `rabbit`*'s recurrence relation to construct an efficient iterative solution*

```
public static int iterativeRabbit(int n) {
// Iterative solution to the rabbit problem.
  // initialize base cases:
  int previous = 1;    // initially rabbit(1)
  int current = 1;     // initially rabbit(2)
  int next = 1;        // result when n is 1 or 2

  // compute next rabbit values when n >= 3
  for (int i = 3; i <= n; i++) {
    // current is rabbit(i-1), previous is rabbit(i-2)
    next = current + previous;  // rabbit(i)

    previous = current;        // get ready for
    current = next;            // next iteration
  }  // end for

  return next;
}  // end iterativeRabbit
```

Thus, an iterative solution can be more efficient than a recursive solution. In certain cases, however, it may be easier to discover a recursive solution than an iterative solution. Therefore, you may need to convert a recursive solution to an iterative solution. This conversion process is easier if your recursive method calls itself once, instead of several times. Be careful when deciding whether your method calls itself more than once. Although the method *rabbit* calls itself twice, the method *binarySearch* calls itself

Convert from recursion to iteration if it is easier to discover a recursive solution but more efficient to use an iterative solution

once, even though you see two calls in the Java code. Those two calls appear within an *if* statement; only one of them will be executed.

Converting a recursive solution to an iterative solution is even easier when the solitary recursive call is the last *action* that the method takes. This situation is called **tail recursion.** For example, the method *write-Backward* exhibits tail recursion because its recursive call is the last action that the method takes. Before you conclude that this is obvious, consider the method *fact*. Although its recursive call appears last in the method definition, *fact*'s last action is the multiplication. Thus, *fact* is not tail recursive.

A tail-recursive method

Recall the definition of *writeBackward*:

```java
public static void writeBackward(String s, int size) {
   if (size > 0) {
      // write the last character
      System.out.println(s.substring(size-1, size));
      writeBackward(s, size - 1);        // write rest
   } // end if
} // end writeBackward
```

Because this method is tail recursive, its last recursive call simply repeats the method's action with altered arguments. You can perform this repetitive action by using an iteration that will be straightforward and often more efficient. For example, the following definition of *writeBackward* is iterative:

Removing tail recursion is often straightforward

```java
public static void writeBackward(String s, int size) {
// Iterative version.
   while (size > 0) {
      System.out.println(s.substring(size-1, size));
      --size;
   } // end while
} // end writeBackward
```

Because tail-recursive methods are often less efficient than their iterative counterparts and because the conversion of a tail-recursive method to an equivalent iterative method is rather mechanical, some compilers automatically replace tail recursion with iteration. Eliminating other forms of recursion is usually more complex, as you will see in Chapter 6, and is a task that *you* would need to undertake, if necessary.

Some recursive algorithms, such as *rabbit*, are inherently inefficient, while other recursive algorithms, such as the binary search,[3] are extremely efficient. You will learn how to determine the relative efficiency of a recursive algorithm in more advanced courses concerned with the analysis of algorithms. Chapter 9 introduces some of these techniques briefly.

Chapter 5 will continue the discussion of recursion by examining several difficult problems that have straightforward recursive solutions. Other chapters in this book use recursion as a matter of course.

---

[3]The binary search algorithm also has an iterative formulation.

SUMMARY

1. Recursion is a technique that solves a problem by solving a smaller problem of the same type.

2. When constructing a recursive solution, keep the following four questions in mind:

   a. How can you define the problem in terms of a smaller problem of the same type?

   b. How does each recursive call diminish the size of the problem?

   c. What instance of the problem can serve as the base case?

   d. As the problem size diminishes, will you reach this base case?

3. When constructing a recursive solution, you should assume that a recursive call's postcondition is true if its precondition is true.

4. You can use the box trace to trace the actions of a recursive method. These boxes resemble activation records, which many compilers use to implement recursion. (Chapter 6 discusses implementing recursion further.) Although the box trace is useful, it cannot replace an intuitive understanding of recursion.

5. Recursion allows you to solve problems—such as the Towers of Hanoi—whose iterative solutions are difficult to conceptualize. Even the most complex problems often have straightforward recursive solutions. Such solutions can be easier to understand, describe, and implement than iterative solutions.

6. Some recursive solutions are much less efficient than a corresponding iterative solution, due to their inherently inefficient algorithms and the overhead of method calls. In such cases, the iterative solution can be preferable. You can use the recursive solution, however, to derive the iterative solution.

7. If you can easily, clearly, and efficiently solve a problem by using iteration, you should do so.

CAUTIONS

1. A recursive algorithm must have a base case, whose solution you know directly without making any recursive calls. Without a base case, a recursive method will generate an infinite sequence of calls. When a recursive method contains more than one recursive call, you will often need more than one base case.

2. A recursive solution must involve one or more smaller problems that are each closer to a base case than is the original problem. You must be sure that these smaller problems eventually reach the base case. Failure to do so could result in an algorithm that does not terminate.

3. When developing a recursive solution, you must be sure that the solutions to the smaller problems really do give you a solution to the original problem. For example, *binarySearch* works because each smaller array is sorted and the value sought is between its first and last items.

4. The box trace, together with well-placed *System.out.println* statements, can be a good aid in debugging recursive methods. Such statements should report the point in the program from which each recursive call occurs as well as the values of input arguments and local variables at both entry to and exit from the methods. Be sure to remove these statements from the final version of the method.

5. A recursive solution that recomputes certain values frequently can be quite inefficient. In such cases, iteration may be preferable to recursion.

SELF-TEST EXERCISES

1. The following method computes the product of the first $n \geq 1$ real numbers in an array. Show how this method satisfies the properties of a recursive method.

```
public static double product(double anArray[], int n) {
// Precondition: 1 <= n <= max size of anArray.
// Postcondition: Returns the product of the first n
// items in anArray; anArray is unchanged.
  if (n == 1) {
    return anArray[0];
  }
  else {
      return anArray[n-1] * product(anArray, n-1);
  }  // end if
}  // end product
```

2. Given an integer $n > 0$, write a recursive method *countDown* that writes the integers n, $n - 1$, . . . , 1. *Hint*: What task can you do and what task can you ask a friend to do for you?

3. Write a recursive method that computes the product of the items in the array *anArray[first..last]*.

4. Of the following recursive methods that you saw in this chapter, identify those that exhibit tail recursion: *fact*, *writeBackward*, *writeBackward2*, *rabbit*, *c* in the Spock problem, *p* in the parade problem, *maxArray*, *binarySearch*, and *kSmall*. Are the methods in Self-Test Exercises 1 through 3 tail recursive?

5. Compute *c(4,2)* in the Spock problem.

6. Trace the execution of the method *solveTowers* to solve the Towers of Hanoi problem for two disks.

EXERCISES

1. The following recursive method *getNumberEqual* searches the array *x* of *n* integers for occurrences of the integer *val*. It returns the number of integers in *x* that are equal to *val*. For example, if *x* contains the 9 integers 1, 2, 4, 4, 5, 6, 7, 8, and 9, then *getNumber Equal(x, 9, 4)* returns the value 2 because 4 occurs twice in *x*.

```java
public static int getNumberEqual(int x[], int n,
                                        int val) {
  int count;
  if (n <= 0) {
    return 0;
  }
  else {
    if (x[n-1] == val) {
      count = 1;
    }
    else {
      count = 0;
    }  // end if

    return getNumberEqual(x, n-1, val) + count;
  }  // end if
}  // end getNumberEqual
```

   Demonstrate that this method is recursive by listing the criteria of a recursive solution and stating how the method meets each criterion.

2. Perform a box trace of the following calls to recursive methods that appear in this chapter. Clearly indicate each subsequent recursive call.

   a. *rabbit(5)*
   b. *countDown(5)* (You wrote *countDown* in Self-Test Exercise 2.)

3. Write a recursive method that will compute the sum of the first *n* integers in an array of at least *n* integers. *Hint*: Begin with the nth integer.

4. Revise the method *writeBackward*, discussed in the section "A Recursive *void* Method: Writing a String Backward," so that its base case is a string of length 1.

5. Given an integer *n* > 0, write a recursive Java method that writes the integers 1, 2, . . . , *n*.

6. Write a recursive Java method that writes the digits of a positive decimal integer in reverse order.

7. a. Write a recursive Java method *writeLine* that writes a character repeatedly to form a line of *n* characters. For example, *writeLine('*', 5)* produces the line *****.

b. Now write a recursive method *writeBlock* that uses *writeLine* to write *m* lines of *n* characters each. For example, *writeBlock('*',* *5, 3)* produces the output

```
*****
*****
*****
```

8. What output does the following program produce?

```java
public class Exercise8 {
  public static int getValue(int a, int b, int n) {
    int returnValue;
    System.out.println("Enter: a = " + a + " b = " + b);

    int c = (a + b)/2;
    if (c * c <= n) {
      returnValue = c;
    }
    else {
      returnValue = getValue(a, c-1, n);
    }  // end if
    System.out.println("Leave: a = " + a + " b = " + b);
    return returnValue;
  }  // end getValue

  public static void main(String[] args) {
    System.out.println(getValue(1, 7, 7));
  }  // end main
}  // end Exercise8
```

9. What output does the following program produce?

```java
public class Exercise9 {

  public static int mystery(int n) {
    return search(1, n, n);
  }  // end mystery

  private static int search(int first, int last, int n) {
    int returnValue;
    System.out.println("Enter: first = " + first +
                       " last = " + last);
    int mid = (first + last)/2;
    if ((mid * mid <= n) && (n < (mid+1) * (mid+1))) {
      returnValue = mid;
    }
    else if (mid * mid > n) {
      returnValue = search(first, mid-1, n);
    }
```

```
      else {
        returnValue = search(mid+1, last, n);
      } // end if
      System.out.println("Leave: first = " + first +
                          " last = " + last);
      return returnValue;
    } // end search

    public static void main(String[] args) {
      System.out.println(mystery(30));
    } // end main
  } //end Exercise9
```

10. Consider the following method that converts a positive decimal number to base 8 and displays the result.

```
public static void displayOctal(int n) {
  if (n > 0) {
    if (n/8 > 0) {
        displayOctal(n/8);
    } // end if
    System.out.println(n%8);
  } // end if
} // end displayOctal
```

Describe how the algorithm works. Trace the method with $n = 100$.

11. Consider the following program:

```
public class Exercise11 {

  public static int f(int n) {
  // Precondition: n >= 0.
    System.out.println("Method f entered, n = " + n);
    switch (n) {
      case 0: case 1: case 2:
        return n + 1;
      default:
        return f(n-2) * f(n-4);
    } // end switch
  } // end f

  public static void main(String[] args) {
    System.out.println("f(8) is equal to " + f(8));
  } // end main
} // end Exercise11
```

Show the exact output of the program. What argument values, if any, could you pass to the method f to cause the program to run forever?

12. Consider the following method:

```
public static void recurse(int x, int y) {
  if (y > 0) {
    ++x;
    --y;
    System.out.println(x + " " + y);
    recurse(x, y);
    System.out.println(x + " " + y);
  }  // end if
}  // end recurse
```

Execute the method with $x = 5$ and $y = 3$.

13. Perform a box trace of the recursive method *binarySearch*, which appears in the section "Binary Search," with the array 1, 5, 9, 12, 15, 21, 29, 31 for each of the following search values:

a. 5   b. 13   c. 16

14. Imagine that you have 101 dalmatians; no two dalmatians have the same number of spots. Suppose that you create an array of 101 integers: The first integer is the number of spots on the first dalmatian, the second integer is the number of spots on the second dalmatian, and so on.

Your friend wants to know whether you have a dalmatian with 99 spots. Thus, you need to determine whether the array contains the integer 99.

a. If you plan to use a binary search to look for the 99, what, if anything, would you do to the array before searching it?

b. What is the index of the integer in the array that a binary search would examine first?

c. If all your dalmatians have more than 99 spots, exactly how many comparisons will a binary search require to determine that 99 is not in the array?

15. This problem considers several ways to compute x^n for some $n \geq 0$.

a. Write an iterative method *power1* to compute x^n for $n \geq 0$.

b. Write a recursive method *power2* to compute x^n by using the following recursive formulation:

$$x^0 = 1$$
$$x^n = x * x^{n-1} \quad \text{if } n > 0$$

c. Write a recursive method *power3* to compute x^n by using the following recursive formulation:

$$x^0 = 1$$
$$x^n = (x^{n/2})^2 \qquad \text{if } n > 0 \text{ and } n \text{ is even}$$
$$x^n = x * (x^{n/2})^2 \qquad \text{if } n > 0 \text{ and } n \text{ is odd}$$

d. How many multiplications will each of the methods *power1*, *power2*, and *power3* perform when computing 3^{32}? 3^{19}?

   e. How many recursive calls will *power2* and *power3* make when
      computing 3^{32}? 3^{19}?

16. Modify the recursive *rabbit* method so that it is visually easy to
    follow the flow of execution. Instead of just adding "Enter" and
    "Leave" messages, indent the trace messages according to how
    "deep" the current recursive call is. For example, the call *rabbit*
    (4) should produce the output

```
Enter rabbit:    n = 4
    Enter rabbit:    n = 3
        Enter rabbit:    n = 2
        Leave rabbit:    n = 2    value = 1
        Enter rabbit:    n = 1
        Leave rabbit:    n = 1    value = 1
    Leave rabbit:    n = 3    value = 2
    Enter rabbit:    n = 2
    Leave rabbit:    n = 2    value = 1
Leave rabbit:    n = 4    value = 3
```

    Note how this output corresponds to figures such as Figure 2-11.

17. Consider the following recurrence relation:

    $f(1) = 1; f(2) = 1; f(3) = 1; f(4) = 3; f(5) = 5;$

    $f(n) = f(n-1) + 3 * f(n-5)$ for all $n > 5$.

    a. Compute $f(n)$ for the following values of *n*: 6, 7, 12, 15.
    b. If you were careful, rather than computing $f(15)$ from scratch
       (the way a recursive Java method would compute it), you would
       have computed $f(6)$, then $f(7)$, then $f(8)$, and so on up to $f(15)$,
       recording the values as you computed them. This ordering
       would have saved you the effort of ever computing the same
       value more than once. (Recall the nonrecursive version of the
       rabbit method discussed at the end of this chapter.)

       Note that during the computation, you never need to
       remember all the previously computed values—only the last
       five. By taking advantage of these observations, write a Java
       method that computes $f(n)$ for arbitrary values of *n*.

18. Write iterative versions of the following recursive methods: *fact*,
    writeBackward, *binarySearch*, *kSmall*.

19. Prove that the method *iterativeRabbit*, which appears in the
    section "Recursion and Efficiency," is correct by using invariants.

*20. Consider the problem of finding the **greatest common divisor
     (gcd)** of two positive integers *a* and *b*. The algorithm presented
     here is a variation of Euclid's algorithm, which is based on the fol-
     lowing theorem:[4]

---

[4]This book uses mod as an abbreviation for the mathematical operation modulo. In
Java, the modulo operator is %.

THEOREM. If a and b are positive integers with $a > b$ such that b is not a divisor of a, then $gcd(a, b) = gcd(b, a \bmod b)$.

This relationship between $gcd(a, b)$ and $gcd(b, a \bmod b)$ is the heart of the recursive solution. It specifies how you can solve the problem of computing $gcd(a, b)$ in terms of another problem of the same type. Also, if b does divide a, then $b = gcd(a, b)$, so an appropriate choice for the base case is $(a \bmod b) = 0$.

This theorem leads to the following recursive definition:

$$gcd(a, b) = \begin{cases} b & \text{if } (a \bmod b) = 0 \\ gcd(b, a \bmod b) & \text{otherwise} \end{cases}$$

The following method implements this recursive algorithm:

```java
public static int gcd(int a, int b) {
    if (a % b == 0) { // base case
        return b;
    }
    else {
        return gcd(b, a % b);
    } // end if
} // end gcd
```

a. Prove the theorem.
b. What happens if $b > a$?
c. How is the problem getting smaller? (That is, do you always approach a base case?) Why is the base case appropriate?

*21. Let $C(n)$ be the number of different groups of integers that can be chosen from the integers 1 through $n - 1$ so that the integers in each group add up to n (for example, $4 = 1 + 1 + 1 + 1 = 1 + 1 + 2 = 2 + 2 \cdots$). Write recursive definitions for $C(n)$ under the following variations:

   a. You count permutations. For example, 1, 2, 1 and 1, 1, 2 are two groups that each add up to 4.
   b. You ignore permutations.

22. Consider the following recursive definition:

$$Acker(m, n) = \begin{cases} n + 1 & \text{if } m = 0 \\ Acker(m - 1, 1) & \text{if } n = 0 \\ Acker(m - 1, Acker(m, n - 1)) & \text{otherwise} \end{cases}$$

This function, called **Ackermann's function,** is of interest because it grows rapidly with respect to the sizes of m and n. What is $Acker(1, 2)$? Implement the function as a method in Java and do a box trace of $Acker(1, 2)$. (*Caution:* Even for modest values of m and n, Ackermann's function requires *many* recursive calls.)

PROGRAMMING PROBLEMS

1. Implement *maxArray*, discussed in the section "Finding the Largest Item in an Array," as a Java method. What other recursive definitions of *maxArray* can you describe?

2. Implement *kSmall*, discussed in the section "Finding the kth Smallest Item in an Array," as a Java method. Use the first item of the array as the pivot.

Data Abstraction: The Walls

PREVIEW This chapter elaborates on data abstraction, which was introduced in Chapter 1 as a technique for increasing the modularity of a program—for building "walls" between a program and its data structures. During the design of a solution, you will discover that you need to support several operations on the data and therefore need to define abstract data types (ADTs). This chapter introduces some simple abstract data types and uses them to demonstrate the advantages of abstract data types in general. In Part II of this book, you will see several other important ADTs.

Only after you have clearly specified the operations of an abstract data type should you consider data structures for implementing it. This chapter explores implementation issues and introduces Java classes as a way to hide the implementation of an ADT from its users.

ABSTRACT DATA TYPES

Modularity is a technique that keeps the complexity of a large program manageable by systematically controlling the interaction of its components. You can focus on one task at a time in a modular program without other distractions. Thus, a modular program is easier to write, read, and modify. Modularity also isolates errors and eliminates redundancies.

A modular program is easier to write, read, and modify

You can develop modular programs by piecing together existing software components with methods that have yet to be written. In doing so, you should focus on *what* a module does and not on *how* it does it. To use existing software, you need a clear set of specifications that details how the modules behave. To write new methods, you need to decide what you would like them to do and proceed under the assumption that they exist and work. In this way you can write the methods in relative isolation from one another, knowing what each one will do but not necessarily *how* each will eventually do it. That is, you should practice **procedural abstraction**.

Write specifications for each module before implementing it

While writing a module's specifications, you must identify details that you can hide within the module. The principle of **information hiding** involves not only hiding these details, but also making them *inaccessible* from outside a module. One way to understand information hiding is to imagine **walls** around the various tasks a program performs. These walls prevent the tasks from becoming entangled. The wall around each task T prevents the other tasks from "seeing" how T is performed. Thus, if task Q uses task T, and if the method for performing task T changes, task Q will not be affected. As Figure 3-1 illustrates, the wall prevents task Q's method of solution from depending on task T's method of solution.

Isolate the implementation details of a module from other modules

The isolation of the modules cannot be total, however. Although task Q does not know *how* task T is performed, it must know *what* task T is and how to initiate it. For example, suppose that a program needs to operate on a sorted array of names. The program may, for instance, need to search the array for a given name or display the names in alphabetical order. The program thus needs a method S that sorts an array of names. Although

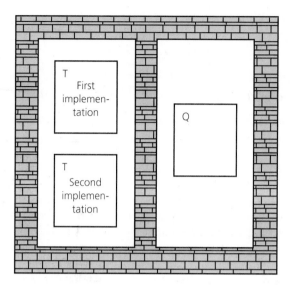

Figure 3-1

Isolated tasks: the implementation of task *T* does not affect task *Q*

the rest of the program knows that method *S* will sort an array, it should not care how *S* accomplishes its task. Thus, imagine a tiny slit in each wall, as Figure 3-2 illustrates. The slit is not large enough to allow the outside world to see the method's inner workings, but things can pass through the slit into and out of the method. For example, you can pass the array into the sort method, and the method can pass the sorted array out to you. What goes in and comes out is governed by the terms of the method's specifications, or **contract**: *If you use the method in this way, this is exactly what it will do for you.*

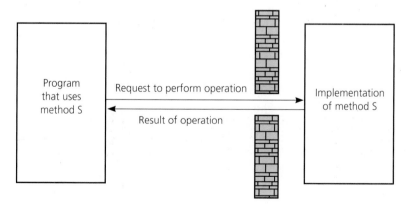

Figure 3-2

A slit in the wall

Often the solution to a problem requires operations on data. Such operations are broadly described in one of three ways:

Typical operations on data

- **Add** data to a data collection.
- **Remove** data from a data collection.
- **Ask questions** about the data in a data collection.

The details of the operations, of course, vary from application to application, but the overall theme is the management of data. Realize, however, that not all problems use or require these operations.

Both procedural and data abstraction ask you to think "what," not "how"

Data abstraction asks that you think in terms of *what* you can do to a collection of data independently of *how* you do it. Data abstraction is a technique that allows you to develop each data structure in relative isolation from the rest of the solution. The other modules of the solution will "know" what operations they can perform on the data, but they should not depend on how the data is stored or how the operations are performed. Again, the terms of the contract are *what* and not *how*. Thus, data abstraction is a natural extension of procedural abstraction.

An ADT is a collection of data and a set of operations on that data

A collection of data together with a set of operations on that data are called an **abstract data type**, or **ADT**. For example, suppose that you need to store a collection of names in a manner that allows you to search rapidly for a given name. The binary search algorithm described in Chapter 2 enables you to search an array efficiently, if the array is sorted. Thus, one solution to this problem is to store the names sorted in an array and to use a binary search algorithm to search the array for a specified name. You can view the *sorted array together with the binary search algorithm* as an ADT that solves this problem.

Specifications indicate what ADT operations do, but not how to implement them

The description of an ADT's operations must be rigorous enough to specify completely their effect on the data, yet it must not specify how to store the data nor how to carry out the operations. For example, the ADT operations should not specify whether to store the data in consecutive memory locations or in disjoint memory locations. You choose a particular **data structure** when you **implement** an ADT.

Data structures are part of an ADT's implementation

Recall that a data structure is a construct that you can define within a programming language to store a collection of data. For example, arrays, which are built into Java, are data structures. However, you can invent other data structures. For example, suppose that you wanted a data structure to store both the names and salaries of a group of employees. You could use the following Java statements:

```
final int MAX_NUMBER = 500;
String[] names = new String[MAX_NUMBER];
double[] salaries = new double[MAX_NUMBER];
```

Here the employee *names[i]* has a salary of *salaries[i]*. The two arrays *names* and *salaries* together form a data structure, yet Java has no single data type to describe it.

When a program must perform data operations that are not directly supported by the language, you should first design an abstract data type and carefully specify what the ADT operations are to do (the contract). Then—*and only then*—should you implement the operations with a data structure. If you implement the operations properly, the rest of the program will be able to assume that the operations perform as specified—that is, that the terms of the contract are honored. However, the program must not depend on a particular approach for supporting the operations.

Carefully specify an ADT's operations before you implement them

An abstract data type is not another name for a data structure.

ADTs Versus Data Structures

- An abstract data type is a collection of data and a set of operations on that data.

- A data structure is a construct within a programming language that stores a collection of data.

ADTs and data structures are not the same

To give you a better idea of the conceptual difference between an ADT and a data structure, consider a refrigerator's ice dispenser, as Figure 3-3 illustrates. It has water as input and produces as output either chilled water, crushed ice, or ice cubes, according to which one of the three buttons you push. It also has an indicator that lights when no ice is presently available. The dispenser is analogous to an abstract data type. The water is analogous to data; the operations are *chill*, *crush*, *cube*, and *isEmpty*. At this level of design, you are not concerned with how the dispenser will perform its operations, only that it performs them. If you want crushed ice, do you really care how the dispenser accomplishes its task as long as it does so correctly? Thus, after you have specified the dispenser's methods, you can design many uses for crushed ice without knowing how the dispenser accomplishes its tasks and without the distraction of engineering details.

Eventually, however, someone must build the dispenser. Exactly how will this machine produce crushed ice, for example? It could first make ice cubes and then either crush them between two steel rollers or

Out-of-ice indicator

Chilled water Crushed ice Ice cubes

Water

Figure 3-3

A dispenser of chilled water, crushed ice, and ice cubes

smash them into small pieces by using hammers. Many other techniques are possible. The internal structure of the dispenser corresponds to the implementation of the ADT in a programming language—that is, to a data structure.

Although the owner of the dispenser does not care about its inner workings, he or she does want a design that is as efficient in its operation as possible. Similarly, the dispenser's manufacturer wants a design that is as easy and cheap to build as possible. You should have these same concerns when you choose a data structure to implement an ADT in Java. Even if you do not implement the ADT yourself, but instead use an already implemented ADT, you—like the person who buys a refrigerator—should care at least about the ADT's efficiency.

Notice that the dispenser is surrounded by steel walls. The only breaks in the walls accommodate the input (water) to the machine and its output (chilled water, crushed ice, or ice cubes). Thus, the machine's interior mechanisms are not only hidden from the user but also are inaccessible. In addition, the mechanism of one operation is hidden from and inaccessible to another operation.

This modular design has benefits. For example, you can improve the operation *crush* by modifying its module without affecting the other modules. You could also add an operation by adding another module to the machine without affecting the original three operations. Thus, both abstraction and information hiding are at work here.

A program should not depend on the details of an ADT's implementation

To summarize, data abstraction results in a wall of ADT operations between data structures and the program that accesses the data within these data structures, as Figure 3-4 illustrates. If you are on the program's

Figure 3-4

A wall of ADT operations isolates a data structure from the program that uses it

side of the wall, you will see an **interface** that enables you to communicate with the data structure. That is, you request the ADT operations to manipulate the data in the data structure, and they pass the results of these manipulations back to you.

This process is analogous to using a vending machine. You press buttons to communicate with the machine and obtain something in return. The machine's external design dictates how you use it, much as an ADT's specifications govern what its operations are and what they do. As long as you use a vending machine according to its design, you can ignore its inner technology. As long as you agree to access data only by using ADT operations, your program can be oblivious to any change in the data structures that implement the ADT.

Using an ADT is like using a vending machine

The following pages describe how to use an abstract data type to realize data abstraction's goal of separating the operations on data from the implementation of these operations. In doing so, we will look at several examples of ADTs.

SPECIFYING ADTs

To elaborate on the notion of an abstract data type, consider a list that you might encounter, such as a list of chores, a list of important dates, a list of addresses, or the grocery list pictured in Figure 3-5. As you write a grocery list, where do you put new items? Assuming that you write a neat one-column list, you probably add new items to the end of the list. You could just as well add items to the beginning of the list or add them so that your list is sorted alphabetically. Regardless, the items on a list appear in a sequence. The list has one first item and one last item. Except for the first and last items, each item has a unique **predecessor** and a unique **successor.** The first item—the **head** or **front** of the list—does not have a predecessor, and the last item—the **tail** or **end** of the list—does not have a successor.

Lists contain items of the same type: You can have a list of grocery items or a list of phone numbers. What can you do to the items on a list? You might count the items to determine the length of the list, add an

Figure 3-5
A grocery list

milk
eggs
butter
apples
bread
chicken

item to the list, remove an item from the list, or look at (**retrieve**) an item. The items on a list, together with operations that you can perform on the items, form an abstract data type. You must specify the behavior of the ADT's operations on its data, that is, the list items. It is important that you focus only on specifying the operations and not on how you will implement them. In other words, do not bring to this discussion any preconceived notion of a data structure that the term "list" might suggest.

Where do you add a new item and which item do you want to look at? The various answers to these questions lead to several kinds of lists. You might decide to add, delete, and retrieve items only at the end of the list or only at the front of the list or at both the front and end of the list. The specifications of these lists are left as an exercise; next we will discuss a more general list.

The ADT List

Once again, consider the grocery list pictured in Figure 3-5. The previously described lists, which manipulate items at one or both ends of the list, are not really adequate for an actual grocery list. You would probably want to access items anywhere on the list. That is, you might look at the item at position *i*, delete the item at position *i*, or insert an item at position *i* on the list. Such operations are part of the ADT **list.**

KEY CONCEPTS

ADT List Operations

1. Create an empty list.

2. Determine whether a list is empty.

3. Determine the number of items on a list.

4. Add an item at a given position in the list.

5. Remove the item at a given position in the list.

6. Remove all the items from the list.

7. Retrieve (get) the item at a given position in the list.

Note that it is customary to include an initialization operation that creates an empty list. Other operations that determine whether the list is empty or the length of the list are also useful.

Although the six items on the list in Figure 3-5 have a sequential order, they are not necessarily sorted by name. Perhaps the items appear in the order in which they occur on the grocer's shelves, but more likely they appear in the order in which they occurred to you as you wrote the list. The ADT list is simply an ordered collection of items that you reference by position number.

The following pseudocode specifies the operations for the ADT list in more detail.

You reference list items by their position within the list

Pseudocode for the ADT List Operations

```
createList()
// Creates an empty list.

isEmpty()
// Determines whether a list is empty.

size()
// Returns the number of items that are in a list.

add(index, item)
// Inserts item at position index of a list, if
// 1 <= index <= size()+1.
// If index <= size(), items are renumbered as
// follows: The item at index becomes the item at
// index+1, the item at index+1 becomes the
// item at index+2, and so on.
// Throws an exception when index is out of range or if
// the item cannot be placed on the list (list full).

remove(index)
// Removes the item at position index of a list, if
// 1 <= index <= size(). If index < size(), items are
// renumbered as follows: The item at index+1 becomes
// the item at index, the item at index+2 becomes the
// item at index+1, and so on.
// Throws an exception when index is out of range or if
// the list is empty.

removeAll()
// Removes all the items in the list.

get(index)
// Returns the item at position index of a list
// if 1 <= index <= size(). The list is
// left unchanged by this operation.
// Throws an exception if index is out of range.
```

To get a more precise idea of how the operations work, apply them to the grocery list

> *milk, eggs, butter, apples, bread, chicken*

where milk is the first item on the list and chicken is the last item. To begin, consider how you can construct this list by using the operations of the ADT list. One way is first to create an empty list *myList* and then use a series of insertion operations to append successively the items to the list as follows:

```
aList.createList()
aList.add(1, milk)
aList.add(2, eggs)
aList.add(3, butter)
aList.add(4, apple)
aList.add(5, bread)
aList.add(6, chicken)
```

The notation[1] $aList.O$ indicates that an operation O applies to the list $aList$.

Notice that the list's insertion operation can insert new items into any position of the list, not just at its front or end. According to add's specification, if a new item is inserted into position i, the position of each item that was at a position of i or greater is increased by 1. Thus, for example, if you start with the previous grocery list and you perform the operation

```
aList.add(4, nuts)
```

the list $aList$ becomes

milk, eggs, butter, nuts, apples, bread, chicken

All items that had position numbers greater than or equal to 4 before the insertion now have their position numbers increased by 1 after the insertion.

Similarly, the deletion operation specifies that if an item is deleted from position i, the position of each item that was at a position greater than i is decreased by 1. Thus, for example, if $aList$ is the list

milk, eggs, butter, nuts, apples, bread, chicken

and you perform the operation

```
aList.remove(5)
```

the list becomes

milk, eggs, butter, nuts, bread, chicken

All items that had position numbers greater than 5 before the deletion now have their position numbers decreased by 1 after the deletion.

An ADT specification should not include implementation issues

These examples illustrate that an ADT can specify the effects of its operations without having to indicate how to store the data. The specifications of the seven operations are the sole terms of the contract for the ADT list: *If you request that these operations be performed, this is what will happen.* The specifications contain no mention of how to store the list or how to perform the operations; they tell you only what you can do to the list. It is of fundamental importance that the specification of an ADT *not* include implementation issues. This restriction on the specification of an

---

[1] This notation is compatible with the planned Java implementation of the ADT.

ADT is what allows you to build a wall between an implementation of an ADT and the program that uses it. (Such a program is called a **client**.) The behavior of the operations is the only thing on which a program should depend.

A program should depend only on the behavior of the ADT

Note that the insertion, deletion, and retrieval operations throw an exception when the argument *index* is out of range. This technique provides the ADT with a simple mechanism to communicate operation failure to its client. For example, if you try to delete the tenth item from a five-item list, *remove* can throw an exception indicating that *index* is out of range. Exceptions enable the client to handle error situations in an implementation-independent way.

What does the specification of the ADT list tell you about its behavior? It is apparent that the list operations fall into the three broad categories presented earlier in this chapter.

- The operation *add* **adds** data to a data collection.
- The operations *remove* and *removeAll* **remove** data from a data collection.
- The operations *isEmpty*, *size*, and *get* **ask questions** about the data in a data collection.

Once you have satisfactorily specified the behavior of an ADT, you can design applications that access and manipulate the ADT's data solely in terms of its operations and without regard for its implementation. As a simple example, suppose that you want to display the items in a list. Even though the wall between the implementation of the ADT list and the rest of the program prevents you from knowing how the list is stored, you can write a method *displayList* in terms of the operations that define the ADT list. The pseudocode for such a method follows:[2]

```
displayList(aList)
// Displays the items on the list aList.

    for (index = 1 through aList.size()) {
        dataItem = aList.get(index)
        Display dataItem
    } // end for
```

An implementation-independent application of the ADT list

Notice that as long as the ADT list is implemented correctly, the *displayList* method will perform its task. In this case, *get* successfully retrieves each list item, because *index*'s value is always valid.

The method *displayList* does not depend on *how* you implement the list. That is, the method will work regardless of whether you use an array or some other data structure to store the list's data. This feature is a definite advantage of abstract data types. In addition, by thinking in terms of the available ADT operations, you will not be distracted by

---

[2]In this example, *displayList* is not an ADT operation, so a procedural notation that specifies *aList* as a parameter is used.

implementation details. Figure 3-6 illustrates the wall between *display-List* and the implementation of the ADT list.

As another application of the ADT operations, suppose that you want a method *replace* that replaces the item in position *i* with a new item. If the *i*th item exists, *replace* deletes the item and inserts the new item at position *i*, as follows:

```
replace(aList, i, newItem)
// Replaces the iᵗʰ item on the list aList with
// newItem.

    if (i >=1 and i <= aList.size()) {
        aList.remove(i)
        aList.add(i, newItem)
    }  // end if
```

impulat to lower it inside

You can use ADT operations in an application without the distraction of implementation details

In both of the preceding examples, notice how you can focus on the task at hand without the distraction of implementation details such as arrays. With less to worry about, you are less likely to make an error in your logic when you use the ADT operations in applications such as *displayList* and *replace*. Likewise, when you finally implement the ADT operations in Java, you will not be distracted by these applications. In addition, because *displayList* and *replace* do not depend on any implementation decisions that you make for the ADT list, they are not

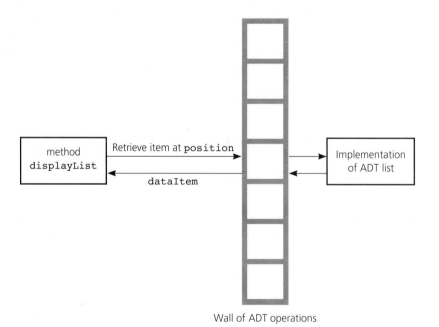

Figure 3-6

The wall between *displayList* and the implementation of the ADT list

altered by your decisions. These assertions assume that you do not change the specifications of the ADT operations when you implement them. However, as Chapter 1 pointed out, developing software is not a linear process. You may realize during implementation that you need to refine your specifications. Clearly, changes to the specification of any module affect any already-designed uses of that module.

To summarize, you can specify the behavior of an ADT independently of its implementation. Given such a specification, and without any knowledge of how the ADT will be implemented, you can design applications that use the ADT's operations to access its data.

The ADT Sorted List

One of the most frequently performed computing tasks is the maintenance, in some *specified* order, of a collection of data. Many examples immediately come to mind: students placed in order by their names, baseball players listed in order by their batting averages, and corporations listed in order by their assets. These orders are called **sorted.** In contrast, the items on a grocery list might be ordered—the order in which they appear on the grocer's shelves, for example—but they are probably not sorted by name.

The problem of *maintaining* sorted data requires more than simply sorting the data. Often you need to insert some new data item into its proper, sorted place. Similarly, you often need to delete some data item. For example, suppose your university maintains an alphabetical list of the students who are currently enrolled. The registrar must insert names into and delete names from this list because students constantly enroll in and leave school. These operations should preserve the sorted order of the data.

The following specifications define the operations for the ADT **sorted list.**

The ADT sorted list maintains items in sorted order

KEY CONCEPTS

Pseudocode for the ADT Sorted List Operations

```
createSortedList()
// Creates an empty sorted list.

sortedIsEmpty()
// Determines whether a sorted list is empty.

sortedSize()
// Returns the number of items that are in a sorted list.

sortedAdd(item)
// Inserts item into its proper sorted position in a
```

```
// sorted list. Throws an exception if the item
// cannot be placed on the list (list full).

sortedRemove(item)
// Deletes item from a sorted list.
// Throws an exception if the item is not found.

sortedGet(index)
// Returns the item at position index of a
// sorted list, if 1 <= index <= sortedSize().
// The list is left unchanged by this operation.
// Throws an exception if the index is out of range.

locateIndex(item)
// Returns the position where item belongs or
// exists in a sorted list; item and the list are
// unchanged.
```

The ADT sorted list differs from the ADT list in that a sorted list inserts and deletes items by their values and not by their positions. For example, *sortedAdd* determines the proper position for *item* according to its value. Also, *locateIndex*—which determines the position of any item, given its value—is a sorted list operation but not a list operation. However, *sortedGet* is like list's *get*: Both operations retrieve an item, given its position. The method *sortedGet* enables you, for example, to retrieve and then display each item in a sorted list.

Designing an ADT

The design of an abstract data type should evolve naturally during the problem-solving process. As an example of how this process might occur, suppose that you want to determine the dates of all the holidays in a given year. One way to do this is to examine a calendar. That is, you could consider each day in the year and ascertain whether that day is a holiday. The following pseudocode is thus a possible solution to this problem:

```
listHolidays(year)
// Displays the dates of all holidays in a given year.

    date = date of first day of year
    while (date is before the first day of year+1) {
        if (date is a holiday) {
            write (date + " is a holiday")
        }  // end if
        date = date of next day
    }  // end while
```

What data is involved here? Clearly, this problem operates on dates, where a date consists of a month, day, and year. What operations will you need to solve the holiday problem? Your ADT must specify and restrict the legal operations on the dates just as the fundamental data type *int* restricts you to operations such as addition and comparison. You can see from the previous pseudocode that you must

What data does a problem require?

- Determine the date of the first day of a given year
- Determine whether a date is before another date
- Determine whether a date is a holiday
- Determine the date of the day that follows a given date

What operations does a problem require?

Thus, you could define the following operations for your ADT:

```
firstDay(year)
// Returns the date of the first day of a given year.

isBefore(date1, date2)
// Returns true if date1 is before date2,
// otherwise returns false.

isHoliday(date)
// Returns true if date is a holiday,
// otherwise returns false.

nextDay(date)
// Returns the date of the day after a given date.
```

The *listHolidays* pseudocode now appears as follows:

```
listHolidays(year)
// Displays the dates of all holidays in a given year.

    date = firstDay(year)
    while (isBefore(date, firstDay(year+1))) {
       if (isHoliday(date)) {
          write (date + " is a holiday ")
       }  // end if
       date = nextDay(date)
    }  // end while
```

Thus, you can design an ADT by identifying data and choosing operations that are suitable to your problem. After specifying the operations, you use them to solve your problem independently of the implementation details of the ADT.

An appointment book. As another example of an ADT design, imagine that you want to create a computerized appointment book that spans a one-year period. Suppose that you make appointments only on the hour and half hour between 8 a.m. and 5 p.m. For simplicity, assume that all appointments are 30 minutes in duration. You want your system to store a brief notation about the nature of each appointment along with the date and time.

To solve this problem, you can define an ADT appointment book. The data items in this ADT are the appointments, where an appointment consists of a date, time, and purpose. What are the operations? Two obvious operations are

- Make an appointment for a certain date, time, and purpose. (You will want to be careful that you do not make an appointment at an already occupied time.)
- Cancel the appointment for a certain date and time.

In addition to these operations, it is likely that you will want to

- Ask whether you have an appointment at a given time.
- Determine the nature of your appointment at a given time.

Finally, ADTs typically have initialization operations.

Thus, the ADT appointment book can have the following operations:

```
createAppointmentBook()
// Creates an empty appointment book.

isAppointment(date, time)
// Returns true if an appointment exists for the date
// and time specified; otherwise returns false.

makeAppointment(date, time, purpose)
// Inserts the appointment for the date, time, and purpose
// specified as long as it does not conflict with an
// existing appointment.
// Returns true if successful, false otherwise.

cancelAppointment(date, time)
// Deletes the appointment for the date and time specified.
// Returns true if successful, false otherwise.

checkAppointment(date, time)
// Returns the purpose of the appointment at
// the given date/time, if one exists. Otherwise, returns
// null.
```

You can use these ADT operations to design other operations on the appointments. For example, suppose that you want to change the date or time of a particular appointment within the existing appointment book *apptBook*. The following pseudocode indicates how to accomplish this task by using the previous ADT operations:

```
// change the date or time of an appointment

read (oldDate, oldTime, newDate, newTime)
```

```
// get purpose of appointment
purpose = apptBook.checkAppointment(oldDate, oldTime)
if (purpose exists) {
  // see if new date/time is available
  if (apptBook.isAppointment(newDate, newTime)) {
    // new date/time is booked
    write ("You already have an appointment at " + newTime +
           " on " + newDate)
  }
  else { // new date/time is available
    apptBook.cancelAppointment(oldDate, oldTime))
    if (apptBook.makeAppointment(newDate, newTime,
       purpose)){
      write ("Your appointment has been rescheduled to" +
             newTime + " on " + newDate)
    } //end if
  } // end if
}
else {
  write ("You do not have an appointment at " + oldTime +
         " on " + oldDate)
} // end if
```

Again notice that you can design applications of ADT operations without knowing how the ADT is implemented. The exercises at the end of this chapter provide examples of other tasks that you can perform with this ADT.

You can use an ADT without knowledge of its implementation

ADTs that suggest other ADTs. Both of the previous examples require you to represent a date; the appointment book example also requires you to represent the time. Java has a *java.util.Date* class that you can use to represent the date and time. You can also design ADTs to represent these items. It is not unusual for the design of one ADT to suggest other ADTs. In fact, you can use one ADT to implement another ADT. The programming problems at the end of this chapter ask you to design and implement the simple ADTs date and time.

You can use an ADT to implement another ADT

This final example also describes an ADT that suggests other ADTs for its implementation. Suppose that you want to design a database of recipes. You could think of this database as an ADT: The recipes are the data items, and some typical operations on the recipes could include the following:

```
insertRecipe(recipe)
// Inserts recipe into the database.

deleteRecipe(recipe)
// Deletes recipe from the database.

retrieveRecipe(name)
// Retrieves the named recipe from the database.
```

This level of the design does not indicate such details as where *insert-Recipe* will place a recipe into the database.

Now imagine that you want to write a method that scales a recipe retrieved from the database: If the recipe is for *n* people, you want to revise it so that it will serve *m* people. Suppose that the recipe contains measurements such as 2½ cups, 1 tablespoon, and ¼ teaspoon. That is, the quantities are given as mixed numbers—integers and fractions—in units of cups, tablespoons, and teaspoons.

This problem suggests another ADT—measurement—with the following operations:

```
readMeasure()
// Reads a measure.

writeMeasure()
// Writes a measure.

scaleMeasure(scaleFactor)
// Multiplies measure by a fractional scaleFactor, which
// has no units, and returns the result.

convertMeasure(oldUnits, newUnits)
// Converts measure from its old units to a measure in
// new units, and returns the result.
```

Suppose that you want the ADT measurement to perform exact fractional arithmetic. Because our planned implementation language Java does not have a data type *fraction* and floating-point arithmetic is not exact, another ADT called fraction is in order. Its operations could include addition, subtraction, multiplication, and division of fractions. For example, you could specify addition as

```
addFractions(first, second)
// Adds two fractions and returns the sum reduced to lowest
// terms.
```

Moreover, you could include operations to convert a mixed number to a fraction and to convert a fraction to a mixed number when feasible.

When you finally implement the ADT measurement, you can use the ADT fraction. That is, you can use one ADT to implement another ADT.

Axioms (Optional)

The previous specifications for ADT operations have been stated rather informally. For example, they rely on your intuition to know the meaning of "an item is at position *i*" in an ADT list. This notion is simple, and most people will understand its intentions. However, some abstract data types are much more complex and less intuitive than a list. For such ADTs, you should use a more rigorous method of defining the behavior of their operations: You must supply a set of mathematical rules—called **axioms**—that precisely specify the behavior of each ADT operation.

An axiom is a mathematical rule

An axiom is actually an invariant—a true statement—for an ADT operation. For example, you are familiar with axioms for algebraic operations; in particular, you know the following rules for multiplication:

$$(a \times b) \times c = a \times (b \times c)$$
$$a \times b = b \times a$$
$$a \times 1 = a$$
$$a \times 0 = 0$$

Axioms for multiplication

These rules, or axioms, are true for any numeric values of a, b, and c, and they describe the behavior of the multiplication operator $\times$.

In a similar fashion, you can write a set of axioms that completely describes the behavior of the operations for the ADT list. For example,

Axioms specify the behavior of an ADT

> *A newly created list is empty*

is an axiom since it is true for all newly created lists. You can state this axiom succinctly in terms of the operations of the ADT list as follows:

> `(aList.createList()).isEmpty()` *is true*

That is, the list `aList` is empty.

The statement

> *If you insert an item x into the ith position of an ADT list, retrieving the ith item will result in x*

is true for all lists, and so it is an axiom. You can state this axiom in terms of the operations of the ADT list as follows:[3]

> `(aList.add(i, x)).get(i) = x`

That is, `get` retrieves from position i of list `aList` the item x that `add` has put there.

The following axioms formally define the ADT list:

KEY CONCEPTS

Axioms for the ADT List

1. `(aList.createList()).size() = 0`

2. `(aList.add(i, x)).size() = aList.size() + 1`

3. `(aList.remove(i)).size() = aList.size() - 1`

4. `(aList.createList()).isEmpty() = true`

5. `(aList.add(i, item)).isEmpty() = false`

6. `(aList.createList()).remove(i) = error`

7. `(aList.add(i, x)).remove(i) = aList`

8. `(aList.createList()).get(i) = error`

9. `(aList.add(i, x)).get(i) = x`

10. `aList.get(i) = (aList.add(i, x)).get(i+1)`

11. `aList.get(i+1) = (aList.remove(i)).get(i)`

---

[3] The = notation within these axioms denotes algebraic equality.

A set of axioms does not make the pre- and postconditions for an ADT's operations unnecessary. For example, the previous axioms do not describe *add*'s behavior when you try to insert an item into position 50 of a list of 2 items. One way to handle this situation is to include the restriction

```
1 <= index <= size()+1
```

in *add*'s precondition. Another way—which you will see when we implement the ADT list later in this chapter—does not restrict *index*, but rather throws an exception if *index* is outside the previous range. Thus, you need both a set of axioms and a set of pre- and postconditions to define the behavior of an ADT's operations completely.

Use axioms to determine the effect of a sequence of ADT operations

You can use axioms to determine the outcome of a sequence of ADT operations. For example, if *aList* is a list of characters, how does the sequence of operations

```
aList.add(1, b)
aList.add(1, a)
```

affect *aList*? We will show that *a* is the first item in this list and that *b* is the second item by using *get* to retrieve these items.

You can write the previous sequence of operations in another way as

```
(aList.add(1, b)).add(1, a)
```

or

```
tempList.add(1, a)
```

where *tempList* represents *aList.add(1, b)*. Now retrieve the first and second items in the list *tempList.add(1, a)*, as follows:

```
(tempList.add(1, a)).get(1) = a   by axiom 9
```

and

```
(tempList.add(1, a)).get(2)
    = tempList.get(1)                by axiom 10
    = (aList.add(1, b)).get(1)       by definition of tempList
    = b                              by axiom 9
```

Thus, *a* is the first item in the list and *b* is the second item.

Axioms are treated further in exercises in the rest of the book.

IMPLEMENTING ADTS

The previous sections emphasized the specification of an abstract data type. When you design an ADT, you concentrate on what its operations do, but you ignore how you will implement them. The result should be a set of clearly specified ADT operations.

Data structures are part of an ADT's implementation

How do you implement an ADT once its operations are clearly specified? That is, how do you store the ADT's data and carry out its operations? Earlier in this chapter you learned that when implementing an

ADT, you choose data structures to represent the ADT's data. Thus, your first reaction to the implementation question might be to choose a data structure and then to write methods that access it in accordance with the ADT operations. Although this point of view is not incorrect, hopefully you have learned not to jump right into code. In general, you should refine an ADT through successive levels of abstraction. That is, you should use a top-down approach to designing an algorithm for each of the ADT operations. You can view each of the successively more concrete descriptions of the ADT as implementing its more abstract predecessors. The refinement process stops when you reach data structures that are available in your programming language. The more primitive your language, the more levels of implementation you will require.

The choices that you make at each level of the implementation can affect its efficiency. For now, our analyses will be intuitive, but Chapter 9 will introduce you to quantitative techniques that you can use to weigh the trade-offs involved.

Recall that the program that uses the ADT should see only a wall of available operations that act on data. Figure 3-7 illustrates this wall once again. Both the data structure that you choose to contain the data and the implementations of the ADT operations are hidden behind the wall. By now, you should realize the advantage of this wall.

In a non-object-oriented implementation, both the data structure and the ADT operations are distinct pieces. The client agrees to honor the wall by using only the ADT operations to access the data structure. Unfortunately, the data structure is hidden only if the client does not look over the wall! Thus, the client can violate the wall—either intentionally or accidentally—by accessing the data structure directly, as Figure 3-8 illustrates. Why is such an action undesirable? Later, this chapter will use an array *items* to store an ADT list's items. In a program

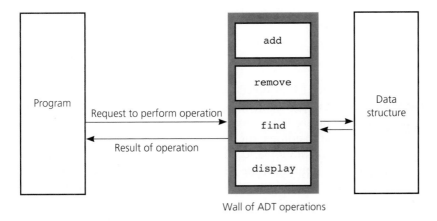

Wall of ADT operations

Figure 3-7

ADT operations provide access to a data structure

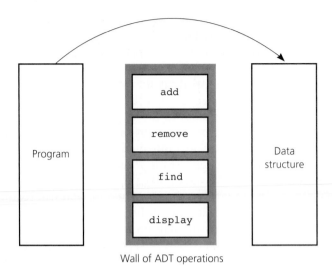

Wall of ADT operations

Figure 3-8

Violating the wall of ADT operations

that uses such a list, you might, for example, accidentally access the first item in the list by writing

```
firstItem = items[0];
```

instead of by invoking the list operation *get*. If you changed to another implementation of the list, your program would be incorrect. To correct your program, you would need to locate and change all occurrences of *items[0]*—but first you would have to realize that *items[0]* is in error!

Object-oriented languages such as Java provide a way for you to enforce the wall of an ADT, thereby preventing access of the data structure in any way other than by using the ADT operations. We will spend some time now exploring this aspect of Java by discussing classes, interfaces, and exceptions.

Java Classes

Recall from Chapter 1 that object-oriented programming, or OOP, views a program not as a sequence of actions but as a collection of components called objects. Encapsulation—one of OOP's three fundamental principles[4]—enables you to enforce the walls of an ADT. It is, therefore, essential to an ADT's implementation and our main focus here.

Encapsulation combines an ADT's data with its operations—called **methods**—to form an **object.** Rather than thinking of the many components of the ADT in Figure 3-7, you can think at a higher level of abstrac-

---

[4] The other principles are inheritance and polymorphism, which Chapter 8 will discuss.

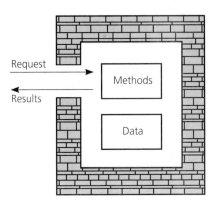

Figure 3-9

An object's data and methods are encapsulated

Request

Methods

Results

Data

tion when you consider the object in Figure 3-9 because it is a single entity. The object hides its inner detail from the programmer who uses it. Thus, an ADT's operations become an object's behaviors.

Encapsulation hides implementation details

We could use a ball as an example of an object. Because thinking of a basketball, volleyball, tennis ball, or soccer ball probably suggests images of the game rather than the object itself, let's abstract the notion of a ball by picturing a sphere. A sphere of a given radius has attributes such as volume and surface area. A sphere as an object should be able to report its radius, volume, surface area, and so on. That is, the sphere object has methods that return such values. This section will develop the notion of a sphere as an object. Later, in Chapter 8, you will see how to derive a ball from a sphere.

In Java, a class is a new data type whose instances are objects. A class contains **data fields** and **methods**, collectively known as class members. Methods typically act on the data fields. By default, all members in a class are **private**—they are not directly accessible by your program—unless you designate them as **public.** The implementations of a class's methods, however, can use any private members of that class.

A Java class defines a new data type

An object is an instance of a class

You should almost always declare a class's data fields as private. Typically, as was mentioned in Chapter 1, you provide methods—such as *setDataField* and *getDataField*—to access the data fields. In this way, you control how and whether the rest of the program can access the data fields. This design principle should lead to programs that not only are easier to debug, but also have fewer logical errors from the beginning.

A class's data fields should be private

You should also distinguish between a class's data fields and any local variables that the implementation of a method requires. In Java, data fields are variables that are shared by all of the methods in the class. Data fields have initial default values,based on their type, and thus do not need to be explicitly initialized. But it is considered to be good programming practice to explicitly initialize data fields in the constructors when necessary. Local variables are used only within a single method and must be initialized explicitly before they are used.

The ADTs that you saw earlier had an operation for their creation. Classes have such methods, called **constructors**. A constructor creates

A constructor creates and initializes an object

and initializes new instances of a class. A typical class has several constructors. A constructor has the same name as the class. Constructors have no return type—not even *void*—and cannot use *return* to return a value. They can, however, have parameters. We will discuss constructors in more detail shortly, after we look at an example of a class definition.

Java destroys objects that a program no longer references

Java has a garbage collection mechanism to destroy objects that a program no longer needs. When a program no longer references an object, the Java runtime environment marks it for garbage collection. Periodically, the Java runtime environment executes a method that returns the memory used by these marked objects to the system for future use. Sometimes when an object is destroyed, other tasks beyond memory deallocation are necessary. In these cases, you define a *finalize* method for the object. Appendix A discusses this situation further.

Other features of classes that will be useful throughout this text include the ability to display objects and to check whether two objects are equal. To facilitate the discussion of constructors and these other features, consider a class of sphere objects called *Sphere*:

```java
public class Sphere {
  private double theRadius;

  public Sphere() {
  // Default constructor: Creates a sphere and
  // initializes its radius to a default value.
  // Precondition: None.
  // Postcondition: A sphere of radius 1 exists.
    setRadius(1.0);
  } // end default constructor

  public Sphere(double initialRadius) {
  // Constructor: Creates a sphere and initializes
  // its radius.
  // Precondition: initialRadius is the desired radius.
  // Postcondition: A sphere of radius initialRadius
  // exists.
    setRadius(initialRadius);
  } // end constructor

  public void setRadius(double newRadius) {
  // Sets (alters) the radius of an existing sphere.
  // Precondition: newRadius is the desired radius.
  // Postcondition: The sphere's radius is newRadius.
    if (newRadius >= 0.0) {
      theRadius = newRadius;
    }  // end if
  } // end setRadius

  public double radius() {
  // Determines a sphere's radius.
```

```
  // Precondition: None.
  // Postcondition: Returns the radius.
    return theRadius;
  } // end radius

  public double diameter() {
  // Determines a sphere's diameter.
  // Precondition: None.
  // Postcondition: Returns the diameter.
    return 2.0 * theRadius;
  } // end diameter

  public double circumference() {
  // Determines a sphere's circumference.
  // Precondition: None.
  // Postcondition: Returns the circumference.
    return Math.PI * diameter();
  } // end circumference

  public double area() {
  // Determines a sphere's surface area.
  // Precondition: None.
  // Postcondition: Returns the surface area.
    return 4.0 * Math.PI * theRadius * theRadius;
  } // end area

  public double volume() {
  // Determines a sphere's volume.
  // Precondition: None.
  // Postcondition: Returns the volume.
    return (4.0*Math.PI * Math.pow(theRadius, 3.0)) / 3.0;
  } // end volume

  public void displayStatistics() {
  // Displays statistics of a sphere.
  // Precondition: Assumes System.out is available.
  // Postcondition: None.
    System.out.println("\nRadius = " + radius() +
                "\nDiameter = " + diameter() +
                "\nCircumference = " + circumference() +
                "\nArea = " + area() +
                "\nVolume = " + volume());
  }  // end displayStatistics
} // end Sphere
```

Constructors. A constructor allocates memory for an object and can initialize the object's data to particular values. A class can have more than one constructor, as is the case for the class *Sphere*.

A default constructor has no parameters

The first constructor in *Sphere* is the **default constructor.** A default constructor by definition has no parameters. Typically, a default constructor initializes data fields to values that the class implementation chooses. For example, the implementation

```
public Sphere() {
    setRadius(1.0);
} // end default constructor
```

sets *theRadius* to 1.0. The following statement invokes the default constructor, which creates the object *unitSphere* and sets its radius to 1.0:

```
Sphere unitSphere = new Sphere();
```

The next constructor in *Sphere* is

```
public Sphere(double initialRadius) {
    setRadius(initialRadius);
} // end constructor
```

It creates a sphere object of radius *initialRadius*. You invoke this constructor by writing a declaration such as

```
Sphere mySphere = new Sphere(5.1);
```

In this case, the object *mySphere* has a radius of 5.1.

If you omit all constructors from your class, the compiler will generate a default constructor—that is, one with no parameters—for you. A **compiler-generated default constructor**, however, might not initialize data fields to values that you will find suitable.

If you define a constructor that has parameters, but you omit the default constructor, the compiler will not generate one for you. Thus, you will not be able to write statements such as

```
Sphere defaultSphere = new Sphere();
```

Using *Sphere*.   The following simple program demonstrates the use of the class *Sphere*:

```
public static void main(String args[]) {
    // unitSphere radius is 1.0
    Sphere unitSphere = new Sphere();
    // mySphere radius is 5.1
    Sphere mySphere = new Sphere(5.1);

    unitSphere.displayStatistics();
    mySphere.setRadius(4.2);   // resets radius to 4.2
    System.out.println(mySphere.diameter());
} // end main
```

*A reference to the private data field **theRadius** would be illegal within this program*

An object such as *mySphere* can, upon request, reset the value of its radius; return its radius; compute its diameter, surface area, circumference, and volume; and display these statistics. These requests to an object are called **messages** and are simply calls to methods. Thus, an object responds to a message by acting on its data. To invoke an object's method, you qualify the method's name—such as *setRadius*—with the object variable—such as *mySphere*.

The previous program is an example of a **client** of a class. A client of a particular class is simply a program or module that uses the class. We will reserve the term **user** for the person who uses a program.

Inheritance. A brief discussion of inheritance is provided here, since it is a common way to create new classes in Java. A more complete discussion of inheritance appears in Chapter 8.

Suppose that we want to create a class for colored spheres, knowing that we have already developed the class *Sphere*. We could write an entirely new class for the colored spheres, but if the colored spheres are actually like the spheres in the class *Sphere*, we can reuse the *Sphere* implementation and add color operations and characteristics by using inheritance. Here is an implementation of the class *ColoredSphere* that uses inheritance:

```java
import java.awt.Color;
public class ColoredSphere extends Sphere {
   private Color color;

   public ColoredSphere(Color c) {
   // Constructor: Creates a sphere and initializes its
   // radius to 1.
   // Precondition: c is the desired color.
   // Postcondition: A sphere of radius 1.0
   // and color c exists.
     super();
     color = c;
   }  // end default constructor

   public ColoredSphere(Color c, double initialRadius) {
   // Constructor: Creates a sphere and initializes its
   // radius.
   // Precondition: initialRadius is the desired radius,
   // c is the desired color.
   // Postcondition: A sphere of radius initialRadius
   // and color c exists.

     super(initialRadius);
     color = c;
   } // end constructor

   public void setColor(Color c) {
   // Sets the color of the sphere.
```

A class derived from the class **Sphere**

```
// Precondition: c is the desired color.
// Postcondition: The sphere color is now c.
  color = c;
}  // end setColor

public Color getColor() {
// Returns the color of the sphere.
// Precondition: c is the desired color.
// Postcondition: None.
  return color;
}  // end getColor
}  // end ColoredSphere
```

Sphere is called the **base class** or **superclass**, and *ColoredSphere* is called the **derived class** or **subclass** of the class *Sphere*. The definition of the subclass includes an *extends* clause that indicates the superclass to be used. When you declare a class without an *extends* clause, you are implicitly extending the class *Object*, so *Object* is its superclass.

Public members of the superclass are available in the subclass

The subclass inherits the contents of the superclass, details of which are discussed in Chapter 8. For the moment, suffice it to say that the subclass will have all of the public members of the superclass available. Any instance of the subclass is also considered to be an instance of the superclass and can be used in a program anywhere that an instance of the superclass can be used. Also, any of the publicly defined methods or variables that can be used with instances of the superclass can be used with instances of the subclass. The subclass instances also have the methods and variables that are publicly defined in the subclass definition.

*A constructor in a subclass should invoke **super** to call the constructor of the superclass*

In the constructor for the *ColoredSphere* class, notice the use of the keyword **super**. You use this keyword to call the constructor of the superclass, so *super()* calls the constructor *Sphere()*, and *super(initialRadius)* calls the constructor *Sphere(double initialRadius)*. If the subclass constructor uses the superclass constructor, the call to *super* must precede all other statements in the subclass constructor.

Here is a method that uses the *ColoredSphere* class:

```
public void useColoredSphere() {
  ColoredSphere ball =
        new ColoredSphere(java.awt.Color.white);
  ball.setRadius(5.0);
  System.out.println("The ball diameter is " +
                            ball.diameter());
  System.out.println("The ball color is " +
                            ball.getColor());
  // other code here...
}  // end useColorSphere
```

An instance of a subclass can invoke public methods of the superclass

This method uses the constructor and the method *getColor* from the subclass *ColoredSphere*. It also uses the methods *setRadius* and *diameter* that are defined in the superclass *Sphere*.

Object equality. Another task that can be useful in program development is to determine whether two objects are equal to one another. The *Object* class provides a method *equals* that compares two objects and returns *true* if they are actually the same object. For example,

Default `equals` as defined in the class `Object` compares two references

```
Sphere sphere1 = new Sphere();
Sphere sphere2 = sphere1;
if (sphere1.equals(sphere2)) {
   System.out.println("sphere1 and sphere2 are the " +
                      "same object");
}
else {
   System.out.println("sphere1 and sphere2 are " +
                      "different objects");
}  // end if
```

will produce the output

```
sphere1 and sphere2 are the same object
```

since both *sphere1* and *sphere2* reference the same object.

Suppose, however, that you want to determine whether two spheres have the same radius. For example,

```
Sphere sphere1 = new Sphere(2.0);
Sphere sphere3 = new Sphere(2.0);
if (sphere1.equals(sphere3)) {
   System.out.println("sphere1 and sphere3 have " +
                      "the same radius");
}
else {
   System.out.println("sphere1 and sphere3 have " +
                      "different radii");
}  // end if
```

will produce the output

```
sphere1 and sphere3 have different radii
```

which is not true! Both *sphere1* and *sphere3* have a radius of 2.0. Remember that the default *equals* compares two references; they differ here because they reference two distinct objects. If you want to have *equals* check the values contained in the object for equality, you must redefine *equals* in the class. Here is an example of such an *equals* for the class *Sphere*:

Customizing `equals` for a class

```
public boolean equals(Object rhs) {
   return ((rhs instanceof Sphere) &&
           (theRadius == ((Sphere)rhs).theRadius));
}  // end equals
```

An `equals` method that determines whether two spheres have the same radius

Notice that the parameter of *equals* is of type *Object*. Remember, we are overriding this method as inherited from the class *Object*, and the parameter list and return value must match. Also notice that we are explicitly checking to make sure that the object parameter *rhs* is an instance of the class *Sphere* by using the *instanceof* operator. If the incoming object *rhs* is an instance of the class *Sphere* (or one of its subclasses), *instanceof* will return *true;* otherwise, the operator returns *false*. Thus, the *equals* method will return *false* when *rhs* is of a class other than *Sphere*. If the *instanceof* operator returns *true*, the boolean expression proceeds to check whether the data fields are equal.

In this example, the data field of the class *Sphere* is a primitive type. If an object is used as a data field, *equals* may have to be defined for that object's class as well. It is up to the designer to decide how "deep" the equality checks must be for a particular class.

Java Interfaces

Often it is convenient to be able to specify a set of methods that you might want to provide in many different classes. One way to do this is to define a superclass that contains these methods and then use inheritance to create the different classes that need to provide those methods. This could pose a problem, however, if the subclass also needs to extend another superclass. Java allows only one class to appear in the *extends* clause.

An interface specifies methods and constants but supplies no implementations

To address this situation, Java provides interfaces. An **interface** provides a way to specify methods and constants, but supplies no implementation details for the methods. Interfaces enable you to specify some desired common behavior that may be useful over many different types of objects. You can then design a method to work with a variety of object types that exhibit this common behavior by specifying the interface as the parameter type for the method, instead of a class. This allows the method to use the common behavior in its implementation, as long as the arguments to the method have implemented the interface.

The Java API has many predefined interfaces. For example, *java.util.Collection* is an interface that provides methods for managing a collection of objects. Here are two of the methods specified in the *Collection* interface:

```
public boolean add(Object o);
public boolean contains(Object o);
```

If you want to have your class provide the methods in this interface, you must indicate your intent to implement the interface by including an ***implements*** clause in your class definition and provide implementations of the methods:

A class that implements an interface

```
public class CardCollection
                        implements java.util.Collection {
    ...
    public boolean add(Object o) {
      // implementation of add method
    } // end add
```

```
    public boolean contains(Object o) {
      // implementation of contains method
    }  // end contains

    // and so on...
  }  // end CardCollection
```

Suppose there is a *print(Collection c)* method. Instances of *Card-Collection* are now eligible to be used as arguments to this method, since *CardCollection* implements the interface *Collection* .

To define your own interface, you use the keyword *interface* instead of *class*, and you provide only method specifications and constants in the interface definition. For example,

```
    public interface MyInterface {
      public final int f1 = 0;
      public void method1();
      public int method2(int a, int b);
    }  // end MyInterface
```

An example of an interface

This defines an interface *MyInterface* that has one constant *f1* and two methods *method1* and *method2*. Note that the name of the interface ends with *Interface*. This is another coding convention that we will use throughout this text.

Interfaces will be used to specify the ADTs that are developed in this text. The implementation of the ADT *list* presented later in this chapter will provide a more complete example of a user-defined interface and how it can be used.

Java Exceptions

Many programming languages, including Java, support a mechanism known as an **exception**, which handles an error during execution. A method indicates that an error has occurred by **throwing** an exception. The exception returns to the point at which you invoked the method, where you **catch** the exception and deal with the error condition.

An exception is a mechanism for handling an error during execution

Catching exceptions.   To catch an exception, Java provides **try-catch** blocks. You place a statement that might throw an exception within a *try* block. The *try* block must be followed by one or more *catch* blocks. Each *catch* block indicates the type of exception you want to handle. A *try* block can have many *catch* blocks associated with it, since even a single statement is capable of throwing more than one type of exception. Also, the *try* block can contain many statements, any of which may throw an exception. Here is the general syntax for a *try* block:

```
    try {
     statement(s);
    }  // end try
```

*Use a **try** block for statements that can throw an exception*

And here is the syntax for a *catch* block:

*Use a **catch** block for each
type of exception that you
handle*

```
catch (exceptionClass identifier) {
  statement(s)
} // end catch
```

When a statement in the *try* block actually throws an exception, the remainder of the *try* block is abandoned and control passes to the statements in the *catch* block that corresponds to the type of exception thrown. The statements in the *catch* block then execute, and, upon completion of the *catch* block, execution resumes at the point following the last *catch* block.

Some exceptions from the Java API cannot be totally ignored. You *must* provide a *catch* block for these exceptions. For example, in the class *java.io.FileInputStream*, the constructor may throw the *FileNotFoundException* if the file specified cannot be found. In this case, the compiler will complain if no *catch* block is provided.

Java has two types of exceptions: checked exceptions and runtime exceptions. The exception *FileNotFoundException* is an example of a checked exception. **Checked exceptions** are instances of classes that are subclasses of the *java.lang.Exception* class. They must be handled locally or explicitly thrown from the method. They are typically used in situations where the method has encountered a serious problem. In some cases, the error may be considered serious enough that the program should be terminated.

*You cannot ignore checked
exceptions*

*You can ignore runtime
exceptions*

Runtime exceptions are used in situations where the error is not considered as serious. These types of exceptions can often be prevented by fail-safe programming. For example, it is fairly easy to avoid allowing an array index to go out of range, a situation that causes the runtime exception *ArrayIndexOutOfBoundsException* to be thrown. Runtime exceptions are instances of classes that are subclasses of the *RuntimeException* class. *RuntimeException* is a subclass of *Exception* that relaxes the requirement of forcing the exception to be caught locally or explicitly thrown again by the method.

Throwing exceptions.   An exception is thrown with the *throw* statement. A typical *throw* statement appears as follows:

*Use a **throw** statement to
throw an exception*

```
throw new exceptionClass(stringArgument);
```

where *exceptionClass* is the type of exception you want to throw and *stringArgument* is an argument to the *exceptionClass* constructor that specifies the detail message, a more detailed description of what may have caused the exception. When a *throw* statement executes, the remaining code in the method does not execute.

*You can define your own excep-
tion class*

The Java API may have an exception class already defined that suits the exception needs of your program. You may also want to define your own exception class. *Exception* or *RuntimeException* is usually used as the superclass for the exception. The one you use will depend on how you want other parts of the program to treat the exception. If you don't want the exception to be ignored, extend *Exception*. If you don't care whether the exception is ignored, or if you have indicated in your precondition how the exception could be avoided, you might choose to extend *RuntimeException*. In either case, your class inherits the same set of methods. Often, no modification of the superclass is done.

If you throw an exception that is not an instance of *RuntimeException* or one of its subclasses, you must either handle the exception within the method by using *try-catch* blocks or throw the exception explicitly from the method. To indicate that a method can throw an exception, include a *throws* clause in the method's specification as follows:

```
public void myMethod() throws MyException {
    // some code here...
    throw new MyException("MyException raised: reason");
}  // end myMethod
```

A method whose code can throw an exception

If the method can throw more than one type of exception, each is listed after the *throws* clause, separated by commas. Thus, the *throws* clause indicates that some error condition can occur during the execution of that method.

Any method that calls *myMethod* must either provide a *catch* clause for instances of *MyException* or contain a *throws* clause of its own for *MyException*.

An Array-Based Implementation of the ADT List

We will now implement the ADT list as a class. Recall that the ADT list operations are

```
createList()
isEmpty()
size()
add(newPosition, newItem)
remove(index)
removeAll()
get(index, dataItem)
```

You need to represent the items in the ADT list and its length. Your first thought is probably to store the list's items in an array *items*. In fact, you might believe that the list is simply a fancy name for an array. This belief is not quite true, however. An **array-based implementation** is a natural choice because both an array and a list identify their items by number. However, the ADT list has operations such as *removeAll* that an array does not. In the next chapter you will see another implementation of the ADT list that does not use an array.

In any case, you can store a list's k^{th} item in *items[k-1]*. How much of the array will the list occupy? Possibly all of it, but probably not. That is, you need to keep track of the array elements that you have assigned to the list and those that are available for use in the future. The maximum

length of the array—its **physical size**—is a known, fixed value such as
MAX_LIST. You can keep track of the current number of items in the list—
that is, the list's length or **logical size**—in a variable $numItems$. An
obvious benefit of this approach is that implementing the operation
$size$ will be easy. Thus, we could use the following statements to implement a list of integers:

```
private final int MAX_LIST = 100; // max length of list
private int items[MAX_LIST];      // array of list items
private int numItems;             // length of list
```

Shift array elements to insert an item

Figure 3-10 illustrates the data fields for an array-based implementation of an ADT list of integers. To insert a new item at a given position in
the array of list items, you must shift to the right the items from this
position on, and insert the new item in the newly created opening.
Figure 3-11 depicts this insertion.

Now consider how to delete an item from the list. You could blank it
out, but this strategy can lead to gaps in the array, as Figure 3-12a illustrates. An array that is full of gaps has three significant problems:

- $numItems - 1$ is no longer the index of the last item in the array.
  You need another variable, $lastPosition$, to contain this index.

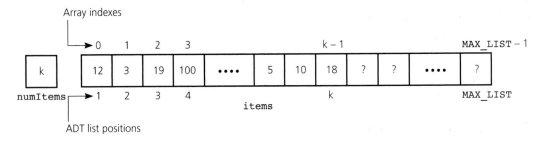

Figure 3-10

An array-based implementation of the ADT list

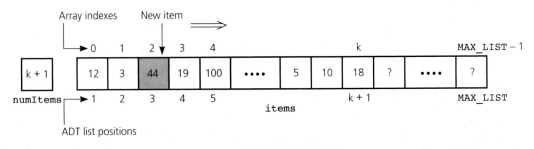

Figure 3-11

Shifting items for insertion at position 3

- Because the items are spread out, the method *get* might have to look at every cell of the array even when only a few items are present.

- When *items[MAX_LIST - 1]* is occupied, the list could appear full, even when fewer than *MAX_LIST* items are present.

Thus, what you really need to do is shift the elements of the array to fill the gap left by the deleted item, as shown in Figure 3-12b.

You should implement each ADT operation as a method of a class. Each operation will require access to both the array *items* and the list's length *numItems*, so make *items* and *numItems* data fields of the class. To hide *items* and *numItems* from the clients of the class, make these data fields private. Although it is not obvious why at this point, it will be convenient to define the method *translate(position)*, which returns the index of the array element that contains the list item at position *index*. That is, *translate(position)* returns the index value *position* – 1. Such a method is not one of the ADT operations and should not be available to the client. It simply makes the implementor's task easier. Thus, you should hide *translate* from the client by defining it as a private method.

If one of the operations is provided an index value that is out of range, an exception should be thrown. Here is a definition of an exception that can be used for an out-of-bounds list index called *ListIndexOutOf-BoundsException*. It is based upon the more general *IndexOutOf-BoundsException* from the Java API:

Shift array elements to delete an item

Implement the ADT list as a class

items and numItems are private data fields

translate is a private method

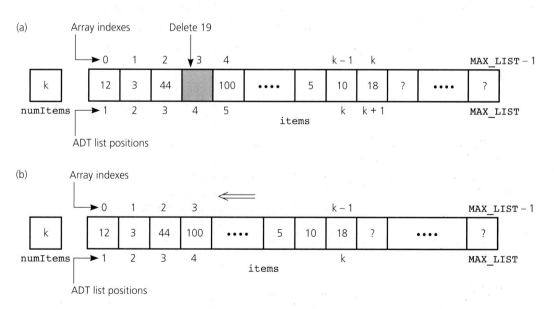

Figure 3-12

(a) Deletion causes a gap; (b) fill gap by shifting

```
public class ListIndexOutOfBoundsException
              extends IndexOutOfBoundsException {
  public ListIndexOutOfBoundsException(String s) {
    super(s);
  }  // end constructor
}  // end ListIndexOutOfBoundsException
```

Also, the exception *ListException* is needed when the array storing the list becomes full. Here is the exception *ListException*:

```
public class ListException extends RuntimeException {
  public ListException(String s) {
    super(s);
  }  // end constructor
}  // end ListException
```

The following interface *IntegerListInterface* provides the specifications for the list operations. The ADT operation *createList* does not appear in the interface because it will be implemented as a constructor.

Interface for a list of integers

```
// **********************************************************
// Interface IntegerListInterface for the ADT list.
// **********************************************************
public interface IntegerListInterface {
  public boolean isEmpty();
  // Determines whether a list is empty.
  // Precondition: None.
  // Postcondition: Returns true if the list is empty,
  // otherwise returns false.
  // Throws: None.

  public int size();
  // Determines the length of a list.
  // Precondition: None.
  // Postcondition: Returns the number of items that are
  // currently in the list.
  // Throws: None.

  public void removeAll();
  // Deletes all the items from the list.
  // Precondition: None.
  // Postcondition: The list is empty.
  // Throws: None.

  public void add(int index, int item)
          throws ListIndexOutOfBoundsException,
                  ListException;
  // Adds an item to the list at position index.
  // Precondition: index indicates the position at which
  // the item should be inserted in the list.
```

```
// Postcondition: If insertion is successful, item is
// at position index in the list, and other items are
// renumbered accordingly.
// Throws: ListIndexOutOfBoundsException if index < 1 or
// index > size()+1.
// Throws: ListException if item cannot be placed on
// the list.


public int get(int index) throws
          ListIndexOutOfBoundsException;
// Retrieves a list item by position.
// Precondition: index is the number of the item to be
// retrieved.
// Postcondition: If 1 <= index <= size(), the item at
// position index in the list is returned.
// Throws: ListIndexOutOfBoundsException if index < 1 or
// index > size().


public void remove(int index)
          throws ListIndexOutOfBoundsException;
// Deletes an item from the list at a given position.
// Precondition: index indicates where the deletion
// should occur.
// Postcondition: If 1 <= index <= size(), the item at
// position index in the list is deleted, and other items
// are renumbered accordingly,
// Throws: ListIndexOutOfBoundsException if index < 1 or
// index > size().
```

```
} // end IntegerListInterface
```

The notion of a list and of the operations that you perform on the list are really independent of the type of items that are stored in the list. The definition just given is very limiting in that it will support only a list of integers. If you use the class *Object* as the type for the list's elements, the specification will be far more flexible. Every class in Java is ultimately derived from the class *Object* through inheritance. This means that any class created in Java could be used as an item in the list class that implements the new list interface.

Use **Object** *as the type of list elements*

What happens if you want to have a list of integers? If the list item type is *Object*, you can no longer use the primitive type *int* as the item type, since *int* is not derived from the class *Object*. In cases where you want a list to contain items of a primitive type, you will need to use a corresponding wrapper class from the Java API. For example, instead of using items of type *int* in the list, the items would be of the type *java.lang.Integer*, a subclass of *Object*.

Here is a revised version, called *ListInterface*, that uses the class *Object* for the list elements. The comments, which are the same as those in *IntegerListInterface*, are left out to save space:

Interface for a list of objects

```
// ********************************************************
// Interface ListInterface for the ADT list.
// ********************************************************
public interface ListInterface {
  public boolean isEmpty();
  public int size();
  public void add(int index, Object item)
                     throws ListIndexOutOfBoundsException;
                       ListException;
  public Object get(int index)
                     throws ListIndexOutOfBoundsException,
  public void remove(int index)
                     throws ListIndexOutOfBoundsException;
  public void removeAll();
}  // end ListInterface
```

The following class implements the interface *ListInterface*, using arrays.

Implementation file

```
// ********************************************************
// Array-based implementation of the ADT list.
// ********************************************************
public class ListArrayBased implements ListInterface {

  private static final int MAX_LIST = 50;
  private Object items[];  // an array of list items
  private int numItems;  // number of items in list

  public ListArrayBased() {
    items = new Object[MAX_LIST];
    numItems = 0;
  }  // end default constructor

  public boolean isEmpty() {
    return (numItems == 0);
  } // end isEmpty

  public int size() {
    return numItems;
  }  // end size

  public void removeAll() {
    // Creates a new array; marks old array for
    // garbage collection.
    items = new Object[MAX_LIST];
```

```
    numItems = 0;
  } // end removeAll

public void add(int index, Object item)
                throws ListIndexOutOfBoundsException {
  if (numItems > MAX_LIST) {
    throw new ListException("ListException on add");
  }  // end if
  if (index >= 1 && index <= numItems+1) {
    // make room for new element by shifting all items at
    // positions >= index toward the end of the
    // list (no shift if index == numItems+1)
    for (int pos = numItems; pos >= index; pos--) {
        items[translate(pos+1)] = items[translate(pos)];
    } // end for
    // insert new item
    items[translate(index)] = item;
    numItems++;
  }
  else {  // index out of range
    throw new ListIndexOutOfBoundsException(
         "ListIndexOutOfBoundsException on add");
  }  // end if
} //end add

public Object get(int index)
                throws ListIndexOutOfBoundsException {
  if (index >= 1 && index <= numItems) {
    return items[translate(index)];
  }
  else {  // index out of range
    throw new ListIndexOutOfBoundsException(
         "ListIndexOutOfBoundsException on get");
  }  // end if
} // end get

public void remove(int index)
                throws ListIndexOutOfBoundsException {
  if (index >= 1 && index <= numItems) {
    // delete item by shifting all items at
    // positions > index toward the beginning of the list
    // (no shift if index == size)
    for (int pos = index+1; pos <= size(); pos++) {
      items[translate(pos-1)] = items[translate(pos)];
    }  // end for
    numItems--;
  }
```

translate?

```
    else {  // index out of range
        throw new ListIndexOutOfBoundsException(
            "ListIndexOutOfBoundsException on remove");
    }  // end if
} // end remove


private int translate(int position) {
  return position - 1;
}  // end translate
}  // end ListArrayBased
```

The following program segment demonstrates the use of *ListArray-Based*:

```
static public void main(String args[]) {
    . . .

    ListArrayBased aList = new ListArrayBased();
    String dataItem;

    aList.add(1, "Cathryn");
    . . .

    dataItem = aList.get(1);
    . . .
```

A client of the class cannot access the class's private members directly

Note that references within this program such as *aList.numItems*, *aList.items[4]*, and *aList.translate(6)* would be illegal because *numItems*, *items*, and *translate* are private members of the class.

In summary, to implement an ADT, given implementation-independent specifications of the ADT operations, you first must choose a data structure to contain the data. Next, you define and implement a class within a Java source file. The ADT operations are public methods within the class, and the ADT data is represented as data fields that are typically private. You then implement the class's methods within an implementation file. The program that uses the class will be able to access the data only by using the ADT operations.

SUMMARY

1. Data abstraction is a technique for controlling the interaction between a program and its data structures. It builds walls around a program's data structures, just as other aspects of modularity build walls around a program's algorithms. Such walls make programs easier to design, implement, read, and modify.

2. The specification of a set of data-management operations together with the data values upon which they operate define an abstract data type (ADT).

3. The formal mathematical study of ADTs uses systems of axioms to specify the behavior of ADT operations.

4. Only after you have fully defined an ADT should you think about how to implement it. The proper choice of a data structure to implement an ADT depends both on the details of the ADT operations and on the context in which you will use the operations.

5. Even after you have selected a data structure as an implementation for an ADT, the remainder of the program should not depend on your particular choice. That is, you should access the data structure by using only the ADT operations. Thus, you hide the implementation behind a wall of ADT operations. To enforce the wall within Java, you define the ADT as a class, thus hiding the ADT's implementation from the program that uses the ADT.

6. An object encapsulates both data and operations on that data. In Java, objects are instances of a class, which is a programmer-defined data type.

7. A Java class contains at least one constructor, which is an initialization method.

8. If you do not define a constructor for a class, the compiler will generate a default constructor—that is, one without parameters—for you. Members of a class should be declared as public or private. The client of the class, that is, the program that uses the class, cannot use members that are private. However, the implementations of methods can use them. Typically, you should make the data fields of a class private and provide public methods to access some or all of the data fields.

CAUTIONS

1. After you design a class, try writing some code that uses your class before you commit to your design. Not only will you see whether your design works for the problem at hand, but you will also test your understanding of your own design and check the comments that document your specifications.

2. When you implement a class, you might discover problems with either your class design or your specifications. If these problems occur, change your design and specifications, try using the class again, and continue implementing. These comments are consistent with the discussion of software life cycle in Chapter 1.

3. A program should not depend upon the particular implementations of its ADTs. By using a class to implement an ADT, you encapsulate the ADT's data and operations. In this way, you can

hide implementation details from the program that uses the ADT. In particular, by making the class's data fields private, you can change the class's implementation without affecting the client.

4. By making a class's data fields private, you make it easier to locate errors in a program's logic. An ADT—and hence a class—is responsible for maintaining its data. If an error occurs, you look at the class's implementation for the source of the error. If the client could manipulate this data directly because the data was public, you would not know where to look for errors.

5. Variables that are local to a method's implementation should not be data fields of the class.

6. If you define a constructor for a class but do not also define a default constructor, the compiler will not generate one for you. In this case, a statement such as

```
ListArrayBased aList = new ListArrayBased();
```

is illegal.

7. An array-based implementation of an ADT restricts the number of items that you can store. Chapter 4 will discuss a way to avoid this problem.

SELF-TEST EXERCISES

1. What is the significance of "wall" and "contract"? Why do these notions help you to become a better problem solver?

2. Write a pseudocode method *swap(aList, i, j)* that interchanges the items currently in positions *i* and *j* of a list. Define the method in terms of the operations of the ADT list, so that it is independent of any particular implementation of the list. Assume that the list, in fact, has items at positions *i* and *j*. What impact does this assumption have on your solution? (See Exercise 2.)

3. What grocery list results from the following sequence of ADT list operations?

```
aList.createList()
aList.add(1, butter)
aList.add(1, eggs)
aList.add(1, milk)
```

4. Write specifications for a list whose insertion, deletion, and retrieval operations are at the end of the list.

5. Write preconditions and postconditions for each of the operations of the ADT sorted list.

6. Write a pseudocode method that creates a sorted list *sortedList* from the list *aList* by using the operations of the ADTs list and sorted list.

7. The specifications of the ADTs list and sorted list do not mention the case in which two or more items have the same value. Are these specifications sufficient to cover this case, or must they be revised?

EXERCISES

1. Consider an ADT list of integers. Write a method that computes the sum of the integers in the list *aList*. The definition of your method should be independent of the list's implementation.

2. Implement the method *swap*, as described in Self-Test Exercise 2, but remove the assumption that the ith and j^{th} items in the list exist. Throw an exception *ListIndexOutOfBoundsException* if *i* or *j* is out of range.

3. Use the method *swap* that you wrote in Exercise 2 to write a method that reverses the order of the items in a list *aList*.

4. The section "The ADT List" describes the methods *displayList* and *replace*. As given in this chapter, these operations exist outside of the ADT; that is, they are not operations of the ADT list. Instead, their implementations are written in terms of the ADT list's operations.

   a. What is an advantage and a disadvantage of the way that *displayList* and *replace* are implemented?
   b. What is an advantage and a disadvantage of adding the operations *displayList* and *replace* to the ADT list?

5. In mathematics, a **set** is a group of distinct items. Specify operations such as equality, subset, union, and intersection as a part of the ADT set.

6. Specify operations that are a part of the ADT fraction. Include typical operations such as addition, subtraction, and reduce (reduce fraction to lowest terms).

7. Write a pseudocode method in terms of the ADT appointment book, described in the section "Designing an ADT," for each of the following tasks:

   a. Change the purpose of the appointment at a given date and time.
   b. Display all the appointments for a given date.

   Do you need to add operations to the ADT to perform these tasks?

8. Consider the ADT polynomial—in a single variable *x*—whose operations include the following:

   degree()
   // Returns the degree of a polynomial.
   getCoefficient(power)
   // Returns the coefficient of the x^{power} term.
   changeCoefficient(newCoefficient, power)

```
// Replaces the coefficient of the x^power term
// with newCoefficient.
```

For this problem, consider only polynomials whose exponents are nonnegative integers. For example,

$$p = 4x^5 + 7x^3 - x^2 + 9$$

The following examples demonstrate the ADT operations on this polynomial.

$p.degree()$ is 5 (the highest power of a term with a nonzero coefficient)

$p.getCoefficient(3)$ is 7 (the coefficient of the x^3 term)

$p.getCoefficient(4)$ is 0 (the coefficient of a missing term is implicitly 0)

$p.changeCoefficient(-3, 7)$ produces the polynomial

$$p = -3x^7 + 4x^5 + 7x^3 - x^2 + 9$$

Using these ADT operations, write statements to perform the following tasks:

a. Display the coefficient of the term that has the highest power.
b. Increase the coefficient of the x^3 term by 8.
c. Compute the sum of two polynomials.

9. Write pseudocode implementations of the operations of the ADT polynomial, as defined in Exercise 8, in terms of the operations of the ADT list.

10. Imagine an unknown implementation of an ADT sorted list of integers. This ADT organizes its items into ascending order. Suppose that you have just read N integers into a one-dimensional array of integers called data. Write some Java statements that use the operations of the ADT sorted list to sort the array into ascending order.

11. Use the axioms for the ADT list, as given in this chapter in the section "Axioms," to prove that the sequence of operations

```
Insert A into position 2
Insert B into position 2
Insert C into position 2
```

has the same effect on a nonempty list of characters as the sequence

```
Insert C into position 2
Insert B into position 3
Insert A into position 4
```

12. Define a set of axioms for the ADT sorted list and use them to prove that the sorted list of characters, which is defined by the sequence of operations

```
Create an empty sorted list
Insert S
Insert T
```

```
Insert R
Delete T
```

is exactly the same as the sorted list defined by the sequence

```
Create an empty sorted list
Insert T
Insert R
Delete T
Insert S
```

13. Repeat Exercise 17 in Chapter 2, using a variation of the ADT list to implement the method $f(n)$.

14. Write pseudocode that merges two sorted lists into a new third sorted list by using only operations of the ADT sorted list.

PROGRAMMING PROBLEMS

1. Design and implement an ADT that represents a triangle. The data for the ADT should include the three sides of the triangle but could also include the triangle's three angles. This data should be declared private in the class that implements the ADT.

   Include at least two initialization operations: One that provides default values for the ADT's data, and another that sets this data to client-supplied values. These operations are the class's constructors.

   The ADT also should include operations that look at the values of the ADT's data; change the values of the ADT's data; compute the triangle's area; and determine whether the triangle is a right triangle, an equilateral triangle, or an isosceles triangle.

2. Design and implement an ADT that represents the time of day. Represent the time as hours and minutes on a 24-hour clock. The hours and minutes are the private data fields of the class that implements the ADT.

   Include at least two initialization operations: One that provides a default value for the time, and another that sets the time to a client-supplied value. These operations are the class's constructors.

   Include operations that set the time, increase the present time by a number of minutes, and display the time in 12-hour and 24-hour notations.

3. Design and implement an ADT that represents a calendar date. You can represent a date's month, day, and year as integers (for example, 4/1/2002). Include operations that advance the date by one day and display the date by using either numbers or words for the months. As an enhancement, include the name of the day.

4. Design and implement an ADT that represents a price in U.S. currency as dollars and cents. After you complete the implementation, write a client method that computes the change due a customer who pays x for an item whose price is y.

5. Define a class for an array-based implementation of the ADT sorted list. Consider a recursive implementation for *locateIndex*. Should *sortedAdd* and *sortedRemove* call *locateIndex*?

6. Write recursive array-based implementations of the insertion, deletion, and retrieval operations for the ADTs list and sorted list.

7. Implement the ADT set that you specified in Exercise 5 by using only arrays and simple variables.

8. Implement the ADT polynomial that Exercise 8 describes.

9. Implement the ADT appointment book, described in the section "Designing an ADT." Add operations as necessary. For example, you should add operations to read and write appointments.

10. **a.** Implement the ADT fraction that you specified in Exercise 6. Provide operations that read, write, add, subtract, multiply, and divide fractions. The results of all arithmetic operations should be in lowest terms, so include a private method *reduceToLowestTerms*. Exercise 20 in Chapter 2 will help you with the details of this method. (Should your read and write operations call *reduceToLowestTerms*?) To simplify the determination of a fraction's sign, you can assume that the denominator of the fraction is positive.

     b. Specify and implement an ADT for mixed numbers, each of which contains an integer portion and a fractional portion in lowest terms. Assume the existence of the ADT fraction (see part a). Provide operations that read, write, add, subtract, multiply, and divide mixed numbers. The results of all arithmetic operations should have fractional portions that are in lowest terms. Also include an operation that converts a fraction to a mixed number.

11. Implement the recipe database as described in the section "Designing an ADT" and, in doing so, implement the ADTs recipe and measurement. Add operations as necessary. For example, you should add operations to the ADT recipe book to read, write, and scale recipes.

12. Repeat Programming Problem 2 of Chapter 1 in light of your knowledge of ADTs and classes.

13. Repeat Programming Problem 3 of Chapter 1 in light of your knowledge of ADTs and classes.

CHAPTER 4

Linked Lists

PREVIEW This chapter reviews Java references and introduces you to the data structure linked list. You will see algorithms for fundamental linked list operations such as insertion and deletion. The chapter also describes several variations of the basic linked list. As you will see, you can use a linked list and its variations when implementing many of the ADTs that appear throughout the remainder of this book. The material in this chapter is thus essential to much of the presentation in the following chapters.

PRELIMINARIES

The ADT list, as described in the previous chapter, has operations to insert, delete, and retrieve items, given their positions within the list. A close examination of the array-based implementation of the ADT list reveals that an array is not always the best data structure to use to maintain a collection of data. An array has a **fixed size**—at least in most commonly used programming languages—but the ADT list can have an arbitrary length. Thus, in the strict sense, you cannot use an array to implement a list because it is certainly possible for the number of items in the list to exceed the fixed size of the array. When developing implementations for ADTs, you often are confronted with this fixed-size problem. In many contexts, you must reject an implementation that has a fixed size in favor of one that can grow dynamically.

In addition, although the most intuitive means of imposing an order on data is to sequence it physically, this approach has its disadvantages. In a physical ordering, the successor of an item *x* is the next data item in sequence after *x*, that is, the item "to the right" of *x*. An array orders its items physically and, as you saw in the previous chapter, when you use an array to implement a list, you must shift data when you insert or delete an item at a specified position. Shifting data can be a time-consuming process that you should avoid, if possible. What alternatives to shifting data are available?

To get a conceptual notion of a list implementation that does not involve shifting, consider Figure 4-1. This figure should help free you from the notion that the only way to maintain a given order of data is to store the data in that order. In these diagrams, each item of the list is actually *linked to* the next item. Thus, if you know where an item is, you can determine its successor, which can be anywhere physically. This flexibility not only allows you to insert and delete data items without shifting data, but it also allows you to increase the size of the list easily. If you need to insert a new item, you simply find its place in the list and set two **links.** Similarly, to delete an item, you find the item and change a link to bypass the item.

An item in a linked list references its successor

Because the items in this data structure are *linked* to one another, it is called a **linked list.** As you will see shortly, *a linked list is able to grow as needed*, whereas an array can hold only a fixed number of data items. In many applications, this flexibility gives a linked list a significant advantage.

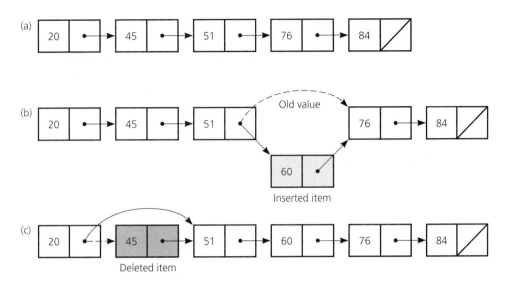

Figure 4-1

(a) A linked list of integers; (b) insertion; (c) deletion

Before we examine linked lists and their use in the implementation of an ADT, we will examine how Java references can be used to implement a linked list. Like many programming languages, Java allows one object to reference another, and you can use this ability to build a linked list. The next section reviews the mechanics of these references.

Object References

When you declare a variable that refers to an object of a given class, you are creating a reference to the object. Note that an object of that class does not come into existence until you apply the *new* operator. A **reference variable**, or simply a **reference**, contains the location, or **address** in memory, of an object. By using a reference to a particular object, you can locate the object and, for example, access the object's public members.

A reference contains the address of an object

Let's look at an example using the class *java.lang.Integer* to help us visualize this scenario:

```
Integer intRef;
intRef = new Integer(5);
```

The first line declares a reference variable *intRef* that can be used to locate an *Integer* object. The second line actually instantiates an *Integer* object and assigns its location to *intRef*. Figure 4-2 illustrates that there are now two separate entities in our program: a reference variable *intRef* that provides the location of an *Integer* object and an *Integer* object.

*intRef references the newly instantiated **Integer** object*

When you declare a reference variable as a data field within a class but do not instantiate an object for it in a constructor, it is initialized to

*A reference variable as a data field of a class has the default value **null***

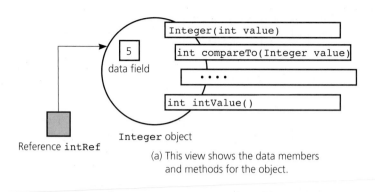

Reference intRef   Integer object

(a) This view shows the data members
and methods for the object.

Integer object

(b) This view only shows the data
members for simplicity. This
is the view used throughout
Reference intRef   the text.

Figure 4-2

A reference to an *Integer* object

null. You can use this constant *null* as the value of a reference to any
type of object. This use indicates that the reference variable does not currently reference any object. For example, if *intRef* is declared as a data
field, and you attempt to use it before you instantiate an *Integer* object
for it, the exception *java.lang.NullPointerException* will be thrown
at runtime. This exception indicates that you attempted to access an
object by using a reference variable that contains a *null* value.

A local reference variable has no
default value

    When you declare a reference variable to be local to a method, no
default value is provided. For example, let *p* be declared as a reference to
an *Integer* object. If you attempt to use *p* to access an object before *p* is
initialized, the compiler will give you the error message *"Variable p*
may not have been initialized."

    When one reference variable is assigned to another reference variable,
both references then refer to the same object. For example,

```
Integer p, q;
p = new Integer(6);
q = p;
```

Figure 4-3d illustrates the result of this assignment. Now the *Integer*
object has two references to it, *p* and *q*. The effect of the assignment

Figure 4-3

(a) Declaring reference variables; (b) allocating an object; (c) allocating another object, with the dereferenced object marked for garbage collection; (d) assigning a reference; (e) allocating an object; (f) assigning *null* to a reference variable; (g) assigning a reference with a *null* value

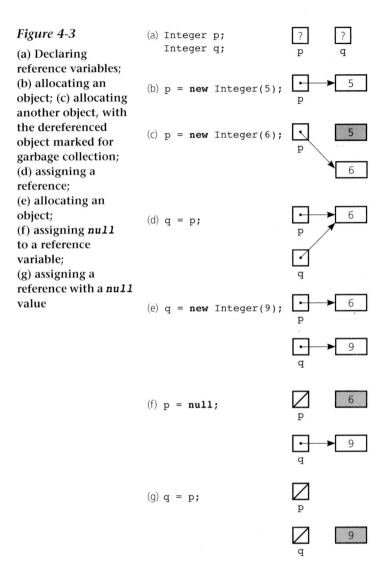

operator is to cause the reference variable on the left side of the assignment to reference the same object as referenced by the right side of the assignment operator. Alternatively, you could let *q* reference a new object, as Figure 4-3e shows.

Suppose that you no longer need the value in a reference variable. That is, you do not want the reference variable to locate any particular object. You can explicitly assign the constant value *null*, discussed earlier, to a reference variable to indicate that it no longer references any object. When you remove all references to an object, the system marks the object for garbage collection, as shown in Figures 4-3c and 4-3f. The Java runtime environment will periodically run a method that returns the memory allocated to the marked objects back to the system for future

The system marks unreferenced objects for garbage collection

use. In other programming languages, such as C++, the programmer must explicitly deallocate memory using special language constructs.

When you declare an array of objects and apply the *new* operator, an array of references is actually created, not an array of objects. For example,

An array of objects is actually an array of references to the objects

```
Integer[] scores = new Integer[30];
```

creates an array of 30 references for *Integer* objects. You must instantiate actual *Integer* objects for each of the array references. For example, you might instantiate objects for the array just created as follows:

```
scores[0] = new Integer(7);
scores[1] = new Integer(9); // and so on ...
```

When you use the equality operators (== and !=), you are actually comparing the values of the reference variables, not the objects that they reference. Suppose that you have the following class definition:

Equality operators compare values of reference variables, not the objects that they reference

```
public class MyNumber {
   private int num;

   public MyNumber(int n) {
      num = n;
   } // end constructor

   public String toString() {
      return "My number is " + num;
   } // end toString
} // end class MyNumber
```

and you declare the following:

```
MyNumber x = new MyNumber(9);
MyNumber y = new MyNumber(9);
MyNumber z = x;
```

Although objects x and y contain the same data, the == operator returns *false*, since x and y refer to different objects. The expression $x == z$ is *true* because the assignment statement $z = x$ causes z to refer to the same object that x references. If you need to be able to compare objects field by field, you must redefine the *equals* method for the class, as discussed in Chapter 3.

Parameter passing in Java can also be discussed in terms of reference variables. When a method is called and has parameters that are objects, the reference value of the actual argument is copied to a formal parameter reference variable. During the execution of the method, the object is accessed through the formal parameter reference variable. This provides the same result as if the original reference was used. Upon completion of the method, the references stored in these formal parameters are discarded, although the objects that the parameters reference may be retained.

When you pass an object to a method as an argument, the reference to the object is copied to the method's formal parameter

This method of parameter passing helps to explain why the use of the *new* operator with a formal parameter in a method can produce

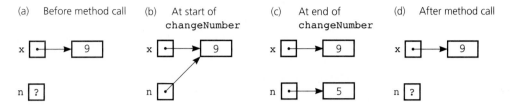

Figure 4-4

The value of a parameter does not affect the argument's value

unexpected results. For example, suppose you have the following method *changeNumber*, which uses the *MyNumber* class:

```
public void changeNumber(MyNumber n) {
  n = new MyNumber(5);
} // end changeNumber
```

and the following Java statements:

```
MyNumber x = new MyNumber(9);
changeNumber(x); // attempts to assign 5 to x
System.out.println(x);
```

The output is "My number is 9". Figure 4-4 demonstrates why this is the case. When the *changeNumber* method is invoked, the reference to object *x* is copied to the formal parameter reference *n* of *changeNumber*. During the execution of *changeNumber*, a new object is created for *n* to reference. But when the *changeNumber* method completes execution, the reference variable *n* is discarded. This causes the newly created object containing 5 to be marked for garbage collection. The value of the reference variable *x* remains unchanged; it still references the same object (containing 9) that it did before the *changeNumber* method was executed.

Note that ADT implementations and data structures that use Java references are said to be **reference based**.

KEY CONCEPTS

Java Reference Variables

1. The declaration

```
Integer intRef;
```

statically allocates a reference variable *intRef* whose value is *null*. When a reference variable contains *null*, it does not reference anything.

2. *intRef* can reference an *Integer* object. The statement

```
intRef = new Integer(5);
```

dynamically allocates an *Integer* object referenced by *intRef*. (However, see item 3 on this list.)

3. If, for some reason, *new* cannot instantiate an object of the class represented, it may throw a `java.lang.InstantiationException` or a `java.lang.IllegalAccessException`. Thus, you can place the following statement within a `try` block to test whether memory was successfully allocated:

    ```
    intRef = new Integer(5);
    ```

4. When the last reference to an object is removed, the object is marked for garbage collection.

Resizeable Arrays

When you declare an array in Java by using statements such as

The number of references in a Java array is of a fixed size

```
final int MAX_SIZE = 50;
double[] myArray = new double[MAX_SIZE];
```

the Java runtime environment reserves a specific number—*MAX_SIZE*, in this case—of references for the array. Once the array has been instantiated, it has a fixed size for the remainder of its lifetime. We have already discussed the problem this fixed-size data structure causes when your program has more than *MAX_SIZE* items to place into the array.

You can create the illusion of a resizeable array—an array that grows and shrinks as the program executes—by using an allocate and copy strategy with fixed-size arrays. If the array that you are currently using in the program reaches its capacity, you allocate a larger array and copy the references stored in the original array to the larger array. How much larger should the new array be? The increment size can be a fixed number of elements or a multiple of the current array size. The following statements demonstrate how you could accomplish this task for an array *myArray*:

Allocate a larger array

Copy the original array to the new larger array

```
if (capacityIncrement == 0) {
  capacity *= 2;
}
else {
  capacity += capacityIncrement;
}
// now create a new array using the updated
// capacity value
double [] newArray = new double[capacity];
// copy the contents of the original array
// to the new array
for (int i = 0; i < myArray.length; i++) {
  newArray[i] = myArray[i];
} // end for
// now change the reference to the original array
// to the new array
myArray = newArray;
```

In this example, *capacity* and *capacityIncrement* represent the capacity of the array and the size of the increment, respectively. Once you exceed the capacity of *myArray*, you allocate a larger array *newArray* according to the value of *capacityIncrement*. Note that if the *capacityIncrement* is zero, the array capacity doubles instead of increasing by a fixed amount. You must copy the values from the original array to the new array and then change the original array reference to reference the new array.

The class *java.util.Vector* uses a similar technique to implement a growable array of objects. The underlying implementation of *java.util.Vector* uses a fixed array of size *capacity* and has a *capacityIncrement* that you can change to suit your needs. Exercise 16 asks you to explore the *java.util.Vector* class to determine when resizing the underlying array will occur.

Subsequent discussion in this book will refer to both fixed-sized and resizeable arrays. Our array-based ADT implementations will use fixed-sized arrays for simplicity. The programming problems will ask you to create array-based implementations that use resizeable arrays.

Reference-Based Linked Lists

A linked list, such as the one in Figure 4-1, contains components that are linked to one another. Each component—usually called a **node**—contains both data and a "link" to the next item. Typically, such links are Java reference variables; another possibility is mentioned at the end of this section. Although you have seen most of the mechanics of references, using references to implement a linked list is probably not yet completely clear to you. Consider now how you can set up such a linked list.

Each node of the list can be implemented as an object. For example, if you want to create a linked list of integers, you could use the following class definition, as Figure 4-5 illustrates:

A node in a linked list is an object

```java
public class IntegerNode {
  public int item;
  public IntegerNode next;
} // end class IntegerNode
```

A node definition that is not desirable because its data fields are public

However, this type of definition violates our rule that data fields must be declared private. We could rewrite this class with accessor and mutator methods as follows:

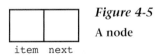

Figure 4-5
A node

item next

```java
public class IntegerNode {
  private int item;
  private IntegerNode next;

  public void setItem(int newItem) {
    item = newItem;
  } // end setItem

  public int getItem() {
```

A node for a linked list of integers

```
      return item;
    } // end getitem

    public void setNext(IntegerNode nextNode) {
      next = nextNode;
    } // end setNext

    public IntegerNode getNext() {
      return next;
    } // end getNext

  } // end class IntegerNode
```

and use this class as follows:

Defining a reference to a node

```
IntegerNode n1 = new IntegerNode();
IntegerNode n2 = new IntegerNode();
n1.setItem(5); // set item in first node
n2.setItem(9); // set item in second node
n1.setNext(n2); // link the nodes
```

This scenario is depicted in Figure 4-6. The mutator methods *setItem* and *setNext* initialize the data fields of the two nodes. Note how *setNext* links the nodes by making the first node reference the second.

We could improve this class by adding constructors, as follows:

```
public class IntegerNode {
  private int item;
  private IntegerNode next;
```

Constructors

```
  public IntegerNode(int newItem) {
    item = newItem;
    next = null;
  } // end constructor

  public IntegerNode(int newItem, IntegerNode nextNode) {
    item = newItem;
```

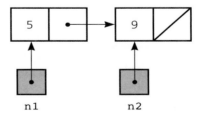

Figure 4-6

The result of linking two instances of *IntegerNode*

```
      next = nextNode;
   } // end constructor
      // setItem, getItem, setNext, getNext as before
      ...
   }    // end class IntegerNode
```

This definition of a node restricts the data to a single integer field. Since we would like to have this class be as reusable as possible, it would be better to change the data field to be of type *Object*. Recall that every class in Java is ultimately derived from the class *Object* through inheritance. This means that any class created in Java could use this node definition for storing objects. Let's first examine the revised class, using objects for data:

A node for a linked list of objects

```
public class Node {
   private Object item;
   private Node next;

   public Node(Object newItem) {
      item = newItem;
      next = null;
   } // end constructor

   public Node(Object newItem, Node nextNode) {
      item = newItem;
      next = nextNode;
   } // end constructor

   public void setItem(Object newItem) {
      item = newItem;
   } // end setItem

   public Object getItem() {
      return item;
   } // end getItem

   public void setNext(Node nextNode) {
      next = nextNode;
   } // end setNext

   public Node getNext() {
      return next;
   } // end getNext
} // end class Node
```

You can use this class as follows:

```
Node n = new Node(new Integer(6));
Node first = new Node(new Integer(9), n);
```

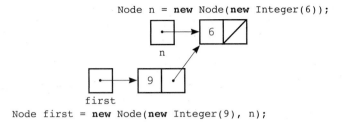

```
              Node n = new Node(new Integer(6));
```

```
Node first = new Node(new Integer(9), n);
```

Figure 4-7

Using the *Node* constructor to initialize a data field and
a link value

Figure 4-7 illustrates this scenario. The constructors are used to initialize the data field and a link value that is either *null* or provided as an
argument. Although the data portion of each node in a linked list can
reference an instance of any class, the figure illustrates data items that
are instances of the class *java.lang.Integer*.

To complete our general description of the linked list, we must consider two other issues. First, what is the value of the data field *next* in the
last node in the list? By setting this field to *null*, you can easily detect
when you are at the end of the linked list.

Second, nothing so far references the beginning of the linked list. If
you cannot get to the beginning of the list, you cannot get to the second
node in the list, and if you cannot get to the second node in the list, you
cannot get to the third node in the list, and so on. The solution is to
have an additional reference variable whose sole purpose is to locate the
first node in the linked list. Such a variable is often called **head**.

The head of a linked list refer-
ences the list's first node

Observe in Figure 4-8 that the reference variable *head* is different
from the other reference variables in the diagram in that it is not within
one of the nodes. Rather, it is a simple reference variable that is external
to the linked list, whereas the *next* data fields are internal reference variables within the nodes of the list. The variable *head* simply enables you
to access the list's beginning. Also, note that *head* always exists, even at
times when there are no nodes in the linked list. The statement

```
Node head = null;
```

creates the variable *head*, whose value is initially *null*. This indicates that
head does not reference anything, and therefore that this list is empty.

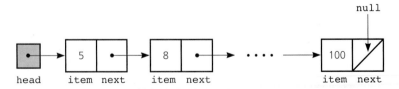

Figure 4-8

A **head** reference to a linked list

Figure 4-9

A lost node

```
head = new Node(new Integer(5));     head = null;
```

It is a common mistake to think that before you can assign *head* a value, you must execute the statement *head = new Node()*. This misconception is rooted in the belief that the variable *head* does not exist unless you create a new node. This is not at all true; *head* is a reference variable waiting to be assigned a value. Thus, for example, you can assign *null* to *head* without first using *new*. In fact, the sequence

```
head = new Node();  // Don't really need to use new here
head = null;    // since we lose the new Node object here
```

A common misconception

destroys the contents of the only reference—*head*—to the newly created node, as Figure 4-9 illustrates. Thus, you have needlessly created a new node and then made it inaccessible. Remember that when you remove the last reference from a node, the system marks it for garbage collection.

As was mentioned earlier, you do not need references to implement a linked list. Programming Problem 9 at the end of this chapter discusses an implementation that uses an array to represent the items in a linked list. Although sometimes useful, such implementations are unusual.

PROGRAMMING WITH LINKED LISTS

The previous section illustrated how you can use reference variables to implement a linked list. This section begins by developing algorithms for displaying the data portions of such a linked list and for inserting items into and deleting items from a linked list. These linked list operations are the basis of many of the data structures that appear throughout the remainder of the book. Thus, the material in this section is essential to much of the discussion in the following chapters.

Displaying the Contents of a Linked List

Suppose now that you have a linked list, as was pictured in Figure 4-8, and that you want to display the data in the list. A high-level pseudocode solution is

```
Let a variable curr reference the first node in
    the linked list
while (the curr reference is not null) {
  Display the data portion of the current node
  Set the curr reference to the next field of the
      current node
} // end while
```

This solution requires that you keep track of the current position within the linked list. Thus, you need a reference variable *curr* that references the current node. Initially, *curr* must reference the first node. Since *head* references the first node, simply copy *head* into *curr* by writing

```
Node curr = head;
```

To display the data portion of the current node, you can use the statement[1]

```
System.out.println(curr.getItem());
```

Finally, to advance the current position to the next node, you write

```
curr = curr.getNext();
```

Figure 4-10 illustrates this action. If the previous assignment statement is not clear, consider

```
temp = curr.getNext();
curr = temp;
```

and then convince yourself that the intermediate variable *temp* is not necessary.

These ideas lead to the following loop in Java:

```
// Display the data in a linked list that head
// references.
// Loop invariant: curr references the next node to be
// displayed
for (Node curr = head; curr != null; curr = curr.getNext()) {
   System.out.println(curr.getItem());
} // end for
```

The variable *curr* references each node in a nonempty linked list during the course of the *for* loop's execution, and so the data portion of each node is displayed. After the last node is displayed, *curr* becomes

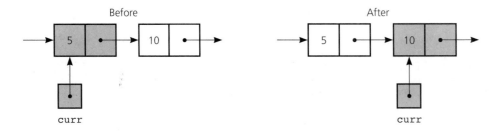

Figure 4-10

The effect of the assignment ***curr = curr.getNext()***

---

[1]See Appendix A for a discussion of *System.out.println* with object parameters.

null and the *for* loop terminates. When the list is empty—that is, when *head* is *null*—the *for* loop is correctly skipped.

A common error in the *for* statement is to compare *curr.getNext()* instead of *curr* with *null*. When *curr* references the last node of a non-empty linked list, *curr.getNext()* is *null*, and so the *for* loop would terminate before displaying the data in the last node. In addition, when the list is empty—that is, when *head* and therefore *curr* are *null*—*curr.getNext()* will throw a *NullPointerException*. Such references are incorrect and should be avoided.

Displaying a linked list is an example of a common operation, **list traversal**. A traversal sequentially **visits** each node in the list until it reaches the end of the list. Our example displays the data portion of each node when it visits the node. Later in this book, you will see that you can do other useful things to a node during a visit.

A traverse operation visits each node in the linked list

Displaying a linked list does not alter it; you will now see operations that modify a linked list by deleting and inserting nodes. These operations assume that the linked list has already been created. Ultimately, you will see how to build a linked list by inserting nodes into an initially empty list.

Deleting a Specified Node from a Linked List

So that you can focus on how to delete a particular node from a linked list, assume that the linked list shown in Figure 4-11 already exists. Notice that, in addition to *head*, the diagram includes two external reference variables, *curr* and *prev*. The task is to delete the node that *curr* references. As you soon will see, you also need *prev* to complete the deletion. For the moment, do not worry about how to establish *curr* and *prev*.

As Figure 4-11 indicates, you can delete a node *N*, which *curr* references, by altering the value of the reference *next* in the node that precedes *N*. You need to set this data field to reference the node that follows *N*, thus bypassing *N* on the chain. (The dashed line indicates the old reference value.) Notice that this reference change does not directly affect node *N*. Since *curr* still references node *N*, the node remains in existence,

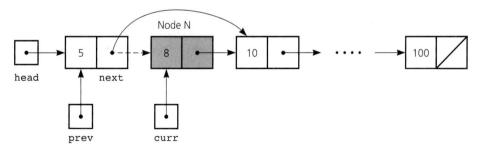

Figure 4-11

Deleting a node from a linked list

and it references the same node that it referenced before the deletion. However, the node has effectively been deleted from the linked list. For example, the method *displayList* from the previous section would not display the contents of node *N*. If *curr* is the only reference to node *N*, when we change *curr* to reference another node or set it equal to *null*, node *N* is marked for garbage collection.

To accomplish this deletion, notice first that if only the reference *curr* points to *N*, you would have no direct way to access the node that precedes *N*. After all, you cannot follow the links in the list backward. However, notice that the reference variable *prev* in Figure 4-11 references the node that precedes *N* and makes it possible for you to alter that node's *next* data field. Doing so deletes node *N* from the linked list. The following assignment statement is all that you need to delete the node that *curr* references:

Deleting an interior node

```
prev.setNext(curr.getNext());
```

A question comes to mind at this point:

- Does the previous method work for any node *N*, regardless of where in the linked list it appears?

No, the method does not work if the node to be deleted is the *first* node in the list, because it certainly does not make sense to assert that *prev* references the node that precedes this node! Thus, *deletion of the first node in a linked list is a special case,* as Figure 4-12 depicts. In this case, *curr* references the first node and *prev* is *null*.

When you delete the first node of the list, you must change the value of *head* to reflect the fact that, after the deletion, the list has a new first node. That is, the node that was second prior to the deletion is now first. You make this change to *head* by using the assignment statement

Deleting the first node is a special case

```
head = head.getNext();
```

As was the case for the deletion of an interior node, the *head* reference now bypasses the old first node. Notice also that if the node to be deleted is the *only* node in the list—and thus it is both the first node and the last node—the previous assignment statement assigns the value *null* to the

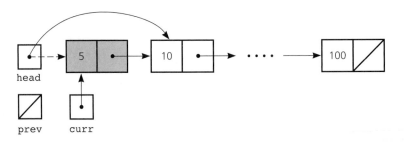

Figure 4-12

Deleting the first node

variable *head*. Recall that the value *null* in *head* indicates an empty list, and so this assignment statement handles the deletion of the only node in a list correctly.

If the node *N* is no longer needed, you should change the *next* data field of the node *N* to *null* and also the value of *curr* to *null*, as the following statements show:

```
curr.setNext(null);
curr = null;
```

This serves two purposes. First, the reference variables *curr* and *next* (in node *N*) can't be inadvertently followed, leading to subtle errors later in the program. Second, the system can now use this returned memory and possibly even reallocate it to your program as a result of the *new* operator.

So far, we have deleted the node *N* that *curr* references, given a reference variable *prev* to the node that precedes *N*. However, another question remains:

- How did the variables *curr* and *prev* come to reference the appropriate nodes?

To answer this question, consider the context in which you might expect to delete a node. In one common situation, you need to delete a node that you specify by position. Such is the case if you use a linked list to implement an ADT list. In another situation, you need to delete a node that contains a particular data value. Such is the case if you use a linked list to implement an ADT sorted list. In both of these situations, you do not pass the values of *curr* and *prev* to the deletion method, but instead the method establishes these values as its first step by searching the linked list for the node *N* that either is at a specified position or contains the data value to be deleted. Once the method finds the node *N*—and the node that precedes *N*—the deletion of *N* proceeds as described previously. The details of determining *curr* and *prev* for deletion are actually the same as for insertion, and they appear in the next section.

To summarize, the deletion process has three high-level steps:

1. Locate the node that you want to delete.
2. Disconnect this node from the linked list by changing references.
3. Return the node to the system.

Three steps to delete a node from a linked list

Later in this chapter, we will incorporate this deletion process into the implementation of the ADT list.

Inserting a Node into a Specified Position of a Linked List

Figure 4-13 illustrates the technique of inserting a new node into a specified position of a linked list. You insert the new node, which the reference

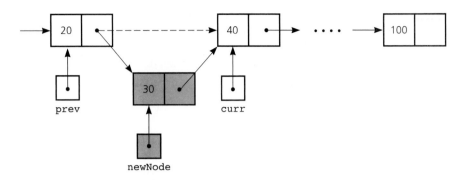

Figure 4-13

Inserting a new node into a linked list

variable *newNode* references, between the two nodes that *prev* and *curr* reference. As the diagram suggests, you can accomplish the insertion by using the following pair of assignment statements:

Inserting a node between nodes

```
newNode.setNext(curr);
prev.setNext(newNode);
```

The following two questions are analogous to those previously asked about the deletion of a node:

- How did the variables *newNode*, *curr*, and *prev* come to reference the appropriate nodes?
- Does the method work for inserting a node into any position of a linked list?

The answer to the first question, like the answer to the analogous question for deletion, is found by considering the context in which you will use the insertion operation. You establish the values of *curr* and *prev* by traversing the linked list until you find the proper position for the new item. You then use the *new* operator to create a new node that references the item as follows:

Creating a node for the new item

```
newNode = new Node(item);
```

You can now insert the node into the list, as was just described.

The answer to the second question is that *insertion, like deletion, must account for special cases*. First, consider the insertion of a node at the beginning of the linked list, as shown in Figure 4-14. You must make *head* reference the new node, and the new node must reference the node that had been at the beginning of the list. You accomplish this by using these statements:

Inserting a node at the beginning of a linked list

```
newNode.setNext(head);
head = newNode;
```

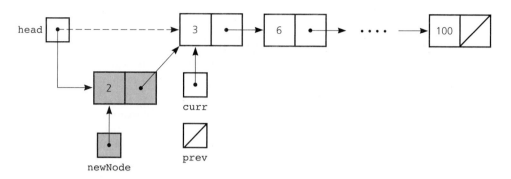

Figure 4-14

Inserting at the beginning of a linked list

Observe that if the list is empty before the insertion, *head* is *null*, so the *next* reference of the new item is set to *null*. This step is correct because the new item is the last item—as well as the first item—on the list.

   Figure 4-15 shows the insertion of a new node at the end of a linked list. This insertion is potentially a special case because the intention of the pair of assignment statements

```
newNode.setNext(curr);
prev.setNext(newNode);
```

is to insert the new node *between* the node that *curr* references and the node that *prev* references. If you are to insert the new node at the end of the list, what node should *curr* reference? In this situation, it makes sense to view the value of *curr* as *null* because, as you traverse the list, *curr* becomes *null* as it moves past the end of the list. Observe that if *curr* has the value *null* and *prev* references the last node on the list, the previous pair of assignment statements will indeed insert the new node at the end of the list. Thus, insertion at the end of a linked list is not a special case.

*If **curr** is **null**, inserting at the end of a linked list is not a special case*

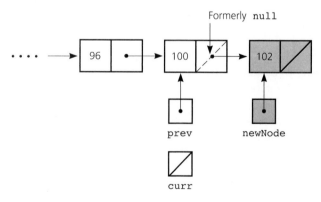

Figure 4-15

Inserting at the end of a linked list

To summarize, the insertion process requires three high-level steps:

Three steps to insert a new node
into a linked list

1. Determine the point of insertion.

2. Create a new node and store the new data in it.

3. Connect the new node to the linked list by changing references.

Determining *curr* and *prev*.   Let us now examine in more detail how to determine the references *curr* and *prev* for the insertion operation just described. As was mentioned, this determination depends on the context in which you will insert a node. As an example, consider a linked list of integers that are sorted into ascending order using the *IntegerNode* class in the previous section. To simplify the discussion, assume that the integers are distinct; that is, no duplicates are present in the list.

To determine the point at which the value *newValue* should be inserted into a sorted linked list, you must traverse the list from its beginning until you find the appropriate place for *newValue*. This appropriate place is just before the node that contains the first data item greater than *newValue*. You know that you will need a reference *curr* to the node that is to follow the new node; that is, *curr* references the node that contains the first data item greater than *newValue*. You also need a reference *prev* to the node that is to precede the new node; that is, *prev* references the node that contains the last data item smaller than *newValue*. Thus, as you traverse the linked list, you keep both a current reference *curr* and a *trailing* reference *prev*. When you reach the node that contains the first value larger than *newValue*, the trailing reference *prev* references the previous node. At this time, you can insert the new node between the two nodes that *prev* and *curr* reference, as was described earlier.

A first attempt at some pseudocode follows:

A first attempt at a solution

```
// determine the point of insertion into a sorted
// linked list

// initialize prev and curr to start the traversal
// from the beginning of the list
prev = null
curr = head

// advance prev and curr as long as
// newValue > the current data item
// Loop invariant: newValue > data items in all
// nodes at and before the node that prev references
while (newValue > curr.getItem()) { // causes a problem!
  prev = curr
  curr = curr.getNext()
}  // end while
```

Unfortunately, the *while* loop causes a problem when the new value is greater than all the values in the list, that is, when the insertion will be at the end of the linked list (or when the linked list is empty). Eventually, the *while* statement compares *newValue* to the value in the last node. During that execution of the loop, *curr* is assigned the value *null*. After this iteration, *newValue* is again compared to *curr.getItem()*, which, when *curr* is *null*, will throw the exception *NullPointerException*.

To solve this problem, you need another test in the termination condition of the *while* statement so that the loop exits when *curr* becomes *null*. Thus, you replace the *while* statement with

while (curr != **null** && newValue > curr.getItem())

The revised pseudocode is

```
// determine the point of insertion into a sorted
// linked list

// initialize prev and curr to start the traversal
// from the beginning of the list
prev = null
curr = head

// advance prev and curr as long as newValue > the
// current data item; do not go beyond end of list
// Loop invariant: newValue > data items in all
// nodes at and before the node that prev references
while (curr != null && newValue > curr.getItem()) {
  prev = curr
  curr = curr.getNext()
}  // end while
```

The correct solution

Notice how the *while* statement also solves the problem of inserting a node at the end of the linked list. In the case where *newValue* is greater than all the values in the list, *prev* references the last node in the list and *curr* becomes *null*, thus terminating the *while* loop. (See Figure 4-16.) Therefore, as you saw earlier, you can insert the new node at the end of the list by using the standard pair of assignment statements

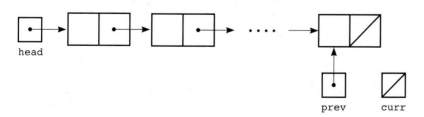

Figure 4-16

When *prev* references the last node and *curr* is *null*, insertion will be at the end of the linked list

```
newNode.setNext(curr);
prev.setNext(newNode);
```

Now consider the insertion of a node at the beginning of the linked list. This situation arises when the value to be inserted is *smaller* than all the values currently in the list. In this case, the `while` loop in the previous pseudocode is never entered, so `prev` and `curr` maintain their original values, as Figure 4-17 illustrates. In particular, `prev` maintains its original

value of `null`. This is the only situation in which the value of `prev` is equal to `null` after execution of the `while` loop ends. Thus, you can detect an insertion at the beginning of the list by comparing `prev` to `null`.

Observe that the solution also correctly handles insertion into an empty linked list as an insertion at the beginning of the list. When the list is empty, the statement `curr = head` assigns `curr` an initial value of

`null`, and thus the `while` loop is never entered. Therefore, `prev` maintains its original value of `null`, indicating an insertion at the beginning of the list.

A little thought should convince you that the solution that determines the point of insertion also works for deletion. If you want to delete a given integer from a linked list of sorted integers, you obviously want to traverse the list until you find the node that contains the value sought. The previous pseudocode will do just that: `curr` will reference the desired node and `prev` either will reference the preceding node or, if the desired node is first on the list, will be `null`, as shown in Figure 4-17.

The following Java statements implement the previous pseudocode:

```
// determine the point of insertion or deletion
// for a sorted linked list
// Loop invariant: newValue > data items in all
// nodes at and before the node that prev references
for ( prev = null, curr = head;
      (curr != null) && (newValue > curr.getItem())
      prev = curr, curr = curr.getNext() ) {
  // no statements in loop body
} // end for
```

Recall that the `&&` (*and*) operator in Java does not evaluate its second operand if its first operand is `false`. Thus, when `curr` becomes `null`, the loop exits without attempting to evaluate `curr.getItem()`. It is, therefore, essential that `curr != null` be first in the logical expression.

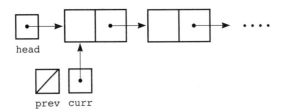

Figure 4-17

When **prev** is **null** and **curr** references the first node, insertion or deletion will be at the beginning of the linked list

head

prev curr

Notice that this implementation relies on the ability to compare one value to another by using the built-in greater than (>) operation for the primitive data type *int*. Suppose instead that the items in the list are of data type *Object*. You can compare objects if they implement the interface *java.lang.Comparable* and have an implementation of the method *compareTo*. For example, suppose that we define the following class to represent a person's first and last names:

```java
public class FullName implements java.lang.Comparable {
  private String firstName;
  private String lastName;

  public FullName(String first, String last) {
    firstName = first;
    lastName = last;
  } // end constructor

  public int compareTo(Object rhs) {
    // returns 0 if all fields match
    // returns 1 if lastName greater than rhs.lastName or
    //      if lastName equals rhs.lastName and
    //      firstName is greater than rhs.firstName
    // returns -1 if lastName is less than rhs.lastName or
    //      if lastName equals rhs.lastName and
    //      firstName is less than rhs.firstName
    if (lastName.compareTo(((FullName)rhs).lastName)==0){
      return firstName.compareTo(((FullName)rhs).firstName);
    }
    else {
      return lastName.compareTo(((FullName)rhs).lastName);
    } // end if
  } // end compareTo
} // end class FullName
```

You can use the following code to find the location of the item *newValue* of type *Comparable* within the list:

```java
// determine the point of insertion or deletion
// for a sorted linked list of objects
// Loop invariant: newValue > data items (using
// compareTo method) in all nodes at and before
// the node that prev references
for ( prev = null, curr = head;
      (curr != null ) &&
      (newValue.compareTo(curr.getItem()) > 0);
      prev = curr, curr = curr.getNext() ) {
} // end for
```

Determining the point of insertion or deletion for a sorted linked list of objects

*Use **compareTo** to compare objects*

The *compareTo* method defines the criteria to decide when objects are equal or when one object is less than or greater than another. This in turn can be used to create a sorted list of objects based upon the criteria defined by the new comparison method.

Determining the values of *curr* and *prev* is simpler when you insert or delete a node by position instead of by its value. This determination is necessary when you use a linked list to implement the ADT list, as you will see next.

A Reference-Based Implementation of the ADT List

This section considers how you can use Java references instead of an array to implement the ADT list. Unlike the array-based implementation, a reference-based implementation does not shift items during insertion and deletion operations. It also does not impose a fixed maximum length on the list—except, of course, as imposed by the storage limits of the system.

As in Chapter 3, and as we will do in the rest of the book, we will implement this ADT as a Java class. For the array-based implementation, we wrote declarations for public methods corresponding to the operation of the ADT list. These declarations will appear unchanged in the reference-based implementation.

You need to represent the items in the ADT list and its length. Figure 4-18 indicates one possible way to represent this data by using references. The variable *head* references a linked list of the items in the ADT list, where the first node in the linked list contains the first item in the ADT list and so on. The variable *numItems* is an integer that is the current number of items in the list. Both *head* and *numItems* will be private data fields of our class.

*head and **numItems** are private data fields*

As you saw previously, you use two references—*curr* and *prev*—to manipulate a linked list. These reference variables will be local to the methods that need them; they are not appropriate data fields of the class.

*curr and **prev** should not be data fields of the class*

Recall that the ADT list operations for insertion, deletion, and retrieval specify the position number *i* of the relevant item. In an attempt to obtain values for *curr* and *prev* from *i*, suppose that you define a method *find(i)* that returns a reference to the ith node in the linked list. If *find* provides a reference *curr* to the ith node, how will you get a reference *prev* to the previous node, that is, to the $(i-1)^{th}$ node? You can get the value of *prev* by invoking *find(i-1)*. Instead of calling *find* twice, however, note that once you have *prev*, *curr* is simply

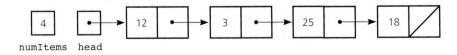

Figure 4-18

A reference-based implementation of the ADT list

prev.getNext(). The only exception to using *find* in this way is for the first node, but you know immediately from *i* whether the operation involves the first node. If it does, you know the reference to the first node, namely *head*, without invoking *find*.

The method *find* is not an ADT operation. Because *find* returns a reference, you would not want any client to call it. Such clients should be able to use the ADT without knowledge of the references that the implementation uses. It is perfectly reasonable for the implementation of an ADT to define variables and methods that the rest of the program should not access. Therefore, *find* is a private method that only the implementations of the ADT operations call.

***find** is a private method*

The following interface specification developed in Chapter 3 will be used for the reference-based implementation of the ADT list. The pre- and postconditions for the ADT list operations are the same as for the array-based implementation that you saw in Chapter 3; they are omitted here to save space.

```
// ***************************************************
// Interface for the ADT list
// ***************************************************
public interface ListInterface {
  // list operations:
  public boolean isEmpty();
  public int size();
  public void add(int index, Object item)
                      throws ListIndexOutOfBoundsException;
  public void remove(int index)
                      throws ListIndexOutOfBoundsException;
  public Object get(int index)
                      throws ListIndexOutOfBoundsException;
  public void removeAll();
} // end ListInterface
```

The implementation of the list begins as follows:

```
// ***************************************************
// Reference-based implementation of ADT list.
// ***************************************************
public class ListReferenceBased implements ListInterface {
  // reference to linked list of items
  private Node head;
  private int numItems; // number of items in list

  // definitions of constructors and methods
    . . .
```

You include the implementations of the class's methods at this point in the class as well as any private methods that may be needed. We now examine each of these implementations.

Default constructor.   The default constructor simply initializes the data fields *numItems* and *head*:

```
public ListReferenceBased() {
    numItems = 0;
    head = null;
}   // end default constructor
```

Since the variables *numItems* and *head* are initialized to these same values by default, this constructor is really not necessary. But if you have other constructors defined and you want to allow for a constructor without parameters, it must be defined explicitly. In general, it's a good idea to define all constructors explicitly.

List operations.   The methods *isEmpty* and *size* have straightforward implementations:

```
public boolean isEmpty() {
    return numItems == 0;
}   // end isEmpty

public int size() {
    return numItems;
}   // end size
```

Because a linked list does not provide direct access to a specified position, the retrieval, insertion, and deletion operations must all traverse the list from its beginning until the specified point is reached. The method *find* performs this traversal and has the following implementation:

```
private Node find(int index) {
// --------------------------------------------------
// Locates a specified node in a linked list.
// Precondition: index is the number of the desired
// node. Assumes that 1 <= index <= numItems+1
// Postcondition: Returns a reference to the desired
// node.
// --------------------------------------------------
    Node curr = head;
    for (int skip = 1; skip < index; skip++) {
        curr = curr.getNext();
    } // end for
    return curr;
} // end find
```

The precondition for *find* requires the *index* to be in the proper range. The *get* operation calls *find* to locate the desired node:

```
public Object get(int index)
                throws ListIndexOutOfBoundsException {
    if (index >= 1 && index <= numItems) {
        // get reference to node, then data in node
        Node curr = find(index);
```

```
      Object dataItem = curr.getItem();
      return dataItem;
    }
    else {
      throw new ListIndexOutOfBoundsException(
                    "List index out of bounds on get");
    } // end if
  } // end get
```

The reference-based implementations of the insertion and deletion operations use the linked list processing techniques developed earlier in this chapter. To insert an item after the first item of a list, you must first obtain a reference to the preceding item. Insertion into the first position of a list is a special case.

```
  public void add(int index, Object item)                    Insertion at a given position
                throws ListIndexOutOfBoundsException {
    if (index >= 1 && index <= numItems+1) {
      if (index == 1) {
        // insert the new node containing item at
        // beginning of list
        Node newNode = new Node(item, head);
        head = newNode;
      }
      else {
        Node prev = find(index-1);

        // insert the new node containing item after
        // the node that prev references
        Node newNode = new Node(item, prev.getNext());
        prev.setNext(newNode);
      } // end if
      numItems++;
    }
    else {
      throw new ListIndexOutOfBoundsException(
                    "List index out of bounds on add"););
    } // end if
  }  // end add
```

The *remove* operation is analogous to insertion. To delete an item that occurs after the first item of a list, you must first obtain a reference to the item that precedes it. Removal from the first position of a list is a special case.

```
  public void remove(int index)                              Deletion from a given position
                throws ListIndexOutOfBoundsException {
    if (index >= 1 && index <= numItems) {
      if (index == 1) {
        // delete the first node from the list
        head = head.getNext();
      }
```

```
      else {
        Node prev = find(index-1);
        // delete the node after the node that prev
        // references, save reference to node
        Node curr = prev.getNext();
        prev.setNext(curr.getNext());
      } // end if
      numItems--;
    } // end if
    else {
      throw new ListIndexOutOfBoundsException(
                  "List index out of bounds on remove");
    } // end if
  }    // end remove
```

The *removeAll* operation simply sets the head reference to *null*, making the nodes in the list unreachable and thus marking them for garbage collection.

```
public void removeAll() {
  // setting head to null causes list to be
  // unreachable and thus marked for garbage
  // collection
  head = null;
  numItems = 0;
} // end removeAll
```

Comparing Array-Based and Reference-Based Implementations

Typically, the various implementations that a programmer contemplates for a particular ADT have advantages and disadvantages. When you must select an implementation, you should weigh these advantages and disadvantages before you make your choice. As you will see, the decision among possible implementations of an ADT is one that you must make time and time again. This section compares the two implementations of the ADT list that you have seen as an example of how you should proceed in general.

Arrays are easy to use, but they have a fixed size

The array-based implementation that you saw in Chapter 3 appears to be a reasonable approach. An array behaves like a list, and arrays are easy to use. However, as was already mentioned, an array has a fixed size; it is possible for the number of items in the list to exceed this fixed size. In practice, when choosing among implementations of an ADT, you must ask the question, does the fixed-size restriction of an array-based implementation present a problem in the context of a particular application? The answer to this question depends on two factors. The obvious factor is whether or not, for a given application, you can predict in advance the maximum number of items in the ADT at any one time. If you cannot, it is quite possible that an operation—and hence the entire program—will fail because the ADT in the context of a particular application requires more storage than the array can provide.

Can you predict the maximum number of items in the ADT?

On the other hand, if, for a given application, you can predict in advance the maximum number of items in the ADT list at any one time, you must explore a more subtle factor: Would you waste storage by declaring an array to be large enough to accommodate this maximum number of items? Consider a case in which the maximum number of items is large, but you suspect that this number rarely will be reached. For example, suppose that your list could contain as many as 10,000 items, but the actual number of items in the list rarely exceeds 50. If you declare 10,000 array locations at compilation time, at least 9,950 array locations will be wasted most of the time. In both of the previous cases, the array-based implementation given in Chapter 3 is not desirable.

Will an array waste storage?

What if you used a resizeable array? Because you would use the *new* operator to allocate a larger array dynamically, you would be able to provide as much storage as the list needs (within the bounds of the particular computer, of course). Thus, you would not have to predict the maximum size of the list. However, if you doubled the size of the array each time you reached the end of the array—which is a reasonable approach to enlarging the array—you still might have many unused array locations. In the example just given, you could allocate an array of 50 locations initially. If you actually have 10,000 items in your list, array doubling will eventually give you an array of 12,800 locations, 2,800 more than you need. Remember also that you waste time by copying the array each time you need more space.

Increasing the size of a resizeable array can waste storage and time

Now suppose that your list will never contain more than 25 items. You could allocate enough storage in the array for the list and know that you would waste little storage when the list contained only a few items. With respect to its size, an array-based implementation is perfectly acceptable in this case.

An array-based implementation is a good choice for a small list

A reference-based implementation can solve any difficulties related to the fixed size of an array-based implementation. You use the *new* operator to allocate storage dynamically, so you do not need to predict the maximum size of the list. Because you allocate memory one item at a time, the list will be allocated only as much storage as it needs. Thus, you will not waste storage.

Linked lists do not have a fixed size

There are other differences between the array-based and reference-based implementations. These differences affect both the time and memory requirements of the implementations. Any time you store a collection of data in an array or a linked list, the data items become ordered; that is, there is a first item, a second item, and so on. This order implies that a typical item has a predecessor and a successor. In an array *anArray*, the location of the next item after the item in *anArray[i]* is *implicit*—it is in *anArray[i+1]*. In a linked list, however, you *explicitly* determine the location of the next item by using the reference in the current node. This notion of an implicit versus explicit next item is one of the primary differences between an array and a linked list. Therefore, an advantage of an array-based implementation is that it does not have to store explicit information about where to find the next data item, thus requiring less memory than a reference-based implementation.

The item after an array item is implied; in a linked list, an item explicitly references the next item

An array-based implementation requires less memory than a reference-based implementation

You can access array items directly with equal access time

Another, more important advantage of an array-based implementation is that it can provide **direct access** to a specified item. For example, if you use the array `items` to implement the ADT list, you know that the item associated with list position i is stored in `items[i-1]`. Accessing either `items[0]` or `items[49]` takes the same amount of time. That is, the **access time** is constant for an array.

You must traverse a linked list to access its ith node

On the other hand, if you use a linked list to implement the ADT list, you have no way of immediately accessing the node that contains the ith item. To get to the appropriate node, you use the `next` data fields to traverse the linked list from its beginning until you reach the ith node. That is, you access the first node and get the reference to the second node, access the second node and get the reference to the third node, and so on until you finally access the ith node. Clearly, the time it takes you to access the first node is less than the time it takes to access the 50th node. The access time for the ith node depends on i.

The time to access the ith node in a linked list depends on i

The type of implementation chosen will affect the efficiency of the operations of the ADT list. An array-based `get` is almost instantaneous, regardless of which list item you access. A reference-based retrieval operation like `get`, however, requires i steps to access the ith item in the list.

You already know that the array-based implementation of the ADT list requires you to shift the data when you insert items into or delete items from the list. For example, if you delete the first item of a 20-item list, you must shift 19 items. In general, deleting the ith item of a list of n items requires $n - i$ shifts. Thus, `remove` requires n-1 shifts to delete the first item, but zero shifts to delete the last item. The list insertion operation `add` has similar requirements.

Insertion into and deletion from a linked list do not require you to shift data

In contrast, you do not need to shift the data when you insert items into or delete items from the linked list of a reference-based implementation. The methods `add` and `remove` require essentially the same effort, regardless of the length of the list or the position of the operation within the list, once you know the point of insertion or deletion. Finding this point, however, requires a list traversal, the time for which will vary depending on where in the list the operation will occur. Recall that the private method `find` performs this traversal. If you examine the definition of `find`, you will see that `find(i)` requires i assignment operations. Thus, `find`'s effort increases with i.

Insertion into and deletion from a linked list require a list traversal

We will continue to compare various solutions to a problem throughout this book. Chapter 9 will introduce a more formal way to discuss the efficiency of algorithms. Until then, our discussions will be informal.

Passing a Linked List to a Method

*A method with access to a linked list's **head** reference has access to the entire list*

How can a method access a linked list? It is sufficient for the method to have access to the list's head reference. From this variable alone, the method can access the entire linked list. In the reference-based implementation of the ADT list that you saw earlier in this chapter, the head reference `head` to the linked list that contains the ADT's items is a private data field of the class *ListReferenceBased.* The methods of this class use *head* directly to manipulate the linked list.

Would you ever want *head* to be an argument of a method? Certainly not for methods outside of the class, because such methods should not have access to the class's underlying data structure. Although on the surface, it would seem that you would never need to pass the head reference to a method, that is not the case. Recursive methods, for example, might need the head reference as an argument. You will see examples of such methods in the next section. Realize that these methods must not be public members of their class. If they were, clients could access the linked list directly, thereby violating the ADT's wall.

As Figure 4-19 illustrates, when *head* is an actual argument to a method, its value is copied into the corresponding formal parameter. The method then can access and alter the nodes in the list. However, the method cannot modify *head*'s value (recall our earlier example in Figure 4-4). This is fine for situations, such as a search method, that do not modify the list. But what should you do if you want to write a method that may need to modify the *head* reference? For example, a method that inserts a node at the beginning of the list will need to modify the *head* reference. One solution is for the return value of the method to be the new value for the *head* reference. Such an example will appear in the next section.

Processing Linked Lists Recursively

It is possible, and sometimes desirable, to process linked lists recursively. This section examines recursive traversal and insertion operations on a linked list. If the recursive methods in this section are members of a class, they should not be public because they require the linked list's head reference as an argument.

Traversal. Suppose that you want to display the elements in a list referenced by *head*. That is, you want to write the objects in the order in which they appear in the linked list. The recursive strategy is simply

```
Write the first node of the list
Write the list minus its first node
```

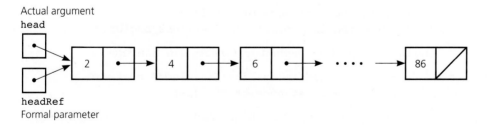

Figure 4-19

A head reference as an argument

The following Java method implements this strategy:

A recursive traversal method

```java
private static void writeList(Node nextNode) {
// ----------------------------------------------------------
// Writes a list of objects.
// Precondition: The linked list is referenced by nextNode.
// Postcondition: The list is displayed. The linked list
// and nextNode are unchanged.
// ----------------------------------------------------------
  if (nextNode != null) {
    // write the first data object
    System.out.println(nextNode.getItem());
    // write the list minus its first node
    writeList(nextNode.getNext());
  }  // end if
}  // end writeList
```

This method is uncomplicated. It requires that you have direct access only to the first node of the list. The linked list provides this direct access because the list's first node, referenced by *head*, contains the list's first data item. Furthermore, you can easily pass the list minus its first node to *writeList*. If *head* references the beginning of the list, *head.getNext()* references the list minus its first node. You should compare *writeList* to the iterative technique that we used earlier in this chapter to display a linked list.

Compare the recursive **writeList** *to the iterative technique on page 163*

Now suppose that you want to display the list backward. Chapter 2 already developed two recursive strategies for writing a string *s* backward. Recall that the strategy of the method *writeBackward* is

writeBackward *strategy*

> Write the last character of string s
> Write string s minus its last character backward

The strategy of the method *writeBackward2* is

writeBackward2 *strategy*

> Write string s minus its first character backward
> Write the first character of string s

We can easily translate these strategies to linked lists. The method *write-Backward* translates to

writeListBackward *strategy*

> Write the last node of the list
> Write the list minus its last node backward

and the strategy of the method *writeBackward2* translates to

writeListBackward2 *strategy*

> Write the list minus its first node backward
> Write the first node of the list

You saw that these two strategies work equally well when an array is used. However, when a linked list is used, the first strategy is very difficult to implement: If *nextNode* references the node that contains the first node of the list, how do you get to the last node? Even if you had some way to get to the last node in the list quickly, it would be very difficult for you to move toward the front of the list at each recursive call. That is, it would be difficult for you to access the ends of the successively shorter lists that the recursive calls generate. (Later you will see a doubly linked list, which would solve this problem.)

This discussion illustrates one of the primary disadvantages of linked lists: Whereas an array provides direct access to any of its items, a linked list does not. Fortunately, however, the strategy of method *writeBackward2* requires that you have direct access only to the first character of the string. This access is the same that *writeListBackward2* requires: .The list's head reference *nextNode* locates the first node in the list, and *next-Node.getNext()* references the list minus the first node.

The following Java method implements the *writeListBackward2* strategy for a linked list:

writeListBackward2 is much easier to implement recursively than writeListBackward

```
private static void writeListBackward2(Node nextNode) {
// -----------------------------------------------------
// Writes a list of objects backwards.
// Precondition: The linked list is referenced by
// nextNode.
// Postcondition: The list is displayed backwards. The
// linked list and nextNode are unchanged.
// -----------------------------------------------------
  if (nextNode != null) {
    // write the list minus its first node backward
    writeListBackward2(nextNode.getNext());
    // write the data object in the first node
    System.out.println(nextNode.getItem());
  } // end if
}   // end writeListBackward2
```

Self-Test Exercise 7 asks you to trace this method. This trace will be similar to the box trace in Figure 2-9. Exercise 5 asks you to write an iterative version of this method. Which version is more efficient?

Insertion.   Now view the insertion of a node into a sorted linked list from a new perspective—that is, recursively. Later in this book you will need a recursive algorithm to perform an insertion into a linked structure. Interestingly, recursive insertion eliminates the need for both a trailing reference and a special case for inserting into the beginning of the list.

Consider the following recursive view of a sorted linked list: A linked list is sorted if its first data item is less than its second data item and the list that begins with the second data item is sorted. More formally, you can state this definition as follows:

The linked list that *head* references is a sorted linked list if

head is *null* (the empty list is a sorted linked list)

or

head.getNext() is *null* (a list with a single node is a sorted linked list) or

head.getItem() < head.getNext().getItem(), and *head.get-Next()* references a sorted linked list

You can base a recursive insertion on this definition. Notice that the following method inserts the node at one of the base cases—either when the list is empty or when the new data item is smaller than all the data items in the list. In both cases, you need to insert the new data item at the beginning of the list.

```
private static Node insertRecursive(Node headNode,
                        java.lang.Comparable newItem) {
  if ( (headNode == null) ||
      (newItem.compareTo(headNode.getItem()) < 0) ) {
    // base case: insert newItem at the beginning of the
    // linked list that nextNode references
    Node newNode = new Node(newItem, headNode);
    headNode = newNode;
  }
  else { //insert into rest of linked list
    Node nextNode = insertRecursive(headNode.getNext(),newItem);
    headNode.setNext(nextNode);
  } // end if
  return headNode;
}  // end insertRecursive
```

First, consider the context for *insertRecursive*. Recall from Chapter 3 that the ADT operation *sortedAdd(newItem)* inserts *newItem* into its proper order in the sorted list. As a public method of the class, *sortedAdd* would call *insertRecursive* to do the insertion recursively. However, *insertRecursive* requires the linked list's head reference as an argument. Since the reference *head* is private and hidden from the client, you would not want *insertRecursive* to be an ADT operation. Thus, you would make it private.

To see how *insertRecursive* works, consider that *sortedAdd* will invoke *insertRecursive* by using the statement

```
head = insertRecursive(head, newItem);
```

Insertion occurs at the base case

Although *insertRecursive* does not maintain a trailing reference, inserting the new node is easy when the base case is reached,. Note that within *insertRecursive, headNode* references the beginning of the sorted linked list. You use *headNode* to make the new node reference the first node in the original list and then change *headNode* so that it references the new node. Since *insertRecursive* returns *headNode, sortedAdd*'s assignment to *head* makes *head* reference the new node as required.

To understand the previous remarks, consider the case in which the new item is to be inserted at the beginning of the original list that has the external reference *head*. In this case, no recursive calls are made, and consequently when the base case is reached—that is, when *newItem.compareTo (headNode.getItem()) < 0*—the actual argument that corresponds to *headNode* is *head*, as Figure 4-20a illustrates. The assignment *headNode* = *newNode* then sets the method's return value to reference the new node. Upon return of *insertRecursive*, the statement

```
head = insertRecursive(head, newItem);
```

assigns the return value to *head*, as Figure 4-20b shows.

The general case in which the new item is inserted into the interior of the list that *head* references is similar. When *insertRecursive* is first called, the *else* clause of the *if* statement executes, making a recursive call to *insertRecursive*. When the base case is reached, what is the actual argument that corresponds to *headNode*? It is the *next* reference of the node that should precede the new node, as Figure 4-21 illustrates. Therefore, the base case returns a reference to the new node. The *else* clause assigns this reference to *nextNode*, and the call to *setNext* sets the next reference of the appropriate node to reference the new node.

When the original call to *insertRecursive* returns *headNode*, its value is unchanged from its original value of *head*. Thus, the assignment

```
head = insertRecursive(head, newItem);
```

leaves the value of *head* unchanged.

Although it could be argued that you should perform the operations on a sorted linked list recursively (after all, recursion does eliminate special cases and the need for a trailing reference), the primary purpose in presenting the recursive *insertRecursive* is to prepare you for the binary search tree algorithms to be presented in Chapter 10.

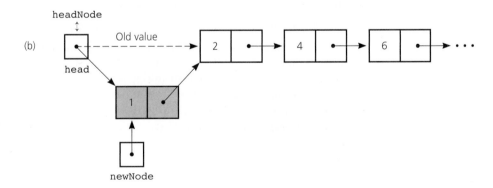

Figure 4-20

(a) A sorted linked list; (b) the assignment made for insertion at the beginning of the list.

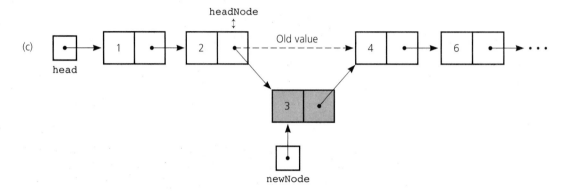

Figure 4-21

(a) The initial call *insertRecursive(head,newItem)*; (b) the first recursive call; (c) the second recursive call inserts at the beginning of the list that *headNode* references

VARIATIONS OF THE LINKED LIST

This section briefly introduces several variations of the linked list that you have just seen. These variations are often useful, and you will encounter them later in this text. Many of the implementation details are left as exercises. Note that in addition to the data structures discussed in this section, it is possible to have other data structures, such as arrays of references to linked lists and linked lists of linked lists. These data structures are also left as exercises.

Tail References

In many situations, you simply want to add an item to the end of a list. For example, maintaining a list of requests for a popular book at the local library would require that new requests for the book be placed at the end of a waiting list. You could use an ADT list called *waitingList* as follows:

```
waitingList.add(request, waitingList.size()+1);
```

This statement adds *request* to the end of *waitingList*. Recall that in implementing *add* to insert an item at the position indicated, we used the method *find* to traverse the list to that position. Note that this statement actually performs these four steps:

1. Allocate a new node for the linked list.
2. Set the reference in the last node in the list to reference the new node.
3. Put the new *request* in the new node.
4. Set the reference in the new node to *null*.

Each time you add a new request, you must get to the last node in the linked list. One way to accomplish this is to traverse the list each time you add a new request. A much more efficient method uses a **tail reference** *tail* to remember where the end of the linked list is—just as *head* remembers where the beginning of the list is. Like *head*, *tail* is external to the list. Figure 4-22 illustrates a linked list of integers that has both *head* and *tail* references.

*Use a **tail** reference to facilitate adding nodes to the end of a linked list*

With *tail* pointing to the end of the linked list, you can perform Steps 1 through 4 by using the single statement

```
tail.setNext(new Node(request, null));
```

This statement sets the *next* reference in the last node in the list to point to a newly allocated node. You then update *tail* so that it references the new last node by writing *tail = tail.getNext();*. You thus have an easy method for adding a new item to the end of the list. Initially, however, when you insert the first item into an empty linked list, *tail*—like *head*—is *null*. We leave the details of a solution as an exercise.

Treat the first insertion as a special case

Circular Linked Lists

When you use a computer that is part of a network, you share the services of another computer—called a **server**—with many other users. A similar sharing of resources occurs when you access a central computer by using a remote terminal. The system must organize the users so that only one user at a time has access to the shared computer. By ordering the users, the system can give each user a turn. Because users regularly

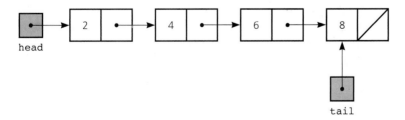

Figure 4-22

A linked list with *head* and *tail* references

enter and exit the system (by logging on or logging off), a linked list of user names allows the system to maintain order without shifting names when it makes insertions to and deletions from the list. Thus, the system can traverse the linked list from the beginning and give each user on the list a turn on the shared computer. What must the system do when it reaches the end of the list? It must return to the beginning of the list. However, the fact that the last node of a linked list does not reference another node can be an inconvenience.

If you want to access the first node of a linked list after accessing the last node, you must resort to the head reference. Suppose that you change the *next* portion of the list's last node so that, instead of containing *null*, it references the first node. The result is a **circular linked list**, as illustrated in Figure 4-23. In contrast, the linked list you saw earlier is said to be **linear.**

Every node in a circular linked list has a successor

Every node in a circular linked list references a successor, so you can start at any node and traverse the entire list. Although you could think of a circular list as not having either a beginning or an end, you still would have an external reference to one of the nodes in the list. Thus, it remains natural to think of both a first and a last node in a circular list. If the external reference locates the "first" node, you still would have to traverse the list to get to the last node. However, if the external reference—call it *list*—references the "last" node, as it does in Figure 4-24, you can access both the first and last nodes without a traversal, because *list.getNext()* references the first node.

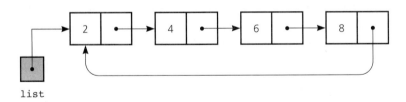

list

Figure 4-23

A circular linked list

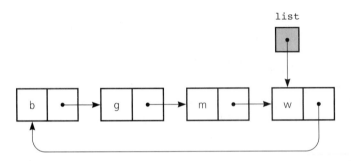

Figure 4-24

A circular linked list with an external reference to the last node

A *null* value in the external reference indicates an empty list, as it did for a linear list. However, no node in a circular list contains *null* in its *next* reference. Thus, you must alter the algorithm for detecting when you have traversed an entire list. By simply comparing the current reference *curr* to the external reference *list*, you can determine when you have traversed the entire circular list. For example, the following Java statements display the data portions of every node in a circular list, assuming that *list* references the "last" node:

No node in a circular linked list contains **null**

```
// display the data in a circular linked list;
// list references its last node
if (list != null) {
  // list is not empty
  Node first = list.getNext(); // reference first node

  Node curr = first;        // start at first node
  // Loop invariant: curr references next node to
  // display
  do {
    // write data portion
    System.out.println(curr.getItem());
    curr = curr.getNext();     // reference next node
  } while (curr != first);     // list traversed?
} // end if
```

Write the data in a circular linked list

Operations such as insertion into and deletion from a circular linked list are left as exercises.

Dummy Head Nodes

Both the insertion and deletion algorithms presented earlier for linear linked lists require a special case to handle action at the first position of a list. Many people prefer a method that eliminates the need for the special case. One such method is to add a **dummy head node**—as Figure 4-25 depicts—that is always present, even when the linked list is empty. In this way, the item at the first position of the list is actually in the second node. Also, the insertion and deletion algorithms initialize *prev* to reference the dummy head node, rather than *null*. Thus, for example, in the deletion algorithm, the statement

```
prev.setNext(curr.getNext());
```

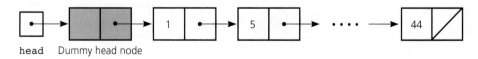

head   Dummy head node

Figure 4-25

A dummy head node

deletes from the list the node that *curr* references, regardless of whether or not this node is the first element in the list.

Despite the fact that a dummy head node eliminates the need for a special case, handling the first list position separately can, in general, be less distracting than altering the list's structure by adding a dummy head node. However, dummy head nodes are useful with doubly linked lists, as you will see in the next section.

Some people like to put global information about the linked list—such as its length and the smallest and largest values in the list—in a dummy head node, as Figure 4-26a shows. This would be possible with the node structure we have specified, since the data field is just a reference to an *Object*. The *Object* that the dummy node references could be a repository for information regarding the list. For example, we could have the following class:

```
public class ListInfo {
    private int length;
    private Object smallestItem, largestItem;
    // methods for accessing the private data appear here
    . . .
} // end class ListInfo
```

The following Java statement establishes the repository of information in the head node:

You can use a head record for global information instead of a dummy head node

```
Node head = new Node(new ListInfo(3,min,max,listNode);
```

where *min* is the smallest item, *max* is the largest item, and *listNode* references the linked list.

Instead of using a dummy head node, you can make *head* be an instance of a class such as *ListInfo* instead of *Node*. The *ListInfo* class

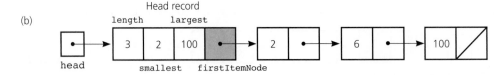

Figure 4-26

(a) A dummy head node with global information; (b) a head record with global information would need one more datafield, *firstItemNode*, to reference the first node of the list. Thus, you could write

```
ListInfo head = new ListInfo(3,min,max,listNode);
```

Figure 4-26b illustrates this situation. In this case, *head* is called a **head record**. Whether you use a dummy head node or a head record is, however, a matter of personal taste.

Doubly Linked Lists

Suppose that you wanted to delete a particular node from a linked list. If you were able to locate the node directly without a traversal, you would not have established a trailing reference to the node that precedes it in the list. Without a trailing reference, you would be unable to delete the node. You could overcome this problem if you had a way to back up from the node that you wished to delete to the node that precedes it. A **doubly linked list** solves this problem because each of its nodes has references to both the next node and the previous node.

Each node in a doubly linked list references both its predecessor and its successor

Consider a sorted linked list of customer names such that each node contains, in addition to its data field, two reference variables, *precede* and *next*. As usual, the *next* reference of node *N* references the node that follows *N* in the list. The *precede* data field references the node that precedes *N* in the list. Figure 4-27 shows the form of this sorted linked list of customers.

Notice that if *curr* references a node *N*, you can get a reference to the node that precedes *N* in the list by using the assignment statement

```
prev = curr.getPrecede();
```

A doubly linked list thus allows you to delete a node without traversing the list to establish a trailing reference.

Because there are more references to set, the mechanics of inserting into and deleting from a doubly linked list are a bit more involved than for a singly linked list. In addition, the special cases at the beginning or the end of the list are more complicated. It is common to eliminate the special cases by using a dummy head node. Although dummy head nodes may not be worthwhile for singly linked lists, the more complicated special cases for doubly linked lists make them very attractive.

Dummy head nodes are useful in doubly linked lists

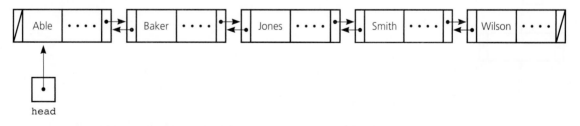

Figure 4-27
A doubly linked list

As Figure 4-28a shows, the external reference $listHead$ always references the dummy head node. Notice that the dummy head node has the
same data type as the other nodes in the list; thus it also contains
$precede$ and $next$ references. You can link the list so that it becomes a
circular doubly linked list. The $next$ reference of the dummy head
node then references the first "real node"—for example, the first customer name—in the list, and the $precede$ reference of the first real node
refers back to the dummy head node. Similarly, the $precede$ reference of
the dummy head node references the last node in the list, and the $next$
reference of the last node references the dummy head node. Note that
the dummy head node is present even when the list is empty. In this
case, both reference variables of the dummy head node reference the
head node itself, as Figure 4-28b illustrates.

A circular doubly linked list
eliminates special cases for
insertion and deletion

By using a circular doubly linked list, you can perform insertions and
deletions without special cases: Inserting into and deleting from the first
or last position is the same as for any other position. Consider, for example, how to delete the node N that $curr$ references. As Figure 4-29 illustrates, you need to

1. Change the $next$ reference of the node that precedes N so that it
    references the node that follows N.

2. Change the $precede$ reference of the node that follows N so that
    it references the node that precedes N.

The following Java statements accomplish these two steps:

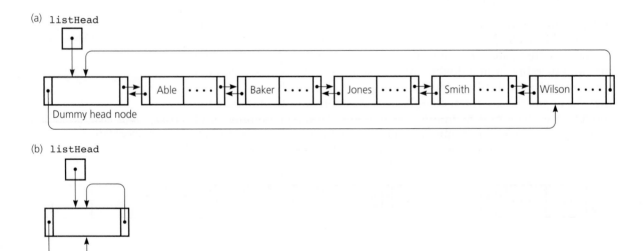

Figure 4-28

**(a) A circular doubly linked list with a dummy head node; (b) an
empty list with a dummy head node**

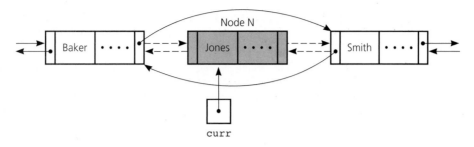

Figure 4-29

Reference changes for deletion

```
// delete the node that curr references
curr.getPrecede().setNext(curr.getNext());
curr.getNext().setPrecede(curr.getPrecede());
```

Deleting a node

You should convince yourself that these statements work even when the node to be deleted is the first, last, or only data (nonhead) node in the list. Now consider how to insert a node into a circular doubly linked list. In general, the fact that the list is doubly linked does not mean that you avoid traversing the list to find the proper place for the new item. For example, if you insert a new customer name, you must find the proper place within the sorted linked list for the new node. The following pseudocode sets *curr* to reference the node that contains the first name greater than *newName*. Thus, *curr* will reference the node that is to follow the new node on the list:

```
// find the insertion point
curr = listHead.getNext() // reference first node, if any
while (curr ≠ listHead and newName > curr.getItem()) {
  curr.getNext()
} // end while
```

Traverse the list to locate the insertion point

Notice that if you want to insert the new node either at the end of the list or into an empty list, the loop will set *curr* to reference the dummy head node. As Figure 4-30 illustrates, once *curr* references the node that is to follow the new node, you need to

1. Set the *next* reference in the new node to reference the node that is to follow it.

2. Set the *precede* reference in the new node to reference the node that is to precede it.

3. Set the *precede* reference in the node that is to follow the new node so that it references the new node.

4. Set the *next* reference in the node that is to precede the new node so that it references the new node.

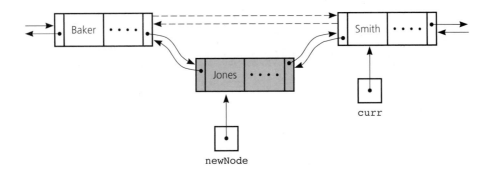

Figure 4-30

Reference changes for insertion

The following Java statements accomplish these four steps, assuming that *newNode* references the new node:

Inserting a node

```
// insert the new node that newNode references before
// the node referenced by curr
newNode.setNext(curr);
newNode.setPrecede(curr.getPrecede());
curr.setPrecede(newNode);
newNode.getPrecede().setNext(newNode);
```

You should convince yourself that these statements work even when you insert the node into the beginning of a list; at the end of a list, in which case *curr* references the head node; or into an empty list, in which case *curr* also references the head node.

APPLICATION: MAINTAINING AN INVENTORY

Imagine that you have a part-time job at the local video store. Realizing that you know a good deal about computers, the store owner asks you to write an interactive program that will maintain the store's inventory of videos that are for sale. The inventory consists of a list of movie titles and the following information associated with each title:

- **Have value:** number of videos currently in stock.
- **Want value:** number of videos that should be in stock. (When the have value is less than the want value, more videos are ordered.)
- **Wait list:** list of names of people waiting for the title if it is sold out.

Because the owner plans to turn off the power to the computer when the store is closed, your inventory program will not be running at all times. Therefore, the program must save the inventory in a file before execution terminates and later restore the inventory when it is run again.

Program input and output are as follows:

Input

- A file that contains a previously saved inventory.
- A file that contains information on an incoming shipment of videos. (See command D.)
- Single-letter commands—with arguments where necessary—that inquire about or modify the inventory and that the user will enter interactively.

Output

- A file that contains the updated inventory. (Note that you remove from the inventory all items whose have values and want values are zero and whose wait lists are empty. Thus, such items do not appear in the file.)
- Output as specified by the individual commands.

The program should be able to execute the following commands:

H	(help)	Provide a summary of the available commands.	*Program commands*
I *<title>*	(inquire)	Display the inventory information for a specified title.	
L	(list)	List the entire inventory (in alphabetical order by title).	
A *<title>*	(add)	Add a new title to the inventory. Prompt for initial want value.	
M *<title>*	(modify)	Modify the want value for a specified title.	
D	(delivery)	Take delivery of a shipment of videos, assuming that the clerk has entered the shipment information (titles and counts) into a file. Read the file, reserve videos for the people on the wait list, and update the have values in the inventory accordingly. Note that the program must add an item to the inventory if a delivered title is not present in the current inventory.	
O	(order)	Write a purchase order for additional videos based on a comparison of the have and want values in the inventory, so that the have value is brought up to the want value.	
R	(return)	Write a return order based on a comparison of the have and want values in the inventory and decrease the have values accordingly (make the return). The purpose is to reduce the have value to the want value.	
S *<title>*	(sell)	Decrease the count for the specified title by 1. If the title is sold out, put a name on the wait list for the title.	
Q	(quit)	Save the inventory and wait lists in a file and terminate execution.	

The problem-solving process that starts with a statement of the problem and ends with a program that effectively solves the problem—that is, a program that meets its specification—has three main stages:

1. The design of a solution
2. The implementation of the solution
3. The final set of refinements to the program

Realize, however, that you cannot complete one stage in total isolation from the others. Also realize that at many steps in the development of a solution, you must make choices. Although the following discussion may give the impression that the choices are clear-cut, this is not always the case. In reality, both the trade-offs between choices and the false starts (wrong choices considered) are often numerous.

This problem primarily involves data management and requires certain program commands. These commands suggest the following operations on the inventory:

Operations on the inventory

- List the inventory in alphabetical order by title (L command).
- Find the inventory item associated with a title (I, M, D, O, and S commands).
- Replace the inventory item associated with a title (M, D, R, and S commands).
- Insert new inventory items (A and D commands).

Recall that each title might have an associated wait list of people who are waiting for that title. You must be able to

- Add new people to the end of the wait list when they want a cassette that is sold out (S command).
- Delete people from the beginning of the wait list when new videos are delivered (D command).
- Display the names on a wait list for a particular title (I and L commands).

In addition, you must be able to

- Save the current inventory and associated wait lists when program execution terminates (Q command).
- Restore the current inventory and associated wait lists when program execution begins again.

You could think of these operations as part of an ADT inventory. Your next step should be to specify each of the operations fully. Since this chapter is about linked lists and implementation issues, the completion of the specifications will be left as an exercise. We will turn our attention to a data structure that could implement the inventory.

Each data item in the ADT inventory represents a movie and contains a title, the number of videos in stock (a have value), the number desired (a want value), and a wait list. How will you represent the wait list? First, you need to decide what information you want to store in the wait list. For example, you might want to keep track of the full name of each person, and create a class *Person* containing data fields for the first and last names of the person. This class might be structured as follows:

```
public class Person {
   private String lastName;
   private String firstName;

   public Person(String first, String last) {
     // to be implemented
     . . .
   } // end constructor

   public String toString() {
     // to be implemented
     . . .
   } // end toString
} // end class Person
```

A person in the wait list

This definition contains the minimum number of methods required to use instances of the *Person* class in our inventory problem. You may also decide that you want to keep additional information about a person, such as the address and phone number. The *toString* method is provided for printing purposes.

Now that you have decided what information to keep in the wait list, how will you implement the wait list itself in the ADT inventory? Could you use any of the implementations of the ADT list we developed previously? To make this decision, you must review the requirements of the wait list as stated in the inventory problem and then see if the ADT list will be able to meet these requirements. The inventory problem requires you to be able to add to the end of the wait list and delete from the beginning of the wait list. Clearly, removing an item from the beginning of the list is easy: You can simply use the ADT list operation *remove* with an index value of 1. Adding an item to the end of the list is also fairly easy. You know the size of the list from the ADT list operation *size()*, and you could use the ADT list operation *add* with an index value of *size() + 1* to place an item at the end of the wait list.

One of the requirements of the inventory problem is that the L command list the inventory in alphabetical order by movie title. Will you be able to use the ADT list in a way that will support this requirement? Not easily, since the ADT list is based on index position, not on a sorted order. A better choice is the ADT sorted list. Not only does it maintain the data in a sorted order for us, but it also provides an operation *locateIndex(item)* that can be used to search for an item in the sorted list.

The ADT list is not the best choice for data that must be in alphabetical order

If the ADT sorted list is not yet implemented, should you use an array-based implementation or a reference-based implementation? If you use an array to contain the items, you can use a binary search. Inserting and deleting items, however, requires you to shift array elements. Using a linked list for the items avoids these data shifts but makes a binary search impractical. (How do you quickly locate the middle item in a linked list?) Weighing these trade-offs, we choose a linked list to implement the ADT sorted list.

To summarize, we have made the following choices:

A sorted list represents the inventory

- The inventory is a sorted list of data items (the ADT sorted list implemented as a linked list of data items), sorted by the title that each item represents.

- Each inventory item contains a title, a have value, a want value, and a list of people's names (the wait list).

Figure 4-31 and the following Java statements summarize these choices:

```
public class StockItem implements java.lang.Comparable {
    public String title;
```

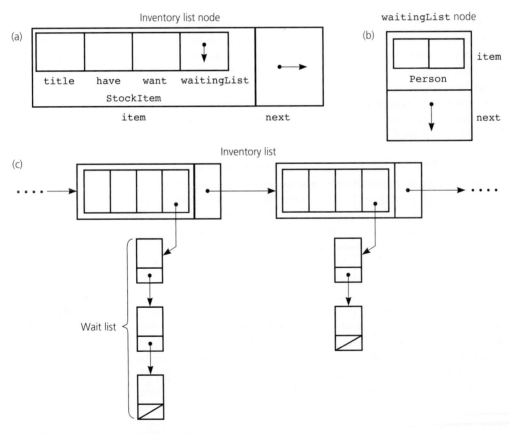

Figure 4-31

(a) Inventory list node; (b) wait list node; (c) orthogonal structure for the inventory

```java
    private int have, want;
    private ListReferenceBased waitingList;

    // various constructors for StockItem
    . . .

    public void addToWaitingList(String lastName,
                                 String firstName) {
    // add a person to the waiting list
      waitingList.addSorted(
                   new Person(lastName, firstName));
    } // end addToWaitingList

    public String toString() {
      // for displaying StockItem instances
      . . .
    } // end toString

    public int compareTo(Object rhs) {
    // define how StockItems are compared
      return title.compareTo(((StockItem)rhs).title);
    } // end compareTo

// mutator and accessor methods for other data fields
    . . .

} // end class StockItem
```

You declare the inventory as follows:

```java
    SortedList inventory = new SortedList();
```

Before you can proceed with the implementation, you must consider how you will save the inventory in a file. Java provides **object serialization**, a process that transforms an object into a stream of bytes that you can save and restore from a file. The most powerful aspect of object serialization is that when you write any object to a file, any other objects that are referenced by that object are also written to the file. To enable this feature, you place an *implements Serializable* clause in each class that has instances that will be written to the file. Thus, to write the inventory successfully, you would include the clause in the classes *ListReferenceBased*, *Node*, *SortedList*, *StockItem*, and *Person*. Then, when you write an inventory object to a file, all of the stock items in the inventory list and their wait lists are also be placed in the file. Here is the code that accomplishes that task:

```java
    try {
      FileOutputStream fos = new
                          FileOutputStream("inventory.dat");
      ObjectOutputStream oos = new ObjectOutputStream(fos);
```

```
            oos.writeObject(inventory);
            fos.close();
        } // end try
    catch (Exception e) {
        System.out.println(e);
    } // end catch
```

Restoring the inventory is also straightforward:

```
    ListReferenceBased restoredInventory;
    try {
        FileInputStream fis = new
                            FileInputStream("inventory.dat");
        ObjectInputStream ois = new ObjectInputStream(fis);
        Object o = ois.readObject();
        restoredInventory = (ListReferencedBased) o;
        System.out.println(restoredInventory);
    } // end try
    catch (Exception e) {
        System.out.println(e);
    } // end catch
```

The completion of this solution is left as an exercise.

SUMMARY

1. You can use reference variables to implement the data structure known as a linked list by using a class definition such as the following:

```
public class Node {
    private Object item;
    private Node next;
    // constructors, accessors, and mutators
    ...
} // end class Node
```

2. Each reference in a linked list is a reference to the next node in the list. For example, if *nodeRef* is a variable of type *Node* that references a node in this linked list,

   • *nodeRef.getItem()* is the data portion of the node.

   • *nodeRef.getNext()* references the next node.

3. Algorithms for inserting data into and deleting data from a linked list both involve these steps: Traverse the list from the beginning until you reach the appropriate position; perform reference changes to alter the structure of the list. In addition, you use the *new* operator to dynamically allocate a new node for insertion. When all references to a node are removed, the node is marked for garbage collection.

4. Inserting a new node at the beginning of a linked list or deleting the first node of a linked list are cases that you treat differently from insertions and deletions anywhere else in the list.

5. An array-based implementation uses an implicit ordering scheme—for example, the item that follows `anArray[i]` is stored in `anArray[i+1]`. A reference-based implementation uses an explicit ordering scheme—for example, to find the item that follows the one in node N, you follow node N's reference.

6. You can access any element of an array directly, but you must traverse a linked list to access a particular node. Therefore, the access time for an array is constant, whereas the access time for a linked list depends upon the location of the node within the list.

7. You can insert items into and delete items from a reference-based linked list without shifting data. This characteristic is an important advantage of a linked list over an array.

8. Although you can use the `new` operator to allocate memory dynamically for either an array or a linked list, you can increase the size of a linked list one node at a time more efficiently than an array. When you increase the size of a resizeable array, you must copy the original array elements into the new array and then deallocate the original array.

9. A binary search of a linked list is impractical because you cannot quickly locate its middle item.

10. You can use recursion to perform operations on a linked list. Such use will eliminate special cases and the need for a trailing reference.

11. The recursive insertion algorithm for a sorted linked list works because each smaller linked list is also sorted. When the algorithm makes an insertion at the beginning of one of these lists, the inserted node will be in the proper position in the original list. The algorithm is guaranteed to terminate because each smaller list contains one fewer node than the preceding list and because the empty list is a base case.

12. A tail reference can be used to facilitate locating the end of a list. This is especially useful when an append operation is required.

13. In a circular linked list, the last node references the first node, so that every node has a successor. If the list's external reference references the last node instead of the first node, you can access both the last node and the first node without traversing the list.

14. Dummy head nodes provide a method for eliminating the special cases for insertion into and deletion from the beginning of a linked list. The use of dummy head nodes is a matter of personal taste for singly linked lists, but it is helpful for a doubly linked list.

15. A head record contains global information about a linked list—such as its length—in addition to a reference to the first node in the list.

16. A doubly linked list allows you to traverse the list in either direction. Each node references its successor as well as its predecessor. Because insertions and deletions with a doubly linked list are more involved than with a singly linked list, it is convenient to use both a dummy head node and a circular organization to eliminate complicated special cases for the beginning and end of the list.

CAUTIONS

1. An uninitialized reference variable has the value *null*. Attempting to use a reference with a value of *null* will cause a *NullPointerException* to be thrown.

2. The sequence

```
Integer intRef = new Integer(5);
intRef = null;
```

allocates a memory cell and then destroys the only means of accessing it. Do not use *new* when you simply want to assign a value to a reference.

3. Insertions into and deletions from the beginning of a linked list are special cases unless you use a dummy head node. Failure to recognize this fact can result in a *null* reference being used, causing a *NullPointerException* to be thrown.

4. When traversing a linked list by using the reference variable *curr*, you must be careful not to reference *curr* after it has "passed" the last node in the list, because it will have the value *null* at that point. For example, the loop

```
while (value > curr.getItem())
  curr.getNext();
```

is incorrect if *value* is greater than all the data values in the linked list, because *curr* becomes *null*. Instead, you should write

```
while ((curr != null) && (value > curr.getItem()))
  curr.getNext();
```

Because Java uses short-circuit evaluation of logical expressions, if *curr* becomes *null*, the expression *curr.getItem()* is not evaluated.

5. A doubly linked list is a data structure that programmers tend to overuse. However, a doubly linked list is appropriate to use when you have direct access to a node. In such cases, you would not have traversed the list from its beginning. If the list were singly linked, you would not have a reference to the preceding node. Because doubly linking the list provides an easy way to get to the node's predecessor as well as its successor, you can, for example, delete the node readily.

SELF-TEST EXERCISES

1. Consider the algorithm for deleting a node from a linked list that this chapter describes.

   a. Is deletion of the last node of a linked list a special case? Explain.
   b. Is deletion of the only node of a one-node linked list a special case? Explain.
   c. Does deleting the first node take more effort than deleting the last node? Explain.

2. a. Write Java statements that create the linked list pictured in Figure 4-32, as follows. Beginning with an empty linked list, first create and attach a node for J, then create and attach a node for E, and finally create and attach a node for B.

   b. Repeat Part *a*, but instead create and attach nodes in the order B, E, J.

3. Consider the sorted linked list of single characters in Figure 4-32. Suppose that *prev* references the first node in this list and *curr* references the second node.

   a. Write Java statements that delete the second node and return it to the system. (*Hint:* First modify Figure 4-32.)
   b. Now assume that *curr* references the first node of the remaining two nodes of the original list. Write Java statements that delete the first node and return it to the system.
   c. Now *head* references the only node that is left in the list. Write Java statements that insert a new node that contains A into the list so that the list remains sorted.
   d. Revise Figure 4-32 so that your new diagram reflects the results of the previous deletions and insertion.

4. Write a Java method that displays only the ith integer in a linked list of integers. Assume that $i \geq 1$ and that the linked list contains at least *i* nodes.

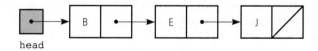

Figure 4-32

Linked list for Self-Test Exercises 2, 3, and 7

5. How many assignment operations does the method that you wrote for Self-Test Exercise 4 require?

6. Write a recursive Java method that retrieves the ith integer in a linked list of integers. Assume that $i \geq 1$ and that the linked list contains at least i nodes. (*Hint:* If $i = 1$, return the first integer in the list; otherwise, retrieve the $(i - 1)^{th}$ integer from the rest of the list.)

7. Trace the execution of `writeListBackward2(head)`, where `head` references the linked list of the characters pictured in Figure 4-32. (`writeListBackward2` appears on page 183 of this chapter.)

EXERCISES

1. This exercise assumes that you have completed Self-Test Exercise 3 and know the final status of the linked list. For each of the following, write the Java statements that perform the requested operation on the list. Also draw a picture of the status of the list after each operation is complete. When you delete a node from the list, return it to the system. All insertions into the list should maintain the list's sorted order. Do not use any of the methods that were presented in this chapter.

    a. Assume that `prev` references the first node and `curr` references the second node. Insert F into the list.

    b. Assume that `prev` references the second node and that `curr` references the third node of the list after you revised it in Part *a*. Delete the last node of the list.

    c. Assume that `prev` references the last node of the list after you revised it in Part *b*, and assume that `curr` is `null`. Insert G into the list.

2. Consider a linked list of items that are in no particular order.

    a. Write a method that inserts a node at the beginning of the linked list and a method that deletes the first node of the linked list.

    b. Repeat Part *a*, but this time perform the insertion and deletion at the end of the list instead of at the beginning.

    c. Repeat Part *b*, but this time assume that the list has a tail reference as well as a head reference.

3. Write a method to count the number of items in a linked list

    a. Iteratively

    b. Recursively

4. Write a method that will delete from a linked list of integers the node that contains the largest integer. Can you do this with a single traversal of the list?

5. The section "Processing Linked Lists Recursively" discussed the traversal of a linked list.

    a. Compare the efficiencies of an iterative method that displays a linked list with the method `writeList`.

    b. Write an iterative method that displays a linked list backward. Compare the efficiencies of your method with the method `writeListBackward2`.

6. Write a method to merge two linked lists of integers that are sorted into ascending order. The result should be a third linked list that is the sorted combination of the original lists. Do not destroy the original lists.

7. Compare the number of operations required to display each node in a linked list of integers with the number of operations required to display each item in an array of integers. A loop that displays the items in a linked list is given in the section "Displaying the Contents of a Linked List."

8. Compare the array-based and reference-based implementations of the ADT list operation `remove(index)`. Describe the work required for various values of `index` under each implementation. What are the implications for efficiency if the cost of shifting data is large compared to the cost of following a reference? When would this situation occur? What if the costs are approximately the same?

9. Assume that the reference `list` references the last node of a circular linked list like the one in Figure 4-24. Write a loop that displays the data portion of every node in the list.

10. Write a method that deletes the ith node from a circular linked list.

11. Imagine a circular linked list of integers that are sorted into ascending order, as Figure 4-33a illustrates. The external reference `list` references the last node, which contains the largest integer. Write a method that revises the list so that its data elements are sorted into descending order, as Figure 4-33b illustrates. Do not allocate new nodes.

12. Revise the implementations of the ADT list operations `add` and `remove` under the assumption that the linked list has a dummy head node.

(a)

(b)

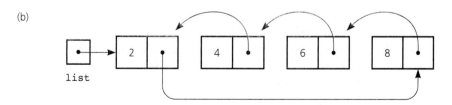

Figure 4-33

Two circular linked lists

13. Add the operations *save* and *restore* to the reference-based implementation of the ADT list. These operations use a file to save and restore the list items.

14. Consider the sorted doubly linked list shown in Figure 4-28. This list is circular and has a dummy head node. Suppose that *newName* contains a name that you want to add to or delete from this list. Write two Java methods: one that inserts a new node containing *newName* into its proper sorted order within the list, and a second that deletes the node containing *newName*.

15. Repeat Exercise 14 for the sorted doubly linked list shown in Figure 4-27. This list is not circular and does not have a dummy head node. Watch out for the special cases at the beginning and end of the list.

16. The class *java.util.Vector* implements a growable array of objects. Here is a subset of the methods available in the class *java.util.Vector*:

Constructors

```
Vector();
// Constructs an empty vector.


Vector(int initialCapacity, int capacityIncrement)
// Constructs an empty vector with the specified
// initial capacity and capacity increment.
```

Methods

```
void addElement(Object obj);
// Adds the specified component to the end of this
// vector, increasing its size by one.


int capacity();
// Returns the current capacity of this vector.


Object elementAt(int index);
// Returns the component at the specified index.


void removeElementAt(int index);
// Deletes the component at the specified index.


int size();
// Returns the number of components in this vector.
```

Complete the following tasks:

a. Declare a vector using the default constructor. Add five string objects to the vector. What do methods *size* and *capacity* return?

b. Write a loop to print the five strings stored in the vector.

c. How many string objects must be added to the vector to cause the capacity to change? Is this answer consistent with Part *a*? What is the new capacity?

d. Remove all of the elements fromt the vector. Does the capacity change? Why do you think the *Vector* class behaves this way?

PROGRAMMING PROBLEMS

1. Chapter 3 introduced the ADT sorted list, which maintains its data in sorted order. For example, a sorted list of names would be maintained in alphabetical order, and a sorted list of numbers would be maintained in either increasing or decreasing order. The operations for a sorted list are summarized on pages 117–118.

Some operations—*sortedIsEmpty*, *sortedSize*, and *sortedGet*, for example—are just like those for the ADT list. Insertion and deletion operations, however, are by value, not by position as they are for a list. For example, when you insert an item into a sorted list, you do not specify where in the list the item belongs. Instead, the insertion operation determines the correct position of the item by comparing its value with those of the existing items on the list. A new operation, *locateIndex*, determines from the value of an item its numerical position within the sorted list.

Note that the specifications given in Chapter 3 do not say anything about duplicate entries in the sorted list. Depending on your application, you might allow duplicates, or you might want to prevent duplicates from entering the list. For example, a sorted list of social security numbers probably should disallow duplicate entries. In this example, an attempt to insert a social security number that already exists in the sorted list would fail.

Write a nonrecursive, reference-based implementation of the ADT sorted list of integers as a Java class such that

a. Duplicates are allowed

b. Duplicates are not allowed, and operations must prevent duplicates from entering the list

2. Repeat Programming Problem 1, but write a recursive, reference-based implementation instead. Recall from this chapter that the recursive methods must be in the private section of the class.

3. Write an implementation of the ADT list that uses a resizeable array to represent the list items.

4. Write a reference-based implementation of the ADT two-ended list, which has insertion and deletion operations at both ends of the list,

a. Without a tail reference

b. With a tail reference

5. Implement the ADT character string by using a linked list of characters. Include typical operations such as append one string to another; extract a substring; find the index of the leftmost occurrence of a character in a string; determine whether one string is a substring of another. Implement the string so that you can obtain its length without traversing the linked list and counting.

6. Consider a sparse implementation of the ADT polynomial that stores only the terms with nonzero coefficients. For example, you can represent the polynomial *p* in Exercise 8 of Chapter 3 with the linked list in Figure 4-34.

   a. Complete the sparse implementation.
   b. Define a traverse operation for the ADT polynomial that will allow you to add two sparse polynomials without having to consider terms with zero coefficients explicitly.

7. When you play a board or card game or when you use a shared computing resource, you get a turn and then wait until everyone else has had a turn. Although the number of players in a game remains relatively static, the number of users of a shared computing service fluctuates. Let's assume that this fluctuation will occur.

   Design an ADT that keeps track of turns within a group of people. You should be able to add or delete people and determine whose turn occurs now.

   Begin with a given group of people; assign these people an initial order. (This order can be random or specified by the user.) The first new person joining the group should get a turn after all others have had an equal number of turns. Each subsequent new person should get a turn after the person who joined the group most recently has a turn.

   Also design an ADT to represent a person. (You can be conservative with the amount of data that this ADT contains.) The data elements that your first ADT stores are instances of the ADT person.

   Implement your ADTs as Java classes. Use a circular linked list as the data structure that keeps track of turns. Implement this linked list by using references and not by using any other class.

   Write a program that uses and, therefore, tests, your ADTs completely. Your program should process several insertion and deletion operations and should demonstrate that people are given turns correctly.

8. Occasionally, a linked structure that does not use references is useful. One such structure uses an array whose items are "linked" by array indexes. Figure 4-35a illustrates an array of nodes that represents the linked list in Figure 4-32. Each node has two data fields, *item* and *next*. The *next* data field is an integer index to the array element that contains the next node in the linked list. Note that the *next* data field of the last node contains –1. The integer variable *head* contains the index of the first node in the list.

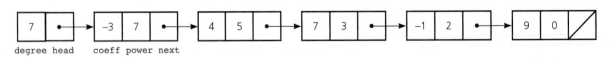

Figure 4-34

A sparse polynomial

The array elements that currently are not a part of the linked list make up a **free list** of available nodes. These nodes form another linked list, with the integer variable *free* containing the index of the first free node. To insert an item into the original linked list, you take a free node from the beginning of the free list and insert it into the linked list (Figure 4-35b). When you delete an item from the linked list, you insert the node into the beginning of the free list (Figure 4-35c). In this way, you can avoid shifting data items.

Implement the ADT list by using this array-based linked list.

9. Write the program for the videocassette inventory problem that this chapter describes.

10. Modify and expand the inventory program that you wrote for the previous programming problem. Here are a few suggestions:

   a. Add the ability to manipulate more than one inventory with the single program.

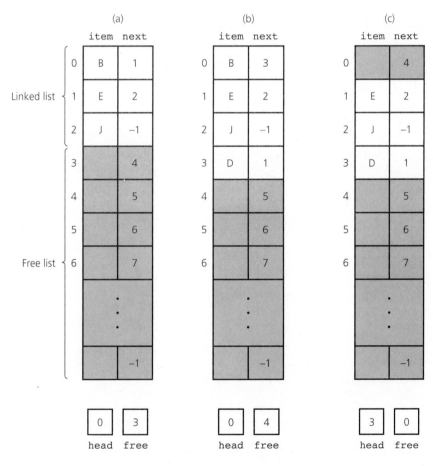

Figure 4-35

(a) An array-based implementation of the linked list in Figure 4-32;
(b) after inserting D in sorted order; (c) after deleting B

b. Add the ability to keep various statistics about each of the inventory items (such as the average number sold per week for the last 10 weeks).

c. Add the ability to modify the have value for an inventory item (for example, when a cassette is damaged or returned by a customer). Consider the implications for maintaining the relationship between a have value and the size of the corresponding wait list.

d. Make the wait lists more sophisticated. For example, keep names and addresses; mail letters automatically when a cassette comes in.

e. Make the ordering mechanism more sophisticated. For instance, do not order videos that have already been ordered but have not yet been delivered.

5

Recursion as a Problem-Solving Technique

PREVIEW Chapter 2 presented the basic concepts of recursion, and now this chapter moves on to some extremely useful and somewhat complex applications in computer science. The recursive solutions to the problems you will see are far more elegant and concise than the best of their nonrecursive counterparts.

This chapter introduces two new concepts, backtracking and formal grammars. Backtracking is a problem-solving technique that involves guesses at a solution. Formal grammars enable you to define, for example, syntactically correct algebraic expressions. The chapter concludes with a discussion of the close relationship between recursion and mathematical induction; you will learn how to use mathematical induction to study properties of algorithms.

More applications of recursion appear in subsequent chapters.

BACKTRACKING

This section considers an organized way to make successive guesses at a solution. If a particular guess leads to a dead end, you back up to that guess and replace it with a different guess. This strategy of retracing steps in reverse order and then trying a new sequence of steps is called **backtracking.** You can combine recursion and backtracking to solve the problem that follows.

Backtracking is a strategy for guessing at a solution and backing up when an impasse is reached

The Eight Queens Problem

A chessboard contains 64 squares that form 8 rows and 8 columns. The most powerful piece in the game of chess is the queen because it can attack any other piece within its row, within its column, or along its diagonal. The Eight Queens problem asks you to place eight queens on the chessboard so that no queen can attack any other queen.

Place eight queens on the chessboard so that no queen can attack any other queen

One strategy is to guess at a solution. However, there are 4,426,165,368 ways to arrange 8 queens on a chessboard of 64 squares— so many ways that it would be exhausting to check all of them for a solution to this problem. Nevertheless, a simple observation eliminates many arrangements from consideration: No queen can reside in a row or a column that contains another queen. In other words, each row and column can contain exactly one queen. Thus, attacks along rows or columns are eliminated, leaving only $8! = 40,320$ arrangements of queens to be checked for attacks along diagonals. A solution now appears more feasible.

Place queens one column at a time

Suppose that you provide some organization for the guessing strategy by placing one queen per column, beginning with the first square of column 1. When you consider column 2, you eliminate its first square because row 1 contains a queen, you eliminate its second square because of a diagonal attack, and you finally place a queen in the third square of column 2. Figure 5-1a shows the placement of five queens as a result of this procedure. The dots in the figure indicate squares that are rejected

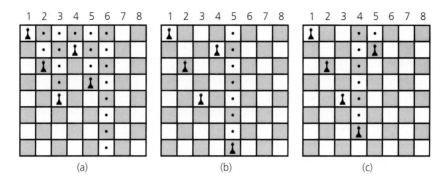

Figure 5-1

(a) Five queens that cannot attack each other, but that can attack all of column 6; (b) backtracking to column 5 to try another square for the queen; (c) backtracking to column 4 to try another square for the queen and then considering column 5 again

because a queen in that square is subject to attack by another queen in an earlier column.

Notice that the five queens in Figure 5-1a can attack any square in column 6. Therefore, you cannot place a queen in column 6, so you must back up to column 5 and move its queen. As Figure 5-1b indicates, the next possible square in column 5 is in the last row. When you consider column 6 once again, there are still no choices for a queen in that column. As you have exhausted the possibilities in column 5, you must back up to column 4. The next possible square in column 4 is in row 7, as Figure 5-1c indicates. You then consider column 5 again and place a queen in row 2.

If you reach an impasse, backtrack to the previous column

How can you use recursion in the solution that was just described? Consider an algorithm that places a queen in a column, given that you have placed queens correctly in the preceding columns. First, if there are no more columns to consider, you are finished; this is the base case. Otherwise, after you successfully place a queen in the current column, you need to consider the next column. That is, you need to solve the same problem with one fewer column; this is the recursive step. Thus, you begin with eight columns, consider smaller problems that decrease in size by one column at each recursive step, and reach the base case when you have a problem with no columns.

This solution appears to satisfy the criteria for a recursive solution. However, you do not know whether you can successfully place a queen in the current column. If you can, you recursively consider the next column. If you cannot place a queen in the current column, you need to backtrack, as has already been described. The following pseudocode describes the algorithm for placing queens in columns, given that the previous columns contain queens that cannot attack one another:

```
placeQueens(currColumn)
// Places queens in columns numbered currColumn through 8.
```

The solution combines recursion with backtracking

```
if (currColumn > 8) {
  The problem is solved
}
else {
  while ( unconsidered squares exist in currColumn
          and the problem is unsolved ) {
    Determine the next square in column currColumn that
        is not under attack by a queen in an earlier
        column
    if (such a square exists) {
      Place a queen in the square
      placeQueens(currColumn+1)  // try next column
      if (no queen is possible in column currColumn+1) {
        Remove queen from column currColumn and consider
            the next square in that column
      }  // end if
    }  // end if
  }  // end while
}  // end if
```

The method *placeQueens* is used in the following context:

Using `placeQueens`

```
Clear all squares on the board
placeQueens(1)              // begin with the first
                           // column
if (a solution exists) {
  Display solution
}
else {
  Display message       // no solution found
}  // end if
```

This context suggests the following class. For simplicity, the class uses a two-dimensional array to represent the board. Each square on the board either contains a queen or is empty.

```java
public class Queens {
  // squares per row or column
  public static final int BOARD_SIZE = 8;

  // used to indicate an empty square
  public static final int EMPTY = 0;

  // used to indicate square contains a queen
  public static final int QUEEN = 1;

  private int board[][]; // chess board
  public Queens() {
    // ------------------------------------------------
    // Constructor: Creates an empty square board.
    // ------------------------------------------------
```

```
      board = new int[BOARD_SIZE][BOARD_SIZE];
   }  // end constructor

   public void clearBoard() {
   // -------------------------------------------------
   // Clears the board.
   // Precondition: None.
   // Postcondition: Sets all squares to EMPTY.
   // -------------------------------------------------
      // To be implemented in Programming Problem 1
   }  // end clearBoard

   public void displayBoard() {
   // -------------------------------------------------
   // Displays the board.
   // Precondition: None.
   // Postcondition: Board is written to standard
   // output; zero is an EMPTY square, one is a square
   // containing a queen (QUEEN).
   // -------------------------------------------------
      // To be implemented in Programming Problem 1
   } // end displayBoard

   public boolean placeQueens(int column) {
   // -------------------------------------------------
   // Places queens in columns of the board beginning
   // at the column specified.
   // Precondition: Queens are placed correctly in
   // columns 1 through column-1.
   // Postcondition: If a solution is found, each
   // column of the board contains one queen and method
   // returns true; otherwise, returns false (no
   // solution exists for a queen anywhere in column
   // specified).
   // -------------------------------------------------
      if (column > BOARD_SIZE) {
        return true;  // base case
      }
      else {
        boolean queenPlaced = false;
        int row = 1;  // number of square in column

        while ( !queenPlaced && (row <= BOARD_SIZE) ) {
          // if square can be attacked
          if (isUnderAttack(row, column)) {
            ++row;  // consider next square in column
          } // end if
          else { // place queen and consider next column
            setQueen(row, column);
```

```
            queenPlaced = placeQueens(column+1);
            // if no queen is possible in next column,
            if (!queenPlaced) {
                // backtrack: remove queen placed earlier
                // and try next square in column
                removeQueen(row, column);
                ++row;
            } // end if
        } // end if
    } // end while
    return queenPlaced;
  } // end if
} // end placeQueens


private void setQueen(int row, int column) {
// ----------------------------------------------------
// Sets a queen at square indicated by row and
// column.
// Precondition: None.
// Postcondition: Sets the square on the board in a
// given row and column to QUEEN.
// ----------------------------------------------------
  // To be implemented in Programming Problem 1
} // end setQueen


private void removeQueen(int row, int column) {
// ----------------------------------------------------
// Removes a queen at square indicated by row and
// column.
// Precondition: None.
// Postcondition: Sets the square on the board in a
// given row and column to EMPTY.
// ----------------------------------------------------
  // To be implemented in Programming Problem 1
} // end removeQueen


private boolean isUnderAttack(int row, int column) {
// ----------------------------------------------------
// Determines whether the square on the board at a
// given row and column is under attack by any queens
// in the columns 1 through column-1.
// Precondition: Each column between 1 and column-1
// has a queen placed in a square at a specific row.
// None of these queens can be attacked by any other
// queen.
// Postcondition: If the designated square is under
// attack, returns true; otherwise, returns false.
// ----------------------------------------------------
```

```
    // To be implemented in Programming Problem 1
}   // end isUnderAttack

private int index(int number) {
// ---------------------------------------------------
// Returns the array index that corresponds to
// a row or column number.
// Precondition: 1 <= number <= BOARD_SIZE.
// Postcondition: Returns adjusted index value.
// ---------------------------------------------------
    // To be implemented in Programming Problem 1
}   // end index
} // end Queens
```

Figure 5-2 indicates the solution that the previous algorithm finds.

By modifying how you use *placeQueens*, you can discover other solutions to the Eight Queens problem. You can also improve this algorithm. Although we used an 8-by-8 array to represent the board because it simplified the implementation, such an array wastes space; after all, only 8 squares out of 64 are used. The programming problems at the end of this chapter consider modifications and improvements to this algorithm.

DEFINING LANGUAGES

English and Java are two languages with which you are familiar. A **language** is nothing more than a set of strings of symbols. For example, if you view a Java program as one long string of characters, you can define the set of all syntactically correct Java programs. This set is the language

$JavaPrograms$ = {strings $w : w$ is a syntactically correct Java program}

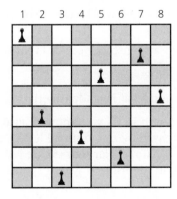

Figure 5-2

A solution to the Eight Queens problem

Notice that whereas all programs are strings, not all strings are programs. A Java compiler is a program that, among other things, determines whether a given string is a member of the language *JavaPrograms;* that is, the compiler determines whether the string is a syntactically correct Java program. Of course, this definition of *JavaPrograms* is not descriptive enough to allow the construction of a compiler. The definition specifies a characteristic of the strings in the set *JavaPrograms:* The strings are syntactically correct Java programs. However, this definition does not give the rules for determining whether a string is in the set or not; that is, the definition does not specify what is meant by a syntactically correct Java program.

The word "language" does not necessarily mean a programming language or a communication language. For example, the set of algebraic expressions forms a language

AlgebraicExpressions = {*w* : *w* is an algebraic expression}

The language *AlgebraicExpressions* is the set of strings that meets certain rules of syntax; however, the set's definition does not give these rules.

In both examples, the rules for forming a string within the language are missing. A **grammar** states the rules of a language. The grammars that you will see in this chapter are recursive in nature. One of the great benefits of using such a grammar to define a language is that you can often write a straightforward recursive algorithm, based on the grammar, that determines whether a given string is in the language. Such an algorithm is called a **recognition algorithm** for the language.

A grammar states the rules for forming the strings in a language

As it is a complex task to present a grammar for the set *JavaPrograms,* we instead will look at grammars for some simpler languages, including several common languages of algebraic expressions.

The Basics of Grammars

A grammar uses several special symbols:

Symbols that grammars use

- *x* | *y* means *x* or *y*.
- *x y* means *x* followed by *y*. (When the context requires clarification, the notation *x* • *y* will be used. The symbol • means concatenate, or append.)
- < *word* > means any instance of *word* that the definition defines.

A grammar for the language

JavaIds = {*w* : *w* is a legal Java identifier}

is simple, so we begin with it. As you know, a legal Java identifier begins with a letter and is followed by zero or more letters and digits. In this context, the underscore (_) and dollar sign ($) are letters. One way to represent this definition of an identifier is with a syntax diagram, as shown in Figure 5-3.

A syntax diagram is convenient for people to use, but a grammar is a better starting point if you want to write a method that will recognize an identifier. A grammar for the language *JavaIds* is

Figure 5-3

A syntax diagram for Java
identifiers

$< identifier > = < letter > \mid < identifier > < letter > \mid < identifier > < digit >$
$< letter > = a \mid b \mid \cdots \mid z \mid A \mid B \mid \cdots \mid Z \mid \_ \mid \$$
$< digit > = 0 \mid 1 \mid \cdots \mid 9$

*A grammar for the language
of Java identifiers*

The definition reads as follows:

> *An identifier is a letter, or an identifier followed by a letter, or an identi-
> fier followed by a digit.*

The most striking aspect of this definition is that *identifier* appears in its
own definition: This grammar is recursive, as are many grammars.

Many grammars are recursive

Given a string *w*, you can determine whether it is in the language
JavaIds by using the grammar to construct the following recognition
algorithm: If *w* is of length 1, it is in the language if the character is a
letter. (This statement is the base case, so to speak.) If *w* is of length
greater than 1, it is in the language if the last character of *w* is either a
letter or a digit, and *w* minus its last character is an identifier.

The pseudocode for a recursive valued method that determines
whether a string is in *JavaIds* follows:

*A recognition algorithm for Java
identifiers*

```
isId(w)
// Returns true if w is a legal Java identifier;
// otherwise returns false.
  if (w is of length 1)  { // base case
    if (w is a letter) {
      return true
    }
    else {
      return false
    }  // end if
  }
  else if (the last character of w is a letter or a digit) {
    return isId(w minus its last character)  // Point X
  }
  else {
  return false
  } // end if
```

Figure 5-4 contains a trace of this method for the string *A2B*.

The initial call is made and the method begins execution.

```
w = "A2B"
```

At point X, a recursive call is made and the new invocation of `isId` begins execution:

At point X, a recursive call is made and the new invocation of `isId` begins execution:

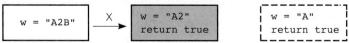

This is the base case, so this invocation of `isId` completes:

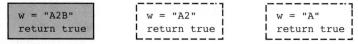

The value is returned to the calling method, which completes execution:

```
w = "A2B"   ──X──▶   w = "A2"        w = "A"
                     return true     return true
```

The value is returned to the calling method, which completes execution:

```
w = "A2B"            w = "A2"         w = "A"
return true          return true      return true
```

Figure 5-4

Trace of `isId("A2B")`

Two Simple Languages

Now consider two more simple examples of languages, their grammars, and resulting recognition algorithms.

Palindromes.   A palindrome is a string that reads the same from left to right as it does from right to left. For example, "radar" and "deed" are both palindromes. You can define the language of palindromes as follows:

Palindromes = {*w* : *w* reads the same left to right as right to left}

How can you use a grammar to define the language *Palindromes*? You need to devise a rule that allows you to determine whether a given string *w* is a palindrome. In the spirit of recursive definitions, you should state this rule in terms of determining whether a *smaller string* is a palindrome. Your first instinct might be to choose *w* minus its last (or first) character for the smaller string. However, this does not work because there is no relationship between the statements

w is a palindrome

and

> *w* minus its last character is a palindrome

That is, *w* might be a palindrome, although *w* minus its last character is not, as is the case for "deed." Similarly, *w* minus its last character might be a palindrome, although *w* is not, as is the case for "deeds."

A little thought reveals that you must consider characters in pairs: There *is* a relationship between the statements

> *w* is a palindrome

and

> *w* minus its first and last characters is a palindrome

Specifically, *w* is a palindrome if and only if

- The first and last characters of *w* are the same

and

- *w* minus its first and last characters is a palindrome

A recursive description of a palindrome

You need a base case that you will reach after stripping away enough pairs of characters. If *w* has an even number of characters, you will eventually be left with two characters, and then, after you strip away another pair, you will be left with zero characters. A string of length zero is called the **empty string** and is a palindrome. If *w* has an odd number of characters, you will eventually be left with one character, after which you cannot strip away another pair. Hence, you must have a second base case: A string of length 1 is a palindrome.

Strings of length 0 or 1 are the base cases

This discussion leads to the following grammar for the language *Palindromes*:

$$< pal > = \text{empty string} \mid < ch > \mid a < pal > a \mid b < pal > b \mid \cdots$$
$$\mid Z < pal > Z$$

$$< ch > = a \mid b \mid \cdots \mid z \mid A \mid B \mid \cdots \mid Z$$

A grammar for the language of palindromes

Based on this grammar, you can construct a recursive valued method for recognizing palindromes. The pseudocode for such a method follows:

```
isPal(w)
// Returns true if the string w of letters is a palindrome;
// otherwise returns false.

  if (w is the empty string or w is of length 1) {
    return true
  }
  else if (w's first and last characters are the same
           letter) {
    return isPal(w minus its first and last characters)
  }
  else {
    return false
  }  // end if
```

A recognition algorithm for palindromes

Strings of the form A"B".   The symbol A^nB^n is standard notation for the string that consists of n consecutive A's followed by n consecutive B's. Another simple language consists of such strings:

$$L = \{w : w \text{ is of the form } A^nB^n \text{ for some } n \geq 0\}$$

The grammar for this language is actually very similar to the grammar for palindromes. You must strip away both the first and last characters and check to see that the first character is an A and the last character is a B. Thus, the grammar is

A grammar for the language of strings $A^n B^n$

$$< legal\text{-}word > = \text{empty string} \mid A < legal\text{-}word > B$$

The pseudocode for a recognition method for this language follows:

A recognition algorithm for strings $A^n B^n$

```
isAnBn(w)
// Returns true if w is of the form AⁿBⁿ;
// otherwise returns false.

  if (the length of w is zero) {
    return true
  }
  else if (w begins with the character A and ends with the
           character B) {
    return isAnBn(w minus its first and last characters)
  }
  else {
    return false
  }  // end if
```

Algebraic Expressions

One of the tasks a compiler must perform is to recognize and evaluate algebraic expressions. For example, consider the Java assignment statement

```
y = x + z * (w/k + z * (7 * 6));
```

A Java compiler must determine whether the right side is a syntactically legal algebraic expression; if so, the compiler must then indicate how to compute the expression's value.

There are several common definitions for a "syntactically legal" algebraic expression. Some definitions force an expression to be *fully parenthesized*, that is, to have parentheses around each pair of operands together with their operator. Thus, you would have to write *((a * b) * c)* rather than *a * b * c*. In general, the stricter a definition, the easier it is to recognize a syntactically legal expression. On the other hand, conforming to overly strict rules of syntax is an inconvenience for programmers.

This section presents three different languages for algebraic expressions. The expressions in these languages are easy to recognize and evaluate but are generally inconvenient to use. However, these languages provide us with good, nontrivial applications of grammars. We will see other languages of algebraic expressions whose members are difficult to recognize and evaluate but are convenient to use. To avoid unnecessary complications, assume that you have only the binary operators +, −, *, and / (no unary operators or exponentiation). Also, assume that all operands in the expression are single-letter identifiers.

Infix, prefix, and postfix expressions. The algebraic expressions you learned about in school are called infix expressions. The term "infix" indicates that every binary operator appears *between* its operands. For example, in the expression

   $a + b$

the operator + is between its operands a and b. This convention necessitates associativity rules, precedence rules, and the use of parentheses to avoid ambiguity. For example, the expression

   $a + b * c$

is ambiguous. What is the second operand of the +? Is it b or is it $(b * c)$? Similarly, the first operand of the * could be either b or $(a + b)$. The rule that * has higher precedence than + removes the ambiguity by specifying that b is the first operand of the * and that $(b * c)$ is the second operand of the +. If you want another interpretation, you must use parentheses:

   $(a + b) * c$

Even with precedence rules, an expression like

   $a / b * c$

is ambiguous. Typically, / and * have equal precedence, so you could interpret the expression either as $(a / b) * c$ or as $a / (b * c)$. The common practice is to *associate from left to right*, thus yielding the first interpretation.

Two alternatives to the traditional infix convention are **prefix** and **postfix.** Under these conventions, an operator appears either before its operands (prefix) or after its operands (postfix). Thus, the infix expression

   $a + b$

is written in prefix form as

   $+ a\, b$

In a prefix expression, an operator precedes its operands

and in postfix form as

   $a\, b +$

In a postfix expression, an operator follows its operands

To further illustrate the conventions, consider the two interpretations of the infix expression $a + b * c$ just considered. You write the expression

   $a + (b * c)$

in prefix form as

   $+ a * b\, c$

The + appears before its operands a and ($*$ b c), and the $*$ appears before its operands b and c. The same expression is written in postfix form as

$$a\ b\ c\ *\ +$$

The $*$ appears after its operands b and c, and the + appears after its operands a and (b c $*$).

Similarly, you write the expression

$$(a + b) * c$$

in prefix form as

$$*\ +\ a\ b\ c$$

The $*$ appears before its operands (+ a b) and c, and the + appears before its operands a and b. The same expression is written in postfix form as

$$a\ b\ +\ c\ *$$

The + appears after its operands a and b, and the $*$ appears after its operands (a b +) and c.

If the infix expression is fully parenthesized, converting it to either prefix or postfix form is straightforward. Because each operator then corresponds to a pair of parentheses, you simply move the operator to the position marked by either the "(" if you want to convert to prefix form or the ")" if you want to convert to postfix form. This position either precedes or follows the operands of the operator. All parentheses would then be removed.

For example, consider the fully parenthesized infix expression

$$((a + b) * c)$$

To convert this expression to prefix form, you first move each operator to the position marked by its corresponding open parenthesis:

Converting to prefix form

$$(\ (\ a\ b\ )\ c\ )$$
$$*\quad +$$

Next, you remove the parentheses to get the desired prefix expression:

$$*\ +\ a\ b\ c$$

Similarly, to convert the infix expression to postfix form, you move each operator to the position marked by its corresponding closing parenthesis:

Converting to postfix form

$$(\ (\ a\ b\ )\ c\ )$$
$$\quad\quad +\quad *$$

Then you remove the parentheses:

$$a\ b\ +\ c\ *$$

When an infix expression is not fully parenthesized, these conversions are more complex. Chapter 6 discusses the general case of converting an infix expression to postfix form.

The advantage of prefix and postfix expressions is that they never need precedence rules, association rules, and parentheses. Therefore, the grammars for prefix and postfix expressions are quite simple. In addition, the algorithms that recognize and evaluate these expressions are relatively straightforward.

Prefix and postfix expressions never need precedence rules, association rules, and parentheses

Prefix expressions.   A grammar that defines the language of all prefix expressions is

$<$ *prefix* $>$ $=$ $<$ *identifier* $>$ $|$ $<$ *operator* $>$ $<$ *prefix* $>$ $<$ *prefix* $>$

$<$ *operator* $>$ $=$ $+$ $|$ $-$ $|$ $*$ $|$ $/$

$<$ *identifier* $>$ $=$ a $|$ b $|$ $\cdots$ $|$ z

From this grammar you can construct a recursive algorithm that recognizes prefix expressions. Suppose that you treat the expression in question as a substring of *strExp* from index *first* through *last*. If the expression is of length 1, it is a prefix expression if and only if *strExp* is a single lowercase letter. Expressions of length 1 can be the base case. If the length of the expression is greater than 1, then for it to be a legal prefix expression, it must be of the form

$<$ *operator* $>$ $<$ *prefix* $>$ $<$ *prefix* $>$

Thus, the algorithm must check to see that

- The first character of *strExp* is an operator

and

- The remainder of *strExp* (index *first* + 1 through *last*) consists of two consecutive prefix expressions

The first task is trivial, but the second is a bit tricky. How can you determine whether you are looking at two consecutive prefix expressions? A key observation is that if you add *any* string of nonblank characters to the end of a prefix expression, you will no longer have a prefix expression. That is, if *E* is a prefix expression and *Y* is any nonempty string of nonblank characters, then *E Y* cannot be a prefix expression. This is a subtle point; Exercise 14 at the end of this chapter asks you to prove it.

If E is a prefix expression, E Y cannot be

Given this observation, you can begin to determine whether the substring of *strExp* starting after the operator consists of two consecutive prefix expressions by identifying a first prefix expression. If you cannot find one, the original string itself is not a prefix expression. If you do find one, you need to know where it ends. Notice that the previous observation implies that only one endpoint is possible for this first expression: Given that the substring of *strExp* from index *first* + 1 through *end1* is a prefix expression, no other prefix expression can begin at position *first* + 1. That is, it is not possible that another substring of *strExp* from index *first* + 1 through *end2* is a prefix expression for any *end2* not equal to *end1*.

If you find that the first prefix expression ends at position *end1*, you then attempt to find a second prefix expression beginning at position

$end1 + 1$ and ending at or before position $last$. If you find the second expression, you must check that you are at the end of the string in question.

By using these ideas, you can show, for example, that $+/ab-cd$ is a prefix expression. For $+/ab-cd$ to be a prefix expression, it must be of the form $+E_1E_2$, where E_1 and E_2 are prefix expressions. Now you can write

$$E_1 = /E_3E_4 \text{ where}$$
$$E_3 = a$$
$$E_4 = b$$

Since E_3 and E_4 are prefix expressions, E_1 is a prefix expression. Similarly, you can write

$$E_2 = -E_5E_6 \text{ where}$$
$$E_5 = c$$
$$E_6 = d$$

and see that E_2 is a prefix expression.

If we assume that the class for prefix expressions has a private data field $strExp$, you can write a method in the same class to determine whether the expression is a prefix expression. First, you construct a recursive valued method $endPre(first, last)$ that returns either the index of the end of the prefix expression $strExp$ or the value -1, which signals that no prefix expression begins at $strExp$. The method appears in pseudocode as follows:

__endPre__ determines the end of a prefix expression

```
endPre(first, last)
// Finds the end of a prefix expression, if one exists.
// Precondition: The substring of strExp from index first
// through last contains no blank characters.
// Postcondition: Returns the index of the last character
// in strExp that begins at index first, if one exists, or
// returns -1 if no such prefix expression exists.

   if (first < 0 or first > last) {
      return -1
   }  // end if
   ch = character at position first of strExp
   if (ch is an identifier) {
      // index of last character in simple prefix expression
      return first
   }
   else if (ch is an operator) {
      // find the end of the first prefix expression
      firstEnd = endPre(first + 1, last)          // Point X

      // if the end of the first expression was found
      // find the end of the second prefix expression
```

```
    if (firstEnd > 0) {
      return endPre(firstEnd + 1, last)           // Point Y
    }
    else {
      return -1
    }  // end if
  }
else {
  return -1
}  // end if
```

Figure 5-5 contains a trace of *endPre* when the initial expression is *+/ab–cd*.

The initial call is made and **endPre** begins execution:

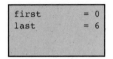

first character of **strExp** is +, so at point X, a recursive call is made and the new invocation of **endPre** begins execution:

Next character of **strExp** is /, so at point X, a recursive call is made and the new invocation of **endPre** begins execution:

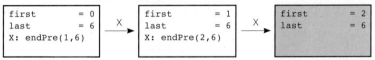

Next character of **strExp** is **a**, which is a base case. The current invocation of **endPre** completes execution and returns its value:

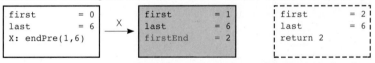

Because **firstEnd** > —1, a recursive call is made from point Y and the new invocation of **endPre** begins execution:

Next character of **strExp** is **b**, which is a base case. The current invocation of **endPre** completes execution and returns its value:

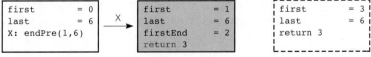

The current invocation of **endPre** completes execution and returns its value:

Figure 5-5

Trace of **endPre(first, last)**, where **strExp** is *+/ab-cd*   *(continues)*

Because `firstEnd > —1`, a recursive call is made from point Y and the new invocation of **endPre** begins execution:

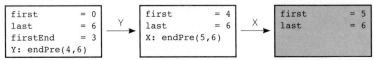

Next character of `strExp` is –, so at point X, a recursive call is made and the new invocation of **endPre** begins execution:

Next character of `strExp` is **c**, which is a base case. The current invocation of **endPre** completes execution and returns its value:

Because `firstEnd > —1`, a recursive call is made from point Y and the new invocation of **endPre** begins execution:

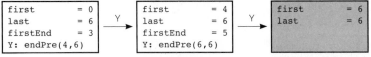

Next character of `strExp` is **d**, which is a base case. The current invocation of **endPre** completes execution and returns its value:

The current invocation of **endPre** completes execution and returns its value:

```
first      = 0      ┌─────────────────┐
last       = 6      │ first      = 4  │
firstEnd   = 3      │ last       = 6  │
return 6            │ firstEnd   = 5  │
                    │ return 6        │
                    └─────────────────┘
```

The current invocation of **endPre** completes execution and returns its value to the original call to **endPre**:

```
┌─────────────────┐
│ first      = 0  │
│ last       = 6  │
│ firstEnd   = 3  │
│ return 6        │
└─────────────────┘
```

Figure 5-5
(continued)

Now you can use the method *endPre* to determine whether the data field *strExp* is a prefix expression as follows:

A recognition algorithm for prefix expressions

```
isPre()
// Determines whether the string expression in this class
// is a prefix expression.
// Precondition: The class has a data field strExp that
// has been initialized with a string expression that
// contains no blank characters.
// Postcondition: Returns true if the expression is in
// prefix form; otherwise returns false.

    size = length of expression strExp
```

```
  lastChar = endPre(0, size - 1)

  if (lastChar >= 0 and lastChar == size-1) {
    return true
  }
  else {
    return false
  }  // end if
```

Having determined that your string is a prefix expression, how can you evaluate it? Since each operator is followed by its two operands, you can look ahead in the expression for them. However, such operands can themselves be prefix expressions, which you must evaluate first. These prefix expressions are subexpressions of the original expression and must therefore be "smaller." A recursive solution to this problem seems natural.

The following method, which appears in pseudocode, evaluates a prefix expression. This algorithm is simpler than one that evaluates infix expressions.

```
evaluatePrefix(strExp)
// Evaluates the prefix expression strExp.
// Precondition: strExp is a string consisting of a valid
// prefix expression containing no blanks.
// Postcondition: Returns the value of the prefix
// expression.
  ch = first character of expression strExp
  Delete first character from strExp
  if (ch is an identifier) {
    // base case - single identifier
    return value of the identifier
  }
  else if (ch is an operator named op) {
    operand1 = evaluatePrefix(strExp)
    operand2 = evaluatePrefix(strExp)
    return operand1 op operand2
  } // end if
```

An algorithm to evaluate a prefix expression

Notice that each recursive call to `evaluatePrefix` removes from `strExp` the most recently evaluated prefix expression. The resulting substring is then used in the next recursive call of `evaluatePrefix`. To implement this method in Java requires that the parameter of `evaluatePrefix` be a mutable string type such as `java.lang.StringBuffer`. (See Appendix A for a discussion of mutable strings.)

Postfix expressions. A grammar that defines the language of all postfix expressions is

> < postfix > = < identifier > | < postfix > < postfix > < operator >
>
> < operator > = + | − | * | /
>
> < identifier > = a | b | · · · | z

Some calculators require that you enter two numbers before you enter the operation that you want to perform. Such calculators, in fact, require you to enter postfix expressions.

Here we will develop an algorithm for converting a prefix expression to a postfix expression. Chapter 6 presents a nonrecursive algorithm for evaluating postfix expressions. Together these two algorithms give you another method for evaluating a prefix expression. To simplify the conversion algorithm, assume that the prefix recognition algorithm has identified this as a syntactically correct prefix expression.

If you think recursively, the conversion from prefix form to postfix form is straightforward. If the prefix expression *exp* is a single letter, then

$$postfix(exp) = exp$$

Otherwise *exp* must be of the form

$$< operator > < prefix1 > < prefix2 >$$

The corresponding postfix expression is then

$$< postfix1 > < postfix2 > < operator >$$

where *< prefix1 >* converts to *< postfix1 >* and *< prefix2 >* converts to *< postfix2 >*. Therefore,

$$postfix(exp) = postfix(prefix1) + postfix(prefix2) + operator$$

Thus, at a high level, the conversion algorithm is

An algorithm that converts a prefix expression to postfix form

```
if (exp is a single letter) {
  return exp
}
else {
  return postfix(prefix1) + postfix(prefix2) + operator

} // end if
```

The following pseudocode method *convert* refines this algorithm. As in *evaluatePrefix*, the parameter *pre* should be a mutable string type.

A recursive algorithm that converts a prefix expression to postfix form

```
convert(pre)
// Converts a prefix expression pre to postfix form.
// Precondition: The expression in the string pre is a
// valid prefix expression.
// Postcondition: Returns the equivalent postfix expression
// as a string.

  // check the first character of the given string
  ch = first character of pre       // get first character
  Delete first character of pre
  if (ch is a lowercase letter) {  // check character
    // base case - single identifier expression
    return ch as a string
  }
```

```
else  { // ch is an operator
  // do the conversion recursively
  postfix1 = convert(pre)
  postfix2 = convert(pre)
  return postfix1 + postfix2 + ch  // concatenate operator
}  // end if
```

Fully parenthesized expressions. Most programmers would object to using prefix or postfix notation for their algebraic expressions, so most programming languages use infix notation. However, infix notation requires precedence rules, rules for association, and parentheses to avoid ambiguity within the expressions.

You can make precedence and association rules unnecessary by placing parentheses around each pair of operands together with their operator, thereby avoiding any ambiguity. A grammar for the language of all fully parenthesized infix expressions is

$< infix > = < identifier > | (< infix > < operator > < infix >)$

$< operator > = + | - | * | /$

$< identifier > = a | b | \cdots | z$

A grammar for the language of fully parenthesized algebraic expressions

Although the grammar is simple, the language is rather inconvenient for programmers.

Therefore, most programming languages support a definition of algebraic expressions that includes both precedence rules for the operators and rules of association so that fully parenthesized expressions are not required. However, the grammars for defining such languages are more involved, and the algorithms for recognizing and evaluating their expressions are more difficult than those you have seen in this section. Programming Problem 7 at the end of this chapter describes such a grammar without left-to-right association rules and asks you to write a recognition algorithm. Chapter 6 presents a nonrecursive evaluation algorithm for algebraic expressions that follows both precedence and left-to-right association rules.

THE RELATIONSHIP BETWEEN RECURSION AND MATHEMATICAL INDUCTION

A very strong relationship exists between recursion and mathematical induction. Recursion solves a problem by specifying a solution to one or more base cases and then demonstrating how to derive the solution to a problem of an arbitrary size from the solutions to smaller problems of the same type. Similarly, mathematical induction proves a property about the natural numbers by proving the property about a base case—usually 0 or 1—and then proving that the property must be true for an arbitrary natural number N if it is true for the natural numbers smaller than N.

Given the similarities between recursion and mathematical induction, it should not be surprising that induction is often employed to

You can use induction to prove
that a recursive algorithm either
is correct or performs
a certain amount of work

prove properties about recursive algorithms. What types of properties? You can, for example, prove that an algorithm actually performs the task that you intended. As an illustration, we will prove that the recursive *factorial* algorithm of Chapter 2 does indeed compute the factorial of its argument. Another use of mathematical induction is to prove that a recursive algorithm performs a certain amount of work. For example, we will prove that the solution to the Towers of Hanoi problem—also from Chapter 2—makes exactly $2^N - 1$ moves when it starts with N disks.

The Correctness of the Recursive Factorial Method

The following pseudocode describes a recursive method that computes the factorial of a nonnegative integer *n:*

```
fact(n)

  if (n is 0) {
    return 1
  }
  else {
    return n * fact(n - 1)
  }  // end if
```

You can prove that the method `fact` returns the values

$$fact(0) = 0! = 1$$
$$fact(n) = n! = n * (n - 1) * (n - 2) * \cdots * 1 \quad \text{if } n > 0$$

The proof is by induction on n.

Basis. *Show that the property is true for n = 0.* That is, you must show that `fact(0)` returns 1. But this result is simply the base case of the method: `fact(0)` returns 1 by its definition.

You now must establish that

property is true for an arbitrary k $\Rightarrow$ property is true for k + 1

Inductive hypothesis. *Assume that the property is true for n = k.* That is, assume that

$$fact(k) = k * (k - 1) * (k - 2) * \cdots * 2 * 1$$

Inductive conclusion. *Show that the property is true for n = k + 1.* That is, you must show that `fact(k + 1)` returns the value

$$(k + 1) * k * (k - 1) * (k - 2) * \cdots * 2 * 1$$

By definition of the method `fact`, `fact(k + 1)` returns the value

$$(k + 1) * fact(k)$$

But by the inductive hypothesis, `fact(k)` returns the value

$$k * (k - 1) * (k - 2) * \cdots * 2 * 1$$

Thus, $fact(k + 1)$ returns the value

$$(k + 1) * k * (k – 1) * (k – 2) * \cdots * 2 * 1$$

which is what you needed to show to establish that

property is true for an arbitrary k $\Rightarrow$ *property is true for k + 1*

The inductive proof is thus complete.

The Cost of Towers of Hanoi

In Chapter 2, you saw the following solution to the Towers of Hanoi problem:

```
solveTowers(count, source, destination, spare)

  if (count is 1) {
    Move a disk directly from source to destination
  }
  else {
    solveTowers(count-1, source, spare, destination)
    solveTowers(1, source, destination, spare)
    solveTowers(count-1, spare, destination, source)
  }  // end if
```

We now pose the following question: If you begin with N disks, how many moves does $solveTowers$ make to solve the problem?

Let $moves(N)$ be the number of moves made starting with N disks. When $N = 1$, the answer is easy:

$$moves(1) = 1$$

When $N > 1$, the value of $moves(N)$ is not so apparent. An inspection of the $solveTowers$ algorithm, however, reveals three recursive calls. Therefore, if you knew how many moves $solveTowers$ made starting with $N - 1$ disks, you could figure out how many moves it made starting with N disks; that is,

$$moves(N) = moves(N – 1) + moves(1) + moves(N – 1)$$

Thus, you have a recurrence relation for the number of moves required for N disks:

$$moves(1) = 1$$
$$moves(N) = 2 * moves(N – 1) + 1 \qquad \text{if } N > 1$$

A recurrence relation for the number of moves that **solveTowers** *requires for N disks*

For example, you can determine $moves(3)$ as follows:

$$moves(3)\ = 2 * moves(2) + 1$$
$$= 2 * (2 * moves(1) + 1) + 1$$
$$= 2 * (2 * 1 + 1) + 1$$
$$= 7$$

Although the recurrence relation gives you a way to compute *moves*(*N*), a **closed-form formula**—such as an algebraic expression—would be more satisfactory because you could substitute any given value for *N* and obtain the number of moves made. However, the recurrence relation is useful because there are techniques for obtaining a closed-form formula from it. Since these techniques are not relevant to us right now, we simply pull the formula out of the blue and use mathematical induction to prove that it is correct.

A closed-form formula for the number of moves that `solveTowers` *requires for N disks*

The solution to the previous recurrence relation is

$$moves(N) = 2^N - 1, \text{ for all } N \geq 1$$

Notice that $2^3 - 1$ agrees with the value 7 that was just computed for *moves*(3).

The proof that $moves(N) = 2^N - 1$ is by induction on *N*.

Basis.   *Show that the property is true for N = 1.* Here, $2^1 - 1 = 1$, which is consistent with the recurrence relation's specification that *moves*(1) = 1.

You now must establish that

property is true for an arbitrary k $\Rightarrow$ property is true for k + 1

Inductive hypothesis.   *Assume that the property is true for N = k.* That is, assume

$$moves(k) = 2^k - 1$$

Inductive conclusion.   *Show that the property is true for N = k + 1.* That is, you must show that $moves(k + 1) = 2^{k+1} - 1$. Now

$$
\begin{aligned}
moves(k + 1) &= 2 * moves(k) + 1 &&\text{from the recurrence relation} \\
&= 2 * (2^k - 1) + 1 &&\text{by the inductive hypothesis} \\
&= 2^{k+1} - 1
\end{aligned}
$$

which is what you needed to show to establish that

property is true for an arbitrary k $\Rightarrow$ property is true for k + 1

The inductive proof is thus complete.

Do not get the false impression that proving properties of programs is an easy matter. These two proofs are about as easy as any will be. However, well-structured programs are far more amenable to these techniques than are poorly structured programs.

Appendix D provides more information about mathematical induction.

SUMMARY

1. **Backtracking is a solution strategy that involves both recursion and a sequence of guesses that ultimately lead to a solution. If a particular guess leads to an impasse, you retrace your steps in**

reverse order, replace that guess, and try to complete the solution again.

2. A grammar is a device for defining a language, which is a set of strings of symbols. By using a grammar to define a language, you often can construct a recognition algorithm that is directly based on the grammar. Grammars are frequently recursive, thus allowing you to describe vast languages concisely.

3. To illustrate the use of grammars, we defined several different languages of algebraic expressions. These different languages have their relative advantages and disadvantages. Prefix and postfix expressions, while difficult for people to use, have simple grammars and eliminate problems of ambiguity. On the other hand, infix expressions are easier for people to use but require parentheses, precedence rules, and rules of association to eliminate ambiguity. Therefore, the grammar for infix expressions is more involved.

4. A close relationship between mathematical induction and recursion exists. You can use induction to prove properties about a recursive algorithm. For example, you can prove that a recursive algorithm is correct, and you can derive the amount of work it requires.

CAUTIONS

1. The subproblems that a recursive solution generates eventually must reach a base case. Failure to do so could result in an algorithm that does not terminate. Solutions that involve backtracking are particularly subject to this kind of error.

2. Grammars, like recursive algorithms, must have carefully chosen base cases. You must ensure that when a string is decomposed far enough, it will always reach the form of one of the grammar's base cases.

3. The subtleties of some of the algorithms you encountered in this chapter indicate the need for mathematical techniques to prove their correctness. The application of these techniques during the design of the various components of a solution can help to eliminate errors in logic before they appear in the program. One such technique is mathematical induction; another is the use of loop invariants, which we discussed in Chapter 1 and will discuss again in subsequent chapters.

SELF-TEST EXERCISES

1. Consider a Four Queens problem, which has the same rules as the Eight Queens problem but uses a 4-by-4 board. Find all solutions to this new problem by applying backtracking by hand.

2. Write the prefix expression that represents the following infix expression: $(a/b)*c-(d+e)*f$

3. Write the postfix expression that represents the following infix expression: $(a*b-c)/d+(e-f)$

4. Write the infix and postfix expressions that represent the following prefix expression: $--a/b+c*def$

5. Is the following string a prefix expression? $+-/abc*+def*gh$

6. Consider the language of these strings: $, cc$d, cccc$dd, cccccc$ddd, and so on. Write a recursive grammar for this language.

7. Use mathematical induction to show that the recurrence relation $f(n) = 2n + f(n-1)$ has the closed-form solution $f(n) = n(n-1)$.

EXERCISES

1. Trace the following recursive methods:

   a. `isPal` with the string abcdeba

   b. `isAnBn` with the string AABB

   c. `endPre` with the expression $-*/abcd$

2. Consider the language that the following grammar defines:

   $<S> = \$ \mid <W> \mid \$<S>$

   $<W> = abb \mid a<W>bb$

   Write all strings that are in this language and that contain seven or fewer characters.

3. Write a recursive grammar for the language of strings of one or more letters. The first letter of each string must be uppercase and all other letters in the string must be lowercase.

4. Consider a language of strings that contain only dots and dashes. All strings in this language contain at least four characters and begin with either two dots or two dashes. If the first two characters are dots, the last one must be a dash; if the first two characters are dashes, the last one must be a dot. Write a recursive grammar for this language.

5. Consider a language of words, where each word is a string of dots and dashes. The following grammar describes this language:

   $<word> = <dot> \mid <dash><word> \mid <word><dot>$

   $<dot> = \bullet$

   $<dash> = -$

   a. Write all three-character strings that are in this language.

   b. Is the string $\bullet\bullet\bullet\bullet--$ in this language? Explain.

    c. Write a seven-character string that contains more dashes than dots and is in the language. Show how you know that your answer is correct.

    d. Write pseudocode for a recursive recognition method `isIn(str)` that returns `true` if the string `str` is in this language and returns `false` otherwise.

6. Let L be the language

$L = \{S : S \text{ is of the form } A^n B^{2n}, \text{ for some } n > 0\}$

Thus, a string is in L if and only if it starts with a sequence of A's and is followed by a sequence of twice as many B's. For example, AABBBB is in L, but ABBB, ABBABB, and the empty string are not.

    a. Give a grammar for the language L.

    b. Write a recursive method that determines whether the string `str` is in L.

7. Is $+*a{-}b/c{+}{+}de{-}fg$ a prefix expression? Explain in terms of the grammar for prefix expressions.

8. Is $ab/c*efg*h/{+}d{-}{+}$ a postfix expression? Explain in terms of the grammar for postfix expressions.

9. Consider the language that the following grammar defines:

$<S> = <L> \mid <D><S><S>$

$<L> = A \mid B$

$<D> = 1 \mid 2$

    a. Write all three-character strings that are in this language.

    b. Write one string in this language that contains more than three characters.

10. Consider a language of the following strings: The letter A, the letter B, the letter C followed by a string that is in the language, the letter D followed by a string in the language. For example, these strings are in this language: A, CA, CCA, DCA, B, CB, CCB, DB, and DCCB.

    a. Write a grammar for this language.

    b. Is CAB in this language? Explain.

    c. Write a recursive recognition algorithm for this language.

11. Consider the language that the following grammar defines:

$< word > = \$ \mid a< word >a \mid b< word >b \mid \cdots \mid y< word >y \mid z< word >z$

Equivalently,

$L = \{w\$\text{reverse}(w) : w \text{ is a string of letters of length} \geq 0\}$

Note that this language is very similar to the language of palindromes, but there is a special middle character here.

    The algorithm that this chapter gave for recognizing palindromes can be adapted easily to this language. The algorithm, which is recursive and processes the string `str` from both ends toward the middle, is based on the following facts:

- A string with no characters is not in the language.
- A string with exactly one character is in the language if the character is a $.
- A longer string is in the language if the ends are identical letters and the inner substring (from the second character to the next to the last character of `str`) is in the language.

Describe a recursive recognition algorithm that processes the string from left to right, reading one character at a time and not explicitly saving the string for future reference. Write a Java method that implements your algorithm.

12. Consider the following recursive method:

```
public static int p(int x) {
   if (x < 3) {
      return x;
   }
   else {
      return p(x-1) * p(x-3);
   } // end if
} // end p
```

Let $m(x)$ be the number of multiplication operations that the execution of `p(x)` performs.

   a. Write a recursive definition of $m(x)$.

   b. Prove that your answer to Part *a* is correct by using mathematical induction.

13. Consider palindromes that consist only of lowercase letters, such as "level" and "deed," but not "RadaR," "ADA," or "101." Let $c(n)$ be the number of palindromes of length n.

   a. Write a recursive definition of $c(n)$.

   b. Prove that your answer to Part *a* is correct by using mathematical induction.

14. Prove the following for single-letter operands: If E is a prefix expression and Y is a nonempty string of nonblank characters, then $E\ Y$ cannot be a legal prefix expression. (*Hint*: Use a proof by induction on the length of E.)

15. Suppose we have the following recurrence relation for $f(n)$:

$$f(0) = 0 \qquad\qquad \text{for } n = 0;$$
$$f(n) = f(n-1) + n \qquad \text{for } n > 0;$$

Prove by induction on n that the following is a closed-form formula for f:

$$f(n) = n(n+1)/2$$

16. Chapter 2 gave the following definition for $c(n, k)$, where n and k are assumed to be nonnegative integers:

$$c(n, k) = \begin{cases} 1 & \text{if } k = 0 \\ 1 & \text{if } k = n \\ 0 & \text{if } k > n \\ c(n-1, k-1) + c(n-1, k) & \text{if } 0 < k < n \end{cases}$$

Prove by induction on n that the following is a closed form for $c(n, k)$:

$$c(n, k) = \frac{n!}{(n-k)!k!}$$

PROGRAMMING PROBLEMS

1. Complete the program that solves the Eight Queens problem.

2. Revise the program that you just wrote for the Eight Queens problem so that it answers the following questions:

   a. How many backtracks occur? That is, how many times does the program remove a queen from the board?

   b. How many calls to *isUnderAttack* are there?

   c. How many recursive calls to *placeQueens* are there?

   d. Can you make *isUnderAttack* more efficient? For example, as soon as you detect that a queen can attack a given square, do you still look for another queen?

*3. You can begin the Eight Queens problem by placing a queen in the second square of the first column instead of the first square. You can then call *placeQueens* to begin with the second column. This revision should lead you to a new solution. Write a program that finds all solutions to the Eight Queens problem.

4. Instead of using an 8-by-8 array to represent the board in the Eight Queens program, you can use a one-dimensional array to represent only the squares that contain a queen. Let *col* be an array of eight integers such that

   col[k] = row index of the queen in column $k + 1$

   For example, if *col[2]* is 3, then a queen is in the fourth row (square) of the third column—that is, in *board[3][2]*. Thus, you use *col[k]* to represent a queen instead of *board[col[k]][k]*.

   This scheme requires that you also store information about whether each queen is subject to attack. Because only one queen per column is permitted, you do not have to check columns. To check for a row attack, define an array *rowAttack* such that *rowAttack[k]* is nonzero if the queen in column $k + 1$ can be attacked by a queen in its row.

To check for diagonal attacks, observe that diagonals have either a positive slope or a negative slope. Those with a positive slope are parallel to the diagonal that runs from the lower left corner of the board to the upper right corner. Diagonals with a negative slope are parallel to the diagonal that runs from the upper left corner to the lower right corner. Convince yourself that if $board[i][j]$ represents a square, then $i + j$ is constant for squares that are in a diagonal with a positive slope, and $i - j$ is constant for squares that are in a diagonal with a negative slope. You will find that $i + j$ ranges from 0 to 14 and that $i - j$ ranges from –7 to +7. Thus, define arrays $posDiagonal$ and $negDiagonal$ such that

$posDiagonal[k]$ is true if the queen in column $k + 1$ can be attacked by a queen in its positive-sloped diagonal, and

$negDiagonal[k]$ is true if the queen in column $k + 1$ can be attacked by a queen in its negative-sloped diagonal.

Use these ideas to write a program that solves the Eight Queens problem.

5. Do you know how to find your way through a maze? After you write this program, you will never be lost again!

Assume that a maze is a rectangular array of squares, some of which are blocked to represent walls. The maze has one entrance and one exit. For example, if x's represent the walls, a maze could appear as:

```
xxxxxxxxxxxxxxxxx x
x       x       xxxx x
x xxxxx xxxxx    xx x
x xxxxx xxxxxxx xx x
x x             xx xx x
x xxxxxxxxxx xx     x
xxxxxxxxxxxxxoxxxxxx
```

A creature, indicated in the previous diagram by o, sits just inside the maze at the entrance. Assume that the creature can move in only four directions: north, south, east, and west. In the diagram, north is up, south is down, east is to the right, and west is to the left. The problem is to move the creature through the maze from the entrance to the exit, if possible. As the creature moves, it should mark its path. At the conclusion of the trip through the maze, you should see both the correct path and incorrect attempts.

Squares in the maze have one of several states: CLEAR (the square is clear), WALL (the square is blocked and represents part of the wall), PATH (the square lies on the path to the exit), and VISITED (the square was visited, but going that way led to an impasse).

This problem uses two ADTs that must interact. The ADT creature represents the creature's current position and contains operations that move the creature. The creature should be able to move north, south, east, and west one square at a time. It should also be able to report its position and mark its trail.

The ADT maze represents the maze itself, which is a two-dimensional rectangular arrangement of squares. Suppose that we number the rows of squares from the top beginning with zero, and we number the columns of squares from the left beginning with zero. Thus, you can use a row number and a column number to identify uniquely any square within the maze. The ADT clearly needs a data structure to represent the maze. It also needs such data as the height and width of the maze, given in numbers of squares; the length of a side of a square; and the row and column coordinates of both the entrance to and the exit from the maze.

The ADT maze should also contain, for example, operations that create a specific maze, given a text file of data; display a maze; determine whether a particular square is part of the wall; determine whether a particular square is part of the path; and so on.

The text file that you will use to represent a maze is simple. An example of how this can be done for the previously given maze is:

```
20   7     width and height of maze in squares
0   18     row and column coordinate of maze exit
6   12     row and column coordinate of maze entrance
XXXXXXXXXXXXXXXXX X
X      X        XXXX X
X XXXXX XXXXX    XX X
X XXXXX XXXXXXX XX X
X X            XX XX X
X XXXXXXXXXX XX      X
XXXXXXXXXXXX XXXXXXX
```

Each line in the file corresponds to a row in the maze; each character in a line corresponds to a column in the maze. X's indicate blocked squares (the walls), and blanks indicate clear squares. This notation is convenient because you can see what the maze looks like as you design it.

If you are at the maze's entrance, you can systematically find your way out of the maze by using the following search algorithm. It involves backtracking—that is, retracing your steps when you reach an impasse.

1. First, check whether you are at the exit. If you are, you're done (a very simple maze); if you are not, go to Step 2.

2. Try to move to the square directly to the north by calling the method *goNorth* (described later).

3. If *goNorth* was successful, you are done. If it was unsuccessful, try to move to the square directly to the west by calling the method *goWest* (described later).

4. If *goWest* was successful, you are done. If it was unsuccessful, try to move to the square directly to the south by calling the method *goSouth* (described later).

5. If *goSouth* was successful, you are done. If it was unsuccessful, try to move to the square directly to the east by calling the method *goEast* (described later).

6. If *goEast* was successful, you are done. If it was unsuccessful, you are still done, because no path exists from the entrance to the exit.

The method *goNorth* will examine all the paths that start at the square to the north of the present square as follows. If the square directly to the north is clear, is inside the maze, and has not been visited before, move into this square and mark it as part of the path. (Note that you are moving from the south.) Check whether you are at the exit. If you are, you're done. Otherwise, try to find a path to the exit from here by trying all paths leaving this square except the one going south (going south would put you back in the square from which you just came) as follows. Call *goNorth*; if it is not successful, call *goWest* and, if it is not successful, call *goEast*. If *goEast* is not successful, mark this square as visited, move back into the square to the south, and return.

The following pseudocode describes the *goNorth* algorithm:

```
goNorth(maze, creature)

    if (the square to the north is clear,
        inside the maze, and unvisited) {
      Move to the north
      Mark the square as part of the path
      if (at exit) {
        success = true
      }
      else {
        success = goNorth(maze, creature)
        if (!success) {
          success = goWest(maze, creature)
          if (!success) {
            success = goEast(maze, creature)
            if (!success) {
              Mark square visited
              Backtrack south
            } // end if
          } // end if
        } // end if
      } // end if
    }
    else {
      success = false
    }  // end if
    return success
```

The *goWest* method will examine all the paths that start at the square to the west of the present square as follows. If the square directly to the west is clear, is inside the maze, and has not been visited before, move into this square and mark it as part of the path. (Note that you are moving from the east.) Check whether you are at the exit. If you are, you're done. Otherwise, try to find a path to the exit from here by trying all paths leaving this square except the one going east (this would put you back in the square from which you just came) as follows. Call *goNorth*; if it is not successful, call *go West* and, if it is not successful, call *goSouth*. If *goSouth* is not successful, mark this square as visited, move back into the square to the east, and return.

The methods *goEast* and *goSouth* are analogous to the methods just described.

6. Write a program that will recognize and evaluate prefix expressions. First design and implement a class of prefix expressions. This class should contain methods to recognize and evaluate prefix expressions. This chapter discusses the algorithms you will need to implement these methods.

7. The following is a grammar that allows you to omit parentheses in infix algebraic expressions when the precedence rules remove ambiguity. For example, $a + b * c$ means $a + (b * c)$. However, the grammar requires parentheses when ambiguity would otherwise result. That is, the grammar does not permit left-to-right association when several operators have the same precedence. For example, $a/b * c$ is illegal. Notice that the definitions introduce factors and terms.

< *expression* > = < *term* > | < *term* > + < *term* > | < *term* > − < *term* >

< *term* > = < *factor* > | < *factor* > * < *factor* > | < *factor* > / < *factor* >

< *factor* > = < *letter* > | (< *expression* >)

< *letter* > = a | b | · · · | z

The recognition algorithm is based on a recursive chain of subtasks: *find an expression → find a term → find a factor*. What makes this a recursive chain is that *find an expression* uses *find a term*, which in turn uses *find a factor*. *Find a factor* either detects a base case or uses *find an expression*, thus forming the recursive chain.

The pseudocode for the recognition algorithm follows:

```
FIND AN EXPRESSION
// The grammar specifies that an expression is either
// a single term or a term followed by a + or a -,
// which then must be followed by a second term.

  Find a term
  if (the next symbol is a + or a -) {
    Find a term
  } // end if
```

FIND A TERM
```
// The grammar specifies that a term is either a
// single factor or a factor followed by a * or a /,
// which must then be followed by a second factor.

  Find a factor
  if (the next symbol is a * or a /) {
    Find a factor
  }  // end if
```

FIND A FACTOR
```
// The grammar specifies that a factor is either a
// single letter (the base case) or an
// expression enclosed in parentheses.

  if (the first symbol is a letter) {
    Done
  }
  else if (the first symbol is a '(') {
    Find an expression starting at character after '('
    Check for ')'
  }
  else {
    No factor exists
  }  // end if
```

Design and implement a class of infix expressions, as described by the given grammar. Include a method to recognize a legal infix expression.

Problem Solving with Abstract Data Types

Part I of this book reviewed aspects of problem solving that are closely related to programming issues, presented data abstraction as a technique for solution design that permeates our approach to problem solving, introduced Java classes as a way to hide a solution's implementation details and to increase its modularity, introduced the linked list as a data structure that you will see throughout this book, and developed recursion as a problem-solving technique that is useful in the construction of algorithms. The primary concerns of the remainder of this book are the aspects of problem solving that involve the *management of data*—that is, the identification and implementation of some of the more common data-management operations.

You saw in Part I that you can organize data either by position—as in the ADT list—or by value—as in the ADT sorted list. In general, these organizations are appropriate for applications of rather different natures. For example, if an application needs to ask a question about the first person in a line, you should organize the data by position. On the other hand, if an application needs to ask a question about the employee named Smith, you should organize the data by value. In Part II, you will see other ADTs that use these two data organizations.

Our study of data management has three goals. The first is to identify useful sets of operations—that is, to identify abstract data types. The second goal is to examine applications that use these abstract data types. The third goal is to construct implementations for the abstract data types—that is, to develop data structures and classes. As you will discover, the nature of the operations of an abstract data type, along with the application in which you will use it, greatly influences the choice of its implementation.

CHAPTER 6

Stacks

PREVIEW　This chapter introduces a well-known ADT called a stack and presents both its applications and implementations. You will see how the operations on a stack give it a last-in, first-out behavior. Two of the several applications of a stack that the chapter considers are evaluating algebraic expressions and searching for a path between two points. Finally, the chapter discusses the important relationship between stacks and recursion.

THE ABSTRACT DATA TYPE

The specification of an abstract data type that you can use to solve a particular problem can emerge during the design of the problem's solution. The ADT developed in the following example happens to be an important one: the ADT stack.

Developing an ADT during the Design of a Solution

When you type a line of text on a keyboard, you are likely to make mistakes. If you use the backspace key to correct these mistakes, each backspace erases the previous character entered. Consecutive backspaces are applied in sequence and so erase several characters. For instance, if you type the line

    abcc←ddde←←←ef←fg

where ← represents the backspace character, the corrected input would be

    abcdefg

How can a program read the original line and get the correct input? In designing a solution to this problem, you eventually must decide how to store the input line. In accordance with the ADT approach, you should postpone this decision until you have a better idea of what operations you will need to perform on the data.

A first attempt at a solution leads to the following pseudocode:

Initial draft of a solution

```
// read the line, correcting mistakes along the way
while (not end of line) {
  Read a new character ch
  if (ch is not a '←') {
    Add ch to the ADT
  }
  else {
    Remove from the ADT the item added most recently
  } // end if
} // end while
```

This solution calls to attention two of the operations that the ADT will have to include:

- Add a new item to the ADT.
- Remove from the ADT the item that was added most recently.

Two ADT operations that are required

Notice that potential trouble lurks if you type a ← when the ADT is empty, that is, when the ADT contains no characters. If this situation should occur, you have two options: (1) have the program terminate and write an error message, or (2) have the program ignore the ← and continue. Either option is reasonable, so let's suppose that you decide to ignore the ← and continue. Therefore, the algorithm becomes

```
// read the line, correcting mistakes along the way
while (not end of line) {
  Read a new character ch
  if (ch is not a '←') {
    Add ch to the ADT
  }
  else if (the ADT is not empty) {
    Remove from the ADT the item added most recently
  }
  else {
    Ignore the '←'
  }  // end if
}  // end while
```

The "read and correct" algorithm

From this pseudocode you can identify a third operation required by the ADT:

- Determine whether the ADT is empty.

Another required ADT operation

This solution places the corrected input line in the ADT. Now suppose that you want to display the line. At first, it appears that you can accomplish this task by using the ADT operations already identified, as follows:

```
// write the line
while (the ADT is not empty) {
  Remove from the ADT the item added most recently
  Write .....Uh-oh!
}  // end while
```

A false start at writing the line

This pseudocode is incorrect for two reasons:

1. When you remove an item from the ADT, the item is gone, so you cannot write it. What you should have done was to *retrieve* from the ADT the item that was added most recently. A retrieval operation means to *look at, but leave unchanged.* Only after retrieving and writing the item should you remove it from the ADT.

Reasons why the attempted solution is incorrect

2. The most recently added item is the last character of the input line. You certainly do not want to write it first. The resolution of this particular difficulty is left to you as an exercise.

If we address only the first difficulty, the following pseudocode writes the input line in reversed order:

The write-backward algorithm

```
// write the line in reversed order
while (the ADT is not empty) {
    Retrieve from the ADT the item that was
        added most recently and put it in ch
    Write ch
    Remove from the ADT the item added most recently
}  // end while
```

Thus, a fourth operation is required by the ADT:

Another required ADT operation

- Retrieve from the ADT the item that was added most recently.

Although you have yet to think about an implementation of the ADT, you know that you must be able to perform four specific operations.[1] These operations define the required ADT, which happens to be well known: It is usually called a **stack.** As you saw in Chapter 3, is it customary to include initialization operations in an ADT. Thus, the following operations define the ADT stack.

ADT Stack Operations

1. Create an empty stack.

2. Determine whether a stack is empty.

3. Add a new item to the stack.

4. Remove from the stack the item that was added most recently.

5. Remove all the items from the stack.

6. Retrieve from the stack the item that was added most recently.

The term "stack" is intended to conjure up visions of things encountered in daily life, such as a stack of dishes in the school cafeteria, a stack of books on your desk, or a stack of assignments waiting for you to work on them. In common English usage, "stack of" and "pile of" are synonymous. To computer scientists, however, a stack is not just any old pile. A stack has the property that the last item placed on the stack will be the first item removed. This property is commonly referred to as **last-in, first-out,** or simply **LIFO.**

Last-in, first-out

---

[1]As you will learn if you complete Exercise 5 at the end of this chapter, the final algorithm to write the line correctly instead of in reversed order does not require additional ADT operations.

A stack of dishes in a cafeteria makes a very good analogy of the abstract data type stack, as Figure 6-1 illustrates. As new dishes are added, the old dishes drop farther into the well beneath the surface. At any particular time, only the dish last placed on the stack is above the surface and visible. This dish is at the **top** of the stack and is the one that must be removed next. In general, the dishes are removed in exactly the opposite order from that in which they were added.

The LIFO property of stacks seems inherently unfair. Think of the poor person who finally gets the last dish on the cafeteria's stack, a dish that may have been placed there six years ago. Or how would you like to be the first person to arrive on the stack for a movie—as opposed to the line for a movie. You would be the last person allowed in! These examples demonstrate the reason that stacks are not especially prevalent in everyday life. The property that we usually desire in our daily lives is **first in, first out**, or **FIFO**. A **queue**, which you will study in the next chapter, is the abstract data type with the FIFO property. Most people would much prefer to wait in a movie *queue*—as a line is called in Britain—than in a movie *stack*. However, while the LIFO property of stacks is not appropriate for very many day-to-day situations, it is precisely what is needed for a large number of problems that arise in computer science.

Notice how well the analogy holds between the abstract data type stack and the stack of cafeteria dishes. The operations that manipulate data in the ADT stack are the *only* such operations, and they correspond to the only things that you can do to a stack of dishes. You can determine whether the stack of dishes is empty but not how many dishes are on the stack; you can inspect the top dish but no other dish; you can place a dish on top of the stack but at no other position; and you can remove a dish from the top of the stack but from no other position. If any of these operations was not available, or if you were permitted to perform any other operations, the ADT would not be a stack.

Although the stack of cafeteria dishes suggests that, as you add or remove dishes, the other dishes move, do not have this expectation of the ADT stack. The stack operations involve only the top item and imply only that the other items in the stack remain in sequence. Implementations of the ADT stack operations might or might not move the stack's items. The implementations given in this chapter do not move data items.

Refining the definition of the ADT stack.   Before we specify the details of the stack operations, consider the removal and retrieval operations more carefully. The current definition enables you to remove the stack's top without inspecting it, or to inspect the stack's top without removing it. Both tasks are reasonable and occur in practice. However, if you wanted to inspect *and* remove the top item of a stack—a task that is not unusual—you would need the sequence of operations

- Retrieve from the stack the item that was added most recently.
- Remove from the stack the item that was added most recently.

Figure 6-1

Stack of cafeteria dishes

An operation that retrieves and then removes the top of a stack would allow you to perform this common task in one operation.

The following pseudocode specifies the operations for the ADT stack in more detail, and includes a combined retrieval and removal operation. The names given here for the operations that add and remove items are conventional for stacks.

Pseudocode for the ADT Stack Operations

```
createStack()
// Creates an empty stack.

isEmpty()
// Determines whether a stack is empty.

push(newItem) throws StackException
// Adds newItem to the top of the stack. Throws
// StackException if the insertion is not successful.

pop() throws StackException
// Retrieves and then removes the top of the stack (the
// item that was added most recently). Throws
// StackException if the deletion is not successful.

popAll()
// Removes all items from the stack.

peek() throws StackException
// Retrieves the top of the stack. That is, peek
// retrieves the item that was added most recently.
// Retrieval does not change the stack. Throws
// StackException if the retrieval is not successful.
```

Recall that Chapter 1 urged you to focus on the specification of a module before you considered its implementation. After specifying an ADT's operations in pseudocode, you should try to use them as a check of your design. Such a test can highlight any deficiencies in your specifications or design. For example, you can use the previous stack operations to refine the algorithms developed earlier in this chapter.

Using the ADT stack in a solution. You now can refine the algorithms developed earlier in this chapter by using the stack operations:

The refined algorithms

```
displayBackward(stack)
// Displays the input line in reversed order by
// writing the contents of stack.
  stack = readAndCorrect()
```

```
  while (!stack.isEmpty()) {
    newChar = stack.pop()
    Write newChar
  }  // end while

  Advance to new line


readAndCorrect()
// Reads the input line and returns the corrected
// version as a stack. For each character read,
// either enters it into the stack or, if it
// is '←', corrects the contents of stack.

  stack.createStack()²
  Read newChar
  while (newChar is not the end-of-line symbol) {
    if (newChar is not '←') {
      stack.push(newChar)
    }
    else if (!stack.isEmpty()) {
      oldChar = stack.pop()
    }  // end if
    Read newChar
  }  // end while
  return stack
```

We have used the stack operations without knowing their implementations or even what a stack looks like. Because the ADT approach builds a wall around the implementation of the stack, your program can use a stack independently of the stack's implementation. As long as the program correctly uses the ADT operations—that is, as long as it honors the contract—it will work regardless of how you implement the ADT.

The contract, therefore, must be written precisely. That is, before you implement any ADT operations, you should specify both their preconditions and their postconditions. Realize, however, that during program design, the first attempt at specification is often informal and is only later made precise by the writing of preconditions and postconditions.

Axioms (*optional*).   As Chapter 3 noted, intuitive specifications, such as those given previously for the stack operations, are not really sufficient to define an ADT formally. For example, to capture formally the intuitive notion that the last item inserted into *stack* is the first item to be removed, you could write an axiom such as

$$(stack.push(newItem)).pop() = stack$$

An example of an axiom

---

[2]You implement the step `stack.createStack()` in Java by declaring `stack` as an instance of the stack class, since `createStack` is implemented as the class's constructor.

That is, if you push *newItem* onto *stack* and then pop it, you are left with the original stack *stack*. Exercise 12 at the end of this chapter discusses the axioms for a stack further.

SIMPLE APPLICATIONS OF THE ADT STACK

This section presents two rather simple examples for which the LIFO property of stacks is appropriate. Note that we will be using the operations of the ADT stack, even though we have not discussed their implementations yet.

Checking for Balanced Braces

Java uses curly braces, "{" and "}", to delimit groups of statements. For example, braces begin and end a method's body. If you treat a Java program as a string of characters, you can use a stack to verify that a program contains balanced braces. For example, the braces in the string

    abc{defg{ijk}{l{mn}}op}qr

are balanced, while the braces in the string

    abc{def}}{ghij{kl}m

are not balanced. You can check whether a string contains balanced braces by traversing it from left to right. As you move from left to right, you match each successive close brace "}" with the most recently encountered unmatched open brace "{"; that is, the "{" must be to the left of the current "}". The braces are balanced if

Requirements for balanced braces

1. Each time you encounter a "}", it matches an already encountered "{"

2. When you reach the end of the string, you have matched each "{"

The solution requires that you keep track of each unmatched "{" and discard one each time you encounter a "}". One way to perform this task is to push each "{" encountered onto a stack and pop one off each time you encounter a "}". Thus, a first-draft pseudocode solution is

Initial draft of a solution

```
while (not at the end of the string) {
  if (the next character is a '{') {
    stack.push('{')
  }
  else if (the character is a '}') {
    openBrace = stack.pop()
  }  // end if
}  // end while
```

Although this solution correctly keeps track of braces, missing from it are the checks that conditions 1 and 2 are met—that is, that the braces are indeed balanced. To verify condition 1 when a "}" is encountered, you must check to see whether the stack is empty before popping from it. If it is empty, you terminate the loop and report that the string is not balanced. To verify condition 2, you must check that the stack is empty when the end of the string is reached.

   Thus, the pseudocode solution to check for balanced braces in *aString* becomes

```
stack.createStack()
balancedSoFar = true
i = 0

while (balancedSoFar and i < length of aString) {
  ch = character at position i in aString
  ++i
  // push an open brace
  if (ch is '{') {
    stack.push('{')
  }
  // close brace
  else if (ch is '}') {
    if (!stack.isEmpty()) {
      openBrace = stack.pop()    // pop a matching open brace
    }
    else {                       // no matching open brace
      balancedSoFar = false
    }  // end if
  }  // end if
  // ignore all characters other than braces
}  // end while


if (balancedSoFar and stack.isEmpty()) {
  aString has balanced braces
}
else {
  aString does not have balanced braces
}  // end if
```

A detailed pseudocode solution to check a string for balanced braces

Figure 6-2 shows the stacks that result when this algorithm is applied to several simple examples.

   It may have occurred to you that a simpler solution to this problem is possible. You need only keep a count of the current number of unmatched open braces.[3] You need not actually store the open braces in

---

[3] Each time you encounter an open brace, you increment the count; each time you encounter a close brace, you decrement the count. If this count ever falls below zero or if it is greater than zero when the end of the string is reached, the string is unbalanced.

Figure 6-2

Traces of the algorithm that checks for balanced braces

a stack. However, the stack-based solution is conceptually useful as it previews more legitimate uses of stacks. For example, Exercise 6 at the end of this chapter asks you to extend the algorithm given here to check for balanced parentheses and square brackets in addition to braces.

The exception *StackException*. Although the previous algorithm—in its present state of refinement—ignores the exception *StackException*, a Java implementation should not. The implementation either should take precautions to avoid an exception or should provide *try* and *catch* blocks to handle a possible exception. Suppose that *push* or *pop* throws *StackException*. Exactly how should you interpret this event?

    The informality of the ADT specifications given earlier complicates the interpretation of *StackException*. For example, as it is specified, *StackException* is thrown if *pop* is not successful. Later, this chapter will clarify this particular specification: *pop* will be unsuccessful if it tries to delete an item from an empty stack. Under this assumption, you can refine the pseudocode

This section of the previous algorithm ignores Stack-Exception

```
// close brace
else if (ch is '}') {
  if (!stack.isEmpty()) {
    openBrace = stack.pop()   // pop open brace
  }
  else {                      // no open brace
    balancedSoFar = false
  }  // end if
}  // end if
```

in the previous algorithm to

```
    // close brace
    else if (ch is '}') {
      try {
        // try to pop open brace
        openBrace = stack.pop()
      } // end try
      catch (StackException e) {
        balancedSoFar = false  // no open brace
      } // end catch
    } // end if
```

Revision that makes use of `StackException`

The *push* operation can fail for implementation-dependent reasons. For example, *push* throws *StackException* if the array in an array-based implementation is full. In the spirit of fail-safe programming, a method that implements this balanced-braces algorithm should check for a thrown *StackException* after *push* and report an unsuccessful insertion.

Recognizing Strings in a Language

Consider the problem of recognizing whether a particular string is in the language

$$L = \{w\$w' : w \text{ is a possibly empty string of characters other than } \$, \\ w' = reverse(w) \}$$

For example, the strings A\$A, ABC\$CBA, and \$ are in *L*, but AB\$AB and ABC\$CB are not. (Exercise 11 in Chapter 5 introduced a similar language.) This language is like the language of palindromes that you saw in Chapter 5, but strings in this language have a special middle character.

A stack is useful in determining whether a given string is in *L*. Suppose you traverse the first half of the string and push each character onto a stack. When you reach the \$, you can undo the process: For each character in the second half of the string, you pop a character off the stack. However, you must match the popped character with the current character in the string to ensure that the second half of the string is the reverse of the first half. The stack must be empty when—and only when—you reach the end of the string; otherwise, one "half" of the string is longer than the other, and so the string is not in *L*.

The following algorithm uses this strategy. To avoid unnecessary complications, assume that *aString* contains exactly one \$.

```
stack.createStack()

// push the characters before $, that is, the
// characters in w, onto the stack
i = 0
ch = character at position i in aString
while (ch is not '$') {
```

A pseudocode recognition algorithm for the language L

```
    stack.push(ch)
    ++i
    ch = character at position i in aString
}  // end while

// skip the $
++i

// match the reverse of w
inLanguage = true   // assume string is in language
while (inLanguage and i < length of aString) {
  ch = character at position i in aString
  try {
    stackTop = stack.pop()
    if (stackTop equals ch) {
      ++i  // characters match
    }
    else {
      //  top of stack is not ch (characters do not match)
      inLanguage = false  // reject string
    }  // end if
  }  // end try
  catch (StackException e) {
    // stack.pop() failed, stack is empty (first half of
    // string is shorter than second half)
    inLanguage = false
  }  // end catch
}  // end while

if (inLanguage and stack.isEmpty()) {
  aString is in language
}
else {
  aString is not in language
}  // end if
```

Notice that the two algorithms presented in this section depend only on the specifications of the stack operations and not on their implementations.

IMPLEMENTATIONS OF THE ADT STACK

This section develops three Java implementations of the ADT stack. The first implementation uses an array to represent the stack, the second uses a linked list, and the third uses the ADT list. Figure 6-3 illustrates these three implementations. The following interface *StackInterface* is used to provide a common specification for the three implementations.

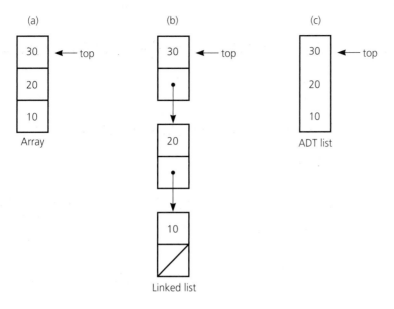

Figure 6-3

Implementations of the ADT stack that use (a) an array; (b) a linked
list; (c) an ADT list

```
public interface StackInterface {
  public boolean isEmpty();
  // Determines whether the stack is empty.
  // Precondition: None.
  // Postcondition: Returns true if the stack is empty;
  // otherwise returns false.

  public void popAll();
  // Removes all the items from the stack.
  // Precondition: None.
  // Postcondition: Stack is empty.

  public void push(Object newItem) throws StackException;
  // Adds an item to the top of a stack.
  // Precondition: newItem is the item to be added.
  // Postcondition: If insertion is successful, newItem
  // is on the top of the stack.
  // Exception: Some implementations may throw
  // StackException when newItem cannot be placed on
  // the stack.

  public Object pop() throws StackException;
  // Removes the top of a stack.
```

```
// Precondition: None.
// Postcondition: If the stack is not empty, the item
// that was added most recently is removed from the
// stack and returned.
// Exception: Throws StackException if the stack is
// empty.

public Object peek() throws StackException;
// Retrieves the top of a stack.
// Precondition: None.
// Postcondition: If the stack is not empty, the item
// that was added most recently is returned. The
// stack is unchanged.
// Exception: Throws StackException if the stack is
// empty.
}  // end StackInterface
```

Here is the class *StackException* that is used in *StackInterface*:

```
public class StackException
            extends java.lang.RuntimeException {
  public StackException(String s) {
    super(s);
  }  // end constructor
}  // end StackException
```

Note that *StackException* extends *java.lang.RuntimeException*, so that the calls to methods that throw *StackException* do not have to be enclosed in *try* blocks. This is a reasonable choice for the operations *pop* and *peek*, since you can avoid the exception by checking to see whether the stack is empty before calling these operations. But *push* can also throw *StackException* in an array-based implementation when a fixed-size array is used and becomes full. You can avoid this exception in an array-based implementation by providing a method *isFull* that determines whether the stack is full; you call *isFull* before you call *push*.

In a reference-based implementation, this *isFull* method would not be necessary. Also, although the *push* method throws *StackException* in the interface specification, the *throws* clause could be omitted in a reference-based implementation of *push*.

An Array-Based Implementation of the ADT Stack

Figure 6-4 suggests that you use an array of *Object*s called *items* to represent the items in a stack and an index *top* such that *items[top]* is the stack's top. We want to define a class whose instances are stacks and whose private data fields are *items* and *top*.

The following class is an array-based implementation of the ADT stack. The default constructor for this class corresponds to and replaces the ADT operation *createStack*. Note that the preconditions and postconditions

Figure 6-4

An array-based implementation

given earlier in *StackInterface* apply here as well, and so are omitted to save space.

```java
public class StackArrayBased implements StackInterface {
  final int MAX_STACK = 50;   // maximum size of stack
  private Object items[];
  private int top;

  public StackArrayBased() {
    items = new Object[MAX_STACK];
    top = -1;
  }  // end default constructor

  public boolean isEmpty() {
    return top < 0;
  }  // end isEmpty

  public boolean isFull() {
    return top == MAX_STACK-1;
  }  // end isFull

  public void push(Object newItem) throws StackException {
    if (!isFull()) {
      items[++top] = newItem;
    }
    else {
      throw new StackException("StackException on " +
                              "push: stack full");
    }  // end if
  }  // end push

  public void popAll() {
    items = new Object[MAX_STACK];
    top = -1;
  }  // end popAll

  public Object pop() throws StackException {
    if (!isEmpty()) {
      return items[top--];
    }
```

```
      else {
         throw new StackException("StackException on " +
                                    "pop: stack empty");
      }  // end if
   }  // end pop

   public Object peek() throws StackException {
      if (!isEmpty()) {
         return items[top];
      }
      else {
         throw new StackException("Stack exception on " +
                                    "peek - stack empty");
      }  // end if
   }  // end peek
}  // end StackArrayBased
```

A program that uses a stack could begin as follows:

```
public class StackTest {
   public static final int MAX_ITEMS = 15;

   public static void main(String[] args) {
      StackArrayBased stack = new StackArrayBased();
      Integer items[] = new Integer[MAX_ITEMS];
      for (int i=0; i<MAX_ITEMS; i++) {
         items[i] = new Integer(i);
         if (!stack.isFull()) {
            stack.push(items[i]);
         }  // end if
      }  // end for
   while (!stack.isEmpty()) {
      // cast result of pop to Integer
      System.out.println((Integer)(stack.pop()));
   }  // end while

      ...
```

*Private data fields are hidden
from the client*

By implementing the stack as a class, and by declaring *items* and *top* as private, you ensure that the client cannot violate the ADT's walls. If you did not hide your implementation within a class, or if you made the array *items* public, the client could access the elements in *items* directly instead of by using the operations of the ADT stack. Thus, the client could access any elements in the stack, not just its top element. You might find this capability attractive, but in fact it violates the specifications of the ADT stack. If you truly need to access all the items of your ADT randomly, do not use a stack!

*StackException provides a
simple way to indicate unusual
events*

Again, note that *StackException* provides a simple way for the implementer to indicate to the stack's client unusual circumstances, such as an attempted insertion into a full stack or a deletion from an empty stack.

Also, note that instances of *StackArrayBased* cannot contain items of a primitive type such as *int*, because *int* is not derived from *Object*. If you need a stack of integers, for example, you will have to use the corresponding wrapper class, which in this case is *Integer*. Finally, *pop* and *peek* return an item that is an instance of *Object*. You must cast this item back to the subtype of *Object* that you pushed onto the stack. Otherwise, methods available for the subtype will not be accessible.

A Reference-Based Implementation of the ADT Stack

Many applications require a reference-based implementation of a stack so that the stack can grow and shrink dynamically. Figure 6-5 illustrates a reference-based implementation of a stack where *top* is a reference to the head of a linked list of items. The implementation uses the same node class developed for the linked list in Chapter 4.

Note that the preconditions and postconditions given earlier in *StackInterface* apply here as well, and so are omitted to save space.

Figure 6-5

A reference-based implementation

```java
public class StackReferenceBased
                    implements StackInterface {
  private Node top;

  public StackReferenceBased() {
    top = null;
  }  // end default constructor

  public boolean isEmpty() {
    return top ==  null;
  }  // end isEmpty

  public void push(Object newItem) {
    top = new Node(newItem, top);
  }  // end push

  public Object pop() throws StackException {
    if (!isEmpty()) {
      Node temp = top;
      top = top.getNext();
      return temp.getItem();
    }
    else {
      throw new StackException("StackException on " +
                               "pop: stack empty");
    }  // end if
  }  // end pop

  public void popAll() {
    top = null;
  }  // end popAll
```

```
        public Object peek() throws StackException {
          if (!isEmpty()) {
            return top.getItem();
          }
          else {
            throw new StackException("StackException on " +
                                       "peek: stack empty");
          }  // end if
        }  // end peek
      }  // end StackReferenceBased
```

An Implementation That Uses the ADT List

You can use the ADT list to represent the items in a stack, as Figure 6-6 illustrates. If the item in position 1 of a list represents the top of the stack, you can implement the stack operation *push(newItem)* as *add(1, newItem)*. Similarly, you can implement the stack operation *pop()* using *get(1)* and *remove(1)* and the stack operation *peek()* as *get(1)*.

Recall that Chapter 4 presented the ADT list as the class *List-ReferenceBased*. (See page 171.) The following class for the ADT stack uses an instance of *ListReferenceBased* to represent the stack.

```
      public class StackListBased implements StackInterface {
        private ListInterface list;

        public StackListBased() {
          list = new ListReferenceBased();
        }  // end default constructor

        public boolean isEmpty() {
          return list.isEmpty();
        }  // end isEmpty

        public void push(Object newItem) {
```

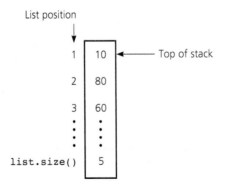

Figure 6-6

An implementation that uses the ADT list

```
    list.add(1, newItem);
  }  // end push

  public Object pop() throws StackException {
    if (!list.isEmpty()) {
      Object temp = list.get(1);
      list.remove(1);
      return temp;
    }
    else {
      throw new StackException("StackException on " +
                               "pop: stack empty");
    }  // end if
  }  // end pop

  public void popAll() {
    list.removeAll();
  }  // end popAll

  public Object peek() throws StackException {
    if (!isEmpty()) {
      return list.get(1);
    }
    else {
      throw new StackException("StackException on " +
                               "peek: stack empty");
    }  // end if
  }  // end peek
}  // end StackListBased
```

The data field *list* is an instance of the class *ListReferenceBased*. Also, the class *ListReferenceBased*'s constructor is called by *StackList-Based*'s constructor.

Comparing Implementations

You have seen implementations of the ADT stack that use an array, a linked list, and the ADT list to represent the items in a stack. We have treated the array and linked list as data structures, but the list is an ADT that we have implemented by using either an array or a linked list. Thus, all our implementations of the ADT stack are ultimately array based or reference based.

Once again the reasons for making the choice between array-based and reference-based implementations are the same as those discussed in earlier chapters. The array-based implementation given in this chapter uses fixed-sized arrays. As such, it prevents the *push* operation from adding an item to the stack if the stack's size limit, which is the size of the array, has been reached. If this restriction is not acceptable, you must

Fixed size versus dynamic size

use either a resizeable array or a reference-based implementation. For the problem that reads and corrects an input line, for example, the fixed-size restriction might not present a difficulty: If the system allows a line length of only 80 characters, you could reasonably use a statically allocated array to represent the stack.

Suppose that you decide to use a reference-based implementation. Should you choose the implementation that uses a linked list or the one that uses a reference-based implementation of the ADT list? Because a linked list actually represents the items on the ADT list, you might feel that using an ADT list to represent a stack is not as efficient as using a linked list directly. You would be right, but notice that the ADT list approach is much simpler to write. If you have battled references to produce a correct reference-based implementation of the ADT list, why do so again when you can *reuse* your work in the implementation of the stack? Which approach would you choose to produce a correct implementation of the stack in the least time? Chapter 8 discusses further the reuse of previously written classes.

Reuse of an already implemented class saves you time

APPLICATION: ALGEBRAIC EXPRESSIONS

This section contains two more problems that you can solve neatly by using the ADT stack. Keep in mind throughout that you are using the ADT stack to solve the problems. You can use the stack operations, but you may not assume any particular implementation. You choose a specific implementation only as a last step.

Your use of an ADT's operations should not depend on its implementation

Chapter 5 presented recursive grammars that specified the syntax of algebraic expressions. Recall that prefix and postfix expressions avoid the ambiguity inherent in the evaluation of infix expressions. We will now consider stack-based solutions to the problems of evaluating infix and postfix expressions. To avoid distracting programming issues, we will allow only the binary operators *, /, +, and −, and disallow exponentiation and unary operators.

The strategy we shall adopt here is first to develop an algorithm for evaluating postfix expressions and then to develop an algorithm for transforming an infix expression into an equivalent postfix expression. Taken together, these two algorithms provide a way to evaluate infix expressions. This strategy eliminates the need for an algorithm that directly evaluates infix expressions, a somewhat more difficult problem that Programming Problem 6 at the end of this chapter considers.

To evaluate an infix expression, first convert it to postfix form and then evaluate the postfix expression

Evaluating Postfix Expressions

As we mentioned in Chapter 5, some calculators require you to enter postfix expressions. For example, to compute the value of

$$2 * (3 + 4)$$

by using a postfix calculator, you would enter the sequence 2, 3, 4, +, *, which corresponds to the postfix expression

    2 3 4 + *

Recall that an operator in a postfix expression applies to the two operands that immediately precede it. Thus, the calculator must be able to retrieve the operands entered most recently. The ADT stack provides this capability. In fact, each time you enter an operand, the calculator pushes it onto a stack. When you enter an operator, the calculator applies it to the top two operands on the stack, pops the operands from the stack, and pushes the result of the operation onto the stack. Figure 6-7 shows the action of the calculator for the previous sequence of operands and operators. The final result, 14, is on the top of the stack.

You can formalize the action of the calculator to obtain an algorithm that evaluates a postfix expression, which is entered as a string of characters. To avoid issues that cloud the algorithm with programming details, assume that

- The string is a syntactically correct postfix expression
- No unary operators are present
- No exponentiation operators are present
- Operands are single lowercase letters that represent integer values

Simplifying assumptions

The pseudocode algorithm is then

```
for (each character ch in the string) {
  if (ch is an operand) {
    Push value that operand ch represents onto stack
  }
}
```

A pseudocode algorithm that evaluates postfix expressions

Key entered	Calculator action		Stack (bottom to top)
2	push 2		2
3	push 3		2 3
4	push 4		2 3 4
+	operand2 = pop stack	(4)	2 3
	operand1 = pop stack	(3)	2
	result = operand1 + operand2	(7)	2
	push result		2 7
*	operand2 = pop stack	(7)	2
	operand1 = pop stack	(2)	
	result = operand1 * operand2	(14)	
	push result		14

Figure 6-7

The action of a postfix calculator when evaluating the expression 2 * (3 + 4)

```
else {  // ch is an operator named op
  // evaluate and push the result
  operand2 = Pop the top of the stack
  operand1 = Pop the top of the stack
  result = operand1 op operand2
  Push result onto stack
}  // end if
}  // end for
```

Upon termination of the algorithm, the value of the expression will be on the top of the stack. Programming Problem 3 at the end of this chapter asks you to implement this algorithm.

Converting Infix Expressions to Equivalent Postfix Expressions

Now that you know how to evaluate a postfix expression, you will be able to evaluate an infix expression, if you first can convert it into an equivalent postfix expression. The infix expressions here are the familiar ones, such as $(a + b) * c / d - e$. They allow parentheses, operator precedence, and left-to-right association.

Will you ever want to evaluate an infix expression? Certainly, you have written such expressions in programs. The compiler that translated your programs had to generate machine instructions to evaluate the expressions. To do so, the compiler first transformed each infix expression into postfix form. Knowing how to convert an expression from infix to postfix notation not only will lead to an algorithm to evaluate infix expressions, but also will give you some insight into the compilation process.

If you manually convert a few infix expressions to postfix form, you will discover three important facts:

Facts about converting from infix to postfix

- The operands always stay in the same order with respect to one another.
- An operator will move only "to the right" with respect to the operands; that is, if, in the infix expression, the operand x precedes the operator *op,* it is also true that in the postfix expression, the operand x precedes the operator *op.*
- All parentheses are removed.

As a consequence of these three facts, the primary task of the conversion algorithm is determining where to place each operator.

The following pseudocode describes a first attempt at converting an infix expression to an equivalent postfix expression *postfixExp:*

First draft of an algorithm to convert an infix expression to postfix form

```
Initialize postfixExp to the null string
for (each character ch in the infix expression) {
  switch (ch) {
    case ch is an operand:
      Append ch to the end of postfixExp
```

```
        break
    case ch is an operator:
        Store ch until you know where to place it
        break
    case ch is '(' or ')':
        Discard ch
        break
    } // end switch
} // end for
```

You may have guessed that you really do not want to simply discard the parentheses, as they play an important role in determining the placement of the operators. In any infix expression, a set of matching parentheses defines an isolated subexpression that consists of an operator and its two operands. Therefore, the algorithm must evaluate the subexpression independently of the rest of the expression. Regardless of what the rest of the expression looks like, the operator within the subexpression belongs with the operands in that subexpression. The parentheses tell the rest of the expression

> *You can have the value of this subexpression after it is evaluated; simply ignore everything inside.*

Parentheses, operator precedence, and left-to-right association determine where to place operators in the postfix expression

Parentheses are thus one of the factors that determine the placement of the operators in the postfix expression. The other factors are precedence and left-to-right association.

In Chapter 5, you saw a simple way to convert a fully parenthesized infix expression to postfix form. Because each operator corresponded to a pair of parentheses, you simply moved each operator to the position marked by its closing parenthesis, and finally removed the parentheses.

The actual problem is more difficult, however, because the infix expression is not always fully parenthesized. Instead, the problem allows precedence and left-to-right association, and therefore requires a more complex algorithm. The following is a high-level description of what you must do when you encounter each character as you read the infix string from left to right.

Five steps in the process to convert from infix to postfix form

1. When you encounter an operand, append it to the output string `postfixExp`. *Justification*: The order of the operands in the postfix expression is the same as the order in the infix expression, and the operands that appear to the left of an operator in the infix expression also appear to its left in the postfix expression.

2. Push each "(" onto the stack.

3. When you encounter an operator, if the stack is empty, push the operator onto the stack. However, if the stack is not empty, pop operators of greater or equal precedence from the stack and append them to `postfixExp`. You stop when you encounter either a "(" or an operator of lower precedence or when the stack becomes empty. You then push the new operator onto the stack.

Thus, this step orders the operators by precedence and in accordance with left-to-right association. Notice that you continue popping from the stack until you encounter an operator of strictly lower precedence than the current operator in the infix expression. You do not stop on equality, because the left-to-right association rule says that in case of a tie in precedence, the leftmost operator is applied first—and this operator is the one that is already on the stack.

4. When you encounter a ")", pop operators off the stack and append them to the end of *postfixExp* until you encounter the matching "(". *Justification:* Within a pair of parentheses, precedence and left-to-right association determine the order of the operators, and Step 3 has already ordered the operators in accordance with these rules.

5. When you reach the end of the string, you append the remaining contents of the stack to *postfixExp*.

For example, Figure 6-8 traces the action of the algorithm on the infix expression $a - (b + c * d)/e$, assuming that the stack and the string *postfixExp* are initially empty. At the end of the algorithm, *postfixExp* contains the resulting postfix expression *abcd*+e/–.

You can use the previous five-step description of the algorithm to develop a fairly concise pseudocode solution, which follows. The symbol + means concatenate (append), so *postfixExp* + *x* means concatenate the string currently in *postfixExp* and the character *x*—that is, follow the string in *postfixExp* with the character *x*. Both the stack *stack* and the postfix expression *postfixExp* are initially empty.

ch	stack (bottom to top)	postfixExp	
a		a	
–	–	a	
(	– (	a	
b	– (	ab	
+	– (+	ab	
c	– (+	abc	
*	– (+ *	abc	
d	– (+ *	abcd	
)	– (+	abcd*	Move operators
	– (	abcd*+	from stack to
	–	abcd*+	postfixExp until " ("
/	– /	abcd*+	
e	– /	abcd*+e	Copy operators from
		abcd*+e/–	stack to postfixExp

Figure 6-8

A trace of the algorithm that converts the infix expression
$a - (b + c * d)/e$ **to postfix form**

```
for (each character ch in the infix expression) {
  switch (ch) {
    case operand:  // append operand to end of postfixExp
      postfixExp = postfixExp + ch
      break
    case '(':       // save '(' on stack
      stack.push(ch)
      break
    case ')':       // pop stack until matching '('
      while (top of stack is not '(') {
        postfixExp = postfixExp + stack.pop()
      } // end while
      openParen = stack.pop() // remove the open parenthesis
      break

    case operator:              // process stack operators of
                                // greater precedence
      while ( !stack.isEmpty() and
              top of stack is not '(' and
              precedence(ch) <= precedence(top of stack) ) {
        postfixExp = postfixExp + stack.pop()
      } // end while

      stack.push(ch)  // save new operator
      break
  } // end switch
} // end for

// append to postfixExp the operators remaining in the stack
while (!stack.isEmpty()) {
  postfixExp = postfixExp + stack.pop()
} // end while
```

A pseudocode algorithm that converts an infix expression to postfix form

Because this algorithm assumes that the given infix expression is syntactically correct, it can ignore the possibility of a *StackException* on *pop*. Programming Problem 5 at the end of this chapter asks you to remove this assumption. In doing so, you will find that you must provide *try* and *catch* blocks for the stack operations.

APPLICATION: A SEARCH PROBLEM

This final application of stacks will introduce you to a general type of **search problem**. In this particular problem, you must find a path from some point of origin to some destination point. We will solve this problem first by using stacks and then by using recursion. The recursive solution will bring to light the close relationship between stacks and recursion.

The High Planes Airline Company (HPAir) wants a program to process customer requests to fly from some origin city to some destination city. So that you can focus on the issue at hand—the use of stacks during problem solving—we will simplify the problem: For each customer request, just indicate whether a sequence of HPAir flights exists from the origin city to the destination city. The more realistic problem of actually producing an itinerary—that is, the sequence of flights—is considered in Programming Problem 11 at the end of this chapter.

Determine whether HPAir flies from one city to another

Imagine three input text files that specify all of the flight information for the airline as follows:

- The names of the cities that HPAir serves
- Pairs of city names; each pair represents the origin and destination of one of HPAir's flights
- Pairs of city names; each pair represents a request to fly from some origin to some destination

The program should then produce output such as

```
Request is to fly from Providence to San Francisco.
HPAir flies from Providence to San Francisco.

Request is to fly from Philadelphia to Albuquerque.
Sorry. HPAir does not fly from Philadelphia to
Albuquerque.

Request is to fly from Salt Lake City to Paris.
Sorry. HPAir does not serve Paris.
```

C_2 is adjacent to C_1 if there is a directed path from C_1 to C_2

Representing the flight data.   The flight map in Figure 6-9 represents the routes that HPAir flies. An arrow from city C_1 to city C_2 indicates a flight from C_1 to C_2. In this case C_2 is **adjacent** to C_1 and the path from C_1 to C_2 is called a **directed path.** Notice that if C_2 is adjacent to C_1, it does not follow that C_1 is adjacent to C_2. For example, in Figure 6-9, there is a flight from city R to city X, but not from city X to city R. As you will see in Chapter 13, the map in Figure 6-9 is called a **graph.**

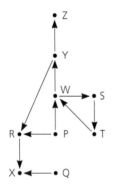

Figure 6-9

Flight map for HPAir

A Nonrecursive Solution That Uses a Stack

When processing a customer's request to fly from some origin city to some destination city, you must determine from the flight map whether there is a route from the origin to the destination. For example, by examining the flight map in Figure 6-9, you can see that a customer could fly from city P to city Z by flying first to city W, then to city Y, and finally to city Z; that is, there is a directed path from P to Z: $P \rightarrow W, W \rightarrow Y, Y \rightarrow Z$. Thus, you must develop an algorithm that searches the flight map for a directed path from the origin city to the destination city. Such a path might involve either a single flight or a sequence of flights. The solution developed here performs an **exhaustive search.** That is, beginning at the origin city, the solution will try every possible sequence of flights until either it finds a sequence that gets to the destination city or it determines that no such sequence exists. You will see that the ADT stack is useful in organizing this search.

Use a stack to organize an exhaustive search

First consider how you might perform the search by hand. One approach is to start at the origin city C_0 and select an arbitrary path to travel—that is, select an arbitrary flight departing from the origin city. This flight will lead you to a new city, C_1. If city C_1 happens to be the destination city, you are done; otherwise, you must attempt to get from C_1 to the destination city. To do this, you select a path to travel out of C_1. This path will lead you to a city C_2. If C_2 is the destination, you are done; otherwise, you must attempt to get from C_2 to the destination city, and so on.

Consider the possible outcomes of applying the previous strategy:

1. You eventually reach the destination city and can conclude that it is possible to fly from the origin to the destination.

2. You reach a city C from which there are no departing flights.

3. You go around in circles. For example, from C_1 you go to C_2, from C_2 you go to C_3, and from C_3 you go back to C_1. You might continue this tour of the three cities forever; that is, the algorithm might enter an infinite loop.

Possible outcomes of the exhaustive search strategy

If you always obtained the first outcome, everyone would be happy. However, because HPAir does not fly between all pairs of cities, you certainly cannot expect that the algorithm will always find a path from the origin city to the destination. For example, if city P in Figure 6-9 is the origin city and city Q is the destination city, the algorithm could not possibly find a path from city P to city Q.

Even if there were a sequence of flights from the origin city to the destination, it would take a bit of luck for the previous strategy to discover it—the algorithm would have to select a "correct" flight at each step. For example, even though there is a way to get from city P to city Z in Figure 6-9, the algorithm might not find it and instead might reach outcome 2 or 3. That is, suppose that from city P the algorithm chose to go to city R. From city R, the algorithm would have to go to city X, from which there are no flights out (outcome 2). On the other hand, suppose that the algorithm chose to go to city W from city P. From city W, the algorithm might choose to go to city S. It would then have to go to city T and then back to W. From W it might once again choose to go to city S and continue to go around in circles (outcome 3).

You thus need to make the algorithm more sophisticated, so that it always finds a path from the origin to the destination, if such a path exists, and otherwise terminates with the conclusion that there is no such path. Suppose that the earlier strategy results in outcome 2: You reach a city C from which there are no departing flights. This certainly does not imply that there is no way to get from the origin to the destination; it implies only that there is no way to get from city C to the destination. In other words, it was a mistake to go to city C. After discovering such a mistake, the algorithm can retrace its steps, or *backtrack*, to the city C' that was visited just before city C was visited. Once back at city C', the algorithm can select a flight to some city other than C. Notice that it is possible that there are no other flights out of city C'. If this were the case, it would mean that it was a mistake to visit city C', and thus you would want to backtrack again, this time to the city that was visited just before city C'.

For example, you saw that, in trying to get from city P to city Z in Figure 6-9, the algorithm might first choose to go from city P to city R and then on to city X. As there are no departing flights from city X, the algorithm must backtrack to city R, the city visited before city X. Once back at city R, the algorithm would attempt to go to some city other than city X, but would discover that this is not possible. The algorithm would thus backtrack once more, this time to city P, which was visited just before city R. From city P, the algorithm would choose to go to city W, which is a step in the right direction!

For the algorithm to implement this new strategy, it must maintain information about the order in which it visits the cities. First notice that when the algorithm backtracks from a city C, it must retreat to the city that it visited most recently before C. This observation suggests that you maintain the sequence of visited cities in a stack. That is, each time you decide to visit a city, you push its name onto the stack, as parts *a*, *b*, and *c* of Figure 6-10 illustrate for the flights from P to R to X in the previous example. You select the next city to visit from those adjacent to the city on the top of the stack. When you need to backtrack from the city C at the top of the stack (for example, because there are no flights out of the city), you simply pop a city from the stack, as shown in Figure 6-10d. After the pop, the city on the top of the stack is the city on the current path that you visited most recently before C. Parts *e* and *f* of Figure 6-10 illustrate the backtrack to city P and the subsequent flight to W.

The algorithm, as developed so far, is

```
stack.createStack()

stack.push(originCity)   // push origin city onto stack

while (a sequence of flights from the origin to the
                        destination has not been found){
   if (you need to backtrack from the city on the
         top of the stack) {
      temp = stack.pop()
   }
```

Figure 6-10

The stack of cities as you
travel (a) from P; (b) to R;
(c) to X; (d) back to R;
(e) back to P; (f) to W

```
    else {
      Select a destination city C for a flight from
      the city on the top of the stack
      stack.push(C)
    }  // end if
  }  // end while
```

Notice that at any point in the algorithm, the contents of the stack correspond to the sequence of flights currently under consideration. The city on the top of the stack is the city you are visiting currently, directly "below" it is the city visited previously, and so forth down to the bottom city, which is the first city visited in the sequence, or the origin city. In other words, an invariant of the *while* loop is that

> *The stack contains a directed path from the origin city at the bottom of the stack to the city at the top of the stack.*

Invariant

You can therefore always retrace your steps as far back through the sequence as needed.

Now consider the question of when to

```
    Backtrack from the city on the top of the stack.
```

You have already seen one case when backtracking is necessary. You must backtrack from the city on the top of the stack when there are no flights out of that city. Another time when you need to backtrack is related to the problem of going around in circles, described previously as the third possible outcome of the original strategy.

A key observation that will tell you when to backtrack is, *You never want to visit a city that the search has already visited.* As a consequence, you must backtrack from a city whenever there are no more unvisited cities to fly to. To see why you never want to visit a city a second time, consider two cases:

Backtrack when there are no more unvisited cities

- If you have visited city C and it is still somewhere in the stack—that is, it is part of the sequence of cities that you are exploring currently—you do not want to visit C again. Any sequence that goes from C through $C_1, C_2, \ldots, C_k$, back to C, and then to C' might just as well skip the intermediate cities and go from C directly to C'.

  Two reasons for not visiting a city more than once

  For example, suppose that the algorithm starts at P in Figure 6-9 and, in trying to find a path to Y, visits W, S, and T. There is now no reason for the algorithm to consider the flight from T to W because W is already in the stack. Anywhere you could fly to by going from W to S, from S to T, and then back to W, such as city Y, you could fly to directly from W without first going through S and T. Because you do not allow the algorithm to visit W a second time, it will backtrack from S and T to W and then go from W directly to Y. Figure 6-11 shows how the stack would appear if revisits were allowed and how it looks after backtracking when revisits are not allowed. Notice that backtracking to W is very different from visiting W for a second time.

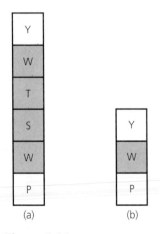

Figure 6-11

The stack of cities
(a) allowing revisits and
(b) after backtracking when
revisits are not allowed

- If you have visited city C, but it is no longer in the stack—because you backtracked from it and popped it from the stack—you do not want to visit C again. This situation is subtle; consider two cases that depend on why you backtracked from the city.

  If you backtracked from C because there were no flights out of it, then you certainly do not ever want to try going through C again. For example, if, starting at P in Figure 6-9, the algorithm goes to R and then to X, it will backtrack from X to R. At this point, although X is no longer in the stack, you certainly do not want to visit it again, because you know there are no flights out of X.

  Now suppose that you backtracked from city C because all cities adjacent to it had been visited. This situation implies that you have already tried all possible flights from C and have failed to find a way to get to the destination city. There is thus no reason to go to C again. For example, suppose that starting from P in Figure 6-9, the algorithm executes the following sequence: Visit R, visit X, backtrack to R (because there are no flights out of X), backtrack to P (because there are no more unvisited cities adjacent to R), visit W, visit Y. At this point the stack contains P-W-Y, with Y on top, as Figure 6-11b shows. You need to choose a flight out of Y. You do not want to fly from Y to R, because you have visited R already and tried all possible flights out of R.

  In both cases, visiting a city a second time does not gain you anything, and in fact it may cause you to go around in circles.

Mark the visited cities

To implement the rule of not visiting a city more than once, you simply mark a city when it has been visited. When choosing the next city to visit, you restrict consideration to unmarked cities adjacent to the city on the top of the stack. The algorithm thus becomes

Next draft of the search algorithm

```
stack.createStack()
Clear marks on all cities
stack.push(originCity)  // push origin city onto stack
Mark the origin as visited

while (a sequence of flights from the origin to the
                        destination has not been found) {
    // loop invariant: The stack contains a directed path
    // from the origin city at the bottom of the stack to
    // the city at the top of the stack
    if (no flights exist from the city on the
          top of the stack to unvisited cities) {
        temp = stack.pop()  // backtrack
    }
    else {
        Select an unvisited destination city C for a
           flight from the city on the top of the stack
```

```
        stack.push(C)
        Mark C as visited
    }  // end if
}  // end while
```

Finally, you need to refine the condition in the *while* statement. That is, you need to refine the algorithm's final determination of whether a path exists from the origin to the destination. The loop invariant, which states that the stack contains a directed path from the origin city to the city on the top of the stack, implies that the algorithm can reach an affirmative conclusion if the city at the top of the stack is the destination city. On the other hand, the algorithm can reach a negative conclusion only after it has exhausted all possibilities—that is, after the algorithm has backtracked to the origin and there remain no unvisited cities to fly to from the origin. At that point, the algorithm will pop the origin city from the stack and the stack will become empty.

With this refinement, the algorithm appears as follows:

```
searchS(originCity, destinationCity)
// Searches for a sequence of flights from
// originCity to destinationCity

  stack.createStack()
  Clear marks on all cities

  stack.push(originCity)  // push origin onto stack
  Mark the origin as visited

  while (!stack.isEmpty() and
         destinationCity is not at the top of the stack) {
    // loop invariant: The stack contains a directed path
    // from the origin city at the bottom of the stack to
    // the city at the top of the stack
    if (no flights exist from the city on the
          top of the stack to unvisited cities) {
      temp = stack.pop()  // backtrack
    }
    else {
      Select an unvisited destination city C for a
          flight from the city on the top of the stack
      stack.push(C)
      Mark C as visited
    }  // end if
  }  // end while

  if (stack.isEmpty()) {
    return false  // no path exists
  }
```

The final version of the search algorithm

```
else {
   return true    // path exists
}  // end if
```

Notice that the algorithm does not specify the order of selection for the unvisited cities. It really does not matter what selection criteria the algorithm uses, because the choice will not affect the final outcome: Either a sequence of flights exists or it does not. The choice, however, will affect the specific flights that the algorithm considers. For example, suppose that the algorithm always flies to the alphabetically earliest unvisited city from the city on the top of the stack. Under this assumption, Figure 6-12 contains a trace of the algorithm's action, given the map in Figure 6-9, with *P* as the origin city and *Z* as the destination city. The algorithm terminates with success.

Now consider the operations that the search algorithm must perform on the flight map. The algorithm marks cities as it visits them, determines whether a city has been visited, and determines which cities are adjacent to a given city. You can treat the flight map as an ADT that has at least these operations, in addition to the search operation itself. Other desirable operations include placing data into the flight map, inserting a city adjacent to another city, displaying the flight map, displaying a list of all cities, and displaying all cities that are adjacent to a given city. Thus, the ADT flight map could include the following operations:

ADT flight map operations

```
createFlightMap()
// Creates an empty flight map.

readFlightMap(cityFileName, flightFileName)
// Reads flight information into the flight map.

displayFlightMap()
// Displays flight information.
```

Action	Reason	Contents of stack (bottom to top)
Push P	Initialize	P
Push R	Next unvisited adjacent city	P R
Push X	Next unvisited adjacent city	P R X
Pop X	No unvisited adjacent city	P R
Pop R	No unvisited adjacent city	P
Push W	Next unvisited adjacent city	P W
Push S	Next unvisited adjacent city	P W S
Push T	Next unvisited adjacent city	P W S T
Pop T	No unvisited adjacent city	P W S
Pop S	No unvisited adjacent city	P W
Push Y	Next unvisited adjacent city	P W Y
Push Z	Next unvisited adjacent city	P W Y Z

Figure 6-12

A trace of the search algorithm, given the flight map in Figure 6-9

```
displayAllCities()
// Displays the names of all cities that HPAir serves.

displayAdjacentCities(city)
// Displays all cities that are adjacent to a given city.

markVisited(city)
// Marks a city as visited.

unvisitAll()
// Clears marks on all cities.

isVisited(city)
// Determines whether a city was visited.

insertAdjacent(city, adjCity)
// Inserts a city adjacent to another city in a
// flight map.

getNextCity(fromCity)
// Returns the next unvisited city, if any, that
// is adjacent to a given city.  Returns null if no
// unvisited adjacent city was found.

isPath(originCity, destinationCity)
// Determines whether a sequence of flights between
// two cities exists.
```

The following Java method implements the *isPath* operation by using the *searchS* algorithm. It assumes that the class *StackReference-Based* implements the stack operations and the class *Map* implements the ADT flight map operations just described. Notice that you must represent the cities by creating a class *City* that implements the *java.lang.Comparable* interface.

```
public boolean isPath(City originCity,
            City destinationCity) {
// ----------------------------------------------------
// Determines whether a sequence of flights between
// two cities exists. Nonrecursive stack version.
// Precondition: originCity and destinationCity are
// the origin and destination cities, respectively.
// Postcondition: Returns true if a sequence of
// flights exists from originCity to destinationCity,
// otherwise returns false. Cities visited during the
// search are marked as visited in the flight map.
// Implementation notes: Uses a stack for the cities
// of a potential path. Calls unvisitAll, markVisited,
```

Java implementation of searchS

```
      // and getNextCity.
      // ---------------------------------------------------
        StackReferenceBased stack = new StackReferenceBased();

        City topCity, nextCity;
        unvisitAll();  // clear marks on all cities

        // push origin city onto stack, mark it visited
        stack.push(originCity);
        markVisited(originCity);

        topCity = (City)(stack.peek());
        while (!stack.isEmpty() &&
               (topCity.compareTo(destinationCity) != 0)) {
          // loop invariant: stack contains a directed path
          // from the origin city at the bottom of the stack
          // to the city at the top of the stack

          // find an unvisited city adjacent to the city on
          // the top of the stack
          nextCity = getNextCity(topCity);

          if (nextCity == null) {
            stack.pop();   // no city found; backtrack
          }
          else {                        // visit city
            stack.push(nextCity);
            markVisited(nextCity);
          }  // end if
          topCity = (City)stack.peek();
        }  // end while
        if (stack.isEmpty()) {
          return false;  // no path exists
        }
        else {
          return true;   // path exists
        }  // end if
      }  // end isPath
```

Programming Problem 9 at the end of this chapter provides implementation details that will enable you to complete the solution to the HPAir problem.

A Recursive Solution

Recall the initial attempt at a solution to the HPAir problem of searching for a sequence of flights from some origin city to some destination city. Consider how you might perform the search "by hand." One approach is to start at the origin city and select an arbitrary flight that departs from the origin city. This flight will lead you to a new city, C_1. If city C_1 happens to be the destination city, you are done; otherwise, you must attempt to get from C_1 to the destination city by selecting a flight out of C_1. This flight will lead you to city C_2. If C_2 is the destination, you are done; otherwise, you must attempt to get from C_2 to the destination city, and so on. There is a distinct recursive flavor to this search strategy, which can be restated as follows:

```
To fly from the origin to the destination:
  Select a city C adjacent to the origin
  Fly from the origin to city C
  if (C is the destination city) {
    Terminate -- the destination is reached
  }
  else {
    Fly from city C to the destination
  } // end if
```

A recursive search strategy

This statement of the search strategy makes its recursive nature very apparent. The first step in flying from the origin city to the destination city is to fly from the origin city to city C. Once at city C, you are confronted with another problem of the same type—you now must fly from city C to the destination.

This recursive formulation is nothing more than a restatement of the initial (incomplete) strategy developed previously. As such it has the same three possible outcomes:

1. You eventually reach the destination city and can conclude that it is possible to fly from the origin to the destination.

Possible outcomes of the recursive search strategy

2. You reach a city C from which there are no departing flights.

3. You go around in circles.

The first of these outcomes corresponds to a base case of the recursive algorithm. If you ever reach the destination city, no additional problems of the form "fly from city C to the destination" are generated, and the algorithm terminates. However, as was observed previously, the algorithm might not produce this outcome; that is, it might not reach this base case. The algorithm might reach a city C that has no departing flights. (Notice that the algorithm does not specify what to do in this case—in this sense the algorithm is incomplete.) Or the algorithm might repeatedly cycle through the same sequence of cities and thus never terminate.

You can resolve these problems by mirroring what you did in the previous solution. Consider the following refinement, in which you mark visited cities and never fly to a city that has been visited already:

```
searchR(originCity, destinationCity)
// Searches for a sequence of flights from
// originCity to destinationCity.
```

A refinement of the recursive search algorithm

```
Mark originCity as visited

if (originCity is destinationCity) {
  Terminate -- the destination is reached
}
else {
  for (each unvisited city C adjacent to originCity) {
    searchR(C, destinationCity)
  }  // end for
}  // end if
```

Now consider what happens when the algorithm reaches a city that has no unvisited city adjacent to it. For example, consider the piece of a flight map in Figure 6-13. When *searchR* reaches city *X*—that is, when the parameter *originCity* has the value *X*—the *for* loop will not be entered, because no unvisited cities are adjacent to *X*. Hence, the method *searchR* returns. This return has the effect of backtracking to city *W*, from which the flight to *X* originated. In terms of the previous pseudocode, the return is made to the point from which the call *searchR(X, destinationCity)* occurred. This point is within the *for* loop, which iterates through the unvisited cities adjacent to *W*; that is, the parameter *originCity* has the value *W*.

After backtracking from *X* to *W*, the *for* loop will again execute. This time the loop chooses city *V*, resulting in the recursive call *searchR(V, destinationCity)*. From this point, the algorithm either will eventually reach the destination city and terminate, or it will backtrack once again to city *W*. If it backtracks to *W*, the *for* loop will terminate because there are no more unvisited cities adjacent to *W*, and a return from *searchR* will occur. The effect is to backtrack to the city where the flight to *W* originated. If the algorithm ever backtracks to the origin city and no remaining unvisited cities are adjacent to it, the algorithm will terminate, and you can conclude that no sequence of flights from the origin to the destination exists. Notice that the algorithm will always terminate in one way or another, because it will either reach the destination city or run out of unvisited cities to try.

The following Java method implements the *searchR* algorithm:

Figure 6-13

A piece of a flight map

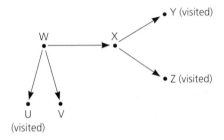

```
   public boolean isPath(City originCity,
                         City destinationCity) {
 City  nextCity;
 boolean done;

 // mark the current city as visited
 markVisited(originCity);

 // base case: the destination is reached
 if (originCity.compareTo(destinationCity) == 0) {
   return true;
 }
 else { // try a flight to each unvisited city
   done = false;
   nextCity = getNextCity(originCity);

   while (nextCity != null && !done) {
     done = isPath(nextCity, destinationCity);
     if (!done) {
       nextCity = getNextCity(originCity);
     }  // end if
   }  // end while

   return done;
 }  // end if
}  // end isPath
```

Java implementation of searchR

You have probably noticed a close parallel between this recursive algorithm and the earlier stack-based algorithm *searchS*. In fact, the two algorithms simply employ different techniques to implement the identical search strategy. The next section will elaborate on the relationship between the two algorithms.

THE RELATIONSHIP BETWEEN STACKS AND RECURSION

The previous section solved the HPAir problem once by using the ADT stack and again by using recursion. The goal of this section is to relate the way that the stack organizes the search for a sequence of flights to the way a recursive algorithm organizes the search. You will see that the ADT stack has a hidden presence in the concept of recursion and, in fact, that stacks have an active role in most computer implementations of recursion.

Consider how the two search algorithms implement three key aspects of their common strategy.

A comparison of key aspects of two search algorithms

- **Visiting a new city.** The recursive algorithm `searchR` visits a new city C by calling `searchR(C, destinationCity)`. The algorithm `searchS` visits city C by pushing C onto a stack. Notice that if you were to use the box trace to trace the execution of `searchR`, the call `searchR(C, destinationCity)` would generate a box in which the city C is associated with the formal parameter `origin-City` of `searchR`.

  For example, Figure 6-14 shows both the state of the box trace for `searchR` and the stack for `searchS` at corresponding points of their search for a path from city P to city Z in Figure 6-9.

- **Backtracking.** Both search algorithms attempt to visit an unvisited city that is adjacent to the current city. Notice that this current city is the value associated with the formal parameter `originCity` in the deepest (rightmost) box of `searchR`'s box trace. Similarly, the current city is on the top of `searchS`'s stack. In Figure 6-14, this current city is X. If no unvisited cities are adjacent to the current city, the algorithms must backtrack to the previous city. The algorithm `searchR` backtracks by returning from the current recursive call. You represent this action in the box trace by crossing off the deepest box. The algorithm `searchS` backtracks by explicitly popping from its stack. For example, from the state depicted in Figure 6-14, both algorithms backtrack to city R and then to city P, as Figure 6-15 illustrates.

- **Termination.** The search algorithms terminate either when they reach the destination city or when they exhaust all possibilities. All possibilities are exhausted when, after backtracking to the origin city, no unvisited adjacent cities remain. This situation occurs for `searchR` when all boxes have been crossed off in the box trace and a return occurs to the point of the original call to the method. For `searchS`, no unvisited cities are adjacent to the origin when the stack becomes empty.

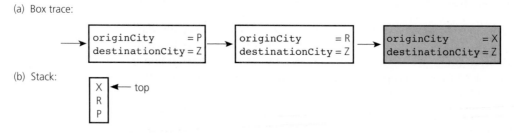

Figure 6-14

Visiting city P, then R, then X: (a) box trace versus (b) stack

(a) Box trace:

originCity   = P
destinationCity = Z

originCity   = R
destinationCity = Z

originCity   = X
destinationCity = Z

(b) Stack:

X
R
P

R
P

P

← top

Figure 6-15

Backtracking from city *X* to *R* to *P*: (a) box trace versus (b) stack

Thus, the two search algorithms really do perform the identical action. In fact, provided that they use the same rule to select an unvisited city—for example, traverse the current city's list of adjacent cities alphabetically—they will always visit the identical cities in the identical order. The similarities between the algorithms are far more than coincidence. In fact, it is always possible to capture the actions of a recursive method by using a stack.

An important context in which the close tie between stacks and recursion is explicitly utilized is a compiler's implementation of a recursive method. It is common for a compiler to use a stack to implement a recursive method in a manner that greatly resembles the box trace. When a recursive call to a method occurs, the implementation must remember certain information. This information consists essentially of the same local environment that you place in the boxes—values of both parameters and local variables, and a reference to the point from which the recursive call was made.

Typically, stacks are used to implement recursive methods

During execution, the compiled program must manage these boxes of information, or **activation records**, just as you must manage them on paper. As the HPAir example has indicated, the operations needed to manage the activation records are those that a stack provides. When a recursive call occurs, a new activation record is created and pushed onto a stack. This action corresponds to the creation of a new box at the deepest point in the sequence. When a return is made from a recursive call, the stack is popped, bringing the activation record that contains the appropriate local environment to the top of the stack. This action corresponds to crossing off the deepest box and following the arrow back to the preceding box. Although we have greatly simplified the process, most implementations of recursion are based on stacks of activation records.

Each recursive call generates an activation record that is pushed onto a stack

You can use a similar strategy to implement a nonrecursive version of a recursive algorithm. You might need to recast a recursive algorithm into a nonrecursive form to make it more efficient, as mentioned in Chapter 2. The previous discussion should give you a taste of the techniques for removing recursion from a program. You will encounter recursion removal as a formal topic in more advanced courses, such as compiler construction.

You can use stacks when implementing a nonrecursive version of a recursive algorithm

SUMMARY

1. The ADT stack operations have a last-in, first-out (LIFO) behavior.

2. Algorithms that operate on algebraic expressions are an important application of stacks. The LIFO nature of stacks is exactly what the algorithm that evaluates postfix expressions needs to organize the operands. Similarly, the algorithm that transforms infix expressions to postfix form uses a stack to organize the operators in accordance with precedence rules and left-to-right association.

3. You can use a stack to determine whether a sequence of flights exists between two cities. The stack keeps track of the sequence of visited cities and enables the search algorithm to backtrack easily. However, displaying the sequence of cities in their normal order from origin to destination is awkward, because the origin city is at the bottom of the stack and the destination is at the top.

4. A strong relationship between recursion and stacks exists. Most implementations of recursion maintain a stack of activation records in a manner that resembles the box trace.

CAUTIONS

1. Operations such as *peek* and *pop* must take reasonable action when the stack is empty. One possibility is to ignore the operation and throw an exception *StackException*.

2. Algorithms that evaluate an infix expression or transform one to postfix form must determine which operands apply to a given operator. Doing so allows for precedence and left-to-right association so that you can omit parentheses.

3. When searching for a sequence of flights between cities, you must take into account the possibility that the algorithm will make wrong choices. For example, the algorithm must be able to backtrack when it hits a dead end, and you must eliminate the possibility that the algorithm will cycle.

SELF-TEST EXERCISES

1. If you push the letters A, B, C, and D in order onto a stack of characters and then pop them, in what order will they be deleted from the stack?

2. What do the initially empty stacks *stack1* and *stack2* "look like" after the following sequence of operations:

```
stack1.push(1)
stack1.push(2)
```

```
stack2.push(3)
stack2.push(4)
stackTop = stack1.pop()
stackTop = stack2.peek()
stack1.push(stackTop)
stack1.push(5)
stackTop = stack2.pop()
stack2.push(6)
```

3. The algorithms that appear in the section "Simple Applications of the ADT Stack" involve strings. Under what conditions would you choose an array-based implementation for the stack in these algorithms? Under what conditions would you choose a reference-based implementation?

4. List the changes that you must make to convert a program that uses an array-based implementation of a stack to one that uses a reference-based implementation of a stack.

5. For each of the following strings, trace the execution of the balanced-braces algorithm and show the contents of the stack at each step.

   a. x{{yz}}}
   b. {x{y{{z}}}
   c. {{{x}}}

6. Use the stack algorithms in this chapter to evaluate the postfix expression *ab−c+*. Assume the following values for the identifiers: *a* = 7; *b* = 3; *c* = −2. Show the status of the stack after each step.

7. Use the stack algorithms in this chapter to convert the infix expression *a/b*c* to postfix form. Be sure to account for left-to-right association. Show the status of the stack after each step.

8. Explain the significance of the precedence tests in the infix-to-postfix conversion algorithm. Why is a $\geq$ test used rather than a $>$ test?

9. Execute the HPAir algorithm with the map in Figure 6-16 for the following requests. Show the state of the stack after each step.

   a. Fly from *A* to *B*.
   b. Fly from *A* to *D*.
   c. Fly from *C* to *G*.

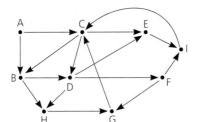

Figure 6-16

Flight map for Self-Test Exercise 9 and Exercise 11

EXERCISES

1. Suppose that you have a stack *stack* and an empty auxiliary stack *auxStack*. Show how you can do each of the following tasks by using only the operations of the ADT stack:

    a. Display the contents of *stack* in reverse order; that is, display the top last.

    b. Count the number of items in *stack*, leaving *stack* unchanged.

    c. Delete every occurrence of a specified item from *stack*, leaving the order of the remaining items unchanged.

2. The diagram of a railroad switching system in Figure 6-17 is commonly used to illustrate the notion of a stack. Identify three stacks in the figure and show how they relate to one another. How can you use this system to construct any possible permutation of railroad cars?

3. An operation that displays the contents of a stack can be useful during program debugging. Add a *display* method to the ADT stack such that

    a. The method uses only ADT stack operations; that is, it is independent of the stack's implementation.

    b. The method assumes and uses the reference-based implementation of the ADT stack.

4. Discuss the efficiency of the implementation of the ADT stack that uses the ADT list, when the list has an array-based implementation.

5. The section "Developing an ADT During the Design of a Solution" described an algorithm *readAndCorrect* that reads a string of characters, correcting mistakes along the way.

    a. For the following input line, trace the execution of *readAndCorrect* and show the contents of the stack at each step:
        abc←de←←fg←h

    b. The nature of the stack-based algorithm makes it simple to display the string in reverse order, but somewhat harder to display it in its correct order. Write a pseudocode algorithm that displays the string in its correct forward order.

Figure 6-17

Railroad switching system for Exercise 2

    c. Implement `readAndCorrect` as a Java method. Use a stack to construct a string that contains the corrected input characters in forward order. Return the string instead of the stack.

6. Revise the solution to the balanced-braces problem so that the expression can contain three types of delimiters: `()`, `[ ]`, and `{ }`. Thus, `{ab(c[d])e}` is valid, but `{ab(c)}` is not.

7. For each of the following strings, trace the execution of the language-recognition algorithm described in the section "Recognizing Strings in a Language," and show the contents of the stack at each step.

    a. xy\$xy   c. y\$yx   e. xy\$y
    b. xy\$x   d. xx\$xx

8. Write a pseudocode method that uses a stack to determine whether a string is in the language L, where

    a. $L = \{w : w$ contains equal numbers of A's and B's$\}$
    b. $L = \{w : w$ is of the form A^nB^n for some $n \geq 0\}$

9. Evaluate the following postfix expressions by using the algorithm given in this chapter. Show the status of the stack after each step of the algorithm. Assume the following values for the identifiers: $a = 7; b = 3; c = 12; d = -5; e = 1$.

    a. *abc+−*   b. *abc−d∗+*   c. *ab+c−de∗+*

10. Convert the following infix expressions to postfix form by using the algorithm given in this chapter. Show the status of the stack after each step of the algorithm.

    a. *a−b+c*   e. *a−(b/c∗d)*
    b. *a/(b∗c)*   f. *a/b/c−(d+e)∗f*
    c. *(a+b)∗c*   g. *a∗(b/c/d)+e*
    d. *a−(b+c)*   h. *a−(b+c∗d)/e*

11. Execute the HPAir algorithm with the map in Figure 6-16 (see Self-Test Exercise 9) for the following requests. Show the state of the stack after each step.

    a. Fly from *A* to *F*.   c. Fly from *A* to *G*.   e. Fly from *F* to *H*.
    b. Fly from *D* to *A*.   d. Fly from *I* to *G*.

*12. As Chapter 3 pointed out, you can define ADT operations in a mathematically formal way by using axioms. For example, the following axioms formally define the ADT stack, where `stack` is an arbitrary stack and `item` is an arbitrary stack item.

```
(stack.createStack()).isEmpty() = true
(stack.push(item)).isEmpty() = false
(stack.createStack()).pop() = error
(stack.push(item)).pop() = stack
(stack.createStack()).peek() = error
(stack.push(item)).peek() = item
```

You can use these axioms, for example, to prove that the stack defined by the sequence of operations

```
Create an empty stack
Push a 5
Push a 7
Push a 3
Pop (the 3)
Push a 9
Push a 4
Pop (the 4)
```

which you can write as

```
(((((((stack.createStack()).push(5)).push(7)).push(3)).
  pop()).push(9)).push(4)).pop()
```

is exactly the same as the stack defined by the sequence

```
Create an empty stack
Push a 5
Push a 7
Push a 9
```

which you can write as

```
(((stack.createStack()).push(5)).push(7)).push(9)
```

Similarly, you can use the axioms to show that

```
(((((((stack.createStack()).push(1)).push(2)).pop()).
  push(3)).pop()).pop()).isEmpty()
```

is true.

a. The following representation of a stack as a sequence of *push* operations without any *pop* operations is called a **canonical form:**

    ```
    (...(stack.createStack()).push()).push()...).push()
    ```

    Prove that any stack is equal to a stack that is in canonical form.

b. Prove that the canonical form is unique. That is, a stack is equal to exactly one stack that is in canonical form.

c. Use the axioms to show formally that

    ```
    (((((((((((stack.createStack()).push(6)).push(9)).
    pop()).pop()).push(2)).pop()).push(3)).push(1)).
    pop()).peek()
    ```

    equals 3.

PROGRAMMING PROBLEMS

1. Write an implementation of the ADT stack that uses a resizeable array to represent the stack items. Anytime the stack becomes full, double the size of the array.

2. The section "Recognizing Strings in a Language" describes a recognition algorithm for the language

$$L = \{w\$w' : \ w \text{ is a possibly empty string of characters other than \$,}$$
$$w' = \text{reverse}(w)\ \}$$

Implement this algorithm.

3. Design and implement a class of postfix calculators. Use the algorithm given in this chapter to evaluate postfix expressions, as entered into the calculator. Use only the operators +, −, *, and /. Assume that the postfix expressions are syntactically correct.

4. Consider simple infix expressions that consist of single-digit operands; the operators +, −, *, and /; and parentheses. Assume that unary operators are illegal and that the expression contains no embedded spaces.

   Design and implement a class of infix calculators. Use the algorithms given in this chapter to evaluate infix expressions, as entered into the calculator. You must first convert the infix expression to postfix form and then evaluate the resulting postfix expression.

5. The infix-to-postfix conversion algorithm described in this chapter assumes that the given infix expression is syntactically correct. Repeat Programming Problem 4 without this assumption.

6. Repeat Programming Problem 4, but use the following algorithm to evaluate an infix expression *infixExp*. The algorithm uses two stacks: One stack, *opStack*, contains operators, and the other stack, *valStack*, contains values of operands and intermediate results. Note that the algorithm treats parentheses as operators with the lowest precedence.

```
for (each character ch in infixExp) {
  switch (ch) {
    case ch is an operand, that is, a digit
      valStack.push(ch)
      break
    case ch is '('
      opStack.push(ch)
      break
    case ch is an operator
      if (opStack.isEmpty()) {
        opStack.push(ch)
      }
      else if (precedence(ch) >
                  precedence(top of opStack)) {
        opStack.push(ch)
      }
      else {
        while (!opStack.isEmpty() and
          precedence(ch) <= precedence(top of opStack)) {
          Execute
        }  // end while
```

```
            opStack.push(ch)
        }  // end if
        break

    case ch is ')'
        while (top of opStack is not '(') {
            Execute
        }  // end while
        opStack.pop()
        break
    }  // end switch
}  // end for

while (!opStack.isEmpty()) {
    Execute
}  // end while
result = valStack.peek()
```

Note that *Execute* means

```
    operand2 = valStack.pop()
    operand1 = valStack.pop()
    op = opStack.pop()
    result = operand1 op operand2
    valStack.push(result)
```

7. The infix evaluation algorithm given in Programming Problem 6 assumes that the given infix expression is syntactically correct. Repeat Programming Problem 6 without this assumption.

8. Using stacks, write a nonrecursive version of the method *solveTowers*, as defined in Chapter 2.

9. Complete the solution to the HPAir problem. The input to the program consists of three text files, as follows:

cityFile	Each line contains the name of a city that HPAir serves. The names are in alphabetical order.
flightFile	Each line contains a pair of city names that represents the origin and destination of one of HPAir's flights.
requestFile	Each line contains a pair of city names that represents a request to fly from some origin to some destination.

   You can make the following assumptions:

   • Each city name contains at most 15 characters. Pairs of city names are separated by a comma.

   • HPAir serves at most 20 cities.

   • The input data is correct.

For example, the input files could appear as

```
cityFile:      Albuquerque
               Chicago
               San Diego

flightFile:    Chicago,      San Diego
               Chicago,      Albuquerque
               Albuquerque,  Chicago

requestFile:   Albuquerque,  San Diego
               Albuquerque,  Paris
               San Diego,    Chicago
```

For this input, the program should produce the following output:

```
Request is to fly from Albuquerque to San Diego.
HPAir flies from Albuquerque to San Diego.

Request is to fly from Albuquerque to Paris.
Sorry. HPAir does not serve Paris.

Request is to fly from San Diego to Chicago.
Sorry. HPAir does not fly from San Diego to Chicago.
```

Begin by implementing the ADT flight map as the Java class *Map*. Use the nonrecursive version of *isPath*. Since *getNextCity* is the primary operation that the search algorithm performs on the flight map, you should choose an implementation that will efficiently determine which cities are adjacent to a given city. If there are *N* cities, you can use *N* linked lists to represent the flight map. You place a node on list *i* for city *j* if and only if there is a directed path from city *i* to city *j*. Such a data structure is called an **adjacency list**; Figure 6-18 illustrates an adjacency list for the flight map in Figure 6-9. Chapter 13 discusses adjacency lists further when it presents ways to represent graphs. At that time, you will learn why an adjacency list is a good choice for the present program.

Although you can implement the adjacency list from scratch, you should also consider using *N* instances of *ListReferenceBased*, which has a reference-based implementation.

You must also create a class *City* that implements the *java.lang.Comparable* interface to store the city name. The class *City* and the previously described adjacency list are the underlying data structures for the ADT flight map.

To simplify reading the input text files, define a class that includes the following methods:

getName(name)
// Gets a name from the next line in a text file.

getNamePair(name1, name2)
// Gets two names from the next line in a text file.

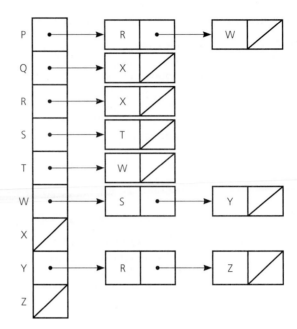

Figure 6-18

Adjacency list for the flight map in Figure 6-9

10. In the implementation of the HPAir problem (see Programming Problem 9), the search for the next unvisited city adjacent to a city *i* always starts at the beginning of the ith linked list in the adjacency list. This approach is actually a bit inefficient, because once the search visits a city, the city can never become unvisited. Modify the program so that the search for the next city begins where the last search left off. That is, maintain an array of *tryNext* references into the adjacency list.

11. Implement an expanded version of the HPAir problem. In addition to the "from" and "to" cities, each line of input contains a flight number (an integer) and the cost of the flight (an integer). Modify the HPAir program so that it will produce a complete itinerary for each request, including the flight number of each flight, the cost of each flight, and the total cost of the trip.

For example, the input files could appear as

cityFile:	Albuquerque			
	Chicago			
	San Diego			
flightFile:	Chicago,	San Diego	703	325
	Chicago,	Albuquerque	111	250
	Albuquerque,	Chicago	178	250
requestFile:	Albuquerque,	San Diego		
	Albuquerque,	Paris		
	San Diego,	Chicago		

For this input, the program should produce the following output:

```
Request is to fly from Albuquerque to San Diego.
Flight #178 from Albuquerque to Chicago    Cost: $250
Flight #703 from Chicago to San Diego      Cost: $325
Total Cost ............  $575
Request is to fly from Albuquerque to Paris.
Sorry. HPAir does not serve Paris.
Request is to fly from San Diego to Chicago.
Sorry. HPAir does not fly from San Diego to Chicago.
```

When the nonrecursive *isPath* method finds a sequence of flights from the origin city to the destination city, its stack contains the corresponding path of cities. The stumbling block to reporting this path is that the cities appear in the stack in reverse order; that is, the destination city is at the top of the stack and the origin city is at the bottom. For example, if you use the program to find a path from city *P* to city *Z* in Figure 6-9, the final contents of the stack will be *P-W-Y-Z*, with *Z* on top. You want to display the origin city *P* first, but it is at the bottom of the stack. If you restrict yourself to the stack operations, the only way that you can write the path in its correct order is first to reverse the stack by popping it onto a temporary stack and then to write the cities as you pop them off the temporary stack. Note that this approach requires that you process each city on the path twice.

Evidently a stack is not the appropriate ADT for the problem of writing the path of cities in the correct order; the appropriate ADT is a **traversable stack.** In addition to the standard stack operations, *isEmpty*, *push*, *pop*, and *peek*, a traversable stack includes the operation *traverse*. This operation begins at one end of the stack and *visits* each item in the stack until it reaches the other end of the stack. For this project, you want *traverse* to begin at the bottom of the stack and move toward the top.

12. What modifications to Programming Problem 11 are required to find a least-cost trip for each request? How can you incorporate time considerations into the problem?

7

Queues

PREVIEW Whereas a stack's behavior is characterized as last-in, first-out, a queue's behavior is characterized as first-in, first-out. This chapter defines the queue's operations and discusses strategies for implementing them. As you will see, queues are common in everyday life. Their first-in, first-out behavior makes them appropriate ADTs for situations that involve waiting. Queues are also important in simulation, a technique for analyzing the behavior of complex systems. This chapter uses a queue to model the behavior of people in a line.

THE ABSTRACT DATA TYPE QUEUE

FIFO: The first item inserted into a queue is the first item out

A **queue** is like a line of people. The first person to join a line is the first person served and is thus the first to leave the line. New items enter a queue at its **back**, or **rear**, and items leave a queue from its **front.** Operations on a queue occur only at its two ends. This characteristic gives a queue its **first-in, first-out (FIFO)** behavior. In contrast, you can think of a stack as having only one end, because all operations are performed at the top of the stack. This characteristic gives a stack its last-in, first-out behavior.

As an abstract data type, the queue has the following operations:

KEY CONCEPTS

ADT Queue Operations

1. Create an empty queue.

2. Determine whether a queue is empty.

3. Add a new item to the queue.

4. Remove from the queue the item that was added earliest.

5. Remove all the items from the queue.

6. Retrieve from the queue the item that was added earliest.

Queues occur in everyday life

Queues are appropriate for many real-world situations. You wait in a queue—that is, a line—to buy a movie ticket, to check out at the book store, or to use an automatic teller machine. The person at the front of the queue is served, while new people join the queue at its back. Even when you call an airline to make a reservation, your call actually enters a queue while you wait for the next available agent.

Queues have applications in computer science

Queues also have applications in computer science. When you print an essay, the computer sends lines faster than the printer can print them. The lines are held in a queue for the printer, which removes them in FIFO order. If you share the printer with other computers, your request to print enters a queue to wait its turn.

Since all of these applications involve waiting, people study them to see how to reduce the wait. Such studies are called **simulations**, and they typically use queues. Later, this chapter examines a simulation of a line of customers at a bank.

The following pseudocode describes the operations for the ADT queue in more detail. As we did for the ADT stack, we specify that the remove operation both retrieves and then removes the item at the front of the queue.

Pseudocode for the ADT Queue Operations

```
createQueue()
// Creates an empty queue.

isEmpty()
// Determines whether a queue is empty.

enqueue(newItem) throws QueueException
// Adds NewItem at the back of a queue. Throws
// QueueException if the operation is not successful.

dequeue() throws QueueException
// Retrieves and removes the front of a queue—the
// item that was added earliest. Throws QueueException
// if the operation is not successful.

dequeueAll()
// Removes all items from a queue

peek() throws QueueException
// Retrieves the front of a queue. That is,
// retrieves the item that was added earliest.
// Throws QueueException if the retrieval is not
// successful. The queue is unchanged.
```

Figure 7-1 illustrates these operations with a queue of integers. Notice that *enqueue* inserts an item at the back of the queue and that *peek*

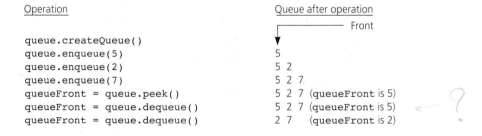

Operation	Queue after operation
	┌──────── Front
queue.createQueue()	▼
queue.enqueue(5)	5
queue.enqueue(2)	5 2
queue.enqueue(7)	5 2 7
queueFront = queue.peek()	5 2 7 (queueFront is 5)
queueFront = queue.dequeue()	5 2 7 (queueFront is 5)
queueFront = queue.dequeue()	2 7 (queueFront is 2)

Figure 7-1

Some queue operations

looks at the item at the front of the queue, whereas *dequeue* deletes the item at the front of the queue.

SIMPLE APPLICATIONS OF THE ADT QUEUE

This section presents two simple applications of the ADT queue. The applications use the operations of the ADT queue independently of their implementations.

Reading a String of Characters

When you enter characters at a keyboard, the system must retain them in the order in which you typed them. It could use a queue for this purpose, as the following pseudocode indicates:

A queue can retain characters in the order in which you type them

```
// read a string of characters from a
// single line of input into a queue
queue.createQueue()
while (not end of line) {
    Read a new character ch
    queue.enqueue(ch)
}   // end while
```

Once the characters are in a queue, the system can process them as necessary. For example, if you had typed an integer—without any mistakes, but possibly preceded or followed by blanks—the queue would contain digits and possibly blanks. If the digits are 2, 4, and 7, the system could convert them into the decimal value 247 by computing

$$10 * (10 * 2 + 4) + 7$$

The following pseudocode performs this conversion in general:

```
// convert digits in queue into a decimal integer n

// get first digit, ignoring any leading blanks
do  {
  ch = queue.dequeue()
}  while (ch is blank)

// Assertion: ch contains first digit
// compute n from digits in queue
n = 0
done = false
do  {
  n = 10 * n + integer that ch represents
  if (!queue.isEmpty()) {
    ch = queue.dequeue()
  }
```

```
    else {
      done = true
    } // end if
} while (!done and ch is a digit)
// Assertion: n is result
```

Recognizing Palindromes

Recall from Chapter 5 that a palindrome is a string of characters that reads the same from left to right as it does from right to left. In the previous chapter, you learned that you can use a stack to reverse the order of occurrences. You should realize by now that you can use a queue to preserve the order of occurrences. Thus, you can use both a queue and a stack to determine whether a string is a palindrome.

As you traverse the character string from left to right, you can insert each character into both a queue and a stack. Figure 7-2 illustrates the result of this action for the string abcbd, which is not a palindrome. You can see that the first character in the string is at the front of the queue and the last character in the string is at the top of the stack. Thus, characters removed from the queue will occur in the order in which they appear in the string; characters removed from the stack will occur in the opposite order.

Knowing this, you can compare the characters at the front of the queue and the top of the stack. If the characters are the same, you can delete them. You repeat this process until either the ADTs become empty, in which case the original string is a palindrome, or the two characters are not the same, in which case the string is not a palindrome.

The following is a pseudocode version of a nonrecursive recognition algorithm for the language of palindromes:

```
isPal(str)
// Determines whether str is a palindrome.

   // create an empty queue and an empty stack
   queue.createQueue()
   stack.createStack()

   // insert each character of the string into both
   // the queue and the stack
   length = the length of str
   for (i = 1 through length) {
      nextChar = iᵗʰ character of str
      queue.enqueue(nextChar)
      stack.push(nextChar)
   } // end for

   // compare the queue characters with the stack
   // characters
   charactersAreEqual = true
```

You can use a queue in conjunction with a stack to recognize palindromes

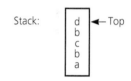

Figure 7-2

The results of inserting a string into both a queue and a stack

A nonrecursive recognition algorithm for palindromes

```
while (queue is not empty and charactersAreEqual is true) {
    queueFront = queue.dequeue()
    stackTop = stack.pop()
    if (queueFront not equal to stackTop) {
        charactersAreEqual = false
    }  // end if
}  // end while
return charactersAreEqual
```

IMPLEMENTATIONS OF THE ADT QUEUE

Like stacks, queues can have an array-based or a reference-based implementation. For queues, the reference-based implementation is a bit more straightforward than the array-based one, so we start with it.

A Reference-Based Implementation

A reference-based implementation of a queue could use a linear linked list with two external references, one to the front and one to the back, as Figure 7-3a illustrates.[1] However, as Figure 7-3b shows, you can actually

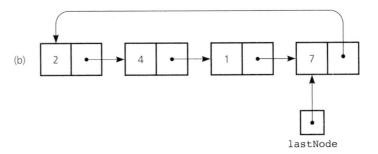

Figure 7-3

A reference-based implementation of a queue: (a) a linear linked list with two external references; (b) a circular linear linked list with one external reference

---

[1] Programming Problem 1 asks you consider the details of this implementation.

get by with a single external reference—to the back—if you make the linked list circular.

When a circular linked list represents a queue, the node at the back of the queue references the node at the front. Thus,

A circular linked list can represent a queue

> *lastNode* references the node at the back of the queue, and
>
> *lastNode.getNext()* references the node at the front

Insertion at the back and deletion from the front are straightforward. Figure 7-4 illustrates the addition of an item to a nonempty queue. Inserting the new node, which *newNode* references, at the back of the queue requires three reference changes: the next reference in the new node, the next reference in the back node, and the external reference *lastNode*. Figure 7-4 depicts these changes and indicates the order in which they must occur. (The dashed lines indicate reference values before the changes.) The addition of an item to an empty queue is a special case, as Figure 7-5 illustrates.

Deletion from the front of the queue is simpler than insertion at the back. Figure 7-6 illustrates the removal of the front item of a queue that contains more than one item. Notice that you need to change only one reference within the queue. Deletion from a queue of one item is a special case that sets the external reference *lastNode* to *null*.

The following is the interface specification for queues. Note that *enqueue*, *dequeue*, and *peek* may throw *QueueException*.

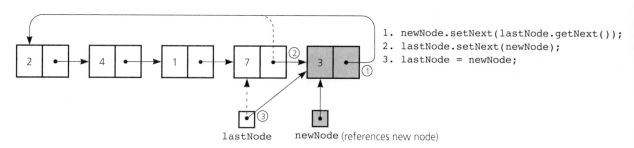

```
1. newNode.setNext(lastNode.getNext());
2. lastNode.setNext(newNode);
3. lastNode = newNode;
```

Figure 7-4

Inserting an item into a nonempty queue

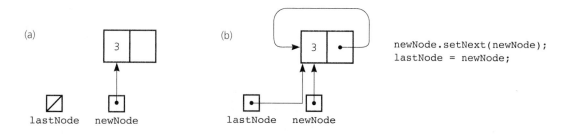

```
newNode.setNext(newNode);
lastNode = newNode;
```

Figure 7-5

Inserting an item into an empty queue: (a) before insertion; (b) after insertion

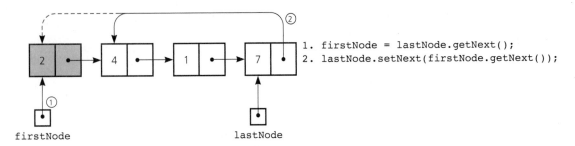

Figure 7-6

Deleting an item from a queue of more than one item

```java
public interface QueueInterface {

  public boolean isEmpty();
  // Determines whether a queue is empty.
  // Precondition: None.
  // Postcondition: Returns true if the queue is empty;
  // otherwise returns false.

  public void enqueue(Object newItem) throws QueueException;
  // Adds an item at the back of a queue.
  // Precondition: newItem is the item to be inserted.
  // Postcondition: If the operation was successful, newItem
  // is at the back of the queue. Some implementations
  // may throw QueueException if newItem cannot be added
  // to the queue.

  public Object dequeue() throws QueueException;
  // Retrieves and removes the front of a queue.
  // Precondition: None.
  // Postcondition: If the queue is not empty, the item
  // that was added to the queue earliest is returned and
  // the item is removed. If the queue is empty, the
  // operation is impossible and QueueException is thrown.

  public void dequeueAll();
  // Removes all items of a queue.
  // Precondition: None.
  // Postcondition: The queue is empty.

  public Object peek() throws QueueException;
  // Retrieves the item at the front of a queue.
  // Precondition: None.
  // Postcondition: If the queue is not empty, the item
  // that was added to the queue earliest is returned.
  // If the queue is empty, the operation is impossible
  // and QueueException is thrown.
} // end QueueInterface
```

The *QueueException* class, which is similar to the *StackException* class developed in Chapter 6, appears next.

```java
public class QueueException extends RuntimeException {

  public QueueException(String s) {
    super(s);
  }  // end constructor
}  // end QueueException
```

The following class is a reference-based implementation of the ADT queue. The implementation uses the *Node* class developed in Chapter 4.

```java
public class QueueReferenceBased implements QueueInterface {
  private Node lastNode;

  public QueueReferenceBased() {
    lastNode = null;
  }  // end default constructor

  // queue operations:
  public boolean isEmpty() {
    return lastNode == null;
  }  // end isEmpty

  public void dequeueAll() {
    lastNode = null;
  }  // end dequeueAll

  public void enqueue(Object newItem) {
    Node newNode = new Node(newItem);

    // insert the new node
    if (isEmpty()) {
      // insertion into empty queue
      newNode.setNext(newNode);
    }
    else {
      // insertion into nonempty queue
      newNode.setNext(lastNode.getNext());
      lastNode.setNext(newNode);
    }  // end if

    lastNode = newNode;  // new node is at back
  }  // end enqueue

  public Object dequeue() throws QueueException {
    if (!isEmpty()) {
      // queue is not empty; remove front
      Node firstNode = lastNode.getNext();
```

```
      if (firstNode == lastNode) { // special case?
        lastNode = null;              // yes, one node in queue
      }
      else {
        lastNode.setNext(firstNode.getNext());
      }  // end if
      return firstNode.getItem();
    }
    else {
      throw new QueueException("QueueException on dequeue:"
                                    + "queue empty");
    }  // end if
  }  // end dequeue

  public Object peek() throws QueueException {
    if (!isEmpty()) {
      // queue is not empty; retrieve front
      Node firstNode = lastNode.getNext();
      return firstNode.getItem();
    }
    else {
      throw new QueueException("QueueException on peek:"
                                    + "queue empty");
    }  // end if
  }  // end peek

} // end QueueReferenceBased
```

A program that uses this implementation could begin as follows:

```
    public class QueueTest {
      public static void main(String[] args) {
        QueueReferenceBased aQueue =
                                    new QueueReferenceBased();
        for (int i = 0; i < 9; i++) {
          aQueue.enqueue(new Integer(i));
        }  // end for
        . . .
      }  // end main
    }  // end QueueTest
```

An Array-Based Implementation

For applications in which a fixed-sized queue does not present a problem, you can use an array to represent a queue. As Figure 7-7a illustrates, a naive array-based implementation of a queue might include the following definitions:

Figure 7-7

(a) A naive array-based implementation of a queue; (b) rightward drift can cause the queue to appear full

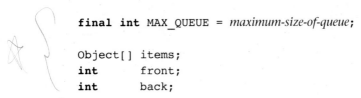

```
final int MAX_QUEUE = maximum-size-of-queue;

Object[] items;
int      front;
int      back;
```

A naive array-based implementation of a queue

The indexes of the front and back items in the queue are, respectively, *front* and *back*. Initially, *front* is 0 and *back* is –1. To insert a new item into the queue, you increment *back* and place the item in *items[back]*. To delete an item, you simply increment *front*. The queue is empty whenever *back* is less than *front*. The queue is full when *back* equals *MAX_QUEUE* – 1.

The problem with this strategy is **rightward drift**—that is, after a sequence of additions and removals, the items in the queue will drift toward the end of the array, and *back* could equal *MAX_QUEUE* – 1 even when the queue contains only a few items. Figure 7-7b illustrates this situation.

Rightward drift can cause a queue-full condition even though the queue contains few entries

One possible solution to this problem is to shift array elements to the left, either after each deletion or whenever *back* equals *MAX_QUEUE* – 1. This solution guarantees that the queue can always contain up to *MAX_QUEUE* items. Shifting is not really satisfactory, however, as it would dominate the cost of the implementation.

Shifting elements to compensate for rightward drift is expensive

A much more elegant solution is possible by viewing the array as circular, as Figure 7-8 illustrates. You advance the queue indexes *front* (to delete an item) and *back* (to insert an item) by moving them clockwise around the array. Figure 7-9 illustrates the effect of a sequence of three queue operations on *front*, *back*, and the array. When either *front* or *back* advances past *MAX_QUEUE* – 1, it wraps around to 0. This wraparound eliminates the problem of rightward drift, which occurred in the previous implementation, because here the circular array has no end.

A circular array eliminates rightward drift

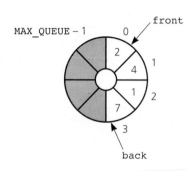

Figure 7-8

A circular implementation of a queue

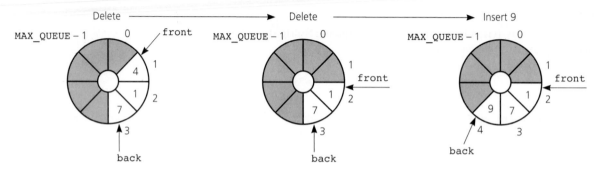

Figure 7-9

The effect of some operations on the queue in Figure 7-8

The only difficulty with this scheme involves detecting the queue-empty and queue-full conditions. It seems reasonable to select as the queue-empty condition

> *front* is one slot ahead of *back*

since this appears to indicate that *front* "passes" *back* when the queue becomes empty, as Figure 7-10a depicts. However, it is also possible that this condition signals a full queue: Because the queue is circular, *back* might in fact "catch up" with *front* as the queue becomes full; Figure 7-10b illustrates this situation.

Obviously, you need a way to distinguish between the two situations. One such way is to keep a count of the number of items in the queue. Before inserting into the queue, you check to see if the count is equal to *MAX_QUEUE*; if it is, the queue is full. Before deleting an item from the queue, you check to see if the count is equal to zero; if it is, the queue is empty.

To initialize the queue, you set *front* to 0, *back* to *MAX_QUEUE* − 1, and *count* to 0. You obtain the wraparound effect of a circular queue by using modulo arithmetic (that is, the Java % operator) when incrementing

front and *back* cannot be used to distinguish between queue-full and queue-empty conditions

By counting queue items, you can detect queue-full and queue-empty conditions

Initialize *front*, *back*, and *count*

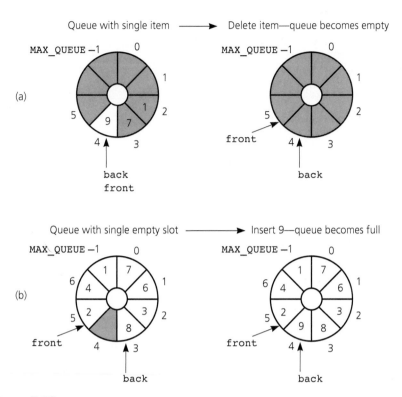

Figure 7-10

(a) **front** passes **back** when the queue becomes empty;
(b) **back** catches up to **front** when the queue becomes full

front and *back*. For example, you can insert *newItem* into the queue by using the statements

```
back = (back+1) % MAX_QUEUE;
items[back] = newItem;
++count;
```

Inserting into a queue

Notice that if *back* equaled *MAX_QUEUE* – 1 before the insertion of *newItem,* the first statement, *back = (back+1) % MAX_QUEUE*, would have the effect of wrapping *back* around to location 0.

Similarly, you can delete the item at the front of the queue by using the statements

```
front = (front+1) % MAX_QUEUE;
--count;
```

Deleting from a queue

The following Java class is an array-based implementation of the ADT queue that uses a circular array as just described. Preconditions and post-conditions have been omitted to save space but are the same as those given in the *QueueInterface* specification.

```java
public class QueueArrayBased implements QueueInterface {
  private final int MAX_QUEUE = 50; // maximum size of queue
  private Object[] items;
  private int front, back, count;


  public QueueArrayBased() {
    items = new Object[MAX_QUEUE];
    front = 0;
    back = MAX_QUEUE-1;
    count = 0;
  }  // end default constructor


  // queue operations:
  public boolean isEmpty() {
    return count == 0;
  }  // end isEmpty


  public boolean isFull() {
    return count == MAX_QUEUE;
  }  // end isFull


  public void enqueue(Object newItem) throws QueueException {
    if (!isFull()) {
      back = (back+1) % (MAX_QUEUE);
      items[back] = newItem;
      ++count;
    }
    else {
      throw new QueueException("QueueException on enqueue: "
                               + "Queue full");
    }  // end if
  }  // end enqueue

  public Object dequeue() throws QueueException {
    if (!isEmpty()) {
      // queue is not empty; remove front
      Object queueFront = items[front];
      front = (front+1) % (MAX_QUEUE);
      --count;
      return queueFront;
    }
    else {
      throw new QueueException("QueueException on dequeue: "
                               + "Queue empty");
    }   // end if
  }  // end dequeue
```

```
public void dequeueAll() {
  items = new Object[MAX_QUEUE];
  front = 0;
  back = MAX_QUEUE-1;
  count = 0;
} // end dequeueAll

public Object peek() throws QueueException {
  if (!isEmpty()) {
    // queue is not empty; retrieve front
    return items[front];
  }
  else {
    throw new QueueException("Queue exception on peek: " +
                             + "Queue empty");
  } // end if
} // end peek

} // end QueueArrayBased
```

Several commonly used variations of this implementation do not require a count of the number of items in the queue. One approach uses a flag *full* to distinguish between the full and empty conditions. The expense of maintaining a *full* flag is about the same as that of maintaining a counter, however. A faster implementation declares *MAX_QUEUE* + 1 locations for the array *items*, but uses only *MAX_QUEUE* of them for queue items. You sacrifice one array location and make *front* the index of the location before the front of the queue. As Figure 7-11 illustrates, the queue is full if

*A **full** flag can replace the counter*

front equals *(back+1)* % *(MAX_QUEUE+1)*

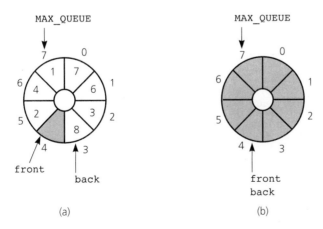

(a)   (b)

Figure 7-11

A more efficient circular implementation: (a) a full queue; (b) an empty queue

but the queue is empty if

> *front* equals *back*

Using an extra array location is more time-efficient

This implementation does not have the overhead of maintaining a counter or flag, and so is more efficient time-wise. For the standard data types, the implementation requires the same space as either the counter or the flag implementation (why?). Programming Problems 3 and 4 discuss these two alternate implementations further.

An Implementation That Uses the ADT List

You can use the ADT list to represent the items in a queue, as Figure 7-12 illustrates. If the item in position 1 of a list *list* represents the front of the queue, you can implement the operation *dequeue()* as *list .remove(1)* and the operation *peek()* as *list.get(1)*. Similarly, if you let the item at the end of the list represent the back of the queue, you can implement the operation *enqueue(newItem)* as *list.add(list .size()+1, newItem)*.

Recall that Chapters 3 and 4 presented the ADT list as an implementation of the interface *ListInterface*. (See, for example, page 171.) The following class for the ADT queue uses an instance of the reference-based implementation *ListReferenceBased* to represent the queue. Preconditions and postconditions are omitted to save space but are the same as those given earlier in this chapter.

```
public class QueueListBased implements QueueInterface {
  private ListInterface list;

  public QueueListBased() {
    list = new ListReferenceBased();
  } // end default constructor

  // queue operations:
  public boolean isEmpty() {
    return list.isEmpty();
  } // end isEmpty

  public void enqueue(Object newItem) {
    list.add(list.size()+1, newItem);
  } // end enqueue
```

Figure 7-12

An implementation that uses the ADT list

```
public Object dequeue() throws QueueException {
  if (!isEmpty()) {
    // queue is not empty; remove front
    Object queueFront = list.get(1);
    list.remove(1);
    return queueFront;
  }
  else {
    throw new QueueException("Queue exception on dequeue: "
                        + " queue empty");
  }  // end if
}  // end dequeue

public void dequeueAll() {
  list.removeAll();
}  // end dequeueAll

public Object peek() throws QueueException {
  if (!isEmpty()) {
    // queue is not empty; retrieve front
    return list.get(1);
  }
  else {
    throw new QueueException("Queue exception on peek "
                        + "queue empty");
  }  // end if
}  // end peek

}  // end QueueListBased
```

As was true for the analogous implementation of the ADT stack in Chapter 6, implementing the queue is simple once you have implemented the ADT list. Exercise 4 at the end of this chapter asks you to consider the efficiency of this implementation.

Comparing Implementations

We have suggested implementations of the ADT queue that use either a linear linked list, a circular linked list, an array, a circular array, or the ADT list to represent the items in a queue. You have seen the details of three of these implementations. All of our implementations of the ADT queue are ultimately either array based or reference based.

The reasons for making the choice between array-based and reference-based implementations are the same as those discussed in earlier chapters. The discussion here is similar to the one in Chapter 6 in the section "Comparing Implementations." We repeat the highlights here in the context of queues.

Fixed size versus dynamic size

An implementation based on a statically allocated array prevents the *enqueue* operation from adding an item to the queue if the array is full. If this restriction is not acceptable, you must use either a resizeable array or a reference-based implementation.

Reuse of an already implemented class saves you time

Suppose you decide to use a reference-based implementation. Should you choose the implementation that uses a linked list, or should you choose a reference-based implementation of the ADT list? Because a linked list actually represents the items on the ADT list, using the ADT list to represent a queue is not as efficient as using a linked list directly. However, the ADT list approach is much simpler to write.

If you decide to use a linked list instead of the ADT list to represent the queue, should you use a linear linked list or a circular linked list? We leave this question for you to answer in Programming Problem 1.

A SUMMARY OF POSITION-ORIENTED ADTs

So far, we have seen three abstract data types—the list, the stack, and the queue—that have a common theme: All of their operations are defined in terms of the positions of their data items. Stacks and queues greatly restrict the positions that their operations can affect; only their end positions can be accessed. The list removes this restriction.

Operations for the ADTs list, stack, and queue reference the position of items

Stacks are really quite similar to queues. This similarity becomes apparent if you pair off their operations, as follows:

A comparison of stack and queue operations

- **createStack** and **createQueue**. These operations create an empty ADT of the appropriate type.

- Stack **isEmpty** and queue **isEmpty**. These operations determine whether any items exist in the ADT.

- **push** and **enqueue**. These operations insert a new item into one end (the top and back, respectively) of the ADT.

- **pop** and **dequeue**. The *pop* operation deletes the most recent item, which is at the top of the stack, and *dequeue* deletes the first item, which is at the front of the queue.

- Stack **peek** and queue **peek**. Stack *peek* retrieves the most recent item, which is at the top of the stack, and queue *peek* retrieves the first item, which is at the front of the queue.

The ADT list, introduced in Chapter 3, allows you to insert into, delete from, and inspect the item at any position of the list. Thus, it has the most flexible operations of the three **position-oriented** ADTs. You can view the list operations as general versions of the stack and queue operations, as follows:

ADT list operations generalize stack and queue operations

- **length**. If you remove the restriction that the stack and queue versions of *isEmpty* can tell only when an item is present, you obtain an operation that can count the number of items that are present.

- **add**. If you remove the restriction that *push* and *enqueue* can insert new items into only one position, you obtain an operation that can insert a new item into any position of the list.

- **remove**. If you remove the restriction that *pop* and *dequeue* can delete items from only one position, you obtain an operation that can delete an item from any position of the list.

- **get**. If you remove the restriction that the stack and queue versions of *peek* can retrieve items from only one position, you obtain an operation that can retrieve the item from any position of the list.

Because each of these three ADTs defines its operations in terms of an item's position in the ADT, this book has presented implementations for them that can provide easy access to specified positions. For example, the stack implementations allow the first position (top) to be accessed quickly, while the queue implementations allow the first position (front) and the last position (back) to be accessed quickly.

APPLICATION: SIMULATION

Simulation—a major application area for computers—is a technique for modeling the behavior of both natural and human-made systems. Generally, the goal of a simulation is to generate statistics that summarize the performance of an existing system or to predict the performance of a proposed system. In this section, we will consider a simple example that illustrates one important type of simulation.

Simulation models the behavior of systems

Consider the following problem. Ms. Simpson, president of the First City Bank of Springfield, has heard her customers complain about how long they have to wait for service. Because she fears that they may move their accounts to another bank, she is considering whether to hire a second teller.

Before Ms. Simpson hires another teller, she would like an approximation of the average time that a customer has to wait for service from First City's only teller. How can Ms. Simpson obtain this information? She could stand with a stopwatch in the bank's lobby all day, but she does not find this prospect particularly exciting. Besides, she would like to use a method that also allows her to predict how much improvement she could expect if the bank hired a given number of additional tellers. She certainly does not want to hire the tellers on a trial basis and monitor the bank's performance before making a final decision.

Ms. Simpson concludes that the best way to obtain the information she wants is to use a computer model to simulate the behavior of her bank. The first step in simulating a system such as a bank is to construct a mathematical model that captures the relevant information about the system. For example, how many tellers does the bank employ? How often do customers arrive? If the model accurately describes the real-world system, a simulation can derive accurate predictions about the system's overall performance. For example, a simulation could predict the average time a customer has to wait before receiving service. A simulation can also evaluate proposed changes to the real-world system. For example, it could predict the effect of hiring more tellers in the bank. A large decrease in the time predicted for the average wait of a customer might justify the cost of hiring additional tellers.

Simulated time

Central to a simulation is the concept of simulated time. Envision a stopwatch that measures time elapsed during a simulation. For example, suppose that the model of the bank specifies only one teller. At time 0, which is the start of the banking day, the simulated system would be in its initial state with no customers. As the simulation runs, the stopwatch ticks away units of time—perhaps minutes—and certain events occur. At time 12, the bank's first customer arrives. Since there is no line, the customer goes directly to the teller and begins her transaction. At time 20, a second customer arrives. Because the first customer has not yet completed her transaction, the second customer must wait in line. At time 38, the first customer completes her transaction and the second customer can begin his. Figure 7-13 illustrates these four times in the simulation.

To gather the information you need, you run this simulation for a specified period of simulated time. During the course of the run, you need to keep track of certain statistics, such as the average time a customer has to wait for service. Notice that in the small example of Figure 7-13, the first customer had to wait 0 minutes to begin a transaction and the second customer had to wait 18 minutes to begin a transaction—an average wait of 9 minutes.

One point not addressed in the previous discussion is how to determine when certain events occur. For example, why did we say that the first customer arrived at time 12 and the second at time 20? By studying real-world systems like our bank, mathematicians have learned to model events such as the arrival of people, using techniques from probability theory. This statistical information is incorporated into the mathematical model of the system and is used to generate events in a way that reflects the real world. The simulation uses these events and is thus called an **event-driven simulation**. Note that the goal is to reflect the long-term average behavior of the system rather than to predict occurrences of specific events. This goal is sufficient for the needs of the simulation.

Although the techniques for generating events to reflect the real world are interesting and important, they require a good deal of mathematical sophistication. Therefore, simply assume that you already have a list of events available for your use. In particular, for the bank problem, assume that a file contains the time of each customer's arrival—an **arrival event**—and the duration of that customer's transaction once the customer reaches the teller. For example, the data

Sample arrival and transaction times

20	5
22	4
23	2
30	3

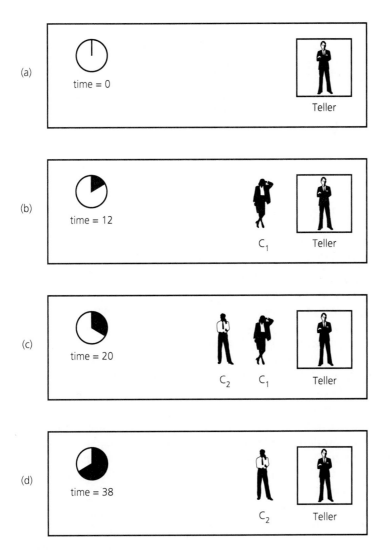

Figure 7-13

A bank line at time (a) 0; (b) 12; (c) 20; (d) 38

indicates that the first customer arrives 20 minutes into the simulation and that the transaction—once begun—requires 5 minutes; the second customer arrives 22 minutes into the simulation and the transaction requires 4 minutes; and so on. Assume that the input file is ordered by arrival time.

Notice that the file does not contain **departure events**; the data does not specify when a customer will complete the transaction and leave. Instead, the simulation must determine when departures occur. By using the arrival time and the transaction length, the simulation can easily determine the time at which a customer departs. To see how to make this determination, you can conduct a simulation by hand with the previous data as follows:

The results of a simulation

Time	Event
20	Customer 1 enters bank and begins transaction
22	Customer 2 enters bank and stands at end of line
23	Customer 3 enters bank and stands at end of line
25	Customer 1 departs; customer 2 begins transaction
29	Customer 2 departs; customer 3 begins transaction
30	Customer 4 enters bank and stands at end of line
31	Customer 3 departs; customer 4 begins transaction
34	Customer 4 departs

A customer's wait time is the elapsed time between arrival in the bank and the start of the transaction. The average of this wait time over all the customers is the statistic that you want to obtain.

To summarize, this simulation is concerned with two types of events:

- **Arrival events.** These events indicate the arrival at the bank of a new customer. The input file specifies the times at which the arrival events occur. As such, they are **external events.** When a customer arrives at the bank, one of two things happens. If the teller is idle when the customer arrives, the customer enters the line and begins the transaction immediately. If the teller is busy, the new customer must stand at the end of the line and wait for service.

- **Departure events.** These events indicate the departure from the bank of a customer who has completed a transaction. The simulation determines the times at which the departure events occur. As such, they are **internal events.** When a customer completes the transaction, he or she departs and the next person in line—if there is one—begins a transaction.

The main tasks of an algorithm that performs the simulation are to determine the times at which the events occur and to process the events when they do occur. The algorithm is stated at a high level as follows:

A first attempt at a simulation algorithm

```
// initialize
currentTime = 0
Initialize the line to "no customers"

while (currentTime ≤ time of the final event) {

  if (an arrival event occurs at time currentTime) {
    Process the arrival event
  }  // end if
  if (a departure event occurs at time currentTime) {
    Process the departure event
  }  // end if
  // when an arrival event and departure event
  // occur at the same time, arbitrarily process
  // the arrival event first
```

```
    ++currentTime
  } // end while
```

But do you really want to increment `currentTime` by 1? You would
for a **time-driven simulation**, where you would determine arrival and
departure times at random and compare those times to `currentTime`. In
such a case, you would increment `currentTime` by 1 to simulate the
ticking of a clock. Recall, however, that this simulation is event driven, so
you have a file of arrival times and transaction times. Because you are
interested only in those times at which arrival and departure events occur
and because no action is required between events, you can advance `cur-
rentTime` from the time of one event directly to the time of the next.

*A time-driven simulation simu-
lates the ticking of a clock*

*An event-driven simulation con-
siders only times of certain
events, in this case, arrivals and
departures*

Thus, you can revise the pseudocode solution as follows:

```
  // initialize the line to "no customers"

  while (events remain to be processed) {
    currentTime = time of next event
    if (event is an arrival event) {
      Process the arrival event
    }
    else {
      Process the departure event
    } // end if
    // when an arrival event and departure event
    // occur at the same time, arbitrarily process
    // the arrival event first
  } // end while
```

*First revision of the simulation
algorithm*

You must determine the time of the next arrival or departure event so
that you can implement the statement

```
  currentTime = time of next event
```

To make this determination, you must maintain an **event list.** An event
list contains all arrival and departure events that will occur but have not
occurred yet. The times of the events in the event list are in ascending
order, and thus the next event to be processed is always at the beginning of
the list. The algorithm simply gets the event from the beginning of the list,
advances to the time specified, and processes the event. The difficulty,
then, lies in successfully managing the event list.

*An event list contains all
future events*

Since each arrival event generates exactly one departure event, you
might think that you should read the entire input file and create an
event list of all arrival and departure events sorted by time. Self-Test
Exercise 5 asks you to explain why this approach is impractical. As you
will see, you can instead manage the event list for this particular
problem so that it always contains at most one event of each kind.

*This event list contains at
most one arrival event and
one departure event*

Recall that the arrival events are specified in the input file in ascending time order. You thus never need to worry about an arrival event until
you have processed all the arrival events that precede it in the file. You
simply keep the earliest unprocessed arrival event in the event list. When

you eventually process this event—that is, when it is time for this customer to arrive—you replace it in the event list with the next unprocessed arrival event, which is the next item in the input file.

Similarly, you need to place only the next departure event to occur on the event list. But how can you determine the times for the departure events? Observe that the next departure event always corresponds to the customer that the teller is currently serving. As soon as a customer begins service, the time of his or her departure is simply

time of next departure = time service begins + length of transaction

Recall that the length of the customer's transaction is in the input file, along with the arrival time. Thus, as soon as a customer begins service, you place a departure event corresponding to this customer in the event list. Figure 7-14 illustrates a typical instance of the event list for this simulation.

Now consider how you can process an event when it is time for the event to occur. You must perform two general types of actions:

Two tasks are required to process each event

- **Update the line:** Add or remove customers.
- **Update the event list:** Add or remove events.

As customers arrive, they go to the back of the line. The current customer, who is at the front of the line, is being served, and it is this customer that you remove from the system next. It is thus natural to use a queue to represent the line of customers in the bank. For this problem, the only information that you must store in the queue about each customer is the time of arrival and the length of the transaction. The event list, since it is sorted by time, is not a queue. We will examine it in more detail shortly.

A queue represents the customers in line

The event list is not a queue

To summarize, you process an event as follows:

The algorithm for arrival events

```
TO PROCESS AN ARRIVAL EVENT

// update the event list
Delete the arrival event for customer C from
    the event list
```

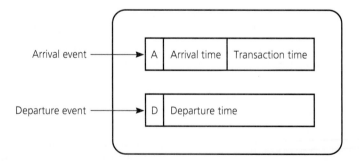

Figure 7-14

A typical instance of the event list

```
if (new customer C begins transaction immediately) {
   Insert a departure event for customer C into the
      event list (time of event = current time +
      transaction length)
}  // end if
if (not at the end of the input file) {
   Read a new arrival event and add it to the event list
      (time of event = time specified in file)
}  // end if
```

Because a customer is served while at the front of the queue, a new customer always enters the queue, even if the queue is empty. You then delete the arrival event for the new customer from the event list. If the new customer is served immediately, you insert a departure event into the event list. Finally, you read a new arrival event into the event list. This arrival event can occur either before or after the departure event.

A new customer always enters the queue and is served while at the queue's front

TO PROCESS A DEPARTURE EVENT

The algorithm for departure events

```
// update the line
Delete the customer at the front of the queue
if (the queue is not empty) {
   The current front customer begins transaction
}  // end if
// update the event list
Delete the departure event from the event list
if (the queue is not empty) {
   Insert into the event list the departure event for
      the customer now at the front of the queue
      (time of event = current time + transaction length)
}  // end if
```

After processing the departure event, you do not read another arrival event from the file. Assuming that the file has not been read completely, the event list will contain an arrival event whose time is earlier than any arrival still in the input file.

Examining the event list more closely will help explain the workings of the algorithm. There is no typical form that an event list takes. For this simulation, however, the event list has four possible configurations:

- Initially, the event list contains an arrival event *A* after you read the first arrival event from the input file but before you process it:

  Four configurations of the event list for this simulation

  Event list: *A* (initial state)

- Generally, the event list for this simulation contains exactly two events: one arrival event *A* and one departure event *D*. Either the departure event is first or the arrival event is first as follows:

  Event list: *D A* (general case—next event is a departure)

  or

  Event list: *A D* (general case—next event is an arrival)

- If the departure event is first and that event leaves the teller's line empty, a new departure event does not replace the just-processed event. Thus, in this case, the event list appears as

  Event list: *A* (a departure leaves the teller's line empty)

  Notice that this instance of the event list is the same as its initial state.

- If the arrival event is first and if, after it is processed, you are at the end of the input file, the event list contains only a departure event:

  Event list: *D* (the input has been exhausted)

Other situations result in an event list that has one of the previous four configurations.

You insert new events either at the beginning of the event list or at the end, depending on the relative times of the new event and the event currently in the event list. For example, suppose that the event list contains only an arrival event *A* and that another customer is now at the front of the line and beginning a transaction. You need to generate a departure event *D* for this customer. If the customer's departure time is before the time of the arrival event *A*, you must insert the departure event *D* before the event *A* in the event list. However, if the departure time is after the time of the arrival event, you must insert the departure event *D* after the arrival event *A*. In the case of a tie, you need a rule to determine which event should take precedence. In this solution, we arbitrarily choose to place the departure event after the arrival event.

You can now combine and refine the pieces of the solution into an algorithm that performs the simulation by using the ADT queue operations to manage the bank line:

The final pseudocode for the event-driven simulation

```
simulate()
// Performs the simulation.

    Create an empty queue bankQueue to represent the bank line
    Create an empty event list eventList

    Get the first arrival event from the input file
    Place the arrival event in the event list

    while (the event list is not empty) {
      newEvent = the first event in the event list

      if (newEvent is an arrival event) {
        processArrival(newEvent, arrivalFile,
                       eventList, bankQueue)
      }
      else {
        processDeparture(newEvent, eventList, bankQueue)
      }  // end if
    }  // end while
```

```
processArrival(arrivalEvent, arrivalFile,
                  eventList, bankQueue)
// Processes an arrival event.

  atFront = bankQueue.isEmpty()  // present queue status

  // update the bankQueue by inserting the customer, as
  // described in arrivalEvent, into the queue
  bankQueue.enqueue(arrivalEvent)

  // update the event list
  Delete arrivalEvent from event list

  if (atFront) {
    // the line was empty, so new customer is at front
    // of line and begins transaction immediately
    Insert into the event list a departure event that
        corresponds to the new customer and has
    currentTime = currentTime + transaction length
  }  // end if

  if (not at end of input file) {
    Get the next arrival event from arrivalFile
    Add the event -- with time as specified in the input
        file -- to the event list
  }  // end if

processDeparture(departureEvent, eventList, bankQueue)
// Processes a departure event.

  // update the line by deleting the front customer
  bankQueue.dequeue()

  // update the event list
  Delete departureEvent from event list
  if (!bankQueue.isEmpty())
    // customer at front of line begins transaction
    Insert into the event list a departure event that
        corresponds to the customer now at the front of the
        line and has currentTime = currentTime
        + transaction length
  }  // end if
```

Figure 7-15 begins a trace of this algorithm for the data on page 316 and shows the changes to the queue and event list. Self-Test Exercise 6 at the end of this chapter asks you to complete the trace.

The event list is, in fact, an ADT. By examining the previous pseudocode, you can see that this ADT must include at least the following operations:

ADT event list operations

```
createEventList()
// Creates an empty event list.

eventListIsEmpty()
// Determines whether an event list is empty.

eventListInsert(event)
// Inserts event into an event list so that events
// are ordered by time. If an arrival event and a
// departure event have the same time, the arrival
// event precedes the departure event.

eventListDelete()
// Deletes the first event from an event list.

eventListRetrieve()
// Retrieves the first event in an event list.
```

Time	Action	bankQueue (front to back)	eventList (beginning to end)
0	Read file, place event in `eventList`	*(empty)*	A 20 5
20	Update `eventList` and `bankQueue`: Customer 1 enters bank	20 5	*(empty)*
	Customer 1 begins transaction, create departure event	20 5	D 25
	Read file, place event in `eventList`	20 5	A 22 4 D 25
22	Update `eventList` and `bankQueue`: Customer 2 enters bank	20 5 22 4	D 25
	Read file, place event in `eventList`	20 5 22 4	A 23 2 D 25
23	Update `eventList` and `bankQueue`: Customer 3 enters bank	20 5 22 4 23 2	D 25
	Read file, place event in `eventList`	20 5 22 4 23 2	D 25 A 30 3
25	Update `eventList` and `bankQueue`: Customer 1 departs	22 4 23 2	A 30 3
	Customer 2 begins transaction, create departure event	22 4 23 2	D 29 A 30 3

Self-Test Exercise 6 asks you to complete this trace.

Figure 7-15

A partial trace of the bank simulation algorithm for the data
   20 5
   22 4
   23 2
   30 3

Programming Problem 6 at the end of this chapter asks you to complete the implementation of this simulation.

SUMMARY

1. The definition of the queue operations gives the ADT queue first-in, first-out (FIFO) behavior.

2. The insertion and deletion operations for a queue require efficient access to both ends of the queue. Therefore, a reference-based implementation of a queue uses either a circular linked list or a linear linked list that has both a head reference and a tail reference.

3. An array-based implementation of a queue is prone to rightward drift. This phenomenon can make a queue look full when it really is not. Shifting the items in the array is one way to compensate for rightward drift. A more efficient solution uses a circular array.

4. If you use a circular array to implement a queue, you must be able to distinguish between the queue-full and queue-empty conditions. You can make this distinction by either counting the number of items in the queue, using a *full* flag, or leaving one array location empty.

5. Models of real-world systems often use queues. The event-driven simulation in this chapter uses a queue to model a line of customers in a bank.

6. Central to a simulation is the notion of simulated time. In a time-driven simulation, simulated time is advanced by a single time unit, whereas in an event-driven simulation, simulated time is advanced to the time of the next event. To implement an event-driven simulation, you maintain an event list that contains events that have not yet occurred. The event list is ordered by the time of the events so that the next event to occur is always at the head of the list.

CAUTIONS

1. If you use a linear linked list with only a head reference to implement a queue, the insertion operation will be inefficient. Each insertion requires a traversal to the end of the linked list. As the queue increases in length, the traversal time—and hence the insertion time—will increase.

2. The management of an event list in an event-driven simulation is typically more difficult than it was in the example presented in this chapter. For instance, if the bank had more than one teller line, the structure of the event list would be much more complex.

SELF-TEST EXERCISES

1. If you add the letters A, B, C, and D in sequence to a queue of characters and then remove them, in what order will they be deleted from the queue?

2. What do the initially empty queues *queue1* and *queue2* "look like" after the following sequence of operations?

   ```
   queue1.enqueue(1)
   queue1.enqueue(2)
   queue2.enqueue(3)
   queue2.enqueue(4)
   queueFront = queue1.dequeue()
   queueFront = queue2.peek()
   queue1.enqueue(queueFront)
   queue1.enqueue(5)
   queueFront = queue2.dequeue()
   queue2.enqueue(6)
   ```

   Compare these results with Self-Test Exercise 2 in Chapter 6.

3. Trace the palindrome-recognition algorithm described in the section "Simple Applications of the ADT Queue" for each of the following strings:
   a. abcda
   b. radar

4. For each of the following situations, which of these ADTs (1 through 4) would be most appropriate: (1) a queue; (2) a stack; (3) a list; (4) none of these?
   a. The customers at a deli counter who take numbers to mark their turn
   b. An alphabetic list of names
   c. Integers that need to be sorted
   d. The boxes in a box trace of a recursive method
   e. A grocery list ordered by the occurrence of the items in the store
   f. The items on a cash register tape
   g. A word processor that allows you to correct typing errors by using the backspace key
   h. A program that uses backtracking
   i. A list of ideas in chronological order
   j. Airplanes that stack above a busy airport, waiting to land
   k. People who are put on hold when they call an airline to make reservations
   l. An employer who fires the most recently hired person

5. In the bank simulation problem that this chapter discusses, why is it impractical to read the entire input file and create a list of all the arrival and departure events before the simulation begins?

6. Complete the hand trace of the bank-line simulation that Figure 7-15 began with the data given on page 316. Show the state of the queue and the event list at each step.

EXERCISES

1. Consider the palindrome-recognition algorithm described in the section "Simple Applications of the ADT Queue." Is it necessary for the algorithm to look at the entire queue and stack? That is, can you reduce the number of times that the loop must execute?

2. Consider the language

$L = \{w\$w' : w$ is a possibly empty string of characters other than \$,
$\quad w' = \text{reverse}(w)\}$

as defined in Chapter 6. Write a recognition algorithm for this language that uses both a queue and a stack. Thus, as you traverse the input string, you insert each character of w into a queue and each character of w' into a stack. Assume that each input string contains exactly one \$.

3. Revise the infix-to-postfix conversion algorithm of Chapter 6 so that it uses a queue to represent the postfix expression.

4. Consider the queue implementation that uses the ADT list to represent the items in the queue. Discuss the efficiency of the queue's insertion and deletion operations when the ADT list's implementation is

a. Array based
b. Reference based

5. An operation that displays the contents of a queue can be useful during program debugging. Add a *display* operation to the ADT queue such that

a. *display* uses only ADT queue operations, so it is independent of the queue's implementation
b. *display* assumes and uses the reference-based implementation of the ADT queue

6. Consider a slight variation of the ADT queue. In this variation, new items can be added to and deleted from either end. This ADT is commonly called a **doubly ended queue**, or **deque**. Use a deque to solve the read-and-correct problem that Chapter 6 describes. In that problem, you enter text at a keyboard and correct typing mistakes by using the backspace key. Each backspace erases the most recently entered character. Your pseudocode solution should provide a corrected string of characters in the order in which they were entered at the keyboard.

7. With the following data, hand-trace the execution of the bank-line simulation that this chapter describes. Each line of data contains an arrival time and a transaction time. Show the state of the queue and the event list at each step.

5	9
7	5
14	5
30	5
32	5
34	5

Note that at time 14 there is a tie between the execution of an arrival event and a departure event.

8. In the solution to the bank simulation problem, can the event list be an ADT queue? Can the event list be an ADT list or sorted list?

9. Consider the stack-based search of the flight map in the HPAir problem of Chapter 6. You can replace the stack that *searchS* uses with a queue. That is, you can replace every call to *push* with a call to *enqueue*, every call to *pop* with a call to *dequeue*, and every call to the stack version of *peek* with a call to the queue version of *peek*. Trace the resulting algorithm when you fly from *P* to *Z* in the flight map in Figure 6-9. Indicate the contents of the queue after every operation on it.

*10. As Chapter 3 pointed out, you can define ADT operations in a mathematically formal way by using axioms. Consider the following axioms for the ADT queue, where *queue* is an arbitrary queue and *item* is an arbitrary queue item.

```
(queue.createQueue()).isEmpty() = true
(queue.enqueue(item)).isEmpty() = false
(queue.createQueue()).dequeue() = error
((queue.createQueue()).enqueue(item)).dequeue() =
                                    queue.createQueue()
queue.isEmpty() = false ⇒
    (queue.enqueue(item)).dequeue() =
                        (queue.dequeue()).enqueue(item)
(queue.createQueue()).peek() = error
((queue.createQueue()).enqueue(item)).peek() = item
queue.isEmpty() = false ⇒
    (queue.enqueue(item)).peek() = queue.peek()
```

   a. Note the recursive nature of the definition of *peek*. What is the base case? What is the recursive step? What is the significance of the *isEmpty* test? Why is *peek* recursive in nature while the operation *peek* for the ADT stack is not?

   b. The representation of a stack as a sequence of *push* operations without any *pop* operations was called a canonical form. (See Exercise 12a in Chapter 6.) Is there a canonical form for the ADT queue that uses only *enqueue* operations? That is, is every queue equal to a queue that can be written with only *enqueues*? Prove your answer.

PROGRAMMING PROBLEMS

1. Write a reference-based implementation of a queue that uses a linear linked list to represent the items in the queue. You will need both a head reference and a tail reference. When you are done, compare your implementation to the one given in this chapter that uses a circular linked list with one external reference. Which implementation is easier to write? Which is easier to understand? Which is more efficient?

2. Write an array-based implementation of a queue that uses a resizeable, circular array to represent the items in the queue.

3. Consider the array-based implementation of a queue given in the text. Instead of counting the number of items in the queue, you could maintain a flag *full* to distinguish between the full and empty conditions. Revise the array-based implementation by using the *full* flag.

4. This chapter described another array-based implementation of a queue that uses no special data field—such as *count* or *full* (see Programming Problem 3)—to distinguish between the full and empty conditions. In this implementation, you declare *MAX_QUEUE* + 1 locations for the array *items*, but use only *MAX_QUEUE* of them for queue items. You sacrifice one array location by making *front* the index of the location before the front of the queue. The queue is full if *front* equals *(back+1) % (MAX_QUEUE+1)*, but the queue is empty if *front* equals *back*.

   a. Does this implementation have the same space requirements as the *count* or *full* implementations? Why?

   b. Implement this array-based approach.

5. Exercise 6 mentioned the doubly ended queue, or deque. New items can be added to and deleted from either end of a deque. Construct array-based and reference-based implementations of the deque.

6. Implement the event-driven simulation of a bank that this chapter described. A queue of arrival events will represent the line of customers in the bank. Maintain the arrival events and departure events in an ADT event list, sorted by the time of the event. Use a reference-based implementation for the ADT event list.

   The input is a text file of arrival and transaction times. Each line of the file contains the arrival time and required transaction time for a customer. The arrival times are ordered by increasing time.

   Your program must count customers and keep track of their cumulative waiting time. These statistics are sufficient to compute the average waiting time after the last event has been processed.

   Display a trace of the events executed and a summary of the computed statistics (total number of arrivals and average time spent waiting in line). For example, the input file shown in the left columns of the following table should produce the output shown in the right column.

Input File		Output
1	5	Simulation Begins
2	5	Processing an arrival event at time: 1
4	5	Processing an arrival event at time: 2
20	5	Processing an arrival event at time: 4
22	5	Processing a departure event at time: 6
24	5	Processing a departure event at time: 11
26	5	Processing a departure event at time: 16
28	5	Processing an arrival event at time: 20
30	5	Processing an arrival event at time: 22
88	3	Processing an arrival event at time: 24
		Processing a departure event at time: 25
		Processing an arrival event at time: 26
		Processing an arrival event at time: 28
		Processing an arrival event at time: 30
		Processing a departure event at time: 30
		Processing a departure event at time: 35
		Processing a departure event at time: 40
		Processing a departure event at time: 45
		Processing a departure event at time: 50
		Processing an arrival event at time: 88
		Processing a departure event at time: 91
		Simulation Ends

```
Final Statistics:
    Total number of people processed: 10
Average amount of time spent waiting: 5.6
```

7. Modify and expand the event-driven simulation program that you wrote in Programming Problem 6. Here are a few suggestions:

   a. Add an operation that displays the event list, and use it to check your hand trace in Exercise 7.

   b. Add some statistics to the simulation. For example, compute the maximum wait in line, the average length of the line, and the maximum length of the line.

   c. Modify the simulation so that it accounts for three tellers, each with a distinct line. You should keep in mind that there should be

      • Three queues, one for each teller

      • A rule that chooses a line when processing an arrival event (for example, enter the shortest line)

      • Three distinct departure events, one for each line

      • Rules for breaking ties in the event list

      Run both this simulation and the original simulation on several sets of input data. How do the statistics compare?

a. The bank is considering the following change: Instead of having three distinct lines (one for each teller), there will be a single line for the three tellers. The person at the front of the line will go to the first available teller. Modify the simulation of Part *c* to account for this variation. Run both simulations on several sets of input data. How do the various statistics compare (averages and maximums)? What can you conclude about having a single line as opposed to having distinct lines?

8. The people that run the Motor Vehicle Department (MVD) have a problem. They are concerned that people do not spend enough time waiting in lines to appreciate the privilege of owning and driving an automobile. The current arrangement is as follows:

- When people walk in the door, they must wait in a line to sign in.
- Once they have signed in, they are told either to stand in line for registration renewal or to wait until they are called for license renewal.
- Once they have completed their desired transaction, they must go and wait in line for the cashier.
- When they finally get to the front of the cashier's line, if they expect to pay by check, they are told that all checks must get approved. To do this, it is necessary to go to the check-approver's table and then reenter the cashier's line at the end.

Write an event-driven simulation to help the Motor Vehicle Department gather statistics.

Each line of input will contain

- A desired transaction code (L for license renewal, R for registration renewal)
- A method-of-payment code ($ for cash, C for check)
- An arrival time (integer)
- A name

Write out the specifics of each event (when, who, what, and so on). Then display these final statistics:

- The total number of license renewals and the average time spent in MVD (arrival until completion of payment) to renew a license
- The total number of registration renewals and the average time spent in MVD (arrival until completion of payment) to renew a registration

Incorporate the following details into your program:

- Define the following events: arrive, sign in, renew license, renew registration, and cope with the cashier (make a payment or find out about check approval).

- In the case of a tie, let the order of events be determined by the list of events just given—that is, arrivals have the highest priority.
- Assume that the various transactions take the following amounts of time:

Sign in	10 seconds
Renew license	90 seconds
Register automobile	60 seconds
See cashier (payment)	30 seconds
See cashier (check not approved)	10 seconds

- As ridiculous as it may seem, the people waiting for license renewal are called in alphabetical order. Note, however, that people are not pushed back once their transactions have started.
- For the sake of this simulation, you can assume that checks are approved instantly. Therefore, the rule for arriving at the front of the cashier's line with a check that has not been approved is to go to the back of the cashier's line with a check that has been approved.

8

Class Relationships

PREVIEW Java classes provide a way to enforce the walls of data abstraction by encapsulating an abstract data type's data and operations. An object-oriented approach, however, goes well beyond encapsulation. Inheritance and polymorphism allow you to derive new classes from existing classes. This chapter describes techniques that make collections of reusable software components possible. It also discusses some of the useful components that exist in the Java API and how they can be used. Realize that much more can and should be said about these techniques. Consider this chapter as an introduction to this material.

INHERITANCE REVISITED

When you think of inheritance, you might imagine a bequest of one million dollars from some long-lost wealthy relative. In the object-oriented world, however, **inheritance** describes the ability of a class to derive properties from a previously defined class. These properties are like the genetic characteristics you received from your parents: Some traits are the same, some are similar but different, and some are new.

A class can derive the behavior and structure of another class

Inheritance, in fact, is a relationship among classes. One class can derive the behavior and structure of another class. For example, Figure 8-1 illustrates some relationships among various timepieces. Digital clocks, for example, include the clock in the dashboard of your car, the clock on the sign of the downtown bank, and the clock on your microwave oven.

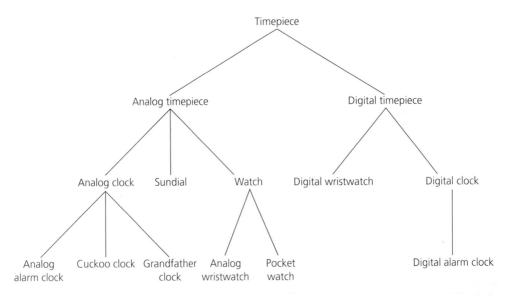

Figure 8-1

Inheritance: Relationships among timepieces

All digital clocks have the same underlying structure and perform operations such as

```
Set the time
Advance the time
Display the time
```

A digital alarm clock is a digital clock that also has alarm methods, such as

A digital alarm clock is a digital clock

```
Set the alarm
Enable the alarm
Sound the alarm
Silence the alarm
```

That is, a digital alarm clock has the structure and operations of a digital clock and, in addition, has an alarm and operations to manipulate the alarm.

You can think of the group of digital clocks and the group of digital alarm clocks as classes. The class of digital alarm clocks is a **subclass** or a **derived class** of the class of digital clocks. The class of digital clocks is a **superclass** or **base class** of the class of digital alarm clocks.

A subclass **inherits** all the members of its superclass, except the constructors. That is, a subclass has the data fields and methods of the superclass in addition to the data fields and methods it defines. A subclass can also have its own version of an inherited method. For example, according to Figure 8-1, a cuckoo clock is a **descendant**, or subclass, of an analog clock, like the one on a classroom wall. The cuckoo clock inherits the structure and behavior of the analog clock, but revises the way it reports the time each hour by adding a cuckoo.

A subclass inherits the members of its superclass

Inheritance enables you to **reuse** software components when you define a new class. For example, you can reuse your design and implementation of an analog clock when you design a cuckoo clock. A simpler example will demonstrate the details of such reuse and show you how Java implements inheritance.

Inheritance enables the reuse of existing classes

Chapter 3 spoke of volleyballs and soccer balls as objects. While designing a class of balls—*Ball*—you might decide that a ball is simply a sphere with a name. This realization is significant in that *Sphere*—the class of spheres—already exists. Thus, if you let *Sphere* be a superclass of *Ball*, you can implement *Ball* without reinventing the sphere. Toward that end, recall the definition of *Sphere* from Chapter 3:

Inheritance reduces the effort necessary to add features to an existing object

```java
public class Sphere {
  private double theRadius;

  public Sphere() {
    setRadius(1.0);
  } // end default constructor

  public Sphere(double initialRadius) {
    setRadius(initialRadius);
  } // end constructor
```

```
public boolean equals(Object rhs) {
  return ((rhs instanceof Sphere) &&
            (theRadius == ((Sphere)rhs).theRadius));
} // end equals

public void setRadius(double newRadius) {
  if (newRadius >= 0.0) {
    theRadius = newRadius;
  } // end if
} // end setRadius

public double radius() {
  return theRadius;
} // end radius

public double diameter() {
  return 2.0 * theRadius;
} // end diameter

public double circumference() {
  return Math.PI * diameter();
} // end circumference

public double area() {
  return 4.0 * Math.PI * theRadius * theRadius;
} // end area

public double volume() {
  return (4.0*Math.PI * Math.pow(theRadius, 3.0)) / 3.0;
} // end volume

public void displayStatistics() {
  System.out.println("\nRadius = " + radius() +
              "\nDiameter = " + diameter() +
              "\nCircumference = " + circumference() +
              "\nArea = " + area() +
              "\nVolume = " + volume());
} // end displayStatistics
} // end Sphere
```

The subclass *Ball* will inherit all the members of the class *Sphere*—except the constructor—and define additional methods and data fields. The *Ball* class could add:

A subclass can add new members to those it inherits

- A data field that names the ball
- Methods to access this name and set this name

- A method to alter an existing ball's radius and name
- A revised method *displayStatistics* to display the ball's name in addition to its statistics as a sphere

You can add as many new members to a subclass as you like. Although you cannot revise a superclass's private data fields and should not reuse their names, you can **override** methods in the superclass. A method in a subclass overrides a method in the superclass if the two methods have the same declarations. Here, the class *Ball* overrides *displayStatistics*. Figure 8-2 illustrates the relationship between *Sphere* and *Ball*.

A subclass can override an inherited method of its superclass

You can declare *Ball* as follows:

```
public class Ball extends Sphere {
   private String theName;  // the ball's name

   // constructors:
   public Ball() {
   // Creates a ball with radius 1.0 and
   // name "unknown".
      setName("unknown");
   }  // end default constructor

   public Ball(double initialRadius, String initialName) {
   // Creates a ball with radius initialRadius and
   // name initialName.
```

*This constructor calls **Sphere**'s default constructor implicitly*

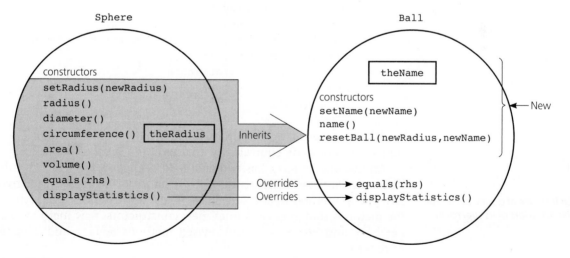

Figure 8-2

The subclass **Ball** inherits members of the superclass **Sphere** and overrides and adds methods

```
          super(initialRadius);
          setName(initialName);
       }  // end constructor

       // additional or revised operations:
       public boolean equals(Object rhs) {
          return ((rhs instanceof Ball) &&
                  (radius() == ((Ball)rhs).radius()) &&
                  (theName.compareTo(((Ball)rhs).theName)==0) );
       }  // end equals

       public String name() {
       // Determines the name of a ball.
          return theName;
       }  // end name

       public void setName(String newName) {
       // Sets (alters) the name of an existing ball.
          theName = newName;
       }  // end setName

       public void resetBall(double newRadius, String newName) {
       // Sets (alters) the radius and name of an existing
       // ball to newRadius and newName, respectively.
          setRadius(newRadius);
          setName(newName);
       }  // end resetBall

       public void displayStatistics() {
       // Displays the statistics of a ball.
          System.out.print("\nStatistics for a "+ name());
          super.displayStatistics();
       }  // end displayStatistics

    }  // end Ball
```

Adding *extends Sphere* after *class Ball* indicates that *Sphere* is a superclass of *Ball* or, equivalently, that *Ball* is a subclass of *Sphere*.

An instance of *Ball* has two data fields—*theRadius*, which is inherited, and *theName*, which is new. An instance of a subclass can invoke any public method in the superclass. Thus, an instance of *Ball* has all the methods that *Sphere* defines; new constructors; new methods *name*, *setName*, and *resetBall*; and revised methods *equals* and *displayStatistics*.

An instance of a subclass has all the behaviors of its superclass

A subclass cannot access the private members of the superclass directly, even though they are inherited. Inheritance does not imply access. After all, you can inherit a locked vault but not be able to open it. In the current example, the data field *theRadius* of *Sphere* is private, so

A subclass inherits private members from the superclass, but cannot access them directly

you can reference it only within the definition of *Sphere* and not within the definition of *Ball*. However, *Ball* can use *Sphere*'s public methods *setRadius* and *radius* to set or obtain the value of *theRadius* indirectly.

Within the implementation of *Ball*, you can use the methods that *Ball* inherits from *Sphere*. For example, the new method *resetBall* calls the inherited method *setRadius*. Also, *Ball*'s *displayStatistics* calls the inherited version of *displayStatistics*, which you indicate by writing *super.displayStatistics()*. The word *super* represents the object reference for the superclass and is necessary to differentiate between the two versions of the method. Thus, you can access a superclass method, even though it has been overridden, by using the *super* reference. *A subclass's methods can call the superclass's public methods*

In the version of *displayStatistics* in the *Ball* class, the subclass partially overrides the superclass version of the method. The subclass version calls the superclass version of the method and performs additional tasks as well.

Clients of a subclass can invoke the public members of the superclass. For example, if you write *Clients of a subclass can invoke the superclass's public methods*

```
Ball myBall = new Ball(5.0, "Volleyball");
```

myBall.diameter() returns *myBall*'s diameter, 10.0 (2 times *myBall*'s radius), by using the method *diameter* that *Ball* inherits from *Sphere*. If a new method has the same name as a superclass method—*displayStatistics*, for example—instances of the new class will use the new method, while instances of the superclass will use the original method. Therefore, if *mySphere* is an instance of *Sphere*, the call *mySphere.displayStatistics()* will invoke *Sphere*'s *displayStatistics*, whereas *myBall.displayStatistics()* will invoke *Ball*'s *displayStatistics*, as Figure 8-3 illustrates.

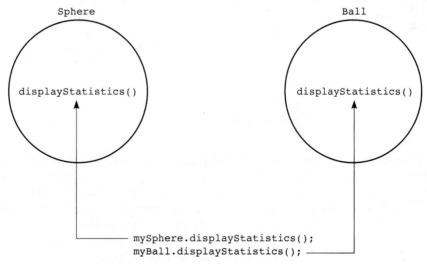

Figure 8-3

An object invokes the correct version of a method.

Finally, note that before any constructor in the subclass is executed, the default constructor (the constructor with no parameters) of the superclass will be executed unless you've specified an alternative constructor from the superclass. To call an alternative constructor, invoke the method with the arguments for the superclass constructor you want to use. For example, the class *Ball* constructor *Ball(double initialRadius, String initial-Name)* calls the single-parameter constructor *Sphere(double initial-Radius)* by using the statement *super(initialRadius)*. This call must appear as the first statement of the subclass's constructor.

Because the default constructor for the class *Ball* does not specify an alternative constructor, the *Sphere* constructor with no parameters is automatically called. Hence, if an instance of the class *Ball* is created using the following statement:

```
Ball myBall = new Ball();
```

myBall will have a radius of 1.0 and *"unknown"* as its name.

Java Packages

Java **packages** provide a way to group related classes together. To create a package, you place a *package* statement at the top of each class file that is part of the package. For example, Java source files that are part of a drawing package would include the following line at the top of the file (Java package names usually begin with a lowercase letter):

```
package drawingPackage;
```

*To include a class in a package, begin the class's source file with a **package** statement*

Just as you must use the same name for both a Java class and the file that contains the class, you must use the same name for a package and the directory that contains all the classes in the package. Thus, the source files for the drawing package must be contained in a directory called *drawingPackage*.

Place the files that contain a package's classes in the same directory

When declaring classes within a package, the keyword *public* must appear in front of the *class* keyword to make the class available to clients of the package. If the drawing package contains a class *Palette*, the source file for *Palette* begins as follows:

```
package drawingPackage;
public class Palette {
    ...
```

Access to a package's classes can be public or restricted

Omitting the keyword *public* will make the class available only to other classes within the package. Sometimes, such restricted access is desirable.

When a class is publicly available within a package, it can also be used as a superclass for any new class, even those appearing in other packages. This is actually done often within the Java API. For example, the exception class *java.lang.RuntimeException* is the superclass for the class *java.util.NoSuchElementException*.

A package can contain other packages as well. If *shapePackage* is a package in *drawingPackage*, the directory for *shapePackage* must be a subdirectory of the *drawingPackage* directory. The package name consists of the hierarchy of package names, separated by periods. For example, if the Java source file for the class *Sphere* is part of *shapePackage*, the following line must appear at the top of the file *Sphere.java*:

> **package** drawingPackage.shapePackage;

You already use packages in your programs when you place an *import* statement in your code. When you write a statement such as

> **import** java.io.*;

Using a package

you indicate to the compiler that you want to use classes in the package *java.io*. The * is a way to indicate that you might use any class in *java.io*, but if you know the specific class from the *java.io* package that you plan to use, you replace the * with the name of that class. For example, the statement

> **import** java.io.DataStream;

indicates that you will use the class *DataStream* from the package *java.io*.

If you omit the package declaration from the source file for a class, the class is added to a default, unnamed package. If all the classes in a group are declared this way, they are all considered to be within this same unnamed package and hence do not require an *import* statement. But if you are developing a package, and you want to use a class that is contained in the unnamed package, you will need to import the class. In this case, since the package has no name, the class name itself is sufficient in the *import* statement.

Java Access Modifiers

The keywords *public* and *private* are called **access modifiers**. They are used to control the visibility of the members of a class. When no access modifier is specified on a member declaration, the member is visible only to classes in the same package. In addition to the *public* and *private* access modifiers, the *protected* access modifier allows a class designer to hide the members from a class's clients but make them available to a subclass or to another class within the same package. That is, a subclass can reference the protected members of its superclass directly, but clients of the superclass or subclass cannot. Also, classes within the same package can access protected members directly.

A class with no access modifier is available to other classes within the same package

For example, *Sphere* has a private field *theRadius*, which the subclass *Ball* cannot reference directly. If, instead, you declared *theRadius* as protected, the class *Ball* would be able to access *theRadius* directly. Any other classes within the same package would also be able to access *theRadius* directly. Clients of *Ball* or *Sphere*, however, would not have direct access to *theRadius*. Figure 8-4 illustrates public, private, protected, and package (default) access for members of a class.

Figure 8-4

Access to public, protected, package access, and private members of a class by a client and a subclass

In general, a class's data fields should be private

As a general stylistic guideline, you should make all data fields of a class private and, if desired, provide indirect access to them by defining methods that are either public or protected. Although a class's public members are available to anyone, its protected members are available exclusively to either its own methods, members of other classes in the same package, or the methods of a subclass. The following summary distinguishes among the access modifiers for members of a class:

KEY CONCEPTS

Membership Categories of a Class

1. Public members can be used by anyone.

2. Members declared without an access modifier (the default) are available to methods of the class and methods of other classes in the same package.

3. Private members can be used only by methods of the class.

4. Protected members can be used only by methods of the class, methods of other classes in the same package, and methods of the subclasses.

Is-a and Has-a Relationships

As you just saw, inheritance provides for superclass/subclass relationships among classes. Other relationships are also possible. When designing new classes from existing ones, it is important to identify their relationship so that you can determine whether to use inheritance. Two basic kinds of relationships are possible: *is-a* and *has-a*.

Is-a relationships. Earlier in this chapter, we used inheritance to derive the class *Ball* from *Sphere*. You should use inheritance only when an *is-a* relationship exists between the superclass and the subclass. In this example, a ball *is a* sphere, as Figure 8-5 illustrates. That is, whatever is true of the superclass *Sphere* is also true of the subclass *Ball*. Wherever you can use an object of type *Sphere*, you can also use an object of type *Ball*. This feature is called **object type compatibility**. In general, a subclass is type-compatible with all of its superclasses. Thus, you can use an instance of a subclass instead of an instance of its superclass, but not the other way around.

Inheritance should imply an is-a relationship

You can use an instance of a subclass anywhere you can use an instance of the superclass

The object type of an actual argument in a call to a method can be a subclass of the object type of the corresponding formal parameter. As you've seen in many of the implementations of ADTs presented earlier, you can use the class *Object* as the type of the formal parameter, and since all classes are derived from the *Object* class, you can use any object type as the actual argument.

As another example, suppose your program uses *Sphere* and *Ball* and contains the following static method:

```
public static void displayDiameter(Sphere thing) {
    System.out.println("The diameter is "
                        + thing.diameter() + ".");
}  // end displayDiameter
```

If you define *mySphere* and *myBall* as

```
Sphere mySphere = new Sphere(2.0);
Ball myBall = new Ball(5.0, "Volleyball");
```

the following calls to *displayDiameter* are legal:

```
displayDiameter(mySphere);  // mySphere's diameter
displayDiameter(myBall);    // myBall's diameter
```

Figure 8-5

A ball "is a" sphere

The first call is unremarkable because both the actual argument *mySphere* and the formal parameter *thing* have the same data type. The second call is more interesting: The type of the actual argument *myBall* is a subclass of the data type of the formal parameter *thing*. Because a ball is a sphere, it can behave like a sphere. That is, *myBall* can perform sphere behaviors, so you can use *myBall* anywhere you can use *mySphere*.

Since a ball is a sphere, you can use it anywhere you can use a sphere

***Has-a* relationships.**   A ball-point pen *has a* ball as its point, as Figure 8-6 illustrates. Although you would want to use *Ball* in your definition of a class *Pen*, you should not use inheritance, because a pen is not a ball. In fact, you do not use inheritance at all to implement a *has-a* relationship. Instead, you can define a data field *point*—whose type is *Ball*—within the class *Pen*, as follows:

If the relationship between two classes is not is-a, you should not use inheritance

```
public class Pen {
    private Ball point;
    ...
}  // end Pen
```

An instance of *Pen* has, or *contains*, an instance of *Ball*. Thus, another name for the *has-a* relationship is **containment**.

You have already seen two other examples of the *has-a* relationship among classes in the preceding two chapters: Chapter 6 presented an implementation of *StackInterface* that used the ADT list to represent the items in a stack, while Chapter 7 used a similar implementation for the ADT queue. The class *StackListBased*, for example, contains a private data field *list* of type *ListReferenceBased*. That is, an instance of *StackListBased* has, or contains, an instance of *ListReferenceBased* that manages the stack's items.

The *has-a* relationship between two classes is possible when inheritance is inappropriate. Later, this chapter implements the ADT sorted list by using the two relationships just discussed.

Figure 8-6

A pen "has a" or "contains a" ball

class Pen

class Ball

DYNAMIC BINDING AND ABSTRACT CLASSES

As you saw earlier, if *mySphere* is an instance of *Sphere* and *myBall* is an instance of *Ball*, *mySphere.displayStatistics()* invokes *Sphere's* version of *displayStatistics*, whereas *myBall.displayStatistics()* invokes *Ball's* version of *displayStatistics*. (See Figure 8-3.) Suppose, however, that the following statements are executed:

```
Ball myBall = new Ball(1.25, "golfball");
Sphere mySphere = myBall;
mySphere.displayStatistics();
```

Since *mySphere* actually references an instance of *Ball*, the *Ball* version of *displayStatistics* is executed. Thus, the appropriate version of a method is decided at execution time, instead of at compilation time, based on the type of object referenced. This situation is called **late binding**, or **dynamic binding**, and a method such as *displayStatistics* is called **polymorphic**. We also say that *Ball's* version of *displayStatistics* **overrides** *Sphere's* version.

A polymorphic method has multiple meanings

We will now examine a more subtle example of late binding. Suppose you wanted the class *Ball* to have a method *area* that behaved differently than *Sphere's* area. Just as *Ball* overrides *displayStatistics*, it could override *area* to compute, for example, the ball's cross-sectional area. Thus, you would add

```
public double area() {
   double r = radius();
   return Math.PI * r * r;  // Math.PI is a constant
} // end area
```

as a public member of the class *Ball*, overriding *Sphere's* area. Consider

```
public class Sphere {
   · · ·       // everything as before
 public double area() {  // surface area
   return 4.0 * Math.PI * theRadius * theRadius;
 } // end area

 public void displayStatistics() {
   System.out.println("\nRadius = " + radius()
           + "\nDiameter = " + diameter()
           + "\nCircumference = " + circumference()
           + "\nArea = " + area()
           + "\nVolume = " + volume());
 } // end displayStatistics

 · · ·

} // end Sphere
```

```
public class Ball extends Sphere {
    · · · // everything as before, except
          // displayStatistics is omitted
          // and area is revised:
  public double area() {
    double r = radius();
    return Math.PI * r * r;
  }  // end area
  · · ·
}  // end Ball
```

Now when an instance of *Sphere* calls *displayStatistics*, *display-Statistics* will call *Sphere*'s *area* (Figure 8-7a), yet when an instance of *Ball* calls *displayStatistics*, *displayStatistics* will call *Ball*'s *area* (Figure 8-7b). Thus, the meaning of *displayStatistics* depends on the type of object that invokes it.

You can control whether a subclass can override a superclass method

The designer of a superclass does have some control over whether a subclass is allowed to override a superclass method. If the field modifier *final* is specified in the method definition (typically after other field modifiers such as *public* and *static*), the method cannot be overridden by a subclass. On the other hand, the field modifier *abstract* requires the subclass to override the method. Abstract methods are discussed in more detail in the next section.

Methods that are **final** *or* **static** *use static binding*

When a method is defined as *final*, the compiler can determine which form of a method to use at compilation time—as opposed to at execution time. This situation is called **early binding**, or **static binding.** Methods declared *static* also use static binding, since only one version of the method is available for all classes.

Overloading methods. When you override a method, you create a method that has the same name and same set of parameters as the original method. Sometimes it is convenient to define another method with the same name as the first but with a different set of parameters. Such a method **overloads** the first method. Frequently you overload constructors so that each constructor has a different set of parameters. Often the choice of which constructor to use depends on the information available when you create an instance. Some of the constructors require fewer parameters and will set some of the data fields to default values.

For another example of overloading, consider the class *Ball* and the method *resetBall*, defined as follows:

```
public void resetBall(double newRadius, String newName) {
// Sets (alters) the radius and name of an existing
// ball to newRadius and newName, respectively.
  setRadius(newRadius);
  setName(newName);
}  // end resetBall
```

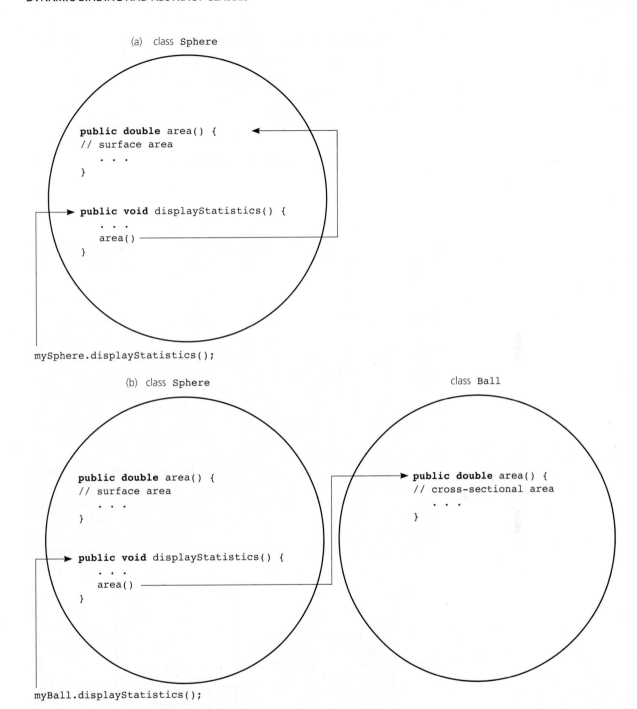

Figure 8-7

area is overridden: (a) ***mySphere.displayStatistics()*** calls ***area*** in
Sphere; (b) ***myBall.displayStatistics()*** calls ***area*** in ***Ball***

You could define two other methods to reset the data fields:

```
public void resetBall(double newRadius) {
// Sets (alters) the radius of an existing
// ball to newRadius.
  setRadius(newRadius);
}  // end resetBall

public void resetBall(String newName) {
// Sets (alters) the name of an existing
// ball to newName.
  setName(newName);
}  // end resetBall
```

All three methods have the same name but different sets of parameters. The arguments in each call to *resetBall* determine which version of the method will be used.

Abstract Classes

Suppose you have a videocassette recorder (VCR) for your videotapes and a Walkman®—which we will call an audiocassette recorder, or ACR—for your audio tapes. ACRs and VCRs share several characteristics. Both devices use magnetic tape in a cassette. You can insert, eject, play, record, fast-forward, rewind, and stop such cassettes. Some of these operations are essentially the same for both devices, while others—in particular, the play and record methods—are different but similar. You could say that a VCR is like an ACR that also plays and records video material.

If ACR and VCR were classes, VCR could be a **subclass** of ACR. An instance of VCR has all of ACR's members, but overrides the play and record operations to suit videotapes, as Figure 8-8 illustrates. VCR could also add new operations, such as one to set the recording time.

Even though the ACR's play and record operations differ from those of the VCR, these operations all transport the tape in a forward direction

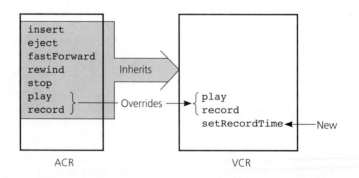

Figure 8-8
VCR is a subclass of ACR

at a slow speed. ACRs and VCRs also have some other operations in common. Recognizing these facts, you can define another class—the tape transport—as a basis for ACR and VCR. It has the following operations:

Tape transport operations

```
insert()
// Inserts a cassette into the transport.

eject()
// Ejects a cassette from the transport.

fastForward()
// Moves the tape forward at a high speed.

rewind()
// Moves the tape backward at a high speed.

goForward()
// Moves the tape forward at a slow speed.

stop()
// Stops the tape.
```

Except for *goForward*, ACRs and VCRs also have these tape transport operations. Although ACRs and VCRs do not have a *goForward* operation, their *play* and *record* operations could certainly use it. Thus, we have the following observations:

- An ACR is a tape transport that plays and records sound.
- A VCR is an ACR that also plays and records video material.

In terms of classes, the class tape transport is the superclass for the class ACR, which in turn is the superclass for the class VCR, as Figure 8-9 illustrates.

Do you really want instances of the tape transport class? Although you might find most of the tape transport's operations useful—after all, the tape transport is a tape rewinder, if you omit the *goForward* operation—the *goForward* operation simply moves the tape without recording or playing, making it a feature without consumer demand! We can conclude, therefore, that the tape transport is a class without instances that forms the basis of other classes.

An **abstract class** has no instances and is used only as the basis of other classes. Thus, the tape transport class is an abstract class. In Java, you declare an abstract class by including the keyword *abstract* in the class definition.

A class that contains at least one abstract method is an abstract class

An abstract class, like other classes, can contain both data fields and methods. Although an abstract class contains the methods and data fields common to all of its subclasses, some of its methods might have their implementations deferred to the subclasses. In these cases, you also declare the methods themselves to be abstract by including the field modifier *abstract* in the method definition. An abstract method does not have a body; instead, the method heading ends with a semicolon. For example, the following is a declaration for an abstract method:

```
public abstract void displayStatistics();
```

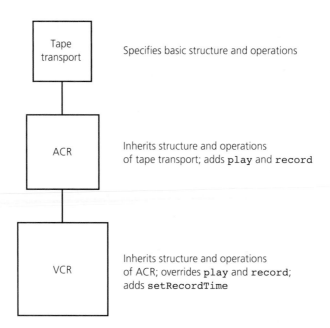

Figure 8-9

ACR has an abstract class (tape transport) and a derived class (VCR)

*An abstract class has subclasses
but no instances*

Any class that contains at least one abstract method must itself be declared abstract. Any subclass that fails to implement all of the abstract methods in its superclass must also be declared as an abstract class.

Another example.   The previous classes *Sphere* and *Ball* describe points that are equidistant from the origin of a three-dimensional coordinate system. The following class, *EquidistantShape*, which declares operations to set and return the distance of a point from the origin, could be an abstract class of *Sphere*:

*An abstract class of **Sphere***

```
public abstract class EquidistantShape {
  private double theRadius;

  public void setRadius(double newRadius) {
    if (newRadius >= 0.0) {
      theRadius = newRadius;
    }  // end if
  }  // end setRadius

  public double radius() {
    return theRadius;
  }  // end radius
```

```
    public abstract void displayStatistics();
} // end EquidistantShape
```

This class declares a private data field *theRadius* with the public methods *setRadius* and *radius* to access *theRadius*. The class also contains one abstract method *displayStatistics*.

Now you could define the class *Sphere* as a subclass of *Equidistant-Shape*:

```
public class Sphere extends EquidistantShape {
    public Sphere() {
        setRadius(1.0);
    } // end default constructor

    public Sphere(double initialRadius) {
        setRadius(initialRadius);
    } // end constructor

    // Implementation of abstract method
    public void displayStatistics() {
        System.out.println("\nRadius = " + radius()
                    + "\nDiameter = " + diameter()
                    + "\nCircumference = " + circumference()
                    + "\nArea = " + area()
                    + "\nVolume = " + volume());
    } // end displayStatistics

    // Remaining methods for class appear here
    . . .

} // end Sphere
```

By including the abstract method *displayStatistics* in the abstract class *EquidistantShape*, you force some subclass—like *Sphere*—to implement it. The class *Ball* can now be a subclass of *Sphere*, just as it appeared earlier in this chapter.

Note that *theRadius* is a private data field of *EquidistantShape* instead of *Sphere*. This means that subclasses of *Sphere* will be unable to access *theRadius* directly by name. Thus, the class *EquidistantShape* must contain the methods *setRadius* and *radius*, and you must provide default implementations for the subclasses to inherit. Alternatively, you could define *theRadius* to be a protected data field of *EquidistantShape*, enabling the subclass to both access *theRadius* directly and define *setRadius* and *radius*. Although data fields are generally private, a protected data field within an abstract class is reasonable, since the class is always a superclass of another class. That is, an abstract class has no other purpose but to form the basis of another class.

An abstract class can provide a constructor, but the constructors cannot be abstract. The key points about abstract classes are summarized as follows:

Abstract Classes

1. An abstract class is used only as the basis for subclasses and thus defines a minimum set of methods and data fields for its subclasses.

2. An abstract class has no instances.

3. An abstract class should, in general, omit implementations except for the methods that provide access to private data fields or that express functionality common to all of the subclasses.

4. A class that contains at least one abstract method must be declared as an abstract class.

5. A subclass of an abstract class must be declared abstract if it does not provide implementations for all abstract methods in the superclass.

Java Interfaces Revisited

Inheritance is one way to have a common set of methods (or common behavior) available for a group of classes. Inheritance also allows the subclasses to inherit the structure of the superclass. In some instances, however, it is only the behavior that is of interest. Java interfaces provide another mechanism for specifying common behavior for a set of (perhaps unrelated) classes.

A Java interface specifies the common behavior of a set of classes

You have already seen how to use Java interfaces to specify the methods for a class. The methods were then implemented by using a variety of techniques, including array-based and reference-based implementations. Clients of the class could use one of these implementations. To facilitate moving from one implementation to another, you can declare references to the class by using the interface definition instead of the class definition. For example, the class *StackArrayBased* implements *StackInterface*. A client of the ADT stack could contain the following statement:

A client can reference a class's interface instead of the class itself

```
StackInterface stack = new StackArrayBased();
```

Since *stack* has the type *StackInterface*, you can use only methods that appear in the interface definition with *stack*—for example, *stack.pop()*. The interface definition should also be used whenever the stack appears as a formal parameter in a method. If you do this throughout the client, all you will need to do to move to the reference-based implementation will be to change the places where instances of the stack are created. For example, the previous definition of *stack* would change to

```
StackInterface stack = new StackReferenceBased();
```

and method calls that adhere to the interface, such as *stack.pop()*, would continue to work in the client.

An interface specifies behaviors that are common to a group of classes

As was mentioned earlier, another common use of interfaces is to specify behavior that is common to a group of unrelated classes. For example, you could define an interface called *AnimateInterface*, as follows:

```
public interface AnimateInterface {
  public void move(int x, int y);
  public void paint();
}  // end AnimateInterface
```

The intent is to provide a common set of methods needed for screen animation. Thus, many different classes, such as the class *Ball*, could implement this interface so that instances of *Ball* could be animated on the screen. If the class *Ball* does not implement all of the methods in the interface, with the intent that a subclass will implement the missing methods, the *Ball* class must be declared as abstract.

Just as you can use inheritance to derive new classes, you can use inheritance to derive new interfaces, often called **subinterfaces**. The Java API provides many interfaces and has many examples of subinterfaces as well. For example, *java.util.Iterator* is an interface that specifies operations for iterating through a collection of objects. An **iterator** is a class that you use to provide access to another class that contains many objects (sometimes referred to as a container class). Thus, the iterator class is a separate class that implements one of the iterator interfaces. The *java.util.Iterator* interface is defined as follows:

You can use inheritance to define a subinterface

An iterator class provides access to another class

```
public interface Iterator {
  public boolean hasNext();
  // Returns true if the iteration has more elements.

  public Object next()
              throws java.util.NoSuchElementException;
  // Returns the next element in the iteration.

  public void remove()
              throws UnsupportedOperationException,
                     IllegalStateException;
  // Removes from the underlying collection the last
  // element returned by the iterator (optional operation).
}  // end Iterator
```

Notice that one of the operations, *remove*, can throw the exception *UnsupportedOperationException*. The expectation is that the *remove* operation will simply throw this exception if the operation is not to be available in the class that implements the interface.

The Java API also has a subinterface of *Iterator*, called *ListIterator*:

```
interface ListIterator extends Iterator {
  public void add(Object o) throws
                  UnsupportedOperationException,
                  ClassCastException,
                  IllegalArgumentException;
```

```
// Inserts the specified element into the list
// (optional operation).

public boolean hasPrevious();
// Returns true if this list iterator has more
// elements when traversing the list in the reverse
// direction.

public Object previous()
            throws java.util.NoSuchElementException;
// Returns the previous element in the list.

public int nextIndex();
// Returns the index of the element that would be
// returned by a subsequent call to next.

public int previousIndex();
// Returns the index of the element that would be
// returned by a subsequent call to previous.

public void set(Object o);
// Replaces the last element returned by next or
// previous with the specified element (optional
// operation).
}   // end ListIterator
```

The methods *hasNext*, *next*, and *remove* are inherited from *Iterator*. Classes that implement the *ListIterator* interface also implement the *Iterator* interface, since *ListIterator* is derived from *Iterator*. The list example in the next section will demonstrate an implementation of this interface in creating an iterator for a list.

THE ADTs LIST AND SORTED LIST REVISITED

Chapter 3 introduced the ADT list and the ADT sorted list. As you know, these lists have some characteristics and operations in common. For example, each ADT can determine its length, determine whether it is empty, and remove all items from the list. Both ADTs also provide a retrieval operation that returns an object at a given index position in the list. You can organize such commonalities into an interface, which can be the basis of these and other list operations. For example,

An interface for lists and sorted lists

```
public interface BasicListInterface {
    public int size();
    public boolean isEmpty();
    public void removeAll();
    public Object get(int index)
                throws ListIndexOutOfBoundsException;
}   // end BasicListInterface
```

THE ADTS LIST AND SORTED LIST REVISITED

All of the members of *BasicListInterface* represent the operations common to both the ADT list and the ADT sorted list. As with classes, inheritance can be used to derive new interfaces. For example, here is a new interface definition based upon *BasicListInterface* for the ADT list presented in Chapter 3:

An interface for a list

```
public interface ListInterface extends BasicListInterface {
  public void add(int index, Object item)
                  throws ListIndexOutOfBoundsException;

  public void remove(int index)
                  throws ListIndexOutOfBoundsException;
}  // end ListInterface
```

Because the class *ListArrayBased* in Chapter 3 and the class *ListReferenceBased* in Chapter 4 are consistent with this interface, their implementation is omitted here.

Implementation of a List Iterator

Because the ADT list contains a group of like objects, you can develop an iterator class by implementing the *java.util.ListIterator* interface. The basic operations needed to iterate through the list are provided in the interface *BasicListInterface*, and so you can use it as the object type for the list in the iterator implementation. Note that *java.util.ListIterator* starts the list indexing at zero, so if a call is made to *nextIndex* immediately after the iterator is created (or at the beginning of the list), it returns zero. The method *previousIndex* returns –1 when the iterator is at the beginning of the list. When the iterator has reached the end of the list, the method *nextIndex* returns the size of the list. Here is the implementation of *BasicListIterator*:

```
public class BasicListIterator
                implements java.util.ListIterator {
  private BasicListInterface list;
  private int loc; // location of iterator in list

  public BasicListIterator(BasicListInterface list) {
    this.list = list;
    loc = 0;
  }  // end constructor

  protected BasicListInterface getList() {
  // This method will be needed by subclasses to access
  // the private data field list.
    return list;
  }  // end getList

  protected void setLoc(int newLoc) {
  // This method will be needed by subclasses to set
```

```java
// the private data field loc.   The method nextIndex
// can be used to get the loc value.
  loc = newLoc;
}   // end setLoc

public boolean hasNext() {
// Returns true if this list iterator has more
// elements when traversing the list in the forward
// direction.
  return (loc < list.size());
}   // end hasNext

public Object next() throws java.util.NoSuchElementException {
// Returns the next element in the list.
  if (hasNext()) {
    Object item = list.get(loc+1);
    loc++;
    return item;
  }
  else {
    throw new java.util.NoSuchElementException();
  }   // end if
}   // end next

public boolean hasPrevious() {
// Returns true if this list iterator has more
// elements when traversing the list in the reverse
// direction.
  return (loc > 0);
}   // end hasPrevious

public Object previous() throws java.util.NoSuchElementException {
// Returns the previous element in the list.
  if (hasPrevious()) {
    Object item = list.get(loc);
    loc--;
    return item;
  }
  else {
    throw new java.util.NoSuchElementException();
  }   // end if
}   // end previous

public int nextIndex() {
// Returns the index of the element that would be
// returned by a subsequent call to next. Returns
// list size if the list iterator is at the end of
// the list.
```

```
      return loc;
   }  // end nextIndex


   public int previousIndex() {
   // Returns the index of the element that would be
   // returned by a subsequent call to previous.
   // Returns -1 if the list iterator is at the
   // beginning of the list.
      return loc-1;
   }  // end previousIndex


   public void add(Object o) throws UnsupportedOperationException {
   // Inserts the specified element into the list
   // (optional operation).
      throw new UnsupportedOperationException();
   }  // end add


   public void remove() throws UnsupportedOperationException {
   // Removes from the underlying collection the last
   // element returned by the iterator (optional
   // operation).
      throw new UnsupportedOperationException();
   }  // end remove


   public void set(Object o) throws UnsupportedOperationException {
   // Replaces the last element returned by next or
   // previous with the specified element (optional
   // operation).
      throw new UnsupportedOperationException();
   }  // end set


}  // end BasicListIterator
```

The implementation of *BasicListIterator* uses the object type *BasicListInterface*. Because *BasicListInterface* does not contain the methods *add* and *remove*, no operations are available for manipulating the contents of the list to support the iterator methods *add*, *remove*, and *set*. If these methods are not implemented in the class *BasicListIterator*, you would need to declare *BasicListIterator* as abstract. But since this iterator class could be used with any class that implements *BasicListInterface*, it makes more sense for the class not to be abstract. Thus, simple implementations that throw *UnsupportedOperationException* are provided for the methods *add*, *remove*, and *set*.

Since *ListInterface* does provide operations for adding items to and removing items from a list, you can create an iterator that supports the operations *add*, *remove*, and *set*. Note that the behavior of an iterator is unspecified if the underlying collection is modified while the iteration is

*A list iterator can support the operations **add**, **remove**, and **set***

in progress in any way other than by calling the *remove*, *set*, and *add* methods provided by the iterator. The new iterator class is a subclass of *BasicListIterator* and overrides the inherited methods *add, remove,* and *set*. The iterator asumes that the actual list to be iterated supports the interface *ListInterface*. The method *add* follows; *remove* and *set* are left as a programming exercise.

```java
public class MyListIterator extends BasicListIterator {

  public MyListIterator(ListInterface list) {
    super(list);
  }  // end constructor


  public void add(Object item) throws UnsupportedOperationException {
  // Inserts the specified element into the list.
  // The element is inserted immediately before
  // the next element that would be returned by next, if
  // any, and after the next element that would be returned
  // by previous, if any. (If the list contains no elements,
  // the new element becomes the sole element on the list.)
  // The new element is inserted before the implicit cursor:
  // a subsequent call to next would be unaffected, and a
  // subsequent call to previous would return the new
  // element. (This call increases by 1 the value that
  // would be returned by a call to nextIndex or
  // previousIndex.)
    ((ListInterface)getList()).add(nextIndex()+1, item);
    setLoc(nextIndex()+1);
  }  // end add


  public void remove() throws UnsupportedOperationException {
  // Removes from the underlying collection the last element
  // returned by the iterator (optional operation).
    // See Programming Problem 8.
  }  // end remove


  public void set(Object item) throws UnsupportedOperationException {
  // Replaces the last element returned by next or
  // previous with the specified element (optional
  // operation).
    // See Programming Problem 8.
  }  // end set
}  // end MyListIterator
```

Here is an example that demonstrates the use of an iterator:

```java
ListInterface names = new ListReferenceBased();
names.add(1, new String("Doug"));
```

```java
names.add(1, new String("Andrew"));
names.add(1, new String("Sarah"));
names.add(1, new String("Michael"));
names.add(1, new String("Frank"));
MyListIterator iter = new MyListIterator(names);
iter.add("Janet");  // adds Janet to beginning of list
iter.previous();  // moves iterator back one location
while (iter.hasNext())  {
   System.out.print("index: " + iter.nextIndex());
   System.out.println("   value: " + iter.next());
}  // end while
```

When you create a new instance of the iterator, you provide an instance of a class that implements *ListInterface* as an argument to its constructor. Values can be added to the list *names* by using the list operations directly—for example, *names.add*—or through the iterator, *iter.add*. Here is the output produced by the code segment just given:

```
index: 0     value: Janet
index: 1     value: Frank
index: 2     value: Michael
index: 3     value: Sarah
index: 4     value: Andrew
index: 5     value: Doug
```

Note that the iterator index starts at zero.

Implementations of the ADT Sorted List That Use the ADT List

Now suppose you want to define and implement a class for the ADT sorted list, whose operations are

```
createSortedList()
isEmpty()
size()
sortedAdd(newItem)
sortedRemove(anItem)
removeAll()
get(index)
locateIndex(anItem)
```

ADT sorted list operations

The method *createSortedList* is implemented as a constructor for the class. The methods *isEmpty*, *size*, *removeAll*, and *get* have already been specified in the interface *BasicListInterface*. The interface definition for the ADT sorted list extends *BasicListInterface* to include the other methods. The elements of the sorted list have one additional requirement: They must implement the *Comparable* interface, as discussed in Chapter 4, so that the sorted list can order the elements. Thus, we have

```
public interface SortedListInterface extends BasicListInterface {
  public void sortedAdd(Comparable newItem) throws ListException;
  public int locateIndex(Comparable anItem);
  public void sortedRemove(Comparable anItem) throws ListException;
} // end SortedListInterface
```

You could, of course, use an array or a linked list to implement a sorted list, but such an approach would force you to repeat much of the corresponding implementations of *ListArrayBased* and *ListReferenceBased*. Fortunately, you can avoid this repetition by using one of the previously defined classes, *ListReferenceBased* or *ListArrayBased*, to implement the class *SortedList*. For the purposes of this discussion, we will use the class *ListReferenceBased*, but *ListArrayBased* could also be used.

*You can reuse **ListArray-Based** or **ListReference-Based** to implement **SortedList***

Two approaches are possible by using the *is-a* and *has-a* relationships between the new class *SortedList* and the existing class *ListReferenceBased*. In most cases, one of the approaches will be best. However, we will use the sorted list to demonstrate both approaches.

A sorted list *is a* list.   Chapter 3 stated that the ADT list is simply a list of items that you reference by position number. If you maintained those items in sorted order, would you have a sorted list? Ignoring name differences, most operations for the ADT list *are* the same as the corresponding operations for the ADT sorted list. The insertion and deletion operations differ, however, and the ADT sorted list has an additional operation, *locateIndex*.

You can insert an item into a sorted list by first using *locateIndex* to determine the position in the sorted list where the new item belongs. You then use *ListReferenceBased*'s *add* method to insert the item into that position in the list. You use a similar approach to delete an item from a sorted list.

An is-a relationship implies inheritance

Thus, a sorted list *is a* list, so you can use inheritance. That is, the class *SortedList* can be a subclass of the class *ListReferenceBased*, inheriting *ListReferenceBased*'s members and implementing the additional methods specified in the interface *SortedListInterface*. Thus, we have the following:

```
public class SortedList extends ListReferenceBased
                              implements SortedListInterface{
  public SortedList() {
    // invokes default constructor of superclass
  } // end default constructor

  public void sortedAdd(Comparable newItem) {
  // Adds an item to the list.
  // Precondition: None.
  // Postcondition: The item is added to the list in
  // sorted order.
    int newPosition = locateIndex(newItem);
    add(newPosition, newItem);
  } // end sortedAdd
```

```
    public void sortedRemove(Comparable anItem)
                                      throws ListException {
// Removes an item from the list.
// Precondition: None.
// Postcondition: The item is removed from the list
// and the sorted order maintained.
      int position = locateIndex(anItem);
      if ((anItem.compareTo(get(position))==0) {
        remove(position);
    }
      else {
        throw new ListException("Sorted remove failed");
      }  // end if
    }  // end sortedRemove

    public int locateIndex(Comparable anItem) {
// Finds an item in the list.
// Precondition: None.
// Postcondition: If the item is in the list, its
// index position in the list is returned.  If the
// item is not in the list, the index of where it
// belongs in the list is returned.
      int index = 1;
      // Loop invariant: anItem belongs after all the
      // elements up to the element referenced by index
      while ( (index <= size()) &&
              (anItem.compareTo(get(index)) > 0 ) ) {
        ++index;
      }  // end while
      return index;
    }  // end locateIndex
  }  // end SortedList
```

Note that by carefully designing the method implementations, especially *locateIndex*, we do not need access to any of the private data fields of the class *ListReferenceBased*. This means that we could just as easily have used *ListArrayBased* as the superclass.

The class *SortedList* now has operations such as *isEmpty*, *size*, and *get*—which it inherits from *ListReferenceBased*—and *sortedAdd* and *sortedRemove*. Note also, however, that *SortedList* has inherited the *add* and *remove* methods from *ListReferenceBased*. The availability of all of the methods from the superclass may or may not be desirable. In this case, the *add* method could potentially destroy the sorted list by making inappropriate insertions into the sorted list. In general, there are two techniques that you can use to solve this problem:

1. You can override the unwanted method with one that provides the correct semantics.

2. You can override the unwanted method with one that simply raises an exception indicating that the method is not supported.

In the present situation, the first technique does not provide a satisfactory solution. The *add* method in the superclass *ListReferenceBased* has a parameter that designates the position of the insertion, whereas the *add* method in the subclass *SortedList* does not. Even if we change the name *sortedAdd* to *add*, the subclass's *add* could not override the superclass's *add*, because the two *add* methods have different sets of parameters.

The second technique, however, does provide a solution. The subclass overrides the superclass's *add* method with a method that throws an *UnsupportedOperationException*. For example, the subclass could contain the following method:

```java
public void add(int index, Object item)
                            throws UnsupportedOperationException {
   throw new UnsupportedOperationException();
}
```

When the *add* method is overridden in this way, the exception *UnsupportedOperationException* is thrown if an instance of *SortedList* invokes *add*.

One advantage of implementing the class *SortedList* using *SortedListInterface* is that the class *BasicListIterator* uses a list of type *BasicListInterface*. The interface *SortedListInterface* is a subinterface of *BasicListInterface*, so instances of *SortedList* are of type *BasicListInterface*. For example, if *sortedNames* is an instance of *SortedList*, you can declare an iterator for *sortedNames* as follows:

```java
BasicListIterator sortedIter = new
                    BasicListIterator(sortedNames);
```

and use it to iterate through the sorted list.

A sorted list *has a* list as a member.   If you do not have an *is-a* relationship between your new class and an existing class, inheritance is inappropriate. You may, however, be able to use an instance of the existing class to implement the new class. The following declaration of the class *SortedList has a* private data field that is an instance of *ListInterface* and that contains the items in the sorted list:

*An instance of **List-Interface** can implement the sorted list*

```java
public class SortedList implements SortedListInterface {
  private ListInterface aList;

// constructors:
  public sortedListClass() {
    aList = new ListReferenceBased();
  }  // end default constructor

// sorted list operations:
  public boolean isEmpty() {
    // To be implemented in Programming Problem 1
  }  // end isEmpty
```

```
   public int size() {
      // To be implemented in Programming Problem 1
   }  // end size


   public void sortedAdd(Comparable newItem) {
      int newPosition = locatePosition(newItem);
      aList.add(newPosition, newItem);
   }  // end sortedAdd


   public void sortedRemove(Comparable anItem) {
      // To be implemented in Programming Problem 1
   }  // end sortedRemove


   public Object get(int position) {
      // To be implemented in Programming Problem 1
   }  // end get


   public int locateIndex(Comparable anItem) {
      // To be implemented in Programming Problem 1
   }  // end locateIndex
}  // end SortedList
```

The data field *aList* is an instance of *ListInterface* and is a member of *SortedList*. The constructor and the *sortedAdd* method are implemented. The notation *aList.add* indicates an invocation to the insertion operation of the ADT list.

Programming Problem 1 at the end of this chapter asks you to complete this implementation. In doing so, you will realize that *locatePosition* needs *get* to access items in *aList*; that is, *ListInterface*'s implementation is hidden from *SortedList*. Notice also that a client of *SortedList* cannot access *aList* and has only the sorted list operations available.

THE ADVANTAGES OF AN OBJECT-ORIENTED APPROACH

The time that you expend on program design can increase when you use object-oriented programming. In addition, the solution that OOP techniques produce will typically be more general than is absolutely necessary to solve the problem at hand. The extra effort that OOP requires, however, is usually worth it.

To design a solution to a problem, you need to identify classes that fit the problem. More likely, you will want a family of related classes. This stage of the design process is time-consuming, particularly if you have no existing classes upon which to build. Once you have implemented a class, however, the implementation of each subclass proceeds more rapidly than if it did not inherit its superclass's methods. For example, the implementation of the previous class *SortedList* would have been much more

A family of related classes

Reuse already existing classes

time-consuming if we did not have the class *ListReferenceBased* on which to base it. Looking ahead, you can reuse previously implemented classes in future programs, either as is or with modifications that can include new classes derived from your existing ones. This reuse of classes can actually reduce the time requirements of an object-oriented design.

OOP also has a positive effect on other phases of the software life cycle, such as program maintenance and verification. You can make one modification to a superclass and affect all of its subclasses. Without inheritance, you would need to make the same change to many modules. In addition, you can add new features to a program by adding subclasses that do not affect their superclasses and, therefore, do not introduce errors into the rest of the program. You can also add a subclass that modifies its superclass's original behavior, even though that superclass was written and compiled long ago.

Program maintenance and verification are easier when you use inheritance

SUMMARY

1. A subclass inherits all members of its previously defined superclass, but can access only the public and protected members. Private members of a class are accessible only by its methods. Protected members can be accessed by methods of both the class and any subclasses, but not by clients of these classes.

2. With inheritance, the public and protected members of the superclass remain, respectively, public and protected members of the subclass. Such a subclass is type-compatible with its superclass. That is, you can use an instance of a subclass wherever you can use an instance of its superclass. This relationship between superclasses and subclasses is an *is-a* relationship.

3. A method in a subclass overrides a method in the superclass if they have the same parameter declarations. If the superclass has defined the method to be *final*, the subclass cannot override the method.

4. An abstract method in a class is a method that you can override in a subclass. When a method is abstract, you can either implement it or defer it to a further subclass.

5. A subclass inherits the interface of each method that is in its superclass. A subclass also inherits the implementation of each nonabstract method that is in its superclass.

6. An abstract class specifies only the essential members necessary for its subclasses and, therefore, can serve as the superclass for a family of classes. A class with at least one abstract method must also be declared abstract and is referred to as an abstract superclass.

7. Early, or static, binding describes a situation whereby a compiler can determine at compilation time the correct method to invoke.

Late, or dynamic, binding describes a situation whereby the system makes this determination at execution time.

8. When you invoke a method that is not declared *final*—for example, *mySphere.displayStatistics()*—the type of object is the determining factor under late binding.

CAUTIONS

1. If a method is abstract, and an implementation is not provided by the subclass, the subclass must also be declared abstract.

2. If a class fails to implement all of the methods in an interface, it must be declared abstract.

3. You should use inheritance only if the relationship between two classes is *is-a*.

SELF-TEST EXERCISES

Self-Test Exercises 1, 2, and 3 consider the classes *Sphere* and *Ball*, which this chapter describes in the section "Inheritance Revisited."

1. Write Java statements for the following tasks:
   a. Declare an instance *mySphere* of *Sphere* with a radius 2.
   b. Declare an instance *myBall* of *Ball* whose radius is 6 and whose name is *Beach ball*.
   c. Display the diameters of *mySphere* and *myBall*.

2. Define a class *Planet* that inherits *Ball*, as defined in this chapter. Your new class should have a private data field that specifies a planet's distance from the sun and public methods that access or alter this distance.

3. a. Can *resetBall*, which is a method of *Ball*, access *Sphere*'s data field *theRadius* directly, or must *resetBall* call *Sphere*'s *setRadius*? Explain.
   b. Repeat Part *a*, but assume that *theRadius* is a protected data field instead of a private data field of the class *Sphere*.

4. Consider the interface *SortedListInterface*, as described in this chapter.
   a. When can a reference be declared as type *SortedListInterface*?
   b. When must a class that implements *SortedListInterface* be used?

5. a. What are the similarities between abstract classes and interfaces?
   b. What are the differences between abstract classes and interfaces?

6. Why should a class's private methods never be abstract?

EXERCISES

1. Recall the classes *Sphere* and *Ball*, as described in this chapter in the section "Inheritance Revisited," and consider the following variation:

   ```
   public class Sphere {
      . . .
      public double area() {  // surface area
      . . .
      } // end area

      public void displayStatistics() {
      . . .
      }  // end displayStatistics
      . . .
   }  // end Sphere

   class Ball extends Sphere {
      . . .
      public double area() {  // cross-sectional area
      . . .
      } // end area

      public void displayStatistics() {
      . . .
      }  // end displayStatistics
      . . .
   }  // end Ball
   ```

   Suppose that the implementation of each version of *displayStatistics* invokes the method *area*.

   a. If *mySphere* is an instance of *Sphere* and *myBall* is an instance of *Ball*, which version of *area* does each of the following calls to *displayStatistics* invoke? Explain your answer.

      ```
      mySphere.DisplayStatistics();
      myBall.DisplayStatistics();
      ```

   b. If the statements

      ```
      Sphere s1 = new Sphere();
      Ball b1 = new Ball();
      ```

      declare *s1* and *b1*, which version of *area* does each of the following calls to *displayStatistics* invoke? Explain your answer.

      ```
      s1.displayStatistics();
      s1 = b1;
      s1.displayStatistics();
      b1.displayStatistics();
      ```

2. Define and implement a class *Pen* that has an instance of *Ball* as one of its data fields. Provide several members for the class *Pen*, such as the data field *color* and methods *isEmpty* and *write*.

3. The section "Abstract Classes" gives a version of the abstract class *EquidistantShape* that contains a private data field *theRadius*.

   a. Define a class of circles as a subclass of *EquidistantShape*.

   b. Revise the abstract class *EquidistantShape* so that *theRadius* is a protected data field instead of a private data field. Which methods are abstract and which methods must you implement?

   c. Repeat Part *a*, assuming the revision you made in Part *b*.

4. Consider the following classes:

   Expression represents algebraic expressions, including prefix, postfix, and infix expressions. Its public methods include *characterAt*. Its protected methods include *isOperator* and *isIdentifier*. It also has several private methods.

   InfixExpression is derived from *Expression* and represents infix expressions. Its public methods include *isLegal* and *evaluate*. It also has several protected and private methods.

   a. What methods can the implementation of *isIdentifier* invoke?

   b. What methods can the implementation of *isLegal* invoke?

5. Assume the classes described in the previous question and consider a main method that contains

   ```
   Expression algExp;
   InfixExpression infixExp;
   ```

   a. Which of these objects can correctly invoke the method *CharacterAt*?

   b. Which of these objects can correctly invoke the method *isOperator*?

   c. Which of these objects can correctly invoke the method *isLegal*?

6. Consider an ADT front list, which restricts insertions, deletions, and retrievals to the first item in the list.

   a. Define an interface *FrontListInterface* that is a subclass of the interface *BasicListInterface*. Provide a reference-based implementation of the interface *FrontListInterface* called *FrontList*.

   b. Define and implement a class for the ADT stack that is a subclass of *FrontList*.

7. Define an abstract class *Person* that describes a typical person. Next, define a subclass *Student* that describes a typical student. Finally, derive from *Student* a class *GradStudent* for a typical graduate student.

PROGRAMMING PROBLEMS

1. Complete the implementation of *SortedList* that has a reference of type *ListInterface* as a data field, as described in the section "Implementations of the ADT Sorted List that Use the ADT List."

2. The interface *ListInterface*, as described in this chapter, does not contain a method *position* that returns the number of a particular item, given the item's value. Such a method enables you to pass the node's number to *remove*, for example, to delete the item.

   Define a subinterface of *ListInterface* that has *position* as a method as well as methods that insert, delete, and retrieve items by their values instead of their positions. Write a class that implements this interface. Always make insertions at the beginning of the list. Although the items in this list are not sorted, the new ADT is analogous to *SortedList*, which contains the method *locatePosition*.

3. Consider an ADT circular list, which is like the ADT list but treats its first item as being immediately after its last item. For example, if a circular list contains six items, retrieval or deletion of the eighth item actually involves the list's second item. Let insertion into a circular list, however, behave exactly like insertion into a list. Define and implement the ADT circular list as a subclass of *ListReferenceBased*, as described in Chapter 4.

4. Programming Problem 11 in Chapter 6 describes the ADT traversable stack. In addition to the standard stack operations—*isEmpty*, *push*, *pop*, and *peek*—a traversable stack includes the operation *traverse*. The *traverse* operation is an iterator that begins at the bottom of the stack and displays each item in the stack until it reaches the top of the stack.

   Alternatively, you could create a *StackIterator* class based on the *StackInterface*, as given in Chapter 6. However, the iterator would then only have access to the methods contained in ther interface, such as *push*, *pop*, and *peek*. Since the iterator should not change the contents of the stack, the implementation would be quite inefficient.

   The *StackIterator* class would be more efficient if it had access to the underlying stack implementation (either *StackArrayBased* or *StackReferenceBased*). Implement a *Stack* class within a package that provides package access to the stack's underlying data structure. Then, in the same package, create a *StackIterator* class that uses this new *Stack* class.

5. Exercise 6 in Chapter 7 defined the double ended queue, or deque. Define and implement the ADT deque as a subinterface of *QueueInterface*, as given in Chapter 7.

6. Algebraic expressions are character strings, but since *String* is a *final* class, you cannot derive a class of expressions from *String*. Instead, define an abstract class *Expression* that can be the basis of other classes of algebraic expressions. Provide methods such as *characterAt*, *isOperator*, and *isIdentifier*. Next design and implement a class *InfixExpression* derived from the class *Expression*.

   Programming Problem 7 of Chapter 5 describes a grammar and a recognition algorithm for infix algebraic expressions. That grammar makes left-to-right association illegal when consecutive operators have the same precedence. Thus, *a/b*c* is illegal, but both *a/(b*c)* and *(a/b)*c* are legal.

Programming Problem 6 of Chapter 6 describes an algorithm to evaluate an infix expression that is syntactically correct by using two stacks.

Include in the class *InfixExpression* an *isLegal* method—based on the recognition algorithm given in Chapter 5—and an *evaluate* method—based on the evaluation algorithm given in Chapter 6. Use one of the ADT stack implementations presented in Chapter 6.

7. Chapter 5 described the class *Queens* that was used in a solution to the Eight Queens problem. A two-dimensional array represented the chessboard and was a data field of the class. Programming Problem 1 of Chapter 5 asked you to write a program to solve the Eight Queens problem based on these ideas. Revise that program by replacing the two-dimensional array with a class that represents the chessboard.

8. Implement the methods *remove* and *set* for the class *MyList-Iterator*. These methods should behave as follows (these descriptions are consistent with the behavior specified in *java.util.ListIterator*):

a. **public void** remove()
   Removes from the list the last element that was returned by *next* or *previous*. This call can be made only once per call to *next* or *previous*. It can be made only if the *add* method in *MyList-Iterator* has not been called after the last call to *next* or *previous*.

   Throws *IllegalStateException* if neither *next* nor *previous* has been called, or if *remove* or *add* has been called after the last call to *next* or *previous*.

b. **public void** set(Object o)
   Replaces the last element returned by *next* or *previous* with the specified element. This call can be made only if neither *remove* nor *add* have been called after the last call to *next* or *previous*.

   Throws *IllegalStateException* if neither *next* nor *previous* has been called, or if *remove* or *add* has been called after the last call to *next* or *previous*.

Note that *remove* and *set* require you to keep track of the state of the iterator; in other words, you must know whether or not *next* and *previous* are called immediately before the use of *remove* or *set*. You may also need to keep track of whether *previous* or *next* was called last to make sure that the correct element is deleted from or replaced in the list when *remove* and *set* are called.

Implement the operations *set* and *remove* for the class *List-Iterator*. Note that you will also need to modify the class *BasicListIterator* to provide support for keeping track of the state of the iterator.

CHAPTER 9

Algorithm Efficiency and Sorting

PREVIEW This chapter will show you how to analyze the efficiency of algorithms. The basic mathematical techniques for analyzing algorithms are central to more advanced topics in computer science and give you a way to formalize the notion that one algorithm is significantly more efficient than another. As examples, you will see analyses of some algorithms that you have studied before, including those that search data. In addition, this chapter examines the important topic of sorting data. You will study some simple algorithms, which you may have seen before, and some more-sophisticated recursive algorithms. Sorting algorithms provide varied and relatively easy examples of the analysis of efficiency.

DETERMINING THE EFFICIENCY OF ALGORITHMS

The comparison of algorithms is a topic that is central to computer science. Determining an algorithm's efficiency is quite important because your choice of algorithm for a given application often has a great impact. Responsive word processors, grocery checkout systems, automatic teller machines, video games, and life support systems all depend on efficient algorithms.

Suppose two algorithms perform the same task, such as searching. What does it mean to compare the algorithms and conclude that one is better? Chapter 1 discussed the several components that contribute to the cost of a computer program. Some of these components involve the cost of human time—the time of the people who develop, maintain, and use the program. The other components involve the cost of program execution—that is, the program's efficiency—measured by the amount of computer time and space that the program requires to execute.

We have, up to this point, emphasized the human cost of a computer program. The early chapters of this book stressed style and readability. They pointed out that well-designed algorithms reduce the human costs of implementing the algorithm with a program, of maintaining the program, and of modifying the program. The primary concern has been to develop good problem-solving skills and programming style. Although we will continue to concentrate our efforts in that direction, the efficiency of

Consider efficiency when selecting an algorithm

algorithms is also important. Efficiency is one criterion that you should use when selecting an algorithm and its implementation. The solutions in this book, in addition to illustrating good programming style, are frequently based on relatively efficient algorithms.

The **analysis of algorithms** is the area of computer science that provides tools for contrasting the efficiency of different methods of solution. Notice the use of the term *methods of solution* rather than *programs*; it is important to emphasize that the analysis concerns itself primarily with *significant* differences in efficiency—differences that you can usually obtain only through superior methods of solution and rarely through clever tricks in coding. Reductions in computing costs due to clever coding tricks are often more than offset by reduced program readability, which increases human costs. An analysis should focus on gross differences in the efficiency of algorithms that are likely to dominate the overall cost of a solution. To do otherwise could lead you to select an algorithm that runs a small fraction of a second faster than another algorithm yet requires many more hours of your time to implement and maintain.

A comparison of algorithms should focus on significant differences in efficiency

The efficient use of both time and memory is important. Computer scientists use similar techniques to analyze an algorithm's time and space efficiency. Since none of the algorithms covered in this text has significant space requirements, our focus will be primarily on time efficiency.

How do you compare the time efficiency of two algorithms that solve the same problem? One possible approach is to implement the two algorithms in Java and run the programs. This approach has at least three fundamental difficulties:

1. **How are the algorithms coded?** If algorithm A_1 runs faster than algorithm A_2, it could be the result of better programming. Thus, if you compare the running times of the programs, you are really comparing implementations of the algorithms rather than the algorithms themselves. You should not compare implementations, because they are sensitive to factors such as programming style that tend to cloud the issue of which algorithm is inherently more efficient.

Three difficulties with comparing programs instead of algorithms

2. **What computer should you use?** The particular computer on which the programs are run also obscures the issue of which algorithm is inherently more efficient. One computer may simply be much faster than the other, so clearly you should use the same computer for both programs. Which computer should you choose? The particular operations that the algorithms require can cause A_1 to run faster than A_2 on one computer, while the opposite is true on another computer. You should compare the efficiency of the algorithms independently of a particular computer.

3. **What data should the programs use?** Perhaps the most important difficulty on this list is the selection of the data for the programs to use. There is always the danger that you will select instances of the problem for which one of the algorithms runs uncharacteristically fast. For example, when comparing a sequential search and a binary search of a sorted array, you might search for an item that happens to be the smallest item in the array. In such a case, the sequential search will find the item more quickly than the binary search because the item is first in the array and so is the first item that the sequential search will examine. Any analysis of efficiency must be independent of specific data.

To overcome these difficulties, computer scientists employ mathematical techniques that analyze algorithms independently of specific implementations, computers, or data. You begin this analysis by counting the number of significant operations in a particular solution, as the next section describes.

Algorithm analysis should be independent of specific implementations, computers, and data

The Execution Time of Algorithms

Counting an algorithm's operations is a way to assess its efficiency

Previous chapters have informally compared different solutions to a given problem by looking at the number of operations that each solution required. For example, Chapter 4 compared array-based and reference-based implementations of the ADT list and found that an array-based `list.get(n)` could access the nth item in a list directly in one step, because the item is stored in `items[n-1]`. A reference-based `list.get(n)`, however, must traverse the list from its beginning until the nth node is reached, and so would require n steps.

An algorithm's execution time is related to the number of operations it requires. Counting an algorithm's operations—if possible—is a way to assess its efficiency. Consider a few other examples.

Traversal of a linked list.   Recall from Chapter 4 that you can display the contents of a linked list that `head` references by using the following statements:[1]

```
Node curr = head;                              ← 1 assignment
while (curr != null) {                          ← n+1 comparisons
   System.out.println(curr.getItem());        ← n writes
   curr.setNext(curr.getNext());              ← n assignments
}   // end while
```

Assuming a linked list of n nodes, these statements require $n + 1$ assignments, $n + 1$ comparisons, and n write operations. If each assignment, comparison, and write operation requires, respectively, a, c, and w time units, the statements require $(n + 1) * (a + c) + n * w$ time units.[2] Thus, the time required to write n nodes is proportional to n. This conclusion makes sense intuitively: It takes longer to display, or traverse, a linked list of 100 items than it does a linked list of 10 items.

Displaying the data in a linked list of n nodes requires time proportional to n

The Towers of Hanoi.   Chapter 5 proved recursively that the solution to the Towers of Hanoi problem with n disks requires $2^n - 1$ moves. If each move requires the same time m, the solution requires $(2^n - 1) * m$ time units. As you will soon see, this time requirement increases rapidly as the number of disks increases.

Nested loops.   Consider an algorithm that contains nested loops of the following form:

```
for (i = 1 through n) {
   for (j = 1 through i) {
      for (k = 1 through 5) {
         Task T
```

---

[1] Chapter 4 actually used a `for` statement. We use an equivalent `while` statement here to clarify the analysis.

[2] Although omitting multiplication operators is common in algebra, we indicate them explicitly here to facilitate counting them.

```
        }  // end for
      }  // end for
    }  // end for
```

If task T requires t time units, the innermost loop on k requires $5 * t$ time units. The loop on j requires $5 * t * i$ time units, and the outermost loop on i requires

$$\sum_{i=1}^{n} (5 * t * i) = 5 * t * (1 + 2 + \cdots + n) = 5 * t * n * (n + 1)/2$$

time units.

Algorithm Growth Rates

As you can see, the previous examples derive an algorithm's time requirement as a function of the problem size. The way to measure a problem's size depends on the application—typical examples are the number of nodes in a linked list, the number of disks in the Tower of Hanoi problem, the size of an array, or the number of items in a stack. Thus, we reached conclusions such as

Measure an algorithm's time requirement as a function of the problem size

> *Algorithm A requires $n^2/5$ time units to solve a problem of size n*

> *Algorithm B requires $5 * n$ time units to solve a problem of size n*

The time units in these two statements must be the same before you can compare the efficiency of the two algorithms. Perhaps we should have written

> *Algorithm A requires $n^2/5$ seconds to solve a problem of size n*

Our earlier discussion indicates the difficulties with such a statement: On what computer does the algorithm require $n^2/5$ seconds? What implementation of the algorithm requires $n^2/5$ seconds? What data caused the algorithm to require $n^2/5$ seconds?

What specifically do you want to know about the time requirement of an algorithm? The most important thing to learn is how quickly the algorithm's time requirement grows as a function of the problem size. Statements such as

> *Algorithm A requires time proportional to n^2*

> *Algorithm B requires time proportional to n*

each express an algorithm's proportional time requirement, or **growth rate**, and enable you to compare algorithm A with another algorithm B. Although you cannot determine the exact time requirement for either algorithm A or algorithm B from these statements, you can determine that for large problems, B will require significantly less time than A. That is, B's time requirement—as a function of the problem size n—increases at a slower rate than A's time requirement, because n increases at a slower rate than n^2. Even if B actually requires $5 * n$ seconds and A actually requires $n^2/5$ seconds, B eventually will require significantly less time than A, as n

Compare algorithm efficiencies for large problems

increases. Figure 9-1 illustrates this fact. Thus, an assertion like "A requires time proportional to n^2" is exactly the kind of statement that characterizes the inherent efficiency of an algorithm independently of such factors as particular computers and implementations.

Figure 9-1 also shows that A's time requirement does not exceed B's until n exceeds 25. Algorithm efficiency is typically a concern for large problems only. The time requirements for small problems are generally not large enough to matter. Thus, our analyses assume large values of n.

Order-of-Magnitude Analysis and Big O Notation

If

> *Algorithm A requires time proportional to f(n)*

Algorithm A is said to be **order** $f(n)$, which is denoted as $O(f(n))$. The function $f(n)$ is called the algorithm's **growth-rate function**. Because the notation uses the capital letter O to denote *order*, it is called the **Big O notation**. If a problem of size n requires time that is directly proportional to n, the problem is $O(n)$—that is, order n. If the time requirement is directly proportional to n^2, the problem is $O(n^2)$, and so on.

The following definition formalizes these ideas:

KEY CONCEPTS

Definition of the Order of an Algorithm

Algorithm A is order $f(n)$—denoted $O(f(n))$—if constants k and n_0 exist such that A requires no more than $k * f(n)$ time units to solve a problem of size $n \geq n_0$.

The requirement $n \geq n_0$ in the definition of $O(f(n))$ formalizes the notion of sufficiently large problems. In general, many values of k and n can satisfy the definition.

Figure 9-1

Time requirements as a function of the problem size *n*

The following examples illustrate the definition:

- Suppose that an algorithm requires $n^2 - 3 * n + 10$ seconds to solve a problem of size n. If constants k and n_0 exist such that

  $$k * n^2 > n^2 - 3 * n + 10 \text{ for all } n \geq n_0$$

  the algorithm is order n^2. In fact, if k is 3 and n_0 is 2,

  $$3 * n^2 > n^2 - 3 * n + 10 \text{ for all } n \geq 2$$

  as Figure 9-2 illustrates. Thus, the algorithm requires no more than $k * n^2$ time units for $n \geq n_0$, and so is $O(n^2)$.

- Previously, we found that displaying a linked list's first n items requires $(n + 1) * (a + c) + n * w$ time units. Since $2 * n \geq n + 1$ for $n \geq 1$,

  $$(2 * a + 2 * c + w) * n \geq (n + 1) * (a + c) + n * w \text{ for } n \geq 1$$

  Thus, this task is $O(n)$. Here, k is $2 * a + 2 * c + w$, and n_0 is 1.

- Similarly, the solution to the Towers of Hanoi problem requires $(2^n - 1) * m$ time units. Since

  $$m * 2^n > (2^n - 1) * m \text{ for } n \geq 1$$

  the solution is $O(2^n)$.

The requirement $n \geq n_0$ in the definition of $O(f(n))$ means that the time estimate is correct for sufficiently large problems. In other words, the time estimate is too small for at most a finite number of problem sizes. For example, the function $\log n$ takes on the value 0 when n is 1. Thus, the fact that $k * \log 1$ is 0 for all constants k implies an unrealistic time requirement; presumably, all algorithms require more than 0 time units even to solve a problem of size 1. Thus, you can discount problems of size $n = 1$ if $f(n)$ is $\log n$.

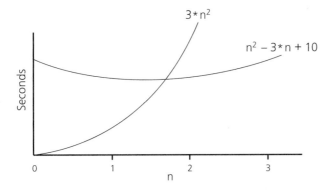

Figure 9-2

When $n \geq 2$, $3 * n^2$ exceeds $n^2 - 3 * n + 10$

To dramatize further the significance of an algorithm's proportional growth rate, consider the table and graph in Figure 9-3. The table (Figure 9-3a) gives, for various values of *n*, the approximate values of some common growth-rate functions, which are listed in order of growth:

Order of growth of some common functions

$$O(1) < O(\log_2 n) < O(n) < O(n * \log_2 n) < O(n^2) < O(n^3) < O(2^n)$$

The table demonstrates the relative speed at which the values of the functions grow. (Figure 9-3b represents the growth-rate functions graphically.[3])

(a)

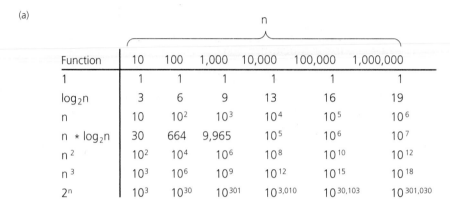

| | n | | | | | |
Function	10	100	1,000	10,000	100,000	1,000,000
1	1	1	1	1	1	1
$\log_2 n$	3	6	9	13	16	19
n	10	10^2	10^3	10^4	10^5	10^6
$n * \log_2 n$	30	664	9,965	10^5	10^6	10^7
n^2	10^2	10^4	10^6	10^8	10^{10}	10^{12}
n^3	10^3	10^6	10^9	10^{12}	10^{15}	10^{18}
2^n	10^3	10^{30}	10^{301}	$10^{3,010}$	$10^{30,103}$	$10^{301,030}$

(b)

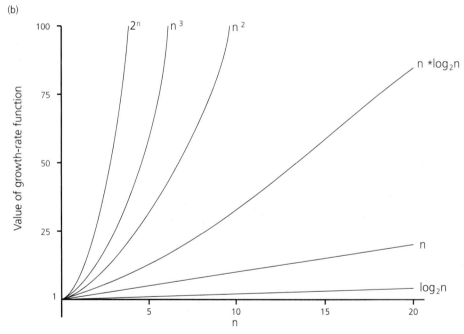

Figure 9-3

A comparison of growth-rate functions: (a) in tabular form; (b) in graphical form

---

[3]The graph of $f(n) = 1$ is omitted because the scale of the figure makes it difficult to draw. It would, however, be a straight line parallel to the *x* axis through $y = 1$.

These growth-rate functions have the following intuitive interpretations:

1
    A growth-rate function of 1 implies a problem whose time requirement is constant and, therefore, independent of the problem's size n.

Intuitive interpretations of growth-rate functions

$\log_2 n$
    The time requirement for a **logarithmic** algorithm increases slowly as the problem size increases. If you square the problem size, you only double its time requirement. Later you will see that the recursive binary search algorithm that you studied in Chapter 2 has this behavior. Recall that a binary search halves an array and then searches one of the halves. Typical logarithmic algorithms solve a problem by solving a smaller constant fraction of the problem.

    The base of the log does not affect a logarithmic growth rate, so you can omit it in a growth-rate function. Exercise 6 at the end of this chapter asks you to show why this is true.

n
    The time requirement for a **linear** algorithm increases directly with the size of the problem. If you square the problem size, you also square its time requirement.

$n * \log_2 n$
    The time requirement for an $n * \log_2 n$ algorithm increases more rapidly than a linear algorithm. Such algorithms usually divide a problem into smaller problems that are each solved separately. You will see an example of such an algorithm— the mergesort—later in this chapter.

n^2
    The time requirement for a **quadratic** algorithm increases rapidly with the size of the problem. Algorithms that use two nested loops are often quadratic. Such algorithms are practical only for small problems. Later in this chapter, you will study several quadratic sorting algorithms.

n^3
    The time requirement for a **cubic** algorithm increases more rapidly with the size of the problem than the time requirement for a quadratic algorithm. Algorithms that use three nested loops are often cubic, and are practical only for small problems.

2^n
    As the size of a problem increases, the time requirement for an **exponential** algorithm usually increases too rapidly to be practical.

If algorithm *A* requires time that is proportional to function *f* and algorithm *B* requires time that is proportional to a slower-growing function *g*, it is apparent that *B* will always be significantly more efficient than *A* for large enough problems. For large problems, the proportional growth rate dominates all other factors in determining an algorithm's efficiency.

Several mathematical properties of Big O notation help to simplify the analysis of an algorithm. As we discuss these properties, you should keep in mind that $O(f(n))$ means "is of order $f(n)$" or "has order $f(n)$." O is not a function.

Some properties of growth-rate functions

1. **You can ignore low-order terms in an algorithm's growth-rate function.** For example, if an algorithm is $O(n^3 + 4 * n^2 + 3 * n)$, it is also $O(n^3)$. By examining the table in Figure 9-3a, you can see that the n^3 term is significantly larger than either $4 * n^2$ or $3 * n$, particularly for large values of *n*. For large *n*, the growth rate of $n^3 + 4 * n^2 + 3 * n$ is the same as the growth rate of n^3. It is the growth rate of $f(n)$, not the value of $f(n)$, that is important here. Thus, even if an algorithm is $O(n^3 + 4 * n^2 + 3 * n)$, we say that it is simply $O(n^3)$. In general, you can usually conclude that an algorithm is $O(f(n))$, where *f* is a function similar to the ones listed in Figure 9-3.

2. **You can ignore a multiplicative constant in the high-order term of an algorithm's growth-rate function.** For example, if an algorithm is $O(5 * n^3)$, it is also $O(n^3)$. This observation follows from the definition of $O(f(n))$, if you let $k = 5$.

3. $O(f(n)) + O(g(n)) = O(f(n) + g(n))$. You can combine growth-rate functions. For example, if an algorithm is $O(n^2) + O(n)$, it is also $O(n^2 + n)$, which you write simply as $O(n^2)$ by applying property 1. Analogous rules hold for multiplication.

These properties imply that you need only an estimate of the time requirement to obtain an algorithm's growth rate; you do not need an exact statement of an algorithm's time requirement, which is fortunate because deriving the exact time requirement is often difficult and sometimes impossible.

An algorithm can require different times to solve different problems of the same size

Worst-case and average-case analyses. A particular algorithm might require different times to solve different problems of the same size. For example, the time that an algorithm requires to search *n* items might depend on the nature of the items. Usually you consider the maximum amount of time that an algorithm can require to solve a problem of size *n*—that is, the worst case. **Worst-case analysis** concludes that algorithm *A* is $O(f(n))$ if, in the worst case, *A* requires no more than $k * f(n)$ time units to solve a problem of size *n* for all but a finite number of values of *n*. Although a worst-case analysis can produce a pessimistic time estimate, such an estimate does not mean that your algorithm will always be slow. Instead, you have shown that the algorithm will never be slower than your estimate. Realize, however, that an algorithm's worst case might happen rarely, if at all, in practice.

An **average-case analysis** attempts to determine the average amount of time that an algorithm requires to solve problems of size n. In an average-case analysis, A is $O(f(n))$ if the average amount of time that A requires to solve a problem of size n is no more than $k * f(n)$ time units for all but a finite number of values of n. Average-case analysis is, in general, far more difficult to perform than worst-case analysis. One difficulty is determining the relative probabilities of encountering various problems of a given size; another is determining the distributions of various data values. Worst-case analysis is easier to calculate and is thus more common.

Keeping Your Perspective

Before continuing with additional order-of-magnitude analyses of specific algorithms, a few words about perspective are appropriate. For example, consider an ADT list of n items. You saw earlier that an array-based `list.get(n)` operation can access the nth item in the list directly. This access is independent of n; `get` takes the same time to access the hundredth item as it does to access the first item in the list. Thus, the array-based implementation of the retrieval operation is $O(1)$. However, the reference-based implementation of `get` in the class `ListReferenceBased` requires n steps to traverse the list until it reaches the nth item, and so is $O(n)$.

*An array-based **get** is O(1)*

*A reference-based **get** is O(n)*

Throughout the course of an analysis, you should always keep in mind that you are interested only in *significant* differences in efficiency. Is the difference in efficiency for the two implementations of `get` significant? As the size of the list grows, the reference-based implementation might require more time to retrieve the desired node, because the node can be farther away from the beginning of the list. In contrast, regardless of how large the list is, the array-based implementation always requires the same constant amount of time to retrieve any particular item. Thus, no matter what your notion of a significant difference in time is, you will reach this time difference if the list is large enough. In this example, observe that the difference in efficiency for the two implementations is worth considering only when the problem is large enough. If the list never has more than 25 items, for example, the difference in the implementations is not significant at all.

Now consider an application—such as a word processor's spelling checker—that frequently retrieves items from a list but rarely inserts or deletes an item. Since an array-based `get` is faster than a reference-based `get`, you should choose an array-based implementation of the list for the application. On the other hand, if an application requires frequent insertions and deletions but rarely retrieves an item, you should choose a reference-based implementation of the list. The most appropriate implementation of an ADT for a given application strongly depends on how frequently the application will perform the operations. You will see more examples of this point in the next chapter.

When choosing an ADT's implementation, consider how frequently particular ADT operations occur in a given application

The response time of some ADT operations, however, can be crucial, even if you seldom use them. For example, an air traffic control system

Some seldom-used but critical operations must be efficient

could include an emergency operation to resolve the impending collision of two airplanes. Clearly, this operation must occur quickly, even if it is rarely used. Thus, before you choose an implementation for an ADT, you should know what operations a particular application requires, approximately how often the application will perform each operation, and the response times that the application requires of each operation.

Soon we will compare a searching algorithm that is $O(n)$ with one that is $O(\log_2 n)$. While it is true that an $O(\log_2 n)$ searching algorithm requires significantly less time on large arrays than an $O(n)$ algorithm requires, on small arrays—say, $n < 25$—the time requirements might not be significantly different at all. In fact, it is entirely possible that, because of factors such as the size of the constant k in the definition of Big O, the $O(n)$ algorithm will run faster on small problems. It is only on large problems that the slower growth rate of an algorithm necessarily gives it a significant advantage. Figure 9-1 illustrated this phenomenon.

If the problem size is always small, you can probably ignore an algorithm's efficiency

Thus, in general, if the maximum size of a given problem is small, the time requirements of any two solutions for that problem likely will not differ significantly. If you know that your problem size will always be small, do not overanalyze; simply choose the algorithm that is easiest to understand, verify, and code.

Weigh the trade-offs between an algorithm's time requirements and its memory requirements

Frequently, when evaluating an algorithm's efficiency, you have to weigh carefully the trade-offs between a solution's execution time requirements and its memory requirements. You are rarely able to make a statement as strong as "This method is the best one for performing the task." A solution that requires a relatively small amount of computer time often also requires a relatively large amount of memory. It may not even be possible to say that one solution requires less time than another. Solution A may perform some components of the task faster than solution B, while solution B performs other components of the task faster than solution A. Often you must analyze the solutions in light of a particular application.

Compare algorithms for both style and efficiency

In summary, it is important to examine an algorithm for both style and efficiency. The analysis should focus only on gross differences in efficiency and not reward coding tricks that save milliseconds. Any finer differences in efficiency are likely to interact with coding issues, which you should not allow to interfere with the development of your programming style. If you find a method of solution that is significantly more efficient than others, you should select it, unless you know that the maximum problem size is quite small. If you will be solving only small problems, it is possible that a less efficient algorithm would be more appropriate. That is, other factors, such as the simplicity of the algorithm, could become more significant than minor differences in efficiency. In fact, performing an order-of-magnitude analysis implicitly

Order-of-magnitude analysis focuses on large problems

assumes that an algorithm will be used to solve large problems. This assumption allows you to focus on growth rates because, regardless of other factors, an algorithm with a slow growth rate will require less time than an algorithm with a fast growth rate, provided that the problems to be solved are sufficiently large.

The Efficiency of Searching Algorithms

As another example of order-of-magnitude analysis, consider the efficiency of two search algorithms: the sequential search and the binary search of an array.

Sequential search. In a sequential search of an array of n items, you look at each item in turn, beginning with the first one, until either you find the desired item or you reach the end of the data collection. In the best case, the desired item is the first one that you examine, so only one comparison is necessary. Thus, in the best case, a sequential search is $O(1)$. In the worst case, the desired item is the last one you examine, so n comparisons are necessary. Thus, in the worst case, the algorithm is $O(n)$. In the average case, you would find the desired item in the middle of the collection, making $n/2$ comparisons. Thus, the algorithm is $O(n)$ in the average case.

Sequential search. Worst case: $O(n)$; average case: $O(n)$; best case: $O(1)$

What is the algorithm's order when you do not find the desired item? Does the algorithm's order depend on whether or not the initial data is sorted? These questions are left for you in Self-Test Exercise 4 at the end of this chapter.

Binary search. Is a binary search of an array more efficient than a sequential search? The binary search algorithm, which Chapter 2 presents, searches a sorted array for a particular item by repeatedly dividing the array in half. The algorithm determines which half the item must be in—if it is indeed present—and discards the other half. Thus, the binary search algorithm searches successively smaller arrays: The size of a given array is approximately one-half the size of the array previously searched.

At each division, the algorithm makes a comparison. How many comparisons does the algorithm make when it searches an array of n items? The exact answer depends, of course, on where the sought-for item resides in the array. However, you can compute the maximum number of comparisons that a binary search requires—that is, the worst case. The number of comparisons is equal to the number of times that the algorithm divides the array in half. Suppose that $n = 2^k$ for some k. The search requires the following steps:

1. Inspect the middle item of an array of size n.
2. Inspect the middle item of an array of size $n/2$.
3. Inspect the middle item of an array of size $n/2^2$, and so on.

To inspect the middle item of an array, you must first divide the array in half. If you divide an array of n items in half, then divide one of those halves in half, and continue dividing halves until only one item remains, you will have performed k divisions. This is true because $n/2^k = 1$. (Remember, we assumed that $n = 2^k$.) In the worst case, the algorithm performs k divisions and, therefore, k comparisons. Because $n = 2^k$,

$$k = \log_2 n$$

Thus, the algorithm is $O(\log_2 n)$ in the worst case when $n = 2^k$.

What if n is not a power of 2? You can easily find the smallest k such that

$$2^{k-1} < n < 2^k$$

(For example, if n is 30, then $k = 5$, because $2^4 = 16 < 30 < 32 = 2^5$.) The algorithm still requires at most k divisions to obtain a subarray with one item. Now it follows that

$$k - 1 < \log_2 n < k$$
$$k < 1 + \log_2 n < k + 1$$
$$k = 1 + \log_2 n \text{ rounded down}$$

Binary search is $O(\log_2 n)$ in the worst case

Thus, the algorithm is still $O(\log_2 n)$ in the worst case when $n \neq 2^k$. In general, the algorithm is $O(\log_2 n)$ in the worst case for any n.

Is a binary search better than a sequential search? Much better! For example $\log_2 1{,}000{,}000 = 19$, so a sequential search of one million sorted items can require one million comparisons, but a binary search of the same items will require at most 20 comparisons. For large arrays, the binary search has an enormous advantage over a sequential search.

Realize, however, that maintaining the array in sorted order requires an overhead cost, which can be substantial. The next section examines the cost of sorting an array.

SORTING ALGORITHMS AND THEIR EFFICIENCY

Sorting is a process that organizes a collection of data into either ascending[4] or descending order. The need for sorting arises in many situations. You may simply want to sort a collection of data before including it in a report. Often, however, you must perform a sort as an initialization step for certain algorithms. For example, searching for data is one of the most common tasks performed by computers. When the collection of data to be searched is large, an efficient method for searching—such as the binary search algorithm—is desirable. However, the binary search algorithm requires that the data be sorted. Thus, sorting the data is a step that must precede a binary search on a collection of data that is not already sorted. Good sorting algorithms, therefore, are quite valuable.

The sorts in this chapter are internal sorts

You can organize sorting algorithms into two categories. An **internal sort** requires that the collection of data fit entirely in the computer's main memory. The algorithms in this chapter are internal sorting algorithms. You use an **external sort** when the collection of data will not fit in the computer's main memory all at once but must reside in secondary storage, such as on a disk. Chapter 14 examines external sorts.

The data items to be sorted might be integers, character strings, or even objects. It is easy to imagine the results of sorting a collection of

---

[4] To allow for duplicate data items, "ascending" is used here to mean nondecreasing and "descending" to mean nonincreasing.

integers or character strings, but consider a collection of objects. If each object contains only one data field, sorting the objects is really no different than sorting a collection of integers. However, when each object contains several data fields, you must know which data field determines the order of the entire object within the collection of data. This data field is called the **sort key.** For example, if the objects represent people, you might want to sort on their names, their ages, or their zip codes. Regardless of your choice of sort key, the sorting algorithm orders entire objects based on only one data field, the sort key.

For simplicity, this chapter assumes that the data items are instances of a class that has implemented the *Comparable* interface. The *Comparable* interface method *compareTo* returns either a negative integer, zero, or a positive integer based upon whether the sort key is less than, equal to, or greater than the sort key of the specified object. All algorithms in this chapter sort the data into ascending order. Modifying these algorithms to sort data into descending order is simple. Finally, each example assumes that the data resides in an array.

Selection Sort

Imagine some data that you can examine all at once. To sort it, you could select the largest item and put it in its place, select the next largest and put it in its place, and so on. For a card player, this process is analogous to looking at an entire hand of cards and ordering it by selecting cards one at a time in their proper order. The **selection sort** formalizes these intuitive notions. To sort an array into ascending order, you first search it for the largest item. Because you want the largest item to be in the last position of the array, you swap the last item with the largest item, even if these items happen to be identical. Now, ignoring the last—and largest—item of the array, you search the rest of the array for its largest item and swap it with its last item, which is the next-to-last item in the original array. You continue until you have selected and swapped $n - 1$ of the n items in the array. The remaining item, which is now in the first position of the array, is in its proper order, so it is not considered further.

Select the largest item

Figure 9-4 provides an example of a selection sort. Beginning with five integers, you select the largest—37—and swap it with the last integer—13. (As the items in this figure are ordered, they appear in boldface. This convention will be used throughout this chapter.) Next you select the largest integer—29—from among the first four integers in the array and swap it with the next-to-last integer in the array—13. Notice that the next selection—14—is already in its proper position, but the algorithm ignores this fact and performs a swap of 14 with itself. It is more efficient in general to occasionally perform an unnecessary swap than it is to continually ask whether the swap is necessary. Finally, you select the 13 and swap it with the item in the second position of the array—10. The array is now sorted into ascending order.

Shaded elements are selected;
boldface elements are in order.

Figure 9-4

**A selection sort of an array
of five integers**

Initial array:	29	10	14	**37**	13
After 1st swap:	29	10	14	13	**37**
After 2nd swap:	13	10	14	**29**	**37**
After 3rd swap:	13	10	**14**	**29**	**37**
After 4th swap:	**10**	**13**	**14**	**29**	**37**

A Java method that performs a selection sort on an array called `the-Array` with *n* items follows:

```
public static void selectionSort(Comparable[] theArray,
                                 int n) {
// ----------------------------------------------------
// Sorts the items in an array into ascending order.
// Precondition: theArray is an array of n items.
// Postcondition: theArray is sorted into
// ascending order.
// Calls: indexOfLargest.
// ----------------------------------------------------
  // last = index of the last item in the subarray of
  //        items yet to be sorted
  // largest = index of the largest item found

  for (int last = n-1; last >= 1; last--) {
    // Invariant: theArray[last+1..n-1] is sorted
    // and > theArray[0..last]

    // select largest item in theArray[0..last]
    int largest = indexOfLargest(theArray, last+1);

    // swap largest item theArray[largest] with
    // theArray[last]
    Comparable temp = theArray[largest];
    theArray[largest] = theArray[last];
    theArray[last] = temp;
  }  // end for
}  // end selectionSort
```

The *selectionSort* method calls the following method:

```
private static int indexOfLargest(Comparable[] theArray,
                                  int size) {
// ----------------------------------------------------
// Finds the largest item in an array.
// Precondition: theArray is an array of size items;
```

```
// size >= 1.
// Postcondition: Returns the index of the largest
// item in the array.
// ---------------------------------------------------
   int indexSoFar = 0; // index of largest item found so far

   // Invariant: theArray[indexSoFar]>=theArray[0..currIndex-1]
   for (int currIndex = 1; currIndex < size; ++currIndex) {
     if (theArray[currIndex].compareTo(theArray[indexSoFar])>0) {
        indexSoFar = currIndex;
     } // end if
   } // end for

   return indexSoFar;  // index of largest item
}  // end indexOfLargest
```

Analysis. As you can see from the previous algorithm, sorting in general compares, exchanges, or moves items. Depending on the programming language and implementation used for storing the data, the cost associated with each of these operations varies. For example, in Java, an array stores references to objects, not the objects themselves. Thus, moving or exchanging data is not expensive in Java, because only the references are moved or exchanged, rather than entire objects. Other languages, however, such as C++, could use an implementation in which the actual objects are stored in an array. In this case, moving and exchanging data becomes much more expensive since entire objects are actually moved around memory.

The comparison operation is typically more involved, since actual data values must be compared. In Java, comparison is done by a call to either *equals* or *compareTo*. Even in cases where the data objects are large and complex, however, the actual comparison is usually based upon a portion of the object, that is, the sort key. Other programming languages, such as C++, use a similar approach of allowing the programmer to specify the comparison operation.

As a first step in analyzing sorting algorithms, you should count the move, exchange, and compare operations. In Java, the comparison operation is usually the most expensive and is thus often the only operation analyzed. However, since other programming languages may incur more expense in moving or exchanging data, we provide some analysis of these operations here. Generally, move, exchange, and compare operations are more expensive than the ones that control loops or manipulate array indexes, particularly when the data to be sorted is more complex than integers or characters. Thus, our approach ignores these less expensive operations. You should convince yourself that ignoring such operations does not affect our final result. (See Exercise 7.)

Clearly, the *for* loop in the method *selectionSort* executes $n - 1$ times. Thus, *selectionSort* calls the method *indexOfLargest* $n - 1$ times. Each call to *indexOfLargest* causes its loop to execute *last* times (that is, *size* – 1 times when *size* is *last* + 1). Thus, the $n - 1$ calls to *indexOfLargest*, for values of *last* that range from $n - 1$ down to 1, cause the loop in *indexOfLargest* to execute a total of

$$(n - 1) + (n - 2) + \cdots + 1 = n * (n - 1)/2$$

times. Because each execution of *indexOfLargest*'s loop performs one comparison, the calls to *indexOfLargest* require

$$n * (n - 1)/2$$

comparisons.

At the end of the *for* loop in *selectionSort*, an exchange is performed between elements *theArray[largest]* and *theArray[last]*. Each exchange requires three assignments, or

$$3 * (n - 1)$$

data moves.

Together, a selection sort of *n* items requires

$$n * (n - 1)/2 + 3 * (n - 1)$$
$$= n^2/2 + 5 * n/2 - 3$$

Selection sort is O(n^2)

major operations. By applying the properties of growth-rate functions (see page 380), you can ignore low-order terms to get $O(n^2/2)$ and then ignore the multiplier 1/2 to get $O(n^2)$. Thus, selection sort is $O(n^2)$.

Although a selection sort does not depend on the initial arrangement of the data, which is an advantage of this algorithm, it is appropriate only for small *n* because $O(n^2)$ grows rapidly. While the algorithm requires $O(n^2)$ comparisons, it requires only $O(n)$ data moves. A selection sort could be a good choice over other methods when data moves are costly but comparisons are not. As we mentioned earlier, there really is no such thing as an expensive data move in a normal sorting situation in Java, because it would surely be references, not entire objects, that are copied in the process of performing the move.

Bubble Sort

The next sorting algorithm is one that you may have seen already. That is precisely why it is analyzed here, because it is not a particularly good algorithm. The **bubble sort** compares adjacent items and exchanges them if they are out of order. This sort usually requires several passes over the data. During the first pass, you compare the first two items in the array. If they are out of order, you exchange them. You then compare the items in the next pair—that is, in positions 2 and 3 of the array. If they are out of order, you exchange them. You proceed, comparing and exchanging items two at a time until you reach the end of the array.

Figure 9-5a illustrates the first pass of a bubble sort of an array of five integers. You compare the items in the first pair—29 and 10—and exchange them because they are out of order. Next you consider the second pair—29 and 14—and exchange these items because they are out

Figure 9-5

The first two passes of a bubble sort of an array of five integers:
(a) pass 1; (b) pass 2

of order. The items in the third pair—29 and 37—are in order, and so you do not exchange them. Finally, you exchange the items in the last pair—37 and 13.

Although the array is not sorted after the first pass, the largest item has "bubbled" to its proper position at the end of the array. During the second pass of the bubble sort, you return to the beginning of the array and consider pairs of items in exactly the same manner as the first pass. You do not, however, include the last—and largest—item of the array. That is, the second pass considers the first $n-1$ items of the array. After the second pass, the second largest item in the array will be in its proper place in the next-to-last position of the array, as Figure 9-5b illustrates. Now, ignoring the last two items, which are in order, you continue with subsequent passes until the array is sorted.

When you order successive pairs of items, the largest item bubbles to the top (end) of the array

Although a bubble sort requires at most $n-1$ passes to sort the array, fewer passes might be possible to sort a particular array. Thus, you could terminate the process if no exchanges occur during any pass. The following Java method *bubbleSort* uses a flag to signal when an exchange occurs during a particular pass.

Bubble sort usually requires several passes through the array

```
public static void bubbleSort(Comparable[] theArray, int n) {
// ----------------------------------------------------
// Sorts the items in an array into ascending order.
// Precondition: theArray is an array of n items.
// Postcondition: theArray is sorted into ascending
// order.
// ----------------------------------------------------
  boolean sorted = false;  // false when swaps occur

  for (int pass = 1; (pass < n) && !sorted; ++pass) {
    // Invariant: theArray[n+1-pass..n-1] is sorted
    //            and > theArray[0..n-pass]
    sorted = true;  // assume sorted
```

```
for (int index = 0; index < n-pass; ++index) {
  // Invariant: theArray[0..index-1] <= theArray[index]
  int nextIndex = index + 1;
  if (theArray[index].compareTo(theArray[nextIndex]) > 0) {
    // exchange items
    Comparable temp = theArray[index];
    theArray[index] = theArray[nextIndex];
    theArray[nextIndex] = temp;
    sorted = false;  // signal exchange
  }  // end if
}  // end for

  // Assertion: theArray[0..n-pass-1] < theArray[n-pass]
}  // end for
}  // end bubbleSort
```

Analysis. As was noted earlier, the bubble sort requires at most $n - 1$ passes through the array. Pass 1 requires $n - 1$ comparisons and at most $n - 1$ exchanges; pass 2 requires $n - 2$ comparisons and at most $n - 2$ exchanges. In general, pass i requires $n - i$ comparisons and at most $n - i$ exchanges. Therefore, in the worst case, a bubble sort will require a total of

$$(n - 1) + (n - 2) + \cdots + 1 = n * (n - 1)/2$$

comparisons and the same number of exchanges. Recall that each exchange requires three data moves. Thus, altogether there are

$$2 * n * (n - 1) = 2 * n^2 - 2 * n$$

major operations in the worst case. Therefore, the bubble sort algorithm is $O(n^2)$ in the worst case.

Bubble sort. Worst case: O(n²); best case: O(n)

The best case occurs when the original data is already sorted: `bubble-Sort` uses one pass, during which $n - 1$ comparisons and no exchanges occur. Thus, the bubble sort is $O(n)$ in the best case.

Insertion Sort

Imagine once again arranging a hand of cards, but now you pick up one card at a time and insert it into its proper position; in this case you are performing an **insertion sort.** Chapter 4 introduced the insertion sort algorithm in the context of a linked list: You can create a sorted linked list from a file of unsorted integers, for example, by repeatedly calling a method that inserts an integer into its proper sorted order in a linked list.

You can use the insertion sort strategy to sort items that reside in an array. This version of the insertion sort partitions the array into two regions: sorted and unsorted, as Figure 9-6 depicts. Initially, the entire array is the unsorted region, just as the cards dealt to you sit in an unsorted pile on the table. At each step, the insertion sort takes the first item of the unsorted region and places it into its correct position in the sorted region. This step is analogous to taking a card from the table and inserting it into its proper position in your hand. The first step, however,

Take each item from the unsorted region and insert it into its correct order in the sorted region

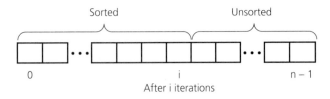

Figure 9-6

An insertion sort partitions the array into two regions

is trivial: Moving `theArray[0]` from the unsorted region to the sorted region really does not require moving data. Therefore, you can omit this first step by considering the initial sorted region to be `theArray[0]` and the initial unsorted region to be `theArray[1..n-1]`. The fact that the items in the sorted region are sorted among themselves is an invariant of the algorithm. Because at each step the size of the sorted region grows by 1 and the size of the unsorted region shrinks by 1, the entire array will be sorted when the algorithm terminates.

Figure 9-7 illustrates an insertion sort of an array of five integers. Initially, the sorted region is `theArray[0]`, which is 29, and the unsorted region is the rest of the array. You take the first item in the unsorted region—the 10—and insert it into its proper position in the sorted region. This insertion requires you to shift array items to make room for the inserted item. You then take the first item in the new unsorted region—the 14—and insert it into its proper position in the sorted region, and so on.

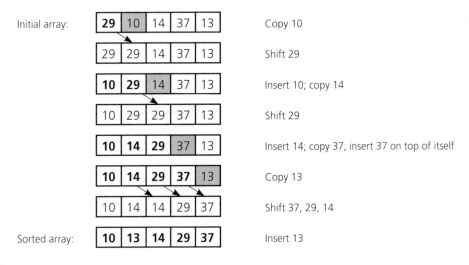

Figure 9-7

An insertion sort of an array of five integers

A Java method that performs an insertion sort on an array of *n* items follows:

```java
public static void insertionSort(Comparable[] theArray,
                                 int n) {
// ------------------------------------------------------
// Sorts the items in an array into ascending order.
// Precondition: theArray is an array of n items.
// Postcondition: theArray is sorted into ascending
// order.
// ------------------------------------------------------
  // unsorted = first index of the unsorted region,
  // loc = index of insertion in the sorted region,
  // nextItem = next item in the unsorted region

  // initially, sorted region is theArray[0],
  //          unsorted region is theArray[1..n-1];
  // in general, sorted region is theArray[0..unsorted-1],
  //          unsorted region is theArray[unsorted..n-1]

  for (int unsorted = 1; unsorted < n; ++unsorted) {
    // Invariant: theArray[0..unsorted-1] is sorted

    // find the right position (loc) in
    // theArray[0..unsorted] for theArray[unsorted],
    // which is the first item in the unsorted
    // region; shift, if necessary, to make room
    Comparable nextItem = theArray[unsorted];
    int loc = unsorted;

    while ((loc > 0) &&
           (theArray[loc-1].compareTo(nextItem) > 0)) {
      // shift theArray[loc-1] to the right
      theArray[loc--] = theArray[loc-1];
    }  // end while
    // Assertion: theArray[loc] is where nextItem belongs
    // insert nextItem into sorted region
    theArray[loc] = nextItem;
  }  // end for
}  // end insertionSort
```

Analysis.   The outer *for* loop in the method *insertionSort* executes $n - 1$ times. This loop contains an inner *for* loop that executes at most *unsorted* times for values of *unsorted* that range from 1 to $n - 1$. Thus, in the worst case, the algorithm's comparison occurs

$$1 + 2 + \cdots + (n - 1) = n * (n - 1)/2$$

times. In addition, the inner loop moves data items at most the same number of times.

The outer loop moves data items twice per iteration, or $2 * (n - 1)$ times. Together, there are

$$n * (n - 1) + 2 * (n - 1) = n^2 + n - 2$$

major operations in the worst case.

Therefore, the insertion sort algorithm is $O(n^2)$ in the worst case. For small arrays—say, fewer than 25 items—the simplicity of the insertion sort makes it an appropriate choice. For large arrays, however, an insertion sort can be prohibitively inefficient.

Insertion sort is $O(n^2)$ in the worst case

Mergesort

Two important divide-and-conquer sorting algorithms, mergesort and quicksort, have elegant recursive formulations and are highly efficient. The presentations here are in the context of sorting arrays, but—as you will see in Chapter 14—mergesort generalizes to external files. It will be convenient to express the algorithms in terms of the array *theArray[first..last]*.

Divide and conquer

Mergesort is a recursive sorting algorithm that always gives the same performance, regardless of the initial order of the array items. Suppose that you divide the array into halves, sort each half, and then **merge** the sorted halves into one sorted array, as Figure 9-8 illustrates. In the figure, the halves <1, 4, 8> and <2, 3> are merged to form the array <1, 2, 3, 4, 8>. This merge step compares an item in one half of the array with an item in the other half and moves the smaller item to a temporary array. This process continues until there are no more items to consider in one half. At that time, you simply move the remaining items to the tempo-

Halve the array, recursively sort its halves, and then merge the halves

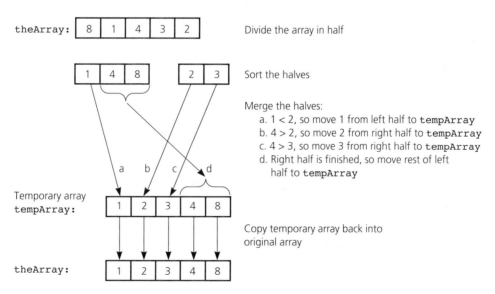

Figure 9-8

A mergesort with an auxiliary temporary array

rary array. Finally, you copy the temporary array back into the original array.

Although the merge step of mergesort produces a sorted array, how do you sort the array halves prior to the merge step? Mergesort sorts the array halves by using mergesort—that is, by calling itself recursively. Thus, the pseudocode for mergesort is

```
mergesort(theArray, first, last)
// Sorts theArray[first..last] by
//   1. sorting the first half of the array
//   2. sorting the second half of the array
//   3. merging the two sorted halves

if (first < last) {
  mid = (first + last)/2    // get midpoint
  // sort theArray[first..mid]
  mergesort(theArray, first, mid)
  // sort theArray[mid+1..last]
  mergesort(theArray, mid + 1, last)
  // merge sorted halves theArray[first..mid]
  // and theArray[mid+1..last]
  merge(theArray, first, mid, last)
}  // end if
// if first >= last, there is nothing to do
```

Clearly, most of the effort in the mergesort algorithm is in the merge step, but does this algorithm actually sort? The recursive calls continue dividing the array into pieces until each piece contains only one item; obviously an array of one item is sorted. The algorithm then merges these small pieces into larger sorted pieces until one sorted array results. Figure 9-9 illustrates both the recursive calls and the merge steps in a mergesort of an array of six integers.

The following Java methods implement the mergesort algorithm. To sort an array *theArray* of *n* items, you would invoke the method *mergesort* by writing *mergesort(theArray, 0, n-1)*.

```
private static void merge(Comparable[] theArray,
                          int first, int mid, int last) {
// ----------------------------------------------------------
// Merges two sorted array segments theArray[first..mid] and
// theArray[mid+1..last] into one sorted array.
// Precondition: first <= mid <= last. The subarrays
// theArray[first..mid] and theArray[mid+1..last] are
// each sorted in increasing order.
// Postcondition: theArray[first..last] is sorted.
// Implementation note: This method merges the two
// subarrays into a temporary array and copies the result
// into the original array anArray.
// ----------------------------------------------------------
```

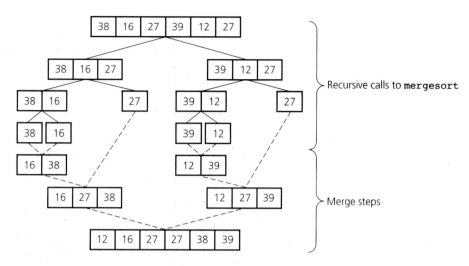

Figure 9-9

A mergesort of an array of six integers

```
int maxSize = theArray.length;
// temporary array
Comparable[] tempArray = new Comparable[maxSize];

// initialize the local indexes to indicate the subarrays
int first1 = first;    // beginning of first subarray
int last1  = mid;      // end of first subarray
int first2 = mid + 1;  // beginning of second subarray
int last2  = last;     // end of second subarray
// while both subarrays are not empty, copy the
// smaller item into the temporary array
int index = first1;    // next available location in
                       // tempArray
while ((first1 <= last1) && (first2 <= last2)) {
  // Invariant: tempArray[first1..index-1] is in order
  if (theArray[first1].compareTo(theArray[first2])<0) {
    tempArray[index] = theArray[first1];
    first1++;
  }
  else {
    tempArray[index] = theArray[first2];
    first2++;
  }  // end if
  index++;
}  // end while

// finish off the nonempty subarray
```

```
      // finish off the first subarray, if necessary
      while (first1 <= last1) {
        // Invariant: tempArray[first1..index-1] is in order
        tempArray[index] = theArray[first1];
        first1++;
        index++;
      }   // end while

      // finish off the second subarray, if necessary
      while (first2 <= last2) {
        // Invariant: tempArray[first1..index-1] is in order
        tempArray[index] = theArray[first2];
        first2++;
        index++;
      }   // end while

      // copy the result back into the original array
      for (index = first; index <= last; ++index) {
        theArray[index] = tempArray[index];
      }   // end for
    }   // end merge

    public static void mergesort(Comparable[] theArray,
                                  int first, int last) {
    // ---------------------------------------------------------
    // Sorts the items in an array into ascending order.
    // Precondition: theArray[first..last] is an array.
    // Postcondition: theArray[first..last] is sorted in
    // ascending order.
    // Calls: merge.
    // ---------------------------------------------------------
      if (first < last) {
        // sort each half
        int mid = (first + last)/2;   // index of midpoint
        // sort left half theArray[first..mid]
        mergesort(theArray, first, mid);
        // sort right half theArray[mid+1..last]
        mergesort(theArray, mid+1, last);

        // merge the two halves
        merge(theArray, first, mid, last);
      }   // end if
    }   // end mergesort
```

Analysis. Because the merge step of the algorithm requires the most effort, let's begin the analysis there. Each merge step merges *the-Array[first..mid]* and *theArray[mid+1..last]*. Figure 9-10 provides an example of a merge step that requires the maximum number of

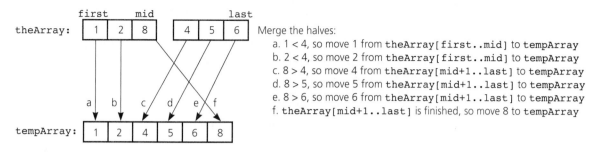

Merge the halves:
a. 1 < 4, so move 1 from `theArray[first..mid]` to `tempArray`
b. 2 < 4, so move 2 from `theArray[first..mid]` to `tempArray`
c. 8 > 4, so move 4 from `theArray[mid+1..last]` to `tempArray`
d. 8 > 5, so move 5 from `theArray[mid+1..last]` to `tempArray`
e. 8 > 6, so move 6 from `theArray[mid+1..last]` to `tempArray`
f. `theArray[mid+1..last]` is finished, so move 8 to `tempArray`

Figure 9-10

A worst-case instance of the merge step in *mergesort*

comparisons. If the total number of items in the two array segments to be merged is n, then merging the segments requires at most $n - 1$ comparisons. (For example, in Figure 9-10 there are six items in the segments and five comparisons.) In addition, there are n moves from the original array to the temporary array, and n moves from the temporary array back to the original array. Thus, each merge step requires $3 * n - 1$ major operations.

Each call to *mergesort* recursively calls itself twice. As Figure 9-11 illustrates, if the original call to *mergesort* is at level 0, two calls to *mergesort* occur at level 1 of the recursion. Each of these calls then calls *mergesort* twice, so four calls to *mergesort* occur at level 2 of the recursion, and so on. How many levels of recursion are there? We can count them as follows.

Each call to *mergesort* halves the array. Halving the array the first time produces two pieces. The next recursive calls to *mergesort* halve each of these two pieces to produce four pieces of the original array; the next recursive calls halve each of these four pieces to produce eight pieces, and so on. The recursive calls continue until the array pieces each

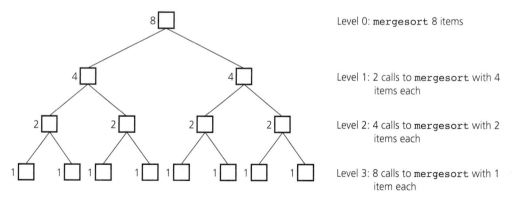

Level 0: mergesort 8 items

Level 1: 2 calls to mergesort with 4 items each

Level 2: 4 calls to mergesort with 2 items each

Level 3: 8 calls to mergesort with 1 item each

Figure 9-11

Levels of recursive calls to *mergesort*, given an array of eight items contain one item—that is, until there are n pieces, where n is the number of items in the original array. If n is a power of 2 ($n = 2^k$), then the recursion goes $k = \log_2 n$ levels deep. For example, in Figure 9-11, there are three levels of recursive calls to `mergesort` because the original array contains eight items, and $8 = 2^3$. If n is not a power of 2, there are $1 + \log_2 n$ (rounded down) levels of recursive calls to `mergesort`.

The original call to `mergesort` (at level 0) calls `merge` once. When called, `merge` merges all n items and requires $3 * n - 1$ operations, as was shown earlier. At level 1 of the recursion, two calls to `mergesort`, and hence to `merge`, occur. Each of these two calls to `merge` merges $n/2$ items and requires $3 * (n/2) - 1$ operations. Together these two calls to `merge` require $2 * (3 * (n/2) - 1)$, or $3 * n - 2$ operations. At level m of the recursion, 2^m calls to `merge` occur; each of these calls merges $n/2^m$ items and so requires $3 * (n/2^m) - 1$ operations. Together the 2^m calls to `merge` require $3 * n - 2^m$ operations. Thus, each level of the recursion requires $O(n)$ operations. Because there are either $\log_2 n$ or $1 + \log_2 n$ levels, *Mergesort is O(n * log₂n)* `mergesort` is $O(n * \log_2 n)$ in both the worst and average cases. You should look at Figure 9-3 again to convince yourself that $O(n * \log_2 n)$ is significantly faster than $O(n^2)$.

Although mergesort is an extremely efficient algorithm with respect to time, it does have one drawback: To perform the step

```
Merge sorted halves theArray[first..mid]
        and theArray[mid+1..last]
```

Mergesort requires a second array as large as the original array the algorithm requires an auxiliary array whose size equals the size of the original array. In Java, this auxiliary array is simply an array of references and hence has little impact. Other programming languages, however, such as C++, actually store the data items in the array. With such languages, this requirement might not be acceptable in situations where storage is limited.

Quicksort

Another divide-and-conquer algorithm Consider the first two steps of the solution to the problem of finding the kth smallest item of the array `theArray[first..last]` that was discussed in Chapter 2:

```
Choose a pivot item p from theArray[first..last]
Partition the items of theArray[first..last] about p
```

Quicksort partitions an array into items that are less than the pivot and those that are greater than or equal to the pivot Recall that this partition, which is pictured again in Figure 9-12, has the property that all items in $S_1 = $ `theArray[first..pivotIndex-1]` are less than the pivot p, and all items in $S_2 = $ `theArray[pivotIndex+1..last]` are greater than or equal to p. Although this property does not imply that the array is sorted, it does imply an extremely useful fact: The items in positions `first` through `pivotIndex` – 1 remain in positions `first` through `pivotIndex` – 1 when the array is properly sorted, although their positions relative to one another may change. Similarly, the items in positions `pivotIndex` + 1 through `last` will remain in positions `pivotIndex` + 1

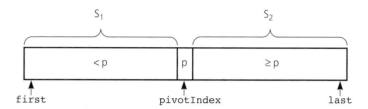

Figure 9-12

A partition about a pivot

through `last` when the array is sorted, although their relative positions may change. Finally, the pivot item remains in its position in the final, sorted array.

Partitioning places the pivot in its correct position within the array

The partition induces relationships among the array items that are the ingredients of a recursive solution. Arranging the array items around the pivot p generates two smaller sorting problems—sort the left section of the array (S_1), and sort the right section of the array (S_2). The relationships between the pivot and the array items imply that once you solve the left and right sorting problems, you will have solved the original sorting problem. That is, partitioning the array before making the recursive calls places the pivot in its correct position and ensures that when the smaller array segments are sorted, their items will be in the proper relation to the rest of the array. Also, the quicksort algorithm will eventually terminate: The left and right sorting problems are indeed smaller problems and are each closer than the original sorting problem to the base case—which is an array containing one item—because the pivot is not part of either S_1 or S_2.

The pseudocode for the quicksort algorithm follows:

```
quicksort(theArray, first, last)
// Sorts theArray[first..last].

   if (first < last) {
      Choose a pivot item p from theArray[first..last]
      Partition the items of theArray[first..last]
        about p
      // the partition is
      // theArray[first..pivotIndex..last]

      // sort S₁
      quicksort(theArray, first, pivotIndex-1)
      // sort S₂
      quicksort(theArray, pivotIndex+1, last)
   } // end if
   // if first >= last, there is nothing to do
```

It is worth contrasting `quicksort` with the pseudocode method given for the kth smallest integer problem in Chapter 2:

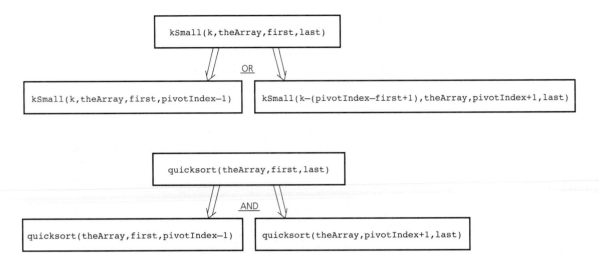

Figure 9-13

kSmall versus **quicksort**

```
kSmall(k, theArray, first, last)
// Returns the kᵗʰ smallest value in
// theArray[first..last].

  Choose a pivot item p from theArray[first..last]
  Partition the items of theArray[first..last] about p
  if (k < pivotIndex - first + 1) {
     return kSmall(k, theArray, first, pivotIndex-1)
  }
  else if (k == pivotIndex - first + 1) {
     return p
  }
  else {
     return kSmall(k-(pivotIndex-first+1),
                   theArray, pivotIndex+1, last)
  }  // end if
```

Difference between kSmall and quicksort

Note that *kSmall* is called recursively only on the section of the array that contains the desired item, and it is not called at all if the desired item is the pivot. On the other hand, *quicksort* is called recursively on both unsorted sections of the array. Figure 9-13 illustrates this difference.

Using an invariant to develop a partition algorithm. Now consider the partition method that both *kSmall* and *quicksort* must call. Partitioning an array section about a pivot item is actually the most difficult part of these two problems.

The partition method will receive an array segment *the-Array[first..last]* as an argument. The method must arrange the items of the array segment into two regions: S_1, the set of items less than the pivot, and S_2, the set of items greater than or equal to the pivot. The method arranges the array so that S_1 is `theArray[first..pivot-Index-1]` and S_2 is `theArray[pivotIndex+1..last]`, as you saw in Figure 9-12.

What pivot should you use? If the items in the array are arranged randomly, you can choose a pivot at random. For example, you can choose `theArray[first]` as the pivot. (The choice of pivot will be discussed in more detail later.) While you are developing the partition, it is convenient to place the pivot in the `theArray[first]` position, regardless of which pivot you choose.

Place your choice of pivot in **`theArray[first]`** *before partitioning*

The items that await placement into either S_1 or S_2 are in another region of the array, called the unknown region. Thus, you should view the array as shown in Figure 9-14. The array indexes `first`, `lastS1`, `firstUnknown`, and `last` divide the array as just described. The relationships between the pivot and the items in the unknown region—which is `theArray[firstUnknown..last]`—are, simply, unknown!

Throughout the entire partitioning process, the following is true:

> *The items in the region S_1 are all less than the pivot, and those in S_2 are all greater than or equal to the pivot.*

Invariant for the partition algorithm

This statement is the invariant for the partition algorithm. For the invariant to be true at the start of the partition algorithm, the array's indexes must be initialized as follows so that the unknown region spans all of the array segment to be partitioned except the pivot:

```
lastS1 = first
firstUnknown = first + 1
```

Initially, all items except the pivot **`theArray[first]`** *constitute the unknown region*

Figure 9-15 shows the initial status of the array.

At each step of the partition algorithm, you examine one item of the unknown region, determine in which of the two regions, S_1 or S_2, it belongs, and place it there. Thus, the size of the unknown region decreases by 1 at each step. The algorithm terminates when the size of the unknown region reaches 0—that is, when `firstUnknown > last`.

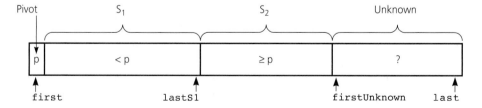

Figure 9-14

Invariant for the partition algorithm

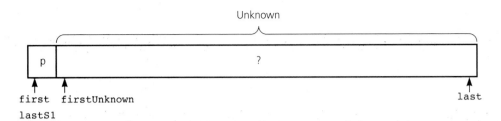

Figure 9-15

Initial state of the array

The following pseudocode describes the partitioning algorithm:

The partition algorithm

```
partition(theArray, first, last)
// Returns the index of the pivot element after
// partitioning theArray[first..last].

    // initialize
    Choose the pivot and swap it with theArray[first]
    p = theArray[first]        // p is the pivot
    lastS₁ = first             // set S₁ and S₂ to empty
    firstUnknown = first + 1   // set unknown region
                               // to theArray[first+1..last]
    // determine the regions S₁ and S₂
    while (firstUnknown <= last) {
       // consider the placement of the "leftmost"
       // item in the unknown region
       if (theArray[firstUnknown] < p) {
         Move theArray[firstUnknown] into S₁
       }
       else {
         Move theArray[firstUnknown] into S₂
       }  // end if
    }  // end while
    // place pivot in proper position between
    // S₁ and S₂, and mark its new location
    Swap theArray[first] with theArray[lastS₁]
    return lastS₁ // the index of the pivot element
```

The algorithm is straightforward enough, but its move operations need clarifying. Consider the two possible actions that you need to take at each iteration of the *while* loop:

> Move **theArray[firstUnknown]** into S_1. S_1 and the unknown region are, in general, not adjacent: S_2 is between the two regions. However, you can perform the required move efficiently. You swap *theArray[firstUnknown]* with the first item of S_2—which is *theArray[lastS1 + 1]*, as Figure 9-16 illustrates. Then you

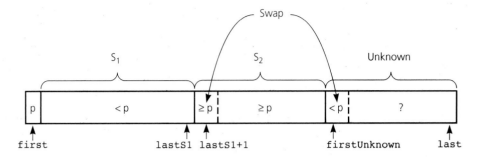

Figure 9-16

Moving **theArray[firstUnknown]** into S_1 by swapping it with
theArray[lastS1+1] and by incrementing both **lastS1** and
firstUnknown

increment `lastS1` by 1. The item that was in `theArray`
`[firstUnknown]` will then be at the rightmost position of S_1.
What about the item of S_2 that was moved to `theAr-`
`ray[firstUnknown]`? If you increment `firstUnknown` by 1, that
item becomes the rightmost member of S_2. Thus, you should
perform the following steps to move `theArray[firstUnknown]`
into S_1:

```
Swap theArray[firstUnknown] with theArray[lastS1+1]
Increment lastS1
Increment firstUnknown
```

This strategy works even when S_2 is empty. In that case,
`lastS1` + 1 equals `firstUnknown`, and thus the swap simply
exchanges an item with itself. *This move preserves the invariant.*

Move theArray[firstUnknown] into S_2. This move is simple to
accomplish. Recall that the rightmost boundary of the region S_2 is
at position `firstUnknown` − 1; that is, regions S_2 and the
unknown region are adjacent, as Figure 9-17 illustrates. Thus, to

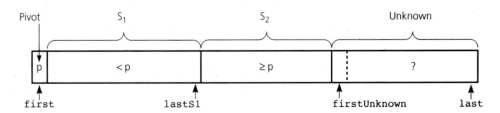

Figure 9-17

Moving **theArray[firstUnknown]** into S_2 by incrementing
firstUnknown

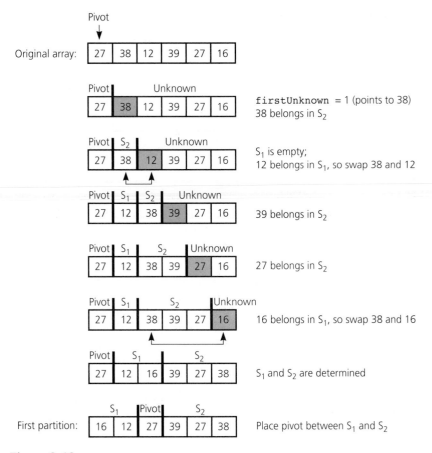

Figure 9-18

Developing the first partition of an array when the pivot is the first item

move *theArray[firstUnknown]* into S_2, simply increment *firstUnknown* by 1: S_2 expands to the right. *This move preserves the invariant.*

After you have moved all items from the unknown region into S_1 and S_2, one final task remains. You must place the pivot between the segments S_1 and S_2. Observe that *theArray[lastS1]* is the rightmost item in S_1. By interchanging this item with the pivot, which is *theArray[first]*, you will place the pivot in its correct location. Then the statement

return *lastS1*

returns the location of the pivot. You can use this index to determine the boundaries of S_1 and S_2. Figure 9-18 traces the partition algorithm for an array of six integers when the pivot is the first item.

Before continuing the implementation of quicksort, we will establish the correctness of the partition algorithm by using invariants. Again, the loop invariant for the algorithm is

> *All items in S_1 (theArray[first+1..lastS1]) are less than the pivot, and all items in S_2 (theArray[lastS1+1..firstUnknown-1]) are greater than or equal to the pivot.*

Recall that when you use invariants to establish the correctness of an iterative algorithm, a four-step process is required:

1. The invariant must be true initially, before the loop begins execution. In the partition algorithm, before the loop that swaps array items is entered, the pivot is theArray[first], the unknown region is theArray[first+1..last], and S_1 and S_2 are empty. The invariant is clearly true initially.

2. An execution of the loop must preserve the invariant. That is, if the invariant is true before any given iteration of the loop, you must show that it is true after the iteration. In the partition algorithm, at each iteration of the loop a single item moves from the unknown region into either S_1 or S_2, depending on whether or not the item is less than the pivot. Thus, if the invariant was true before the move, it will remain true after the move.

3. The invariant must capture the correctness of the algorithm. That is, you must show that if the invariant is true when the loop terminates, the algorithm is correct. In the partition algorithm, the termination condition is that the unknown region is empty. But if the unknown region is empty, each item of theArray[first+1..last] must be in either S_1 or S_2—in which case the invariant implies that the partition algorithm has done what it was supposed to do.

4. The loop must terminate. That is, you must show that the loop will terminate after a finite number of iterations. In the partition algorithm, the size of the unknown region decreases by 1 at each iteration. Therefore, the unknown region becomes empty after a finite number of iterations, and thus the termination condition for the loop will be met.

The proof that the partition algorithm is correct uses an invariant and requires four steps

The following Java methods implement the quicksort algorithm. The method *choosePivot* enables you to try various pivots easily. To sort an array *theArray* of *n* items, you invoke the method *quicksort* by writing quicksort(theArray, 0, n-1).

```
private static void choosePivot(Comparable[] theArray,
                                int first, int last) {
// ------------------------------------------------------------
// Chooses a pivot for quicksort's partition algorithm and
// swaps it with the first item in an array.
// Precondition: theArray[first..last] is an array;
// first <= last.
```

```java
// Postcondition: theArray[first] is the pivot.
// ---------------------------------------------------------
// Implementation left as an exercise.
}  // end choosePivot

private static int partition(Comparable[] theArray,
                             int first, int last) {
// ---------------------------------------------------------
// Partitions an array for quicksort.
// Precondition: theArray[first..last] is an array;
// first <= last.
// Postcondition: Returns the index of the pivot element of
// theArray[first..last]. Upon completion of the method,
// this will be the index value lastS1 such that
//    S1 = theArray[first..lastS1-1] <  pivot
//         theArray[lastS1]          == pivot
//    S2 = theArray[lastS1+1..last]  >= pivot
// Calls: choosePivot.
// ---------------------------------------------------------
   // tempItem is used to swap elements in the array
   Comparable tempItem;
   // place pivot in theArray[first]
   choosePivot(theArray, first, last);
   Comparable pivot = theArray[first];   // reference pivot

   // initially, everything but pivot is in unknown
   int lastS1 = first;          // index of last item in S1

   // move one item at a time until unknown region is empty
   // firstUnknown is the index of first item in unknown region

   for (int firstUnknown = first + 1; firstUnknown <= last;
                               ++firstUnknown) {
     // Invariant: theArray[first+1..lastS1] < pivot
     //            theArray[lastS1+1..firstUnknown-1] >= pivot

     // move item from unknown to proper region
     if (theArray[firstUnknown].compareTo(pivot) < 0) {
       // item from unknown belongs in S1
       ++lastS1;
       tempItem = theArray[firstUnknown];
       theArray[firstUnknown] = theArray[lastS1];
       theArray[lastS1] = tempItem;
     }  // end if
   // else item from unknown belongs in S2
   }  // end for
```

```
  // place pivot in proper position and mark its location
  tempItem = theArray[first];
  theArray[first] = theArray[lastS1];
  theArray[lastS1] = tempItem;
  return lastS1;
}  // end partition

public static void quickSort(Comparable[] theArray,
                             int first, int last) {

// ----------------------------------------------------------
// Sorts the items in an array into ascending order.
// Precondition: theArray[first..last] is an array.
// Postcondition: theArray[first..last] is sorted.
// Calls: partition.
// ----------------------------------------------------------

  int pivotIndex;

  if (first < last) {
    // create the partition: S1, Pivot, S2
    pivotIndex = partition(theArray, first, last);

    // sort regions S1 and S2
    quickSort(theArray, first, pivotIndex-1);
    quickSort(theArray, pivotIndex+1, last);
  }  // end if
}  // end quickSort
```

In the analysis to follow, you will learn that it is desirable to avoid a pivot that makes either S_1 or S_2 empty. A good choice of pivot is one that is near the median of the array items. Exercise 17 at the end of this chapter considers this choice of pivot.

As you can see, *quicksort* and *mergesort* are similar in spirit, but whereas *quicksort* does its work before its recursive calls, *mergesort* does its work after its recursive calls. That is, while *quicksort* has the form

```
quicksort(theArray, first, last)

  if (first < last) {
    Prepare theArray for recursive calls
    quicksort(S₁ region of theArray)
    quicksort(S₂ region of theArray)
  }  // end if
```

mergesort has the general form

```
mergesort(theArray, first, last)

  if (first < last) {
    mergesort(Left half of theArray)
```

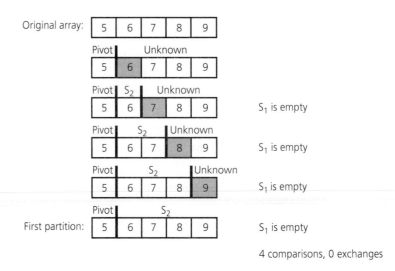

Figure 9-19

A worst-case partitioning with `quicksort`

```
    mergesort(Right half of theArray)
    Tidy up array after the recursive calls
}  // end if
```

The preparation in `quicksort` is to partition the array into regions S_1 and S_2. The algorithm then sorts S_1 and S_2 independently, because every item in S_1 belongs to the left of every item in S_2. In `mergesort,` on the other hand, no work is done before the recursive calls: The algorithm sorts each half of the array with respect to itself. However, the algorithm must still deal with the interaction between the items in the two halves. That is, the algorithm must merge the two halves of the array after the recursive calls.

Analysis.   The major effort in the `quicksort` method occurs during the partitioning step. As you consider each item in the unknown region, you compare `theArray[firstUnknown]` with the pivot and move `the-Array[firstUnknown]` into either S_1 or S_2. It is possible for one of S_1 or S_2 to remain empty. For example, if the pivot is the smallest item in the array segment, S_1 will remain empty. This occurrence is the worst case because S_2 decreases in size by only 1 at each recursive call to `quicksort`. Thus, the maximum number of recursive calls to `quicksort` will occur.

quicksort is slow when the array is already sorted and you choose the smallest item as the pivot

Notice what happens when the array is already sorted into ascending order and you choose the first array item as the pivot. Figure 9-19 shows the results of the first call to `partition` for this situation. The pivot is the smallest item in the array, and S_1 remains empty. In this case, `parti-tion` requires $n - 1$ comparisons to partition the n items in this array. On the next recursive call to `quicksort, partition` is passed $n - 1$ items, so it will require $n - 2$ comparisons to partition them. Again, S_1, will remain

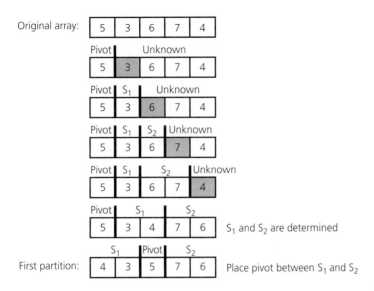

Figure 9-20

An average-case partitioning with `quicksort`

empty. Because the array segment that `quicksort` considers at each level of recursion decreases in size by only 1, $n - 1$ levels of recursion are required. Therefore, `quicksort` requires

$$1 + 2 + \cdots + (n - 1) = n * (n - 1)/2$$

comparisons. However, recall that a move into S_2 does not require an exchange of array items; it requires only a change in the index *first-Unknown*.

Similarly, if S_2 remains empty at each recursive call, $n * (n - 1)/2$ comparisons are required. In addition, however, an exchange is necessary to move each unknown item to S_1. Thus, $n * (n - 1)/2$ exchanges are necessary. (Again, each exchange requires three data moves.) Thus, you can conclude that `quicksort` is $O(n^2)$ in the worst case.

In contrast, Figure 9-20 shows an example in which S_1 and S_2 contain the same number of items. In the average case, when S_1 and S_2 contain the same—or nearly the same—number of items arranged at random, fewer recursive calls to `quicksort` occur. As in the previous analysis of `mergesort`, you can conclude that there are either $\log_2 n$ or $1 + \log_2 n$ levels of recursive calls to `quicksort`. Each call to `quicksort` involves m comparisons and at most m exchanges, where m is the number of items in the subarray to be sorted. Clearly $m \le n - 1$.

A formal analysis of `quicksort`'s average-case behavior would show that it is $O(n * \log_2 n)$. Thus, on large arrays you can expect `quicksort` to run significantly faster than `insertionSort`, although in its worst case, `quicksort` will require roughly the same amount of time as `insertion-Sort`.

Quicksort. Worst case: $O(n^2)$; average case: $O(n * \log_2 n)$

It might seem surprising, then, that `quicksort` is often used to sort large arrays. The reason for `quicksort`'s popularity is that it is usually extremely fast in practice, despite its unimpressive theoretical worst-case behavior. Although a worst-case situation is not typical, even if the worst case occurs, `quicksort`'s performance is acceptable for moderately large arrays.

The fact that `quicksort`'s average-case behavior is far better than its worst-case behavior distinguishes it from the other sorting algorithms considered in this chapter. If the original arrangement of data in the array is "random," `quicksort` performs at least as well as any known sorting algorithm that involves comparisons. Unless the array is already ordered, `quicksort` is best.

On the other hand, `mergesort`'s efficiency is somewhere between the possibilities for `quicksort:` Sometimes `quicksort` is faster, and sometimes `mergesort` is faster. While the worst-case behavior of `mergesort` is of the same order of magnitude as `quicksort`'s average-case behavior, in most situations `quicksort` will run somewhat faster than `mergesort`. However, in its worst case, `quicksort` will be significantly slower than `mergesort`.

Radix Sort

The final sorting algorithm in this chapter is included here because it is quite different from the others.

Imagine one last time that you are sorting a hand of cards. This time you pick up the cards one at a time and arrange them by rank into 13 possible groups in this order: 2, 3, . . . , 10, J, Q, K, A. Combine these groups and place the cards face down on the table so that the 2s are on top and the aces are on the bottom. Now pick up the cards one at a time and arrange them by suit into four possible groups in this order: clubs, diamonds, hearts, and spades. When taken together, the groups result in a sorted hand of cards.

A **radix sort** uses this idea of forming groups and then combining them to sort a collection of data. The sort treats each data item as a character string. As a first simple example of a radix sort, consider this collection of three-letter strings:

ABC, XYZ, BWZ, AAC, RLT, JBX, RDT, KLT, AEO, TLJ

The sort begins by organizing the data according to their rightmost (least significant) letters. Although none of the strings ends in A or B, two strings end in C. Place those two strings into a group. Continuing through the alphabet, you form the following groups:

Group strings by rightmost letter   (ABC, AAC) (TLJ) (AEO) (RLT, RDT, KLT) (JBX) (XYZ, BWZ)

The strings in each group end with the same letter, and the groups are ordered by that letter. The strings within each group retain their relative order from the original list of strings.

Now combine the groups into one as follows. Take the items in the first group in their present order, follow them with the items in the second group in their present order, and so on. The following group results:

ABC, AAC, TLJ, AEO, RLT, RDT, KLT, JBX, XYZ, BWZ *Combine groups*

Next, form new groups as you did before, but this time use the middle letter of each string instead of the last letter:

(AAC) (ABC, JBX) (RDT) (AEO) (TLJ, RLT, KLT) (BWZ) (XYZ) *Group strings by middle letter*

Now the strings in each group have the same middle letter, and the groups are ordered by that letter. As before, the strings within each group retain their relative order from the previous group of all strings.

Combine these groups into one group, again preserving the relative order of the items within each group:

AAC, ABC, JBX, RDT, AEO, TLJ, RLT, KLT, BWZ, XYZ *Combine groups*

Now form new groups according to the first letter of each string:

(AAC, ABC, AEO) (BWZ) (JBX) (KLT) (RDT, RLT) (TLJ) (XYZ) *Group strings by first letter*

Finally, combine the groups, again maintaining the relative order within each group:

AAC, ABC, AEO, BWZ, JBX, KLT, RDT, RLT, TLJ, XYZ *Sorted strings*

The strings are now in sorted order.

In the previous example, all character strings had the same length. If the character strings have varying lengths, you can treat them as if they were the same length by padding them on the right with blanks as necessary.

To sort numeric data, the radix sort treats a number as a character string. You can treat numbers as if they were padded on the left with zeros, making them all appear to be the same length. You then form groups according to the rightmost digits, combine the groups, form groups according to the next-to-last digits, combine them, and so on, just as you did in the previous example. Figure 9-21 shows a radix sort of eight integers.

The following pseudocode describes the algorithm for a radix sort of n decimal integers of d digits each:

```
radixSort(theArray, n, d)
// Sorts n d-digit integers in the array theArray.

  for (j = d down to 1) {
    Initialize 10 groups to empty
    Initialize a counter for each group to 0
    for (i = 0 through n-1) {
      k = jth digit of theArray[i]
      Place theArray[i] at the end of group k
```

0123, 2154, 0222, 0004, 0283, 1560, 1061, 2150	Original integers
(156**0**, 215**0**) (106**1**) (022**2**) (012**3**, 028**3**) (215**4**, 000**4**)	Grouped by fourth digit
1560, 2150, 1061, 0222, 0123, 0283, 2154, 0004	Combined
(00**0**4) (02**2**2, 01**2**3) (21**5**0, 21**5**4) (15**6**0, 10**6**1) (02**8**3)	Grouped by third digit
0004, 0222, 0123, 2150, 2154, 1560, 1061, 0283	Combined
(0**0**04, 1**0**61) (0**1**23, 2**1**50, 2**1**54) (0**2**22, 0**2**83) (1**5**60)	Grouped by second digit
0004, 1061, 0123, 2150, 2154, 0222, 0283, 1560	Combined
(**0**004, **0**123, **0**222, **0**283) (**1**061, **1**560) (**2**150, **2**154)	Grouped by first digit
0004, 0123, 0222, 0283, 1061, 1560, 2150, 2154	Combined (sorted)

Figure 9-21

A radix sort of eight integers

```
          Increase kᵗʰ counter by 1
      }  // end for i


      Replace the items in theArray with all the
          items in group 0, followed by all the
          items in group 1, and so on.
      }  // end for j
```

Analysis. From the pseudocode for the radix sort, you can see that this algorithm requires *n* moves each time it forms groups and *n* moves to combine them again into one group. The algorithm performs these 2 * *n* moves *d* times. Therefore, the radix sort requires 2 * *n* * *d* moves to sort *n* strings of *d* characters each. However, notice that no comparisons are necessary. Thus, radix sort is O(*n*).

A Comparison of Sorting Algorithms

Figure 9-22 summarizes the worst-case and average-case orders of magnitude for the sorting algorithms that appear in this chapter. For reference

	Worst case	Average case
Selection sort	n^2	n^2
Bubble sort	n^2	n^2
Insertion sort	n^2	n^2
Mergesort	n * log n	n * log n
Quicksort	n^2	n * log n
Radix sort	n	n
Treesort	n^2	n * log n
Heapsort	n * log n	n * log n

Figure 9-22

Approximate growth rates of time required for eight sorting algorithms

purposes, two other algorithms—treesort and heapsort—are included here, even though you will not study them until Chapters 10 and 11, respectively.

SUMMARY

1. Order-of-magnitude analysis and Big O notation measure an algorithm's time requirement as a function of the problem size by using a growth-rate function. This approach enables you to analyze the efficiency of an algorithm without regard for such factors as computer speed and programming skill that are beyond your control.

2. When you compare the inherent efficiency of algorithms, you examine their growth-rate functions when the problems are large. Only significant differences in growth-rate functions are meaningful.

3. Worst-case analysis considers the maximum amount of work an algorithm will require on a problem of a given size, while average-case analysis considers the expected amount of work that it will require.

4. You can use order-of-magnitude analysis to help you choose an implementation for an abstract data type. If your application frequently uses particular ADT operations, your implementation should be efficient for at least those operations.

5. Selection sort, bubble sort, and insertion sort are all $O(n^2)$ algorithms. Although, in a particular case, one might be faster than another, for large problems they all are slow.

6. Quicksort and mergesort are two very efficient recursive sorting algorithms. In the "average" case, quicksort is among the fastest known sorting algorithms. However, quicksort's worst-case behavior is significantly slower than mergesort's. Fortunately, quicksort's worst case rarely occurs in practice. Actual execution time for mergesort is not quite as fast as quicksort in the average case, even though they have the same order. However, mergesort's performance is consistently good in all cases. Mergesort has the disadvantage of requiring extra storage equal to the size of the array to be sorted.

CAUTIONS

1. In general, you should avoid analyzing an algorithm solely by studying the running times of a specific implementation. Running times are influenced by such factors as programming style, the particular computer, and the data on which the program is run.

2. When comparing the efficiency of various solutions, look only at significant differences. This rule is consistent with the multidimensional view of the cost of a computer program.

3. While manipulating the Big O notation, remember that $O(f(n))$ represents an inequality. It is not a function but simply a notation that means "is of order $f(n)$" or "has order $f(n)$".

4. If a problem is small, do not overanalyze it. In such a situation, the primary concern should be simplicity. For example, if you are sorting an array that contains only a small number of items—say, fewer than 25—a simple $O(n^2)$ algorithm such as an insertion sort is appropriate.

5. If you are sorting a very large array, an $O(n^2)$ algorithm is probably too inefficient to use.

6. Quicksort is appropriate when you are confident that the data in the array to be sorted is arranged randomly. Although quicksort's worst-case behavior is $O(n^2)$, the worst case rarely occurs in practice.

SELF-TEST EXERCISES

1. How many comparisons of array items do the following loops contain?

    ```
    int temp;
    for (j = 1; j <= n-1; ++j) {
      i = j + 1;
      do {
        if (theArray[i] < theArray[j]) {
          temp = theArray[i];
          theArray[i] = theArray[j];
          theArray[j] = temp;
        }  // end if
        ++i;
      } while (i <= n);
    }  // end for
    ```

2. Repeat Self-Test Exercise 1, replacing the statement $i = j + 1$ with $i = j$.

3. What order is an algorithm that has as a growth-rate function
    a. $8 * n^3 - 9 * n$ b. $7 * \log_2 n + 20$ c. $7 * \log_2 n + n$

4. Consider a sequential search of n data items.
    a. If the data items are sorted into ascending order, how can you determine that your desired item is not in the data collection without always making n comparisons?

    b. What is the order of the sequential search algorithm when the desired item is not in the data collection? Do this for both sorted and unsorted data, and consider the best, average, and worst cases.

    c. Show that if the sequential search algorithm finds the desired item in the data collection, the algorithm's order does not depend upon whether or not the data items are sorted.

5. Trace the selection sort as it sorts the following array into ascending order: 20 80 40 25 60 30.

6. Repeat Self-Test Exercise 5, but instead sort the array into descending order.

7. Trace the bubble sort as it sorts the following array into ascending order: 25 30 20 80 40 60.

8. Trace the insertion sort as it sorts the array in Self-Test Exercise 7 into ascending order.

9. Show that the mergesort algorithm satisfies the four criteria of recursion that Chapter 2 describes.

10. Trace quicksort's partitioning algorithm as it partitions the following array. Use the first item as the pivot.

    38 16 40 39 12 27

11. Suppose that you sort a large array of integers by using mergesort. Next you use a binary search to determine whether a given integer occurs in the array. Finally, you display all the integers in the sorted array.

    a. Which algorithm is faster, in general: the mergesort or the binary search? Explain in terms of Big O notation.

    b. Which algorithm is faster, in general: the binary search or displaying the integers? Explain in terms of Big O notation.

EXERCISES

1. What is the order of each of the following tasks in the worst case?

    a. Computing the sum of the first n even integers by using a `for` loop

    b. Displaying all n integers in an array

    c. Displaying all n integers in a sorted linked list

    d. Displaying all n names in a circular linked list

    e. Displaying one array element

    f. Displaying the last integer in a linked list

    g. Searching an array of n integers for a particular value by using a binary search

    h. Sorting an array of n integers into descending order by using a mergesort

    i. Adding an item to a stack of n items

    j. Adding an item to a queue of n items

2. Suppose that your implementation of a particular algorithm appears in Java as

```java
for (int pass = 1; pass <= n; ++pass) {
  for (int index = 0; index < n; ++index) {
    for (int count = 1; count < 10; ++count) {
      . . .
    } // end for
  } // end for
} // end for
```

The previous code shows only the repetition in the algorithm, not the computations that occur within the loops. These computations, however, are independent of n. What is the order of the algorithm? Justify your answer.

3. Consider the following Java method f. Do not be concerned with f's purpose.

```java
public static void f(int[] theArray, int n) {
  int temp;
  for (int j = 0; j < n; ++j) {
    int i = 0;
    while (i <= j) {
      if (theArray[i] < (theArray[j])) {
        temp = theArray[i];
        theArray[i] = theArray[j];
        theArray[j] = temp;
      }  // end if
      ++i;
    }  // end while
  }  // end for
}  // end f
```

How many comparisons does f perform?

4. For large arrays and in the worst case, is selection sort faster than insertion sort? Explain.

5. Show that any polynomial $f(x) = c_n x^n + c_{n-1} x^{n-1} + \cdots + c_1 x + c_0$ is $O(x^n)$.

6. Show that for all constants $a, b > 1$, $f(n)$ is $O(\log_a n)$ if and only if $f(n)$ is $O(\log_b n)$. Thus, you can omit the base when you write $O(\log n)$. *Hint:* Use the identity $\log_a n = \log_b n / \log_b a$ for all constants $a, b > 1$.

7. This chapter's analysis of selection sort ignored operations that control loops or manipulate array indexes. Revise this analysis by counting *all* operations, and show that the algorithm is still $O(n^2)$.

8. Trace the insertion sort as it sorts the following array into ascending order: 20 80 40 25 60 40.

9. Apply the selection sort, bubble sort, and insertion sort to
   a. An inverted array: 8 6 4 2
   b. An ordered array: 2 4 6 8

10. Find an array that makes the bubble sort exhibit its worst behavior.

11. Write recursive versions of `selectionSort`, `bubbleSort`, and `insertionSort`.

12. Trace the mergesort algorithm as it sorts the following array into ascending order. List the calls to `mergesort` and to `merge` in the order in which they occur.

    20 80 40 25 60 30

13. When sorting an array by using mergesort,

    a. Do the recursive calls to `mergesort` depend on the values in the array, the number of items in the array, or both? Explain.

    b. In what step of `mergesort` are the items in the array actually swapped (that is, sorted)? Explain.

14. Trace the quicksort algorithm as it sorts the following array into ascending order. List the calls to `quicksort` and to `partition` in the order in which they occur.

    20 80 40 25 60 10 15

15. Suppose that you remove the call to `merge` from the `mergesort` algorithm to obtain

    ```
    mystery(theArray, n)
    // mystery algorithm for theArray[0..n-1].

      if (n > 1) {
        mystery(Left half of theArray, n/2)
        mystery(Right half of theArray, n/2)
      }  // end if
    ```

    What does this new algorithm do?

16. You can choose any array item as the pivot for `quicksort`. You then interchange items so that your pivot is in `theArray[first]`. One way to choose a pivot is to take the middle value of the three values `theArray[first]`, `theArray[last]`, and `theArray[(first + last)/2]`. How many comparisons are necessary to sort an array of size n if you always choose the pivot in this way?

17. The partition algorithm that `quicksort` uses moves one item at a time from the unknown region into the appropriate region S_1 or S_2. If the item to be moved belongs in region S_1, and if S_2 is empty, the algorithm will swap an array item with itself. Modify the partition algorithm to eliminate this unnecessary swapping.

18. Use invariants to show that the method `selectionSort` is correct.

*19. Describe an iterative version of `mergesort`. Define an appropriate invariant and show the correctness of your algorithm.

20. One criterion used to evaluate sorting algorithms is stability. A sorting algorithm is **stable** if it does not exchange items that have the same sort key. Thus, items with the same sort key (possibly differing in other ways) will maintain their positions relative to one

another. For example, you might want to take an array of students sorted by name and sort it by year of graduation. Using a stable sorting algorithm to sort the array by year will ensure that within each year the students will remain sorted by name. Some applications mandate a stable sorting algorithm. Others do not. Which of the sorting algorithms described in this chapter are stable?

21. When we discussed the radix sort, we sorted a hand of cards by first ordering the cards by rank and then by suit. To implement a radix sort for this example, you could use two characters to represent a card, if you used T to represent a 10. For example, S2 is the 2 of spades and HT is the 10 of hearts.

   a. Trace the radix sort for this example.
   b. Suppose that you did not use T to represent a 10—that is, suppose that H10 is the 10 of hearts—and that you padded the two-character strings on the right with a blank to form three-character strings. How would a radix sort order the entire deck of cards in this case?

PROGRAMMING PROBLEMS

1. Add a counter to the methods *insertionSort* and *mergesort* that counts the number of comparisons that are made. Run the two methods with arrays of various sizes. On what size does the difference in the number of comparisons become significant? How does this size compare with the size that the orders of these algorithms predict?

2. The method *quicksort* uses the method *choosePivot* to choose a pivot and place it into the first array location. Implement *choosePivot* in two ways:

   a. Always choose the first item in the array as pivot.
   b. Choose a pivot as Exercise 16 describes.

   Add a counter to the method *partition* that counts the number of comparisons that are made. Run *quicksort* with each pivot selection strategy and with arrays of various sizes. On what size array does the difference in the number of comparisons become significant? For which pivot selection strategy does the difference in the number of comparisons become significant?

3. a. Modify the partition algorithm for *quicksort* so that S_1 and S_2 will never be empty.
   b. Another partitioning strategy for *quicksort* is possible. Let an index *low* traverse the array segment *theArray [first..last]* from *first* to *last* and stop when it encounters the first item that is greater than the pivot item. Similarly, let a second index *high* traverse the array segment from *last* to *first* and stop when it encounters the first item that is smaller than the pivot item. Then swap these two items, increment *low*, decrement *high*, and continue until *high* and *low* meet somewhere in the

middle. Implement this version of *quicksort* in Java. How can you ensure that the regions S_1 and S_2 are not empty?

c. There are several variations of this partitioning strategy. What other strategies can you think of? How do they compare to the two that have been given?

4. Implement the radix sort of an array by using an ADT queue for each group.

5. Implement a radix sort of a linked list of integers.

6. a. Implement a mergesort of a linked list of integers.
   b. Implement any other sorting algorithms that are appropriate for a linked list.

7. You can sort a large array of integers that are in the range 1 to 100 by using an array *count* of 100 items to count the number of occurrences of each integer in the array. Fill in the details of this sorting algorithm, which is called a **bucket sort**, and write a Java method that implements it. What is the order of the bucket sort? Why is the bucket sort not useful as a general sorting algorithm?

8. Shellsort (named for its inventor, Donald Shell) is an improved insertion sort. Rather than always exchanging adjacent items—as in insertion sort—Shellsort can exchange items that are far apart in the array. Shellsort arranges the array so that every h^{th} item forms a sorted subarray. For every h in a decreasing sequence of values, Shellsort arranges the array. For example, if h is 5, every fifth item forms a sorted subarray. Ultimately, if h is 1, the entire array will be sorted.

One possible sequence of h's begins at $n/2$ and halves n until it becomes 1. By using this sequence, and by replacing 1 with h and 0 with h–1 in *insertionSort*, we get the following method for Shellsort:

```java
public static void shellsort(Comparable[] theArray, int n) {
  int loc;
  Comparable nextItem;
  for (int h = n/2; h > 0; h = h/2) {
    for (int unsorted = h; unsorted < n; ++unsorted) {
      nextItem = theArray[unsorted];
      loc = unsorted;
      while ((loc >= h) &&
              (theArray[loc-h].compareTo(nextItem) > 0)) {
        theArray[loc] = theArray[loc-h];
        loc = loc - h;
      } // end while
      theArray[loc] = nextItem;
    } // end for unsorted
  } // end for h
} // end shellsort
```

Add a counter to the methods *insertionSort* and *shellsort* that counts the number of comparisons that are made. Run the two methods with arrays of various sizes. On what size does the difference in the number of comparisons become significant?

Trees

PREVIEW   The data organizations presented in previous chapters are linear in that items are one after another. The ADTs in this chapter organize data in a nonlinear, hierarchical form, whereby an item can have more than one immediate successor. In particular, this chapter discusses the specifications, implementations, and relative efficiency of the ADT binary tree and the ADT binary search tree. These ADTs are basic to the next three chapters.

The previous chapters discussed ADTs whose operations fit into at least one of these general categories:

General categories of data-management operations

- Operations that insert data into a data collection
- Operations that delete data from a data collection
- Operations that ask questions about the data in a data collection

The ADTs list, stack, and queue are all **position oriented**, and their operations have the form

The form of operations on position-oriented ADTs

- Insert a data item into the ith *position* of a data collection.
- Delete a data item from the ith *position* of a data collection.
- Ask a question about the data item in the ith *position* of a data collection.

As you have seen, the ADT list places no restriction on the value of i, while the ADTs stack and queue do impose some restrictions. For example, the operations of the ADT stack are restricted to inserting into, deleting from, and asking a question about one end—the top—of the stack. Thus, although they differ with respect to the flexibility of their operations, lists, stacks, and queues manage an association between data items and *positions*.

The ADT sorted list is **value oriented.** Its operations are of the form

The form of operations on value-oriented ADTs

- Insert a data item containing the *value x*.
- Delete a data item containing the *value x*.
- Ask a question about a data item containing the *value x*.

Although these operations, like position-oriented operations, fit into the three general categories of operations listed earlier—they insert data, delete data, and ask questions about data—they are based upon *values* of data items instead of *positions*.

This chapter discusses two major ADTs: the binary tree and the binary search tree. As you will see, the binary tree is a position-oriented ADT, but it is not linear as are lists, stacks, and queues. Thus, you will not reference items in a binary tree by using a position number. Our discussion of the ADT binary tree provides an important background for the more useful binary search tree, which is a value-oriented ADT. Although a binary search tree is also not linear, it has operations similar to those of a sorted list, which is linear.

In the next chapter, you will see two more valued-oriented ADTs: the ADT table and the ADT priority queue. The implementations of both of these ADTs can use the ideas presented in this chapter.

TERMINOLOGY

You use **trees** to represent relationships. Previous chapters informally used tree diagrams to represent the relationships between the calls of a recursive algorithm. For example, the diagram of the *rabbit* algorithm's recursive calls in Figure 2-11 of Chapter 2 is actually a tree. Each call to *rabbit* is represented by a box, or **node**, or **vertex**, in the tree. The lines between the nodes (boxes) are called **edges.** For this tree, the edges indicate recursive calls. For example, the edges from *rabbit*(7) to *rabbit*(6) and *rabbit*(5) indicate that subproblem *rabbit*(7) makes calls to *rabbit*(6) and *rabbit*(5).

All trees are **hierarchical** in nature. Intuitively, hierarchical means that a "parent-child" relationship exists between the nodes in the tree. If an edge is between node *n* and node *m*, and node *n* is above node *m* in the tree, then *n* is the **parent** of *m*, and *m* is a **child** of *n*. In the tree in Figure 10-1, nodes *B* and *C* are children of node *A*. Children of the same parent—for example, *B* and *C*—are called **siblings.** Each node in a tree has at most one parent, and exactly one node—called the **root** of the tree—has no parent. Node *A* is the root of the tree in Figure 10-1. A node that has no children is called a **leaf** of the tree. The leaves of the tree in Figure 10-1 are *C, D, E,* and *F.*

The parent-child relationship between the nodes is generalized to the relationships **ancestor** and **descendant.** In Figure 10-1, *A* is an ancestor of *D,* and thus *D* is a descendant of *A.* Not all nodes are related by the ancestor or descendant relationship: *B* and *C,* for instance, are not so related. However, the root of any tree is an ancestor of every node in that tree. A **subtree** in a tree is any node in the tree together with all of its descendants. A **subtree of a node** *n* is a subtree rooted at a child of *n.* For example, Figure 10-2 shows a subtree of the tree in Figure 10-1. This subtree has *B* as its root and is a subtree of the node *A.*

Because trees are hierarchical in nature, you can use them to represent information that itself is hierarchical in nature—for example, organization charts and family trees, as Figure 10-3 depicts. It may be disconcerting to discover, however, that the nodes in the family tree in Figure 10-3b that represent Caroline's parents (John and Jacqueline) are the children of the node that represents Caroline! That is, the nodes that represent Caroline's ancestors are the descendants of Caroline's node. It's no wonder that computer scientists often seem to be confused by reality.

Formally, a **general tree** *T* is a set of one or more nodes such that *T* is partitioned into disjoint subsets:

- A single node *r*, the root
- Sets that are general trees, called subtrees of *r*

Thus, the trees in Figures 10-1 and 10-3a are general trees.

The primary focus of this chapter will be on binary trees. Formally, a **binary tree** is a set *T* of nodes such that either

- *T* is empty, or

Trees are hierarchical

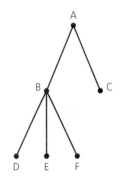

Figure 10-1

A general tree

A subtree is any node and its descendants

Figure 10-2

A subtree of the tree in Figure 10-1

Formal definition of a binary tree

- *T* is partitioned into three disjoint subsets:
  - A single node *r*, the root
  - Two possibly empty sets that are binary trees, called **left** and **right subtrees** of *r*

The trees in Figures 2-11 and 10-3b are binary trees. Notice that each node in a binary tree has no more than two children. A binary tree is not a special kind of general tree, because a binary tree can be empty, whereas a general tree cannot.

The following intuitive restatement of the definition of a binary tree is useful:

T is a binary tree if either

Intuitive definition of a binary tree

- *T* has no nodes, or
- *T* is of the form

$$T_L \overset{r}{\diagup} \diagdown T_R$$

where *r* is a node and T_L and T_R are both binary trees

Notice that the formal definition agrees with this intuitive one: If *r* is the root of *T*, then the binary tree T_L is the left subtree of node *r* and T_R is the right subtree of node *r*. If T_L is not empty, its root is the **left child** of *r*, and if T_R is not empty, its root is the **right child** of *r*. Notice that if both sub-trees of a node are empty, that node is a leaf.

As an example of how you can use a binary tree to represent data in a hierarchical form, consider Figure 10-4. The binary trees in this figure represent algebraic expressions that involve the binary operators +, −, *, and /. To represent an expression such as *a* − *b*, you place the operator in the root node and the operands *a* and *b* into the left and right children, respectively, of the root. (See Figure 10-4a.) Figure 10-4b represents the expression *a* − *b*/*c*; a subtree represents the subexpression *b*/*c*. A similar situation exists in Figure 10-4c, which represents (*a* − *b*) * *c*. The leaves of these trees contain the expressions' operands, while other tree nodes

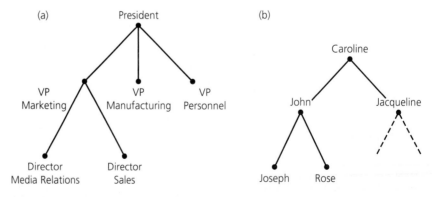

Figure 10-3

(a) An organization chart; (b) a family tree

Figure 10-4

Binary trees that represent algebraic expressions

Figure 10-5

A binary search tree
of names

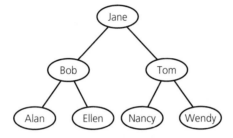

contain the operators. Parentheses do not appear in these trees. The binary tree provides a hierarchy for the operations—that is, the tree specifies an unambiguous order for evaluating an expression.

The nodes of a tree typically contain values. A **binary search tree** is a binary tree that is in a sense sorted according to the values in its nodes. For each node n, a binary search tree satisfies the following three properties:

- n's value is greater than all values in its left subtree T_L.
- n's value is less than all values in its right subtree T_R.
- Both T_L and T_R are binary search trees.

Properties of a binary search tree

Figure 10-5 is an example of a binary search tree. As its name suggests, a binary search tree organizes data in a way that facilitates searching it for a particular data item. Later, this chapter discusses binary search trees in detail.

The height of trees. Trees come in many shapes. For example, although the binary trees in Figure 10-6 all contain the same nodes, their structures are quite different. Although each of these trees has seven nodes, some are "taller" than others. The **height** of any tree is the number of nodes on the

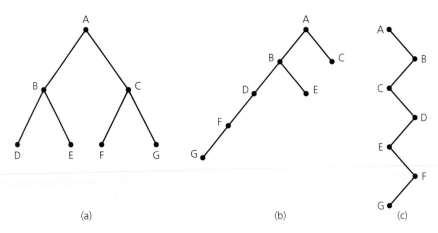

Figure 10-6

Binary trees with the same nodes but different heights

longest path from the root to a leaf. For example, the trees in Figure 10-6 have respective heights of 3, 5, and 7. Many people's intuitive notion of height would lead them to say that these trees have heights of 2, 4, and 6. Indeed, many authors define height to agree with this intuition. However, the definition of height used in this book leads to a cleaner statement of many algorithms and properties of trees.

There are other equivalent ways to define the height of a tree *T*. One way uses the following definition of the **level** of a node *n*:

Level of a node

- If *n* is the root of *T*, it is at level 1.
- If *n* is not the root of *T*, its level is 1 greater than the level of its parent.

For example, in Figure 10-6a, node *A* is at level 1, node *B* is at level 2, and node *D* is at level 3.

The **height** of a tree *T* in terms of the levels of its nodes is defined as follows:

Height of a tree in terms of levels

- If *T* is empty, its height is 0.
- If *T* is not empty, its height is equal to the maximum level of its nodes.

Apply this definition to the trees in Figure 10-6 and show that their heights are, respectively, 3, 5, and 7, as was stated earlier.

For binary trees, it is often convenient to use an equivalent recursive definition of height:

Recursive definition of height

- If *T* is empty, its height is 0.
- If *T* is a nonempty binary tree, then because *T* is of the form

$$T_L \overset{\displaystyle r}{\diagup \diagdown} T_R$$

the height of T is 1 greater than the height of its root's taller sub-tree; that is,

$$height(T) = 1 + max\{height(T_L), height(T_R)\}$$

Later, when we discuss the efficiency of searching a binary search tree, it will be necessary to determine the maximum and minimum heights of a binary tree of n nodes.

Full, complete, and balanced binary trees. In a **full binary tree** of height h, all nodes that are at a level less than h have two children each. Figure 10-7 depicts a full binary tree of height 3. Each node in a full binary tree has left and right subtrees of the same height. Among binary trees of height h, a full binary tree has as many leaves as possible, and they all are at level h. Intuitively, a full binary tree has no missing nodes.

Figure 10-7

A full binary tree of height 3

When proving properties about full binary trees—such as how many nodes they have—the following recursive definition of a full binary tree is convenient:

- If T is empty, T is a full binary tree of height 0.

- If T is not empty and has height $h > 0$, T is a full binary tree if its root's subtrees are both full binary trees of height $h - 1$.

A full binary tree

This definition closely reflects the recursive nature of a binary tree.

A **complete binary tree** of height h is a binary tree that is full down to level $h - 1$, with level h filled in from left to right, as Figure 10-8 illustrates. More formally, a binary tree T of height h is complete if

1. All nodes at level $h - 2$ and above have two children each, and

A complete binary tree

2. When a node at level $h - 1$ has children, all nodes to its left at the same level have two children each, and

3. When a node at level $h - 1$ has one child, it is a left child

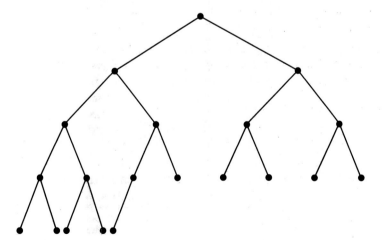

Figure 10-8

A complete binary tree

Full binary trees are complete

Parts 2 and 3 of this definition formalize the requirement that level h be filled in from left to right. Note that a full binary tree is complete.

Finally, a binary tree is **height balanced**, or simply **balanced**, if the height of any node's right subtree differs from the height of the node's left subtree by no more than 1. The binary trees in Figures 10-8 and 10-6a are balanced, but the trees in Figures 10-6b and 10–6c are not balanced. A complete binary tree is balanced.

Complete binary trees are balanced

The following is a summary of the major tree terminology presented so far.

KEY CONCEPTS

Summary of Tree Terminology

General tree	A set of one or more nodes, partitioned into a root node and subsets that are general subtrees of the root.
Parent of node n	The node directly above node n in the tree.
Child of node n	A node directly below node n in the tree.
Root	The only node in the tree with no parent.
Leaf	A node with no children.
Siblings	Nodes with a common parent.
Ancestor of node n	A node on the path from the root to n.
Descendant of node n	A node on a path from n to a leaf.
Subtree of node n	A tree that consists of a child (if any) of n and the child's descendants.
Height	The number of nodes on the longest path from the root to a leaf.
Binary tree	A set of nodes that is either empty or partitioned into a root node and one or two subsets that are binary subtrees of the root. Each node has at most two children, the left child and the right child.
Left (right) child of node n	A node directly below and to the left (right) of node n in a binary tree.
Left (right) subtree of node n	In a binary tree, the left (right) child (if any) of node n plus its descendants.
Binary search tree	A binary tree where the value in any node n is greater than the value in every node in n's left subtree, but less than the value of every node in n's right subtree.
Empty binary tree	A binary tree with no nodes.
Full binary tree	A binary tree of height h with no missing nodes. All leaves are at level h and all other nodes each have two children.

| Complete binary tree | A binary tree of height h that is full to level $h - 1$ and has level h filled in from left to right. |
| Balanced binary tree | A binary tree in which the left and right subtrees of any node have heights that differ by at most 1. |

THE ADT BINARY TREE

As an abstract data type, the binary tree has operations that add and remove nodes and subtrees. By using these basic operations, you can build any binary tree. Other operations set or retrieve the data in the root of the tree and determine whether the tree is empty.

Traversal operations that *visit* every node in a binary tree are also typical. "Visiting" a node means "doing something with or to" the node. Chapter 4 introduced the concept of traversal for a linked list: Beginning with the list's first node, you visit each node sequentially until you reach the end of the linked list. Chapter 8 showed how to implement a Java iterator to facilitate traversal of the list. Traversal of a binary tree, however, visits the tree's nodes in one of several different orders. The three standard orders are called preorder, inorder, and postorder, and they are described in the next section along with an iterator for binary trees.

The operations available for a particular ADT binary tree depend on the type of binary tree being implemented. Thus, we will first develop an abstract class representing a binary tree, containing only the most basic binary tree operations. Later, we will extend this abstract class to provide additional binary tree operations.

Basic Operations of the ADT Binary Tree

The first task is to define the operations that are common to all binary tree implementations. Here is a summary:

Basic Operations of the ADT Binary Tree

1. Create an empty binary tree.
2. Create a one-node binary tree, given an item.
3. Remove all nodes from a binary tree, leaving it empty.
4. Determine whether a binary tree is empty.
5. Determine what data is the binary tree's root.

Notice that we did not include in this basic set of operations an operation that changes the item in the root. For some binary trees, such an operation would not be desirable.

The following pseudocode specifies these basic operations in more detail.

Pseudocode for the Basic Operations of the ADT Binary Tree

```
createBinaryTree()
// Creates an empty binary tree.

createBinaryTree(rootItem)
// Creates a one-node binary tree whose root contains
// rootItem.

makeEmpty()
// Removes all of the nodes from a binary tree, leaving an
// empty tree.

isEmpty()
// Determines whether a binary tree is empty.

getRootItem() throws TreeException
// Retrieves the data item in the root of a nonempty
// binary tree. Throws TreeException if the tree is
// empty.
```

As you can see, we must still specify other operations for building the tree. One possible set of operations is presented next.

General Operations of the ADT Binary Tree

As was mentioned earlier, the particular operations provided for an ADT binary tree depend on the kind of binary tree we are designing. This section specifies some general operations for a binary tree, with the assumption that we are adding these operations to the basic operations of the ADT binary tree specified before.

Pseudocode for the General Operations of the ADT Binary Tree

```
createBinaryTree(rootItem, leftTree, rightTree)
// Creates a binary tree whose root contains rootItem and
// has leftTree and rightTree, respectively, as its left
// and right subtrees.
```

```
setRootItem(newItem)
// Replaces the data item in the root of a binary tree
// with newItem, if the tree is not empty. If the
// tree is empty, creates a root node whose data item
// is newItem and inserts the new node into the tree.

attachLeft(newItem) throws TreeException
// Attaches a left child containing newItem to the root of
// a binary tree. Throws TreeException if the binary
// tree is empty (no root node to attach to) or a left
// subtree already exists (should explicitly
// detach it first).

attachRight(newItem) throws TreeException
// Attaches a right child containing newItem to the root of
// a binary tree. Throws TreeException if the binary
// tree is empty (no root node to attach to) or a left
// subtree already exists (should explicitly
// detach it first).

attachLeftSubtree(leftTree) throws TreeException
// Attaches leftTree as the left subtree of the
// root of a binary tree and makes leftTree empty
// so that it cannot be used as a reference into this tree.
// Throws TreeException if the binary tree is empty
// (no root node to attach to) or a left subtree already
// exists (should explicitly detach it first).

attachRightSubtree(rightTree) throws TreeException
// Attaches rightTree as the right subtree of the
// root of a binary tree and makes rightTree empty
// so that it cannot be used as a reference into this tree.
// Throws TreeException if the binary tree is empty
// (no root node to attach to) or a right subtree already
// exists (should explicitly detach it first).

detachLeftSubtree() throws TreeException
// Detaches and returns the left subtree of a binary tree's
// root. Throws TreeException if the binary
// tree is empty (no root node to detach from).

detachRightSubtree() throws TreeException
// Detaches and returns the right subtree of a binary tree's
// root. Throws TreeException if the binary
// tree is empty (no root node to detach from).
```

You can use these operations, for example, to build the binary tree in Figure 10-6b, in which the node labels represent character data. The following pseudocode constructs the tree from the subtree *tree1* rooted at *"F"*, the subtree *tree2* rooted at *"D"*, the subtree *tree3* rooted at *"B"*, and the subtree *tree4* rooted at *"C"*. Initially, these subtrees exist but are empty.

Using ADT binary tree operations to build a binary tree

```
tree1.setRootItem("F")
tree1.attachLeft("G")

tree2.setRootItem("D")
tree2.attachLeftSubtree(tree1)

tree3.setRootItem("B")
tree3.attachLeftSubtree(tree2)
tree3.attachRight("E")

tree4.setRootItem("C")
// tree in Fig 10-6b
binTree.createBinaryTree("A", tree3, tree4)
```

The traversal operations are considered in detail next.

Traversals of a Binary Tree

A traversal algorithm for a binary tree visits each node in the tree. While visiting a node, you do something with or to the node. For the purpose of this discussion, assume that visiting a node simply means displaying the data portion of the node.

With the recursive definition of a binary tree in mind, you can construct a recursive traversal algorithm as follows. According to the definition, the binary tree T is either empty or is of the form

If T is empty, the traversal algorithm takes no action—an empty tree is the base case. If T is not empty, the traversal algorithm must perform three tasks: It must display the data in the root r, and it must traverse the two subtrees T_L and T_R, each of which is a binary tree smaller than T.

Thus, the general form of the recursive traversal algorithm is

The general form of a recursive traversal algorithm

```
traverse(binTree)
// Traverses the binary tree binTree.

    if (binTree is not empty) {
       traverse(Left subtree of binTree's root)
       traverse(Right subtree of binTree's root)
    }  // end if
```

This algorithm is not quite complete, however. It is missing the instruction to display the data in the root. When traversing any binary tree, the algorithm has three choices of when to visit the root r. It can visit r before it traverses both of r's subtrees, it can visit r after it has traversed r's left subtree T_L but before it traverses r's right subtree T_R, or it can visit r after it has traversed both of r's subtrees. These traversals are called **preorder, inorder**, and **postorder**, respectively. Figure 10-9 shows the results of these traversals for a given binary tree.

The preorder traversal algorithm is as follows:

Preorder traversal

```
preorder(binTree)
// Traverses the binary tree binTree in preorder.
// Assumes that "visit a node" means to display
// the node's data item.

  if (binTree is not empty) {
    Display the data in the root of binTree
    preorder(Left subtree of binTree's root)
    preorder(Right subtree of binTree's root)
  }  // end if
```

The preorder traversal of the tree in Figure 10-9a visits the nodes in this order: 60, 20, 10, 40, 30, 50, 70. If you apply preorder traversal to a binary tree that represents an algebraic expression, such as any tree in Figure 10-4, and display the nodes as you visit them, you will obtain the prefix form of the expression.[1]

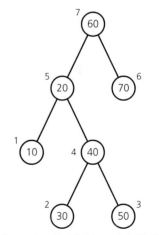

(a) Preorder: 60, 20, 10, 40, 30, 50, 70   (b) Inorder: 10, 20, 30, 40, 50, 60, 70   (c) Postorder: 10, 30, 50, 40, 20, 70, 60

(Numbers beside nodes indicate traversal order.)

Figure 10-9

Traversals of a binary tree: (a) preorder; (b) inorder; (c) postorder

---

[1] The prefix expressions are (a) $-ab$; (b) $-a/bc$; (c) $*-abc$.

The inorder traversal algorithm is as follows:

Inorder traversal

```
inorder(binTree)
// Traverses the binary tree binTree in inorder.
// Assumes that "visit a node" means to display
// the node's data item.

  if (binTree is not empty) {
     inorder(Left subtree of binTree's root)
     Display the data in the root of binTree
     inorder(Right subtree of binTree's root)
  }  // end if
```

The result of the inorder traversal of the tree in Figure 10-9b is 10, 20, 30, 40, 50, 60, 70. If you apply inorder traversal to a binary search tree, you will visit the nodes in order according to their data values. Such is the case for the tree in Figure 10-9b.

Finally, the postorder traversal algorithm is as follows:

Postorder traversal

```
postorder(binTree)
// Traverses the binary tree binTree in postorder.
// Assumes that "visit a node" means to display
// the node's data item.

  if (binTree is not empty) {
     postorder(Left subtree of binTree's root)
     postorder(Right subtree of binTree's root)
     Display the data in the root of binTree
  }  // end if
```

The result of the postorder traversal of the tree in Figure 10-9c is 10, 30, 50, 40, 20, 70, 60. If you apply postorder traversal to a binary tree that represents an algebraic expression, such as any tree in Figure 10-4, and display the nodes as you visit them, you will obtain the postfix form of the expression.[2]

Each of these traversals visits every node in a binary tree exactly once. Thus, *n* visits occur for a tree of *n* nodes. Each visit performs the same operations on each node, independently of *n*, so it must be O(1). Thus, each traversal is O(*n*).

Traversal is O(n)

As we discussed in Chapter 8, an iterator class can be developed in conjunction with a collection of objects. In this case, the objects are stored in the nodes of a binary tree, and the order in which this collection is iterated could be based on preorder, inorder, or postorder traversal of the tree. This allows users of the binary tree class to visit each node of the tree and specify the action to be performed on each item in the tree.

---

[2]The postfix expressions are (a) *ab*–; (b) *abc*/–; (c) *ab*−*c**.

Possible Representations of a Binary Tree

You can implement a binary tree by using the constructs of Java in one of three general ways. Two of these approaches use arrays, but the typical implementation uses references. In each case, the described data structures would be private data fields of a class of binary trees.

To illustrate the three approaches, we will implement a binary tree of names. Each node in this tree contains a name, and, because the tree is a binary tree, each node has at most two descendant nodes.

An array-based representation. If you use a Java class to define a node in the tree, you can represent the entire binary tree by using an array of tree nodes. Each tree node contains a data portion—a name in this case—and two indexes, one for each of the node's children, as the following Java statements indicate:

```java
public class TreeNode {
    private Object item;        // data item in the tree
    private int leftChild;      // index to left child
    private int rightChild;     // index to right child
    ...
    // constructors and methods appear here
}   // end TreeNode

public abstract class BinaryTreeArrayBased {
    protected final int MAX_NODES = 100;
    protected TreeNode tree[];
    protected int root; // index of tree's root
    protected int free; // index of next unused array
                        // location
    ...
    // constructors and methods
}   // end BinaryTreeArrayBased
```

The class *BinaryTreeArrayBased* is declared *abstract*, since it is the basis for implementing other classes of binary trees. Also, there will be no instances of this base class *BinaryTreeArrayBased*. The constants and data fields are declared *protected* so that they will be directly accessible by the subclasses.

The variable *root* is an index to the tree's root within the array *tree*. If the tree is empty, *root* is –1. Both *leftChild* and *rightChild* within a node are indexes to the children of that node. If a node has no left child, *leftChild* is –1; if a node has no right child, *rightChild* is –1.

As the tree changes due to insertions and deletions, its nodes may not be in contiguous elements of the array. Therefore, this implementation requires you to establish a list of available nodes, which is called a **free list.** To insert a new node into the tree, you first obtain an available node from the free list. If you delete a node from the tree, you place it into the free list so that you can reuse the node at a later time. The variable *free*

A free list keeps track of available nodes

is the index to the first node in the free list and, arbitrarily, the *right–Child* field of each node in the free list is the index of the next node in the free list.[3] Figure 10-10 contains a binary tree and the data fields for its array-based implementation.

An array-based representation of a complete tree.   The previous implementation works for any binary tree, even though the tree in Figure 10-10 is complete. If you know that your binary tree is complete, you can use a simpler array-based implementation that saves memory. As you saw earlier in this chapter, a complete tree of height h is full to level $h - 1$ and has level h filled from left to right.

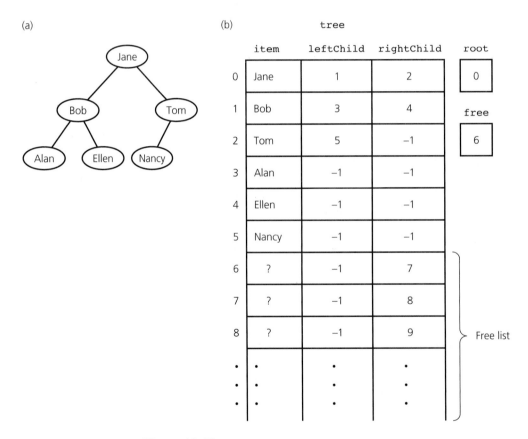

Figure 10-10

(a) A binary tree of names; (b) its array-based implementation

---

[3]This free list is actually an array-based linked list, as Programming Problem 9 of Chapter 4 describes.

Figure 10-11

Level-by-level numbering of a complete binary tree

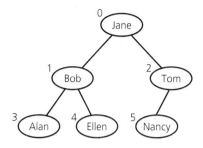

Figure 10-12

An array-based implementation of the complete binary tree in Figure 10-11

0	Jane
1	Bob
2	Tom
3	Alan
4	Ellen
5	Nancy
6	
7	

Figure 10-11 shows the complete binary tree of Figure 10-10a with its nodes numbered according to a standard level-by-level scheme. The root is numbered 0, and the children of the root (the next level of the tree) are numbered, left to right, 1 and 2. The nodes at the next level are numbered, left to right, 3, 4, and 5. You place these nodes into the array `tree` in numeric order. That is, `tree[i]` contains the node numbered *i*, as Figure 10-12 illustrates. Now, given any node `tree[i]`, you can easily locate both of its children and its parent: Its left child (if it exists) is `tree[2*i+1]`, its right child (if it exists) is `tree[2*i+2]`, and its parent (if `tree[i]` is not the root) is `tree[(i-1)/2]`.

This array-based representation requires a complete binary tree. If nodes were missing from the middle of the tree, the numbering scheme would be thrown off, and the parent-child relationship among nodes would be ambiguous. This requirement implies that any changes to the tree must maintain its completeness.

If the binary tree is complete and remains complete, you can use a memory-efficient array-based implementation

As you will see in the next chapter, an array-based representation of a binary tree is useful in the implementation of the ADT priority queue.

A reference-based representation. You can use Java references to link the nodes in the tree. Thus, you can represent a tree by using the following Java classes:

```
public class TreeNode {
  private Object item;
  private TreeNode leftChild;
  private TreeNode rightChild;
  ...
  // constructors and methods, including methods to get
  // the leftChild reference (getLeft()) and the
  // rightChild reference (getRight())
}  // end TreeNode

public abstract class BinaryTreeBasis {
  protected TreeNode root;
  ...
  // constructors and methods appear here
}  // end BinaryTreeBasis
```

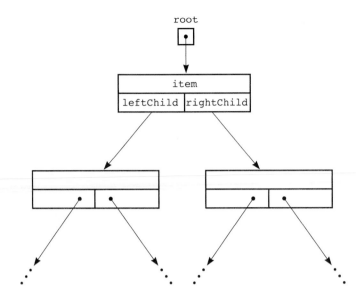

Figure 10-13

A reference-based implementation of a binary tree

The class *TreeNode* is analogous to the class *Node* that we used in Chapter 4 for a linked list. Within the class *BinaryTreeBasis*, the external reference *root* references the tree's root. If the tree is empty, *root* is *null*. Figure 10-13 illustrates this implementation.

The root of a nonempty binary tree has a left subtree and a right subtree, each of which is a binary tree. In a reference-based implementation, *root* references the root *r* of a binary tree, *root.getLeft()* references the root of the left subtree of *r*, and *root.getRight()* references the root of the right subtree of *r*.

The section that follows provides the details for a reference-based implementation of the ADT binary tree.

A Reference-Based Implementation of the ADT Binary Tree

The following classes provide a reference-based implementation for the ADT binary tree described earlier. A discussion of several implementation details follows these classes. The specification of pre- and postconditions is left as an exercise.

A node in a binary tree

```java
public class TreeNode {
  private Object item;
  private TreeNode leftChild;
  private TreeNode rightChild;
```

```java
   public TreeNode(Object newItem) {
   // Initializes tree node with item and no children.
     item = newItem;
     leftChild  = null;
     rightChild = null;
   }  // end constructor

   public TreeNode(Object newItem,
                     TreeNode left, TreeNode right) {
   // Initializes tree node with item and
   // the left and right children references.
     item = newItem;
     leftChild  = left;
     rightChild = right;
   }  // end constructor

   public Object getItem() {
   // Returns the item field.
     return item;
   }  // end getItem

   public void setItem(Object newItem) {
   // Sets the item field to the new value newItem.
     item  = newItem;
   }  // end setItem

   public TreeNode getLeft() {
   // Returns the reference to the left child.
     return leftChild;
   }  // end getLeft

   public void setLeft(TreeNode left) {
   // Sets the left child reference to left.
     leftChild  = left;
   }  // end setLeft

   public TreeNode getRight() {
   // Returns the reference to the right child.
     return rightChild;
   }  // end getRight

   public void setRight(TreeNode right) {
   // Sets the right child reference to right.
     rightChild  = right;
   }  // end setRight
 }  // end TreeNode
```

An exception class

```
public class TreeException extends RuntimeException {
  public TreeException(String s) {
    super(s);
  }  // end constructor
} // end TreeException
```

An abstract class of basic tree operators

```
public abstract class BinaryTreeBasis {
  protected TreeNode root;

  public BinaryTreeBasis() {
    root = null;
  }  // end default constructor

  public BinaryTreeBasis(Object rootItem) {
    root = new TreeNode(rootItem, null, null);
  }  // end constructor

  public boolean isEmpty() {
  // Returns true if the tree is empty, else returns false.
    return root == null;
  }  // end isEmpty

  public void makeEmpty() {
  // Removes all nodes from the tree.
    root = null;
  }  // end makeEmpty

  public Object getRootItem() throws TreeException {
  // Returns the item in the tree's root.
    if (root == null) {
      throw new TreeException("TreeException: Empty tree");
    }
    else {
      return root.getItem();
    }  // end if
  }  // end getRootItem

}  // end BinaryTreeBasis
```

BinaryTreeBasis will be used as the base class for the implementation of particular binary trees. It is declared as an abstract class because it is used for inheritance purposes only; there can be no direct instances of this class. *BinaryTreeBasis* declares the root of the tree as a protected item so that the subclasses will have direct access to the root of the tree. It also provides methods to check for an empty tree, to make the tree empty, and to retrieve the contents of the root node. Setting the contents of the root node is left to a subclass, since different kinds of binary trees may have varying requirements regarding the value in the root node of the tree.

The following class implements the general operations of a binary tree and is derived from *BinaryTreeBasis*.

```java
public class BinaryTree extends BinaryTreeBasis {
  public BinaryTree() {
  }  // end default constructor

  public BinaryTree(Object rootItem) {
    super(rootItem);
  }  // end constructor

  public BinaryTree(Object rootItem,
                    BinaryTree leftTree,
                    BinaryTree rightTree) {
    root = new TreeNode(rootItem, null, null);
    attachLeftSubtree(leftTree);
    attachRightSubtree(rightTree);
  }  // end constructor

  public void setRootItem(Object newItem) {
    if (root != null) {
      root.setItem(newItem);
    }
    else {
      root = new TreeNode(newItem, null, null);
    }  // end if
  }  // end setRootItem

  public void attachLeft(Object newItem) {
    if (!isEmpty() && root.getLeft() == null) {
      // assertion: nonempty tree; no left child
      root.setLeft(new TreeNode(newItem, null, null));
    }  // end if
  }  // end attachLeft

  public void attachRight(Object newItem) {
    if (!isEmpty() && root.getRight() == null) {
      // assertion: nonempty tree; no right child
      root.setRight(new TreeNode(newItem, null, null));
    }  // end if
  }  // end attachRight

  public void attachLeftSubtree(BinaryTree leftTree)
                                  throws TreeException {
    if (isEmpty()) {
      throw new TreeException("TreeException:  Empty tree");
    }
```

A class that extends
BinaryTreeBasis

```java
    else if (root.getLeft() != null) {
      // a left subtree already exists; it should have been
      // deleted first
      throw new TreeException("TreeException: " +
                        "Cannot overwrite left subtree");
    }
    else {
      // assertion: nonempty tree; no left child
      root.setLeft(leftTree.root);
      // don't want to leave multiple entry points into
      // our tree
      leftTree.makeEmpty();
    }  // end if
  }  // end attachLeftSubtree

  public void attachRightSubtree(BinaryTree rightTree)
                              throws TreeException {
    if (isEmpty()) {
      throw new TreeException("TreeException:  Empty tree");
    }
    else if (root.getRight() != null) {
      // a right subtree already exists; it should have been
      // deleted first
      throw new TreeException("TreeException: " +
                        "Cannot overwrite right subtree");
    }
    else {
      // assertion: nonempty tree; no right child
      root.setRight(rightTree.root);
      // don't want to leave multiple entry points into
      // our tree
      rightTree.makeEmpty();
    }  // end if
  }  // end attachRightSubtree

  protected BinaryTree(TreeNode rootNode) {
    root = rootNode;
  }  // end protected constructor

  public BinaryTree detachLeftSubtree()
                         throws TreeException {
    if (isEmpty()) {
      throw new TreeException("TreeException:  Empty tree");
    }
    else {
      // create a new binary tree that has root's left
      // node as its root
      BinaryTree leftTree;
```

```
      leftTree = new BinaryTree(root.getLeft());
      root.setLeft(null);
      return leftTree;
   }  // end if
}  // end detachLeftSubtree


public BinaryTree detachRightSubtree()
                    throws TreeException {
   if (isEmpty()) {
      throw new TreeException("TreeException:  Empty tree");
   }
   else {
      BinaryTree rightTree;
      rightTree = new BinaryTree(root.getRight());
      root.setRight(null);
      return rightTree;
   }  // end if
}  // end detachRightSubtree


} // end BinaryTree
```

The class *BinaryTree* has more constructors than previous classes
you have seen. They allow you to define binary trees in a variety of circumstances. Two of these constructors refer back to the abstract class
BinaryTreeBasis, with a third declared within *BinaryTree*. With these
constructors you can construct a binary tree

- That is empty
- From data for its root, which is its only node
- From data for its root and the root's two subtrees

For example, the following statements invoke these three constructors:

```
BinaryTree tree1 = new BinaryTree();
BinaryTree tree2 = new BinaryTree(root2);
BinaryTree tree3 = new BinaryTree(root3);
BinaryTree tree4 = new BinaryTree(root4, tree2, tree3);
```

Sample uses of public constructors

In these statements, *tree1* is an empty binary tree; *tree2* and *tree3* have
only root nodes, whose data is *root2* and *root3*, respectively; and *tree4* is
a binary tree whose root contains *root4* and has subtrees *tree2* and *tree3*.

The class also contains a protected constructor, which creates a tree
from a reference to a root node. For example,

```
leftTree = new BinaryTree(root.getLeft())
```

constructs a tree *leftTree* whose root is the node that *root.getLeft()*
references. Although the methods *detachLeftSubtree* and *detach-
RightSubtree* use this constructor, it should not be available to clients of
the class, because they do not have access to node references. Thus, this
constructor is not public.

Some methods should not be public

Note that *attachLeftSubtree* and *attachRightSubtree* call *make-Empty* with the subtree as an argument after the subtree has been attached to the invoking tree. This causes the root of the subtree as it existed in the client to be set to *null*. Thus, the client will not be able to access and manipulate the subtree directly, a violation of abstraction of the tree.

Tree Traversals Using an Iterator

We will use the tree traversals to determine the order in which an iterator will visit the nodes of a tree. The tree iterator will implement the Java *Iterator* interface and will provide methods to set the iterator to the type of traversal desired. Since the abstract class *BinaryTreeBasis* has sufficient information to perform a traversal, we will define the iterator using this class. This will allow the iterator class to be used by any subclass of the *BinaryTreeBasis*.

As we mentioned in Chapter 8, a class that implements the *Iterator* interface must provide three methods: *next()*, *hasNext()*, and *remove()*. We will not implement the *remove()* method in this version of the iterator for two reasons: First, the semantics of removing a node from a tree may depend on the type of tree you are working with (for example, a binary search tree). Second, the class *BinaryTree* itself does not provide a method for removing nodes from the tree.

The iterator class for the binary tree should be placed in the same package as *BinaryTreeBasis*. Doing so will give the iterator access to the root of the tree and, in turn, to all of the nodes of the tree. This access is necessary for the implementation of the iterator.

You must implement the recursive traversal operations carefully so that you do not violate the wall of the ADT. For example, the method *inorder*, whose declaration is

void inorder(TreeNode treeNode);

has as a parameter the reference *treeNode*, which eventually references every node in the tree. Because this parameter clearly depends on the tree's reference-based implementation, *inorder* is not suitable as a public method. The method *inorder*, in fact, is a private method, which the public method *setInorder* calls.

The implementation presented here for the iterator of a binary tree assumes that the iteration order will be set by calling *setPreorder*, *set-Inorder*, or *setPostorder*. Until one of these methods is called, the iterator will not provide any items from the tree (*hasNext* returns *false*).

Implement traversals so that the action to be performed remains on the client's side of the wall

Recall from Chapter 8 that the behavior of an iterator is unspecified if the underlying collection is modified in any way other than by calling the method *remove()* while the iteration is in progress. Thus, if the binary tree is altered after the iteration order has been set, the changes to the tree will not be reflected in the iteration.

Here is the definition of the tree iterator class *TreeIterator*:

```java
public class TreeIterator implements java.util.Iterator {
  private BinaryTreeBasis binTree;
  private TreeNode currentNode;
  private QueueInterface queue; // from Chapter 7

  public TreeIterator(BinaryTreeBasis bTree) {
    binTree = bTree;
    currentNode = null;
    // empty queue indicates no traversal type currently
    // selected or end of current traversal has been reached
    queue = new QueueReferenceBased();
  } // end constructor

  public boolean hasNext() {
    return !queue.isEmpty();
  } // end hasNext

  public Object next()
              throws java.util.NoSuchElementException {
    try {
      currentNode = (TreeNode)queue.dequeue();
      return currentNode.getItem();
    } // end try
    catch (QueueException e) {
      throw new java.util.NoSuchElementException();
    } // end catch
  } // end next

  public void remove()
              throws UnsupportedOperationException {
    throw new UnsupportedOperationException();
  } // end remove

  public void setPreorder() {
    queue.dequeueAll();
    preorder(binTree.root);
  } // setPreOrder

  public void setInorder() {
    queue.dequeueAll();
    inorder(binTree.root);
  } // end setInorder

  public void setPostorder() {
    queue.dequeueAll();
    postorder(binTree.root);
  } // end setPostorder
```

```
    private void preorder(TreeNode treeNode) {
      if (treeNode != null) {
        queue.enqueue(treeNode);
        preorder(treeNode.getLeft());
        preorder(treeNode.getRight());
      } // end if
    }   // end preorder

    private void inorder(TreeNode treeNode) {
      if (treeNode != null) {
        inorder(treeNode.getLeft());
        queue.enqueue(treeNode);
        inorder(treeNode.getRight());
      } // end if
    }   // end inorder

    private void postorder(TreeNode treeNode) {
      if (treeNode != null) {
        postorder(treeNode.getLeft());
        postorder(treeNode.getRight());
        queue.enqueue(treeNode);
      } // end if
    }   // end postorder
}   // end TreeIterator
```

The class *TreeIterator* uses a queue to maintain the current traversal of the nodes in the tree. This traversal order is placed in a queue when the client selects the desired traversal method. If a new traversal is set in the middle of an iteration, the queue is cleared first, and then the new traversal is generated.

The following statements create an iterator that will perform a preorder traversal of a tree *tree4*:

```
    TreeIterator treeIterator = new TreeIterator(tree4);
    treeIterator.setPreorder();
```

Here is an example that uses the iterator to print out the nodes of the tree using the preorder traversal:

```
        System.out.println("Preorder traversal:");
        while (treeIterator.hasNext()) {
          System.out.println(treeIterator.next());
        }   // end while
```

To demonstrate how to use *BinaryTree* and *TreeIterator*, we build and then traverse the binary tree in Figure 10-9:

A sample program
```
public static void main(String[] args) {
    BinaryTree tree3 = new BinaryTree(new Integer(70));

    // build the tree in Figure 10-9
```

```
BinaryTree tree1 = new BinaryTree();
tree1.setRootItem(new Integer(40));
tree1.attachLeft(new Integer(30));
tree1.attachRight(new Integer(50));

BinaryTree tree2 = new BinaryTree();
tree2.setRootItem(new Integer(20));
tree2.attachLeft(new Integer(10));
tree2.attachRightSubtree(tree1);

BinaryTree binTree =    // tree in Figure 10-9
        new BinaryTree(new Integer(60), tree2, tree3);

TreeIterator btIterator = new TreeIterator(binTree);
btIterator.setInorder();

while (btIterator.hasNext()) {
  System.out.println(btIterator.next());
} // end while

BinaryTree leftTree = binTree.detachLeftSubtree();
TreeIterator leftIterator = new TreeIterator(leftTree);

// iterate through the left subtree
leftIterator.setInorder();
while (leftIterator.hasNext()) {
  System.out.println(leftIterator.next());
} // end while

// iterate through binTree minus left subtree
btIterator.setInorder();
while (btIterator.hasNext()) {
  System.out.println(btIterator.next());
} // end while
} // end main
```

Here, *binTree* is the tree in Figure 10-9. Its inorder traversal is 10, 20, 30, 40, 50, 60, 70. The inorder traversal of the left subtree of *binTree*'s root (the subtree rooted at 20) is 10, 20, 30, 40, 50. The inorder traversal of *leftTree* produces the same result. Since *leftTree* is actually detached from *binTree*, the final traversal of *binTree* is 60, 70.

One disadvantage of this implementation of the traversal is that it performs a lot of computations that may never be used. Not only is a queue of node references created, but also the recursion stores activation records on an implicit stack. Besides the time requirement, O(n) additional space is used by the recursion for a tree with n nodes. In contrast, the space requirement for a nonrecursive traversal of the tree would be only O(*height of the tree*). Programming Problem 6 asks you to explore this issue further.

Nonrecursive traversal (*optional*).   Before leaving the topic of traversals, let's develop a nonrecursive traversal algorithm to illustrate further the relationship between stacks and recursion that was discussed in Chapter 6. In particular, we will develop a nonrecursive inorder traversal for the reference-based implementation of a binary tree.

The conceptually difficult part of a nonrecursive traversal is determining where to go next after a particular node has been visited. To gain some insight into this problem, consider how the recursive *inorder* method works:

```
inorder(treeNode)
// Recursively traverses a binary tree in inorder.

if (treeNode != null) {
   inorder(treeNode.getLeft())   // point 1
   queue.enqueue(treeNode)
   inorder(treeNode.getRight()) // point 2
} // end if
```

Recursive calls from points 1 and 2

The method has its recursive calls marked as points 1 and 2.

During the course of the method's execution, the value of the reference *treeNode* actually marks the current position in the tree. Each time *inorder* makes a recursive call, the traversal moves to another node. In terms of the stack that is implicit to recursive methods, a call to *inorder* pushes the new value of *treeNode*—that is, a reference to the new current node—onto the stack. At any given time, the stack contains references to the nodes along the path from the tree's root to the current node n, with the reference to n at the top of the stack and the reference to the root at the bottom. Note that n is possibly "empty"—that is, it may be indicated by a *null* value for *treeNode* at the top of the stack.

*Study recursive **inorder**'s implicit stack to gain insight into a nonrecursive traversal algorithm*

Figure 10-14 partially traces the execution of *inorder* and shows the contents of the implicit stack. The first four steps of the trace show the stack as *treeNode* references first 60, then 20, then 10, and then becomes *null*. The recursive calls for these four steps are from point 1 in *inorder*.

Now consider what happens when *inorder* returns from a recursive call. The traversal retraces its steps by backing up the tree from a node n to its parent p, from which the recursive call to n was made. Thus, the reference to n is popped from the stack and the reference to p comes to the top of the stack, as occurs in Step 5 of the trace in Figure 10-14. (n happens to be empty in this case, so *null* is popped from the stack.)

What happens next depends on which subtree of p has just been traversed. If you have just finished traversing p's left subtree (that is, if n is the left child of p and thus the return is made to point 1 in *inorder*), control is returned to the statement that displays the data in node p. Such is the case for Steps 6 and 10 of the trace in Figure 10-14. Figure 10-15a illustrates Steps 9 and 10 in more detail.

After the data in p has been displayed, a recursive call is made from point 2 and the right subtree of p is traversed. However, if, as Figure 10-15b illustrates, you have just traversed p's right subtree (that is, if n is

(The notation →60 means "a reference to the node containing 60.")

Figure 10-14

Contents of the implicit stack as **treeNode** progresses through a
given tree during a recursive inorder traversal

the right child of *p* and thus the return is made to point 2), control is
returned to the end of the method. As a consequence, another return is
made, the reference to *p* is popped off the stack, and you go back up the
tree to *p*'s parent, from which the recursive call to *p* was made. In this
latter case, the data in *p* is not displayed—it was displayed before the
recursive call to *n* was made from point 2.

Thus, two facts emerge from the recursive version of *inorder* when a
return is made from a recursive call:

- The implicit recursive stack of references is used to find the node *Actions at a return from a*
  p to which the traversal must go back. *recursive call to* **inorder**

- Once the traversal backs up to node *p*, it either visits *p* (for example, displays its data) or backs farther up the tree. It visits *p* if *p*'s
  left subtree has just been traversed; it backs up if its right subtree
  has just been traversed. The appropriate action is taken simply as a
  consequence of the point—1 or 2—to which control is returned.

You could directly mimic this action by using an iterative method and
an explicit stack, as long as some bookkeeping device kept track of which
subtree of a node had just been traversed. However, you can use the following observation both to eliminate the need for the bookkeeping device and

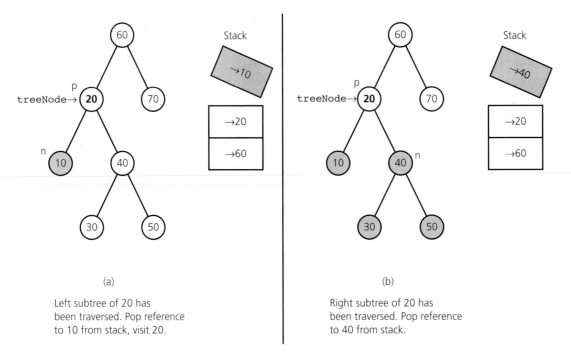

(a)

Left subtree of 20 has
been traversed. Pop reference
to 10 from stack, visit 20.

(b)

Right subtree of 20 has
been traversed. Pop reference
to 40 from stack.

Figure 10-15

Traversing (a) the left and (b) the right subtrees of 20

to speed up the traversal somewhat. Consider the tree in Figure 10-16. After you have finished traversing the subtree rooted at node *R*, there is no need to return to nodes *C* and *B*, because the right subtrees of these nodes have already been traversed. You can instead return directly to node *A*, which is the nearest ancestor of *R* whose right subtree has not yet been traversed.

This strategy of not returning to a node after its right subtree has been traversed is simple to implement: You place a reference to a node in the stack only before the node's left subtree is traversed, but not before its right subtree is traversed. Thus, in Figure 10-16, when you are at node *R*, the stack contains *A* and *R*, with *R* on top. Nodes *B* and *C* are not in the stack, because you have visited them already and are currently traversing their right subtrees. On the other hand, *A* is in the stack because you are currently traversing its left subtree. When you return from node *R*, nodes *B* and *C* are thus bypassed because you have finished with their right subtrees and do not need to return to these nodes. Thus, you pop *R*'s reference from the stack and go directly to node *A*, whose left subtree has just been traversed. You then visit *A*, pop its reference from the stack, and traverse *A*'s right subtree.

This nonrecursive traversal strategy is captured by the following pseudocode, assuming a reference-based implementation. Exercise 14 at the end of this chapter asks you to trace this algorithm for the tree in Figure 10-14.

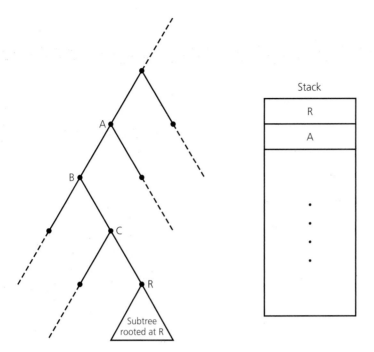

Stack

R
A

Figure 10-16

Avoiding returns to nodes *B* and *C*

```
inorderTraverse(treeNode)                              Nonrecursive inorder traversal
// Nonrecursively traverses a binary tree in inorder.

  // initialize
  Create an empty stack visitStack
  curr = treeNode          // start at root treeNode
  done = false

  while (!done) {
    if (curr != null) {
      // place reference to node on stack before
      // traversing node's left subtree
      visitStack.push(curr)

      // traverse the left subtree
      curr = curr.getLeft()
    }

    else {// backtrack from the empty subtree and visit
          // the node at the top of the stack; however,
          // if the stack is empty, you are done
```

```
if (!visitStack.isEmpty()) {
  curr = visitStack.pop()
  queue.enqueue(curr)

  // traverse the right subtree
  // of the node just visited
  curr = curr.getRight()
}

  else {
    done = true
  }  // end if
}  // end if
}  // end while
```

Eliminating recursion can be more complicated than the example given here. However, the general case is beyond the scope of this book.

THE ADT BINARY SEARCH TREE

Searching for a particular item is one operation for which the ADT binary tree is ill suited. The binary search tree is a binary tree that corrects this deficiency by organizing its data by value. Recall that each node n in a binary search tree satisfies the following three properties:

- n's value is greater than all values in its left subtree T_L.
- n's value is less than all values in its right subtree T_R.
- Both T_L and T_R are binary search trees.

This organization of data enables you to search a binary search tree for a particular data item, given its value instead of its position. As you will see, certain conditions make this search efficient.

A binary search tree is often used in situations where the instances stored in the tree contain many different fields of information. For example, each item in a binary search tree might contain a person's name, ID number, address, telephone number, and so on. In general, such an item is called a **record** and will be an instance of a Java class. To determine whether a particular person is in the tree, you could provide the data for all components, or **fields,** of the record, but typically you would provide only one field—the ID number, for example. Thus, the request

```
Find the record for the person whose ID number is
123456789
```

is feasible if the ID number uniquely describes the person. By making this request, not only can you determine whether a person is in a binary search tree, but, once you find the person's record, you can also access the other data about the person.

A field such as an ID number is called a **search key**, or simply a **key**, because it identifies the record that you seek. This portion of the record may involve more than one field, and it will need to be compared to the key of other records. It is important that the value of the search key remain the same as long as the item is stored in the tree. Changing the search key of an existing element in the tree could make that element or other tree elements impossible to find. Thus, the search-key value should not be modifiable. This suggests the use of a *KeyedItem* class for items of the tree. The class *KeyedItem* will contain the search key as a data field and a method for accessing the search key. The class appears as follows:

A data item in a binary search tree has a specially designated search key

```
public abstract class KeyedItem {
   private Comparable searchKey;

   public KeyedItem(Comparable key) {
      searchKey = key;
   }  // end constructor

   public Comparable getKey() {
      return searchKey;
   } // end getKey
} // end KeyedItem
```

Classes for the items that are in a binary search tree must extend *KeyedItem*. Such classes will have only the constructor available for initializing the search key. Thus, the search-key value cannot be modified once an item is created.

As an example of a class that extends *KeyedItem*, suppose we want to create a class *Person* as just described, in which the person's ID number is used as the search key.

```
public class Person extends KeyedItem {
   // inherits method getKey that returns the search key
   private FullName name;
   private String phoneNumber;
   private Address address;

   public Person(String id, FullName name, String phone,
               Address addr) {
     super(id);   // sets the key value to id
     this.name = name;
     phoneNumber = phone;
     address = addr;
   }  // end constructor

   public String toString() {
     return getKey() + " # " + name;
   } // end toString

   // other methods would appear here
}  // end Person
```

Notice that the class *Person* inherits the *getKey* method to return the field that has been designated as the key. This will be the value that is used to search for a record in the tree. The *Person* class could easily be designed to use a key that involves more than one value. For example, if the key is the person's first name and last name, you can use the class *FullName* as presented on page 173 of Chapter 4, since it implements the *Comparable* interface. The class *Person* would then provide the person's full name as the key by replacing the constructor with the following:

```
public Person(String id, FullName name,
                 String phone, Address addr) {

    super(name);
    idNumber = id; // idNumber declared as a private
                   // data field
    phoneNumber = phone;
    address = addr;
} // end constructor
```

You also would revise the data fields of *Person* by omitting *name* and adding *idNumber*.

For simplicity, we will assume that the search key uniquely identifies the records in your binary search tree. In this case, you can restate the recursive definition of a binary search tree as follows:

For each node n, a binary search tree satisfies the following three properties:

A recursive definition of a binary search tree

- n's search key is greater than all search keys in n's left subtree T_L.
- n's search key is less than all search keys in n's right subtree T_R.
- Both T_L and T_R are binary search trees.

As an ADT, the binary search tree has operations that are like the operations for the ADTs you studied in previous chapters in that they involve inserting, deleting, and retrieving data. In the implementations of the position-oriented ADTs list, stack, and queue, insertion and deletion into the ADT was independent of the value of the data. In the binary search tree, however, the insertion, deletion, and retrieval operations are by search-key value, not by position. The search key facilitates the search process, since we need to know only the key information to find a particular record or to determine the proper position for a data item in the tree. The traversal operations that you just saw for a binary tree apply to a binary search tree without change, because a binary search tree is a binary tree.

The operations that extend the basic ADT binary tree to the ADT binary search tree are as follows:

KEY CONCEPTS

Operations of the ADT Binary Search Tree

1. Insert a new item into a binary search tree.

2. Delete the item with a given search key from a binary search tree.

3. Retrieve the item with a given search key from a binary search tree.

4. Traverse the items in a binary search tree in preorder, inorder, or postorder.

The following pseudocode specifies the first three operations in more detail. As you soon will see, you can use the class *TreeIterator* developed earlier to perform traversals of a binary search tree.

KEY CONCEPTS

Pseudocode for the Operations of the ADT Binary Search Tree

```
insert(newItem)
// Inserts newItem into a binary search tree whose items
// have distinct search keys that differ from newItem's
// search key.

delete(searchKey) throws TreeException
// Deletes from a binary search tree the item whose search
// key equals searchKey. If no such item exists, the
// operation fails and throws TreeException.

retrieve(searchKey)
// Returns the item in a binary search
// tree whose search key equals searchKey. Returns
// null if no such item exists.
```

Figure 10-17 is a binary search tree *nameTree* of names. Each node in the tree is actually a record that represents the named person. That is, if the search key for each record is the person's name, you see only the search keys in the picture of the tree.

For example,

```
firstRecord = nameTree.retrieve("Nancy")
```

retrieves Nancy's record into *firstRecord*. If you insert a record *second-Record* into *nameTree* that describes Jack by invoking

```
nameTree.insert(secondRecord)
```

you will be able to retrieve that record later and still be able to retrieve Nancy's record. If you delete Jane's record by using

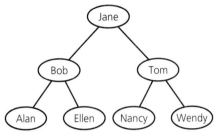

Figure 10-17

A binary search tree

```
nameTree.delete("Jane")
```

you will still be able to retrieve the records for Nancy and Jack. Finally, if an iterator *nameIterator* is declared for *nameTree*, you display the name records as follows:

```
TreeIterator nameIterator = new TreeIterator(nameTree);
nameIterator.setInorder();
System.out.println("Inorder traversal:");
while (nameIterator.hasNext()) {
  System.out.println(nameIterator.next());
}  // end while
```

This will display in alphabetical order the names of the people that *name-Tree* represents.

Algorithms for the Operations of the ADT Binary Search Tree

Consider again the binary search tree in Figure 10-17. Each node in the tree contains data for a particular person. The person's first name is the search key, and that is the only data item you see in the figure.

Because a binary search tree is recursive by nature, it is natural to formulate recursive algorithms for operations on the tree. Suppose that you want to locate Ellen's record in the binary search tree of Figure 10-17. Jane is in the root node of the tree, so if Ellen's record is present in the tree it must be in Jane's left subtree, because the search key Ellen is before the search key Jane alphabetically. From the recursive definition, you know that Jane's left subtree is also a binary search tree, so you use exactly the same strategy to search this subtree for Ellen. Bob is in the root of this binary search tree, and, because the search key Ellen is greater than the search key Bob, Ellen's record must be in Bob's right subtree. Bob's right subtree is also a binary search tree, and it happens that Ellen is in the root node of this tree. Thus, the search has located Ellen's record.

The following pseudocode summarizes this search strategy:

A search algorithm for a binary search tree

```
search(bst, searchKey)
// Searches the binary search tree bst for the item
// whose search key is searchKey.
```

```
if (bst is empty) {
  The desired record is not found
}
else if (searchKey == search key of root's item) {
    The desired record is found
}
else if (searchKey < search key of root's item) {
    search(Left subtree of bst, searchKey)
}
else {
  search(Right subtree of bst, searchKey)
} // end if
```

As you will see, this *search* algorithm is the basis of the insertion, deletion, and retrieval operations on a binary search tree.

Many different binary search trees can contain the names Alan, Bob, Ellen, Jane, Nancy, Tom, and Wendy. For example, in addition to the tree in Figure 10-17, each tree in Figure 10-18 is a valid binary search tree for

Several different binary search trees are possible for the same data

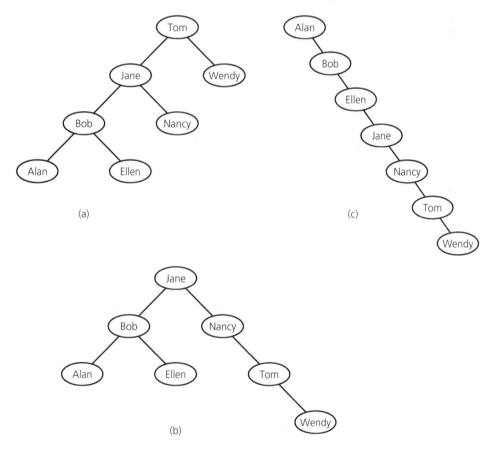

Figure 10-18

Binary search trees with the same data as in Figure 10-17

these names. Although these trees have different shapes, the shape of the tree in no way affects the validity of the *search* algorithm. The algorithm requires only that a tree be a binary search tree.

The method *search* works more efficiently on some trees than on others, however. For example, with the tree in Figure 10-18c, the *search* algorithm inspects every node before locating Wendy. In fact, this binary tree really has the same structure as a sorted linear linked list and offers no advantage in efficiency. In contrast, with the full tree in Figure 10-17, the *search* algorithm inspects only the nodes that contain the names Jane, Tom, and Wendy. These names are exactly the names that a binary search of the sorted array in Figure 10-19 would inspect. Later in this chapter, you will learn more about how the shape of a binary search tree affects *search*'s efficiency and how the insertion and deletion operations affect this shape.

The algorithms that follow for insertion, deletion, retrieval, and traversal assume the reference-based implementation of a binary tree that was discussed earlier in this chapter. With minor changes, the basic algorithms also apply to other implementations of the binary tree. Also keep in mind the assumption that the items in the tree have unique search keys.

Insertion. Suppose that you want to insert a record for Frank into the binary search tree of Figure 10-17. As a first step, imagine that you instead want to *search* for the item with a search key of Frank. The *search* algorithm first searches the tree rooted at Jane, then the tree rooted at Bob, and then the tree rooted at Ellen. It then searches the tree rooted at the right child of Ellen. Because this tree is empty, as Figure 10-20 illustrates, the *search* algorithm has reached a base case and will terminate with the report that Frank is not present. What does it mean that *search* looked for Frank in the right subtree of Ellen? For one thing, it means that if Frank were the right child of Ellen, *search* would have found Frank there.

This observation indicates that a good place to insert Frank is as the right child of Ellen. Because Ellen has no right child, the insertion is simple, requiring only that Ellen's *rightChild* field reference a node containing Frank. More important, Frank belongs in this location—*search* will look for Frank here. Specifically, inserting Frank as the right child of Ellen will preserve the tree's binary search tree property. Because *search*, when searching for Frank, would follow a path that leads to the right child of Ellen, you are assured that Frank is in the proper relation to the names above it in the tree.

Alan	Bob	Ellen	Jane	Nancy	Tom	Wendy
0	1	2	3	4	5	6

Figure 10-19

An array of names in sorted order

Figure 10-20

Empty subtree where **search** terminates

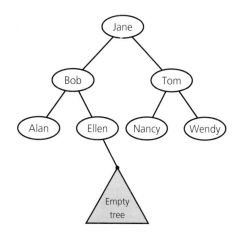

Using *search* to determine where in the tree to insert a new name always leads to an easy insertion. No matter what new item you insert into the tree, *search* will always terminate at an empty subtree. Thus, *search* always tells you to insert the item as a new leaf. Because adding a leaf requires only a change of the appropriate reference in the parent, the work required for an insertion is virtually the same as that for the corresponding search.

*Use **search** to determine the insertion point*

The following high-level pseudocode describes this insertion process:

```
insertItem(treeNode, newItem)
// Inserts newItem into the binary search tree of
// which treeNode is the root.
   Let parentNode be the parent of the empty subtree
        at which search terminates when it seeks
        newItem's search key

   if (Search terminated at parentNode's left subtree) {
      Set leftChild of parentNode to reference newItem
   }
   else {
      Set rightChild of parentNode to reference newItem
   }  // end if
```

First draft of the insertion algorithm

The appropriate reference—*leftChild* or *rightChild*—of node *parentNode* must be set to reference the new node. The recursive nature of the *search* algorithm provides an elegant means of setting the reference, provided that you return *treeNode* as the result of the method, as you will see. Thus, *insertItem* is refined as follows:

```
insertItem(treeNode, newItem)
// Inserts newItem into the binary search tree of
// which treeNode is the root.
```

Refinement of the insertion algorithm

```
if (treeNode is null) {
  Create a new node and let treeNode reference it
  Create a new node with newItem as the data portion
  Set the references in the new node to null
}

else if (newItem.getKey() < treeNode.getItem().getKey()) {
  treeNode.setLeft(insertItem(treeNode.getLeft(), newItem))
}
else {
  treeNode.setRight(insertItem(treeNode.getRight(), newItem))
} // end if

return treeNode
```

How does this recursive algorithm set *leftChild* and *rightChild* to reference the new node? The situation is quite similar to the recursive insertion method for the sorted linked list that you saw in Chapter 4. If the tree was empty before the insertion, the external reference to the root of the tree would be *null* and the method would not make a recursive call. When this situation occurs, a new tree node must be created and initialized. The method then returns the reference to this node, which should be made the new root of the tree. Figure 10-21a illustrates insertion into an empty tree.

The general case of *insertItem* is similar to the special case for an empty tree. When the formal parameter *treeNode* becomes *null,* the corresponding actual argument is the *leftChild* or *rightChild* reference in the parent of the empty subtree; that is, this reference has the value *null*. This reference was passed to the *insertItem* method by one of the recursive calls

```
insertItem(treeNode.getLeft(), newItem)
```

or

```
insertItem(treeNode.getRight(), newItem)
```

As in the case of the empty tree, the method will return the reference to a new node, which then must be set as either the parent's left child or the parent's right child. Thus, you complete the insertion by using either *setLeft* to make the returned node the new left child of the parent, or *setRight* to make the returned node the new right child of the parent. Parts *b* and *c* of Figure 10-21 illustrate the general case of insertion.

To copy a tree, traverse it in pre-order and insert each item visited into a new tree

You can use *insertItem* to create a binary search tree. For example, beginning with an empty tree, if you insert the names Jane, Bob, Alan, Ellen, Tom, Nancy, and Wendy in order, you will get the binary search tree in Figure 10-17. It is interesting to note that the names Jane, Bob, Alan, Ellen, Tom, Nancy, and Wendy constitute the preorder traversal of the tree in Figure 10-17. Thus, if you take the output of a preorder traversal of a binary search tree and use it with *insertItem* to create a binary search tree, you will obtain a duplicate tree.

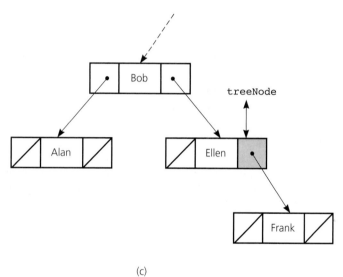

Figure 10-21

**(a) Insertion into an empty tree; (b) search terminates at a leaf;
(c) insertion at a leaf**

By inserting the previous names in a different order, you will get a different binary search tree. For example, by inserting the previous names in alphabetic order, you will get the binary search tree in Figure 10-18c.

Deletion. The deletion operation is a bit more involved than insertion. First, you use the *search* algorithm to locate the item with the specified search key and then, if it is found, you must remove the item from the tree. A first draft of the algorithm follows:

First draft of the deletion algorithm

```
deleteItem(rootNode, searchKey)
// Deletes from the binary search tree with root
// rootNode the item whose search key equals
// searchKey. If no such item exists, the operation
// fails and throws TreeException.
   Locate (by using the search algorithm) the item i
      whose search key equals searchKey

   if (item i is found) {
     Remove item i from the tree
   }
   else {
     throw a tree exception
   }  // end if
```

The essential task here is

```
Remove item i from the tree
```

Assuming that `deleteItem` locates item *i* in a particular node *N*, there are three cases to consider:

Three cases for the node N containing the item to be deleted

1. *N* is a leaf.

2. *N* has only one child.

3. *N* has two children.

Case 1: Set the reference in a leaf's parent to `null`

The first case is the easiest. To remove the leaf containing item *i*, you need only set the reference in its parent to `null`. The second case is a bit more difficult. If *N* has only one child, you have two possibilities:

Case 2: Two possibilities for a node with one child

• *N* has only a left child.

• *N* has only a right child.

The two possibilities are symmetrical, so it is sufficient to illustrate the solution for a left child. In Figure 10-22a, *L* is the left child of *N*, and *P* is the parent of *N*. *N* can be either the left child or the right child of *P*. If you deleted *N* from the tree, *L* would be without a parent, and *P* would be without one of its children. Suppose you let *L* take the place of *N* as one of

Let N's parent adopt N's child

P's children, as in Figure 10-22b. Does this adoption preserve the binary search tree property?

If *N* is the left child of *P*, for example, all of the search keys in the subtree rooted at *N* are less than the search key in *P*. Thus, all of the search keys in the subtree rooted at *L* are less than the search key in *P*. Therefore, after *N* is removed and *L* is adopted by *P*, all of the search keys in *P*'s left subtree are still less than the search key in *P*. This deletion strategy thus preserves the binary search tree property. A parallel argument holds if *N* is a right child of *P*, and therefore the binary search tree property is preserved in either case.

Case 3: N has two children

The most difficult of the three cases occurs when the item to be deleted is in a node *N* that has two children, as in Figure 10-23. As you just saw, when *N* has only one child, the child replaces *N*. However,

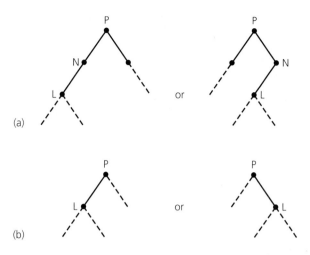

Figure 10-22

(a) *N* with only a left child—*N* can be either the left or right child of *P*;
(b) after deleting node *N*

Figure 10-23

N with two children

when *N* has two children, these children cannot both replace *N*: *N*'s parent has room for only one of *N*'s children as a replacement for *N*. A different strategy is necessary.

In fact, you will not delete *N* at all. You can find another node that is easier to delete and delete it instead of *N*. This strategy may sound like cheating. After all, the programmer who requests

```
nameTree.delete(searchKey)
```

expects that the item whose search key equals `searchKey` will be deleted from the ADT binary search tree. However, the programmer expects only that the *item* will be deleted and has no right, because of the wall between the program and the ADT implementation, to expect a particular *node* in the tree to be deleted.

Consider, then, an alternate strategy. To delete from a binary search tree an item that resides in a node *N* that has two children, take the following steps:

1. Locate another node *M* that is easier to remove from the tree than the node *N*.

2. Copy the item that is in *M* to *N*, thus effectively deleting from the tree the item originally in *N*.

3. Remove the node *M* from the tree.

Deleting an item whose node has two children

What kind of node *M* is easier to remove than the node *N*? Because you know how to delete a node that has no children or one child, *M* could be such a node. You have to be careful, though. Can you choose any node and copy its data into *N*? No, because you must preserve the tree's status as

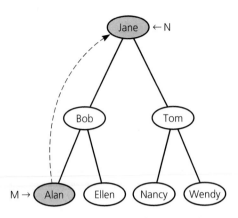

Figure 10-24

Not any node will do

a binary search tree. For example, if in the tree of Figure 10-24, you copied the data from *M* to *N*, the result would no longer be a binary search tree.

What data item, when copied into the node *N*, will preserve the tree's status as a binary search tree? All of the search keys in the left subtree of *N* are less than the search key in *N*, and all of the search keys in the right subtree of *N* are greater than the search key in *N*. You must retain this property when you replace the search key *x* in node *N* with the search key *y*. There are two suitable possibilities for the value *y*: It can come immediately after or immediately before *x* in the sorted order of search keys. If *y* comes immediately after *x*, then clearly all search keys in the left subtree of *N* are smaller than *y*, because they are all smaller than *x*, as Figure 10-25 illustrates. Further, all search keys in the right subtree of *N* are greater than or equal to *y*, because they are greater than *x* and, by assumption, there are no search keys in the tree between *x* and *y*. A similar argument illustrates that if *y* comes immediately before *x* in the sorted order, it is greater than or equal to all search keys in the left subtree of *N* and smaller than all search keys in the right subtree of *N*.

You can thus copy into *N* either the item whose search key is immediately after *N*'s search key[4] or the item whose search key is immediately before it. Suppose that, arbitrarily, you decide to use the node whose search key *y* comes immediately after *N*'s search key *x*. This search key is

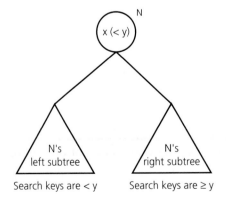

Figure 10-25

Search key *x* can be replaced by *y*

called *x*'s **inorder successor**.[5] How can you locate this node? Because *N* has two children, the inorder successor of its search key is in the leftmost node of *N*'s right subtree. That is, to find the node that contains *y*, you follow *N*'s `rightChild` reference to its right child *R*, which must be present because *N* has two children. You then descend the tree rooted at *R* by taking left branches at each node until you encounter a node *M* with no left child. You copy the item in this node *M* into node *N* and then, because *M* has no left child, you can remove *M* from the tree as one of the two easy cases. (See Figure 10-26.)

The inorder successor of N's search key is in the leftmost node in N's right subtree

A more detailed high-level description of the deletion algorithm follows:

Second draft of the deletion algorithm

```
deleteItem(rootNode, searchKey)
// Deletes from the binary search tree with root
// rootNode the item whose search key equals
// searchKey. If no such item exists, the operation
// fails and throws TreeException.

  Locate (by using the search algorithm) the
     item whose search key equals searchKey; it
     occurs in node i

if (item is found in node i) {
  deleteNode(i)  // defined next
}
else {
  throw a tree exception
}  // end if
```

Figure 10-26

Copying the item whose search key is the inorder successor of *N*'s search key

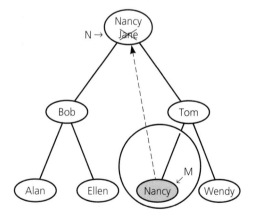

---

[4]*N*'s search key is the search key of the data item in *N*.
[5]We also will use the term *N*'s **inorder successor** to mean the inorder successor of *N*'s search key.

```
deleteNode(treeNode)
// Deletes the item in treeNode. Returns
// the root node of the resulting tree.

  if (treeNode is a leaf) {
    Remove treeNode from the tree
  }
  else if (treeNode has only one child c) {
    if (c was a left child of its parent p){
      Make c the left child of p
    }
    else {
      Make c the right child of p
    }  // end if
  }
  else { // treeNode has two children
    Find the item contained in treeNode's
        inorder successor
    Copy the item into treeNode
    Remove treeNode's inorder successor by using the
        previous technique for a leaf or a node
        with one child
  }  // end if

  return reference to root node of resulting tree
```

In the following refinement, *search*'s algorithm is adapted and inserted directly into *deleteItem*. Also, the method *deleteNode* uses the method *findLeftmost* to find the item in the node *M*, that is, the inorder successor of node *N*. The item in *M* is saved for later replacement of the item in node *N*. Next, *deleteLeftmost* deletes *M* from the tree. The saved item then replaces the item in node *N*, thus deleting it from the binary search tree.

Final draft of the deletion algorithm

```
deleteItem(rootNode, searchKey)
// Deletes from the binary search tree with root
// rootNode the item whose search key equals searchKey.
// Returns the root node of the resulting tree.
// If no such item exists, the operation
// fails and throws TreeException.

  if (rootNode is null) {
    throw TreeException // item not found
  }
  else if (searchKey equals the key in rootNode item) {
    // delete the rootNode; a new root of the tree is
    // returned
    newRoot = deleteNode(rootNode, searchKey)
```

```
      return newRoot
   }
   else if (searchKey is less than the key in rootNode item) {
     newLeft = deleteItem(rootNode.getLeft(), searchKey)
     rootNode.setLeft(newLeft)
     return rootNode // returns rootNode with new left
                     // subtree
   }
   else { // search the right subtree
     newRight = deleteItem(rootNode.getRight(), searchKey)
     rootNode.setRight(newRight)
     return rootNode // returns rootNode with new right
                     // subtree
} // end if


deleteNode(treeNode)
// Deletes the item in the node referenced by treeNode.
// Returns the root node of the resulting tree.

   if (treeNode is a leaf) {
     // remove leaf from the tree
    return null
   }
   else if (treeNode has only one child c) {
     // c replaces treeNode as the child of
     // treeNode's parent
     if (c is the left child of treeNode) {
       return treeNode.getLeft()
     }
     else {
       return treeNode.getRight()
     } // end if
   }
   else { // treeNode has two children
     // find the inorder successor of the search key in
     // treeNode: it is in the leftmost node of the
     // subtree rooted at treeNode's right child
     replacementItem = findLeftMost(treeNode)
     replacementRChild = deleteLeftmost(treeNode.getRight())
     Set treeNode's item to replacementItem
     Set treeNode's right child to replacementRChild
     return treeNode
   } // end if

findLeftmost(treeNode)
// Returns the item that is the leftmost
// descendant of the tree rooted at treeNode.
```

```
  if (treeNode.getLeft() == null) {
    // this is the node you want, so return its item
    return treeNode.getItem()
  }
  else {
    return findLeftmost(treeNode.getLeft())
  }  // end if


deleteLeftmost(treeNode)
// Deletes the node that is the leftmost
// descendant of the tree rooted at treeNode.
// Returns subtree of deleted node.

  if (treeNode.getLeft() == null) {
    // this is the node you want; it has no left
    // child, but it might have a right subtree

    // the return value of this method is a
    // child reference of treeNode's parent; thus, the
    // following "moves up" treeNode's right subtree
    return treeNode.getRight()
  }
  else {
    replacementLChild = deleteLeftmost(treeNode.getLeft())
    treeNode.setLeft(replacementLChild)
    return treeNode
  }  // end if
```

Observe that, as in the case of the *insertItem* method, the actual argument that corresponds to *rootNode* either is one of the references of the parent of *N*, as Figure 10-27 depicts, or is the external reference to the root, in the case where *N* is the root of the original tree. In either case *rootNode* references *N*. Thus, any change you make to *rootNode* by calling the method *deleteNode* with actual argument *rootNode* changes the reference in the parent of *N*. The recursive method *deleteLeftmost*, which is called by *deleteNode* if *N* has two children, also uses this strategy to remove the inorder successor of the node containing the item to be deleted.

Exercise 27 at the end of this chapter describes an easier deletion algorithm. However, that algorithm tends to increase the height of the tree, and, as you will see later, an increase in height can decrease the efficiency of searching the tree.

Retrieval.   By refining the *search* algorithm, you can implement the retrieval operation. Recall that the *search* algorithm is

```
    search(bst, searchKey)
    // Searches the binary search tree bst for the item
    // whose search key is searchKey.
```

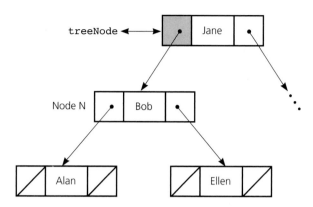

Any change to `treeNode` while deleting node N (Bob) changes `leftChild` of Jane

Figure 10-27

Recursive deletion of node *N*

```
if (bst is empty) {
  The desired record is not found
}
else if (searchKey == search key of bst's root item) {
  The desired record is found
}
else if (searchKey < search key of bst's root item) {
  search(Left subtree of bst, searchKey)
}
else {
  search(Right subtree of bst, searchKey)
}  // end if
```

The retrieval operation must return the item with the desired search key if it exists; otherwise it must return a *null* reference. The retrieval algorithm, therefore, appears as follows:

```
retrieveItem(treeNode, searchKey)
// Returns the item (treeItem) whose search
// key equals searchKey from the binary search tree
// that has treeNode as its root. The operation
// returns a null reference if no such item
// exists.

  if (treeNode == null) {
    treeItem = null  // tree is empty
  }
  else if (searchKey == treeNode.getItem().getKey()) {
```

retrieveItem is a refinement of search

```
            // item is in the root of some subtree
            treeItem = treeNode.getItem()
        }
        else if (searchKey < treeNode.getItem().getKey()) {
            // search the left subtree
            treeItem =
            retrieveItem(treeNode.getLeft(), searchKey)
        }
        else { // search the right subtree
            treeItem =
            retrieveItem(treeNode.getRight(), searchKey)
        }  // end if

    return treeItem
```

Traversal.   The traversals for a binary search tree are the same as the traversals for a binary tree. You should be aware, however, that an inorder traversal of a binary search tree will visit the tree's nodes in sorted search-key order. Before seeing the proof of this statement, recall the inorder traversal algorithm:

```
    inorder(bst)
    // Traverses the binary tree bst in inorder.

      if (bst is not empty) {
        inorder(Left subtree of bst's root)
        Process the root of bst
        inorder(Right subtree of bst's root)
      } // end if
```

THEOREM 10-1.   The inorder traversal of a binary search tree T will visit its nodes in sorted search-key order.

PROOF.   The proof is by induction on h, the height of T.

Basis: $h = 0$. When T is empty, the algorithm does not visit any nodes. This is the proper sorted order for the zero names that are in the tree!

Inductive hypothesis: Assume that the theorem is true for all k, $0 < k < h$. That is, assume for all k $(0 < k < h)$ that the inorder traversal visits the nodes in sorted search-key order.

Inductive conclusion: You must show that the theorem is true for $k = h > 0$. T has the form

Because T is a binary search tree, all the search keys in the left subtree T_L are less than the search key in the root r, and all the search keys in the right subtree T_R are greater than the search key in r. The *inorder* algorithm will visit all the nodes in T_L, then visit r, and then visit all the nodes in T_R. Thus, the only concern is that *inorder* visit the nodes within each of the subtrees T_L and T_R in the correct sorted order. But because T is a binary search tree of height h, each subtree is a binary search tree of height less than h. Therefore, by the inductive hypothesis, *inorder* visits the nodes in each subtree T_L and T_R in the correct sorted search-key order. **(End of proof.)**

It follows from this theorem that *inorder* visits a node's inorder successor immediately after it visits the node.

Use inorder traversal to visit nodes of a binary search tree in search-key order

A Reference-Based Implementation of the ADT Binary Search Tree

A Java reference-based implementation of the ADT binary search tree follows. Notice the protected methods that implement the recursive algorithms. These methods are not public, because clients do not have access to node references. The methods could be private, but making them protected enables a derived class to use them directly.

```java
// ADT binary search tree.
//  Assumption: A tree contains at most one item with a
//              given search key at any time.

public class BinarySearchTree extends BinaryTreeBasis {
// inherits isEmpty(), makeEmpty(), getRootItem(), and
// the use of the constructors from BinaryTreeBasis

  public BinarySearchTree() {
  }  // end default constructor

  public BinarySearchTree(KeyedItem rootItem) {
    super(rootItem);
  }  // end constructor

  public void insert(KeyedItem newItem) {
    root = insertItem(root, newItem);
  }  // end insert

  public KeyedItem retrieve(Comparable searchKey) {
    return retrieveItem(root, searchKey);
  }  // end retrieve

  public void delete(Comparable searchKey) throws TreeException {
    root = deleteItem(root, searchKey);
  }  // end delete

  public void delete(KeyedItem item) throws TreeException {
    root = deleteItem(root, item.getKey());
  }  // end delete
```

```
protected TreeNode insertItem(TreeNode tNode,
                              KeyedItem newItem) {
  TreeNode newSubtree;
  if (tNode == null) {
    // position of insertion found; insert after leaf
    // create a new node
    tNode = new TreeNode(newItem, null, null);
    return tNode;
  }  // end if
  KeyedItem nodeItem = (KeyedItem)tNode.getItem();

  // search for the insertion position
  if (newItem.getKey().compareTo(nodeItem.getKey()) < 0) {
    // search the left subtree
    newSubtree = insertItem(tNode.getLeft(), newItem);
    tNode.setLeft(newSubtree);
    return tNode;
  }
  else { // search the right subtree
    newSubtree = insertItem(tNode.getRight(), newItem);
    tNode.setRight(newSubtree);
    return tNode;
  }  // end if
}  // end insertItem

protected KeyedItem retrieveItem(TreeNode tNode,
                                 Comparable searchKey) {
  KeyedItem treeItem;
  if (tNode == null) {
    treeItem = null;
  }
  else {
    KeyedItem nodeItem = (KeyedItem)tNode.getItem();
    if (searchKey.compareTo(nodeItem.getKey()) == 0) {
      // item is in the root of some subtree
      treeItem = (KeyedItem)tNode.getItem();
    }
    else if (searchKey.compareTo(nodeItem.getKey()) < 0) {
      // search the left subtree
      treeItem = retrieveItem(tNode.getLeft(), searchKey);
    }
    else  { // search the right subtree
      treeItem = retrieveItem(tNode.getRight(), searchKey);
    }  // end if
  }  // end if
  return treeItem;
}  // end retrieveItem
```

```java
protected TreeNode deleteItem(TreeNode tNode,
                             Comparable searchKey) {
// Calls: deleteNode.
  TreeNode newSubtree;
  if (tNode == null) {
    throw new TreeException("TreeException: Item not found");
  }
  else {
    KeyedItem nodeItem = (KeyedItem)tNode.getItem();
    if (searchKey.compareTo(nodeItem.getKey()) == 0) {
      // item is in the root of some subtree
      tNode = deleteNode(tNode);  // delete the item
    }
    // else search for the item
    else if (searchKey.compareTo(nodeItem.getKey()) < 0) {
      // search the left subtree
      newSubtree = deleteItem(tNode.getLeft(), searchKey);
      tNode.setLeft(newSubtree);
    }
    else { // search the right subtree
      newSubtree = deleteItem(tNode.getRight(), searchKey);
      tNode.setRight(newSubtree);
    }  // end if
  }  // end if
  return tNode;
}  // end deleteItem

protected TreeNode deleteNode(TreeNode tNode) {
// Algorithm note: There are four cases to consider:
//    1. The tNode is a leaf.
//    2. The tNode has no left child.
//    3. The tNode has no right child.
//    4. The tNode has two children.
// Calls: findLeftmost and deleteLeftmost
  KeyedItem replacementItem;

  // test for a leaf
  if ( (tNode.getLeft() == null) &&
       (tNode.getRight() == null) ) {
    return null;
  }  // end if leaf

  // test for no left child
  else if (tNode.getLeft() == null) {
    return tNode.getRight();
  }  // end if no left child
```

```
                    // test for no right child
                    else if (tNode.getRight() == null) {
                      return tNode.getLeft();
                    }  // end if no right child

                    // there are two children:
                    // retrieve and delete the inorder successor
                    else {
                      replacementItem = findLeftmost(tNode.getRight());
                      tNode.setItem(replacementItem);
                      tNode.setRight(deleteLeftmost(tNode.getRight()));
                      return tNode;
                    }  // end if
                  }  // end deleteNode

                  protected KeyedItem findLeftmost(TreeNode tNode)  {
                    if (tNode.getLeft() == null) {
                      return (KeyedItem)tNode.getItem();
                    }
                    else {
                      return findLeftmost(tNode.getLeft());
                    }  // end if
                  }  // end findLeftmost

                  protected TreeNode deleteLeftmost(TreeNode tNode) {
                    if (tNode.getLeft() == null) {
                      return tNode.getRight();
                    }
                    else {
                      tNode.setLeft(deleteLeftmost(tNode.getLeft()));
                      return tNode;
                    }  // end if
                  }  // end deleteLeftmost

                }  // end BinarySearchTree
```

The class *TreeIterator* developed earlier in the chapter can be used with *BinarySearchTree*. It would also make sense to implement the *remove* method, since *BinarySearchTree* provides a method for deleting a node from the tree. Exercise 29 at the end of this chapter asks you to explore this possibility.

The Efficiency of Binary Search Tree Operations

You have seen binary search trees in many shapes. For example, even though the binary search trees in Figures 10-17 and 10-18c have seven nodes each, they have radically different shapes and heights. You saw that to locate Wendy in Figure 10-18c, you would have to inspect all seven nodes, but you can locate Wendy in Figure 10-17 by inspecting only three nodes (Jane, Tom, and Wendy). Consider now the relationship between the height of a binary search tree and the efficiency of the retrieval, insertion, and deletion operations.

Each of these operations compares the specified value `searchKey` to the search keys in the nodes along a **path** through the tree. This path always starts at the root of the tree and, at each node *N*, follows the left or right branch, depending on the comparison of `searchKey` to the search key in *N*. The path terminates at the node that contains `searchKey` or, if `searchKey` is not present, at an empty subtree. Thus, each retrieval, insertion, or deletion operation requires a number of comparisons equal to the number of nodes along this path. This means that the maximum number of comparisons that each operation can require is the number of nodes on the longest path through the tree. In other words, the *maximum number of comparisons that these operations can require is equal to the height of the binary search tree*. What, then, are the maximum and minimum heights of a binary search tree of *n* nodes?

The maximum number of comparisons for a retrieval, insertion, or deletion is the height of the tree

The maximum and minimum heights of a binary search tree. You can maximize the height of a binary tree with *n* nodes simply by giving each internal node (nonleaf) exactly one child, as shown in Figure 10-28. This process will result in a tree of height *n*. An *n*-node tree with height *n* strikingly resembles a linear linked list.

n is the maximum height of a binary tree with n nodes

A minimum-height binary tree with *n* nodes is a bit more difficult to obtain. As a first step, consider the number of nodes that a binary tree with a given height *h* can have. For example, if *h* = 3, the possible binary trees include those in Figure 10-29. Thus, binary trees of height 3 can have between 3 and 7 nodes. In addition, Figure 10-29 shows that 3 is the minimum height for a binary tree with 4, 5, 6, or 7 nodes. Similarly, binary trees with more than 7 nodes require a height greater than 3.

Intuitively, to minimize the height of a binary tree given *n* nodes, you must fill each level of the tree as completely as possible. A complete tree meets this requirement (although it does not matter whether the nodes on the last level are filled left to right). In fact, trees *b*, *c*, *d*, and *e* of Figure 10-29 are complete trees. If a complete binary tree of a given height *h* is to have the maximum possible number of nodes, it should be full (as in Figure 10-29e). Figure 10-30 counts these nodes by level and shows the following:

Except for the last level, each level of a minimum-height binary tree must contain as many nodes as possible

THEOREM 10-2. A full binary tree of height $h \geq 0$ has $2^h - 1$ nodes.
A formal proof by induction of this theorem is left as an exercise.
    It follows then that

THEOREM 10-3. The maximum number of nodes that a binary tree of height *h* can have is $2^h - 1$.
You cannot add nodes to a full binary tree of height *h* without increasing its height. The formal proof of this theorem, which closely parallels that of Theorem 10-2, is left as an exercise.

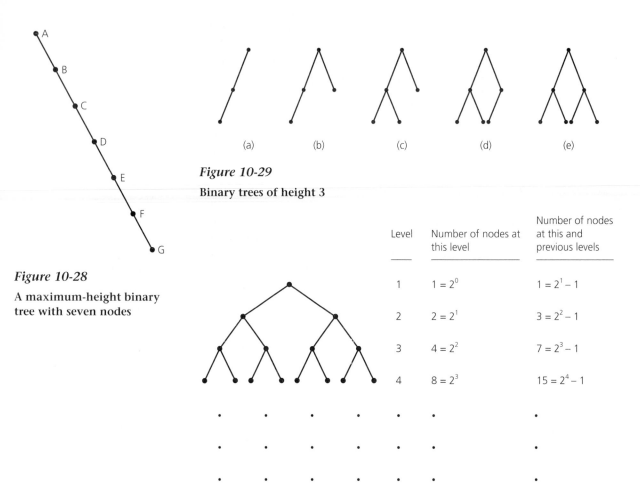

Figure 10-28

A maximum-height binary tree with seven nodes

Figure 10-29

Binary trees of height 3

Level	Number of nodes at this level	Number of nodes at this and previous levels
1	$1 = 2^0$	$1 = 2^1 - 1$
2	$2 = 2^1$	$3 = 2^2 - 1$
3	$4 = 2^2$	$7 = 2^3 - 1$
4	$8 = 2^3$	$15 = 2^4 - 1$
h	2^{h-1}	$2^h - 1$

Figure 10-30

Counting the nodes in a full binary tree of height *h*

The following theorem uses Theorems 10-2 and 10-3 to determine the minimum height of a binary tree that contains some given number of nodes.

THEOREM 10-4. The minimum height of a binary tree with n nodes is $\lceil \log_2(n + 1) \rceil$.[6]

---

[6]The **ceiling of *X*,** which $\lceil X \rceil$ denotes, is X rounded up. For example, $\lceil 6 \rceil = 6$, $\lceil 6.1 \rceil = 7$, and $\lceil 6.8 \rceil = 7$.

PROOF. Let h be the smallest integer such that $n \leq 2^h - 1$. To find the minimum height of a binary tree with n nodes, first establish the following facts:

1. *A binary tree whose height is $\leq h - 1$ has $< n$ nodes.*

   By Theorem 10-3, a binary tree of height $h - 1$ has at most $2^{h-1} - 1$ nodes. If it is possible that $n \leq 2^{h-1} - 1 < 2^h - 1$, then h is not the smallest integer such that $n \leq 2^h - 1$. Therefore, n must be greater than $2^{h-1} - 1$ or, equivalently, $2^{h-1} - 1 < n$. Because a binary tree of height $h - 1$ has at most $2^{h-1} - 1$ nodes, it must have fewer than n nodes.

2. *There exists a complete binary tree of height h that has exactly n nodes.*

   Consider the full binary tree of height $h - 1$. By Theorem 10-2, it has $2^{h-1} - 1$ nodes. As you just saw, $n > 2^{h-1} - 1$ because h was selected so that $n \leq 2^h - 1$. You can thus add nodes to the full tree from left to right until you have n nodes, as Figure 10-31 illustrates. Because $n \leq 2^h - 1$ and a binary tree of height h cannot have more than $2^h - 1$ nodes, you will reach n nodes by the time level h is filled up.

3. *The minimum height of a binary tree with n nodes is the smallest integer h such that $n \leq 2^h - 1$.*

   If h is the smallest integer such that $n \leq 2^h - 1$, and if a binary tree has height $\leq h - 1$, then by fact 1, it has fewer than n nodes. Because by fact 2 there is a binary tree of height h that has exactly n nodes, h must be as small as possible.

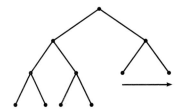

Figure 10-31

Filling in the last level of a tree

The previous discussion implies that

$$2^{h-1} - 1 < n \leq 2^h - 1$$
$$2^{h-1} < n + 1 \leq 2^h$$
$$h - 1 < \log_2(n + 1) \leq h$$

If $\log_2(n + 1) = h$, the theorem is proven. Otherwise, $h - 1 < \log_2(n + 1) < h$ implies that $\log_2(n + 1)$ cannot be an integer. Therefore, round $\log_2(n + 1)$ up to get h.

Thus, $h = \lceil \log_2(n + 1) \rceil$ is the minimum height of a binary tree with n nodes. **(End of proof.)**

Complete trees and full trees with n nodes thus have heights of $\lceil \log_2(n + 1) \rceil$, which, as you just saw, is the theoretical minimum. This minimum height is the same as the maximum number of comparisons a binary search must make to search an array with n elements. Thus, if a binary search tree is complete and therefore balanced, the time it takes to search it for a value is about the same as that required for a binary search of an array. On the other hand, as you go from balanced trees toward trees with a linear structure, the height approaches the number of nodes n. This number is the same as the maximum number of comparisons that you must make when searching a linked list of n nodes.

Complete trees and full trees have minimum height

The height of an n-node binary search tree ranges from $\lceil \log_2(n + 1) \rceil$ to n

Insertion in search-key order produces a maximum-height binary search tree

However, the outstanding efficiency of the operations on a binary search tree hinges on the assumption that the height of the binary search tree is $\lceil \log_2(n + 1) \rceil$. What will the height of a binary search tree actually be? The factor that determines the height of a binary search tree is the order in which you perform the insertion and deletion operations on the tree. Recall that, starting with an empty tree, if you insert names in the order Alan, Bob, Ellen, Jane, Nancy, Tom, Wendy, you would obtain a binary search tree of maximum height, as shown in Figure 10-18c. On the other hand, if you insert names in the order Jane, Bob, Tom, Alan, Ellen, Nancy, Wendy, you would obtain a binary search tree of minimum height, as shown in Figure 10-17.

Insertion in random order produces a near-minimum-height binary search tree

Which of these situations should you expect to encounter in the course of a real application? It can be proven mathematically that if the insertion and deletion operations occur in a random order, the height of the binary search tree will be quite close to $\log_2 n$. Thus, in this sense, the previous analysis is not unduly optimistic. However, in a real-world application, is it realistic to expect the insertion and deletion operations to occur in random order? In many applications, the answer is yes. There are, however, applications in which this assumption would be dubious. For example, the person preparing the previous sequence of names for the insertion operations might well decide to "help you out" by arranging the names to be inserted into sorted order. This arrangement, as has been mentioned, would lead to a tree of maximum height. Thus, while in many applications you can expect the behavior of a binary search tree to be excellent, you should be wary of the possibility of poor performance due to some characteristic of a given application.

Is there anything you can do if you suspect that the operations might not occur in a random order? Similarly, is there anything you can do if you have an enormous number of items and need to ensure that the height of the tree is close to $\log_2 n$? Chapter 12 presents variations of the basic binary search tree that are guaranteed always to remain balanced.

Figure 10-32 summarizes the order of the retrieval, insertion, deletion, and traversal operations for the ADT binary search tree.

Treesort

You can use the ADT binary search tree to sort an array of records efficiently into search-key order. To simplify the discussion, however, we will

Operation	Average case	Worst case
Retrieval	O(log n)	O(n)
Insertion	O(log n)	O(n)
Deletion	O(log n)	O(n)
Traversal	O(n)	O(n)

Figure 10-32

The order of the retrieval, insertion, deletion, and traversal operations for the reference-based implementation of the ADT binary search tree

sort an array of integers into ascending order, as we did with the sorting algorithms in Chapter 9.

The basic idea of the algorithm is simple:

```
treesort(anArray, n)
// Sorts the n integers in array anArray into
// ascending order.

    Insert anArray's elements into a binary search tree
      bTree


    Traverse bTree inorder. As you visit bTree's nodes, copy
        their data items into successive locations of anArray
```

Treesort uses a binary search tree

An inorder traversal of the binary search tree *bTree* visits the integers in *bTree*'s nodes in ascending order.

A treesort can be quite efficient. As Figure 10-32 indicates, each insertion into a binary search tree requires O(log *n*) operations in the average case and O(*n*) operations in the worst case. Thus, *treesort*'s *n* insertions require O(*n* * log *n*) operations in the average case and O(n^2) operations in the worst case. The traversal of the tree involves one copy operation for each of the *n* elements and so is O(*n*). Since O(*n*) is less than O(*n* * log *n*) and O(n^2), treesort is O(*n* * log *n*) in the average case and O(n^2) in the worst case.

*Treesort.
Average case: O(n * log n);
worst case: O(n^2)*

Saving a Binary Search Tree in a File

Imagine a program that maintains the names, addresses, and telephone numbers of your friends and relatives. While the program is running, you can enter a name and get the person's address and phone number. If you terminate program execution, the program must save its database of people in a form that it can recover at a later time.

If the program uses a binary search tree to represent the database, it must save the tree's data in a file so that it can later restore the tree. You could save the tree by simply adding the *java.io.Serializable* interface to the various classes in the implementation of the binary search tree. Exercise 33 at the end of this chapter asks you to decide which classes would need to have this interface specified. Suppose, however, that you want to define the interface *java.io.Serializable* only on the items you are storing in the tree. We will consider two different algorithms for saving and restoring a binary search tree. The first algorithm restores a binary search tree to its original shape. The second restores a binary search tree to a shape that is balanced.

Saving a binary search tree and then restoring it to its original shape.
The first algorithm restores a binary search tree to exactly the same shape it had before it was saved. For example, consider the tree in Figure 10-33a. If you save the tree in preorder, you get the sequence 60, 20, 10, 40, 30, 50, 70. If you then use the binary search tree *insert* to insert these values

*Use a preorder traversal and
insert to save and then
restore a binary search tree in its
original shape*

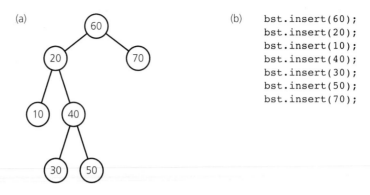

Figure 10-33

(a) A binary search tree *bst* ; (b) the sequence of insertions that
result in this tree

into a tree that is initially empty, you will get the original tree. Figure 10-33b shows this sequence of insertion operations in pseudocode.

Saving a binary search tree and then restoring it to a balanced shape.
Can you do better than the previous algorithm? That is, do you necessarily want the restored tree to have its original shape? Recall that you can organize a given set of data items into binary search trees with many different shapes. Although the shape of a binary search tree has no effect whatsoever on the correctness of the ADT operations, it will affect the efficiency of those operations. Efficient operations are assured if the binary search tree is balanced.

A balanced binary search tree increases the efficiency of the ADT operations

The algorithm that restores a binary search tree to a balanced shape is surprisingly simple. In fact, you can even guarantee a restored tree of minimum height—a condition stronger than balanced. To gain some insight into the solution, consider a full tree, because it is balanced. If you save a full tree in a file by using an inorder traversal, the file will be in sorted order, as Figure 10-34 illustrates. A full tree with exactly $n = 2^h - 1$ nodes for some height h has the exact middle of the data items in its root.

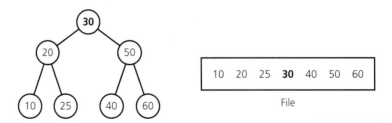

Figure 10-34

A full tree saved in a file by using inorder traversal

The left and right subtrees of the root are full trees of $2^{h-1} - 1$ nodes each (that is, half of $n - 1$, since n is odd or, equivalently, $n/2$). Thus, you can use the following recursive algorithm to create a full binary search tree with n nodes, provided you either know or can determine n beforehand.

```
readFull(inputFile, n)
```

Building a full binary search tree

```
// Builds a full binary search tree from n sorted values
// in a file and returns the tree's root.
  if (n > 0) {
    treeNode = a new node with null child references
    // construct the left subtree
    Set treeNode's left child to readFull(inputFile, n/2)

    // get the root
    Read item from file into treeNode's item

    // construct the right subtree
    Set treeNode's right child to readFull(inputFile, n/2)
  }  // end if
  return treeNode;
```

Surprisingly, you can construct the tree directly by reading the sorted data sequentially from the file.

This algorithm for building a full binary search tree is simple, but what can you do if the tree to be restored is not full (that is, if it does not have $n = 2^h - 1$ nodes for some h)? The first thing that comes to mind is that the restored tree should be complete—full up to the last level, with the last level filled in from left to right. Actually, because you care only about minimizing the height of the restored tree, it does not matter where the nodes on the last level go, as Figure 10-35 shows.

The *readFull* algorithm is essentially correct even if the tree is not full. However, you do have to be a bit careful when computing the sizes of the left and right subtrees of the tree's root. If n is odd, both subtrees are of size $n/2$, as before. (The root is automatically accounted for.) If n is even, however, you have to account for the root and the fact that one of the root's subtrees will have one more node than the other. In this case, you can arbitrarily choose to put the extra node in the left subtree. The following algorithm makes these compensations:

Figure 10-35

A tree of minimum height that is not complete

```
readTree(inputFile, n)
// Builds a minimum-height binary search tree from n sorted
// values in a file. Will return the tree's root.

  if (n > 0) {
    treeNode = reference to new node with null
               child references
```

Building a minimum-height binary search tree

```
    // construct the left subtree
    Set treeNode's left child to readTree(inputFile, n/2)

    // get the root
    Read item from file into treeNode's item

    // construct the right subtree
    Set treeNode's right child to
        readTree(inputFile, (n-1)/2)
  } // end if
```

return *treeNode*

You should trace this algorithm and convince yourself that it is correct for both even and odd values of *n*.

To summarize, you can easily restore a tree as a balanced binary search tree if the data is sorted—that is, if it has been produced from the inorder traversal—and you know the number *n* of nodes in the tree. You need *n* so that you can determine the middle item and, in turn, the number of nodes in the left and right subtrees of the tree's root. Knowing these numbers is a simple matter of counting nodes as you traverse the tree and then saving the number in a file that the restore operation can read.

Note that *readTree* would be an appropriate protected method of *BinarySearchTree*, if you also had a public method to call it.

GENERAL TREES

This chapter ends with a brief discussion of general trees and their relationship to binary trees. Consider the general tree in Figure 10-36. The three children *B*, *C*, and *D* of node *A*, for example, are siblings. The leftmost child *B* is called the **oldest child**, or **first child**, of *A*. One way to implement this tree uses the same node structure that we used for a reference-based binary tree. That is, each node has two references: The left one references the node's oldest child and the right one references the node's

Figure 10-36

A general tree

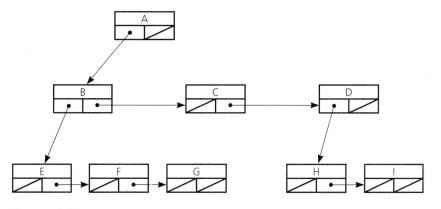

Figure 10-37

A reference-based implementation of the general tree in Figure 10-36

Figure 10-38

The binary tree that Figure
10-37 represents

next sibling. Thus, you can use the data structure in Figure 10-37 to implement the tree in Figure 10-36. Notice that the structure in Figure 10-37 also represents the binary tree pictured in Figure 10-38.

An ***n*-ary tree** is a generalization of a binary tree whose nodes each can have no more than *n* children. The tree in Figure 10-36 is an *n*-ary tree with *n* = 3. You can, of course, use the implementation just described for an *n*-ary tree. However, because you know the maximum number of children for each node, you can let each node reference its children directly. Figure 10-39 illustrates such a representation for the tree in Figure 10-36. This tree is shorter than the tree in Figure 10-38.

Exercise 32 at the end of this chapter discusses general trees further.

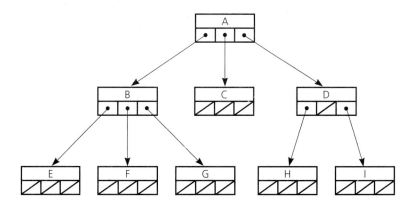

Figure 10-39

An implementation of the *n*-ary tree in Figure 10-36

SUMMARY

1. Binary trees provide a hierarchical organization of data, which is important in many applications.

2. The implementation of a binary tree is usually reference based. If the binary tree is complete, an efficient array-based implementation is possible.

3. Traversing a tree is a useful operation. Intuitively, traversing a tree means to visit every node in the tree. Because the meaning of "visit" is application dependent, the traversal operations are implemented using an iterator.

4. The binary search tree allows you to use a binary search–like algorithm to search for an item with a specified value.

5. Binary search trees come in many shapes. The height of a binary search tree with n nodes can range from a minimum of $\lceil \log_2(n + 1) \rceil$ to a maximum of n. The shape of a binary search tree determines the efficiency of its operations. The closer a binary search tree is to a balanced tree (and the farther it is from a linear structure), the closer the behavior of the *search* algorithm will be to a binary search (and the farther it will be from the behavior of a linear search).

6. An inorder traversal of a binary search tree visits the tree's nodes in sorted search-key order.

7. The treesort algorithm efficiently sorts an array by using the binary search tree's insertion and traversal operations.

8. If you save a binary search tree's data in a file while performing an inorder traversal of its nodes, you can restore the tree as a binary search tree of minimum height. If you save a binary search tree's data in a file while performing a preorder traversal of its nodes, you can restore the tree to its original form.

CAUTIONS

1. If you use an array-based implementation of a complete binary tree, you must be sure that the tree remains complete as a result of insertions or deletions.

2. Operations on a binary search tree can be quite efficient. In the worst case, however—when the tree approaches a linear shape—the performance of its operations degrades and is comparable to that of a linear linked list. If you must avoid such a situation for a given application, you should use the balancing methods presented in Chapter 12.

SELF-TEST EXERCISES

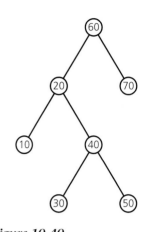

1. Consider the tree in Figure 10-40. What node or nodes are

   a. The tree's root
   b. Parents
   c. Children of the parents in Part *b*
   d. Siblings
   e. Ancestors of 50
   f. Descendants of 20
   g. Leaves

2. What are the levels of all nodes in the tree in

   a. Figure 10-6b
   b. Figure 10-6c

   Figure 10-40

   A tree for Self-Test Exercises 1, 3, 7, and 11 and for Exercises 6 and 11

3. What is the height of the tree in Figure 10-40?

4. Consider the binary trees in Figure 10-29. Which are complete? Which are full? Which are balanced?

5. What are the preorder, inorder, and postorder traversals of the binary tree in Figure 10-6a?

6. Beginning with an empty binary search tree, what binary search tree is formed when you insert the following values in the order given: J, N, B, A, W, E, T?

7. Starting with an empty binary search tree, in what order should you insert items to get the binary search tree in Figure 10-40?

8. Represent the full binary tree in Figure 10-34 with an array.

9. What complete binary tree does the array in Figure 10-41 represent?

Figure 10-41

An array for Self-Test Exercise 9

10. Is the tree in Figure 10-42 a binary search tree?

11. Using the tree in Figure 10-40, trace the algorithm that searches a binary search tree, given a search key of

    a. 30
    b. 15

    In each case, list the nodes in the order in which the search visits them.

12. Trace the treesort algorithm as it sorts the following array into ascending order: 20 80 40 25 60 30.

Figure 10-42

A tree for Self-Test Exercise 10 and for Exercise 2a

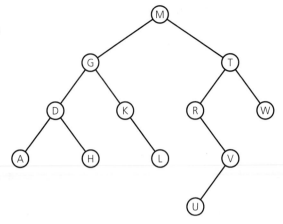

13.   **a.**   What binary search tree results when you execute `readTree` with a file of the six integers 2, 4, 6, 8, 10, 12?

      b.   Is the resulting tree's height a minimum? Is the tree complete? Is it full?

EXERCISES

1.   Write pre- and postconditions for the operations of the ADT binary tree.

2.   What are the preorder, inorder, and postorder traversals of the binary trees in

      a. Figure 10-42   **b.** Figure 10-6b   **c.** Figure 10-6c

3.   Consider the binary search tree in Figure 10-43. The numbers simply label the nodes so that you can reference them; they do not indicate the contents of the nodes.

      a.   Which node must contain the inorder successor of the value in the root? Explain.

      b.   In what order will an inorder traversal visit the nodes of this tree? Indicate this order by listing the labels of the nodes in the order that they are visited.

4.   Beginning with an empty binary search tree, what binary search tree is formed when you insert the following values in the order given?

      a.   W, T, N, J, E, B, A

      b.   W, T, N, A, B, E, J

      c.   A, B, W, J, N, T, E

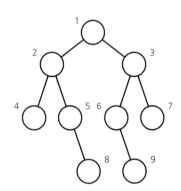

Figure 10-43

A binary search tree for Exercise 3

5. Arrange nodes that contain the letters A, C, E, F, L, V, and Z into two binary search trees: one that has maximum height and one that has minimum height.

6. Consider the binary search tree in Figure 10-40.

    a. What tree results after you insert the nodes 80, 65, 75, 45, 35, and 25, in that order?

    b. After inserting the nodes mentioned in Part *a*, what tree results when you delete the nodes 50 and 20?

7. If you delete an item from a binary search tree and then insert it back into the tree, will you ever change the shape of the tree?

8. Given the ADT binary tree operations as defined in this chapter, what tree or trees does the following sequence of statements produce?

```
BinaryTree t1 = new BinaryTree(new Integer(2));
t1.attachLeft(new Integer(5));
t1.attachRight(new Integer(3));
t1 = new BinaryTree(new Integer(10), t1, null);

BinaryTree t2 = new BinaryTree(new Integer(8));
t2.attachLeft(new Integer(6));
t2.attachRight(new Integer(7));

BinaryTree s = new BinaryTree(new Integer(9), t1, t2);
BinaryTree r = new BinaryTree(new Integer(1));
r.attachLeft(new Integer(2));
r.attachRight(new Integer(3));

BinaryTree t = new BinaryTree(new Integer(4), s, r);
```

9. Consider a method *isLeaf()* that returns *true* if an instance of *BinaryTree* is a one-node tree—that is, if it consists of only a leaf— and returns *false* otherwise.

    a. Add the method of *isLeaf* to *BinaryTree* so that the method is available to clients of the class.

    b. If *isLeaf* were not a member of *BinaryTree*, would a client of the class be able to implement *isLeaf*? Explain.

10. The operation *replace(replacementItem)* locates, if possible, the item in a binary search tree with the same search key as *replacementItem*. If the tree contains such an item, *replace* replaces it with *replacementItem*. Thus, the fields of the original item are updated.

    a. Add the operation *replace* to the reference-based implementation of the ADT binary search tree given in this chapter. The operation should replace an item without altering the tree structure.

    b. Instead of adding *replace* as an operation of the ADT binary search tree, implement it as a client of *BinarySearchTree*. Will the shape of the binary tree remain the same?

11. Suppose that you traverse the binary search tree in Figure 10-40 and write the data item in each node visited to a file. You plan to read this file later and create a new binary search tree by using the ADT binary search tree operation *insert*. In creating the file, in what order should you traverse the tree so that the new tree will have exactly the same shape and nodes as the original tree? What does the file look like after the original tree is traversed?

12. Consider an array-based implementation of a binary search tree *bst*. Figure 10-10 presents such a representation for a particular binary search tree.

   a. Depict the array in an array-based implementation for the binary search tree in Figure 10-18a.

   b. Show the effect of each of the following sequential operations on the array in Part *a* of this exercise. For simplicity, assume that tree items are names.

```
bst.insert(new Name("Doug"));
bst.delete(new Name("Nancy"));
bst.delete(new Name("Bob"));
bst.insert(new Name("Sarah"));
```

   c. Repeat Parts *a* and *b* of this exercise for the tree in Figure 10-18b.

   d. Write an inorder traversal algorithm for this array-based implementation.

13. Duplicates in an ADT could mean either identical items or, more subtly, items that have identical search keys but with differences in other fields. If duplicates are allowed in a binary search tree, it is important to have a convention that determines the relationship between the duplicates. Items that duplicate the root of a tree should either all be in the left subtree or all be in the right subtree, and, of course, this property must hold for every subtree.

   a. Why is this convention critical to the effective use of the binary search tree?

   b. This chapter stated that you can delete an item from a binary search tree by replacing it with the item whose search key either immediately follows or immediately precedes the search key of the item to be deleted. If duplicates are allowed, however, the choice between inorder successor and inorder predecessor is no longer arbitrary. How does the convention of putting duplicates in either the left or right subtree affect this choice?

14. Complete the trace of the nonrecursive inorder traversal algorithm that Figure 10-14 began. Show the contents of the implicit stack as the traversal progresses.

15. Implement in Java the nonrecursive inorder traversal algorithm for a binary tree that was presented in this chapter. (See Exercise 14.)

16. Given the recursive nature of a binary tree, a good strategy for writing a Java method that operates on a binary tree is often first to write a recursive definition of the task. Given such a recursive definition, a Java implementation is often straightforward.

Write recursive definitions that perform the following tasks on arbitrary binary trees. Implement the definitions in Java. Must your methods be members of *BinaryTree*? For simplicity, assume that each data item in the tree is an *integer* object and that there are no duplicates.

 a. Count the number of nodes in the tree. (*Hint*: If the tree is empty, the count is 0. If the tree is not empty, the count is 1 plus the number of nodes in the root's left subtree plus the number of nodes in the root's right subtree.)
 b. Compute the height of a tree.
 c. Find the maximum element.
 d. Find the sum of the elements.
 e. Find the average of the elements.
 f. Find a specific item.
 g. Determine whether one item is an ancestor of another (that is, whether one item is in the subtree rooted at the other item).
 h. Determine the highest level that is full or, equivalently, has the maximum number of nodes for that level. (See Exercise 22.)

17. Consider a nonempty binary tree with two types of nodes: **min** nodes and **max** nodes. Each node has an integer value initially associated with it. You can define the **value** of such a **minimax** tree as follows:

 • If the root is a min node, the value of the tree is equal to the *minimum* of
  ▪ The integer stored in the root
  ▪ The value of the left subtree, but only if it is nonempty
  ▪ The value of the right subtree, but only if it is nonempty

 • If the root is a max node, the value of the tree is equal to the *maximum* of the above three values.

 a. Compute the value of the minimax tree in Figure 10-44. Each node is labeled with its initial value.
 b. Write a general solution in Java for representing and evaluating these trees.

*18. A binary search tree with a given set of data items can have several different structures that conform to the definition of a binary search tree. If you are given a list of data items, does at least one binary search tree whose preorder traversal matches the order of the items on your list always exist? Is there ever more than one binary search tree that has the given preorder traversal?

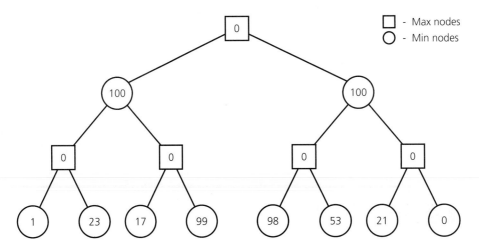

Figure 10-44

A minimax tree for Exercise 17

*19. How many differently shaped, *n*-node binary trees are possible? How many differently shaped, *n*-node binary search trees are possible? (Write recursive definitions.)

20. Write pseudocode for a method that performs a range query for a binary search tree. That is, the method should visit all items that have a search key in a given range of values (such as all values between 100 and 1,000).

21. Prove Theorems 10-2 and 10-3 by using induction.

22. What is the maximum number of nodes that a binary tree can have at level *n*? Prove your answer by using induction. Use this fact to do the following:

   a. Rewrite the formal definition of a complete tree of height *h*.

   b. Derive a closed form for the formula

$$\sum_{i=1}^{h} 2^{i-1}$$

   What is the significance of this sum?

23. Prove by induction that a binary tree with *n* nodes has exactly $n + 1$ empty subtrees (or, in Java terms, $n + 1$ `null` references).

24. A binary tree is **strictly binary** if every nonleaf node has exactly two children. Prove by induction on the number of leaves that a strictly binary tree with *n* leaves has exactly $2n - 1$ nodes.

25. Consider two algorithms for traversing a binary tree. Both are non-recursive algorithms that use an extra ADT for bookkeeping. Both algorithms have the following basic form:

```
Put the root of the tree in the ADT
while (the ADT is not empty) {
  Remove a node from the ADT and call it n
  Visit n
  if (n has a left child) {
    Put the child in the ADT
  } // end if
  if (n has a right child) {
    Put the child in the ADT
  } // end if
} // end while
```

The difference between the two algorithms is the method for choosing a node *n* to remove from the ADT.

Algorithm 1: Remove the newest (most recently added) node from the ADT.

Algorithm 2: Remove the oldest (earliest added) node from the ADT.

a. In what order would each algorithm visit the nodes of the tree in Figure 10-17?

b. For each algorithm, describe an appropriate ADT for doing the bookkeeping. What should the ADT data be? Do not use extra memory unnecessarily for the bookkeeping ADT. Also, note that the traversal of a tree should not alter the tree in any way.

26. Describe how to save a binary tree in a file so that you can later restore the tree to its original shape. Compare the efficiencies of saving and restoring a binary tree and a binary search tree.

27. Design another algorithm to delete nodes from a binary search tree. This algorithm differs from the one described in this chapter when the node *N* has two children. First let *N*'s right child take the place of the deleted node *N* in the same manner in which you delete a node with one child. Next reconnect *N*'s left child (along with its subtree, if any) to the left side of the node containing the inorder successor of the search key in *N*.

28. Write iterative methods to perform insertion and deletion operations on a binary search tree.

29. Use public inheritance to derive the class *BSTTreeIterator* from the class *TreeIterator* and implement the method *remove*. Is the traversal affected when a node of the tree is removed? Does this depend on the implementation of the iterator?

30. If you know in advance that you often access a given item in a binary search tree several times in a row before accessing a different item, you will search for the same item repeatedly. One way to address this problem is to add an extra bookkeeping component to your implementation. That is, you can maintain a last-accessed reference that will always reference the last item that any binary search tree operation accessed. Whenever you perform such an

operation, you can check the search key of the item most recently accessed before performing the operation.

Revise the implementation of the ADT binary search tree to add this new feature by adding the data field *lastAccessed* to the class.

31. The motivation for using a doubly linked list is the need to locate and delete a node in a list without traversing the list. The analogy for a binary search tree is to maintain parent references. That is, every node except the root will have a reference to its parent in the tree. Write insertion and deletion operations for this tree.

32. A node in a general tree, such as the one in Figure 10-36, can have an arbitrary number of children.

   a. Describe a Java implementation of a general tree in which every node contains an array of child references. Write a recursive preorder traversal method for this implementation. What are the advantages and disadvantages of this implementation?

   b. Consider the implementation of a general tree that this chapter described. Each node has two references: The left one references the node's oldest child and the right one references the node's next sibling. Write a recursive preorder traversal method for this implementation.

   c. Every node in a binary tree *T* has at most two children. Compare the oldest-child/next-sibling representation of *T* described in Part *b* to the left-child/right-child representation of a binary tree described in this chapter. Does one representation simplify the implementation of the ADT operations? Are the two representations ever the same?

33. The section "Saving a Binary Search Tree in a File" mentions that you can save a binary search tree in a file by adding the interface *java.io.Serializable* to the various classes involved in the implementation of the tree. Name all of these classes when the binary search tree contains instances of the class *Person* presented in this chapter.

PROGRAMMING PROBLEMS

1. Write an array-based implementation of the ADT binary search tree that uses dynamic memory allocation. Use a data structure like the one in Figure 10-10.

2. Repeat Programming Problem 1 for complete binary trees.

3. Write a Java program that learns about a universe of your choice by asking the user yes/no questions. For example, your program might learn about animals by having the following dialogue with its user. (User responses are in uppercase.)

```
Think of an animal and I will guess it.
Does it have legs? YES
```

```
Is it a cat? YES
I win! Continue? YES

Think of an animal and I will guess it.
Does it have legs? NO
Is it a snake? YES
I win! Continue? YES

Think of an animal and I will guess it.
Does it have legs? NO
Is it a snake? NO
I give up. What is it? EARTHWORM
Please type a question whose answer is yes for an
earthworm and no for a snake:
DOES IT LIVE UNDERGROUND?
Continue? YES

Think of an animal and I will guess it.
Does it have legs? NO
Does it live underground? NO
Is it a snake? NO
I give up. What is it? FISH
Please type a question whose answer is yes for a
fish and no for a snake:
DOES IT LIVE IN WATER?
Continue? NO


Good-bye.
```

The program begins with minimal knowledge about animals: It knows that cats have legs and snakes do not. When the program incorrectly guesses "snake" the next time, it asks for the answer and also asks for a way to distinguish between snakes and earthworms.

The program builds a binary tree of questions and animals. A YES response to a question is stored in the question's left child; a NO response is stored in the question's right child.

4. Write a program that maintains the names, addresses, and telephone numbers of your friends and relatives and thus serves as an address book. You should be able to enter, delete, modify, or search this data. The person's name should be the search key, and initially you can assume that the names are unique. The program should be able to save the address book in a file for use later.

Design a class to represent the people in the address book and another class to represent the address book itself. This class should contain a binary search tree of people as a data field.

You can enhance this problem by adding birth dates to the database and by adding an operation that lists everyone who satisfies a given criterion. For example, it might list people born in a given month or people who live in a given state. You should also be able to list everyone in the database.

5. Write a program that provides a way for you to store and retrieve telephone numbers. Design a user interface that provides the following operations:

Add: Adds a person's name and phone number to the phone book.

Delete: Deletes a given person's name and phone number from the phone book, given only the name.

Find: Locates a person's phone number, given only the person's name.

Change: Changes a person's phone number, given the person's name and new phone number.

Quit: Quits the application, after first saving the address book in a text file.

You can proceed as follows:

- Design and implement the class *Person*, which represents the name and phone number of a person. You will store instances of this class in the phone book.

- Design and implement the class *PhoneBook*, which represents the phone book. The class should contain a binary search tree as a data field. This tree contains the people in the book.

- Add methods that use a text file to save and restore the tree.

- Design and implement the class *Menu*, which provides the program's user interface.

The program should read data from a text file when it begins and save data into a text file when the user quits the program.

6. In this chapter, a single iterator class was created to perform any one of the three binary tree traversals. The user could specify which of the traversals to use by calling *setPreorder*, *setInorder*, or *setPostorder*. An alternative implementation is based on creating a separate iterator class for each of the traversals. Also, as was mentioned in this chapter, the space and time requirements of the traversal can be minimized if the traversals are based on nonrecursive algorithms.

For example, the following pseudocode demonstrates how the method *inorderTraverse* presented in this chapter can be modified slightly and called from the method *next* in the iterator. The original version of *inorderTraverse* used a queue to store the entire traversal. This version of the method will produce the next node in the traversal only as needed. It is therefore slightly different in that the statement that queued a node is replaced with a return of the node.

```
inorderTraverse(treeNode)
// Nonrecursively traverses a binary tree
// inorder.
  curr = treeNode    // start at treeNode
  done = false
  while (!done) {
    if (curr != null) {
      visitStack.push(curr)
      // traverse the left subtree
      curr = curr.getLeft()
    }
    else {
      if (!visitStack.isEmpty()) {
        curr = visitStack.pop()
        return curr.getItem();
      }
      else {
        done = true
      }  // end if
    }  // end if
  }  // end while
```

Implement an iterator class for each of the three traversals using nonrecursive methods such that the storage requirements are never greater than O(*height of the tree*).

CHAPTER 11

Tables and Priority Queues

PREVIEW   This chapter considers the ADT table, which is appropriate for problems that must manage data by value. Several table implementations—which use arrays, linked lists, and binary search trees—will be presented, along with their advantages and disadvantages.

To make an intelligent choice among the various possible table implementations, you must analyze the efficiency with which each of the implementations supports the table operations. For example, this chapter analyzes the efficiency of array-based and reference-based table implementations and concludes that, in many applications, the implementations do not support the table operations as efficiently as possible. This conclusion motivates the use of a more sophisticated table implementation based on the binary search tree.

This chapter also introduces an important variation of the table, the ADT priority queue. This ADT provides operations for easily retrieving and deleting the item with the largest value. Although you can implement a priority queue by using a binary search tree, a simpler tree structure, known as a heap, is often more appropriate for this purpose.

THE ADT TABLE

The previous chapter introduced value-oriented ADTs whose operations are of the form

- Insert a data item containing the value *x*.
- Delete a data item containing the value *x*.
- Ask a question about a data item containing the value *x*.

Applications that require such value-oriented operations are extremely prevalent, as you might imagine. For example, the tasks

- *Find the phone number of John Smith*
- *Delete all the information about the employee with ID number 12908*

involve values instead of positions. This section presents another example of a value-oriented ADT.

The name of an ADT often suggests images of familiar objects that possess properties resembling those of the ADT. For example, the name "stack" might remind you of a stack of dishes. What does the name "table" bring to mind? If you had heard the question before you began reading this book, you might have answered, "My favorite mahogany coffee table." However, your answer now should be something more like, "A table of the major cities of the world," such as the one in Figure 11-1.

This table of cities contains several pieces of information about each city. Its design allows you to look up this information. For example, if you wanted to know the population of London, you could scan the column of city names, starting at the top, until you came to London. Because the cities are listed in alphabetical order, you could also mimic a binary search. You could begin the search near the middle of the table, determine in which half London lies, and recursively apply the binary

City	Country	Population
Athens	Greece	2,500,000
Barcelona	Spain	1,800,000
Cairo	Egypt	9,500,000
London	England	9,400,000
New York	U.S.A.	7,300,000
Paris	France	2,200,000
Rome	Italy	2,800,000
Toronto	Canada	3,200,000
Venice	Italy	300,000

Figure 11-1

An ordinary table of cities

search to the appropriate half. As you know, a binary search is far more efficient than scanning the entire table from the beginning.

If, however, you wanted to find which of the major cities are in Italy, you would have no choice but to scan the entire table. The alphabetical order of the city names does not help you for this problem at all. The table's arrangement facilitates the search for a given city, but other types of questions require a complete scan of the table.

The ADT **table**, or **dictionary**, also allows you to look up information easily and has a special operation for this purpose. Typically, the items in the ADT table are records that contain several pieces of data. You can facilitate the retrieval of an item by basing the search on a specified search key. In the table of cities, for example, you could designate `city` as the search key if you often needed to retrieve the information about a city. You can devise implementations of a table that allow the rapid retrieval of the item(s) whose search key matches some specified value. However, if you need to retrieve item(s) based on a value of a non-search-key portion of each record, you will have to inspect the entire table. Therefore, the choice of a search key sends the ADT implementer the following message:

The ADT table uses a search key to identify its items

> *Arrange the data to facilitate the search for an item, given the value of its search key.*

The basic operations that define the ADT table are as follows:

Operations of the ADT Table

1. Create an empty table.

2. Determine whether a table is empty.

3. Determine the number of items in a table.

4. Insert a new item into a table.

5. Delete the item with a given search key from a table.

6. Retrieve the item with a given search key from a table.

7. Traverse the items in a table in sorted search-key order.

For simplicity, we will assume that all items in the table have distinct search keys. Under this assumption, the insertion operation must reject an attempt to insert an item whose search key is the same as an item already in the table. The following pseudocode specifies in more detail the operations for an ADT table of items with distinct search keys:

KEY CONCEPTS

Pseudocode for the Operations of the ADT Table

```
createTable()
// Creates an empty table.

tableIsEmpty()
// Determines whether a table is empty.

tableLength()
// Determines the number of items in a table.

tableInsert(newItem) throws TableException
// Inserts newItem into a table whose items have distinct
// search keys that differ from newItem's search key.
// Throws TableException if the insertion is not
// successful.

tableDelete(searchKey)
// Deletes from a table the item whose search key equals
// searchKey. Returns false if no such item exists.
// Returns true if the deletion was successful.

tableRetrieve(searchKey)
// Returns the item in a table whose search
// key equals searchKey. Returns null
// if no such item exists.

tableTraverse()
// Traverses a table in sorted search-key order.
```

Various sets of table operations are possible

Our table assumes distinct search keys

Other tables could allow duplicate search keys

You should realize that these operations are only one possible set of table operations. The client may require either a subset of these operations or other operations not listed here to fit the application at hand. It may also be convenient to modify the definitions of some of the operations. For example, these operations assume that no two table items have the same values in their search keys. However, in many applications it is quite reasonable to expect duplicate search-key values. If this is the case, you must redefine several of the operations to eliminate the ambiguity that would arise from duplicate search-key values. For example, which item should *tableRetrieve* return if several items have the specified value in their search keys? You should tailor your definition of the ADT table to the problem at hand.

Although the operations *tableInsert, tableDelete,* and *table-Retrieve* in the previous set of operations are sufficient for some applications, you cannot do several significant things without additional operations. For instance, you cannot perform an important task such as

   Display all the table items

because you cannot retrieve a data item unless you know the value of its search key. Thus, you cannot display the entire table unless you can traverse the table.

In defining the traversal operation, you must specify the order in which *tableTraverse* should visit the items. One common specification is to visit the items sorted by the search key, but perhaps you do not care in what order the traversal visits the items. As you will see, the way you define *tableTraverse*—if you define it at all—may affect the way that you implement the table.

The concept of a search key for the table items is essential to the implementation of the table. It is important that the value of the search key remain the same as long as the item is stored in the table. Changing the search key of an existing element in the table could make that element or other table elements impossible to find. Thus, the search-key value should not be modifiable. This suggests the use of a class for items of the table; the class will contain the search key and a method for accessing the search-key data field. This is the same class that appeared in Chapter 10:

```
package SearchKeys;

public abstract class KeyedItem {
  private Comparable searchKey;

  public KeyedItem(Comparable key) {
    searchKey = key;
  }  // end constructor

  public Comparable getKey() {
    return searchKey;
  }  // end getKey
}  // end KeyedItem
```

Recall that classes that extend *KeyedItem* will have only the constructor available for initializing the search key. Thus, the search-key value cannot be modified once an item is created, which meets our requirement.

Suppose that the items in the table are instances of the following class:

```
import SearchKeys.KeyedItem;

public class City extends KeyedItem {
  private String city;     // city's name
  private String country;  // city's country
  private int    pop;      // city's population
```

```
      . . .
      // implementation of methods for accessing private
      // data fields
   }   // end City
```

and you want to perform tasks on this table such as

- *Display, in alphabetical order, the name of each*
  city and its population
- *Increase the population of each city by 10 percent*
- *Delete all cities with a population of less than*
  1,000,000

Each task suggests that you designate *city* as the search key. The class *City* contains all the information for a city, including the city name (returned by the inherited method *getKey*), country, and population. Here is a Java definition of *City*:

```
import SearchKeys.KeyedItem;

public class City extends KeyedItem {
   // city's name will be designated as search key
   private String country;  // city's country
   private int     pop;     // city's population

   public City(String theCity, String theCountry,
               int newPop) {
     super(theCity); // makes city name the search key
     country = theCountry;
     pop = newPop;
   }  // end constructor

   public String toString() {
     return getKey() + ", " + country + "   " + pop;
   }  // end toString

   // The methods getCountry, setCountry, getPopulation,
   // and setPopulation appear here.

      ...

   }  // end City
```

The first task requires you to write the city names in alphabetical order. Thus, *tableTraverse* must visit items alphabetically by search key. One way to implement *tableTraverse* is to define an iterator for the ADT table. You can use an instance of this iterator class to access each table item and then pass it to a method such as *displayItem*, which appears in pseudocode as follows:

```
displayItem(anItem)

   Display anItem.getCity()
   Display anItem.getPopulation()
```

The iterator's visitation order is immaterial for the other two tasks. To perform the second task, you pass each item that the iterator visits to a method *updatePopulation:*

```
updatePopulation(anItem)
```
Second task

```
   anItem.setPopulation(1.1 * anItem.getPopulation())
```

To perform the third task, you pass each item that the iterator visits to a method *deleteSmall*:

```
deleteSmall(table, anItem)
```
Third task

```
   if (anItem.getPopulation() < 1,000,000)
     table.tableDelete(anItem)
```

However, this task is not as simple as it may seem. By deleting an item, you alter the table during the traversal with the iterator. Which item will the iterator visit next? Clearly, it should visit the one after the deleted item, but will it do so, or will it skip that item? Usually, you use the iterator's *remove* method to perform a deletion when an iterator is in use. Doing so clarifies the semantics of the deletion with respect to the iterator. The definition of the iterators for the two table implementations presented later in this chapter, and in particular the *remove* operation, are left as programming problems.

The following interface *TableInterface* summarizes the table operations:

```
    package Tables;
    import SearchKeys.KeyedItem;

    public interface TableInterface {

    // Table operations:
    // Precondition for all operations:
    // No two items of the table have the same search key.
    // The table's items are sorted by search key.

      public boolean tableIsEmpty();
      // Determines whether a table is empty.
      // Postcondition: Returns true if the table is
      // empty; otherwise returns false.

      public int tableLength();
      // Determines the length of a table.
      // Postcondition: Returns the number of items in the
      // table.

      public void tableInsert(KeyedItem newItem)
                            throws TableException;
      // Inserts an item into a table in its proper sorted
```

```
// order according to the item's search key.
// Precondition: The item to be inserted into the
// table is newItem, whose search key differs from
// all search keys presently in the table.
// Postcondition: If the insertion was successful,
// newItem is in its proper order in the table.
// Otherwise, the table is unchanged, and
// TableException is thrown.

public boolean tableDelete(Comparable searchKey);
// Deletes an item with a given search key from a
// table.
// Precondition: searchKey is the search key of the
// item to be deleted.
// Postcondition: If the item whose search key equals
// searchKey existed in the table, the item was
// deleted and method returns true. Otherwise, the
// table is unchanged and the method returns false.

public KeyedItem tableRetrieve(Comparable searchKey);
// Retrieves an item with a given search key from a
// table.
// Precondition: searchKey is the search key of the
// item to be retrieved.
// Postcondition: If the retrieval was successful,
// the table item with the matching search key is
// returned. If no such item exists, the method
// returns a null reference.

}   // end TableInterface
```

Selecting an Implementation

In the previous chapters, ADT implementations were either array based or reference based. That is, you used either an array or a linked list to store the ADT's items. Such implementations are called **linear** because they represent items one after another in a data structure and thus mirror the flat, listlike appearance of the table of cities in Figure 11-1.

Linear implementations of a table are certainly possible and fall into four categories:

Four categories of linear implementations

- Unsorted, array based
- Unsorted, reference based
- Sorted (by search key), array based
- Sorted (by search key), reference based

The unsorted implementations store the items in no particular order; they can insert a new item into any convenient location. The sorted implementations, however, must insert a new item into its proper position as determined by the value of its search key. Whether sorted or unsorted, the array-based and reference-based linear implementations have the basic structures shown in Figure 11-2. Both implementations maintain a count of the current number of items in the table. As you will see, the unsorted and sorted implementations have their relative advantages and disadvantages.

At this point in your study of ADTs, you have other choices for a table implementation. For instance, you can implement the ADT table by using an ADT list, sorted list, or binary search tree. The binary search tree implementation, as illustrated in Figure 11-3, is an example of a **nonlinear implementation** and offers several advantages over linear implementations. Among these advantages is the opportunity to reuse the implementation of the ADT binary search tree given in Chapter 10. Implementations based on the ADTs list and sorted list also share this advantage, and they are left for you to consider as programming problems.

A binary search tree implementation is nonlinear

A major goal of this chapter is to indicate how the requirements of a particular application influence the selection of an implementation. The discussion here elaborates on the comments made in Chapter 9 in the section "Keeping Your Perspective." Some applications require all of the operations of the ADT table given earlier; others require either a subset of them or additional operations. Before choosing an implementation of the ADT table, you as problem solver should carefully analyze which operations you really need for the application at hand. It is tempting to want all possible operations, but this strategy is a poor one, because often one implementation supports some of the operations more efficiently than another implementation does. Therefore, if you include an operation that you never use, you might end up with an implementation of the ADT that does not best suit your purpose.

What operations are needed?

In addition to knowing what operations are needed for a given application, the ADT implementer should know approximately how often the application will perform each operation. Although some applications may

How often is each operation required?

Figure 11-2

The data fields for two sorted linear implementations of the ADT table for the data in Figure 11-1: (a) array based; (b) reference based

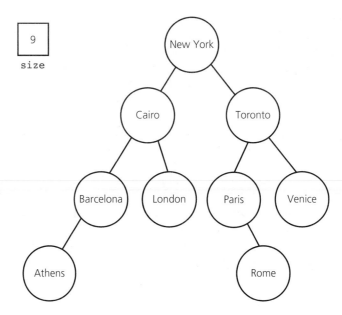

Figure 11-3

The data fields for a binary search tree implementation of the ADT table for the data in Figure 11-1

require many occurrences of every operation, other applications may not. For example, if you maintained a table of major cities such as the one in Figure 11-1, you would expect to perform many more retrieval operations than insertions or deletions. Thus, if you seldom insert items, you can tolerate a table implementation that results in an inefficient insertion operation, as long as frequently used operations are efficient. Of course, as Chapter 9 mentioned, if an ADT operation is to be used in a life-or-death situation, that operation must be efficient, even if you rarely need it. The necessary operations, their expected frequency of occurrence, and their required response times are therefore some factors that influence which implementation of an ADT you should select for a particular application. You should, however, remain conscious of factors other than efficiency, as discussed in Chapter 9.

Consider now several different application scenarios, each of which requires a particular mix of the table operations. The analysis of various implementations of the ADT table will illustrate some of the basic concerns of the analysis of algorithms. You will see, given an application, how to select an implementation that supports in a reasonably efficient manner the required mix of table operations.

Scenario A: Insertion and traversal in no particular order.   Mary's sorority plans to raise money for a local charity. Tired of previous fund-raisers, Mary suggests a brainstorming session to discover a new money-making strategy. As sorority members voice their ideas, Mary records them by inserting each new thought into a table. Later, she will print a report of all the ideas currently in the table. Assume that the organization of the report is irrelevant—the items can be sorted or unsorted. Also assume that operations such as retrieval, deletion, or traversal in sorted order either do not occur or occur so infrequently that they do not influence your choice of an implementation.

For this application, maintaining the items in a sorted order has no advantage. In fact, by not maintaining a sorted order, the `tableInsert` operation can be quite efficient. For either unsorted linear implementation, you can insert a new item into any convenient location. For an unsorted array-based implementation, you can easily insert a new item after the last item in the array—that is, at location `items[size]`. Figure 11-4a shows the result of this insertion after `size` has been updated. For a reference-based implementation, you can simply insert a new item at the beginning of the linked list. As Figure 11-4b illustrates, `head` references the new item, and the new item references the item previously first on the list. Thus, not only can you insert a new item quickly into either unsorted implementation of a table, but also the `tableInsert` operation is O(1): It requires a constant time for either implementation regardless of the table size.

An unsorted order is efficient

Should you choose the array-based or the reference-based implementation? As you have seen with other ADTs, an implementation that uses dynamically allocated memory is appropriate if you do not have a good estimate of the maximum possible size of the table. Mary's brainstorming session likely falls into this category. On the other hand, if you know that the table's maximum size is not drastically larger than its expected size,[1] the choice is mostly a matter of style.

Array based versus reference based

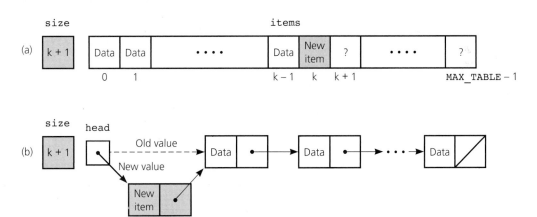

Figure 11-4

Insertion for unsorted linear implementations: (a) array based;
(b) reference based

---

[1]Chapter 4, in the section "Comparing Array-Based and Reference-Based Implementations," discussed how the expected and maximum number of items in an ADT affect an array-based implementation.

Should you consider a binary search tree implementation for this application? Because such an implementation orders the table items, it does more work than the application requires. In fact, as you saw in Chapter 10, insertion into a binary search tree is O(log n) in the average case.

Scenario B: Retrieval.   When you use a word processor's thesaurus to look up synonyms for a word, you use a retrieval operation. If an ADT table represents the thesaurus, each table item is a record that contains both the word—which is the search key—and the word's synonyms. Frequent retrieval operations require a table implementation that allows you to search efficiently for an item, given its search-key value. Typically, you cannot alter the thesaurus, so no insertion or deletion operations are necessary.

A sorted array-based implementation can use a binary search

For an array-based implementation, you can use a binary search to retrieve a particular word's record, if the array is sorted. On the other hand, for a reference-based implementation, you must traverse the linked list from its beginning until you encounter the word in the list. The binary search performs this retrieval in significantly less time than is required to traverse a linked list. Two questions come to mind at this point:

Questions

1. Is a binary search of a linked list possible?
2. How much more efficient is a binary search of an array than a sequential search of a linked list?

A binary search is impractical with a reference-based implementation

Can you perform a binary search under a reference-based implementation? Yes, but too inefficiently to be practical. Consider the very first step of the binary search algorithm:

```
Look at the "middle" item in the table
```

If n items are in a linked list, how can you possibly get to the middle item of the list? You can traverse the list from the beginning until you have visited $n/2$ items. But, as you will see in the answer to the second question, just this first step will often take longer than the entire binary search of an array. Further, you would have the same problem of finding the "middle" element at each recursive step. It is thus not practical to perform a binary search for the linear reference-based implementation. This observation is extremely significant.

On the other hand, if n items are in an array `items`, the middle item is at location $n/2$ and can be accessed directly. Thus, a binary search of an array requires considerably less time than an algorithm that must inspect every item in the table. What does "considerably less time" mean? As you know, without the ability to perform a binary search, you may have to inspect every item in the table, either to locate an item with a particular value in its search key or to determine that such an item is not present. In other words, if a table has size n, you will have to inspect as many as n items; thus, such a search is O(n). How much better can you do with a binary search? Recall from Chapter 9 that a binary search is $O(\log_2 n)$ in its worst case and that an $O(\log_2 n)$ algorithm is substantially more efficient than an $O(n)$ algorithm. For example, $\log_2 1024 = 10$ and $\log_2 1,048,576 = 20$. For a large table, the binary search has an enormous advantage.

Since a thesaurus is probably large, you must choose an implementation for which a binary search is practical. As you have just seen, this observation eliminates the linear reference-based implementations. The sorted array-based implementation is fine here, since you know the size of the thesaurus.

If you know the table's maximum size, a sorted array-based implementation is appropriate for frequent retrievals

The binary search tree implementation is also a good choice for retrieval-dominated applications. As you saw in Chapter 10, searching a binary search tree is $O(\log n)$ if the tree is balanced. Since the thesaurus does not change, you can create a balanced tree that remains balanced and be assured of an efficient search.

If you do not know the table's maximum size, use a binary search tree implementation

Scenario C: Insertion, deletion, retrieval, and traversal in sorted order.

If your local library has computerized its catalog of books, you perform a retrieval operation when you access this catalog. The library staff uses insertion and deletion operations to update the catalog and a traversal to save the entire catalog in a file. Presumably, retrieval is the most frequent operation, but the other operations are not infrequent enough to ignore. (Otherwise, this scenario would be the same as Scenario B!)

To insert into a table an item that has the value X in its search key, you must first determine where the item belongs in the table's sorted order. Similarly, to delete from the table an item that has the value X in its search key, you must first locate the item. Thus, both the *table-Insert* and *tableDelete* operations perform the following steps:

1. Find the appropriate position in the table.
2. Insert into (or delete from) this position.

Both insertion and deletion perform these two steps

Step 1 is far more efficient if the table implementation is array based instead of reference based. For an array-based implementation, you can use a binary search to determine—in the case of insertion—where the new item X belongs and—in the case of deletion—where the item is located. On the other hand, for a reference-based implementation, you know from the discussion in Scenario B that a binary search is impractical, and so you must traverse the list from its beginning until you encounter the appropriate location in the list. You also saw in Scenario B that it takes significantly less time to perform a binary search of an array than it does to traverse a linked list.

Use an array-based implementation for Step 1

Thus, because it facilitates a binary search, the array-based implementation is superior with respect to Step 1 of *tableInsert* and *table-Delete*. However, as you may have guessed, the reference-based implementation is better for Step 2, the actual insertion or deletion of the item. Under the array-based implementation, *tableInsert* must shift array items to make room for the new item (see Figure 11-5a), while

Use a reference-based implementation for Step 2

(a)

(b)

Figure 11-5

Insertion for sorted linear implementations: (a) array based;
(b) reference based

A sorted array-based implementation shifts data during insertions and deletions

tableDelete must shift array items to fill in the gap created when the item is removed. The worst case would require that every array item be shifted. On the other hand, under the reference-based implementation, you can accomplish this second step simply by changing at most two references, as Figure 11-5b illustrates.

The sorted linear implementations are comparable here, but none are suitable

When you take Steps 1 and 2 together, you will find that the sorted array-based and sorted reference-based implementations of *tableInsert* or *tableDelete* both require roughly the same amount of time—they are both $O(n)$. Neither implementation supports these operations particularly well. The binary search tree implementation, however, combines the best features of the two linear implementations. Because it is reference based, you avoid shifting data, and the table can grow dynamically as needed. You can also retrieve items from a binary search tree efficiently.

Summary.   An unsorted array-based implementation of the ADT table can efficiently insert an item at the end of an array. A deletion, however, will usually require shifting data so that no hole remains in the array. Because the items are unsorted, retrieval will require a sequential search.

A sorted array-based implementation usually requires shifting data during both insertions and deletions. Retrieval, however, can use an efficient binary search because the items are sorted.

An unsorted reference-based implementation can efficiently insert an item at the beginning of a linked list. A deletion will require a sequential search but no data shifts. Retrieval will also require a sequential search.

A sorted reference-based implementation requires a sequential search but no data shifts during both insertions and deletions. Retrieval will also require a sequential search.

Although these linear implementations are less sophisticated and generally require more time than the binary search tree implementation, they are nevertheless useful for many applications. Because linear implementations are easy to understand conceptually, they are appropriate for tables that will contain only a small number of items. In such cases, efficiency is not as great a concern as simplicity and clarity. Even when a table is large, a linear implementation may still be appropriate for applications that can use an unsorted table and have few deletions.

Despite certain difficulties, linear implementations of a table can be appropriate

The nonlinear, binary search tree implementation of the ADT table can be a better choice, in general, than the linear implementations. If an n-node binary search tree has minimum height—that is, has height $\lceil \log_2(n + 1) \rceil$—the binary search tree implementation of the ADT table certainly succeeds where the linear implementations failed: You can, with efficiency comparable to that of a binary search, locate an item in both the retrieval operation and the first steps of the insertion and deletion operations. In addition, the reference-based implementation of the binary search tree permits dynamic allocation of its nodes, and so it can handle a table whose maximum size is unknown. This implementation also efficiently performs the second step of the insertion and deletion operations: The actual insertion and removal of a node requires only a few reference changes (plus a short traversal to the inorder successor if the node to be removed has two children) rather than the possible shifting of all the table items, as the array-based implementations require. The binary search tree implementation therefore combines the best aspects of the two linear implementations, yet avoids their disadvantages.

A binary search tree implementation is a better choice, in general

As the previous chapter showed, however, the height of a binary search tree depends on the order in which you perform the insertion and deletion operations on the tree and can be as large as n. If the insertion and deletion operations occur in a random order, the height of the binary search tree will be quite close to its minimum value. You do need to watch for a possible increase in the tree's height, however, and the resulting decrease in performance. If instead you use a variation of the binary search tree that remains balanced—as Chapter 12 describes—you can keep the height of the tree near $\log_2 n$.

A balanced binary search tree increases the efficiency of the ADT table operations

Figure 11-6 summarizes the order of the insertion, deletion, retrieval, and traversal operations for the table implementations discussed in this chapter.

	Insertion	Deletion	Retrieval	Traversal
Unsorted array based	O(1)	O(n)	O(n)	O(n)
Unsorted pointer based	O(1)	O(n)	O(n)	O(n)
Sorted array based	O(n)	O(n)	O(log n)	O(n)
Sorted pointer based	O(n)	O(n)	O(n)	O(n)
Binary search tree	O(log n)	O(log n)	O(log n)	O(n)

Figure 11-6

The average-case order of the operations of the ADT table for various implementations

A Sorted Array-Based Implementation of the ADT Table

Perspective, efficiency, and moti-vation are reasons for studying the linear implementations

If the binary search tree implementation of the ADT table is so good, you might wonder why you needed to study the linear implementations at all. There are three reasons. The first and foremost of these is perspective. Chapter 9 spoke of the dangers of overanalyzing a problem. If the size of the problem is small, the difference in efficiency among the possible solutions is likely insignificant. In particular, if the size of the table is small, a linear implementation is adequate and simple to understand.

The second reason is efficiency: A linear implementation can be quite efficient for certain situations. For example, a linear implementation was best for Scenario A, where the predominant operations are insertion and traversal in no particular order. For Scenario B, where the predominant operation is retrieval, the sorted array-based implementation is ade-quate, if the maximum number of items is known. For these situations, a concern for simplicity suggests that you use a linear implementation and not a binary search tree, even for large tables.

The third reason is motivation. By seeing scenarios for which the linear implementations are not adequate, you are forced to look beyond arrays and consider other implementations, such as the binary search tree. Actually looking at both a linear implementation and a binary search tree implementation allows you to see these inadequacies more clearly.

The following sorted array-based implementation assumes unique search keys. Exercise 7 at the end of this chapter asks you to remove this assumption. The pre- and postconditions are omitted to save space, but they are the same as those given earlier in this chapter in *Table-Interface*.

```
package Tables;
import SearchKeys.KeyedItem;


// ***********************************************************
// ADT table.
// Sorted array-based implementation.
// Assumption: A table contains at most one item with a
//             given search key at any time.
// ***********************************************************

public class TableArrayBased implements TableInterface{
   final int MAX_TABLE = 100;        // maximum size of table;
   protected KeyedItem[] items;      // table items
   private int size;                 // table size

   public TableArrayBased() {
     items = new KeyedItem[MAX_TABLE];
     size = 0;
   }  // default constructor
```

```java
public boolean tableIsEmpty() {
  return size==0;
} // end tableIsEmpty

public int tableLength() {
  return size;
}  // end tableLength

public void tableInsert(KeyedItem newItem)
                    throws TableException {
// Calls: position.
  if (size < MAX_TABLE) {
    // there is room to insert;
    // locate the position where newItem belongs
    int spot = position(newItem.getKey());
    if ((spot < size) &&
        (items[spot].getKey()).compareTo(newItem.getKey())==0) {
        // we have found a duplicate key
        throw new TableException("Table Exception: " +
                  "Insertion failed, duplicate key item");
    }
    else {
      // shift up to make room for the new item
      for (int index = size-1; index >= spot; --index) {
        items[index+1] = items[index];
      } //end for
      // make the insertion
      items[spot] = newItem;
      ++size;
    }  // end if
  }
  else {
    throw new TableException("TableException: Table full");
  } // end if
}  // end tableInsert

public boolean tableDelete(Comparable searchKey) {
// Calls: position.
  // locate the position where searchKey exists/belongs
  int spot = position(searchKey);
  // is searchKey present in the table?
  boolean success = (spot <= size) &&
          (items[spot].getKey().compareTo(searchKey)==0);
  if (success) {
    // searchKey in table
    --size;  // delete the item
    // shift down to fill the gap
```

```
      for (int index = spot; index < size; ++index) {
        items[index] = items[index+1];
      } //end for
    }  // end if
    return success;
  }  // end tableDelete


  public KeyedItem tableRetrieve(Comparable searchKey) {
  // Calls: position.

    // locate the position where searchKey exists/belongs
    int spot = position(searchKey);
    // is searchKey present in table?
    boolean success = (spot <= size) &&
            (items[spot].getKey().compareTo(searchKey)==0);
    if (success) {
      return items[spot];   // item present; retrieve it
    }
    else {
      return null;
    }  // end if
  }  // end tableRetrieve


  protected int position(Comparable searchKey) {
  // Finds the position of a table item or its insertion
  // point.
  // Precondition: searchKey is the value of the search key
  // sought in the table.
  // Postcondition: Returns the index (between 0 and
  // size - 1) of the item in the table whose search key
  // equals searchKey. If no such item exists, returns the
  // position (between 0 and size) that the item would
  // occupy if inserted into the table. The table is
  // unchanged.
    int pos = 0;
    while ((pos < size) &&
            (searchKey.compareTo(items[pos].getKey()) > 0)) {
      pos++;
    }  // end while
    return pos;
  }  // end position
}  // end TableArrayBased
```

A Binary Search Tree Implementation of the ADT Table

Although linear implementations are suited to specific applications, they
are not good as general-purpose implementations of the ADT table.

The following nonlinear reference-based implementation uses a binary search tree to represent the items in the ADT table. That is, class *TableBSTBased* has a binary search tree as one of its data fields. In this way, *TableBSTBased* reuses the class *BinarySearchTree* from the previous chapter. The pre- and postconditions are omitted to save space, but they are the same as those given earlier in this chapter.

```java
package Tables;
import BinaryTrees.*;
import SearchKeys.*;

// Assumes that the binary search tree created in Chapter 10
// is contained in a package called BinaryTrees.
// ********************************************************
// Implementation of a table using a binary search tree.
// Assumption: A table contains at most one item with a
//             given search key at any time.
// ********************************************************
public class TableBSTBased implements TableInterface {
  protected BinarySearchTree bst; // binary search tree that
                                  // contains the table's items
  protected int size;             // number of items in the table

  public TableBSTBased() {
    bst = new BinarySearchTree();
    size = 0;
  }  // end default constructor

// table operations:
  public boolean tableIsEmpty() {
    return size == 0;
  }  // end tableIsEmpty

  public int tableLength() {
    return size;
  }  // end tableLength

  public void tableInsert(KeyedItem newItem)
                          throws TableException {
    if (bst.retrieve(newItem.getKey()) == null) {
      bst.insert(newItem);
      ++size;
    }
    else {
      throw new TableException("Table Exception: Insertion"
                          + " failed, duplicate key item");
    } // end if
  }  // end tableInsert
```

```java
    public KeyedItem tableRetrieve(Comparable searchKey) {
      return bst.retrieve(searchKey);
    }  // end tableRetrieve

    public boolean tableDelete(Comparable searchKey) {
      try {
        bst.delete(searchKey);
      }  // end try
      catch (TreeException e) {
        return false;
      }  // end catch

      --size;
      return true;
    }  // end tableDelete

    protected void setSize(int newSize) {
      size = newSize;
    }  // end setSize

}  // end TableBSTBased
```

The following statements demonstrate how to use this class in a program that requires the ADT table:

A sample program

```java
import Tables.*;

public class TestTable {

  public static void displayCity(City anItem) {
    System.out.println(anItem.getCity());
  }  // end displayCity

  // Main entry point
  public static void main(String[] args) {
    TableInterface chart = new TableBSTBased();
    City anItem;

    anItem = new City("Narragansett", "USA", 12000);
    chart.tableInsert(anItem);
    anItem = new City("Ocracoke", "USA", 3000);
    chart.tableInsert(anItem);

    // If a table iterator class called TableIteratorBST
    // is available for the class TableBSTBased (as created
    // in Programming Problem 2), you also can do the
    // following:
```

```
    TableIteratorBST iter = new TableIteratorBST(chart);
    while (iter.hasNext()) {
      displayCity((City)iter.next());
    }  // end while
  }  // end main
}  // end TestTable
```

THE ADT PRIORITY QUEUE: A VARIATION OF THE ADT TABLE

The ADT table organizes its data by search key, facilitating the retrieval of a particular item, given its search key. Thus, the ADT table is appropriate when you have a database to maintain and search by value, such as the table of cities described earlier in this chapter. Consider now applications for which another ADT, related to the ADT table, would be more appropriate.

Imagine a person who visits a hospital's emergency room (ER). When any patient enters the hospital, a staff member enters a record about that person into a database for later retrieval by nurses, doctors, and the billing department. In addition, the staff must keep track of the emergency room patients and decide when each person will receive care.

The ADT table would be an appropriate choice for the hospital's general database. What ADT should the ER staff use for their patients? The ADT table would facilitate the treatment of ER patients in alphabetic order by name or in numeric order by ID number. A queue would enable the treatment of patients in the order of arrival. In either case, Ms. Zither, who was just rushed to the ER with acute appendicitis, would have to wait for Mr. Able to have a splinter removed. Clearly, the ER staff should assign some measure of urgency, or **priority**, to the patients waiting for treatment. The next available doctor should treat the patient with the highest priority. The ADT that the ER staff needs should produce this patient upon request.

You can organize data by priorities

Another example of the use of priorities is your list of daily or weekly tasks. Suppose that your "to do" list for this week contains the following items:

> Send a birthday card to Aunt Mabel.
>
> Start the research paper for world history.
>
> Finish reading Chapter 11 of *Walls and Mirrors*.
>
> Make plans for Saturday night.

You usually prioritize your list of tasks

When you consult your list, you most likely will attend to the task that, for you, has the highest priority.

A **priority value** indicates, for example, a patient's priority for treatment or a task's priority for completion. What quantity should you use for this priority value? Many reasonable possibilities exist, including a simple ranking from 1 to 10. Let's arbitrarily decide that the largest priority value indicates the highest priority. The priority value becomes a part of the record that represents an item. You insert each item into an ADT and then ask the ADT for the item that has the highest priority.

A priority queue orders by priority values

Such an ADT is known as a **priority queue.** More formally, a priority queue is an ADT that provides the following operations:

KEY CONCEPTS

Operations of the ADT Priority Queue

1. Create an empty priority queue.

2. Determine whether a priority queue is empty.

3. Insert a new item into a priority queue.

4. Retrieve and then delete the item in a priority queue with the highest priority value.

The following pseudocode specifies in more detail the operations for an ADT priority queue:

KEY CONCEPTS

Pseudocode for the Operations of the ADT Priority Queue

```
createPQueue()
// Creates an empty priority queue.

pqIsEmpty()
// Determines whether a priority queue is empty.

pqInsert(newItem) throws PQueueException
// Inserts newItem into a priority queue. Throws
// PQueueException if priority queue is full.

pqDelete()
// Retrieves and then deletes the item in a priority queue
// with the highest priority value.
```

Priority queue pqDelete is the difference between a priority queue and a table

These operations resemble a subset of the operations of the ADT table. The significant difference is the *pqDelete* operation. Whereas the sequence of table operations *tableRetrieve–tableDelete* allows you to retrieve and delete an item that has a specified value in its search key, *pqDelete* allows you to retrieve and delete the item with the highest priority value. Notice that *pqDelete*, unlike *tableRetrieve* and *table-Delete*, is not told the value in question. Because in general you will not know what the highest priority value is, *tableRetrieve* and *table-Delete* could not easily perform this task. On the other hand, you could not use *pqDelete* to retrieve and delete an item with some specified value.

The ADT priority queue and the ADT table are thus both similar and dissimilar, a fact that their implementations reflect. To begin, consider some of the table implementations as implementations for a priority queue. The sorted linear implementations are appropriate if the number of items in the priority queue is small. The array-based implementation maintains the items sorted in ascending order of priority value, so that the item with the highest priority value is at the end of the array, as Figure 11-7a illustrates. Thus, *pqDelete* simply returns the item in *items[size-1]* and decrements *size*. However, the *pqInsert* operation, after using a binary search to find the correct position for the insertion, must shift the array elements to make room for the new item.

Possible implementations

The linear reference-based implementation, shown in Figure 11-7b, maintains the items sorted in descending order of priority value, so that the item with the highest priority value is at the beginning of the linked

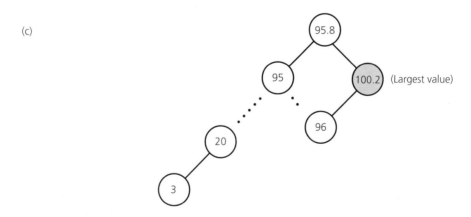

Figure 11-7

Some implementations of the ADT priority queue: (a) array based; (b) reference based; (c) binary search tree

list. Thus, *pqDelete* simply returns the item that *pqHead* references and then changes *pqHead* to reference the next item. The *pqInsert* operation, however, must traverse the list to find the correct position for the insertion. Thus, the linear implementations of priority queues suffer from the same trade-offs as the linear implementations of tables.

Instead, consider a binary search tree as an implementation of a priority queue, as Figure 11-7c illustrates. Although the *pqInsert* operation is the same as *tableInsert*, the *pqDelete* operation has no direct analogue among the table operations. It must locate the item with the highest priority value, without knowing what that value is. The task is not difficult, however, because this item is always in the rightmost node of the tree. (Why?) You thus need only follow *rightChild* references until you encounter a node with a *null rightChild* reference. (Methods analogous to the binary search tree's *findLeftmost* and *deleteLeftmost* can accomplish this task.) Removing this node from the tree is particularly easy because it has at most one child.

A binary search tree implementation is thus good for both a table and a priority queue. Tables and priority queues have different uses, however. Some table applications primarily involve retrieval and traversal operations and thus do not affect the balance of the binary search tree. Priority queues, on the other hand, do not have retrieval and traversal operations, so all their applications involve insertions and deletions, which can affect the shape of the binary search tree. You could use a balanced variation of the binary search tree from Chapter 12; however, if you know the maximum size of the priority queue, a better choice might be an array-based implementation of a heap, which is described next. The heap implementation is often the most appropriate one for a priority queue, but it is not at all appropriate as an implementation of a table.

Heaps

A heap differs from a binary search tree in two ways

A **heap** is an ADT that is similar to a binary search tree, although it differs from a binary search tree in two significant ways. First, while you can view a binary search tree as sorted, a heap is ordered in a much weaker sense. This order, however, is sufficient for the efficient performance of the priority-queue operations. Second, while binary search trees come in many different shapes, heaps are always complete binary trees.

A heap is a special complete binary tree

A heap is a complete binary tree

1. That is empty

or

2. Whose root contains a search key greater than or equal to the search key in each of its children, and

3. Whose root has heaps as its subtrees

In our definition of a heap, the root contains the item with the largest search key. Such a heap is also known as a **maxheap.** A **minheap,** on the other hand, places the item with the smallest search key in its root. Exercise 13 considers the minheap further.

Because a heap is a complete binary tree, you can use an array-based implementation of a binary tree, as you saw in Chapter 10, if you know the maximum size of the heap. For example, Figure 11-8 shows a heap along with its array representation. The search key in a heap node is greater than or equal to the search keys in each of the node's children. Further, in a heap, the search keys of the children have no relationship; that is, you do not know which child contains the larger search key.

KEY CONCEPTS

Pseudocode for the Operations of the ADT Heap

```
createHeap()
// Creates an empty heap.

heapIsEmpty()
// Determines whether a heap is empty.

heapInsert(newItem) throws HeapException
// Inserts newItem into a heap. Throws HeapException
// if heap is full.

heapDelete()
// Retrieves and then deletes a heap's root item.
// This item has the largest search key.
```

An array-based implementation of a heap. Let the following data fields represent the heap:

- *items:* an array of heap items
- *size:* an integer equal to the number of items in the heap

An array and an integer counter are the data fields for an array-based implementation of a heap

The array *items* corresponds to the array-based representation of a tree. (To simplify the following discussion, assume that the heap items are integers.)

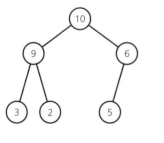

0	10
1	9
2	6
3	3
4	2
5	5

Figure 11-8

A heap with its array representation

heapDelete. First consider the *heapDelete* operation. Where is the largest search key in the heap? Because the search key in every node is greater than or equal to the search key in either of its children, the largest search key must be in the root of the tree. Thus, the first step of the *heap-Delete* operation is

heapDelete's first step

```
// return the item in the root
rootItem = items[0]
```

That was easy, but you must also remove the root. When you do so, you are left with two disjoint heaps, as Figure 11-9a indicates. Therefore, you need to transform the remaining nodes back into a heap. To begin this transformation, you take the item in the last node of the tree and place it in the root, as follows:

heapDelete's second step
produces a semiheap

```
// copy the item from the last node into the root
items[0] = items[size-1]

// remove the last node
--size
```

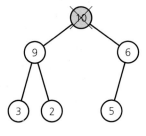

(a)

(b)

Figure 11-9

(a) Disjoint heaps; (b) a semiheap

As Figure 11-9b suggests, the result of this step is *not* necessarily a heap. It is, however, a complete binary tree whose left and right subtrees are both heaps. The only problem is that the item in the root may be (and usually is) out of place. Such a structure is called a **semiheap.** You thus need a way to transform a semiheap into a heap. One strategy allows the item in the root to *trickle down* the tree until it reaches a node in which it will not be out of place; that is, the item will come to rest in the first node where its search key would be greater than (or equal to) the search key of each of its children. To accomplish this, you first compare the search key in the root of the semiheap to the search keys in its children. If the root has a smaller search key than the larger of the search keys in its children, you swap the item in the root with that of the larger child. (The larger child is the child whose search key is greater than the search key of the other child.)

Figure 11-10 illustrates the `heapDelete` operation. Although the value 5 trickles down to its correct position after only one swap, in general more swaps may be necessary. In fact, once the items in the root and the larger child *C* have been swapped, *C* becomes the root of a semiheap. (Notice that node *C* does not move; only its value changes.) This strategy suggests the following recursive algorithm:

```
heapRebuild(items, root, size)
// Converts a semiheap rooted at index root into a heap.

  // Recursively trickle the item at index root down to
  // its proper position by swapping it with its larger
  // child, if the child is larger than the item.
  // If the item is at a leaf, nothing needs to be done.

  if (the root is not a leaf) {
    // root must have a left child
    child = 2 * root + 1            // left child index

    if (the root has a right child) {
      rightChild = child + 1          // right child index
      if (items[rightChild].getKey() > items[child].getKey()) {
```

heapDelete's final step transforms the semiheap into a heap

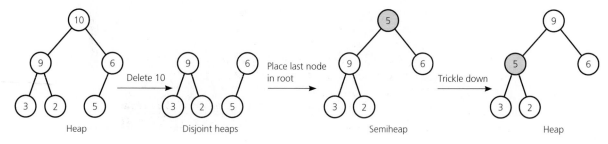

Figure 11-10

Deletion from a heap

```
                    child = rightChild              // larger child index
              }  // end if
          }  // end if

          // if the item in the root has a smaller search key
          // than the search key of the item in the larger
          // child, swap items
          if (items[root].getKey() < items[child].getKey()) {
            Swap items[root] and items[child]

              // transform semiheap rooted at child into a heap
              heapRebuild(items, child, size)
          }  // end if
      }  // end if

      // else root is a leaf, so you are done
```

Figure 11-11 illustrates *heapRebuild*'s recursive calls.

Now the *heapDelete* operation uses *heapRebuild* as follows:

```
          // return the item in the root
          rootItem = items[0]

          // copy the item from the last node into the root
          items[0] = items[size-1]

          // remove the last node
          --size
```

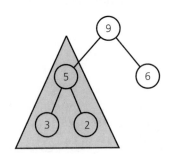

First semiheap passed to heapRebuild   Second semiheap passed to heapRebuild

Figure 11-11

Recursive calls to *heapRebuild*

```
// transform the semiheap back into a heap
heapRebuild(items, 0, size)

return rootItem
```

Consider briefly the efficiency of `heapDelete`. Because the tree is stored in an array, the removal of a node requires you to swap array elements. These swaps may concern you, but they do not necessarily indicate that the algorithm is inefficient. Since array contents are references, swapping will be very fast. The data in the objects need not be copied. At most, how many array elements will you have to swap? After `heapDelete` copies the item in the last node of the tree into the root, `heapRebuild` trickles this item down the tree until its appropriate place is found. This item travels down a single path from the root to, at worst, a leaf. Therefore, the number of array items that `heapRebuild` must swap is no greater than the height of the tree. The height of a complete binary tree with n nodes is always $\lceil \log_2(n + 1) \rceil$, as you know from Chapter 10. Each swap requires three reference changes, so `heapDelete` requires

heapDelete's efficiency

$$3 * \lceil \log_2(n + 1) \rceil + 1$$

reference changes. Thus, `heapDelete` is O(log n), which is, in fact, quite efficient.

heapDelete is O(log n)

heapInsert. The strategy for the `heapInsert` algorithm is the opposite of that for `heapDelete`. A new item is inserted at the bottom of the tree, and it trickles up to its proper place, as Figure 11-12 illustrates. It is easy to trickle up a node, because the parent of the node in `items[i]`— other than a root—is always stored in `items[(i-1)/2]`. The pseudocode for `heapInsert` is

```
// insert newItem into the bottom of the tree
items[size] = newItem
```

Insertion strategy

```
// trickle new item up to appropriate spot in the tree
place = size
parent = (place-1)/2
```

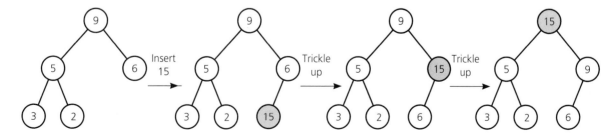

Figure 11-12

Insertion into a heap

```
while ( (parent >= 0) and
        (items[place] > items[parent]) ) {
  Swap items[place] and items[parent]
  place = parent
  parent = (place-1)/2
} // end while
```

```
Increment size
```

The efficiency of *heapInsert* is like that of *heapDelete*. That is, *heap-Insert*, at worst, has to swap array elements on a path from a leaf to the root. The number of swaps, therefore, cannot exceed the height of the tree. Because the height of the tree, which is complete, is always $\lceil \log_2(n + 1) \rceil$, *heapInsert* is also O(log *n*).

heapInsert is O(log n)

The following class is an array-based implementation of the ADT heap:

```java
package Heaps;
import SearchKeys.KeyedItem;

public class Heap {
  private int MAX_HEAP = 100;   //maximum size of heap;
  private KeyedItem[] items;     // array of heap items
  private int size;              // number of heap items

  public Heap() {
    items = new KeyedItem[MAX_HEAP];
    size = 0;
  }  // end default constructor

// heap operations:
  public boolean heapIsEmpty() {
// Determines whether a heap is empty.
// Precondition: None.
// Postcondition: Returns true if the heap is empty;
// otherwise returns false.
    return size == 0;
  } // end heapIsEmpty

  public void heapInsert(KeyedItem newItem)
                        throws HeapException {
// Inserts an item into a heap.
// Precondition: newItem is the item to be inserted.
// Postcondition: If the heap was not full, newItem is
// in its proper position; otherwise HeapException is
// thrown.

    if (size < MAX_HEAP) {
      // place the new item at the end of the heap
      items[size] = newItem;
```

```
      // trickle new item up to its proper position
      int place = size;
      int parent = (place - 1)/2;
      while ( (parent >= 0) && (items[place].getKey().compareTo
                                (items[parent].getKey()))<0){
        // swap items[place] and items[parent]
        KeyedItem temp = items[parent];
        items[parent] = items[place];
        items[place] = temp;

        place = parent;
        parent = (place - 1)/2;
      }  // end while

      ++size;
    }  // end if
    else {
      throw new HeapException("HeapException: Heap full");
    }  // end if
} // end heapInsert


public KeyedItem heapDelete() {
// Retrieves and deletes the item in the root of a heap.
// This item has the largest search key in the heap.
// Precondition: None.
// Postcondition: If the heap is not empty, returns the
// item in the root of the heap and then deletes it.
// However, if the heap is empty, removal is impossible
// and the method returns null.
  KeyedItem rootItem = null;
  if (!heapIsEmpty()) {
    rootItem = items[0];
    items[0] = items[--size];
    heapRebuild(0);
  }  // end if
  return rootItem;
} // end heapDelete


protected void heapRebuild(int root) {
// if the root is not a leaf and the root's search key
// is less than the larger of the search keys in the
// root's children
  int child = 2 * root + 1;  // index of root's left
                             // child, if any
  if ( child < size ) {
    // root is not a leaf, so it has a left child at child
```

```
      int rightChild = child + 1;   // index of right child,
                                     // if any

      // if root has a right child, find larger child
      if ( (rightChild < size) && (items[rightChild].getKey().
                       compareTo(items[child].getKey()))<0) {
        child = rightChild;     // index of larger child
      } // end if

      // if the root's value is smaller than the
      // value in the larger child, swap values
      if (items[root].getKey().
                           compareTo(items[child].getKey())>0){
        KeyedItem temp = items[root];
        items[root] = items[child];
        items[child] = temp;

        // transform the new subtree into a heap
        heapRebuild(child);
      }  // end if
    }  // end if
    // if root is a leaf, do nothing
  } // end heapRebuild

} // end Heap
```

A Heap Implementation of the ADT Priority Queue

Priority-queue operations and heap operations are analogous

Once you have implemented the ADT heap, the implementation of the ADT priority queue is straightforward, because priority-queue operations are exactly analogous to heap operations. The priority value in a priority-queue item corresponds to a heap item's search key. Thus, the implementation of the priority queue can reuse the class *Heap*. That is, the class *PriorityQueue* has an instance of *Heap* as its data field:

```
package PriorityQueues;

import Heaps.*;
import SearchKeys.KeyedItem;
// **********************************************************
// Assumes that Heap implementation is in package Heaps.
// PriorityQueue class implementation.
// **********************************************************

public class PriorityQueue {
  private Heap h;

  public PriorityQueue() {
    h = new Heap();
```

```
   }  // end default constructor

   // priority-queue operations:
   public boolean pqIsEmpty() {
     return h.heapIsEmpty();
   }  // end pqIsEmpty

   public void pqInsert(KeyedItem newItem)
                        throws PQueueException {
     try {
       h.heapInsert(newItem);
     }  // end try
     catch (HeapException e) { throw new PQueueException(
                "PQueueException: Priority queue full");

     }  // end catch
   }  // end pqInsert

   public KeyedItem pqDelete() {
     return h.heapDelete();
   }  // end pqDelete

}  // end PriorityQueue
```

How does a heap compare to a binary search tree as an implementation of a priority queue? If you know the maximum number of items in the priority queue, the heap is the better implementation.

The heap implementation requires knowledge of the priority queue's maximum size

Because a heap is complete, it is always balanced, which is its major advantage. If the binary search tree is balanced, both implementations will have the same average performance for n items: They both will be O(log n). The height of a binary search tree, however, can increase during insertions and deletions, greatly exceeding $\log_2 n$ and degrading the implementation's efficiency to O(n) in the worst case. The heap implementation avoids this decrease in performance.

A heap is always balanced

In the next chapter, you will see how to keep a binary search tree balanced, but the operations that do this are far more complex than the heap operations. Do not think, however, that a heap can replace a binary search tree as a table implementation; as was stated earlier, a heap is not appropriate in this role. If this fact is not apparent to you, try to perform the table operation *tableRetrieve* on a heap, or try to traverse a heap in search-key order.

Finite, distinct priority values.   If you have a finite number of distinct priority values, such as the integers 1 through 20, many items will likely have the same priority value. You could place items whose priority values are the same in the order in which you encounter them.

A heap of queues accommodates this situation, with one queue for each distinct priority value. To insert an item into the priority queue, you add a queue for the item's priority value to the heap, if it is not already there. Then you insert the item into the corresponding queue. To

A heap of queues

delete an item from a priority queue, you delete the item at the front of the queue that corresponds to the highest priority value in the heap. If this deletion leaves the queue empty, you remove it from the heap.

Programming Problem 7 at the end of this chapter treats distinct priority values further.

Heapsort

As its name implies, the heapsort algorithm uses a heap to sort an array *anArray* of items that are in no particular order. The first step of the algorithm transforms the array into a heap. One way to accomplish this transformation is to use the *heapInsert* method to insert the items into the heap one by one.

A more efficient method of building a heap out of the items of *anArray* is possible, however. For example, assume that the initial contents of *anArray* are as shown in Figure 11-13a. First you imagine the array as a binary tree by assigning the items of *anArray* to the tree's nodes, beginning with the root and proceeding left to right down the tree. Figure 11-13b shows the resulting tree. Next, you transform this tree into a heap by calling *heapRebuild* repeatedly. *heapRebuild* transforms a semiheap—a tree whose subtrees are both heaps but whose root may be out of place—into a heap. But are there any semiheaps in the tree for *heapRebuild* to work on? Although the tree in Figure 11-13b is not a semiheap, if you look at its leaves you will find semiheaps—that is, each leaf is a semiheap. (In fact, each leaf is a heap, but for the sake of simplicity, ignore this fact.) You first call *heapRebuild* on the leaves from right to left. You then move up the tree, knowing that by the time you reach a node *s*, its subtrees are heaps, and thus *heapRebuild* will transform the semiheap rooted at *s* into a heap.

The following algorithm transforms the array *anArray* of *n* items into a heap and is the first step of the heapsort algorithm:

Building a heap from an array of items

```
for (index = n - 1 down to 0)
    // Assertion: the tree rooted at index is a semiheap
    heapRebuild(anArray, index, n)
    // Assertion: the tree rooted at index is a heap
```

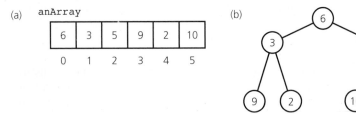

Figure 11-13

(a) The initial contents of **anArray**; (b) **anArray**'s corresponding binary tree

Actually, you can replace $n - 1$ with $n/2$ in the previous *for* statement. Exercise 16 at the end of this chapter asks you to explain why this improvement is possible. Figure 11-14 traces this algorithm for the array in Figure 11-13a.

After transforming the array into a heap, heapsort partitions the array into two regions—the Heap region and the Sorted region—as Figure 11-15 illustrates. The Heap region is in *anArray[0..last]*, and the Sorted region is in *anArray[last+1..n-1]*. Initially, the Heap region is all of *anArray* and the Sorted region is empty—that is, *last* is equal to $n - 1$.

Each step of the algorithm moves an item *I* from the Heap region to the Sorted region. The invariant of the heapsort algorithm is

- After Step k, the Sorted region contains the k largest values in *anArray*, and they are in sorted order—that is, *anArray[n-1]* is the largest, *anArray[n-2]* is the second largest, and so on.

Invariant for heapsort

- The items in the Heap region form a heap.

So that the invariant holds, *I* must be the item that has the largest value in the Heap region, and therefore *I* must be in the root of the heap. To accomplish the move, you exchange the item in the root of the heap with the last item in the heap—that is, you exchange *anArray[0]* with *anArray[last]*—and then decrement the value of *last*. As a result, the item just swapped from the root into *anArray[last]* becomes the smallest item in the Sorted region (and is in the first position of the Sorted

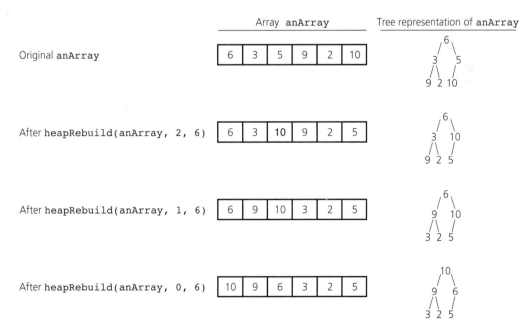

Figure 11-14

Transforming an array *anArray* into a heap

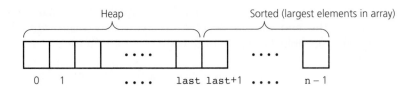

Figure 11-15

Heapsort partitions an array into two regions

region). After the move, you must transform the Heap region back into a heap because the new root may be out of place. You can accomplish this transformation by using *heapRebuild* to trickle down the item now in the root so that the Heap region is once again a heap.

The following algorithm summarizes the steps:

```
heapSort(anArray, n)
// Sorts anArray[0..n-1].

  // build initial heap
  for (index = n - 1 down to 0) {
    // Invariant: the tree rooted at index is a semiheap
    heapRebuild(anArray, index, n)
    // Assertion: the tree rooted at index is a heap
  }  // end for
  // Assertion: anArray[0] is the largest item in heap
  // anArray[0..n-1]

  // initialize the regions
  last = n - 1

  // Invariant: anArray[0..last] is a heap,
  // anArray[last+1..n-1] is
  // sorted and contains the largest items of A

  for (step = 1 through n) {
    // move the largest item in the heap region -- that
    // is, the root anArray[0] -- to the beginning of the
    // Sorted region by swapping items
    Swap anArray[0] and anArray[last]

    // expand the Sorted region, shrink the Heap region
    Decrement last

    // make the Heap region a heap again
    heapRebuild(anArray, 0, last)
  }  // end for
```

Figure 11-16 completes the trace of heapsort that Figure 11-14 began. The Java implementation of heapsort is left as an exercise.

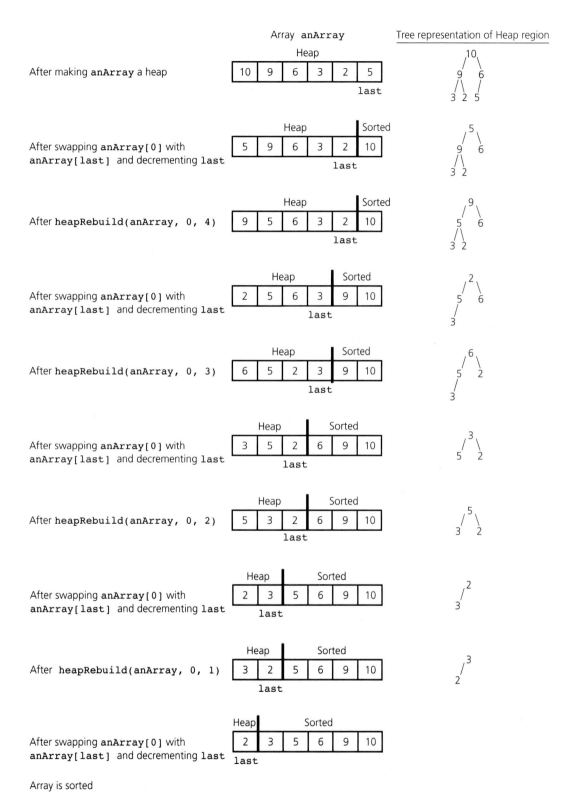

Figure 11-16

A trace of heapsort, beginning with the heap in Figure 11-14

*Heapsort is O(n * log n)*

The analysis of the efficiency of heapsort is similar to that of merge-sort, as given in Chapter 9. Both algorithms are O($n * \log n$) in both the worst and average cases. Heapsort has an advantage over mergesort in that it does not require a second array. Quicksort is also O($n * \log n$) in the average case but is O(n^2) in the worst case. Even though quicksort has poor worst-case efficiency, it is generally the preferred sorting method.

SUMMARY

1. The ADT table supports value-oriented operations, such as

    Retrieve all the information about John Smith

2. The linear implementations (array based and reference based) of a table are adequate only in limited situations, such as when the table is small, or for certain operations. In those situations, the simplicity of a linear implementation may be an advantage. A linear implementation of a table, however, is not suitable as a general-purpose, reusable class.

3. A nonlinear reference-based (binary search tree) implementation of the ADT table provides the best aspects of the two linear implementations. The reference-based implementation allows the table to grow dynamically and allows insertions and dele-tions of data to occur through just a few reference changes. In addition, the binary search tree allows you to use a binary search-like algorithm when searching for an item with a specified value. These characteristics make a nonlinear table implementation far superior to the linear implementations in many applications.

4. A priority queue is a variation of the ADT table. Its operations allow you to retrieve and remove the item with the largest prior-ity value.

5. A heap that uses an array-based representation of a complete binary tree is a good implementation of a priority queue when you know the maximum number of items that will be stored at any one time.

6. Heapsort, like mergesort, has good worst-case and average-case behaviors, but neither algorithm is as good in the average case as quicksort. Heapsort has an advantage over mergesort in that it does not require a second array.

CAUTIONS

1. When defining an ADT to solve a particular problem, do not request unnecessary operations. The proper choice of an imple-mentation depends on the mix of requested operations, and if

you request an operation that you do not need, you might get an implementation that does not best support what you are really doing.

2. A linear array-based implementation of the ADT table must shift the references to the data during a deletion and during an insertion in sorted order. These shifts can be time consuming, particularly for large tables.

3. Although a linear reference-based implementation of the ADT table eliminates the need to shift the references to the data, it does not support the insertion and deletion operations any more efficiently than does an array-based implementation, because you cannot perform a binary search in a reasonable fashion.

4. Usually a binary search tree can support the operations of the ADT table quite efficiently. However, in the worst case, when the tree approaches a linear shape, the performance of the table operations is comparable to that of a linear reference-based implementation. If a given application cannot tolerate poor performance, you should use the table implementations presented in Chapter 12.

5. Although a heap is a good implementation of a priority queue, it is not appropriate for a table. Specifically, a heap does not support the sorted *tableRetrieve* and traversal operations efficiently.

SELF-TEST EXERCISES

1. Using the operations of the ADT table, write pseudocode for a *tableReplace* operation that replaces the table item whose search key is x with another item whose search key is also x.

2. Does the array in Figure 11-17 represent a heap?

3. Is the full binary tree in Figure 10-34 a semiheap? Is it a heap?

4. Consider the heap in Figure 11-8. Draw the heap after you insert 12 and then remove 12.

5. What does the initially empty heap *h* contain after the following sequence of pseudocode operations?

```
h.heapInsert(2)
h.heapInsert(3)
h.heapInsert(4)
h.heapInsert(1)
h.heapInsert(9)
item = h.heapDelete()
h.heapInsert(7)
h.heapInsert(6)
item = h.heapDelete()
h.heapInsert(5)
```

6. What does the heap that represents the initially empty priority queue *pq* contain after the following sequence of pseudocode operations?

```
pq.pqInsert(5)
pq.pqInsert(9)
pq.pqInsert(6)
pq.pqInsert(7)
pq.pqInsert(3)
pq.pqInsert(4)
item = pq.pqDelete()
pq.pqInsert(9)
pq.pqInsert(2)
item = pq.pqDelete()
```

7. Execute the pseudocode statements

```
for (index = n - 1 down to 0)
   heapRebuild(anArray, index, n)
```

on the array in Figure 11-17.

Figure 11-17

Array for Self-Test Exercises 2 and 7 and Exercise 17

EXERCISES

1. Complete the sorted array-based implementation of the ADT table.

2. The operation `tableReplace(replacementItem)` locates, if possible, the item in a table with the same search key as `replacementItem`. If the table contains such an item, `tableReplace` replaces it with `replacementItem`. Thus, the fields of the original item are updated.

    a. Write implementations of `tableReplace` for the five implementations (four linear ones and the binary search tree) of the ADT table described in this chapter.

    b. For the binary search tree implementation of the ADT table, under what circumstances can `tableReplace` replace an item without altering the structure of the binary search tree? (See Exercise 10 in Chapter 10.)

3. Imagine an application program that behaves like an English dictionary. The user types a word and the program provides the word's definition. Thus, the dictionary needs only a retrieval operation. Which implementation of the ADT table would be most efficient as an English dictionary?

4. When you use a word processor's spell checker, it compares the words in your document with words in a dictionary. You can add new words to the dictionary as necessary. Thus, this dictionary needs frequent retrievals and occasional insertions. Which implementation of the ADT table would be most efficient as a spell checker's dictionary?

5. A Java compiler uses a **symbol table** to keep track of the identifiers that a program uses. When the compiler encounters an identifier, it searches the symbol table to see whether that identifier has already been encountered. If the identifier is new, it is inserted into the table. Thus, the symbol table needs only insertion and retrieval operations. Which implementation of the ADT table would be most efficient as a symbol table?

6. The implementations of the ADT table given in this chapter make the following assumption: At any time, a table contains at most one item with a given search key. Although the definition of an ADT required for a specific application may not allow duplicates, it is probably wise to test for them rather than simply to assume that they will not occur. Why?

   Modify the table implementations so that they test for—and disallow—any duplicates. What table operations are affected? What are the implications for the unsorted linear implementations?

7. Although disallowing duplicates in the ADT table (see Exercise 6) is reasonable for some applications, it is just as reasonable to have an application that will allow duplicates.

   a. What are the implications of inserting duplicate items that are identical? What are the implications of duplicate items for the deletion and retrieval operations?

   b. What are the implications of inserting items that are not identical but have the same search key? Specifically, what would the implementations of *tableInsert, tableDelete,* and *tableRetrieve* do?

8. Suppose that you want to support table deletion operations for two different search keys (for example, *tableDeleteN* to delete by name and *tableDeleteS* to delete by social security number). Describe an efficient implementation.

9. Repeat Exercise 8, but instead organize one of the search keys with a binary search tree and the other with a sorted linked list.

10. Prove that the root of a heap contains the largest search key in the tree.

11. Does the order in which you insert items into a heap affect the heap that results? Explain.

12. Suppose that you have two items with the same priority value. How does the order in which you insert these items into a priority queue affect the order in which they will be deleted? What can you

do if you need elements with equal priority value to be served on a first-come, first-served basis?

13. The heap that this chapter described is called a maxheap because the largest element is at the root. This organization is appropriate because the *pqDelete* operation for the heap implementation of the priority queue deletes the element with the highest priority value. Suppose that you wanted the *pqDelete* operation to delete the element with the lowest priority value instead. You would then use a minheap. Convert the maxheap implementation to a minheap implementation.

14. Suppose that you wanted to maintain the index of the item with the smallest priority value in a maxheap. That is, in addition to a *removeMax* operation, you might want to support a *retrieveMin* operation. How difficult would it be to maintain this index within the *pqInsert* and *removeMax* operations?

15. Suppose that after you have placed several items into a priority queue, you need to adjust one of their priority values. For example, a particular task in a priority queue of tasks could become either more or less urgent. How can you adjust a heap if a single priority value changes?

16. Show that within the pseudocode for the method *heapsort* you can replace the statement

    ```
    for (index = n-1 down to 0)
    ```

    with

    ```
    for (index = n/2 down to 0)
    ```

17. Trace the action of *heapSort* on the array in Figure 11-17.

18. Implement *heapSort* in Java.

19. Revise *heapSort* so that it sorts an array into descending order.

PROGRAMMING PROBLEMS

1. Write the sorted reference-based, unsorted array-based, and unsorted reference-based implementations of the ADT table described in this chapter.

2. Write iterator classes for the two table classes presented in this chapter, *TableArrayBased* and *TableBSTBased*. Be sure to include an implementation of the *remove* operation.

3. Write unsorted and sorted implementations of the ADT table that use, respectively, the ADTs list and sorted list, which Chapter 3 described.

4. Repeat Programming Problem 4 of Chapter 10, using the ADT table as the address book.

5. Implement the symbol table described in Exercise 5 by reusing the class *TableArrayBased*.

6. As Figure 11-7 illustrates, you can use data structures other than a heap to implement the ADT priority queue.

   a. Write the Java class for the reference-based implementation that Figure 11-7b represents.

   b. Write the Java class for the binary search tree implementation that Figure 11-7c represents.

   c. Implement the classes that you wrote in Parts *a* and *b*.

7. Suppose that you wanted to implement a priority queue whose priority values are the integers 1 through 20.

   a. Implement the priority queue as a heap of queues, as described in this chapter.

   b. Another solution uses an array of 20 queues, one for each priority value. Use this approach to implement the priority queue.

8. Write an interactive program that will monitor the flow of patients in a large hospital. The program should account for patients checking in and out of the hospital and should allow access to information about a given patient. In addition, the program should manage the scheduling of three operating rooms. Doctors make a request that includes a patient's name and a priority value between 1 and 10 that reflects the urgency of the operation. Patients are chosen for the operating room by priority value, and patients with the same priority are served on a first-come, first-served basis.

   The user should use either one-letter or one-word commands to control the program. As you design your solution, try to identify the essential operations (excuse the pun) that you must perform on the data, and only then choose an appropriate data structure for implementation. This approach will allow you to maintain the wall between the main part of the program and the implementations. An interesting exercise would be to recast this problem as an event-driven simulation.

CHAPTER 12

Advanced Implementations of Tables

PREVIEW   Although Chapter 11 described the advantages of using the binary search tree to implement the ADT table, the efficiency of this implementation suffers when the tree loses its balance. This chapter introduces several advanced implementations of the table. First examined are various other search trees, which remain balanced in all situations and thus enable table operations whose efficiency is comparable to a binary search.

This chapter then considers a completely different implementation of the ADT table that, for many applications, is even more efficient than a search-tree implementation. In principle the algorithm, which is called hashing, locates a data item by performing a calculation on its search-key value, rather than by searching for it.

Finally, the chapter considers data organizations that support diverse kinds of operations simultaneously. For example, you might want to organize data in first-in, first-out order, but you also might require the data to be in sorted order. The challenge is to design cooperative data structures to manage the data.

BALANCED SEARCH TREES

As you saw in the previous chapter, the efficiency of the binary search tree implementation of the ADT table is related to the tree's height. The operations *tableRetrieve*, *tableInsert*, and *tableDelete* follow a path from the root of the tree to the node that contains the desired item (or, in the case of the insertion operation, to the node that is to become the parent of the new item). At each node along the path, you compare a given value to the search key in the node and determine which subtree to search next. Because the maximum number of nodes on such a path is equal to the height of the tree, the maximum number of comparisons that the table operations can require is also equal to this height.

As you know, the height of a binary search tree of n items ranges from a maximum of n to a minimum of $\lceil \log_2(n + 1) \rceil$. As a consequence, locating a particular item in a binary search tree requires between n and $\lceil \log_2(n + 1) \rceil$ comparisons. Thus, a search of a binary search tree can be as inefficient as a sequential search of a linked list or as efficient as a binary search of an array. Efficiency was the primary reason for developing the binary search tree implementation of the table: We wanted to perform a search of a linked structure as efficiently as we could perform a binary search of an array. Thus, we certainly want the most optimistic behavior of the binary search tree.

The height of a binary search tree is sensitive to the order of insertions and deletions

What affects the height of a binary search tree? As you learned in Chapter 10, the height of the tree is quite sensitive to the order in which you insert or delete items. For example, consider a binary search tree that contains the items[1] 10, 20, 30, 40, 50, 60, and 70. If you inserted the

---

[1] As in Chapter 10, tree items are records that each contain a search key. The tree diagrams in this chapter will show only these search keys, and the discussions will often treat an item as if it consisted solely of its search key.

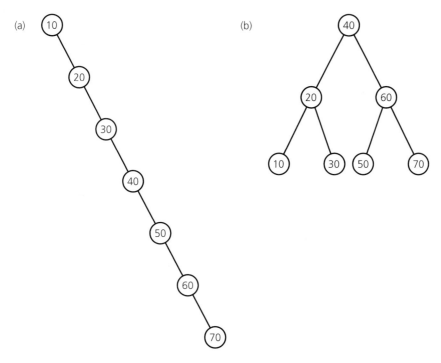

Figure 12-1

A binary search tree of (a) maximum height; (b) minimum height

items into the tree in ascending order, you would obtain a binary search tree of maximum height, as shown in Figure 12-1a. If, on the other hand, you inserted the items in the order 40, 20, 60, 10, 30, 50, 70, you would obtain a balanced binary search tree of minimum height, as shown in Figure 12-1b.

As you can see, if you use the algorithms in Chapter 10 to maintain a binary search tree, insertions and deletions can cause the tree to lose its balance and approach a linear shape. Such a tree is no better than a linked list. For this reason, it is desirable in many applications to use one of several variations of the binary search tree. Such trees can absorb insertions and deletions without a deterioration of their balance and are easier to maintain than a minimum-height binary search tree. In addition, you can search these trees almost as efficiently as you can search a minimum-height binary search tree. This chapter discusses the better-known search trees to give you a sense of the possibilities. We continue to assume that the search keys in a tree are unique, that is, that there are no duplicates.

Various search trees can retain their balance despite insertions and deletions

2-3 Trees

A **2-3 tree** is a tree in which each internal node (nonleaf) has either two or three children, and all leaves are at the same level. For example, Figure 12-2

Figure 12-2

A 2-3 tree of height 3

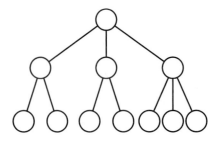

shows a 2-3 tree of height 3. A node with two children is called a **2-node**—the nodes in a binary tree are all 2-nodes—and a node with three children is called a **3-node**.

A 2-3 tree is not binary

A 2-3 tree is not a binary tree, because a node can have three children; nevertheless, a 2-3 tree does resemble a full binary tree. If a particular 2-3 tree does not contain 3-nodes—a possibility, according to the definition—it is like a full binary tree, because all of its internal nodes have two children and all of its leaves are at the same level. If, on the other hand, some of the internal nodes of a 2-3 tree do have three children, the tree will contain more nodes than a full binary tree of the same height. Therefore, a 2-3 tree of height h always has at least as many nodes as a full binary tree of height h; that is, it always has at least $2^h - 1$ nodes.

A 2-3 tree is never taller than a minimum-height binary tree

To put this another way, a 2-3 tree with n nodes never has height greater than $\lceil \log_2(n + 1) \rceil$, the minimum height of a binary tree with n nodes.

Given these observations, a 2-3 tree might be useful as an implementation of the ADT table. Indeed, this is the case if the 2-3 tree orders its nodes to make it useful as a search tree. The following recursive definition[2] of a 2-3 tree specifies this order:

A 2-3 tree

T is a 2-3 tree of height h if

1. T is empty (a 2-3 tree of height 0).

or

2. T is of the form

where r is a node that contains one data item and T_L and T_R are both 2-3 trees, each of height $h - 1$. In this case, the search key in r must be greater than each search key in the left subtree T_L and smaller than each search key in the right subtree T_R.

or

---

[2]Just as we distinguish between a binary tree and a binary search tree, we could distinguish between a 2-3 tree and a "2-3 search tree." The previous description would define a 2-3 tree, and the definition given here would define a 2-3 search tree. Most people, however, do not make such a distinction and use the term "2-3 tree" to mean "2-3 search tree"; we will also.

3. T is of the form

where r is a node that contains two data items and T_L, T_M, and T_R are 2-3 trees, each of height $h - 1$. In this case, the smaller search key in r must be greater than each search key in the left subtree T_L and smaller than each search key in the **middle subtree** T_M. The larger search key in r must be greater than each search key in the middle subtree T_M and smaller than each search key in the right subtree T_R.

This definition implies the following rules for how you may place data items in the nodes of a 2-3 tree.

Rules for Placing Data Items in the Nodes of a 2-3 Tree

1. A 2-node, which has two children, must contain a single data item whose search key is greater than the left child's search key(s) and less than the right child's search key(s), as Figure 12-3a illustrates.

2. A 3-node, which has three children, must contain two data items whose search keys S and L satisfy the following relationships, as Figure 12-3b illustrates: S is greater than the left child's search key(s) and less than the middle child's search key(s); L is greater than the middle child's search key(s) and less than the right child's search key(s).

3. A leaf may contain either one or two data items.

Figure 12-3

**Nodes in a 2-3 tree:
(a) a 2-node; (b) a 3-node**

Thus, the items in a 2-3 tree are ordered by their search keys. For example, the tree in Figure 12-4 is a 2-3 tree.

You can represent any node in a 2-3 tree with the following class:

Items in a 2-3 tree are ordered

A node in a 2-3 tree

```
import SearchKeys.KeyedItem;

public class Tree23Node {
    private KeyedItem smallItem;
    private KeyedItem largeItem;
    private Tree23Node leftChild;
    private Tree23Node midChild;
```

Figure 12-4

A 2-3 tree

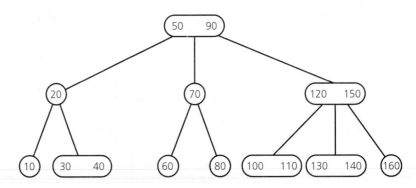

```
      private Tree23Node rightChild;

      // constructors and methods for accessing the private
      // data fields appear here
         .   .   .
      }   // end Tree23Node
```

When a node contains only one data item, you can place it in *smallItem* and use *leftChild* and *midChild* to reference the node's children. To be safe, you can place *null* in *rightChild*.

Now consider the traversal, retrieval, insertion, and deletion operations for a 2-3 tree. The algorithms for these operations are recursive. You can avoid distracting implementation details by defining the base case for these recursive algorithms to be a leaf rather than an empty subtree. As a result, the algorithms must assume that they are not passed an empty tree as an argument.

Traversing a 2-3 tree.   You can traverse a 2-3 tree in sorted search-key order by performing the analogue of an inorder traversal:

Traversal in sorted order

```
inorder(ttTree)
// Traverses the nonempty 2-3 tree, ttTree, in sorted
// search-key order.

  if (ttTree's root node r is a leaf) {
    Visit the data item(s)
  }
  else if (r has two data items) {
    inorder(left subtree of ttTree's root)
    Visit the first data item
    inorder(middle subtree of ttTree's root)
    Visit the second data item
    inorder(right subtree of ttTree's root)
  }
  else  { // r has one data item
    inorder(left subtree of ttTree's root)
    Visit the data item
    inorder(right subtree of ttTree's root)
  }  // end if
```

Searching a 2-3 tree.   The ordering of items in a 2-3 tree is analogous to the ordering for a binary search tree and allows you to search a 2-3 tree efficiently for a particular item. In fact, the retrieval operation for a 2-3 tree is quite similar to the retrieval operation for a binary search tree, as you can see from the following pseudocode:

Searching a 2-3 tree is efficient

```
retrieveItem(ttTree, searchKey)
// Returns from the nonempty 2-3 tree ttTree the
// item whose search key equals searchKey. The operation
// fails and returns null if no such item exists,

  if (searchKey is in ttTree's root node r) {
    // the item has been found
    treeItem = the data portion of r
  }
  else if (r is a leaf) {
    treeItem = null  // failure
  }

  // else search the appropriate subtree
  else if (r has two data items) {
    if (searchKey < smaller search key of r) {
      treeItem = retrieveItem(r's left subtree, searchKey)
    }
    else if (searchKey < larger search key of r) {
     treeItem = retrieveItem(r's middle subtree, searchKey)
    }
    else  {
     treeItem = retrieveItem(r's right subtree, searchKey)
    }  // end if
  }

  else  { // r has one data item
    if (searchKey < r's search key) {
      treeItem = retrieveItem(r's left subtree, searchKey)
    }
    else {
      treeItem = retrieveItem(r's right subtree, searchKey)
    }  // end if
  }  // end if
```

Have you gained anything by using a 2-3 tree rather than a binary search tree to implement the ADT table? You can search the 2-3 tree and the shortest binary search tree with about the same efficiency, because

- A binary search tree with *n* nodes cannot be shorter than $\lceil \log_2(n + 1) \rceil$
- A 2-3 tree with *n* nodes cannot be taller than $\lceil \log_2(n + 1) \rceil$
- A node in a 2-3 tree has at most two items

Searching a 2-3 tree is not *more* efficient than searching a binary search tree, however. This observation may surprise you because, after all, the nodes of a 2-3 tree can have three children, and hence a 2-3 tree might indeed be shorter than the shortest possible binary search tree. Although true, this advantage in height is offset by the extra time required to compare a given value with two search-key values instead of only one. In other words, although you might visit fewer nodes when searching a 2-3 tree, you might have to make more comparisons at each node. As a consequence, the number of comparisons required to search a 2-3 tree for a given item is *approximately equal* to the number of comparisons required to search a binary search tree that is *as balanced as possible.* This number is approximately $\log_2 n$.

Searching a 2-3 tree is $O(\log_2 n)$

If you can search a 2-3 tree and a balanced binary search tree with approximately the same efficiency, why then should you use a 2-3 tree? Although maintaining the balance of a binary search tree is difficult in the face of insertion and deletion operations, maintaining the shape of a 2-3 tree is relatively simple. For example, consider the two trees in Figure 12-5. The first tree is a binary search tree and the second is a 2-3 tree. Both trees contain the same data items. The binary search tree is as balanced as possible, and thus you can search both it and the 2-3 tree for an item with approximately the same efficiency. If, however, you perform a sequence of insertions on the binary search tree—by using the insertion algorithm of Chapter 10—the tree can quickly lose its balance, as Figure 12-6a indicates. As you soon will see, you can perform the same sequence of insertions on the 2-3 tree without a degradation in the tree's shape—it will retain its structure, as Figure 12-6b shows.

Maintaining the shape of a 2-3 tree is relatively easy

The new values (32 through 39) that were inserted into the binary search tree of Figure 12-5a appear along a single path in Figure 12-6a. The insertions increased the height of the binary search tree from 4 to 12—an increase of 8. On the other hand, the new values have been spread throughout the 2-3 tree in Figure 12-6b. As a consequence, the

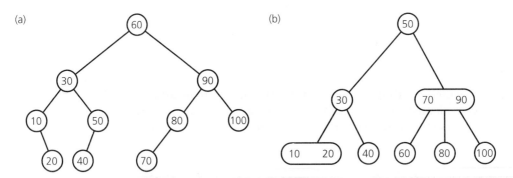

Figure 12-5

(a) A balanced binary search tree; (b) a 2-3 tree with the same elements

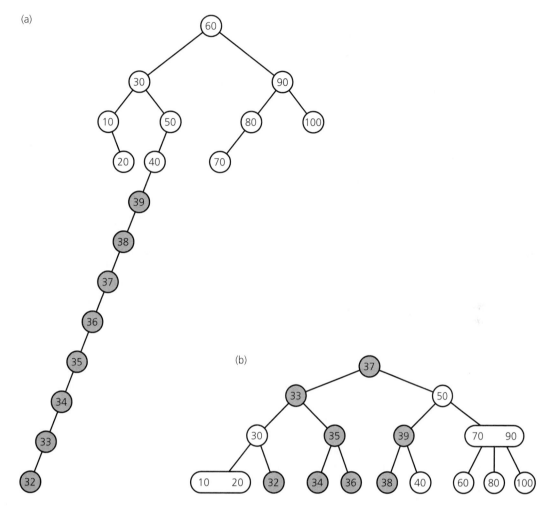

Figure 12-6

(a) The binary search tree of Figure 12-5a after a sequence of insertions;
(b) the 2-3 tree of Figure 12-5b after the same insertions

height of the resulting tree is only 1 greater than the height of the original 2-3 tree in Figure 12-5b. We demonstrate these insertions into the original 2-3 tree next.

Inserting into a 2-3 tree. Because the nodes of a 2-3 tree can have either two or three children and can contain one or two values, you can insert items into the tree while maintaining its shape. The following paragraphs informally describe the sequence of insertions that produced the 2-3 tree shown in Figure 12-6b. Figure 12-5b shows the original tree.

Figure 12-7

After inserting 39

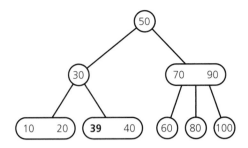

Insertion into a 2-node leaf is simple

Insert 39 As is true with a binary search tree, the first step in inserting a node into a 2-3 tree is to locate the node at which the search for 39 would terminate. To do this, you can use the search strategy of the `retrieveItem` algorithm given previously; an unsuccessful search will always terminate at a leaf. With the tree in Figure 12-5b, the search for 39 terminates at the leaf <40>.[3] Since this node contains only one item, you can simply insert the new item into this node. The result is the 2-3 tree in Figure 12-7.

Insert 38. In a similar manner, you would search the tree in Figure 12-7 for 38 and find that the search terminates at the node <39 40>. As a conceptual first step, you should place 38 in this node, as Figure 12-8a illustrates.

Insertion into a 3-node causes it to divide

This placement is problematic because a node cannot contain three values. You divide these three values, however, into the smallest (38), middle (39), and largest (40) values. You can move the middle value (39) up to the node's parent *p* and separate the remaining values, 38 and 40, into two nodes that you attach to *p* as children, as Figure 12-8b indicates. Since you chose to move up the middle value of <38 39 40>, the parent correctly separates the values of its children; that is, 38 is less than 39, which is less than 40. The result of the insertion is the 2-3 tree in Figure 12-8c.

(a)

(b)

(c)
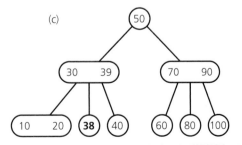

Figure 12-8

(a), (b) The steps for inserting 38; (c) the resulting tree

---

[3] Here, the angle brackets denote a node and its contents.

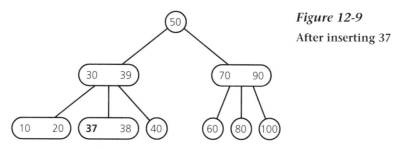

Figure 12-9

After inserting 37

Insert 37. The insertion of 37 into the tree in Figure 12-8c is easy because 37 belongs in a leaf that currently contains only one value, 38. The result of this insertion is the 2-3 tree in Figure 12-9.

Insert 36. The search strategy determines that 36 belongs in the node <37 38> of the tree in Figure 12-9. Again, as a conceptual first step, place it there, as Figure 12-10a indicates.

Because the node <36 37 38> now contains three values, you divide it—as you did previously—into the smallest (36), middle (37), and largest (38) values. You then move the middle value (37) up to the node's parent *p*, and attach to *p*—as children—nodes that contain the smallest (36) and largest (38) values, as Figure 12-10b illustrates.

This time, however, you are not finished: You have a node <30 37 39> that contains three values and has four children. This situation is familiar, with the slight difference that the overcrowded node is not a leaf but rather has four children. As you did before, you divide the node into the smallest (30), middle (37), and largest (39) values and then move the

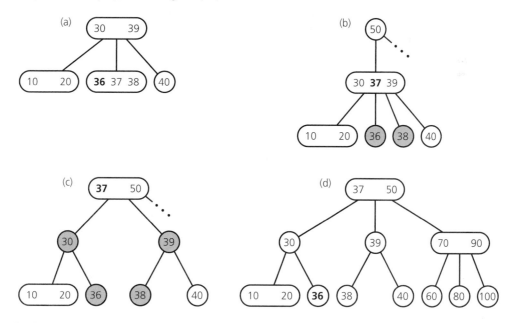

Figure 12-10

(a), (b), (c) The steps for inserting 36; (d) the resulting tree

Figure 12-11

The tree after the insertion
of 35, 34, and 33

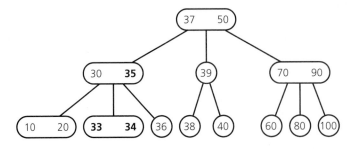

middle value up to the node's parent. Because you are splitting an internal node, you now must account for its four children; that is, what happens to nodes <10 20>, <36>, <38>, and <40>, which were the children of node <30 37 39>? The solution is to attach the left pair of children (nodes <10 20> and <36>) to the smallest value (30) and attach the right pair of children (nodes <38> and <40>) to the largest value (39), as shown in Figure 12-10c. The final result of this insertion is the 2-3 tree in Figure 12-10d.

Insert 35, 34, and 33.   Each of these insertions is similar to the previous ones. Figure 12-11 shows the tree after the three insertions.

Before performing the final insertion of the value 32, consider the 2-3 tree's insertion strategy.

When a leaf contains three items, split it into two nodes

The insertion algorithm.   To insert an item I into a 2-3 tree, you first locate the leaf at which the search for I would terminate. You insert the new item I into the leaf, and if the leaf now contains only two items, you are done. However, if the leaf contains three items, you must **split** it into two nodes, n_1 and n_2. As Figure 12-12 illustrates, you place the smallest[4]

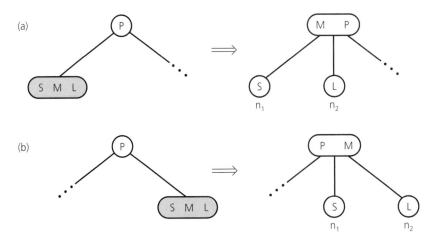

Figure 12-12

Splitting a leaf in a 2-3 tree

---

[4]"Smallest item" means the item with the smallest search key. Analogously, the terms "middle item" and "largest item" will also be used.

item S into n_1, place the largest item L into n_2, and move the middle item M up to the original leaf's parent. Nodes n_1 and n_2 then become children of the parent. If the parent now has only three children (and contains two items)—as is true here—you are finished. On the other hand, if the parent now has four children (and contains three items), you must split it, as follows.

You split an internal node n that contains three items by using the process just described for a leaf, except that you must also take care of n's four children. As Figure 12-13 illustrates, you split n into n_1 and n_2, place n's smallest item S into n_1, attach n's two leftmost children to n_1, place n's largest item L into n_2, attach n's two rightmost children to n_2, and move n's middle item M up to n's parent.

When an internal node contains three items, split it into two nodes and accommodate its children

After this, the process of splitting a node and moving an item up to the parent continues recursively until a node is reached that had only one item before the insertion and thus has only two items after it takes on a new item. Notice in the previous sequence of insertions that the tree's height never increased from its original value of 3. In general, *an insertion will not increase the height of the tree* as long as there is at least one node containing only one item on the path from the root to the leaf into which the new item is inserted. The insertion strategy of a 2-3 tree has thus postponed the growth of the tree's height much more effectively than the strategy of a basic binary search tree did.

When the height of a 2-3 tree does grow, it does so from the top. An increase in the height of a 2-3 tree will occur if every node on the path from the root of the tree to the leaf into which the new item is inserted contains two items. In this case, the recursive process of splitting a node and moving an item up to the node's parent will eventually reach the root r. When this occurs you must split r into r_1 and r_2 exactly as you would any other internal node. However, you must create a new node

When the root contains three items, split it into two nodes and create a new root node

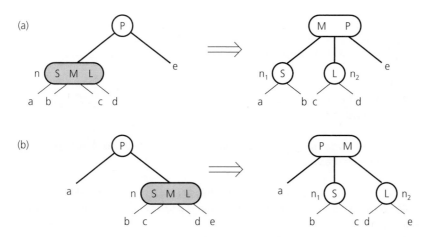

Figure 12-13

Splitting an internal node in a 2-3 tree

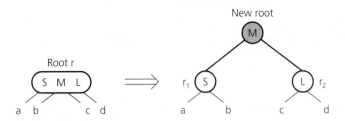

Figure 12-14

Splitting the root of a 2-3 tree

that contains the middle item of *r* and becomes the parent of r_1 and r_2.
Thus, the new node is the new root of the tree, as Figure 12-14 illustrates.
The following algorithm summarizes the entire insertion strategy:

2-3 tree insertion algorithm

```
insertItem(ttTree, newItem)
// Inserts newItem into a 2-3 tree ttTree whose items have
// distinct search keys that differ from newItem's search
// key.

   Let sKey be the search key of newItem
   Locate the leaf leafNode in which sKey belongs
   Add newItem to leafNode

   if (leafNode now has three items) {
      split(leafNode)
   }  // end if


split(n)
// Splits node n, which contains 3 items. Note: if n is
// not a leaf, it has 4 children.

   if (n is the root) {
      Create a new node p
   }
   else {
      Let p be the parent of n
   }  // end if

   Replace node n with two nodes, n₁ and n₂, so that p is
      their parent

   Give n₁ the item in n with the smallest search-key value
   Give n₂ the item in n with the largest search-key value

   if (n is not a leaf) {
      n₁ becomes the parent of n's two leftmost children
```

```
     n₂ becomes the parent of n's two rightmost children
}  // end if


Move the item in n that has the middle
   search-key value up to p

if (p now has three items) {
  split(p)
}  // end if
```

Insert 32. To be sure that you fully understand the insertion algorithm, go through the steps of inserting 32 into the 2-3 tree in Figure 12-11. The result should be the tree shown in Figure 12-6b.

Once again, compare this tree with the binary search tree in Figure 12-6a and notice the dramatic advantage of the 2-3 tree's insertion strategy.

Deleting from a 2-3 tree. The deletion strategy for a 2-3 tree is the inverse of its insertion strategy. Just as a 2-3 tree spreads insertions throughout the tree by splitting nodes when they become too full, it spreads deletions throughout the tree by merging nodes when they become empty. As an illustration of the 2-3 tree's deletion strategy, consider the deletion of 70, 100, and 80 from the tree in Figure 12-5b.

Delete 70. By searching the tree, you will discover that 70 is in the node <70 90>. Because you always want to begin the deletion process at a leaf, the first step is to swap 70 with its inorder successor—the value that follows it in the sorted order. Because 70 is the smaller of the two values in the node, its inorder successor (80) is the smallest value in the node's middle subtree. (The inorder successor of an item in an internal node will always be in a leaf.) After the swap, the tree appears as shown in Figure 12-15a. The value 80 is in a legal position of the search tree because it is larger than all the values in its node's left subtree and smaller than all the values in its node's right subtree. The value 70 is not in a legal position, but this is of no concern, because the next step is to delete this value from the leaf.

Swap the value to be deleted with its inorder successor

In general, after you delete a value from a leaf, another value may remain in the leaf (because the leaf contained two values before the deletion). If this is the case, you are done, because a leaf of a 2-3 tree can contain a single value. In this example, however, once you delete 70 from the leaf, the node is left without a value, as Figure 12-15b indicates.

You then delete the node, as Figure 12-15c illustrates. At this point you see that the parent of the deleted node contains two values (80 and 90) but has two children (60 and 100). This situation is not allowed in a 2-3 tree. (See Rule 1.) You can remedy the problem by moving the smaller value (80) down from the parent into the left child, as Figure 12-15d illustrates. Deleting the leaf node and moving a value down to a sibling of the leaf is called **merging** the leaf with its sibling.

Merge nodes

The 2-3 tree that results from this deletion is shown in Figure 12-15e.

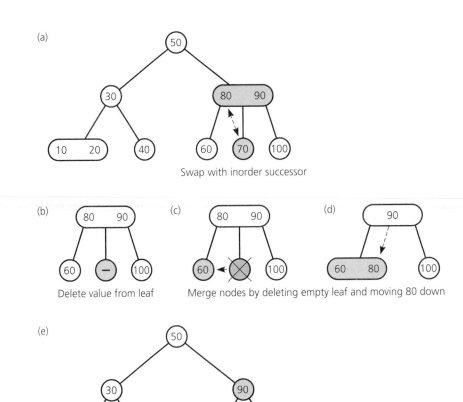

Figure 12-15

(a), (b), (c), (d) The steps for deleting 70; (e) the resulting tree

Redistribute values

Delete 100.   The search strategy discovers that 100 is in the leaf <100> of the tree in Figure 12-15e. When you delete the value from this leaf, the node becomes empty, as Figure 12-16a indicates. In this case, however, no merging of nodes is required, because the sibling <60 80> can spare a value. That is, the sibling has two values, whereas a 2-3 tree requires only that it have at least one value. If you simply move the value 80 into the empty node—as Figure 12-16b illustrates—you find that the search-tree order is destroyed: The value in 90's right child is 80, whereas it should be greater than 90. The solution to this problem is to redistribute the values among the empty node, its sibling, and its parent. Here you can move the larger value (80) from the sibling into the parent and move the value 90 down from the parent into the node that had been empty, as Figure 12-16c shows. This distribution preserves the search-tree order, and you have thus completed the deletion. The resulting 2-3 tree is shown in Figure 12-16d.

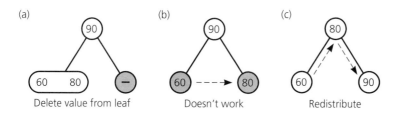

(a) Delete value from leaf (b) Doesn't work (c) Redistribute

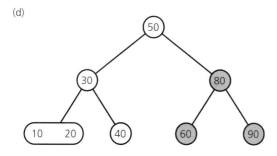

(d)

Figure 12-16

(a), (b), (c) The steps for deleting 100; (d) the resulting tree

Delete 80. The search strategy finds that 80 is in an internal node of the tree in Figure 12-16d. You thus must swap 80 with its inorder successor, 90, as Figure 12-17a illustrates. When you delete 80 from the leaf, the node becomes empty. (See Figure 12-17b.) Because the sibling of the empty node has only one value, you cannot redistribute as you did in the deletion of 100. Instead you must merge the nodes, bringing the value 90 down from the parent and removing the empty leaf, as Figure 12-17c indicates.

You are not yet finished, however, because the parent now contains no values and has only one child. You must recursively apply the deletion strategy to this internal node without a value. First, you should check to see if the node's sibling can spare a value. Because the sibling <30> contains only the single value 30, you cannot redistribute—you must merge the nodes. The merging of two internal nodes is identical to the merging of leaves, except that the child <60 90> of the empty node must be adopted. Because the sibling of the empty node contains only one value (and hence can have only two children, as stated in Rule 1), it can become the parent of <60 90> only if you bring the value 50 down from the sibling's parent. The tree now appears as shown in Figure 12-17d. Note that this operation preserves the search property of the tree.

Now the parent of the merged nodes is left with no values and only a single child. Usually, you would apply the recursive deletion strategy to this node, but this case is special because the node is the root. Because the root is empty and has only one child, you can simply remove it, allowing <30 50> to become the root of the tree, as Figure 12-17e illustrates. This deletion has thus caused the height of the tree to shrink by 1.

Figure 12-17

The steps for deleting 80

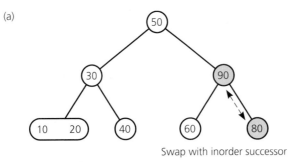

(a)

Swap with inorder successor

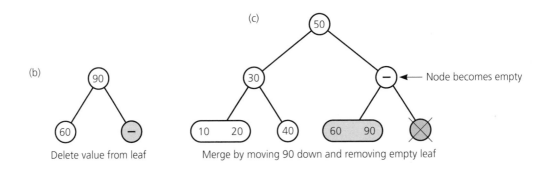

(b)

Delete value from leaf

(c)

Node becomes empty

Merge by moving 90 down and removing empty leaf

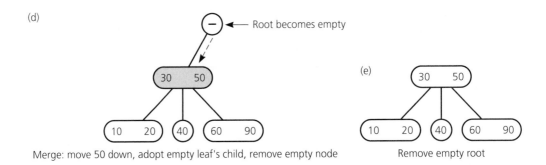

(d)

Root becomes empty

Merge: move 50 down, adopt empty leaf's child, remove empty node

(e)

Remove empty root

To summarize, we have deleted 70, 100, and 80 from the 2-3 tree in Figure 12-5b and obtained the 2-3 tree in Figure 12-18b. In contrast, after deleting 70, 100, and 80 from the balanced binary search tree in Figure 12-5a, you are left with the tree in Figure 12-18a. Notice that the deletions affected only one part of the binary search tree, causing it to lose its balance. The left subtree has not been affected at all, and thus the overall height of the tree has not been diminished.

The deletion algorithm. In summary, to delete an item *I* from a 2-3 tree, you first locate the node *n* that contains it. If *n* is not a leaf, you find *I*'s

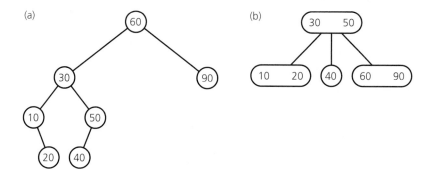

Figure 12-18

Results of deleting 70, 100, and 80 from (a) the binary search tree of Figure 12-5a and (b) the 2-3 tree of Figure 12-5b

inorder successor and swap it with *I*. As a result of the swap, the deletion always begins at a leaf. If the leaf contains an item in addition to *I*, you simply delete *I* and you are done. On the other hand, if the leaf contains only *I*, deleting *I* would leave the leaf without a data item. In this case you must perform some additional work to complete the deletion.

You first check the siblings of the now-empty leaf. If a sibling has two items, you redistribute the items among the sibling, the empty leaf, and the leaf's parent, as Figure 12-19a illustrates. If no sibling of the leaf has two items, you merge the leaf with an adjacent sibling by moving an item down from the leaf's parent into the sibling—it had only one item before, so it has room for another—and removing the empty leaf. This case is shown in Figure 12-19b.

By moving an item down from a node *n*, as just described, you might cause *n* to be left without a data item and with only one child. If so, you recursively apply the deletion algorithm to *n*. Thus, if *n* has a sibling with two items (and three children), you redistribute the items among *n*, the sibling, and *n*'s parent. You also give *n* one of its sibling's children, as Figure 12-19c indicates.

If *n* has no sibling with two items, you merge *n* with a sibling, as Figure 12-19d illustrates. That is, you move an item down from the parent and let the sibling adopt *n*'s one child. (At this point you know that the sibling previously had only one item and two children.) You then remove the empty leaf. If the merge causes *n*'s parent to be without an item, you recursively apply the deletion process to it.

If the merging continues so that the root of the tree is without an item (and has only one child), you simply remove the root. When this step occurs, the height of the tree is reduced by 1, as Figure 12-19e illustrates.

A high-level statement of the algorithm for deleting from a 2-3 tree is shown beginning on page 561.

Redistribute values

Merge nodes

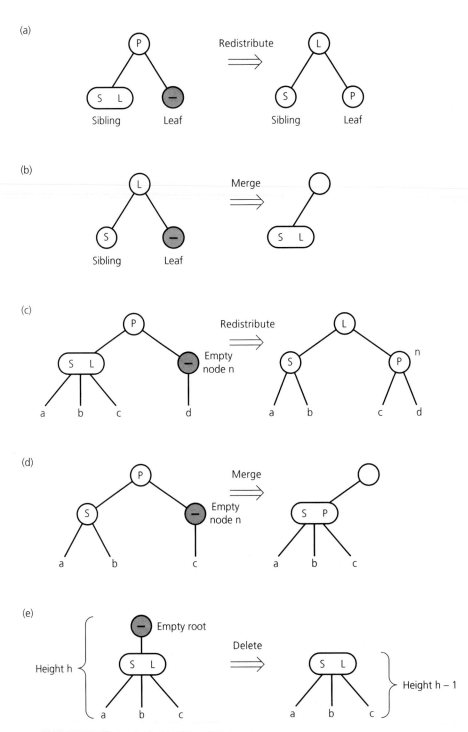

Figure 12-19

(a) Redistributing values; (b) merging a leaf; (c) redistributing values and children; (d) merging internal nodes; (e) deleting the root

```
deleteItem(searchKey)
// Deletes from the 2-3 tree the item whose
// search key equals searchKey. If the deletion is
// successful, the method returns true.
// If no such item exists, the operation fails and
// returns false.

  Attempt to locate item theItem whose search key
      equals searchKey

  if (theItem is present) {
    if (theItem is not in a leaf) {
      Swap item theItem with its inorder successor, which
          will be in a leaf theLeaf
    }  // end if

    // the deletion always begins at a leaf
    Delete item theItem from leaf theLeaf

    if (theLeaf now has no items) {
      fix(theLeaf)
    }  // end if
    return true
  }

  else {
    return false
  }  // end if

fix(n)
// Completes the deletion when node n is empty by either
// removing the root, redistributing values, or merging
// nodes. Note: if n is internal, it has one child.

  if (n is the root) {
    Remove the root
  }
  else {
    Let p be the parent of n

    if (some sibling of n has two items) {
      Distribute items appropriately among n, the
          sibling, and p
      if (n is internal) {
        Move the appropriate child from sibling to n
      }  // end if
    }

    else { // merge the node
      Choose an adjacent sibling s of n
      Bring the appropriate item down from p into s
```

```
if (n is internal) {
  Move n's child to s
}  // end if

Remove node n

if (p is now empty) {
   fix(p)
}  // end if
} // end if


} // end if
```

The details of the Java implementation of the preceding insertion and deletion algorithms for 2-3 trees are rather involved. The implementation is left as a challenging exercise (Programming Problem 2).

You might be concerned about the overhead that the insertion and deletion algorithms incur in the course of maintaining the 2-3 structure of the tree. That is, after the search strategy locates either the item or the position for the new item, the insertion and deletion algorithms sometimes have to perform extra work, such as splitting and merging nodes. However, this extra work is not a real concern. A rigorous mathematical analysis would show that the extra work required to maintain the structure of a 2-3 tree after an insertion or a deletion is not significant. In other words, when analyzing the efficiency of the *insertItem* and *deleteItem* algorithms, it is sufficient to consider only the time required to locate the item (or the position for the insertion). Given that a 2-3 tree is always balanced, you can search a 2-3 tree in all situations with the logarithmic efficiency of a binary search. Thus, the 2-3 tree implementation of the ADT table is guaranteed to provide efficient table operations. Although a binary search tree that is as balanced as possible minimizes the amount of work required to implement the operations of the ADT table, its balance is difficult to maintain. A 2-3 tree is a compromise—although searching it may not be quite as efficient as searching a binary search tree of minimum height, it is relatively simple to maintain.

A 2-3 tree is always balanced

A 2-3 implementation of a table is $O(\log_2 n)$ for all table operations

2-3-4 Trees

If a 2-3 tree is so good, are trees whose nodes can have more than three children even better? To an extent, the answer is yes. A **2-3-4 tree** is like a 2-3 tree, but it also allows **4-nodes**, which are nodes that have four children and three data items. For example, Figure 12-20 shows a 2-3-4 tree of height 3 that has the same items as the 2-3 tree in Figure 12-6b. As you will see, you can perform insertions and deletions on a 2-3-4 tree with fewer steps than a 2-3 tree requires.

T is a 2-3-4 tree of height *h* if

A 2-3-4 tree

1. *T* is empty (a 2-3-4 tree of height 0).

or

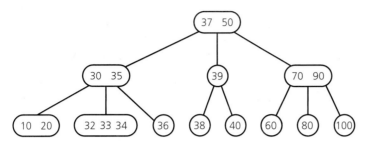

Figure 12-20

A 2-3-4 tree with the same items as the 2-3 tree in Figure 12-6b

2. *T* is of the form

where *r* is a node that contains one data item and T_L and T_R are both 2-3-4 trees, each of height *h* − 1. In this case, the search key in *r* must be greater than each search key in the left subtree T_L and smaller than each search key in the right subtree T_R.

or

3. *T* is of the form

where *r* is a node that contains two data items and T_L, T_M, and T_R are 2-3-4 trees, each of height *h* − 1. In this case, the smaller search key in *r* must be greater than each search key in the left subtree T_L and smaller than each search key in the middle subtree T_M. The larger search key in *r* must be greater than each search key in T_M and smaller than each search key in the right subtree T_R.

or

4. *T* is of the form

where *r* is a node that contains three data items and T_L, T_{ML}, T_{MR}, and T_R are 2-3-4 trees, each of height *h* − 1. In this case, the smallest search key in *r* must be greater than each search key in the left subtree T_L and smaller than each search key in the **middle-left subtree** T_{ML}. The middle search key in *r* must be greater than each search key in T_{ML} and smaller than each search key in the **middle-right subtree** T_{MR}. The largest search key in *r* must be greater than each search key in T_{MR} and smaller than each search key in the right subtree T_R.

This definition implies the following rules for how you may place data items in the nodes of a 2-3-4 tree:

Rules for Placing Data Items in the Nodes of a 2-3-4 Tree

1. A 2-node, which has two children, must contain a single data item whose search keys satisfy the relationships pictured earlier in Figure 12-3a.

2. A 3-node, which has three children, must contain two data items whose search keys satisfy the relationships pictured earlier in Figure 12-3b.

3. A 4-node, which has four children, must contain three data items whose search keys S, M, and L satisfy the following relationships, as Figure 12-21 illustrates: S is greater than the left child's search key(s) and less than the middle-left child's search key(s); M is greater than the middle-left child's search key(s) and less than the middle-right child's search key(s); L is greater than the middle-right child's search key(s) and less than the right child's search key(s).

4. A leaf may contain either one, two, or three data items.

A 2-3-4 tree requires more storage than a 2-3 tree

A node in a 2-3-4 tree

Although a 2-3-4 tree has more efficient insertion and deletion operations than a 2-3 tree, it also has greater storage requirements due to the additional data fields in its 4-nodes, as the following Java class indicates:

```java
import SearchKeys.KeyedItem;

public class Tree234Node {
   private KeyedItem smallItem;
   private KeyedItem middleItem;
   private KeyedItem largeItem;
   private Tree234Node leftChild;
   private Tree234Node lMidChild;
   private Tree234Node rMidChild;
   private Tree234Node rightChild;

   // constructors and methods for accessing the private
   // data fields appear here
     .  .  .
}  // end Tree234Node
```

Figure 12-21

A 4-node in a 2-3-4 tree

As you will see later, however, you can transform a 2-3-4 tree into a special binary tree that reduces the storage requirements.

Searching and traversing a 2-3-4 tree.   The search algorithm and the traversal algorithm for a 2-3-4 tree are simple extensions of the corresponding algorithms for a 2-3 tree. For example, to search the tree in Figure 12-20 given the search key 31, you would search the left subtree of the root, because 31 is less than 37; search the middle subtree of the node <30 35>, because 31 is between 30 and 35; and terminate the search at the left child reference of <32 33 34>, because 31 is less than 32, deducing that no item in the tree has a search key of 31. Exercise 5 at the end of the chapter asks you to complete the details of searching and traversing a 2-3-4 tree.

Inserting into a 2-3-4 tree.   The insertion algorithm for a 2-3-4 tree, like the insertion algorithm for a 2-3 tree, splits a node by moving one of its items up to its parent node. For a 2-3 tree, the search algorithm traces a path from the root to a leaf and then backs up from the leaf as it splits nodes. To avoid this return path after reaching a leaf, the insertion algorithm for a 2-3-4 tree splits 4-nodes as soon as it encounters them on the way down the tree from the root to a leaf. As a result, when a 4-node is split and an item is moved up to the node's parent, the parent cannot possibly be a 4-node and so can accommodate another item.

Split 4-nodes as they are encountered

As an example of the algorithm, consider the tree in Figure 12-22a. This one-node tree is the result of inserting 60, 30, and 10 into an initially empty 2-3-4 tree.

Insert 20.   While determining the insertion point, you begin at the root and encounter the 4-node <10 30 60>, which you split by moving the middle value 30 up. Since the node is the root, you create a new root, move 30 into it, and attach two children, as Figure 12-22b illustrates. You continue the search for 20 by examining the left subtree of the root, since 20 is less than 30. The insertion results in the tree in Figure 12-22c.

Insert 50 and 40.   The insertions of 50 and 40 do not require split nodes and result in the tree in Figure 12-23.

Insert 70.   As you search Figure 12-23 for 70's insertion point, you encounter the 4-node <40 50 60>, since 70 is greater than 30. You split this

Figure 12-23
After inserting 50 and 40

Figure 12-22
Inserting 20 into a one-node 2-3-4 tree

4-node by moving 50 up to the node's parent <30>, to get the tree in Figure 12-24a. You then insert 70 into the leaf <60>, as Figure 12-24b illustrates.

Insert 80 and 15.   These insertions do not require split nodes and result in the tree in Figure 12-25.

Insert 90.   As you search Figure 12-25 for 90's insertion point, you traverse the root's right subtree, since 90 is greater than 50, and encounter the 4-node <60 70 80>. You split this 4-node into two nodes and move 70 up to the root, as Figure 12-26a indicates. Finally, since 90 is greater than 70, you insert 90 into the leaf <80> to get the tree in Figure 12-26b.

Insert 100.   As you begin to search Figure 12-26b, you immediately encounter a 4-node at the tree's root. You split this node into two nodes and move 50 up to a new root, as Figure 12-27a indicates. After continuing the search, you insert 100 into <80 90> to get the tree in Figure 12-27b.

Splitting 4-nodes during insertion.   As you have just seen, you split each 4-node as soon as you encounter it during your search from the root to a leaf that will accommodate the new item to be inserted. The 4-node will either

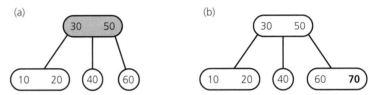

Figure 12-24

The steps for inserting 70

Figure 12-25

After inserting 80 and 15

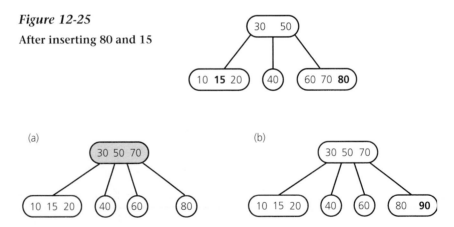

Figure 12-26

The steps for inserting 90

- Be the root, or
- have a 2-node parent, or
- have a 3-node parent.

Figure 12-28 illustrates how to split a 4-node that is the tree's root. You have seen two previous examples of this: We split <10 30 60> in Figure 12-22a, resulting in the tree in Figure 12-22b. We also split <30 50 70> during the insertion of 100 into the tree in Figure 12-26b, giving us the tree in Figure 12-27a.

Figure 12-29 illustrates the two possible situations that you can encounter when you split a 4-node whose parent is a 2-node. For example, when you split <40 50 60> during the insertion of 70 into the tree in Figure 12-23, you get the tree in Figure 12-24a.

Figure 12-30 illustrates the three possible situations that you can encounter when you split a 4-node whose parent is a 3-node. For example, when you split <60 70 80> during the insertion of 90 into the tree in Figure 12-25, you get the tree in Figure 12-26a.

Deleting from a 2-3-4 tree. The deletion algorithm for a 2-3-4 tree has the same beginning as the deletion algorithm for a 2-3 tree. You first locate the node *n* that contains the item *theItem* that you want to delete. You then find *theItem*'s inorder successor and swap it with *theItem* so that the deletion will always be at a leaf. If that leaf is either a 3-node or a 4-node, you simply remove *theItem*. If you can ensure that *theItem* does not occur in a 2-node, you can perform the deletion in one pass through the tree from root to leaf, unlike deletion from a 2-3 tree. That is, you will not have to back away from the leaf and restructure the tree.

To accomplish this goal, you transform each 2-node that you encounter during the search for *theItem* into either a 3-node or a 4-node.

Transform each 2-node into a 3-node or a 4-node

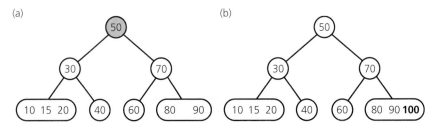

(a)   (b)

Figure 12-27

The steps for inserting 100

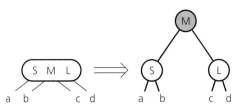

Figure 12-28

Splitting a 4-node root during insertion

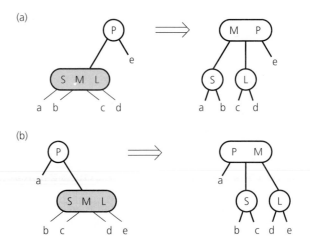

Figure 12-29

Splitting a 4-node whose parent is a 2-node during insertion

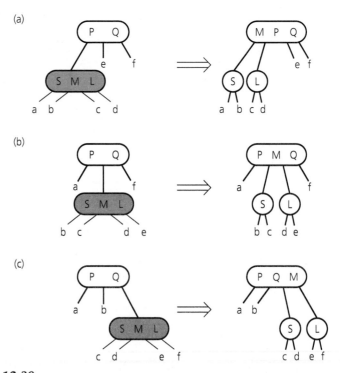

Figure 12-30

Splitting a 4-node whose parent is a 3-node during insertion

Several cases are possible, depending on the configuration of the 2-node's parent and nearest sibling. (Arbitrarily, a node's nearest sibling is its left sibling, unless the node is a left child, in which case its nearest sibling is to its right.) That is, either the parent or the sibling could be a 2-node, a 3-node, or a 4-node. For example, if the next node that you will encounter is a 2-node and both its parent and nearest sibling are 2-nodes, apply the transformation that Figure 12-28 illustrates, but in reverse; if the parent is a 3-node, apply the transformation that Figure 12-29 illustrates, but in reverse; and if the parent is a 4-node, apply the transformation that Figure 12-30 illustrates, but in reverse.

The details of deletion are left to you as a challenging exercise (Exercise 5).

Concluding remarks. The advantage of both 2-3 and 2-3-4 trees is their easy-to-maintain balance, not their shorter height. Even if a 2-3 tree is shorter than a balanced binary search tree, the reduction in height is offset by the increased number of comparisons that the search algorithm may require at each node. The situation is similar for a 2-3-4 tree, but its insertion and deletion algorithms require only one pass through the tree and so are simpler than those for a 2-3 tree. This decrease in effort makes the 2-3-4 tree more attractive than the 2-3 tree.

2-3 and 2-3-4 trees are attractive because their balance is easy to maintain

Insertion and deletion algorithms for a 2-3-4 tree require fewer steps than those for a 2-3 tree

Should we consider trees whose nodes have even more than four children? Although a tree whose nodes can each have 100 children would be shorter than a 2-3-4 tree, its search algorithm would require more comparisons at each node to determine which subtree to search. Thus, allowing the nodes of a tree to have many children is counterproductive. Such a search tree is appropriate, however, when it is implemented in external storage, because moving from node to node is far more expensive than comparing the data values in a node. In such cases, a search tree with the minimum possible height is desirable, even at the expense of additional comparisons at each node. Chapter 14 will discuss external search trees further.

Allowing nodes with more than four children is counterproductive

Red-Black Trees

A 2-3-4 tree is attractive because it is balanced and its insertion and deletion operations use only one pass from root to leaf. On the other hand, a 2-3-4 tree requires more storage than a binary search tree that contains the same data because a 2-3-4 tree has nodes that must accommodate up to three data items. A typical binary search tree is inappropriate, however, because it might not be balanced.

A 2-3-4 tree requires more storage than a binary search tree

You can use a special binary search tree—**a red-black tree**—to represent a 2-3-4 tree and retain the advantages of a 2-3-4 tree without the storage overhead. The idea is to represent each 3-node and 4-node in a 2-3-4 tree as an equivalent binary tree. To distinguish between 2-nodes that appeared in the original 2-3-4 tree and 2-nodes that were generated from 3-nodes and 4-nodes, you use red and black child references. Let all

A red-black tree has the advantages of a 2-3-4 tree but requires less storage

the child references in the original 2-3-4 tree be black; use red child references to link the 2-nodes that result when you split 3-nodes and 4-nodes.

Figures 12-31 and 12-32 indicate how to represent, respectively, a
4-node and a 3-node as binary trees. Because there are two possible ways
to represent a 3-node as a binary tree, a red-black representation of a
2-3-4 tree is not unique. Figure 12-33 gives a red-black representation for
the 2-3-4 tree in Figure 12-20. In all of these figures, a dashed line represents a red reference and a solid line represents a black reference.

A node in a red-black tree is similar to a node in a binary search tree,
but it must also store the reference colors, as the following Java class
indicates:

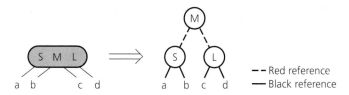

Figure 12-31

Red-black representation of a 4-node

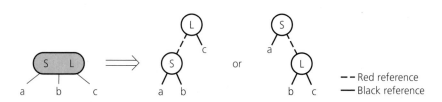

Figure 12-32

Red-black representation of a 3-node

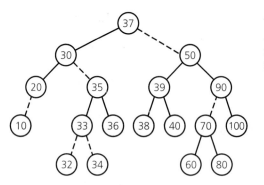

Figure 12-33

**A red-black tree that
represents the 2-3-4 tree
in Figure 12-20**

```
import SearchKeys.KeyedItem;
```
A node in a red-black tree

```
public class RBTreeNode {
  public static final int RED = 0;
  public static final int BLACK = 1;
  private KeyedItem item;
  private RBTreeNode leftChild;
  private RBTreeNode rightChild;
  private int leftColor;
  private int rightColor;

  // constructors and methods for accessing the private
  // data fields appear here
      .  .  .
}  // end RBTreeNode
```

Even with the reference colors, a node in a red-black tree requires less storage than a node in a 2-3-4 tree. (Why? See Self-Test Exercise 6.) Keep in mind that the transformations in Figures 12-31 and 12-32 imply a change in node structure.

Searching and traversing a red-black tree. Since a red-black tree is a binary search tree, you can search and traverse it by using the algorithms for a binary search tree. You simply ignore the color of the references.

Inserting into and deleting from a red-black tree. Because a red-black tree actually represents a 2-3-4 tree, you simply need to adjust the 2-3-4 insertion algorithms to accommodate the red-black representation. Recall that while searching a 2-3-4 tree, you split each 4-node that you encounter, so it is sufficient to reformulate that process in terms of the red-black representation. For example, Figure 12-31 shows the red-black representation of a 4-node. Thus, to identify a 4-node in its red-black form, you look for a node that has two red references.

Suppose that the 4-node is the root of the 2-3-4 tree. Figure 12-28 shows how to split the root into 2-nodes. By comparing this figure with Figure 12-31, you see that to perform an equivalent operation on a red-black tree, you simply change the color of its root's references to black, as Figure 12-34 illustrates.

Splitting the equivalent of a 4-node requires only simple color changes

Figure 12-29 shows how to split a 4-node whose parent is a 2-node. If you reformulate this figure by using the red-black notation given in Figures 12-31 and 12-32, you get Figure 12-35. Notice that this case also requires only color changes within the red-black tree.

Figure 12-34

Splitting a red-black representation of a 4-node that is the root

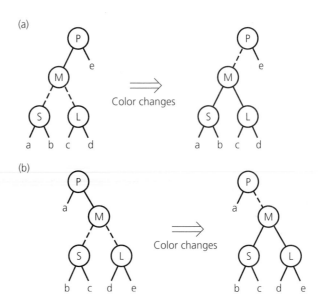

Figure 12-35

Splitting a red-black representation of a 4-node whose parent is a 2-node

Finally, Figure 12-30 shows how to split a 4-node whose parent is a 3-node. Note that each configuration before a split in Figure 12-30 has two red-black representations, as Figure 12-36 illustrates. (Apply the transformations that Figures 12-31 and 12-32 describe to Figure 12-30.) As you can see from Figure 12-36, each pair of representations transforms into the same red-black configuration. Of the six possibilities given in Figure 12-36, only two require simple color changes. The others also require changes to the references themselves. These reference changes, *Reference changes called rotations result in a shorter tree* which are called **rotations**, result in a shorter tree.

The deletion algorithm follows in an analogous fashion from the 2-3-4 deletion algorithm. Since insertion and deletion operations on a red-black tree frequently require only color changes, they are more efficient than the corresponding operations on a 2-3-4 tree.

Exercise 8 asks you to complete the details of the insertion and deletion algorithms.

AVL Trees

An AVL tree is a balanced binary search tree

An **AVL tree**—named for its inventors, Adel'son-Vel'skii and Landis—is a balanced binary search tree. Since the heights of the left and right subtrees of any node in a balanced binary tree differ by no more than 1, you can search an AVL tree almost as efficiently as a minimum-height binary search tree. This section will simply introduce you to the notion of an AVL tree—the oldest form of balanced binary tree—and leave the details for another course.

It is, in fact, possible to rearrange any binary search tree of n nodes to obtain a binary search tree with the minimum possible height $\lceil \log_2(n + 1) \rceil$.

(a)

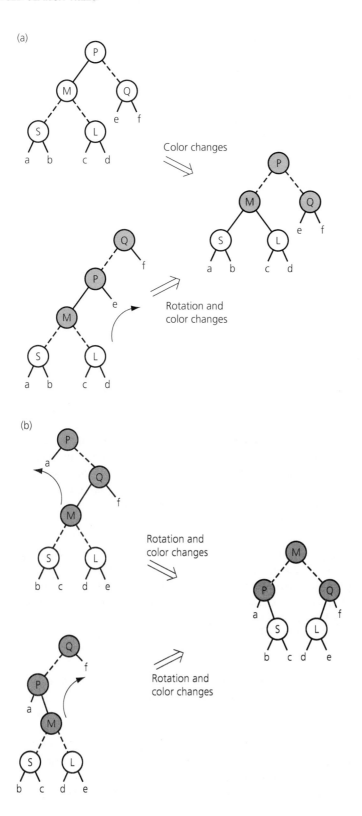

Figure 12-36

Splitting a red-black representation of a 4-node whose parent is a 3-node

(b)

(continues)

Figure 12-36
(continued)

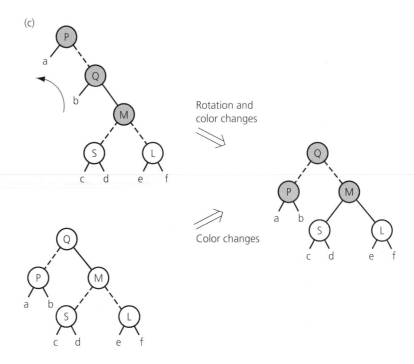

Recall, for example, the algorithms developed in Chapter 10 that use a file to save and restore a binary search tree. You can start with an arbitrary binary search tree, save its values in a file, and then construct from these same values a new binary search tree of minimum height. Although this approach may be appropriate in the context of a table that occasionally is saved and restored, it requires too much work to be performed every time an insertion or deletion leaves the tree unbalanced. The cost of repeatedly rebuilding the tree could very well outweigh the benefit of searching a tree of minimum height.

An AVL tree maintains a height close to the minimum

The AVL method is a compromise. It maintains a binary search tree with a height close to the minimum, but it is able to do so with far less work than would be necessary to keep the height of the tree exactly equal to the minimum. The basic strategy of the AVL method is to monitor the shape of the binary search tree. You insert or delete nodes just as you would for any binary search tree, but after each insertion or deletion, you check that the tree is still an AVL tree. That is, you determine whether any node in the tree has left and right subtrees whose heights differ by more than 1. For example, suppose that the binary search tree in Figure 12-37a is the result of a sequence of insertions and deletions. The heights of the left and right subtrees of the root 30 differ by 2. You can restore this tree's AVL property—that is, its balance—by

Rotations restore the balance

rearranging its nodes. For instance, you can **rotate** the tree so that the node 20 becomes the root, with left child 10 and right child 30, as in Figure 12-37b. Notice that you cannot arbitrarily rearrange the tree's

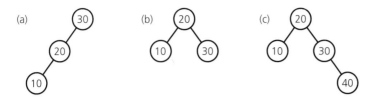

Figure 12-37

(a) An unbalanced binary search tree; (b) a balanced tree after rotation; (c) a balanced tree after insertion

nodes, because you must take care not to destroy the search tree's ordering property in the course of the rebalancing.

Rotations are not necessary after every insertion or deletion. For example, you can insert 40 into the AVL tree in Figure 12-37b and still have an AVL tree. (See Figure 12-37c.) However, when a rotation is necessary to restore a tree's AVL property, the rotation will be one of two possible types. Let's look at an example of each type.

Suppose that you have the tree in Figure 12-38a after the insertion or deletion of a node. (Perhaps you obtained this tree by inserting 60 into an AVL tree.) An imbalance occurs at the node 20; that is, 20's left and right subtrees differ in height by more than 1. A **single rotation** to the left is necessary to obtain the balanced tree in Figure 12-38b: 40 becomes the parent of 20, which adopts 30 as its right child. Figure 12-39 shows this rotation in a more general form. It shows, for example, that before the rotation, the left and right subtrees of the node 40 have heights h and $h + 1$, respectively. After the rotation, the tree is balanced and, in this particular case, has decreased in height from $h + 3$ to $h + 2$. Figures 12-40 and 12-41 show examples of a single left rotation that restores a tree's balance but does not affect its height. An analogous single right rotation would produce a mirror image of these examples.

A more complex rotation may be necessary. For example, consider the tree in Figure 12-42a, which is the result of nodes being added to or

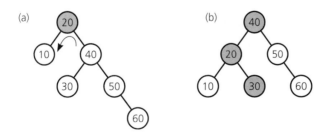

Figure 12-38

(a) An unbalanced binary search tree; (b) a balanced tree after a single left rotation

Figure 12-39

Before and after a single left rotation that decreases the tree's height

 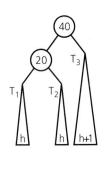

Before rotation   After rotation

Figure 12-40

(a) An unbalanced binary search tree; (b) a balanced tree after a single left rotation

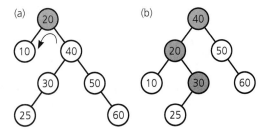

Figure 12-41

Before and after a single left rotation that does not affect the tree's height

Before rotation   After rotation

deleted from an AVL tree. The left and right subtrees of 20 differ in height by more than 1. A **double rotation** is necessary to restore this tree's balance. Figure 12-42b shows the result of a left rotation about 20, and Figure 12-42c shows the result of a right rotation about 40. Figure 12-43 illustrates this double rotation in a more general form. Mirror images of these figures provide examples of other possible double rotations.

It can be proven that the height of an AVL tree with *n* nodes will always be very close to the theoretical minimum of $\lceil \log_2(n + 1) \rceil$. The AVL tree implementation of a table is, therefore, one implementation that guarantees a binary searchlike efficiency. Usually, however, implementations that use either a 2-3-4 tree or a red-black tree will be simpler.

An AVL tree implementation of a table is more difficult than other implementations

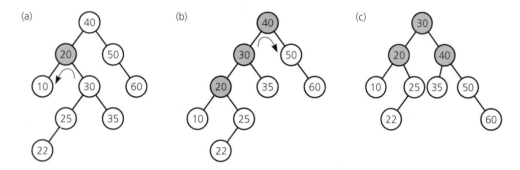

Figure 12-42

(a) Before; (b) during; and (c) after a double rotation

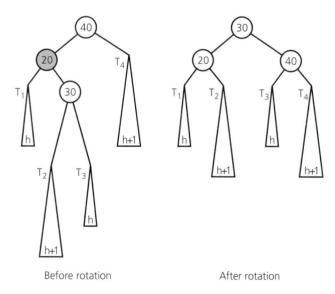

Before rotation   After rotation

Figure 12-43

Before and after a double rotation that decreases the tree's height

HASHING

The binary search tree and its balanced variants, such as 2-3, 2-3-4, red-black, and AVL trees, provide excellent implementations of the ADT table. They allow you to perform all of the table operations quite efficiently. If, for example, a table contains 10,000 items, the operations `tableRetrieve, tableInsert,` and `tableDelete` each require approximately $\log_2 10,000 = 13$ steps. As impressive as this efficiency may be, situations do occur for which the search-tree implementations are not adequate.

As you know, time can be vital. For example, when a person calls the 911 emergency system, the system detects the caller's telephone number and searches a database for the caller's address. Similarly, an air traffic control system searches a database of flight information, given a flight number. Clearly these searches must be rapid.

Table operations without searches

A radically different strategy is necessary to locate (and insert or delete) an item virtually instantaneously. Imagine an array `table` of n items—with each array slot capable of holding a single table item—and a seemingly magical box called an "address calculator." Whenever you have a new item that you want to insert into the table, the address calculator will tell you where you should place it in the array. Figure 12-44 illustrates this scenario.

You can thus easily perform an insertion into the table as follows:

```
tableInsert(newItem)

    i = the array index that the address calculator
            gives you for newItem's search key
    table[i] = newItem
```

An insertion is O(1); that is, it requires constant time.

You also use the address calculator for the `tableRetrieve` and `tableDelete` operations. If you want to retrieve an item that has a particular

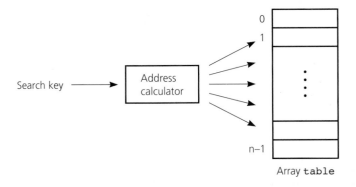

Figure 12-44

Address calculator

search key, you simply ask the address calculator to tell you where it would insert such an item. Because you would have inserted the item earlier by using the `tableInsert` algorithm just given, if the desired item is present in the table, it will be in the array location that the address calculator specifies.

Thus, the retrieval operation appears in pseudocode as follows:

```
tableRetrieve(searchKey)
// Returns table item that has a matching searchKey.
// If not found, returns null.

   i = the array index that the address calculator
          gives you for an item whose search key
          equals searchKey

   if (table[i].getKey() equals searchKey) {
     return table[i]
   }
   else {
     return null
   }  // end if
```

Similarly, the pseudocode for the deletion operation is

```
tableDelete(searchKey)
// Deletes item that has a matching searchKey. If
// successful, returns true; otherwise, returns false.
   i = the array index that the address calculator
          gives you for an item whose search key
          equals searchKey

   success = (table[i].getKey() equals searchKey)
   if (success) {
     Delete the item from table[i]
   }  // end if
   return success
```

It thus appears that you can perform the operations `tableRetrieve`, `tableInsert`, and `tableDelete` virtually instantaneously. You never have to search for an item; instead, you simply let the address calculator determine where the item should be. The amount of time required to carry out the operations is O(1) and depends only on how quickly the address calculator can perform this computation.

If you are to implement such a scheme, you must, of course, be able to construct an address calculator that can, with very little work, tell you where a given item should be. Address calculators are actually not as mysterious as they seem; in fact, many exist that can approximate the idealized behavior just described. Such an address calculator is usually referred to as a **hash function**. The scheme just described is an idealized description of a method known as **hashing**, and the array `table` is called the **hash table**.

A hash function tells you where to place an item in an array called a hash table

To understand how a hash function works, consider the 911 emergency system mentioned earlier. If, for each person, the system had a record whose search key was the person's telephone number, it could store these records in a search tree. Although searching a tree would be fast, faster access to a particular record would be possible by storing the records in an array *table*, as follows. You store the record for a person whose telephone number is *num* into *table[num]*. Retrieval of the record, then, is almost instantaneous given its search key *num*. For example, you can store the record for the telephone number 123-4567 in *table[1234567]*. If you can spare ten million memory locations for *table*, this approach is fine. You need not use memory so extravagantly, however, since 911 systems are regional. If you consider only one telephone exchange, for example, you can store the record for the number 123-4567 in *table[4567]* and get by with an array *table* of 10,000 locations.

The transformation of 1234567 into an array index 4567 is a simple example of a hash function. A hash function h must take an arbitrary integer x and map it into an integer that you can use as an array index. In our example, such indexes would be in the range 0 through 9999. That is, h is a function such that for any integer x,

A hash function maps an integer into an array index

$h(x) = i$, where i is an integer in the range 0 through 9999

Since the database contains records for every telephone number in a particular exchange, the array *table* is completely full. In this sense, our example is not typical of hashing applications and serves only to illustrate the idea of a hash function. What if many fewer records were in the array? Consider, for example, an air traffic control system that stores a record for each current flight according to its four-digit flight number. You could store a record for Flight 4567 in *table[4567]*, but you still would need an array of 10,000 locations, even if only 50 flights were current.

A different hash function would save memory. If you allow space for a maximum of 101 flights, for example, so that the array *table* has indexes 0 through 100, the necessary hash function h should map any four-digit flight number into an integer in the range 0 through 100.

If you have such a hash function h—and you will see several suggestions for hash functions later—the table operations are easy to write. For example, in the *tableRetrieve* algorithm, the step

```
i = the array index that the address calculator
         gives you for an item whose search key
         equals searchKey
```

is implemented simply as

```
i = h(searchKey)
```

In the previous example, *searchKey* would be the flight number.

The table operations appear to be virtually instantaneous. But is hashing really as good as it sounds? If it really were this good, there

would have been little reason for developing all those other table implementations. Hashing would beat them hands down!

Why is hashing not quite as simple as it seems? You might first notice
that since the hashing scheme stores the items in an array, it would
appear to suffer from the familiar problems associated with a fixed-size
implementation. Obviously, the hash table must be large enough to
contain all of the items that you want to store. This requirement is not
the crux of the implementation's difficulty, however, for—as you will see
later—there are ways to allow the hash table to grow dynamically. The
implementation has a major pitfall, even given the assumption that the
number of items to be stored will never exceed the size of the hash table.

Ideally, you want the hash function to map each *x* into a unique
integer *i*. The hash function in the ideal situation is called a **perfect hash
function.** In fact, it is possible to construct perfect hash functions if you
know all of the possible search keys that *actually* occur in the table. You
have this knowledge for the 911 example, since everyone is in the database, but not for the air traffic control example. Usually, you will not
know the values of the search keys in advance.

In practice, a hash function can map two or more search keys *x* and *y*
into the *same* integer. That is, the hash function tells you to store two or
more items in the same array location `table[i]`. This occurrence is
called a **collision.** Thus, even if fewer than 101 items were present in the
hash table `table[0..100]`, *h* could very well tell you to place more than
one item into the same array location. For example, if two items have
search keys 4567 and 7597, and if

$$h(4567) = h(7597) = 22$$

h will tell you to place the two items into the same array location,
`table[22]`. That is, the search keys 4567 and 7597 have collided.

Even if the number of items that can be in the array at any one time
is small, the only way to avoid collisions completely is for the hash table
to be large enough that each possible search-key value can have its own
location. If, for example, social security numbers were the search keys,
you would need an array location for each integer in the range
000000000 through 999999999. This situation would certainly require a
good deal of storage! Because reserving vast amounts of storage is usually
not practical, **collision-resolution schemes** are necessary to make
hashing feasible. Such resolution schemes usually require that the hash
function place items evenly throughout the hash table.

To summarize, a typical hash function must

- Be easy and fast to compute
- Place items evenly throughout the hash table

Note that the size of the hash table affects the ability of the hash function
to distribute the items evenly throughout the table. The requirements of a
hash function will be discussed in more detail later in this chapter.

*A perfect hash function maps
each search key into a unique
location of the hash table*

*A perfect hash function is
possible if you know all the
search keys*

*Collisions occur when the hash
function maps more than one
item into the same array
location*

*Requirements for a hash
function*

Consider now several hash functions and collision-resolution schemes.

Hash Functions

It is sufficient to consider hash functions that have an arbitrary integer as an argument. Why? If a search key is not an integer, you can simply map the search key into an integer, which you then hash. At the end of this section, you will see one way to convert a string into an integer.

There are many ways to convert an arbitrary integer into an integer within a certain range, such as 0 through 100. Thus, there are many ways to construct a hash function. Many of these functions, however, will not be suitable. Here are several simple hash functions that operate on positive integers.

Selecting digits.   If your search key is the nine-digit employee ID number 001364825, you could select the fourth digit and the last digit, to obtain 35 as the index to the hash table. That is,

$$h(001364825) = 35 \quad \textit{(select the fourth and last digits)}$$

Therefore, you would store the item whose search key is 001364825 in `table[35]`.

You do need to be careful about which digits you choose in a particular situation. For example, the first three digits of a social security number are based on the geographic region in which the number was assigned. If you select only these digits, you will map all people from the same state into the same location of the hash table.

Digit-selection hash functions are simple and fast, but generally they do not evenly distribute the items in the hash table. A hash function really should utilize the entire search key.

Folding.   One way to improve upon the previous method of selecting digits is to add the digits. For example, you can add all of the digits in 001364825 to obtain

$$0 + 0 + 1 + 3 + 6 + 4 + 8 + 2 + 5 = 29 \quad \textit{(add the digits)}$$

Therefore, you would store the item whose search key is 001364825 in `table[29]`. Notice that if you add all of the digits from a nine-digit search key,

$$0 \leq h(\text{search key}) \leq 81$$

That is, you would use only `table[0]` through `table[81]` of the hash table. To change this situation or to increase the size of the hash table, you can group the digits in the search key and add the groups. For example, you could form three groups of three digits from the search key 001364825 and add them as follows:

$$001 + 364 + 825 = 1,190$$

For this hash function,

$$0 \leq h(\text{search key}) \leq 3 * 999 = 2{,}997$$

Clearly, if 2,997 is larger than the size of the hash table that you want, you can alter the groups that you choose. Perhaps not as obvious is that you can apply more than one hash function to a search key. For example, you could select some of the digits from the search key before adding them, or you could either select digits from the previous result 2,997 or apply folding to it once again by adding 29 and 97.

You can apply more than one hash function to a single search key

Modulo arithmetic. Modulo arithmetic provides a simple and effective hash function that we will use in the rest of this chapter. For example, consider the function[5]

$$h(x) = x \bmod \textit{tableSize}$$

where the hash table `table` has *tableSize* elements. In particular, if *tableSize* is 101, $h(x) = x \bmod 101$ maps any integer x into the range 0 through 100. For example, h maps 001364825 into 12.

For $h(x) = x \bmod \textit{tableSize}$, many x's map into `table[0]`, many x's map into `table[1]`, and so on. That is, collisions occur. However, you can distribute the table items evenly over all of `table`—thus reducing collisions—by choosing a prime number as *tableSize*. The reasoning behind choosing a prime number is discussed later in this chapter in the section "What Constitutes a Good Hash Function?" For instance, 101 in the previous example is prime. The choice of table size will also be discussed in more detail later in this chapter. For now, realize that 101 is used here as a simple example of a prime table size. For the typical table, 101 is much too small.

The table size should be prime

Converting a character string to an integer. If your search key is a character string—such as a name—you could convert it into an integer before applying the hash function $h(x)$. To do so, you could first assign each character in the string an integer value. For example, for the word "NOTE" you could assign the ASCII values 78, 79, 84, and 69, to the letters N, O, T, and E, respectively. Or, if you assign the values 1 through 26 to the letters A through Z, you could assign 14 to N, 15 to O, 20 to T, and 5 to E.

If you now simply add these numbers, you will get an integer, but it will not be unique to the character string. For example, the string "TONE" will give you the same result. Instead, write the numeric value for each character in binary and concatenate the results. If you assign the values 1 through 26 to the letters A through Z, you obtain the following for the string "NOTE":

N is 14, or 01110 in binary

O is 15, or 01111 in binary

---

[5]Remember that this book uses "mod" as an abbreviation for the mathematical operation modulo. In Java, the modulo operator is `%`.

T is 20, or 10100 in binary

E is 5, or 00101 in binary

Concatenating the binary values gives you the binary integer

01110011111010000101

which is 474,757 in decimal. You can apply the hash function x mod *table-Size* for $x = 474{,}757$.

Now consider a more efficient way to compute 474,757. Rather than converting the previous binary number to decimal, you can evaluate the expression

$$14 * 32^3 + 15 * 32^2 + 20 * 32^1 + 5 * 32^0$$

This computation is possible because we have represented each character as a 5-bit binary number, and 2^5 is 32.

By factoring this expression, you can minimize the number of arithmetic operations. This technique is called **Horner's rule** and results in

Horner's rule minimizes the number of computations

$$((14 * 32 + 15) * 32 + 20) * 32 + 5$$

Although both of these expressions have the same value, the result in either case could very well be larger than a typical computer can represent; that is, an overflow can occur.

Since we plan to use the hash function

$$h(x) = x \bmod tableSize$$

you can prevent an overflow by applying the modulo operator after computing each parenthesized expression in Horner's rule. The implementation of this algorithm is left as an exercise.

Resolving Collisions

Consider the problems caused by a collision. Suppose that you want to insert an item whose search key is 4567 into the hash table `table`, as was described previously. The hash function $h(x) = x \bmod 101$ tells you to place the new item in `table[22]`, because 4567 mod 101 is 22. Suppose, however, that `table[22]` already contains an item, as Figure 12-45 illustrates. If earlier you had placed 7597 into `table[22]` because 7597 mod 101 equals 22, where do you place the new item? You certainly do not want to disallow the insertion on the grounds that the table is full: You could have a collision even when inserting into a table that contains only one item!

Two approaches to collision resolution

Two general approaches to collision resolution are common. One approach allocates another location *within* the hash table to the new item. A second approach changes the structure of the hash table so that each location `table[i]` can accommodate more than one item. The collision-resolution schemes described next exemplify these two approaches.

Approach 1: Open addressing.   During an attempt to insert a new item into a table, if the hash function indicates a location in the hash table that is already occupied, you **probe** for some other empty, or open, location in which to place the item. The sequence of locations that you examine is called the **probe sequence.**

Such schemes are said to use **open addressing**. The concern, of course, is that you must be able to find a table item efficiently after you have inserted it. That is, the `tableDelete` and `tableRetrieve` operations must be able to reproduce the probe sequence that `tableInsert` used and must do so efficiently.

The difference among the various open-addressing schemes is the method used to probe for an empty location. We briefly describe three such methods.

Linear probing. In this simple scheme to resolve a collision, you search the hash table sequentially, starting from the original hash location. More specifically, if `table[h(searchKey)]` is occupied, you check `table [h(searchKey)+1]`, `table[h(searchKey)+2]`, and so on until you find an available location. Figure 12-46 illustrates the placement of four items that all hash into the same location `table[22]` of the hash table, assuming a hash function $h(x) = x \bmod 101$. Typically, you *wrap around* from the last table location to the first table location if necessary.

Begin at the hash location and search the table sequentially

In the absence of deletions, the implementation of `tableRetrieve` under this scheme is straightforward. You need only follow the same probe sequence that `tableInsert` used until you either find the item you are searching for, reach an empty location, which indicates that the item is not present, or visit every table location.

Deletions, however, add a slight complication. The `tableDelete` operation itself is no problem. You merely find the desired item, as in `tableRetrieve`, and delete it, making the location empty. But what happens to `tableRetrieve` after deletions? The new empty locations

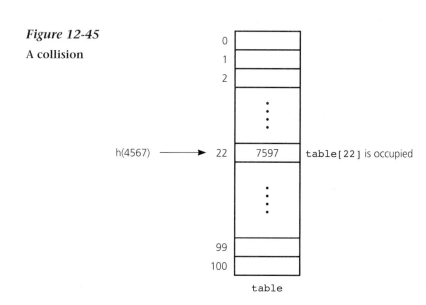

Figure 12-45

A collision

h(4567) ⟶ 22   7597   `table[22]` is occupied

table

Figure 12-46

Linear probing with
$h(x) = x \bmod 101$

```
22    7597        i = 7597 mod 101 = 22
23    4567        i+1
24    0628        i+2
25    3658        i+3
```

table

that `tableDelete` created along a probe sequence could cause `tableRe-trieve` to stop prematurely, incorrectly indicating a failure. You can resolve this problem by allowing a table location to be in one of three states: occupied (currently in use), empty (has not been used), or deleted (was once occupied but is now available). You then modify the `tableRe-trieve` operation to continue probing when it encounters a location in the deleted state. Similarly, you modify `tableInsert` to insert into either empty or deleted locations.

Three states: occupied,
empty, deleted

One of the problems with the linear-probing scheme is that table items tend to **cluster** together in the hash table. That is, the table contains groups of consecutively occupied locations. This phenomenon is called **primary clustering**. Clusters can get close to one another and, in fact, merge into a larger cluster. Large clusters tend to get even larger. ("The rich get richer.") Thus, one part of the table might be quite dense, even though another part has relatively few items. Primary clustering causes long probe searches and therefore decreases the overall efficiency of hashing.

Clustering can be a problem

Quadratic probing.   You can virtually eliminate primary clusters simply by adjusting the linear probing scheme just described. Instead of probing consecutive locations from the original hash location `table[h(search-Key)]`, you check locations `table[h(searchKey)+1²]`, `table[h(search-Key)+2²]`, `table[h(searchKey)+3²]`, and so on until you find an available location. Figure 12-47 illustrates this open-addressing scheme—which is called **quadratic probing**—for the same items that appear in Figure 12-46.

Unfortunately, when two items hash into the same location, quadratic probing uses the same probe sequence for each item. This phenomenon—called **secondary clustering**—delays the resolution of the collision. Although the analysis of quadratic probing remains incomplete, it appears that secondary clustering is not a problem.

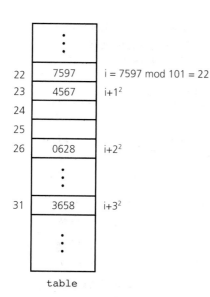

Figure 12-47

Quadratic probing with
$h(x) = x \bmod 101$

22	7597	$i = 7597 \bmod 101 = 22$
23	4567	$i+1^2$
24		
25		
26	0628	$i+2^2$
31	3658	$i+3^2$

table

Double hashing. Double hashing, which is yet another open-addressing scheme, drastically reduces clustering. The probe sequences that both linear probing and quadratic probing use are *key independent*. For example, linear probing inspects the table locations sequentially no matter what the hash key is. In contrast, double hashing defines *key-dependent* probe sequences. In this scheme, the probe sequence still searches the table in a linear order, starting at the location $h_1(key)$, but a second hash function h_2 determines the size of the steps taken.

A hash address and a step size determine the probe sequence

Although you choose h_1 as usual, you must follow these guidelines for h_2:

$h_2(key) \neq 0$
$h_2 \neq h_1$

Guidelines for the step-size function h_2

Clearly, you need a nonzero step size $h_2(key)$ to define the probe sequence. In addition, h_2 must differ from h_1 to avoid clustering.

For example, let h_1 and h_2 be the primary and secondary hash functions defined as

$h_1(key) = key \bmod 11$
$h_2(key) = 7 - (key \bmod 7)$

Primary and secondary hash functions

where a hash table of only 11 items is assumed, so that you can readily see the effect of these functions on the hash table. If *key* = 58, h_1 hashes *key* to table location 3 (58 mod 11), and h_2 indicates that the probe sequence should take steps of size 5 (7 – 58 mod 7). In other words, the probe sequence will be 3, 8, 2 (wraps around), 7, 1 (wraps around), 6, 0, 5, 10, 4, 9. On the other hand, if *key* = 14, h_1 hashes *key* to table location 3 (14 mod 11), and h_2 indicates that the probe sequence should take steps of size 7 (7 – 14 mod 7), and so the probe sequence would be 3, 10, 6, 2, 9, 5, 1, 8, 4, 0.

Each of these probe sequences visits *all* the table locations. This phenomenon always occurs if the size of the table and the size of the probe step are relatively prime, that is, if their greatest common divisor is 1. Because the size of a hash table is commonly a prime number, it will be relatively prime to all step sizes.

Figure 12-48 illustrates the insertion of 58, 14, and 91 into an initially empty hash table. Since $h_1(58)$ is 3, you place 58 into $table[3]$. You then find that $h_1(14)$ is also 3, so to avoid a collision, you step by $h_2(14) = 7$ and place 14 into $table[3 + 7]$, or $table[10]$. Finally, $h_1(91)$ is 3 and $h_2(91)$ is 7. Since $table[3]$ is occupied, you probe $table[10]$ and find that it, too, is occupied. You finally store 91 in $table[(10 + 7) \% 11]$, or $table[6]$.

Using more than one hash function is called **rehashing.** While more than two hash functions can be desirable, such schemes are difficult to implement.

Increasing the size of the hash table.   With any of the open-addressing schemes, as the hash table fills, the probability of a collision increases. At some point, a larger hash table becomes desirable. If you use a resizeable array for the hash table, you can increase its size whenever the table becomes too full.

You cannot simply double the size of the array, as we did in earlier chapters, because the size of the hash table must remain prime. In addition, you do not copy the items from the original hash table to the new hash table. If your hash function is x mod *tableSize*, it changes as *tableSize* changes. Thus, you need to apply your new hash function to every item in the old hash table before placing it into the new hash table.

Approach 2: Restructuring the hash table.   Another way to resolve collisions is to change the structure of the array $table$—the hash table—so that

Each hash-table location can accommodate more than one item

Figure 12-48

Double hashing during the insertion of 58, 14, and 91

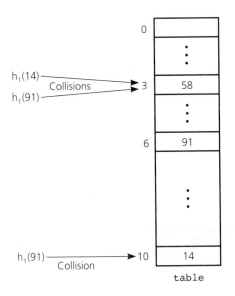

it can accommodate more than one item in the same location. We describe two such ways to alter the hash table.

Buckets. If you define the hash table `table` so that each location `table[i]` is itself an array called a **bucket**, you then can store the items that hash into `table[i]` in this array. The problem with this approach, of course, is choosing the size B of each bucket. If B is too small, you will only have postponed the problem of collisions until $B + 1$ items map into some array location. If you attempt to make B large enough so that each array location can accommodate the largest number of items that might map into it, you are likely to waste a good deal of storage.

A bucket is an element of a hash table that is itself an array

Separate chaining. A better approach is to design the hash table as an array of linked lists. In this collision-resolution method, known as **separate chaining**, each entry `table[i]` is a reference to a linked list—the **chain**—of items that the hash function has mapped into location `i`, as Figure 12-49 illustrates. The following classes for the ADT table assume an implementation that uses a hash table and separate chaining:

Each hash-table location is a linked list

```java
import SearchKeys.KeyedItem;

public class ChainNode {
  private KeyedItem item;
  private ChainNode next;

  public ChainNode(KeyedItem newItem, ChainNode nextNode) {
    item = newItem;
    next = nextNode;
  } // end constructor
```

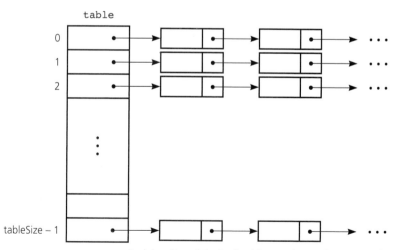

Each location of the hash table contains a reference to a linked list

Figure 12-49

Separate chaining

```java
  public void setItem(KeyedItem newItem) {
    item = newItem;
  }  // end setItem

  public KeyedItem getItem() {
    return item;
  }  // end getItem

  public void setNext(ChainNode nextNode) {
    next = nextNode;
  }  // end setNext

  public ChainNode getNext() {
    return next;
  }  // end getNext
} // end ChainNode


// ***********************************************************
// Hash table implementation.
// Assumption: A table contains at most one item with a
//             given search key at any time.
// ***********************************************************
public class HashTable {
  public final int HASH_TABLE_SIZE = 101;
  private ChainNode[] table;          // hash table
  private int         size;           // size of ADT table

// constructor:
  public HashTable() {
    table = new ChainNode[HASH_TABLE_SIZE];
    size = 0;
  }  // end default constructor

// table operations:
  public boolean tableIsEmpty() {
    return size==0;
  }  // end tableIsEmpty

  public int tableLength() {
    return size;
  }  // end tableLength

// Programming Problem 4 asks you to implement the following
// methods.

  public void tableInsert(KeyedItem newItem)
                            throws HashException {
```

```
        .   .   .

}   // end tableInsert

public boolean tableDelete(Comparable searchKey) {

        .   .   .

}   // end tableDelete

public KeyedItem tableRetrieve(Comparable searchKey) {

        .   .   .

}   // end tableRetrieve

protected int hashIndex(Comparable searchKey) {
    // hash function

        .   .   .

}   // end hashIndex

}   // end HashTable
```

KeyedItem is the base class for the items that are stored in the table. The *KeyedItem* class was first presented in Chapter 10, and provides a data field for the search key, a constructor, and the method *getKey*. The search key is used by the *hashIndex* method in the class *HashTable* to generate a hash index value. Since the *hashIndex* method does not have access to the internal structure of the search key, it must rely on methods available in the class *Object* and the interface *Comparable*. The *Object* class has two methods that are likely to be used in the implementation of *hashIndex*: *toString* and *hashCode*. The *hashIndex* method could use *toString* with the techniques involving strings discussed earlier in the chapter. The *hashIndex* method could also simply call *hashCode*, a method that returns a unique value for each unique object. The *hashIndex* method of the class *HashTable* should take care of ensuring that the value generated is in an appropriate range and should resolve collisions if needed.

When you insert a new item into the table, you simply place it at the beginning of the linked list that the hash function indicates. The following pseudocode describes the insertion algorithm:

tableInsert(newItem)

```
if (table not full) {
    searchKey = the search key of newItem
    i = hashIndex(searchKey)
    node = reference to a new node containing newItem
```

```
    node.setNext(table[i]);
    table[i] = node
}
else { // table full
    throw new HashException()
}  // end if
```

When you want to retrieve an item, you search the linked list that the hash function indicates. The following pseudocode describes the retrieval algorithm:

```
tableRetrieve(searchKey)

    i = hashIndex(searchKey)
    node = table[i]

    while ((node ≠ null) &&
             (node.getItem().getKey() ≠ searchKey)){
      node = node.getNext()
    }  // end while

    if (node != null) {
      return node.getItem()
    }

    else {
      return null
    }  // end if
```

The deletion algorithm is very similar to the retrieval algorithm and is left as an exercise. (See Exercise 11.)

Separate chaining successfully resolves collisions

Separate chaining is thus a successful method of resolving collisions. With separate chaining, the size of the ADT table is dynamic and can exceed the size of the hash table, since each linked list can be as long as necessary. As you will see in the next section, the length of these linked lists affects the efficiency of retrievals and deletions.

The Efficiency of Hashing

An analysis of the average-case efficiency of hashing involves the **load factor** α, which is the ratio of the current number of items in the table to the maximum size of the array `table`. That is,

The load factor measures how full a hash table is

$$\alpha = \frac{Current\ number\ of\ table\ items}{tableSize}$$

α is a measure of how full the hash table `table` is. As `table` fills, α increases and the chance of collision increases, so search times increase. Thus, hashing efficiency decreases as α increases.

Unlike the efficiency of earlier table implementations, the efficiency of hashing does not depend solely on the number *n* of items in the table. While it is true that for a fixed *tableSize*, efficiency decreases as *n* increases, for a given *n* you can choose *tableSize* to increase efficiency. Thus, when determining *tableSize*, you should estimate the largest possible *n* and select *tableSize* so that α is small. As you will see shortly, α should not exceed 2/3.

Hashing efficiency for a particular search also depends on whether the search is successful. An unsuccessful search requires more time in general than a successful search. The following analyses[6] enable a comparison of collision-resolution techniques.

Unsuccessful searches generally require more time than successful searches

Linear probing. For linear probing, the approximate average number of comparisons that a search requires is

$$\frac{1}{2}\left[1 + \frac{1}{1-\alpha}\right] \qquad \text{for a successful search, and}$$

$$\frac{1}{2}\left[1 + \frac{1}{(1-\alpha)^2}\right] \qquad \text{for an unsuccessful search}$$

As collisions increase, the probe sequences increase in length, causing increased search times. For example, for a table that is two-thirds full ($\alpha = 2/3$), an average unsuccessful search might require at most five comparisons, or probes, while an average successful search might require at most two comparisons. To maintain efficiency, it is important to prevent the hash table from filling up.

Do not let the hash table get too full

Quadratic probing and double hashing. The efficiency of both quadratic probing and double hashing is given by

$$\frac{-\log_e(1-\alpha)}{\alpha} \qquad \text{for a successful search, and}$$

$$\frac{1}{1-\alpha} \qquad \text{for an unsuccessful search}$$

On average, both methods require fewer comparisons than linear probing. For example, for a table that is two-thirds full, an average unsuccessful search might require at most three comparisons, or probes, while an average successful search might require at most two comparisons. As a result, you can use a smaller hash table for both quadratic probing and double hashing than you can for linear probing. However, because they are open-addressing schemes, all three methods suffer when you are unable to predict the number of insertions and deletions that will occur. If your hash table is too small, it will fill up, and search efficiency will decrease.

Open-addressing schemes require a good estimate of the number of insertions and deletions

---

[6]D. E. Knuth, *Searching and Sorting*, vol. 3 of *The Art of Computer Programming* (Menlo Park, CA: Addison-Wesley, 1973).

Separate chaining. Since the `tableInsert` operation places the new item at the beginning of a linked list within the hash table, it is O(1). The `tableRetrieve` and `tableDelete` operations, however, are not as fast. They each require a search of the linked list of items, so ideally you would like for these linked lists to be short.

For separate chaining, *tableSize* is the number of linked lists, not the maximum number of table items. Thus, it is entirely possible, and even likely, that the current number of table items *n* exceeds *tableSize*. That is, the load factor α, or *n*/*tableSize*, can exceed 1. Since *tableSize* is the number of linked lists, *n*/*tableSize*—that is, α—is the average length of each linked list.

Some searches of the hash table are unsuccessful because the relevant linked list is empty. Such searches are virtually instantaneous. For an unsuccessful search of a nonempty linked list, however, `tableRetrieve` and `tableDelete` must examine the entire list, that is, α items in the average case. On the other hand, a successful search must examine a nonempty linked list. In the average case, the search will locate the item in the middle of the list. That is, after determining that the linked list is not empty, the search will examine α/2 items.

Thus, the efficiency of the retrieval and deletion operations under the separate-chaining approach is

$$1 + \frac{\alpha}{2} \qquad \text{for a successful search, and}$$

$$\alpha \qquad \text{for an unsuccessful search}$$

Even if the linked lists typically are short, you should still estimate the worst case. If you seriously underestimate *tableSize* or if most of the table items happen to hash into the same location, the number of items in a linked list could be quite large. In fact, in the worst case, all *n* items in the table could be in the same linked list!

As you can see, the time that a retrieval or deletion operation requires can range from almost nothing—if the linked list to be searched either is empty or has only a couple of items in it—to the time required to search a linked list that contains all the items in the table, if all the items hashed into the same location.

Comparing methods. Figure 12-50 plots the relative efficiency of the collision-resolution schemes just discussed. When the hash table `table` is about half full—that is, when α is 0.5—the methods are nearly equal in efficiency. As the table fills and α approaches 1, separate chaining is the most efficient. Does this mean that we should discard all other search methods in favor of hashing with separate chaining?

No. The analyses here are average-case analyses. Although an implementation of the ADT table that uses hashing might often be faster than one that uses a search tree, in the worst case it can be much slower. If you can afford both an occasional slow search and a large *tableSize*—that is, a small α—then hashing can be an attractive table implementation.

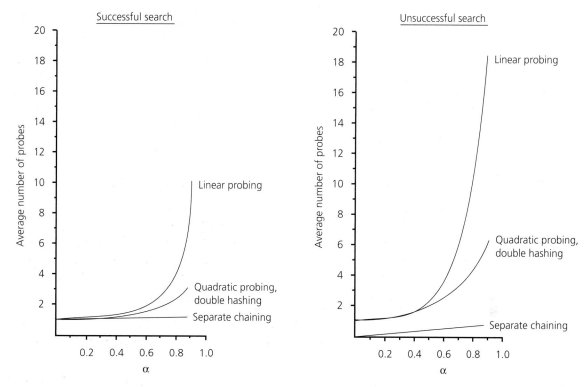

Figure 12-50

The relative efficiency of four collision-resolution methods

However, if you are performing a life-and-death search for your city's poison control center, a search-tree implementation would at least provide you with a guaranteed bound on its worst-case behavior.

What Constitutes a Good Hash Function?

Before concluding this introduction to hashing, consider in more detail the issue of choosing a hash function to perform the address calculations for a given application. A great deal has been written on this subject, most of which is beyond the mathematical level of this book. However, this section will present a brief summary of the major concerns.

- **A hash function should be easy and fast to compute.** If a hashing scheme is to perform table operations almost instantaneously and in constant time, you certainly must be able to calculate the hash function rapidly. Most of the common hash functions require only a single division (like the modulo function), a single multiplication, or some kind of "bit-level" operation on the internal representation of the search key. In all these cases, the requirement that the hash function be easy and fast to compute is satisfied.

You cannot avoid collisions entirely

- **A hash function should scatter the data evenly throughout the hash table.** Unless you use a perfect hash function—which is usually impractical to construct—you typically cannot avoid collisions entirely. For example, to achieve the best performance from a separate-chaining scheme, each entry `table[i]` should contain approximately the same number of items in its chain; that is, each chain should contain approximately *n/tableSize* items (and thus no chain should contain significantly more than *n/tableSize* items). To accomplish this goal, your hash function should scatter the search keys evenly throughout the hash table.

There are two issues to consider with regard to how evenly a hash function scatters the search keys.

- **How well does the hash function scatter random data?** If every search-key value is equally likely, will the hash function scatter the search keys evenly? For example, consider the following scheme for hashing nine-digit ID numbers:

  `table[0..39]` is the hash table, and
  the hash function is $h(x) =$ (first two digits of x) mod 40

  The question is, given the assumption that all employee ID numbers are equally likely, does a given ID number x have equal probability of hashing into any one of the 40 array locations? For this hash function, the answer is no. Only ID numbers that start with 19, 59, and 99 map into `table[19]`, while only ID numbers that start with 20 and 60 map into `table[20]`. In general, three different ID *prefixes*—that is, the first two digits of an ID number—map into each array location 0 through 19, while only two different prefixes map into each array location 20 through 39. Since all ID numbers are equally likely—and thus all prefixes 00 through 99 are equally likely—a given ID number is 50 percent more likely to hash into one of the locations 0 through 19 than it is to hash into one of the locations 20 through 39. As a result, each array location 0 through 19 would contain, on average, 50 percent more items than each location 20 through 39.

  Thus, the hash function

A function that does not scatter random data evenly

  $h(x) =$ (first two digits of x) mod 40

  does not scatter random data evenly throughout the array `table[0..39]`. On the other hand, it can be shown that the hash function

A function that does scatter random data evenly

  $h(x) = x$ mod 101

  does, in fact, scatter random data evenly throughout the array `table[0..100]`.

- **How well does the hash function scatter nonrandom data?** Even if a hash function scatters random data evenly, it may have trouble with nonrandom data. In general, no matter what hash function you select, it is always possible that the data will have some unlucky pattern that will result in uneven scattering.

Although there is no way to guarantee that a hash function will scatter all data evenly, you can greatly increase the likelihood of this behavior.

As an example, consider the following scheme:

`table[0..99]` is the hash table, and
the hash function is $h(x) =$ first two digits of x

If every ID number is equally likely, h will scatter the search keys evenly throughout the array. But what if every ID number is not equally likely? For instance, a company might assign employee IDs according to department, as follows:

10xxxxx	Sales
20xxxxx	Customer Relations
. . .	
90xxxxx	Data Processing

Under this assignment, only 9 out of the 100 array locations would contain any items at all. Further, those locations corresponding to the largest departments (Sales, for example, which corresponds to `table[10]`) would contain more items than those locations corresponding to the smallest departments. This scheme certainly does not scatter the data evenly.

Much research has been done into the types of hash functions that you should use to guard against various types of patterns in the data. The results of this research are really in the province of more advanced courses, but two general principles can be noted here:

1. The calculation of the hash function should *involve the entire search key*. Thus, for example, computing a modulo of the entire ID number is much safer than using only its first two digits.
2. If a hash function uses modulo arithmetic, *the base should be prime;* that is, if h is of the form

$$h(x) = x \text{ mod } tableSize$$

then *tableSize* should be a prime number. This selection of *tableSize* is a safeguard against many subtle kinds of patterns in the data (for example, search keys whose digits are likely to be multiples of one another). Although each application can have its own particular kind of patterns and thus should be analyzed on an individual basis, choosing *tableSize* to be prime is an easy way to safeguard against some common types of patterns in the data.

General requirements of a hash function

Table Traversal: An Inefficient Operation under Hashing

For many applications, hashing provides the most efficient implementation of the ADT table. One important table operation—traversal in sorted order—performs poorly when hashing implements the table. As mentioned earlier, a good hash function scatters items as randomly as possible throughout the array, so that no ordering relationship exists between the search

Items hashed into `table[i]` and `table[i+1]` have no ordering relationship

keys that hash into *table[i]* and those that hash into *table[i + 1]*. As a consequence, if you must traverse the table in sorted order, you first would have to sort the items. If sorting were required frequently, hashing would be a far less attractive implementation than a search tree.

Traversing a table in sorted order is really just one example of a whole class of operations that hashing does not support well. Many similar operations that you often wish to perform on a table require that the items be ordered. For example, consider an operation that must find the table item with the smallest or largest value in its search key. If you use a search-tree implementation, these items are in the leftmost and right-most nodes of the tree, respectively. If you use a hashing implementation, however, you do not know where these items are—you would have to search the entire table. A similar type of operation is a **range query**, which requires that you retrieve all items whose search keys fall into a given range of values. For example, you might want to retrieve all items whose search keys are in the range 129 to 755. This task is relatively easy to perform by using a search tree (see Exercise 3), but if you use hashing, there is no efficient way to answer the range query.

Hashing versus balanced search trees

In general, if an application requires any of these ordered operations, you should probably use a search tree. Although the *tableRetrieve*, *tableInsert*, and *tableDelete* operations are somewhat more efficient when you use hashing to implement the table instead of a balanced search tree, the balanced search tree supports these operations so efficiently itself that, in most contexts, the difference in speed for these operations is negligible (whereas the advantage of the search tree over hashing for the ordered operations is significant).

In the context of external storage, however, the story is different. For data that is stored externally, the difference in speed between hashing's implementation of *tableRetrieve* and a search tree's implementation may well be significant, as you will see in Chapter 14. In an external setting, it is not uncommon to see a hashing implementation of the *tableRetrieve* operation and a search-tree implementation of the ordered operations used simultaneously.

DATA WITH MULTIPLE ORGANIZATIONS

Many applications require a data organization that simultaneously supports several different data-management tasks. One simple example involves a waiting list of customers, that is, a queue of customer records. In addition to requiring the standard queue operations *isEmpty*, *enqueue*, *dequeue*, and *peek*, suppose that the application frequently requires a listing of the customer records in the queue. This listing is more useful if the records appear sorted by customer name. You thus need a traversal operation that visits the customer records in sorted order.

This scenario presents an interesting problem. If you simply store the customer records in a queue, they will not, in general, be sorted by name. If, on the other hand, you just store the records in sorted order, you will be unable to process the customers on a first-come, first-served basis. Apparently, this problem requires you to organize the data in two different ways.

One solution is to maintain two independent data structures, one organized to support the sorted traversal and the other organized to support the queue operations. Figure 12-51 depicts reference-based implementations of a sorted linked list of customer records and a queue of the same records. The reference-based data structures are a good choice because they do not require an estimate of the maximum number of customer records that must be stored. Note that although figures throughout the text have shown the data within the nodes of the data structure, in reality it is the references to the objects that are actually stored in the data structure. As Figure 12-51 shows, the two data structures share one set of data items.

How well does this scheme support the required operations? The operations that only *retrieve* data are easy to perform and require no coordination between the two data structures. You can obtain a sorted list of customer records by traversing the sorted linked list, and you can perform the queue *peek* operation by inspecting the record at the front of the queue.

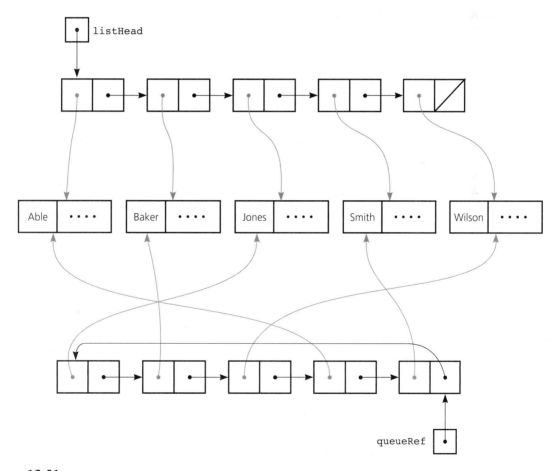

Figure 12-51

Two data structures that share the same data: (a) a sorted linked list;
(b) a reference-based queue

The insertion and deletion operations are, however, more difficult to perform because they must *modify* both data structures. That is, the insertion and deletion operations are done separately on the two data structures. The insertion operation has two steps:

1. Insert the new customer record at the back of the queue. This step requires only a few reference changes.

2. Insert the new customer record into its proper position in the sorted linked list. This step requires a traversal of the sorted linked list.

Similarly, the deletion operation has two steps:

1. Delete the customer at the front of the queue, but retain a copy of the name for the next step. This step requires only a few reference changes. Note that this deletion removes a node from the queue but does not deallocate the customer records as it is still referenced by the sorted list.

2. Search the sorted linked list for the name just removed from the queue, and delete from the list the customer record containing this name. This step requires a traversal of the sorted linked list.

Several independent data structures do not support all operations efficiently

Thus, although the scheme efficiently supports a traversal of the sorted list and the queue *peek* operation, insertion and deletion require a search of the sorted linked list (whereas in a queue alone *enqueue* and *dequeue* require only a small, constant number of steps). Can you improve on this scheme? One possibility is to store the customer records in a binary search tree rather than a sorted linked list. This approach would allow you to perform the second steps of the insertion and deletion operations much more efficiently. While the binary search tree strategy is certainly an improvement over the original scheme, the insertion and deletion operations would still require significantly more work than they would for a normal queue.

A different kind of scheme, one that supports the deletion operation almost as efficiently as if you were maintaining only a queue, is possible by allowing the data structures to communicate with each other. This concept is demonstrated here first with a sorted linked list and a queue, and then with more-complex structures, such as a binary search tree.

Interdependent data structures provide a better way to support a multiple organization of data

In the data structure shown in Figure 12-52, the sorted linked list contains references to customer records, and the queue contains references to the nodes containing the customer records. That is, each entry of the queue references the node in the sorted linked list for the customer at the given queue position. As you will soon see, this scheme significantly improves the efficiency of the *dequeue* operation.

The efficiency of a traversal of the sorted list and the queue's *peek* and *enqueue* operations does not differ significantly from that of the original scheme that Figure 12-51 depicts. You still traverse the sorted linked list as before. However, you perform *peek* and *enqueue* as follows:

peek()

Let nodeRef be the reference stored at the front of

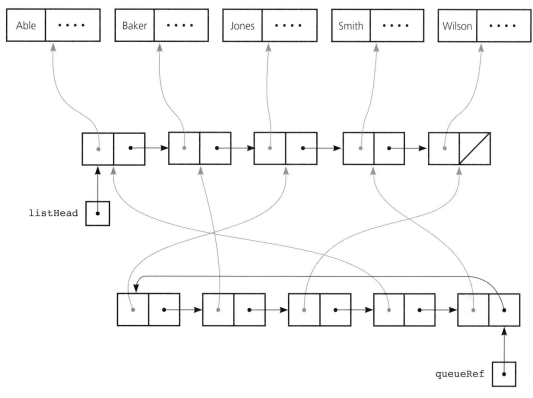

Figure 12-52

A queue referencing a sorted linked list

> the queue (nodeRef references the node, which is
> in the sorted linked list, that contains the
> record for the customer at the front of the
> queue)

  return item in the node that nodeRef references

enqueue(newItem)

  Find the proper position for newItem in the sorted
      linked list
  Insert a node that contains newItem into this
      position
  Insert a reference to the new node at the back of
      the queue

   The real benefit of the new scheme is in the implementation of the
dequeue operation:

dequeue()

  Delete the item at the front of the queue and
      retain its reference nodeRef (nodeRef

> references the node that contains the customer
>   record to be deleted)
>
> Delete from the sorted linked list the node
>   that nodeRef references

Because the front of the queue contains a reference to the node *N* that you want to delete from the sorted linked list, there is no need to search the linked list. You have a reference to the appropriate node, and all you need to do is delete it.

There is one big problem, however. Because you are able to go directly to node *N* without traversing the linked list from its beginning, you have no trailing reference to the node that precedes *N* on the list! Recall that you must have a trailing reference to delete *N*. As the scheme now stands, the only way to obtain the trailing reference is to traverse the linked list from its beginning, but this requirement negates the advantage gained by having the queue reference the linked list. However, as you saw in Chapter 4, you can solve this problem by replacing the *A doubly linked list is required* singly linked list in Figure 12-52 with a doubly linked list, as shown in Figure 12-53. (See Programming Problem 8.)

To summarize, you have seen a fairly good scheme for implementing the queue operations plus a sorted traversal. The only operation whose efficiency you might improve significantly is *enqueue*, since you still

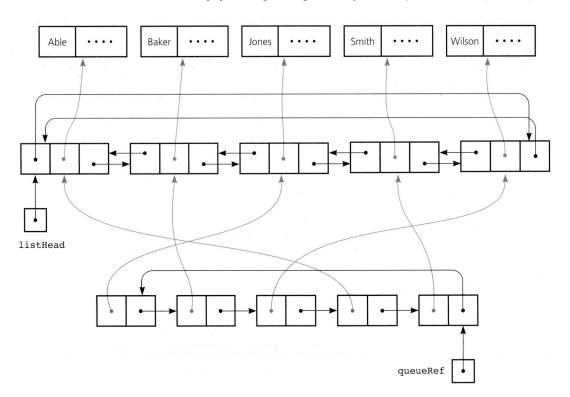

Figure 12-53

A queue referencing into a doubly linked list

must traverse the linked list to find the proper place to insert a new customer record.

The choice to store the customer records in a linear linked list was made to simplify the discussion. A more efficient scheme has the queue reference a binary search tree rather than a linked list. This data structure allows you to perform the *enqueue* operation in logarithmic time, assuming that the tree remains balanced. To support the *dequeue* operation efficiently, however, you need a doubly linked tree. That is, each node in the tree must reference its parent so that you can easily delete the node that the front of the queue references. Figure 12-54 illustrates this data structure; its implementation, which is somewhat difficult, is the subject of Programming Problem 9.

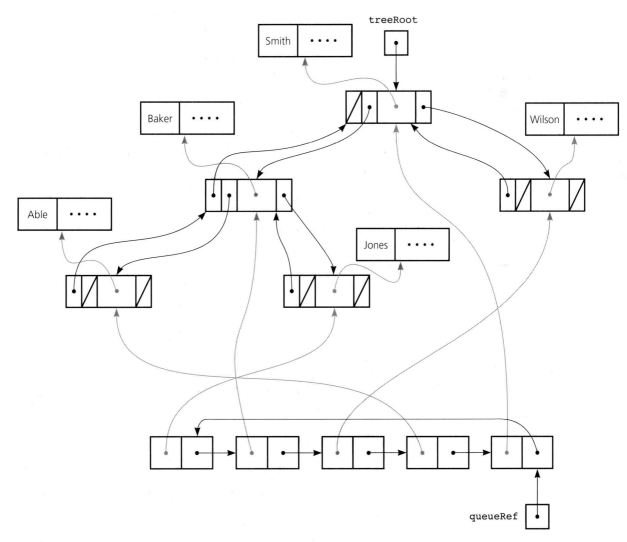

Figure 12-54

A queue referencing a doubly linked binary search tree

In general, you can impose several different organizations simultaneously on a set of data items. This concept is discussed further in Chapter 14 in the context of indexing external storage.

SUMMARY

1. A 2-3 tree and a 2-3-4 tree are variants of a binary search tree. The internal nodes of a 2-3 tree can have either two or three children. The internal nodes of a 2-3-4 tree can have either two, three, or four children. Allowing the number of children to vary permits the insertion and deletion algorithms to maintain easily the balance of the tree.

2. The insertion and deletion algorithms for a 2-3-4 tree require only a single pass from root to leaf and, therefore, are more efficient than the corresponding algorithms for a 2-3 tree.

3. A red-black tree is a binary tree representation of a 2-3-4 tree that requires less storage than a 2-3-4 tree. Insertions and deletions for a red-black tree are more efficient than the corresponding operations on a 2-3-4 tree.

4. An AVL tree is a binary search tree that is guaranteed to remain balanced. The insertion and deletion algorithms perform rotations in the event that the tree starts to stray from a balanced shape.

5. Hashing as a table implementation calculates where the data item should be rather than searching for it. Hashing allows for very efficient retrievals, insertions, and deletions.

6. The hash function should be extremely easy to compute—it should require only a few operations—and it should scatter the search keys evenly throughout the hash table.

7. A collision occurs when two different search keys hash into the same array location. Two ways to resolve collisions are through probing and chaining.

8. Hashing does not efficiently support operations that require the table items to be ordered—for example, traversing the table in sorted order.

9. When table operations such as traversal are not important to a particular application, if you know the maximum number of table items and if you have ample storage, hashing is a table implementation that is simpler and faster than balanced search tree implementations. Tree implementations, however, are dynamic and do not require you to estimate the maximum number of table items.

10. You can impose several independent organizations on a given set of data. For example, you can store records in a sorted doubly

linked list and impose a FIFO order by using a queue of references to the list.

CAUTIONS

1. Even though search trees that allow their nodes to have more than two children are shorter than binary search trees, they are not necessarily easier to search: More comparisons are necessary at each node to determine which subtree should be searched next.

2. A hashing scheme, in general, must provide a means of resolving collisions. Choose a hash function that keeps the number of collisions to a minimum. You should be careful to avoid a hash function that will map more items into one part of the hash table than into another.

3. To improve the performance of hashing, either change the hash function or increase the size of the hash table. Do not use complex collision-resolution schemes.

4. Hashing is not a good table implementation if you frequently require operations that depend on some order of the table's items. For example, if you frequently need to either traverse the table in sorted order or find the item with the largest search-key value, you probably should not use hashing.

SELF-TEST EXERCISES

1. What is the result of inserting 5, 40, 10, 20, 15, and 30—in the order given—into an initially empty 2-3 tree? Note that insertion of one item into an empty 2-3 tree will create a single node that contains the inserted item.

2. a. What is the result of deleting the 10 from the 2-3 tree that you created in Self-Test Exercise 1?
   b. What is the result of inserting 3 and 4 into the 2-3 tree that you created in Self-Test Exercise 1?

3. a. Repeat Self-Test Exercise 1 for a 2-3-4 tree.
   b. Insert 3 and 4 into the tree that you created in Part *a*.

4. What red-black tree represents the 2-3-4 tree in Figure 12-27a?

5. If your application of the ADT table involves only retrieval—such as the application in Scenario B of Chapter 11 that searched a thesaurus—what tree would provide for the most efficient table implementation: a balanced binary search tree, a 2-3 tree, a 2-3-4 tree, or a red-black tree?

6. Why does a node in a red-black tree require less memory than a node in a 2-3-4 tree?

7. Write the pseudocode for the *tableDelete* operation when linear probing is used to implement the hash table.

8. What is the probe sequence that double hashing uses when

   $h_1(key) = key$ mod 11, $h_2(key) = 7 - (key$ mod 7$)$, and $key = 19$

9. If $h(x) = x$ mod 7 and separate chaining resolves collisions, what does the hash table look like after the following insertions occur: 8, 10, 24, 15, 32, 17? Assume that each table item contains only a search key.

EXERCISES

1. Execute the following sequence of operations on an initially empty ADT table *t* that is implemented as

   a. A binary search tree   **d.** A red-black tree
   b. A 2-3 tree   **e.** An AVL tree
   c. A 2-3-4 tree

   and show the underlying tree after each operation:

   t.tableInsert(10)
   t.tableInsert(100)
   t.tableInsert(30)
   t.tableInsert(80)
   t.tableInsert(50)
   t.tableDelete(10)
   t.tableInsert(60)
   t.tableInsert(70)
   t.tableInsert(40)
   t.tableDelete(80)
   t.tableInsert(90)
   t.tableInsert(20)
   t.tableDelete(30)
   t.tableDelete(70)

2. What are the advantages of implementing the ADT table with a 2-3 tree instead of a binary search tree? Why do you not, in general, maintain a completely balanced binary search tree?

3. Write a pseudocode method that performs a range query for a 2-3 tree. That is, the method should visit all items that have a search key in a given range of values (such as all values between 100 and 1,000).

4. Assume that the tree in Figure 12-5b is a 2-3-4 tree, and insert 39, 38, 37, 36, 35, 34, 33, and 32 into it. What 2-3-4 tree results?

*5. Write pseudocode for the insertion, deletion, retrieval, and traversal operations for a 2-3-4 tree.

6. Figure 12-33 is a red-black tree that represents the 2-3-4 tree in Figure 12-20. Draw another red-black tree that also represents the same 2-3-4 tree.

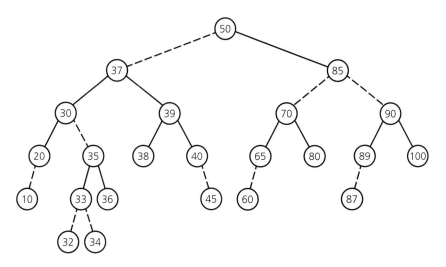

Figure 12-55

A red-black tree for Exercise 7

7. What 2-3-4 tree does the red-black tree in Figure 12-55 represent?

8. Write pseudocode for the insertion, deletion, retrieval, and traversal operations for a red-black tree.

9. Write a Java method that converts a 2-3-4 tree to a red-black tree.

10. Write pseudocode for the table operations `tableInsert`, `tableDelete`, and `tableRetrieve` when the implementation uses hashing and linear probing to resolve collisions.

11. Write pseudocode for the `tableDelete` operation when the implementation uses hashing and separate chaining to resolve collisions.

12. The success of a hash-table implementation of the ADT table is related to the choice of a good hash function. A good hash function is one that is easy to compute and that will evenly distribute the possible data. Comment on the appropriateness of the following hash functions. What patterns would hash to the same location?

   a. The hash table has size 2,048. The search keys are English words. The hash function is

   $h(key)$ = (sum of positions in alphabet of key's letters) mod 2048

   b. The hash table has size 2,048. The keys are strings that begin with a letter. The hash function is

   $h(key)$ = (position in alphabet of first letter of key) mod 2048

   Thus, "BUT" maps to 2. How appropriate is this hash function if the strings are random? What if the strings are English words?

   c. The hash table is 10,000 entries long. The search keys are integers in the range 0 through 9999. The hash function is

$h(key) = (key * random)$ truncated to an integer

where *random* represents a sophisticated random-number generator that returns a real value between 0 and 1.

   d. The hash table is 10,000 entries long (*HASH_TABLE_SIZE* is 10000). The search keys are integers in the range 0 through 9999. The hash function is given by the following Java method:

```java
public int hashIndex(int x) {
  for (int i = 1; i <= 1000000; ++i) {
    x = (x * x) % HASH_TABLE_SIZE;
  }  // end for
  return x;
}  // end hashIndex
```

PROGRAMMING PROBLEMS

1. Implement the ADT table by using a 2-3-4 tree.

2. Implement the ADT table by using a 2-3 tree. (This implementation is more difficult than the 2-3-4 implementation.)

3. Implement the ADT table by using a red-black tree.

4. Exercise 5 in Chapter 11 describes a compiler's symbol table, which keeps track of the program's identifiers. Write an implementation of a symbol table that uses hashing. Use the hash function $h(x) = x$ mod *tableSize* and the algorithm that involves Horner's rule, as described in the section "Hash Functions," to convert a variable into an integer *x*. Resolve collisions by using separate chaining. (See the code given on pages 590 and 591 of this chapter.)

    Since you add an item to the table only if it is not already present, does the time required for an insertion increase?

5. Repeat Programming Problem 4, but this time

   a. Use linear probing as the collision-resolution scheme.
   b. Use double hashing as the collision-resolution scheme.
   c. Use quadratic probing as the collision-resolution scheme.

6. Repeat Programming Problem 4, but allocate the hash table dynamically. If the hash table becomes more than half full, increase its size to the first prime number greater than 2 * *tableSize*.

7. Repeat Programming Problem 4, but experiment with variations of chaining. For example, you could use a binary search tree or a 2-3-4 tree instead of a linked list.

8. Implement the operations of the ADT queue as well as a sorted traversal operation for a queue that references a doubly linked list, as shown in Figure 12-53.

9. Implement the operations of the ADT queue as well as a sorted traversal operation for a queue that references a doubly linked binary search tree, as shown in Figure 12-54. You will need the insertion and deletion operations for a binary search tree that contains parent references, as discussed in Exercise 31 of Chapter 10.

10. Repeat Programming Problem 4 of Chapter 10, using the ADT table as the address book. Use a balanced search tree to implement the table.

11. Implement the symbol table described in Exercise 5 of Chapter 11, using hashing.

13

Graphs

PREVIEW Graphs are an important mathematical concept that have significant applications not only in computer science, but also in many other fields. You can view a graph as a mathematical construct, a data structure, or an abstract data type. This chapter provides an introduction to graphs that allows you to view a graph in any of these three ways. It also presents the major operations and applications of graphs that are relevant to the computer scientist.

TERMINOLOGY

You are undoubtedly familiar with graphs: Line graphs, bar graphs, and pie charts are in common use. The simple line graph in Figure 13-1 is an example of the type of graph that this chapter considers: a set of points that are joined by lines. Clearly, graphs provide a way to illustrate data. However, graphs also represent the relationships among data items, and it is this feature of graphs that is important here.

G = {V, E}; that is, a graph is a set of vertices and edges

A **graph** G consists of two sets: a set V of **vertices**, or **nodes**, and a set E of **edges** that connect the vertices. For example, the campus map in Figure 13-2a is a graph whose vertices represent buildings and whose edges represent the sidewalks between the buildings. This definition of a graph is more general than the definition of a line graph. In fact, a line graph, with its points and lines, is a special case of the general definition of a graph.

Adjacent vertices are joined by an edge

A **subgraph** consists of a subset of a graph's vertices and a subset of its edges. Figure 13-2b shows a subgraph of the graph in Figure 13-2a. Two vertices of a graph are **adjacent** if they are joined by an edge. In Figure 13-2b, the Library and the Student Union are adjacent. A **path** between two vertices is a sequence of edges that begins at one vertex and ends at another vertex. For example, there is a path in Figure 13-2a that begins at the Dormitory, leads first to the Library, then to the Student Union, and finally back to the Library. Although a path may pass through the same vertex more than once, as the path just described does, a **simple path** may not. The path Dormitory–Library–Student Union is a simple path. A **cycle** is a path that begins and ends at the same vertex; a **simple cycle** is a cycle that does not pass through other vertices more than once. The path Library–Student Union–Gymnasium–Dormitory–Library is a simple

A path between two vertices is a sequence of edges

A simple path passes through a vertex only once

A cycle is a path that begins and ends at the same vertex

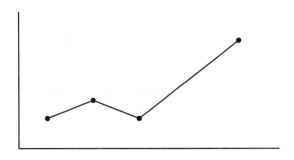

Figure 13-1
An ordinary line graph

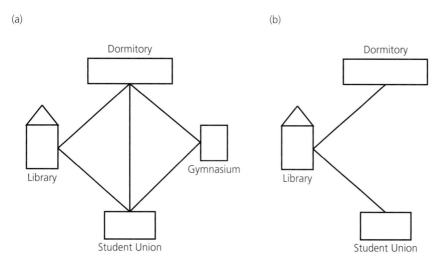

Figure 13-2

(a) A campus map as a graph; (b) a subgraph

cycle in the graph in Figure 13-2a. A graph is **connected** if each pair of distinct vertices has a path between them. That is, in a connected graph you can get from any vertex to any other vertex by following a path. Figure 13-3a shows a connected graph. Notice that a connected graph does not necessarily have an edge between every pair of vertices. Figure 13-3b shows a **disconnected** graph.

A connected graph has a path between each pair of distinct vertices

A graph is **complete** if each pair of distinct vertices has an edge between them. The graph in Figure 13-3c is complete. Clearly, a complete graph is also connected, but the converse is not true; notice that the graph in Figure 13-3a is connected but is not complete.

A complete graph has an edge between each pair of distinct vertices

A complete graph is connected

Since a graph has a *set* of edges, a graph cannot have duplicate edges between vertices. However, a **multigraph**, as illustrated in Figure 13-4a, does allow multiple edges. A graph's edges cannot begin and end at the

A multigraph has multiple edges and so is not a graph

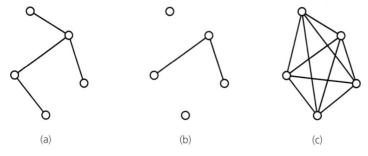

Figure 13-3

Graphs that are (a) connected; (b) disconnected; and (c) complete

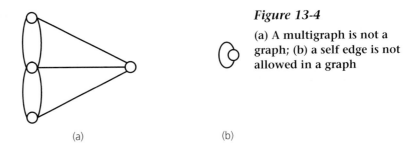

Figure 13-4

(a) A multigraph is not a graph; (b) a self edge is not allowed in a graph

(a)   (b)

same vertex. Figure 13-4b shows such an edge, which is called a **self edge**, or **loop.**

You can label the edges of a graph. When these labels represent numeric values, the graph is called a **weighted graph.** The graph in Figure 13-5a is a weighted graph whose edges are labeled with the distances between cities.

The edges of a weighted graph have numeric labels

All of the previous graphs are examples of **undirected** graphs because the edges do not indicate a direction. That is, you can travel in either direction along the edges between the vertices of an undirected graph. In contrast, each edge in a **directed graph,** or **digraph,** has a direction and is called a **directed edge.** Although each distinct pair of vertices in an undirected graph has only one edge between them, a directed graph can have two edges between a pair of vertices, one in each direction. For example, the airline

Each edge in a directed graph has a direction

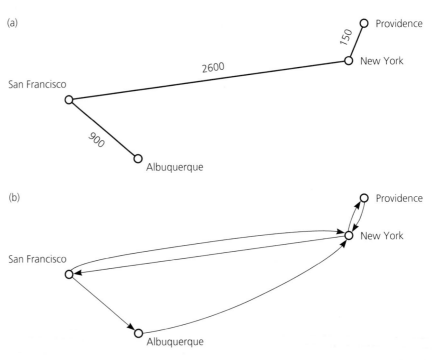

Figure 13-5

(a) A weighted graph; (b) a directed graph

flight map in Figure 13-5b is a directed graph. There are flights in both directions between Providence and New York, but, although there is a flight from San Francisco to Albuquerque, there is no flight from Albuquerque to San Francisco. You can convert an undirected graph to a directed graph by replacing each edge with two edges that point in opposite directions.

The definitions just given for undirected graphs apply also to directed graphs, with changes that account for direction. For example, a **directed path** is a sequence of directed edges between two vertices, such as the directed path in Figure 13-5b that begins in Providence, goes to New York, and ends in San Francisco. However, the definition of adjacent vertices is not quite as obvious for a digraph. If there is a directed edge from vertex x to vertex y, then y is **adjacent** to x. (Alternatively, y is a **successor** of x, and x is a **predecessor** of y.) It does not necessarily follow, however, that x is adjacent to y. Thus, in Figure 13-5b, Albuquerque is adjacent to San Francisco, but San Francisco is not adjacent to Albuquerque.

In a directed graph, vertex y is adjacent to vertex x if there is a directed edge from x to y

GRAPHS AS ADTs

You can treat graphs as abstract data types. Insertion and deletion operations are somewhat different for graphs than for other ADTs that you have studied in that they apply to either vertices or edges. You can define the ADT graph so that its vertices either do or do not contain values. A graph whose vertices do not contain values represents only the relationships among vertices. Such graphs are not unusual, because many problems have no need for vertex values. However, the following operations of the ADT graph do assume that the graph's vertices contain values.

KEY CONCEPTS

Operations of the ADT Graph

1. Create an empty graph.
2. Determine whether a graph is empty.
3. Determine the number of vertices in a graph.
4. Determine the number of edges in a graph.
5. Determine whether an edge exists between two given vertices. For weighted graphs, return weight value.
6. Insert a vertex in a graph whose vertices have distinct search keys that differ from the new vertex's search key.
7. Insert an edge between two given vertices in a graph.
8. Delete a particular vertex from a graph and any edges between the vertex and other vertices.
9. Delete the edge between two given vertices in a graph.
10. Retrieve from a graph the vertex that contains a given search key.

Several variations of this ADT are possible. For example, if the graph is directed, you can replace occurrences of "edges" in the previous operations with "directed edges." You can also add traversal operations to the ADT. This chapter will discuss graph-traversal algorithms shortly.

Implementing Graphs

Adjacency matrix

The two most common implementations of a graph are the adjacency matrix and the adjacency list. An **adjacency matrix** for a graph with n vertices numbered 0, 1, . . . , $n - 1$ is an n by n array $matrix$ such that $matrix[i][j]$ is 1 (or $true$) if there is an edge from vertex i to vertex j, and 0 (or $false$) otherwise. Figure 13-6 shows a directed graph and its adjacency matrix. Notice that the diagonal entries $matrix[i][i]$ are 0, although sometimes it can be useful to set these entries to 1. You should choose the value that is most convenient for your application.

When the graph is weighted, you can let $matrix[i][j]$ be the weight that labels the edge from vertex i to vertex j, instead of simply 1, and let $matrix[i][j]$ equal ∞ instead of 0 when there is no edge from vertex i to vertex j. For example, Figure 13-7 shows a weighted undirected graph and its adjacency matrix. Notice that the adjacency matrix for an undirected graph is symmetrical; that is, $matrix[i][j]$ equals $matrix[j][i]$.

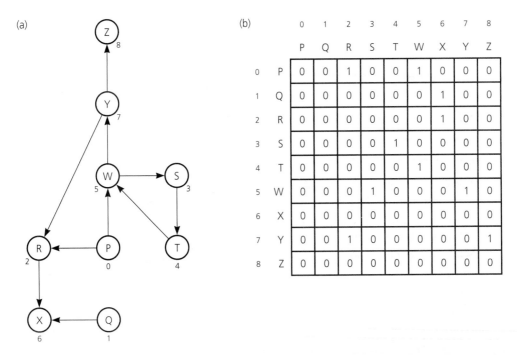

Figure 13-6

(a) A directed graph and (b) its adjacency matrix

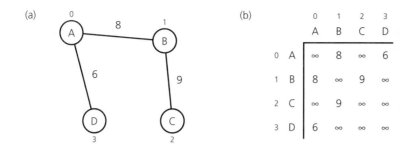

Figure 13-7

(a) A weighted undirected graph and (b) its adjacency matrix

Our definition of an adjacency matrix does not mention the value, if any, in a vertex. If you need to associate values with vertices, you can use a second array, *values,* to represent the *n* vertex values. The *values* array is one-dimensional, and *values[i]* is the value in vertex *i*.

Vertices can have values

An **adjacency list** for a graph with *n* vertices numbered $0, 1, \ldots, n - 1$ consists of *n* linked lists. The ith linked list has a node for vertex *j* if and only if the graph contains an edge from vertex *i* to vertex *j*. This node can contain the vertex *j*'s value, if any. If the vertex has no value, the node needs to contain some indication of the vertex's identity. Figure 13-8

Adjacency list

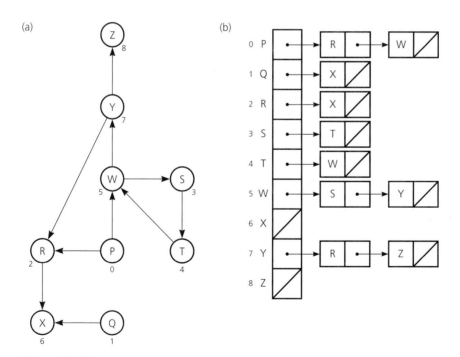

Figure 13-8

(a) A directed graph and (b) its adjacency list

shows a directed graph and its adjacency list. You can see, for example, that vertex 0 (*P*) has edges to vertex 2 (*R*) and vertex 5 (*W*). Thus, the first linked list in the adjacency list contains nodes for *R* and *W*.

Figure 13-9 shows an undirected graph and its adjacency list. The adjacency list for an undirected graph treats each edge as if it were two directed edges in opposite directions. Thus, the edge between *A* and *B* in Figure 13-9a appears as edges from *A* to *B* and from *B* to *A* in Figure 13-9b. The graph in part *a* happens to be weighted; you can include the edge weights in the nodes of the adjacency list, given in part *b*.

Which of these two implementations of a graph—the adjacency matrix or the adjacency list—is better? The answer depends on how your particular application uses the graph. For example, the two most commonly performed graph operations are

Two common operations on graphs

1. Determine whether there is an edge from vertex *i* to vertex *j*

2. Find all vertices adjacent to a given vertex *i*

An adjacency matrix supports operation 1 more efficiently

The adjacency matrix supports the first operation somewhat more efficiently than does the adjacency list. To determine whether there is an edge from *i* to *j* by using an adjacency matrix, you need only examine the value of `matrix[i][j]`. If you use an adjacency list, however, you must traverse the ith linked list to determine whether a vertex corresponding to vertex *j* is present.

An adjacency list supports operation 2 more efficiently

The second operation, on the other hand, is supported more efficiently by the adjacency list. To determine all vertices adjacent to a given vertex *i*, given the adjacency matrix, you must traverse the ith row of the array; however, given the adjacency list, you need only traverse the ith linked list. For a graph with *n* vertices, the ith row of the adjacency matrix always has *n* entries, whereas the ith linked list has only as many nodes as there are vertices adjacent to vertex *i*, a number typically far less than *n*.

Consider now the space requirements of the two implementations. On the surface it might appear that the matrix implementation requires less

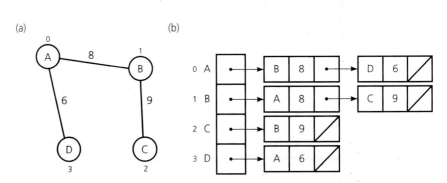

Figure 13-9

(a) A weighted undirected graph and (b) its adjacency list

memory than the linked list implementation, because each entry in the matrix is simply an integer, whereas each linked list node contains both a value to identify the vertex and a reference to the next node. The adjacency matrix, however, always has n^2 entries, whereas the number of nodes in an adjacency list equals the number of edges in a directed graph or twice that number for an undirected graph. Even though the adjacency list also has n head references, it often requires less storage than an adjacency matrix.

An adjacency list often requires less space than an adjacency matrix

Programming Problem 1 at the end of this chapter asks you to implement the ADT graph. When choosing a graph implementation for a particular application, you must consider such factors as what operations you will perform most frequently on the graph and the number of edges that the graph is likely to contain. For example, Chapter 6 presented the HPAir problem, which was to determine whether an airline provided a sequence of flights from an origin city to a destination city. The flight map for that problem, is in fact, a directed graph and appeared earlier in this chapter in Figure 13-8a. Figures 13-6b and 13-8b show, respectively, the adjacency matrix and adjacency list for this graph. Because the most frequent operation was to find all cities (vertices) adjacent to a given city (vertex), the adjacency list would be the more efficient implementation of the flight map. The adjacency list also requires less storage than the adjacency matrix, which you can demonstrate as an exercise.

GRAPH TRAVERSALS

The solution to the HPAir problem in Chapter 6 involved an exhaustive search of the graph in Figure 13-8a to determine a directed path from the origin vertex (city) to the destination vertex (city). The algorithm *searchS* started at a given vertex and traversed edges to other vertices until it either found the desired vertex or determined that no (directed) path existed between the two vertices.

What distinguishes *searchS* from a standard graph traversal is that *searchS* stops when it first encounters the designated destination vertex. A **graph-traversal algorithm**, on the other hand, will not stop until it has visited *all of the vertices that it can reach*. That is, a graph traversal that starts at vertex *v* will visit all vertices *w* for which there is a path between *v* and *w*. Unlike a tree traversal, which always visits *all* of the nodes in a tree, a graph traversal does not necessarily visit all of the vertices in the graph unless the graph is connected. In fact, a graph traversal visits every vertex in the graph if and only if the graph is connected, regardless of where the traversal starts. (See Exercise 15.) Thus, you can use a graph traversal to determine whether a graph is connected.

A graph traversal visits all of the vertices that it can reach

A graph traversal visits all vertices if and only if the graph is connected

If a graph is not connected, a graph traversal that begins at vertex *v* will visit only a subset of the graph's vertices. This subset is called the **connected component** containing *v*. You can determine all of the connected components of a graph by repeatedly starting a traversal at an unvisited vertex.

A connected component is the subset of vertices visited during a traversal that begins at a given vertex

If a graph contains a cycle, a graph-traversal algorithm can loop indefinitely. To prevent such a misfortune, the algorithm must mark each vertex during a visit and must never visit a vertex more than once.

Two basic graph-traversal algorithms, which apply to either directed or undirected graphs, are presented next. These algorithms visit the vertices in different orders, but if they both start at the same vertex, they will visit the same set of vertices. Figure 13-10 shows the traversal order for the two algorithms when they begin at vertex *v*.

Depth-First Search

DFS traversal goes as far as possible from a vertex before backing up

From a given vertex *v*, the **depth-first search (DFS)** strategy of graph traversal proceeds along a path from *v* as deeply into the graph as possible before backing up. That is, after visiting a vertex, a DFS visits, if possible, an unvisited adjacent vertex.

The DFS strategy has a simple recursive form:

Recursive DFS traversal algorithm

```
dfs(v)
// Traverses a graph beginning at vertex v by using a
// depth-first search: Recursive version.

    Mark v as visited
    for (each unvisited vertex u adjacent to v)
        dfs(u)
```

Choose an order in which to visit adjacent vertices

The depth-first search algorithm does not completely specify the order in which it should visit the vertices adjacent to *v*. One possibility is to visit the vertices adjacent to *v* in sorted (that is, alphabetic or numerically increasing) order. This possibility is natural either when an adja-

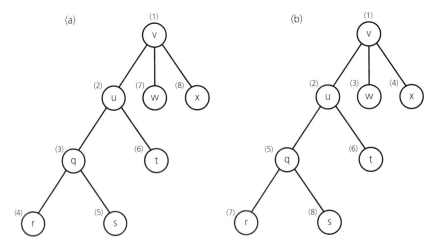

Figure 13-10

Visitation order for (a) a depth-first search; (b) a breadth-first search cency matrix represents the graph or when the nodes in each linked list of an adjacency list are linked in sorted order.

As Figure 13-10a illustrates, the DFS traversal algorithm marks and then visits each of the vertices v, u, q, and r. When the traversal reaches a vertex—such as r—that has no unvisited adjacent vertices, it backs up and visits, if possible, an unvisited adjacent vertex. Thus, the traversal backs up to q and then visits s. Continuing in this manner, the traversal visits vertices in the order given in the figure.

An iterative version of the DFS algorithm is also possible by using a stack:

```
dfs(v)
// Traverses a graph beginning at vertex v by using a
// depth-first search: Iterative version.

  s.createStack()

  // push v onto the stack and mark it
  s.push(v)
  Mark v as visited

  // loop invariant: there is a path from vertex v at the
  // bottom of the stack s to the vertex at the top of s
  while (!s.isEmpty()) {
    if (no unvisited vertices are adjacent to
        the vertex on the top of the stack)
      s.pop()  // backtrack
    }
    else {
      Select an unvisited vertex u adjacent to
          the vertex on the top of the stack
      s.push(u)
      Mark u as visited
    }  // end if
  }  // end while
```

An iterative DFS traversal algorithm uses a stack

The `dfs` algorithm is similar to the `searchS` algorithm of Chapter 6, but the `while` statement in `searchS` terminates when the top of the stack is `destination`.

For another example of a DFS traversal, consider the graph in Figure 13-11. Figure 13-12 shows the contents of the stack as the previous method `dfs` visits vertices in this graph, beginning at vertex a. Because the graph is connected, a DFS traversal will visit every vertex. In fact, the traversal visits the vertices in this order: a, b, c, d, g, e, f, h, i.

The vertex from which a depth-first traversal embarks is the vertex that it visited most recently. This *last visited, first explored* strategy is reflected both in the explicit stack of vertices that the iterative `dfs` uses and in the implicit stack of vertices that the recursive `dfs` generates with its recursive calls.

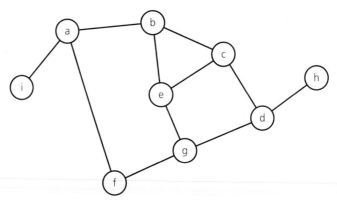

Figure 13-11

A connected graph with cycles

Node visited	Stack (bottom to top)
a	a
b	a b
c	a b c
d	a b c d
g	a b c d g
e	a b c d g e
(backtrack)	a b c d g
f	a b c d g f
(backtrack)	a b c d g
(backtrack)	a b c d
h	a b c d h
(backtrack)	a b c d
(backtrack)	a b c
(backtrack)	a b
(backtrack)	a
i	a i
(backtrack)	a
(backtrack)	(empty)

Figure 13-12

The results of a depth-first traversal, beginning at vertex *a*, of the graph in Figure 13-11

Breadth-First Search

BFS traversal visits all vertices adjacent to a vertex before going forward

After visiting a given vertex *v*, the **breadth-first search (BFS)** strategy of graph traversal visits every vertex adjacent to *v* that it can before visiting any other vertex. As Figure 13-10b illustrates, after marking and visiting *v*, the BFS traversal algorithm marks and then visits each of the vertices *u, w*, and *x*. Since no other vertices are adjacent to *v*, the BFS algorithm visits, if possible, all unvisited vertices adjacent to *u*. Thus, the traversal visits *q* and *t*. Continuing in this manner, the traversal visits vertices in the order given in the figure.

A BFS traversal will not embark from any of the vertices adjacent to *v* until it has visited all possible vertices adjacent to *v*. Whereas a DFS is a *last visited, first explored* strategy, a BFS is a *first visited, first explored* strategy. It is not surprising, then, that a breadth-first search uses a queue. An iterative version of this algorithm follows.

An iterative BFS traversal algorithm uses a queue

```
bfs(v)
// Traverses a graph beginning at vertex v by using a
// breadth-first search: Iterative version.

  q.createQueue()

  // add v to queue and mark it
  q.enqueue(v)
  Mark v as visited

while (!q.isEmpty()) {
    w = q.dequeue()

    // loop invariant: there is a path from vertex w to
    // every vertex in the queue q
    for (each unvisited vertex u adjacent to w) {
       Mark u as visited
       q.enqueue(u)
    } // end for
 } // end while
```

Figure 13-13 shows the contents of the queue as *bfs* visits vertices in the graph in Figure 13-11, beginning at vertex *a*. In general, a breadth-first search will visit the same vertices as a depth-first search, but in a different order. In this example, the BFS traversal visits all of the vertices in this order: *a, b, f, i, c, e, g, d, h*.

A recursive version of BFS traversal is not as simple as the recursive version of DFS traversal. Exercise 16 at the end of this chapter asks you to think about why this is so.

A recursive BFS traversal algorithm is possible, but not simple

APPLICATIONS OF GRAPHS

There are many useful applications of graphs. This section surveys some of these common applications.

Topological Sorting

A directed graph without cycles, such as the one in Figure 13-14, has a natural order. For example, vertex *a* precedes *b*, which precedes *c*. Such a

Figure 13-13

The results of a breadth-first traversal, beginning at vertex *a*, of the graph in Figure 13-11

Node visited	Queue (front to back)
a	a
	(empty)
b	b
f	b f
i	b f i
	f i
c	f i c
e	f i c e
	i c e
g	i c e g
	c e g
	e g
d	e g d
	g d
	d
	(empty)
h	h
	(empty)

Figure 13-14

A directed graph without cycles

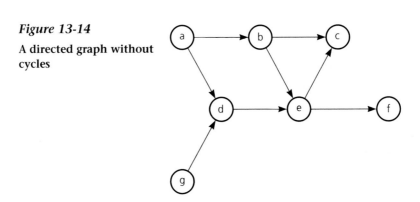

graph has significance in ordinary life. If the vertices represent academic courses, the graph represents the prerequisite structure for the courses. For example, course *a* is a prerequisite to course *b*, which is a prerequisite to both courses *c* and *e*. In what order should you take all seven courses so that you will satisfy all prerequisites? There is a linear order, called a **topological order**, of the vertices in a directed graph without cycles that answers this question. In a list of vertices in topological order, vertex *x* precedes vertex *y* if there is a directed edge from *x* to *y* in the graph.

The vertices in a given graph may have several topological orders. For example, two topological orders for the vertices in Figure 13-14 are

   a, g, d, b, e, c, f

and

   a, b, g, d, e, f, c

If you arrange the vertices of a directed graph linearly and in a topological order, the edges will all point in one direction. Figure 13-15 shows two versions of the graph in Figure 13-14 that correspond to the two topological orders just given.

Arranging the vertices into a topological order is called **topological sorting.** There are several simple algorithms for finding a topological order. First, you could find a vertex that has no successor. You remove from the graph the vertex and all edges that lead to it, and add it to the beginning of a list of vertices. You add each subsequent vertex that has no successor to the beginning of the list. When the graph is empty, the list of vertices will be in topological order. The following pseudocode describes this algorithm:

```
topSort1(theGraph)
// Arranges the vertices in graph theGraph into a
// topological order and places them in list aList
// Returns aList.

   n = number of vertices in theGraph
   for (step = 1 through n) {
      Select a vertex v that has no successors
      aList.add(1, v)
      Delete from theGraph vertex v and its edges
   }  // end for
   return aList
```

A simple topological sorting algorithm

When the traversal ends, the list *aList* of vertices will be in topological order. Figure 13-16 traces this algorithm for the graph in Figure 13-14. The resulting topological order is the one that Figure 13-15a represents.

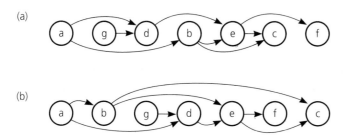

Figure 13-15

The graph in Figure 13-14 arranged according to the topological orders (a) *a, g, d, b, e, c, f* and (b) *a, b, g, d, e, f, c*

Graph `theGraph`   List `aList`   Graph `theGraph`   List `aList`

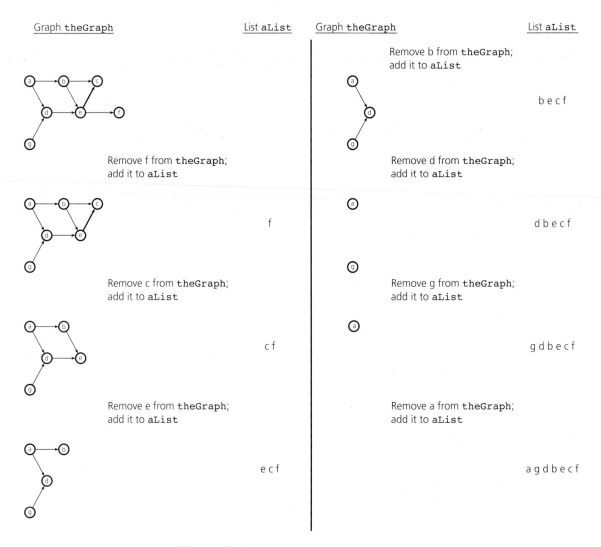

Remove b from `theGraph`;
add it to `aList`

                                                                                                                    b e c f

Remove f from `theGraph`;
add it to `aList`

                                                    f   Remove d from `theGraph`;
                                                                      add it to `aList`

                                                                                                                    d b e c f

Remove c from `theGraph`;
add it to `aList`

                                                                      Remove g from `theGraph`;
                                                                      add it to `aList`

                                                    c f

                                                                                                                    g d b e c f

Remove e from `theGraph`;
add it to `aList`

                                                                      Remove a from `theGraph`;
                                                                      add it to `aList`

                                                    e c f

                                                                                                                    a g d b e c f

Figure 13-16

A trace of *topSort1* for the graph in Figure 13-14

Another algorithm is a simple modification of the iterative depth-first search algorithm. First you push all vertices that have no predecessor onto a stack. Each time you pop a vertex from the stack, you add it to the beginning of a list of vertices. The pseudocode for this algorithm is

The DFS topological sorting algorithm

```
topSort2(theGraph, aList)
// Arranges the vertices in graph theGraph into a
// topological order and places them in list aList.
// Returns aList.

    s.createStack()
    for (all vertices v in the graph theGraph) {
        if (v has no predecessors) {
```

```
        s.push(v)
        Mark v as visited
    } // end if
} // end for

while (!s.isEmpty()) {
    if (all vertices adjacent to the vertex on
          the top of the stack have been visited) {
        v = s.pop()
        aList.add(1, v)
    }

    else {
        Select an unvisited vertex u adjacent to
          the vertex on the top of the stack
        s.push(u)
        Mark u as visited
    } // end if
} // end while
return aList
```

When the traversal ends, the list *aList* of vertices will be in topological order. Figure 13-17 traces this algorithm for the graph in Figure 13-14. The resulting topological order is the one that Figure 13-15b represents.

Action	Stack **s** (bottom to top)	List **aList** (beginning to end)
Push a	a	
Push g	a g	
Push d	a g d	
Push e	a g d e	
Push c	a g d e c	
Pop c, add c to **aList**	a g d e	c
Push f	a g d e f	c
Pop f, add f to **aList**	a g d e	f c
Pop e, add e to **aList**	a g d	e f c
Pop d, add d to **aList**	a g	d e f c
Pop g, add g to **aList**	a	g d e f c
Push b	a b	g d e f c
Pop b, add b to **aList**	a	b g d e f c
Pop a, add a to **aList**	(empty)	a b g d e f c

Figure 13-17

A trace of *topSort2* for the graph in Figure 13-14

Spanning Trees

A tree is an undirected connected graph without cycles

A tree is a special kind of undirected graph, one that is connected but has no cycles. Each vertex in the graph in Figure 13-3a could be the root of a different tree. Although all trees are graphs, not all graphs are trees. The nodes (vertices) of a tree have a hierarchal arrangement that is not required of all graphs.

A **spanning tree** of a connected undirected graph G is a subgraph of G that contains all of G's vertices and enough of its edges to form a tree. For example, Figure 13-18 shows a spanning tree for the graph in Figure 13-11. The dashed lines in Figure 13-18 indicate edges that were omitted from the graph to form the tree. There may be several spanning trees for a given graph.

If you have a connected undirected graph with cycles and you remove edges until there are no cycles, you will obtain a spanning tree for the graph. It is relatively simple to determine whether a graph contains a cycle. One way to make this determination is based on the following observations about undirected graphs:

Observations about undirected graphs that enable you to detect a cycle

1. **A connected undirected graph that has n vertices must have at least $n - 1$ edges.** To establish this fact, recall that a connected graph has a path between every pair of vertices. Suppose that, beginning with n vertices, you choose one vertex and draw an edge between it and any other vertex. Next, draw an edge between this second vertex and any other unattached vertex. If you continue this process until you run out of unattached vertices, you will get a connected graph like the ones in Figure 13-19. If the graph has n vertices, it has $n - 1$ edges. In addition, if you remove an edge, the graph will not be connected.

2. **A connected undirected graph that has n vertices and exactly $n - 1$ edges cannot contain a cycle.** To see this, begin with the previous observation: To be connected, a graph with n vertices must have at least $n - 1$ edges. If a connected graph did have a

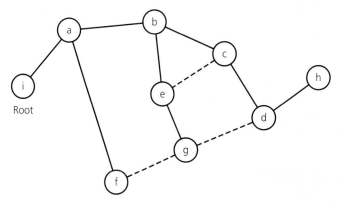

Figure 13-18

A spanning tree for the graph in Figure 13-11

Figure 13-19

Connected graphs that each have four vertices and three edges

cycle, you could remove any edge along that cycle and still have a connected graph. Thus, if a connected graph with n vertices and $n - 1$ edges did contain a cycle, removing an edge along the cycle would leave you with a connected graph with only $n - 2$ edges, which is impossible according to observation 1.

3. **A connected undirected graph that has n vertices and more than $n - 1$ edges must contain at least one cycle.** For example, if you add an edge to any of the graphs in Figure 13-19, you will create a cycle within the graph. This fact is harder to establish and is left as an exercise. (See Exercise 14 at the end of this chapter.)

Thus, you can determine whether a connected graph contains a cycle simply by counting its vertices and edges.

Simply count a graph's vertices and edges to determine whether it contains a cycle

It follows, then, that a tree, which is a connected undirected graph without cycles, must connect its n nodes with $n - 1$ edges. Thus, to obtain the spanning tree of a connected graph of n vertices, you must remove edges along cycles until $n - 1$ edges are left.

Two algorithms for determining a spanning tree of a graph are based on the previous traversal algorithms and are presented next. In general, these algorithms will produce different spanning trees for any particular graph.

The DFS spanning tree.   One way to determine a spanning tree for a connected undirected graph is to traverse the graph's vertices by using a depth-first search. As you traverse the graph, mark the edges that you follow. After the traversal is complete, the graph's vertices and marked edges form a spanning tree, which is called the **depth-first search (DFS) spanning tree.** (Alternatively, you can remove the unmarked edges from the graph to form the spanning tree.) Simple modifications to the previous iterative and recursive versions of *dfs* result in algorithms to create a DFS spanning tree. For example, the recursive algorithm follows:

```
dfsTree(v)
// Forms a spanning tree for a connected undirected graph
// beginning at vertex v by using depth-first search:
// Recursive version.

    Mark v as visited
```

DFS spanning tree algorithm

```
for (each unvisited vertex u adjacent to v) {
   Mark the edge from u to v
   dfsTree(u)
}  // end for
```

When you apply this algorithm to the graph in Figure 13-11, you get the DFS spanning tree rooted at vertex *a* shown in Figure 13-20. The figure indicates the order in which the algorithm visits vertices and marks edges. You should reproduce these results by tracing the algorithm.

The BFS spanning tree.   Another way to determine a spanning tree for a connected undirected graph is to traverse the graph's vertices by using a breadth-first search. As you traverse the graph, mark the edges that you follow. After the traversal is complete, the graph's vertices and marked edges form a spanning tree, which is called the **breadth-first search (BFS) spanning tree**. (Alternatively, you can remove the unmarked edges from the graph to form the spanning tree.) You can modify the previous iterative version of *bfs* by marking the edge between *w* and *u* before you add *u* to the queue. The result is the following iterative algorithm to create a BFS spanning tree.

```
bfsTree(v)
// Forms a spanning tree for a connected undirected graph
// beginning at vertex v by using breadth-first search:
// Iterative version.

   q.createQueue()

   // add v to queue and mark it
   q.enqueue(v)
   Mark v as visited
```

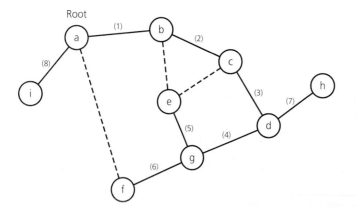

The DFS spanning tree algorithm visits vertices in this order: a, b, c, d, g, e, f, h, i. Numbers indicate the order in which the algorithm marks edges.

Figure 13-20

The DFS spanning tree rooted at vertex *a* for the graph in Figure 13-11

```
while (!q.isEmpty() {
  w = q.dequeue()

  // loop invariant: there is a path from vertex w to
  // every vertex in the queue q
  for (each unvisited vertex u adjacent to w) {
     Mark u as visited
     Mark edge between w and u
     q.enqueue(u)
  } // end for
} // end while
```

When you apply this algorithm to the graph in Figure 13-11, you get the BFS spanning tree rooted at vertex *a* shown in Figure 13-21. The figure indicates the order in which the algorithm visits vertices and marks edges. You should reproduce these results by tracing the algorithm.

Minimum Spanning Trees

Imagine that a developing country hires you to design its telephone system so that all the cities in the country can call one another. Obviously, one solution is to place telephone lines between every pair of cities. However, your engineering team has determined that due to the country's mountainous terrain, it is impossible to put lines between certain pairs of cities. The team's report contains the weighted undirected graph in Figure 13-22. The vertices in the graph represent *n* cities. An edge between two vertices indicates that it is feasible to place a telephone line between the cities that the vertices represent, and each edge's weight represents the installation cost of the telephone line. Note that if this graph is not connected, you will be unable to link all of the cities with a network of tele-

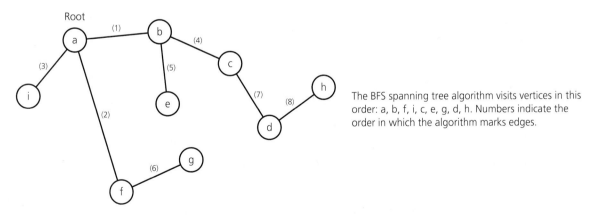

The BFS spanning tree algorithm visits vertices in this order: a, b, f, i, c, e, g, d, h. Numbers indicate the order in which the algorithm marks edges.

Figure 13-21

The BFS spanning tree rooted at vertex *a* for the graph in Figure 13-11

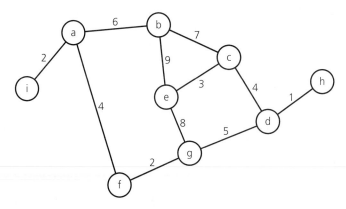

Figure 13-22

A weighted, connected, undirected graph

phone lines. The graph in Figure 13-22 is connected, however, making the problem feasible.

If you install a telephone line between each pair of cities that is connected by an edge in the graph, you will certainly solve the problem. However, this solution may be too costly. From observation 1 in the previous section, you know that $n - 1$ is the minimum number of edges necessary for a graph of n vertices to be connected. Thus, $n - 1$ is the minimum number of lines that can connect n cities.

If the cost of installing each line is the same, the problem is reduced to one of finding any spanning tree of the graph. The total installation cost—that is, the **cost of the spanning tree**—is the sum of the costs of the edges in the spanning tree. However, as the graph in Figure 13-22 shows, the cost of installing each line varies. Because there may be more than one spanning tree, and because the cost of different trees may vary, you need to solve the problem by selecting a spanning tree with the least cost; that is, you must select a spanning tree for which the sum of the edge weights (costs) is minimal. Such a tree is called the **minimum spanning tree**, and it need not be unique. Although there may be several minimum spanning trees for a particular graph, their costs are equal.

A minimum spanning tree of a connected undirected graph has a minimal edge-weight sum

One simple algorithm, called Prim's algorithm, finds a minimum spanning tree that begins at any vertex. Initially, the tree contains only the starting vertex. At each stage, the algorithm selects a least-cost edge from among those that begin with a vertex in the tree and end with a vertex not in the tree. The latter vertex and least-cost edge are then added to the tree. The following pseudocode describes this algorithm:

Minimum spanning tree algorithm

```
PrimsAlgorithm(v)
// Determines a minimum spanning tree for a weighted,
// connected, undirected graph whose weights are
// nonnegative, beginning with any vertex v.
   Mark vertex v as visited and include it in the minimum
      spanning tree
```

```
while (there are unvisited vertices) {
    Find the least-cost edge (v, u) from a visited
        vertex v to some unvisited vertex u
    Mark u as visited
    Add the vertex u and the edge (v, u) to the minimum
        spanning tree
}  // end while
```

Figure 13-23 traces *PrimsAlgorithm* for the graph in Figure 13-22, beginning at vertex *a*. Edges added to the tree appear as solid lines, while edges under consideration appear as dashed lines.

It is not obvious that the spanning tree that *PrimsAlgorithm* determines will be minimal. However, the proof that *PrimsAlgorithm* is correct is beyond the scope of this book.

Shortest Paths

Consider once again a map of airline routes. A weighted directed graph can represent this map: The vertices are cities, and the edges indicate existing flights between cities. The edge weights represent the mileage between cities (vertices); as such, the weights are not negative. For example, you could combine the two graphs in Figure 13-5 to get such a weighted directed graph.

Often for weighted directed graphs you need to know the shortest path between two particular vertices. The **shortest path** between two given vertices in a weighted graph is the path that has the smallest sum of its edge weights. Although we use the term "shortest," realize that the weights could be a measure other than distance, such as the cost of each flight in dollars or the duration of each flight in hours. The sum of the weights of the edges of a path is called the path's **length** or **weight** or **cost**.

The shortest path between two vertices in a weighted graph has the smallest edge-weight sum

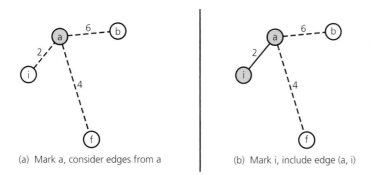

(a) Mark a, consider edges from a   (b) Mark i, include edge (a, i)

Figure 13-23

A trace of *PrimsAlgorithm* for the graph in Figure 13-22, beginning at vertex *a*

(continues)

Figure 13-23
(continued)

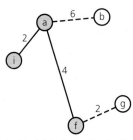

(c) Mark f, include edge (a, f)

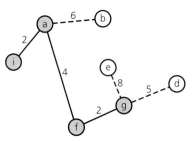

(d) Mark g, include edge (f, g)

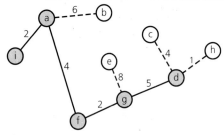

(e) Mark d, include edge (g, d)

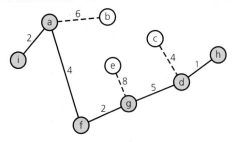

(f) Mark h, include edge (d, h)

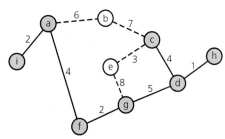

(g) Mark c, include edge (d, c)

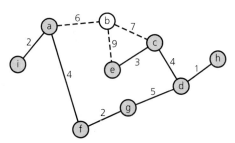

(h) Mark e, include edge (c, e)

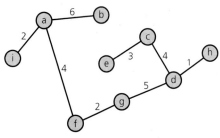

(i) Mark b, include edge (a, b)

For example, the shortest path from vertex 0 to vertex 1 in the graph in Figure 13-24a is not the edge between 0 and 1—its cost is 8—but rather the path from 0 to 4 to 2 to 1, with a cost of 7. For convenience, the starting vertex, or origin, is numbered 0 and the other vertices are numbered from 1 to *n* – 1. Notice the graph's adjacency matrix in Figure 13-24b.

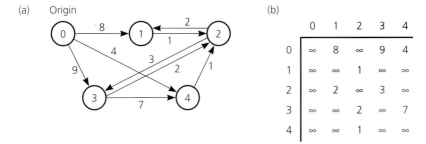

Figure 13-24

(a) A weighted directed graph and (b) its adjacency matrix

An algorithm attributed to E. Dijkstra actually determines the shortest paths between a given origin and *all* other vertices. The algorithm uses a set *vertexSet* of selected vertices and an array *weight*, where *weight*[*v*] is the weight of the shortest (cheapest) path from vertex 0 to vertex *v* that passes through vertices in *vertexSet*.

Finding the shortest paths between vertex 0 and all other vertices

If *v* is in *vertexSet*, the shortest path involves only vertices in *vertexSet*. However, if *v* is not in *vertexSet*, then *v* is the only vertex along the path that is not in *vertexSet*. That is, the path ends with an edge from a vertex in *vertexSet* to *v*.

Initially, *vertexSet* contains only vertex 0, and *weight* contains the weights of the single-edge paths from vertex 0 to all other vertices. That is, *weight*[*v*] equals *matrix*[0][*v*] for all *v*, where *matrix* is the adjacency matrix. Thus, initially *weight* is the first row of *matrix*.

After this initialization step, you find a vertex *v* that is not in *vertexSet* and that minimizes *weight*[*v*]. You add *v* to *vertexSet*. For all (unselected) vertices *u* not in *vertexSet*, you check the values *weight*[*u*] to ensure that they are indeed minimums. That is, can you reduce *weight*[*u*]—the weight of a path from vertex 0 to vertex *u*—by passing through the newly selected vertex *v*?

To make this determination, break the path from 0 to *u* into two pieces and find their weights as follows:

$weight[v]$ = weight of the shortest path from 0 to *v*
$matrix[v][u]$ = weight of the edge from *v* to *u*

Then compare *weight*[*u*] with *weight*[*v*] + *matrix*[*v*][*u*] and let

$weight[u]$ = the smaller of the values *weight*[*u*] and
$weight[v] + matrix[v][u]$

The pseudocode for **Dijkstra's shortest-path algorithm** is as follows:

```
shortestPath(theGraph, weight)
// Finds the minimum-cost paths between an origin vertex
// (vertex 0) and all other vertices in a weighted directed
// graph theGraph. The array weight contains theGraph's
// weights which are nonnegative.
```

The shortest-path algorithm

```
                        // Step 1: initialization
                        Create a set vertexSet that contains only vertex 0
                        n = number of vertices in theGraph
                        for (v = 0 through n - 1) {
                          weight[v] = matrix[0][v]
                        }  // end for
                        // Steps 2 through n
```

Loop invariant

```
                        // Invariant: For v not in vertexSet, weight[v] is the
                        // smallest weight of all paths from 0 to v that pass
                        // through only vertices in vertexSet before reaching v.
                        // For v in vertexSet, weight[v] is the smallest weight
                        // of all paths from 0 to v (including paths outside
                        // vertexSet), and the shortest path from 0 to v lies
                        // entirely in vertexSet.
                        for (step = 2 through n) {
                          Find the smallest weight[v] such that v is not in
                              vertexSet
                          Add v to vertexSet

                          // Check weight[u] for all u not in vertexSet
                          for (all vertices u not in vertexSet) {
                            if (weight[u] > weight[v] + matrix[v][u]) {
                              weight[u] = weight[v] + matrix[v][u]
                            }  // end if
                          }  // end for
                        }  // end for
```

The loop invariant states that once a vertex v is placed in *vertexSet, weight[v]*
is the weight of the absolutely shortest path from 0 to v and will not
change.

Figure 13-25 traces the algorithm for the graph in Figure 13-24a. The
algorithm takes the following steps:

A trace of the shortest-path
algorithm

Step 1. *vertexSet* initially contains vertex 0, and *weight* is initially the first
row of the graph's adjacency matrix, shown in Figure 13-24b.

Step	v	vertexSet	weight[0]	weight[1]	weight[2]	weight[3]	weight[4]
1	–	0	0	8	∞	9	4
2	4	0, 4	0	8	5	9	4
3	2	0, 4, 2	0	7	5	8	4
4	1	0, 4, 2, 1	0	7	5	8	4
5	3	0, 4, 2, 1, 3	0	7	5	8	4

Figure 13-25

**A trace of the shortest-path algorithm applied to the graph in
Figure 13-24a**

Step 2. *weight*[4] = 4 is the smallest value in *weight,* ignoring *weight*[0] because 0 is in *vertexSet.* Thus, *v* = 4, so add 4 to *vertexSet.* For vertices not in *vertexSet*—that is, for *u* = 1, 2, and 3—check whether it is shorter to go from 0 to 4 and then along an edge to *u* instead of directly from 0 to *u* along an edge. For vertices 1 and 3, it is not shorter to include vertex 4 in the path. However, for vertex 2 notice that *weight*[2] = ∞ > *weight*[4] + *matrix*[4][2] = 4 + 1 = 5. Therefore, replace *weight*[2] with 5. You can also verify this conclusion by examining the graph directly, as Figure 13-26a shows.

Step 3. *weight*[2] = 5 is the smallest value in *weight,* ignoring *weight*[0] and *weight*[4] because 0 and 4 are in *vertexSet.* Thus, *v* = 2, so add 2 to *vertexSet.* For vertices not in *vertexSet*—that is, for *u* = 1 and 3—check whether it is shorter to go from 0 to 2 and then along an edge to *u* instead of directly from 0 to *u* along an edge. (See parts *b* and *c* of Figure 13-26.)

Notice that

weight[1] = 8 > *weight*[2] + *matrix*[2][1] = 5 + 2 = 7. Therefore, replace *weight*[1] with 7.

weight[3] = 9 > *weight*[2] + *matrix*[2][3] = 5 + 3 = 8. Therefore, replace *weight*[3] with 8.

Step 4. *weight*[1] = 7 is the smallest value in *weight,* ignoring *weight*[0], *weight*[2], and *weight*[4] because 0, 2, and 4 are in *vertexSet.* Thus, *v* = 1, so add 1 to *vertexSet.* For vertex 3, which is the only vertex not in *vertexSet,* notice that *weight*[3] = 8 < *weight*[1] + *matrix*[1][3] = 7 + ∞, as Figure 13-26d shows. Therefore, leave *weight*[3] as it is.

Step 5. The only remaining vertex not in *vertexSet* is 3, so add it to *vertexSet* and stop.

The final values in *weight* are the weights of the shortest paths. These values appear in the last line of Figure 13-25. For example, the shortest path from vertex 0 to vertex 1 has a cost of *weight*[1], which is 7. This result agrees with our earlier observation about Figure 13-24. We saw then that the shortest path is from 0 to 4 to 2 to 1. Also, the shortest path from vertex 0 to vertex 2 has a cost of *weight*[2], which is 5. This path is from 0 to 4 to 2.

The weights in *weight* are the smallest possible, as long as the algorithm's loop invariant is true. The proof that the loop invariant is true is by induction on `step,` and is left as a difficult exercise. (See Exercise 17.)

Circuits

A **circuit** is simply another name for a type of cycle that is common in the statement of certain problems. Recall that a cycle in a graph is a path that begins and ends at the same vertex. Typical circuits either visit every vertex once or visit every edge once.

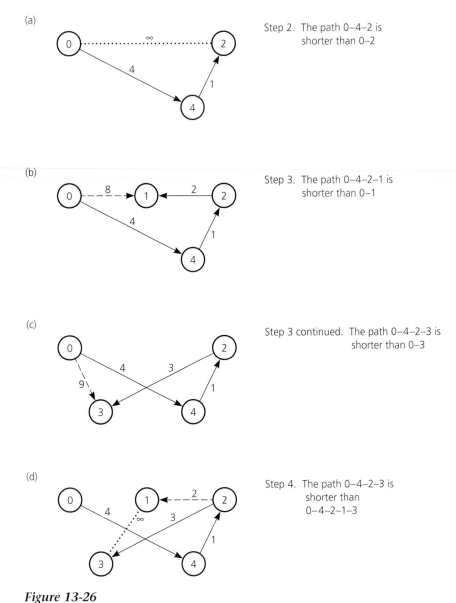

Step 2. The path 0–4–2 is
          shorter than 0–2

Step 3. The path 0–4–2–1 is
          shorter than 0–1

Step 3 continued. The path 0–4–2–3 is
          shorter than 0–3

Step 4. The path 0–4–2–3 is
          shorter than
          0–4–2–1–3

Figure 13-26

Checking *weight*[*u*] by examining the graph: (a) *weight*[2] in Step 2;
(b) *weight*[1] in Step 3; (c) *weight*[3] in Step 3; (d) *weight*[3] in Step 4

Probably the first application of graphs occurred in the early 1700s
when Euler (pronounced "oiler") proposed a bridge problem. Two islands
in a river are joined to each other and to the river banks by several bridges,
as Figure 13-27a illustrates. The bridges correspond to the edges in the
multigraph in Figure 13-27b, and the land masses correspond to the vertices. The problem asked whether you can begin at a vertex *v*, pass through

Figure 13-27

(a) Euler's bridge problem and (b) its multigraph representation

every edge exactly once, and terminate at *v*. Euler demonstrated that no solution exists for this particular configuration of edges and vertices.

For simplicity, we will consider an undirected graph rather than a multigraph. A path in an undirected graph that begins at a vertex *v*, passes through every edge in the graph exactly once, and terminates at *v* is called an **Euler circuit**. Euler showed that an Euler circuit exists if and only if each vertex touches an even number of edges. Intuitively, if you arrive at a vertex along one edge, you must be able to leave the vertex along another edge. If you cannot, you will not be able to reach all of the vertices.

An Euler circuit begins at a vertex v, passes through every edge exactly once, and termi-nates at v

Finding an Euler circuit is like drawing each of the diagrams in Figure 13-28 without lifting your pencil or redrawing a line. No solution is possible for Figure 13-28a, but you should be able to find one easily for Figure 13-28b. Figure 13-29 contains undirected graphs based on Figure 13-28. In Figure 13-29a, vertices *h* and *i* each touch an odd number of edges (three), so no Euler circuit is possible. On the other hand, each vertex in Figure 13-29b touches an even number of edges, making an Euler circuit feasible. Notice also that the graphs are connected. If a graph is not connected, a path through *all* of the vertices would not be possible.

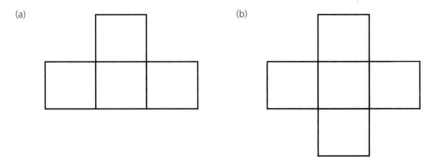

Figure 13-28

Pencil and paper drawings

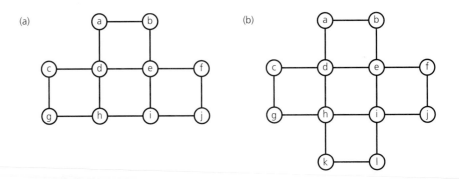

Figure 13-29

Connected undirected graphs based on the drawings in Figure 13-28

Let's find an Euler circuit for the graph in Figure 13-29b, starting arbitrarily at vertex *a*. The strategy uses a depth-first search that marks edges instead of vertices as they are traversed. Recall that a depth-first search traverses a path from *a* as deeply into the graph as possible. By marking edges instead of vertices, you will return to the starting vertex; that is, you will find a cycle. In this example, the cycle is *a, b, e, d, a*, if we visit the vertices in alphabetical order, as Figure 13-30a shows. Clearly this is not the desired circuit, because we have not visited every edge. We are not finished, however.

To continue, find the first vertex along the cycle *a, b, e, d, a* that touches an unvisited edge. In our example, the desired vertex is *e*. Apply our modified depth-first search, beginning with this vertex. The resulting cycle is *e, f, j, i, e*. Next you join this cycle with the one you found previously. That is, when you reach *e* in the first cycle, you travel along the second cycle before continuing in the first cycle. The resulting path is *a, b, e, f, j, i, e, d, a*, as Figure 13-30b shows.

The first vertex along our combined cycle that touches an unvisited edge is *i*. Beginning at *i*, our algorithm determines the cycle *i, l, k, h, i*. Joining this to our combined cycle results in the path *a, b, e, f, j, i, l, k, h, i, e, d, a*. (See Figure 13-30c.) The first vertex along this combined cycle that touches an unvisited edge is *h*. From *h*, we find the cycle *h, g, c, d, h*. Joining this to our combined cycle results in the Euler circuit *a, b, e, f, j, i, l, k, h, g, c, d, h, i, e, d, a*. (See Figure 13-30d.)

Some Difficult Problems

The next three applications of graphs have solutions that are beyond the scope of this book.

A Hamilton circuit begins at a vertex v, passes through every vertex exactly once, and terminates at v

The traveling salesperson problem. A **Hamilton circuit** is a path that begins at a vertex *v*, passes through every vertex in the graph exactly once, and terminates at *v*. Determining whether or not an arbitrary graph contains a Hamilton circuit can be difficult. A well-known variation of this

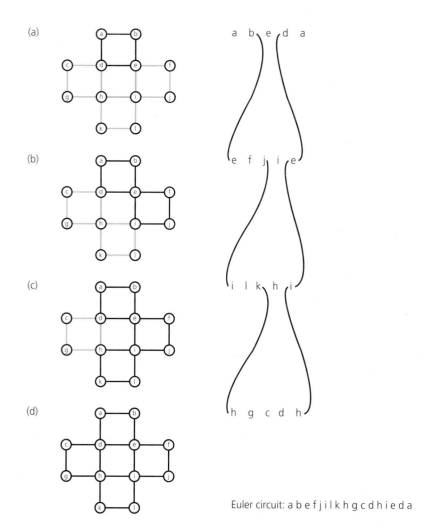

Euler circuit: a b e f j i l k h g c d h i e d a

Figure 13-30

The steps to determine an Euler circuit for the graph in Figure 13-29b

problem—the traveling salesperson problem—involves a weighted graph that represents a road map. Each edge has an associated cost, such as the mileage between cities or the time required to drive from one city to the next. The salesperson must begin at an origin city, visit every other city exactly once, and return to the origin city. However, the circuit traveled must be the least expensive.

Unfortunately for this traveler, solving the problem is no easy task. Although a solution does exist, it is quite slow, and no better solution is known.

The three utilities problem. Imagine three houses *A, B,* and *C* and three utilities *X, Y,* and *Z* (such as telephone, water, and electricity), as Figure 13-31 illustrates. If the houses and the utilities are vertices in a graph, is

Figure 13-31

The three utilities problem

it possible to connect each house to each utility with edges that do not cross one another? The answer to this question is no.

A planar graph can be drawn so that no two edges cross

A graph is **planar** if you can draw it in a plane in at least one way so that no two edges cross. The generalization of the three utilities problem determines whether a given graph is planar. Making this determination has many important applications. For example, a graph can represent an electronic circuit where the vertices represent components and the edges represent the connections between components. Is it possible to design the circuit so that the connections do not cross? The solutions to these problems are also beyond the scope of this book.

The four-color problem.   Given a planar graph, can you color the vertices so that no adjacent vertices have the same color, if you use at most four colors? For example, the graph in Figure 13-11 is planar because none of its edges cross. You can solve the coloring problem for this graph by using only three colors. Color vertices *a, c, g,* and *h* red; color vertices *b, d, f,* and *i* blue; and color vertex *e* green.

The answer to our question is yes, but it is difficult to prove. In fact, this problem was posed more than a century before it was solved in the 1970s with the use of a computer.

SUMMARY

1. The two most common implementations of a graph are the adjacency matrix and the adjacency list. Each has its relative advantages and disadvantages. The choice should depend on the needs of the given application.

2. Graph searching is an important application of stacks and queues. Depth-first search is a graph-traversal algorithm that uses

a stack to keep track of the sequence of visited vertices. It goes as deep into the graph as it can before backtracking. Breadth-first search uses a queue to keep track of the sequence of visited vertices. It visits all possible adjacent vertices before traversing further into the graph.

3. Topological sorting produces a linear order of the vertices in a directed graph without cycles. Vertex x precedes vertex y if there is a directed edge from x to y in the graph.

4. Trees are connected undirected graphs without cycles. A spanning tree of a connected undirected graph is a subgraph that contains all of the graph's vertices and enough of its edges to form a tree. DFS and BFS traversals produce DFS and BFS spanning trees.

5. A minimum spanning tree for a weighted undirected graph is a spanning tree whose edge-weight sum is minimal. Although a particular graph can have several minimum spanning trees, their edge-weight sums will be the same.

6. The shortest path between two vertices in a weighted directed graph is the path that has the smallest sum of its edge weights.

7. An Euler circuit in an undirected graph is a cycle that begins at vertex v, passes through every edge in the graph exactly once, and terminates at v.

8. A Hamilton circuit in an undirected graph is a cycle that begins at vertex v, passes through every vertex in the graph exactly once, and terminates at v.

CAUTIONS

1. When searching a graph, realize that the algorithm might take wrong turns. For example, you must eliminate the possibility of cycling within the algorithm; the algorithm must be able to backtrack when it hits a dead end.

SELF-TEST EXERCISES

1. Describe the graphs in Figure 13-32. For example, are they directed? Connected? Complete? Weighted?

2. Use the depth-first strategy and the breadth-first strategy to traverse the graph in Figure 13-32a, beginning with vertex 0. List the vertices in the order in which each traversal visits them.

3. Write the adjacency matrix for the graph in Figure 13-32a.

4. Add an edge to the directed graph in Figure 13-14 that runs from vertex d to vertex b. Write all possible topological orders for the vertices in this new graph.

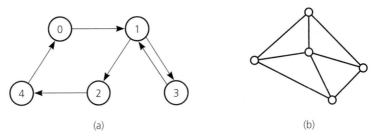

Figure 13-32

Graphs for Self-Test Exercises 1, 2, and 3

5. Is it possible for a connected undirected graph with 5 vertices and 4 edges to contain a simple cycle? Explain.

6. Draw the DFS spanning tree whose root is vertex 0 for the graph in Figure 13-33.

7. Draw the minimum spanning tree whose root is vertex 0 for the graph in Figure 13-33.

Figure 13-33

A graph for Self-Test Exercises 6 and 7 and Exercises 1 and 3

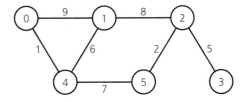

8. What are the shortest paths from vertex 0 to each vertex of the graph in Figure 13-24a? (Note the weights of these paths in Figure 13-25.)

EXERCISES

When given a choice of vertices to visit, the traversals in the following exercises should visit vertices in sorted order.

1. Give the adjacency matrix and adjacency list for
   a. The weighted graph in Figure 13-33
   b. The directed graph in Figure 13-34

2. Show that the adjacency list in Figure 13-8b requires less memory than the adjacency matrix in Figure 13-6b.

3. Use both the depth-first strategy and the breadth-first strategy to traverse the graph in Figure 13-33, beginning with vertex 0, and the graph in Figure 13-35, beginning with vertex *a*. List the vertices in the order in which each traversal visits them.

Figure 13-34

A graph for Exercise 1

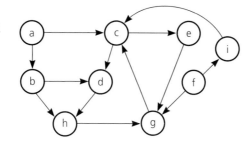

Figure 13-35

A graph for Exercises
3 and 8

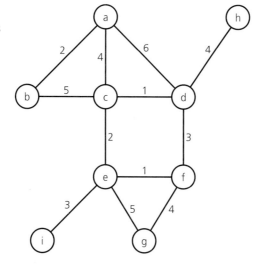

4. By modifying the DFS traversal algorithm, write pseudocode for an algorithm that determines whether a graph contains a cycle.

5. Trace the DFS topological sorting algorithm *topSort2*, and indicate the resulting topological order of the vertices for each graph in Figure 13-36.

6. Revise the topological sorting algorithm *topSort1* by removing predecessors instead of successors. Trace the new algorithm for each graph in Figure 13-36.

7. Trace the DFS and BFS spanning tree algorithms, beginning with vertex *a* of the graph in Figure 13-11, and show that the spanning trees are the trees in Figures 13-20 and 13-21, respectively.

8. Draw the DFS and BFS spanning trees rooted at *a* for the graph in Figure 13-35. Then draw the minimum spanning tree rooted at *a* for this graph.

9. Write pseudocode for an iterative algorithm that determines a DFS spanning tree for an undirected graph. Base your algorithm on the traversal algorithm *dfs*.

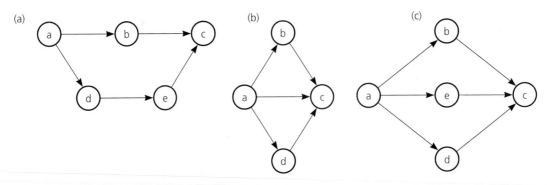

Figure 13-36

Graphs for Exercises 5 and 6

10. Draw the minimum spanning tree for the graph in Figure 13-22 when you start with

a. Vertex *g*   **b.** Vertex *c*

11. Trace the shortest-path algorithm for the graph in Figure 13-37, letting vertex 0 be the origin.

12. Implement the shortest-path algorithm in Java. How can you modify this algorithm so that any vertex can be the origin?

13. Determine an Euler circuit for the graph in Figure 13-38. Why is one possible?

14. Prove that a connected undirected graph with *n* vertices and more than *n* – 1 edges must contain at least one simple cycle. (See observation 3 in the section "Spanning Trees.")

Figure 13-37

A graph for Exercise 11

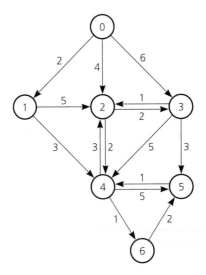

Figure 13-38

A graph for Exercise 13

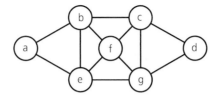

*15. Prove that a graph-traversal algorithm visits every vertex in the graph if and only if the graph is connected, regardless of where the traversal starts.

*16. Although the DFS traversal algorithm has a simple recursive form, a recursive BFS traversal algorithm is not straightforward.

  a. Explain why this fact is true.
  b. Write the pseudocode for a recursive version of the BFS traversal algorithm.

*17. Prove that the loop invariant of Dijkstra's shortest-path algorithm is true by using a proof by induction on *step*.

PROGRAMMING PROBLEMS

1. Implement the ADT graph as a Java class, first by using an adjacency matrix to represent the graph and then by using an adjacency list to represent the graph. Allow the graph to be either weighted or unweighted and either directed or undirected. Include DFS and BFS traversals.

2. Extend Programming Problem 1 by adding ADT operations such as *isConnected* and *hasCycle*. Also, include operations that perform a topological sort for a directed graph without cycles, determine the DFS and BFS spanning trees for a connected graph, and determine a minimum spanning tree for a connected undirected graph.

3. The HPAir problem was the subject of Programming Problems 9, 10, and 11 of Chapter 6. Revise these problems by implementing the ADT flight map as a derived class of the graph class that you wrote for Programming Problem 1.

14

External Methods

A Look at External Storage
Sorting Data in an External File
External Tables

Summary

Cautions

Self-Test Exercises

Exercises

Programming Problems

PREVIEW All of the previous table implementations assume that the data items reside in the computer's internal memory. Many real-world applications, however, require a table so large that it greatly exceeds the amount of available internal memory. In such situations, you must store the table on an external storage device such as a disk and perform table operations there.

This chapter considers the problem of data management in an external environment by using a random access file as a model of external storage. In particular, this chapter discusses how to sort the data in an external file by modifying the mergesort algorithm and how to search an external file by using generalizations of the hashing and search-tree schemes developed previously.

A LOOK AT EXTERNAL STORAGE

You use external storage when your program reads data from and writes data to a file. Also, when you use a word processing program, for example, and choose Save, the program saves your current document in a file. This action enables you to exit the program and then use it later to retrieve your document for revision. This is one of the advantages of external storage: It exists beyond the execution period of a program. In this sense, it is "permanent" instead of volatile like internal memory.

External storage exists after program execution

Another advantage of external storage is that, in general, there is far more of it than internal memory. If you have a table of one million data items, each of which is a record of moderate size, you will probably not be able to store the entire table in internal memory at one time. On the other hand, this much data can easily reside on an external disk. As a consequence, when dealing with tables of this magnitude, you cannot simply read the entire table into memory when you want to operate on it and then write it back onto the disk when you are finished. Instead, you must devise ways to operate on data—for example, sort it and search it—while it resides externally.

Generally, there is more external storage than internal memory

In general, you can create files for either sequential access or random access. To access the data stored at a given position in a **sequential access file**, you must advance the file window beyond all the intervening data. In this sense, a sequential access file resembles a linked list. To access a particular node in the list, you must traverse the list from its beginning until you reach the desired node. In contrast, a **random access file** allows you to access the data at a given position directly. A random access file resembles an array in that you can access the element at $data[i]$ without first accessing the elements before $data[i]$.

Random access files are essential for external tables

Without random access files, it would be impossible to support the table operations efficiently in an external environment. Many programming languages, including Java, support both sequential access and random access of files. However, to permit a language-independent discussion, we will construct a model of random access files that illustrates how a programming language that does not support such files might implement them. This model will be a simplification of reality but will include the features necessary for this discussion.

Imagine that a computer's memory is divided into two parts: internal memory and external memory, as Figure 14-1 illustrates. Assume that an executing program, along with its nonfile data, resides in the computer's internal memory; the permanent files of a computer system reside in the external memory. Further assume that the external storage devices have the characteristics of a disk (although some systems use other devices).

A file consists of **data records.** A data record can be anything from a simple value, such as an integer, to an aggregate structure, such as an employee record. For simplicity, assume that the data records in any one file are all of the same type.

The records of a file are organized into one or more **blocks,** as Figure 14-2 shows. The size of a block—that is, the number of bits of data it can contain—is determined by both the hardware configuration and the system software of the computer. In general, an individual program has no control over this size. Therefore, the number of records in a block is a function of the size of the records in the file. For example, a file of integer records will have more records per block than a file of employee records.

Much as you number the elements of an array, you can number the blocks of a file in a linear sequence. With a random access file, a program can read a given block from the file by specifying its block number, and similarly, it can write data out to a particular block. In this regard a random access file resembles an array of arrays, with each block of the file analogous to a single array entry, which is itself an array that contains several records.

In this random access model, *all input and output is at the block level rather than at the record level.* That is, you can read and write a block of records, but you cannot read or write an individual record. Reading or writing a block is called a **block access.**

The algorithms in this chapter assume commands for reading and writing blocks. The statement

```
buf.readBlock(dataFile, i)
```

will read the *i*th block of the file `dataFile` and place it in an object `buf`. This object must accommodate the many records that each block of the

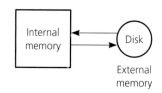

Figure 14-1

Internal and external memory

A file contains records that are organized into blocks

Random access input and output involves blocks instead of records

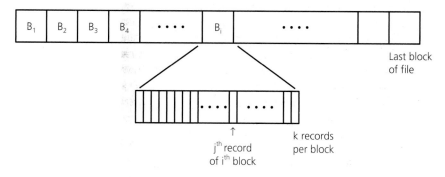

Figure 14-2

A file partitioned into blocks of records

A buffer stores data temporarily

file `dataFile` contains. For example, if each block contains 100 employee records, *buf* must store at least 100 employee records. The object *buf* is called a **buffer**, which is a location that temporarily stores data as it makes its way from one process or location to another.

Once the system has read a block into *buf,* the program can process—for example, inspect or modify—the records in the block. Also, because the records in the object *buf* are only copies of the records in the file `dataFile,` if a program does modify the records in *buf,* it must write *buf* back out to `dataFile,` so that the file also reflects the modifications. We assume that the statement

```
buf.writeBlock(dataFile, i)
```

will write the contents of *buf* to the *i*th block of the file `dataFile`. If `data-File` contains *n* blocks, the statement

```
buf.writeBlock(dataFile, n+1)
```

will append a new block to `dataFile`, and thus the file can grow dynamically, just as a Java file can.

Again, realize that these input and output commands allow you to read and write only entire blocks. As a consequence, even if you need to operate on only a single record of the file, you must access an entire block. For example, suppose that you want to give employee Smith a $1,000 raise. If Smith's record is in block *i* (how to determine the correct block is discussed later in the chapter), you would perform the following steps:

Updating a portion of a record within a block

```
// read block i from file dataFile into buffer buf
buf.readBlock(dataFile, i)

Find the entry buf.getRecord(j) that contains the
    record whose search key is "Smith"

// increase the salary portion of Smith's record
((buf.getRecord(j)).setSalary((buf.getRecord(j)).salary()
            + 1000)

// write changed block back to file dataFile
buf.writeBlock(dataFile, i)
```

Reduce the number of block accesses

The time required to read or write a block of data is typically much longer than the time required to operate on the block's data once it is in the computer's internal memory.[1] For example, you typically can inspect every record in the buffer *buf* in less time than that required to read a block into the buffer. As a consequence, you should reduce the number of required block accesses. In the previous pseudocode, for instance, you should process as many records in *buf* as possible before writing it to the

---

[1]Data enters or leaves a buffer at a rate that differs from the record-processing rate. (Hence, a buffer between two processes compensates for the difference in the rates at which they operate on data.)

file. You should pay little attention to the time required to operate on a block of data once it has been read into internal memory.

Interestingly, several programming languages, including Java, have commands to make it *appear* that you can access records one at a time. In general, however, the system actually performs input and output at the block level and perhaps hides this fact from the program. For example, if a programming language includes the statement

```
rec.readRecord(dataFile, i)
// Reads the i^th record of file dataFile into rec.
```

the system probably accesses the entire block that contains the ith record. Our model of input and output therefore approximates reality reasonably well.

In most external data-management applications, the time required for block accesses typically dominates all other factors. The rest of the chapter discusses how to sort and search externally stored data. The goal will be to reduce the number of required block accesses.

Block access time is the dominant factor when considering an algorithm's efficiency

SORTING DATA IN AN EXTERNAL FILE

This section considers the following problem of sorting data that resides in an external file:

An external file contains 1,600 employee records. You want to sort these records by social security number. Each block contains 100 records, and thus the file contains 16 blocks B_1, B_2, and so on to B_{16}. Assume that the program can access only enough internal memory to manipulate about 300 records (three blocks' worth) at one time.

A sorting problem

Sorting the file might not sound like a difficult task, because you have already seen several sorting algorithms earlier in this book. There is, however, a fundamental difference here in that the file is far too large to fit into internal memory all at once. This restriction presents something of a problem because the sorting algorithms presented earlier assume that all the data to be sorted is available at one time in internal memory (for example, that it is all in an array). Fortunately, however, we can remove this assumption for a modified version of mergesort.

The basis of the mergesort algorithm is that you can easily merge two sorted segments—such as arrays—of data records into a third sorted segment that is the combination of the two. For example, if S_1 and S_2 are sorted segments of records, the first step of the merge is to compare the first record of each segment and select the record with the smaller search key. If the record from S_1 is selected, the next step is to compare the second record of S_1 to the first record of S_2. This process is continued until all of the records have been considered. The key observation is that at any step, the merge never needs to look beyond the *leading edge* of either segment.

This observation makes a mergesort appropriate for the problem of sorting external files, if you modify the algorithm appropriately. Suppose that the 1,600 records to be sorted are in the file F and that you are not permitted to alter this file. You have two work files, F_1 and F_2. One of the work files will contain the sorted records when the algorithm terminates. The algorithm has two phases: Phase 1 sorts each block of records, and Phase 2 performs a series of merges.

External mergesort

Phase 1. Read a block from F into internal memory, sort its records by using an internal sort, and write the sorted block out to F_1 before you read the next block from F. After you process all 16 blocks of F, F_1 contains 16 **sorted runs** R_1, R_2, and so on to R_{16}; that is, F_1 contains 16 blocks of records, with the records within each block sorted among themselves, as Figure 14-3a illustrates.

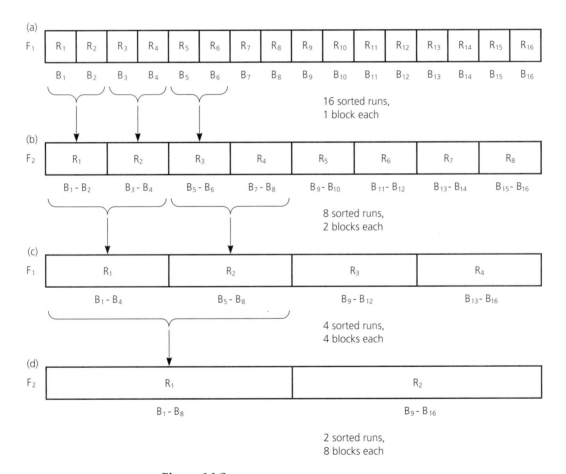

Figure 14-3

(a) 16 sorted runs, 1 block each, in file F_1; (b) 8 sorted runs, 2 blocks each, in file F_2; (c) 4 sorted runs, 4 blocks each, in file F_1; (d) 2 sorted runs, 8 blocks each, in file F_2

Phase 2. Phase 2 is a sequence of merge steps. Each merge step merges pairs of sorted runs to form larger sorted runs. Each merge step doubles the number of blocks in each sorted run and thus halves the total number of sorted runs. For example, as Figure 14-3b shows, the first merge step merges eight pairs of sorted runs from F_1 (R_1 with R_2, R_3 with R_4, . . . , R_{15} with R_{16}) to form eight sorted runs, each two blocks long, which are written to F_2. The next merge step merges four pairs of sorted runs from F_2 (R_1 with R_2, R_3 with R_4, . . . , R_7 with R_8) to form four sorted runs, each four blocks long, which are written back to F_1, as Figure 14-3c illustrates. The next step merges the two pairs of sorted runs from F_1 to form two sorted runs, which are written to F_2. (See Figure 14-3d.) The final step merges the two sorted runs into one, which is written to F_1. At this point, F_1 will contain all of the records of the original file in sorted order.

Given this overall strategy, how can you merge the sorted runs at each step of Phase 2? The statement of the problem provides only sufficient internal memory to manipulate at most 300 records at once. However, in the later steps of Phase 2, runs contain more than 300 records each, so you must merge the runs a piece at a time. To accomplish this merge, you must divide the program's internal memory into three buffers, *in1, in2,* and *out,* each capable of holding 100 records (the block size). You read block-sized pieces of the runs into the two *in* buffers and merge them into the *out* buffer. Whenever an *in* buffer is exhausted—that is, when all of its elements have been copied to *out*—you read the next piece of the run into the *in* buffer; whenever the *out* buffer becomes full, you write this completed piece of the new sorted run to one of the files.

Merging sorted runs in Phase 2

Consider how you can perform the first merge step. You start this step with the pair of runs R_1 and R_2, which are in the first and second blocks, respectively, of the file F_1. (See Figure 14-3a.) Because at this first merge step each run contains only one block, an entire run can fit into one of the *in* buffers. You can thus read R_1 and R_2 into the buffers *in1* and *in2,* and then merge *in1* and *in2* into *out.* However, although the result of merging *in1* and *in2* is a sorted run two blocks long (200 records), *out* can hold only one block (100 records). Thus, when *out* becomes full in the course of the merge, you write its contents to the first block of F_2, as Figure 14-4a illustrates. The merging of *in1* and *in2* into *out* then resumes. The buffer *out* will become full for a second time only after all of the records in *in1* and *in2* are exhausted. At that time, write the contents of *out* to the second block of F_2. You merge the remaining seven pairs from F in the same manner and append the resulting runs to F_2.

This first merge step is conceptually a bit easier than the others because the initial runs are only one block in size, and thus each can fit entirely into one of the *in* buffers. What do you do in the later steps when the runs to be merged are larger than a single block? Consider, for example, the merge step in which you must merge runs of four blocks each to form runs of eight blocks each. (See Figure 14-3c.) The first pair of these runs to be merged is in blocks 1 through 4 and 5 through 8 of F_1.

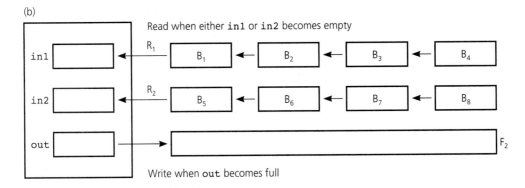

Figure 14-4

(a) Merging single blocks; (b) merging long runs

The algorithm will read the first block of R_1—which is the first block B_1 of the file—into *in1*, and it will read the first block of R_2—which is B_5— into *in2*, as Figure 14-4b illustrates. Then, as it did earlier, the algorithm merges *in1* and *in2* into *out*. The complication here is that as soon as you finish moving all of the records from either *in1* or *in2*, you must read the next block from the corresponding run. For example, if you finish *in2* first, you must read the next block of R_2—which is B_6—into *in2* before the merge can continue. The algorithm thus must detect when the *in* buffers become exhausted as well as when the *out* buffer becomes full.

A high-level description of the algorithm for merging arbitrary-sized sorted runs R_i and R_j from F_1 into F_2 is as follows:

Pseudocode to merge
sorted runs

```
Read the first block of Rᵢ into in1
Read the first block of Rⱼ into in2

while (either in1 or in2 is not exhausted) {
  Select the smaller "leading" record of in1 and in2
              and place it into the next position of out (if
              one of the buffers is exhausted, select the
              leading record from the other)
```

```
    if (out is full) {
      Write its contents to the next block of F₂
    } // end if
    if (in1 is exhausted and blocks remain in Rᵢ) {
      Read the next block into in1
    } // end if
    if (in2 is exhausted and blocks remain in Rⱼ) {
      Read the next block into in2
    } // end if
  } // end while
```

A pseudocode version of the external sorting algorithm follows. Notice that it uses *readBlock* and *writeBlock,* as introduced in the previous section, and assumes a method *copyFile* that copies a file. To avoid further complications, the solution assumes that the number of blocks in the file is a power of 2. This assumption allows the algorithm always to pair off the sorted runs at each step of the merge phase, avoiding special end-of-file testing that would obscure the algorithm. Also note that the algorithm uses two temporary files and copies the final sorted temporary file to the designated output.

```
externalMergesort(unsortedFileName, sortedFileName)
// Sorts a file by using an external mergesort.
// Precondition: unsortedFileName is the name of an external
// file to be sorted. sortedFileName is the name that the
// method will give to the resulting sorted file.
// Postcondition: The new file named sortedFileName is
// sorted. The original file is unchanged. Both files are
// closed.
// Calls: blockSort, mergeFile, and copyFile.
// Simplifying assumption: The number of blocks in the
// unsorted file is an exact power of 2.

  Associate unsortedFileName with the file variable inFile
      and sortedFileName with the file variable outFile

  // Phase 1: sort file block by block and count the blocks
  blockSort(inFile, tempFile1, numberOfBlocks)

  // Phase 2: merge runs of size 1, 2, 4, 8,...,
  // numberOfBlocks/2 (uses two temporary files and a toggle
  // that keeps track of the files for each merge step)
  toggle = 1

  for (size = 1 through numberOfBlocks/2 with
                                      increments of size) {
    if (toggle == 1) {
      mergeFile(tempFile1, tempFile2, size, numberOfBlocks)
    }
```

A pseudocode mergesort method

```
  else {
    mergeFile(tempFile2, tempFile1, size, numberOfBlocks)
  }  // end if
  toggle = -toggle
}  // end for


// copy the current temporary file to outFile
if (toggle == 1) {
  copyFile(tempFile1, outFile)
}
else {
  copyFile(tempFile2, outFile)
}  // end if
```

The method *externalMergesort* calls *blockSort* and *mergeFile,* which calls *mergeRuns.* The pseudocode for these methods follows.

```
blockSort(inFile, outFile, numberOfBlocks)
// Sorts each block of records in a file.
// Precondition: The file variable inFile is associated
// with the file to be sorted.
// Postcondition: The file associated with the file variable
// outFile contains the blocks of inFile. Each block is
// sorted; numberOfBlocks is the number of blocks processed.
// Both files are closed.
// Calls: readBlock and writeBlock to perform random access
// input and output, and sortBuffer to sort a buffer.

  Prepare inFile for input
  Prepare outFile for output

  numberOfBlocks = 0
  while (more blocks in inFile remain to be read) {
    ++numberOfBlocks
    buffer.readBlock(inFile, numberOfBlocks)
    sortBuffer(buffer)  // sort with some internal sort
    buffer.writeBlock(outFile, numberOfBlocks)
  }  // end while

  Close inFile and outFile
// end blockSort


mergeFile(inFile, outFile, runSize, numberOfBlocks)
// Merges blocks from one file to another.
// Precondition: inFile is an external file that contains
// numberOfBlocks sorted blocks organized into runs of
// runSize blocks each.
```

```
// Postcondition: outFile contains the merged runs of
// inFile. Both files are closed.
// Calls: mergeRuns.

  Prepare inFile for input
  Prepare outFile for output

  for (next = 1 through numberOfBlocks with increments
                                        of 2 * runSize) {
    // Invariant: runs in outFile are ordered
    mergeRuns(inFile, outFile, next, runSize)
  }  // end for
  Close inFile and outFile
// end mergeFile


mergeRuns(fromFile, toFile, start, size)
// Merges two consecutive sorted runs in a file.
// Precondition: fromFile is an external file of sorted runs
// open for input. toFile is an external file of sorted runs
// open for output. start is the block number of the first
// run on fromFile to be merged; this run contains size
// blocks.
//     Run 1: block start to block start + size - 1
//     Run 2: block start + size to start + (2 * size) - 1
// Postcondition: The merged runs from fromFile are appended
// to toFile. The files remain open.

  // initialize the input buffers for runs 1 and 2
  in1.readBlock(fromFile, first block of Run 1)
  in2.readBlock(fromFile, first block of Run 2)

  // Merge until one of the runs is finished. Whenever an
  // input buffer is exhausted, the next block is read.
  // Whenever the output buffer is full, it is written.
  while (neither run is finished) {
    // Invariant: out and each block in toFile are ordered
    Select the smaller "leading edge" of in1 and in2, and
        place it in the next position of out

    if (out is full) {
      out.writeBlock(toFile, next block of toFile)
    }  // end if

    if (in1 is exhausted and blocks remain in Run 1) {
      in1.readBlock(fromFile, next block of Run 1)
    }  // end if
```

```
    if (in2 is exhausted and blocks remain in Run 2) {
      in2.readBlock(fromFile, next block of Run 2)
    }  // end if
  }  // end while

  // Assertion: exactly one of the runs is complete

  // append the remainder of the unfinished input
  // buffer to the output buffer and write it

  while (in1 is not exhausted) {
    // Invariant: out is ordered
    Place next item of in1 into the next position of out
  }  // end while

  while (in2 is not exhausted) {
    // Invariant: out is ordered
    Place next item of in2 into the next position of out
  }  // end while

  out.writeBlock(toFile, next block of toFile)

  // finish off the remaining complete blocks

  while (blocks remain in Run 1) {
    // Invariant: each block in toFile is ordered
    in1.readBlock(fromFile, next block of Run 1)
    in1.writeBlock(toFile, next block of toFile)
  }  // end while

  while (blocks remain in Run 2) {
    // Invariant: Each block in toFile is ordered
    in2.readBlock(fromFile, next block of Run 2)
    in2.writeBlock(toFile, next block of toFile)
  }  // end while
// end mergeRuns
```

EXTERNAL TABLES

This section discusses techniques for organizing records in external storage so that you can efficiently perform ADT table operations such as retrieval, insertion, deletion, and traversal. Although this discussion will only scratch the surface of this topic, you do have a head start: Two of the most important external table implementations are variations of the 2-3 tree and hashing, which you studied in Chapter 12.

Suppose you have a random access file of records that are to be table items. The file is partitioned into blocks, as described earlier in this chapter. One of the simplest table implementations stores the records in order by their search key, perhaps sorting the file by using the external mergesort algorithm developed in the previous section. Once it is sorted, you can easily traverse the file in sorted order by using the following algorithm:

A simple external table imple- mentation: records stored in search-key order

```
traverseTable(dataFile, numberOfBlocks, recordsPerBlock)
// Traverses the sorted file dataFile in sorted order,
// visiting each node.

  // read each block of file dataFile into an
  // internal buffer buf
  for (blockNumber = 1 through numberOfBlocks) {
    buf.readBlock(dataFile, blockNumber)
    // visit each record in the block
    for (recordNumber = 1 through recordsPerBlock) {
      Visit record buf.getRecord(recordNumber-1)
    }  // end for
  }  // end for
```

Sorted-order traversal

To perform the `tableRetrieve` operation on the sorted file, you can use a binary search algorithm as follows:

Retrieval by using a binary search

```
tableRetrieve(dataFile, recordsPerBlock, first, last, searchKey)
// Searches blocks first through last of file dataFile and
// returns the record whose search key equals
// searchKey. The operation fails and returns null
// if no such item exists,

  if (first > last or nothing is left to read from dataFile) {
    return null
  }
  else {
    // read the middle block of file dataFile into buffer buf
    mid = (first + last)/2
    buf.readBlock(dataFile, mid)
    if ( (searchKey >= (buf.getRecord(0)).getKey()) &&
         (searchKey <= (buf.getRecord(recordsPerBlock-1)).getKey()) ) {
      // desired block is found
      Search buffer buf for record buf.getRecord(j)
          whose search key equals searchKey
      if (record is found) {
        tableItem = buf.getRecord(j)
        return tableItem
      }
       else {
        return null
```

```
    }  // end if
  }
  // else search appropriate half of the file
  else if (searchKey < (buf.getRecord(0)).getKey()) {
    return tableRetrieve(dataFile, recordsPerBlock,
                         first, mid-1, searchKey)
  }
  else {
    return tableRetrieve(dataFile, recordsPerBlock,
                         mid+1, last, searchKey)
  }  // end if
}  // end if
```

The `tableRetrieve` algorithm recursively splits the file in half and reads the middle block into the object *buf*. Splitting a file segment requires that you know the numbers of the first and last blocks of the segment. You would pass these values as arguments, along with the file variable, to `tableRetrieve`.

Once you have read the middle block of the file segment into *buf*, you determine whether a record whose search key equals *searchKey* could be in this block. You can make this determination by comparing *searchKey* to the smallest search key in *buf*—which is in *buf.getRecord(0)*—and to the largest search key in *buf*, which is in *buf.getRecord(recordsPerBlock-1)*. If *searchKey* does not lie between the values of the smallest and largest search keys in *buf*, you must recursively search one of the halves of the file (which half to search depends on whether *searchKey* is less than or greater than the search keys in the block you just examined). If, on the other hand, *searchKey* does lie between the values of the smallest and largest search keys of the block in *buf*, you must search *buf* for the record. Because the records within the block *buf* are sorted, you could use a binary search on the records within this block. However, the number of records in the block *buf* is typically small, and thus the time required to scan the block sequentially is insignificant compared to the time required to read the block from the file. It is therefore common simply to scan the block sequentially.

This external implementation of the ADT table is not very different from the internal sorted array-based implementation. As such, it has many of the same advantages and disadvantages. Its main advantage is that because the records are sorted sequentially, you can use a binary search to locate the block that contains a given search key. The main disadvantage of the implementation is that, as is the case with an array-based implementa-

tableInsert and tableDelete for an external implementation of the ADT table can require many costly block accesses due to shifting records

tion, the `tableInsert` and `tableDelete` operations must shift table items. Shifting records in an external file is, in general, far more costly than shifting array items. A file may contain an enormous number of large records, which are organized as several thousand blocks. As a consequence, the shifting could require a prohibitively large number of block accesses.

Consider, for example, Figure 14-5. If you insert a new record into block *k*, you must shift the records not only in block *k*, but also in every

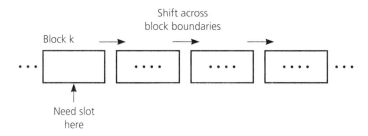

Figure 14-5

Shifting across block boundaries

block after it. As a result, you must shift some records across block boundaries. Thus, for each of these blocks, you must read the block into internal memory, shift its records by using an assignment such as

```
buf.setRecord(i+1, buf.getRecord(i))
```

and write the block to the file so that the file reflects the change. This large number of block accesses makes the external sorted buffer-based implementation practical only for tables in which insertions and deletions are rare. (See Exercise 1 at the end of this chapter.)

Indexing an External File

Two of the best external table implementations are variations of the internal hashing and search-tree schemes. The biggest difference between the internal and external versions of these implementations is that in the external versions, it is often advantageous to organize an **index** to the data file rather than to organize the data file itself. An index to a data file is conceptually similar to other indexes with which you are familiar. For example, consider a library catalog. Rather than looking all over the library for a particular title, you can simply search the catalog. The catalog is typically organized alphabetically by title (or by author), so it is a simple matter to locate the appropriate entry. The entry for each book contains an indication (for example, a Library of Congress number) of where on the shelves you can find the book.

Using a catalog to index the books in a library has at least three benefits:

- Because each catalog entry is much smaller than the book it represents, the entire catalog for a large library can fit into a small space. A patron can thus locate a particular book quickly.

- The library can organize the books on the shelves in any way, without regard to how easy it will be for a patron to scan the shelves for a particular book. To locate a particular book, the patron searches the catalog for the appropriate entry.

Advantages of a library catalog

- The library can have different types of catalogs to facilitate different types of searches. For example, it can have one catalog organized by title and another organized by author.

Now consider how you can use an index to a data file to much the same advantage as the library catalog. As Figure 14-6 illustrates, you can leave the data file in a disorganized state and maintain an organized index to it. When you need to locate a particular record in the data file, you search the index for the corresponding entry, which will tell you where to find the desired record in the data file.

An index to a data file

An index to the data file is simply a file, called the **index file**, that contains an **index record** for each record in the data file, just as a library catalog contains an entry for each book in the library. An index record has two parts: a **key**, which contains the same value as the search key of its corresponding record in the data file, and a **pointer**, which shows the number of the block in the data file that contains this data record. You thus can determine which block of the data file contains the record whose search key equals *searchKey* by searching the index file for the index record whose key equals *searchKey*.

Maintaining an index to a data file has benefits analogous to those provided by the library's catalog:

Advantages of an index file

- In general, an index record will be much smaller than a data record. While the data record may contain many components, an index record contains only two: a key, which is also part of the data record, and a single integer pointer, which is the block number. Thus, just as a library catalog occupies only a small fraction of the space occupied by the books it indexes, an index file is only a fraction of the size of the data file. As you will see, the small size of the index file often allows you to manipulate it with fewer block accesses than you would need to manipulate the data file.

- Because you do not need to maintain the data file in any particular order, you can insert new records in any convenient location, such as at the end of the file. As you will see, this flexibility

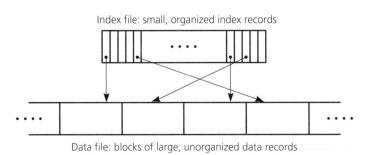

Index file: small, organized index records

Data file: blocks of large, unorganized data records

Figure 14-6

A data file with an index

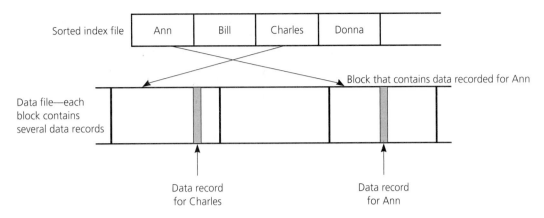

Sorted index file: | Ann | Bill | Charles | Donna | |

Block that contains data recorded for Ann

Data file—each block contains several data records

Data record for Charles

Data record for Ann

Figure 14-7

A data file with a sorted index file

eliminates the need to shift the data records during insertions and deletions.

- You can maintain several indexes simultaneously. Just as a library can have one catalog organized by title and another organized by author, you can have one index file that indexes the data file by one search key (for example, an index file that consists of <*name, pointer*> records), and a second index file that indexes the data file by another search key (for example, an index file that consists of <*socSec, pointer*> records). Such **multiple indexing** is discussed briefly at the end of this chapter.

Organize the index file but not the data file

Although you do not organize the data file, you must organize the index file so that you can search and update it rapidly. Before considering how to organize an index file by using either hashing or search-tree schemes, first consider a less complex organization that illustrates the concepts of indexing. In particular, let the index file simply store the index records sequentially, sorted by their keys, as shown in Figure 14-7.

To perform the *tableRetrieve* operation, for example, you can use a binary search on the index file as follows:

Retrieval by searching an index file

```
tableRetrieve(tIndex, tData, searchKey)
// Returns the record whose search key
// equals searchKey, where tIndex is the index file and
// tData is the data file. The operation fails and returns
// null if no such record exists.

  if (no blocks are left in tIndex to read) {
    return null
  }
```

```
else {
  // read the middle block of index file into buf
  mid = number of middle block of index file tIndex
  buf.readBlock(tIndex, mid)
  num = indexRecordsPerBlock
  if ((searchKey >= (buf.getRecord(0)).getKey()) &&
      (searchKey <= buf.getRecord(indexRecPerBlock-1).getKey())) {

    // desired block of index file found
    Search buf for index file record buf.getRecord(j)
        whose key value equals searchKey

    if (index record buf.getRecord(j) is found) {
      blockNum = number of the data-file block to
                    which buf.getRecord(j) points
      data.readBlock(tData, blockNum)
      Find data record data.getRecord(k) whose search
          key equals searchKey
      tableItem = data.getRecord(k)
      return tableItem
    }
    else {
      return null
    }  // end if
  }

  else if (tIndex is one block in size) {
    return null  // no more blocks in file
  }

  // else search appropriate half of index file
  else if (searchKey < (buf.getRecord(0)).getKey()) {
    return tableRetrieve(first half of tIndex, tData,
                          searchKey)
  }
  else {
    return tableRetrieve(second half of tIndex, tData,
                          searchKey)
  }  // end if
}  // end if
```

Because the index records are far smaller than the data records, the index file contains far fewer blocks than the data file. For example, if the index records are one-tenth the size of the data records and the data file contains 1,000 blocks, the index file will require only about 100 blocks. As a result, the use of an index cuts the number of block accesses in *tableRetrieve* down from about $\log_2 1000 \approx 10$ to about $1 + \log_2 100 \approx 8$. (The one additional block access is into the data file once you have located the appropriate index record.)

An index file reduces the number of required block accesses for table operations

The reduction in block accesses is far more dramatic for the `table-Insert` and `tableDelete` operations. In the implementation of an external table discussed earlier in this section, if you insert a record into or delete a record from the first block of data, for example, you have to shift records in every block, requiring that you access all 1,000 blocks of the data file. (See Figure 14-5.)

However, when you perform an insertion or a deletion by using the index scheme, you have to shift only index records. When you use an index file, you do not keep the data file in any particular order, so you can insert a new data record into any convenient location in the data file. This flexibility means that you can simply insert a new data record at the end of the file or at a position left vacant by a previous deletion (as you will see). As a result, you never need to shift records in the data file. However, you do need to shift records in the index file to create an opening for a corresponding index entry in its proper sorted position. Because the index file contains many fewer blocks than the data file (100 versus 1,000 in the previous example), the maximum number of block accesses required is greatly reduced. A secondary benefit of shifting index records rather than data records is a reduction in the time requirement for a single shift. Because the index records themselves are smaller, the time required for the statement $buf.setRecord(i+1, buf.getRecord(i))$ is decreased.

Shift index records instead of data records

Deletions under the index scheme reap similar benefits. Once you have searched the index file and located the data record to be deleted, you can simply leave its location vacant in the data file, and thus you need not shift any data records. You can keep track of the vacant locations in the data file (see Exercise 2), so that you can insert new data records into the vacancies, as was mentioned earlier. The only shifting required is in the index file to fill the gap created when you remove the index record that corresponds to the deleted data record.

Even though this scheme is an improvement over maintaining a sorted data file, in many applications it is far from satisfactory. The 100 block accesses that could be required to insert or delete an index record often would be prohibitive. Far better implementations are possible when you use either hashing or search trees to organize the index file.

An unsorted data file with a sorted index is more efficient than a sorted data file, but other schemes are even better

External Hashing

The external hashing scheme is quite similar to the internal scheme described in Chapter 12. In the internal hashing scheme, each entry of the array `table` contains a reference to the beginning of the list of items that hash into that location. In the external hashing scheme, each entry of `table` contains a block pointer to the beginning of a list, but here each list consists of *blocks of index records*. In other words, you hash an index file rather than the data file, as Figure 14-8 illustrates. (In many applications the array `table` is itself so large that you must keep it in external storage—for example, in the first K blocks of the index file. To avoid this extra detail, you can assume here that the array `table` is an internal array.)

You hash the index file instead of the data file

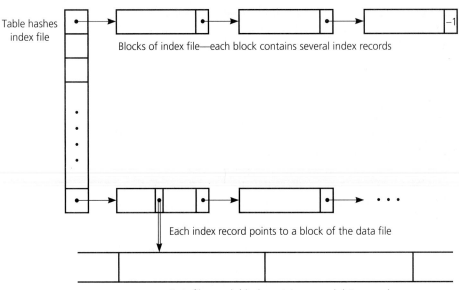

Blocks of index file—each block contains several index records

Each index record points to a block of the data file

Data file—each block contains several data records

Figure 14-8

A hashed index file

Associated with each entry `table[i]` is a linked list of blocks of the index file, as you can see in Figure 14-8. Each block of `table[i]`'s linked list contains index records whose keys (and thus whose corresponding data records' search keys) hash into location `i`. To form the linked lists, you must reserve space in each block for a block pointer—the integer block number of the next block in the chain—as Figure 14-9 illustrates. That is, in this linked list, the block pointers are integers, not Java references. A pointer value of –1 is used as a `null` pointer.

Index records	

Pointer to next
block in chain

Figure 14-9

A single block with a pointer

Retrieval under external hashing of an index file. The `tableRetrieve` operation appears in pseudocode as follows:

```
tableRetrieve(tIndex, tData, searchKey)
// Returns the item whose search key equals searchKey,
// where tIndex is the index file, which is hashed, and
// tData is the data file. The operation fails and returns
// null if no such record exists.

  // apply the hash function to the search key
  i = h(searchKey)

  // find the first block in the chain of index blocks —
  // these blocks contain index records that hash into
  // location i
  p = table[i]
```

```
// if p == -1, no values have hashed into location i
if (p != -1) {
  buf.readBlock(tIndex, p)
}  // end if


// search for the block with the desired index record
while (p != -1 and buf does not contain an index record
                    whose key value equals searchKey) {
  p = number of next block in chain
  // if p == -1, you are at the last block in the chain
  if (p != -1) {
   buf.readBlock(tIndex, p)
  }  // end if
}  // end while


// retrieve the data item if present
if (p != -1) {
  // buf.getRecord(j) is the index record whose
  // key value equals searchKey
  blockNum = number of the data-file block to
             which buf.getRecord(j) points
  data.readBlock(tData, blockNum)
  Find data record data.getRecord(k) whose search key
      equals searchKey
  tableItem = data.getRecord(k)
  return tableItem
}
else {
  return null
}  // end if
```

Insertion under external hashing of an index file.   The external hashing versions of *tableInsert* and *tableDelete* are also similar to the internal hashing versions. The major difference is that, in the external environment, you must insert or delete both a data record and the corresponding index record.

To insert a new data record whose search key is *searchKey*, you take the following steps:

1. Insert the data record into the data file. Because the data file is not ordered, the new record can go anywhere you want. If a previous deletion has left a free slot in the middle of the data file, you can insert it there. (See Exercise 2.)

If no slots are free, you insert the new data record at the end of the last block, or, if necessary, you append a new block to the end of the data file and store the record there. In either case, let p denote the number of the block that contains this new data record.

2. Insert a corresponding index record into the index file. You need to insert into the index file an index record that has key value *searchKey* and reference value *p*. (Recall that *p* is the number of the block in the data file into which you inserted the new data record.) Because the index file is hashed, you first apply the hash function to *searchKey*, letting

$$i = h(searchKey)$$

You then insert the index record <*searchKey*, *p*> into the chain of blocks that the entry *table[i]* points to. You can insert this record into any block in the chain that contains a free slot, or, if necessary, you can allocate a new block and link it to the beginning of the chain.

Deletion under external hashing of an index file.   To delete the data record whose search key is *searchKey*, you take the following steps:

1. Search the index file for the corresponding index record. You apply the hash function to *searchKey*, letting

$$i = h(searchKey)$$

You then search the chain of index blocks pointed to by the entry *table[i]* for an index record whose key value equals *searchKey*. If you do not find such a record, you can conclude that the data file does not contain a record whose search key equals *searchKey*. However, if you find an index record <*searchKey*, *p*>, you delete it from the index file after noting the block number *p*, which indicates where in the data file you can find the data record to be deleted.

2. Delete the data record from the data file. You know that the data record is in block *p* of the data file. You simply access this block, search the block for the record, delete the record, and write the block back to the file.

Observe that for each of the operations *tableRetrieve*, *tableInsert*, and *tableDelete*, the number of block accesses is very low. You never have to access more than one block of the data file, and at worst you have to access all of the blocks along a single hash chain of the index file. You can take measures to keep the length of each of the chains quite short (for example, one or two blocks long), just as you can with internal hashing. You should make the size of the array *table* large enough so that the average length of a chain is near one block, and the hash function should scatter the keys evenly. If necessary, you can even structure each chain as an external search tree—a **B-tree**—by using the techniques described in the next section.

The hashing implementation is the one to choose when you need to perform the operations *tableRetrieve*, *tableInsert*, and *tableDelete* on a large external table. As is the case with internal hashing, however, this implementation is not practical for certain other operations, such as

Choose external hashing for **tableRetrieve***,* **tableInsert***, and* **tableDelete** *operations*

sorted traversal, retrieval of the smallest or largest item, and range queries that require ordered data. When these types of operations are added to the basic table operations *tableRetrieve, tableInsert,* and *tableDelete,* you should use a search-tree implementation instead of hashing.

B-Trees

Another way to search an external table is to organize it as a balanced search tree. Just as you can apply external hashing to the index file, you can organize the index file, not the data file, as an external search tree. The implementation developed here is a generalization of the 2-3 tree of Chapter 12.

You can organize the blocks of an external file into a tree structure by using block numbers for child pointers. In Figure 14-10a, for example, the blocks are organized into a 2-3 tree. Each block of the file is a node in the tree and contains three child pointers, each of which is the integer block number of the child. A child pointer value of –1 plays the role of a *null* pointer, and thus, for example, a leaf will contain three child pointers with the value –1.

If you organized the index file into a 2-3 tree, each node (block of the index file) would contain either one or two index records, each of the

Organize the index file as an external 2-3 tree

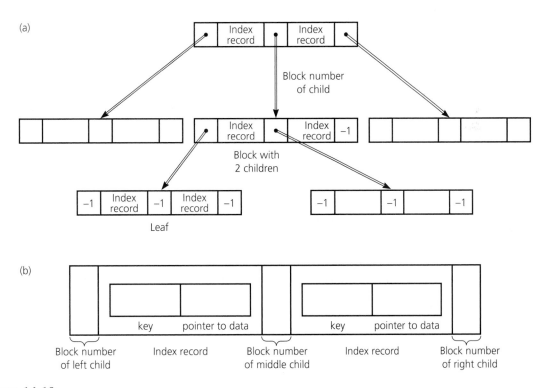

Figure 14-10

(a) Blocks organized into a 2-3 tree; (b) a single node of the 2-3 tree form <*key*, `pointer`>, and three child pointers. The pointer portion of an index record has nothing to do with the tree structure of the index file; *pointer* indicates the block (in the data file) that contains the data record whose search key equals *key*. (See Figure 14-10b.) To help avoid confusion, the pointers in the tree structure of the index file will be referred to as **child pointers**.

You must organize the index records in the tree so that their keys obey the same search-tree ordering property as an internal 2-3 tree. This organization allows you to retrieve the data record with a given value in its search key as follows:

Retrieval when the index file is a 2-3 tree

```
tableRetrieve(tIndex, tData, rootNum, searchKey)
// Returns the record whose search key equals searchKey.
// tIndex is the index file, which is organized as a
// 2-3 tree. rootNum is the block number (of the
// index file) that contains the root of the tree. tData
// is the data file. The operation fails and returns a
// null reference if no such record exists.
  if (no blocks are left in tIndex to read) {
    return null
  }
  else {
    // read from index file into buf the
    // block that contains the root of the 2-3 tree
    buf.readBlock(tIndex, rootNum)

    // search for the index record whose key value
    // equals searchKey
    if (searchKey is in the root) {
      blockNum = number of the data-file block that
                  index record specifies
      data.readBlock(tData, blockNum)
      Find data record data.getRecord(k) whose search key
          equals searchKey
      tableItem = data.getRecord(k)
      return tableItem
    }
    // else search the appropriate subtree
    else if (the root is a leaf) {
      return null
    } // end else if
    else {
      child = block number of root of
                  appropriate subtree
      return tableRetrieve(tIndex, tData, child,
                              searchKey)
    }  // end if
  }  // end if
```

You also can perform insertions and deletions in a manner similar to the internal version, with the addition that you must insert records into and delete records from both the index file and the data file (as was the case in the external hashing scheme described earlier). In the course of insertions into and deletions from the index file, you must split and merge nodes of the tree just as you do for the internal version. You perform insertions into and deletions from the data file—which, recall, is not ordered in any way—exactly as described for the external hashing implementation. You thus can support the table operations fairly well by using an external version of the 2-3 tree.

However, you can generalize the 2-3 tree to a structure that is even more suitable for an external environment. Recall the discussion in Chapter 12 about search trees whose nodes can have many children. Adding more children per node reduces the height of the search tree but increases the number of comparisons at each node during the search for a value.

An external 2-3 tree is adequate, but an improvement is possible

In an external environment, however, the advantage of keeping a search tree short far outweighs the disadvantage of performing extra work at each node. As you traverse the search tree in an external environment, you must perform a block access for each node visited. Because the time required to access a block of an external file is, in general, far greater than the time required to process the data in that block once it has been read in, the overriding concern is to reduce the number of block accesses required. This fact implies that you should attempt to reduce the height of the tree, even at the expense of requiring more comparisons at each node. In an external search tree, you should thus allow each node to have as many children as possible, with only the block size as a limiting factor.

Keep an external search tree short

How many children can a block of some fixed size accommodate? If a node is to have *m* children, clearly you must be able to fit *m* child pointers in the node. In addition to child pointers, however, the node must also contain index records.

Before you can answer the question of how many children a block can accommodate, you must first consider this related question: If a node *N* in a search tree has *m* children, how many key values—and thus how many index records—must it contain?

In a binary search tree, if the node *N* has two children, it must contain one key value, as Figure 14-11a indicates. You can think of the key value in node *N* as separating the key values in *N*'s two subtrees—all of the key values in *N*'s left subtree are less than *N*'s key value, and all of the key values in *N*'s right subtree are greater than *N*'s key value. When you are searching the tree for a given key value, the key value in *N* tells you which branch to take.

Binary search tree: the number of records and children per node

Similarly, if a node *N* in a 2-3 tree has three children, it must contain two key values. (See Figure 14-11b.) These two values separate the key values in *N*'s three subtrees—all of the key values in the left subtree are less than *N*'s smaller key value, all of the key values in *N*'s middle subtree lie between *N*'s two key values, and all of the key values in *N*'s right

2-3 tree: the number of records and children per node

(a)

(c)

Figure 14-11

(a) A node with two children; (b) a node with three children; (c) a node with *m* children

subtree are greater than N's larger key value. As is the case with a binary search tree, this requirement allows a search algorithm to know which branch to take at any given node.

General search tree: the number of records and children per node

In general, if a node N in a search tree is to have m children, it must contain $m - 1$ key values to separate the values in its subtrees correctly. (See Figure 14-11c.) Suppose that you denote the subtrees of N as S_0, S_1, and so on to S_{m-1} and denote the key values in N as K_1, K_2, and so on to K_{m-1} (with $K_1 < K_2 < \cdots < K_{m-1}$). The key values in N must separate the values in its subtrees as follows:

- All the values in subtree S_0 must be less than the key value K_1.

- For all i, $1 \le i \le m - 2$, all the values in subtree S_i must lie between the key values K_i and K_{i+1}.

- All the values in subtree S_{m-1} must be greater than the key value K_{m-1}.

If every node in the tree obeys this property, you can search the tree by using a generalized version of a search tree's retrieval algorithm. Thus, you can perform the `tableRetrieve` operation as follows:

Retrieval with a general external search tree

```
tableRetrieve(tIndex, tData, rootNum, searchKey)
// Returns the record whose search key
// equals searchKey. tIndex is the index file, which is
// organized as a search tree. rootNum is the block number
// (of the index file) that contains the root of the tree.
// tData is the data file. The operation fails and returns
// null if no such record exists.
```

```
if (no blocks are left in tIndex to read) {
  return null
}
else {
  // read from index file into internal buffer buf the
  // block that contains the root of the tree
  buf.readBlock(tIndex, rootNum)

  // search for the index record whose key value
  // equals searchKey
  if (searchKey is one of the Kᵢ in the root) {
    blockNum = number of the data-file block that
                  index record specifies
    data.readBlock(tData, blockNum)
    Find data record data.getRecord(k) whose search key
        equals searchKey
    tableItem = data.getRecord(k)
    return tableItem
  }
  // else search the appropriate subtree
  else if (the root is a leaf) {
    return null
  }
  else {
    Determine which subtree Sᵢ to search
    child = block number of the root of Sᵢ
    return tableRetrieve(tIndex, tData, child, searchKey)
  }  // end if
}  // end if
```

Now return to the question of how many children the nodes of the search tree can have—that is, how big can m be? If you wish to organize the index file into a search tree, the items that you store in each node will be records of the form $<key, pointer>$. Thus, if each node in the tree (which, recall, is a block of the index file) is to have m children, it must be large enough to accommodate m child pointers and $m - 1$ records of the form $<key, pointer>$. You should choose m to be the largest integer such that m child pointers (which, recall, are integers) and $m - 1$ $<key, pointer>$ records can fit into a single block of the file. Actually, the algorithms are somewhat simplified if you always choose an odd number for m. That is, you should choose m to be the largest odd integer such that m child pointers and $m - 1$ index records can fit into a single block.

Ideally, then, you should structure the external search tree so that every internal node has m children, where m is chosen as just described, and all leaves are at the same level, as is the case with full trees and 2-3 trees. For example, Figure 14-12 shows a full tree whose internal nodes each have five children. Although this search tree has the minimum possible height, its balance is too difficult to maintain in the face of insertions

Number of children per node

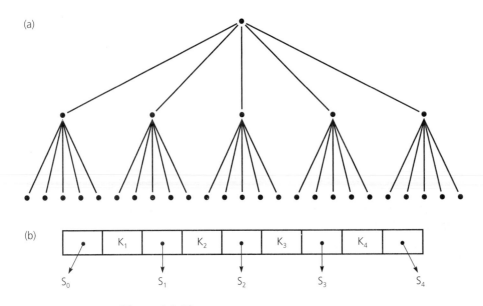

Figure 14-12

**(a) A full tree whose internal nodes have five children; (b) the
format of a single node**

and deletions. As a consequence, you must make a compromise. You can
still insist that all the leaves of the search tree be at the same level—that
is, that the tree be balanced—but you must allow each internal node to
have between m and $[m/2] + 1$ children. (The [ ] notation means *greatest
integer in*. Thus, [5/2] is 2, for example.)

This type of search tree is known as a **B-tree of degree *m*** and has the
following characteristics:

B-tree of degree m

- All leaves are at the same level.

- Each node contains between $m - 1$ and $[m/2]$ records, and each
  internal node has one more child than it has records. An exception to this rule is that the root of the tree can contain as few as
  one record and can have as few as two children. This exception
  is necessitated by the insertion and deletion algorithms
  described next.

A 2-3 tree is a B-tree of degree 3

A 2-3 tree is a B-tree of degree 3. Furthermore, the manner in which the
B-tree insertion and deletion algorithms maintain the structure of the
tree is a direct generalization of the 2-3 tree's strategy of splitting and
merging nodes.

The B-tree insertion and deletion algorithms are illustrated next by
means of an example. Assume that the index file is organized into a B-tree
of degree 5—that is, 5 is the maximum and 3 is the minimum number of
children that an internal node (other than the root) in the tree can have.
(Typically, a B-tree will be of a higher degree, but the diagrams would get
out of hand!)

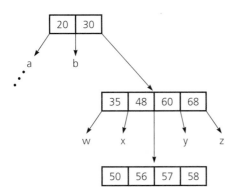

Figure 14-13

A B-tree of degree 5

Insertion into a B-tree. To insert a data record with search key 55 into the tree shown in Figure 14-13, you take the following steps:

1. **Insert the data record into the data file.** First you find block p in the data file into which you can insert the new record. As was true with the external hashing implementation, block p is either any block with a vacant slot or a new block.

2. **Insert a corresponding index record into the index file.** You now must insert the index record <55, p> into the index file, which is a B-tree of degree 5. The first step is to locate the leaf of the tree in which this index record belongs by determining where the search for 55 would terminate.

   Suppose that this is the leaf L shown in Figure 14-14a. Conceptually, you insert the new index record into L, causing it to contain five records (Figure 14-14b). Since a node can contain only four records, you must split L into L_1 and L_2. With an action analogous to the splitting of a node in a 2-3 tree, L_1 gets the two records with the smallest key values, L_2 gets the two records with the largest key values, and the record with the middle key value (56) is moved up to the parent P. (See Figure 14-14c.)

   In this example, P now has six children and five records, so it must be split into P_1 and P_2. The record with the middle key value (56) is moved up to P's parent, Q. Then P's children must be distributed appropriately, as happens with a 2-3 tree when an internal node is split. (See Figure 14-14d.)

   At this point the insertion is complete, since P's parent Q now contains only three records and has only four children. In general, though, an insertion might cause splitting to propagate all the way up to the root (Figure 14-14e). If the root must be split, the new root will contain only one record and have only two children—the definition of a B-tree allows for this eventuality.

Deletion from a B-tree. To delete a data record with a given search key from a B-tree, you take the following steps:

1. **Locate the index record in the index file.** You use the search algorithm to locate the index record with the desired key value.

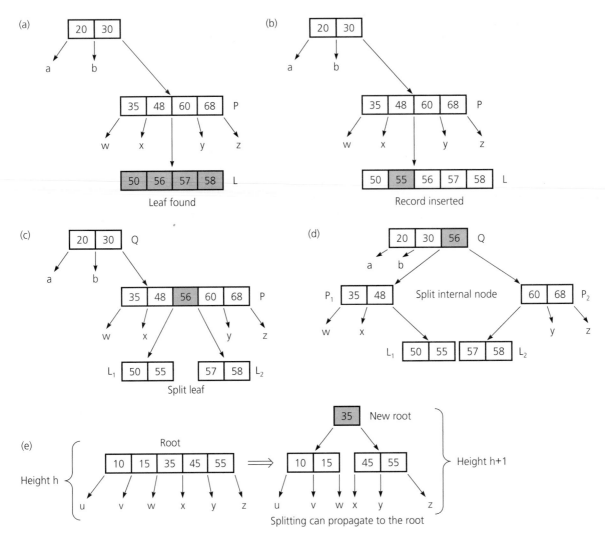

Figure 14-14

The steps for inserting 55

If this record is not already in a leaf, you swap it with its inorder successor. (See Exercise 5.) Suppose that the leaf L shown in Figure 14-15a contains the index record with the desired key value, 73. After noting the value p of the pointer in this index record (you will need p in Step 2 to delete the data record), you remove the index record from L (Figure 14-15b). Because L now contains only one value (recall that a node must contain at least two values) and since L's siblings cannot spare a value, you merge L with one of the siblings and bring down a record from the parent P (Figure 14-15c). Notice that this step is analogous to the merge step for a 2-3 tree. However, P now has only one value and two children, and since its siblings cannot spare a record and child, you must merge P with its sibling P_1 and bring a record down from P's parent, Q. Since P is an internal node, its children must be adopted by P_1. (See Figure 14-15d.)

After this merge, P's parent Q is left with only two children and one record. In this case, however, Q's sibling Q_1 can spare a record and a child, so you redistribute children and records among Q_1, Q, and the parent S to complete the deletion. (See Figure 14-15e.) If a deletion ever propagates all the way up to the root, leaving it with only one record and only two children, you are finished because the definition of a B-tree allows this situation. If a future deletion causes the root to have a single child and no records, you remove the root so that the tree's height decreases by 1, as Figure 14-15f illustrates. The deletion of the index record is complete, and you now must delete the data record.

2. **Delete the data record from the data file.** Prior to deleting the index record, you noted the value p of its pointer. Block p of the data file contains the data record to be deleted. Thus, you simply access block p, delete the data record, and write the block back to the file. The high-level pseudocode for the insertion and deletion algorithms parallels that of the 2-3 tree and is left as an exercise.

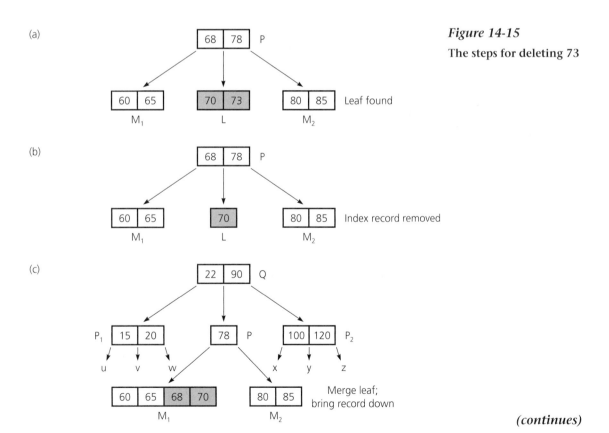

Figure 14-15

The steps for deleting 73

(continues)

Figure 14-15
(continued)

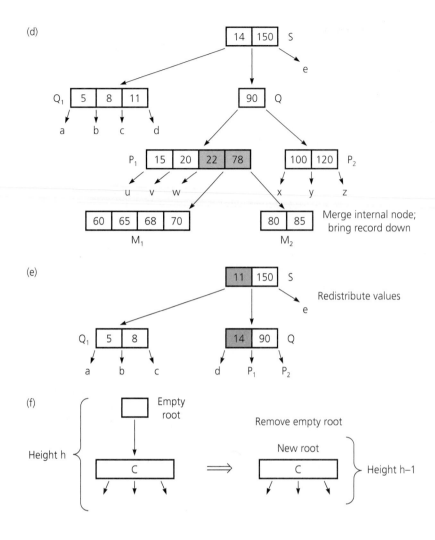

Traversals

Now consider the operation `traverseTable` in sorted order, which is one of the operations that hashing does not support at all efficiently. Often an application requires only that the traversal display the search keys of the records. If such is the case, the B-tree implementation can efficiently support the operation, because you do not have to access the data file. You can visit the search keys in sorted order by using an inorder traversal of the B-tree, as follows:

Accessing only the search key of each record, but not the data file

Inorder traversal of a B-tree index file

```
traverseTable(blockNum, m)
// Traverses in sorted order an index file that is organized
// as a B-tree of degree m. blockNum is the block number of
// the root of the B-tree in the index file.
```

```
if (blockNum != -1) {
   // read the root into internal buffer buf
   buf.readBlock(indexFile, blockNum)

   // traverse the children

   // traverse S₀
   Let p be the block number of the 0ᵗʰ child of buf
   traverseTable(p, m)

   for (i = 1 through m - 1) {
      Display key Kᵢ of buf

      // traverse Sᵢ
      Let p be the block number of the iᵗʰ child of buf
      traverseTable(p, m)
   }  // end for
}  // end if
```

This traversal accomplishes the task with the minimum possible number of block accesses because each block of the index file is read only once. This algorithm, however, assumes that enough internal memory is available for a recursive stack of h blocks, where h is the height of the tree. In many situations this assumption is reasonable—for example, a 255-degree B-tree that indexes a file of 16 million data records has a height of no more than 3. When internal memory cannot accommodate h blocks, you must use a different algorithm. (See Exercise 9.)

Accessing the entire data record

If the traversal must display the entire data record (and not just the search key), the B-tree implementation is less attractive. In this case, as you traverse the B-tree, you must access the appropriate block of the data file. The traversal becomes

Sorted-order traversal of a data file indexed with a B-tree

```
traverseTable(blockNum, m)
// Traverses in sorted order a data file that is indexed
// with a B-tree of degree m. blockNum is the block number
// of the root of the B-tree.

if (blockNum != -1) {
   // read the root into internal buffer buf
   buf.readBlock(indexFile, blockNum)

   // traverse S₀
   Let p be the block number of the 0ᵗʰ child of buf
   traverseTable(p, m)
   for (i = 1 through m - 1) {
      Let p_i be the pointer in the iᵗʰ index record of buf
      data.readBlock(dataFile, p_i)
      Extract from data the record whose search key equals Kᵢ
      Display the data record
```

```
        // traverse Sᵢ
        Let p be the block number of the iᵗʰ child of buf
        traverseTable(p, m)
    } // end for
} // end if
```

Generally, the previous traversal is unacceptable

This traversal requires you to read a block of the data file before you display each data record; that is, the number of data-file block accesses is equal to the number of data records. In general, such a large number of block accesses would not be acceptable. If you must perform this type of traversal frequently, you probably would modify the B-tree scheme so that the data file itself was kept nearly sorted.

Multiple Indexing

Before concluding the discussion of external implementations, let's consider the multiple indexing of a data file. Chapter 12 presented a problem in which you had to support multiple organizations for data stored in internal memory. Such a problem is also common for data stored externally. For example, suppose that a data file contains a collection of employee records on which you need to perform two types of retrievals:

```
retrieveN(aName)
// Retrieves the item whose search key contains the
// name aName.
```

```
retrieveS(ssn)
// Retrieves the item whose search key contains the
// Social Security number ssn.
```

Multiple index files allow multiple data organizations

One solution to this problem is to maintain two independent index files to the data file. For example, you could have one index file that contains index records of the form <*name, pointer*> and a second index file that contains index records of the form <*socSec, pointer*>. These index files could both be hashed, could both be B-trees, or could be one of each, as Figure 14-16 indicates. The choice would depend on the operations you wanted to perform with each search key. (Similarly, if an application required extremely fast retrievals on *socSec* and also required operations such as traverse in sorted *socSec* order and range queries on *socSec,* it might be reasonable to have two *socSec* index files—one hashed, the other a B-tree.)

While you can perform each retrieval operation by using only one of the indexes (that is, use the *name* index for *retrieveN* and the *socSec* index for *retrieveS*), insertion and deletion operations must update both indexes. For example, the delete-by-name operation *deleteN(Jones)* requires the following steps:

A deletion by name must update both indexes

1. Search the *name* index file for Jones and delete the index record.
2. Delete the appropriate data record from the data file, noting the *socSec* value *ssn* of this record.
3. Search the *socSec* index file for *ssn* and delete this index record.

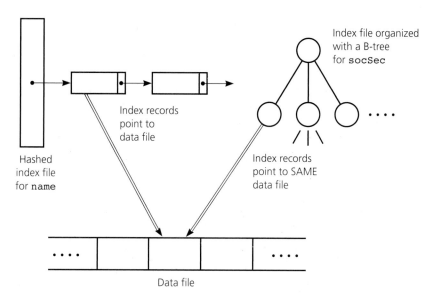

Figure 14-16

Multiple index files

In general, the price paid for multiple indexing is more storage space and an additional overhead for updating each index whenever you modify the data file.

This chapter has presented, at a very high level, the basic principles of managing data in external storage. The details of implementing the algorithms depend heavily on your specific computing system. Particular situations often mandate either variations of the methods described here or completely different approaches. In future courses and work experience, you will undoubtedly learn much more about these techniques.

SUMMARY

1. An external file is partitioned into blocks. Each block typically contains many data records, and a block is generally the smallest unit of transfer between internal and external memory. That is, to access a record, you must access the block that contains it.

2. You can access the ith block of a random access file without accessing the blocks that precede it. In this sense, random access files resemble arrays.

3. You can modify the mergesort algorithm, presented in Chapter 9, so that it can sort an external file of records without requiring all of the records to be in internal memory at one time.

4. An index to a data file is a file that contains an index record for each record in the data file. An index record contains both the search key of the corresponding data record and the number of the block in the data file that contains the data record.

5. You can organize the index file by using either hashing or a B-tree. These schemes allow you to perform the basic table operations by using only a few block accesses.

6. You can have several index files for the same data file. Such multiple indexing allows you to perform different types of operations efficiently, such as retrieve by name and retrieve by social security number.

CAUTIONS

1. Before you can process (for example, inspect or update) a record, you must read it from an external file into internal memory. Once you modify a record, you must write it back to the file.

2. Block accesses are typically quite slow when compared to other computer operations. Therefore, you must carefully organize a file so that you can perform tasks by using only a few block accesses. Otherwise, response time can be very poor.

3. If a record is inserted into or deleted from a data file, you must make the corresponding change to the index file. If a data file has more than one index file, you must update each index file. Thus, multiple indexing has an overhead.

4. Although external hashing generally permits retrievals, insertions, and deletions to be performed more quickly than does a B-tree, it does not support such operations as sorted traversals or range queries. This deficiency is one motivation for multiple indexing.

SELF-TEXT EXERCISES

1. Consider two files of 1,600 employee records each. The records in each file are organized into sixteen 100-record blocks. One file is sequential access and the other is random access. Describe how you would append one record to the end of each file.

2. Trace *externalMergesort* with an external file of 16 blocks. Assume that the buffers *in1*, *in2*, and *out* are each one block long. List the calls to the various methods in the order in which they occur.

3. Trace the retrieval algorithm for an indexed external file when the search key is less than all keys in the index. Assume that the index file stores the index records sequentially, sorted by their search keys, and contains 20 blocks of 50 records each. Also, assume that the data file contains 100 blocks, and each block contains 10 employee

records. List the calls to the various methods in the order in which they occur.

4. Repeat Self-Test Exercise 3, but this time assume that the search key equals the key in record 26 of block 12 of the index. Also assume that record 26 of the index points to block 98 of the data file.

EXERCISES

1. Assuming the existence of `readBlock` and `writeBlock` methods, write a pseudocode program for shifting data to make a gap at some specified location of a sorted file. Pay particular attention to the details of shifting the last item out of one block and into the first position of the next block. You can assume that the last record of the file is in record `lastRec` of block `lastBlock` and that `lastBlock` is not full. (Note that this assumption permits shifting without allocating a new block to the file.)

2. The problem of managing the blocks of an external data file indexed by either a B-tree or an external hashing scheme is similar to that of managing memory for internal structures. When an external structure such as a data file needs more memory (for example, to insert a new record), it gets a new block from a **free list** that the system manages. That is, if the file contains N blocks, the system can allocate to it an $(N + 1)^{\text{th}}$ block. When the file no longer needs a block, you can deallocate it and return it to the system.

The complication in the management of external storage is that a block allocated to a file may have available space interspersed with data. For example, after you have deleted a record from the middle of a data file, the block that contained that record will have space available for at least one record. Therefore, you must be able to keep track of blocks that have space available for one or more records as well as recognize when blocks are completely empty (so that you can return them to the system).

Assuming the existence of `allocateBlock` and `returnBlock` methods that get empty blocks from and return empty blocks to the system, write pseudocode implementations of the following external memory-management methods:

```
getSlot(dataFile, blockNum, recNum)
// Determines the block number (blockNum) and record
// number (recNum) of an available slot in file
// dataFile. A new block is allocated to the file from
// the system if necessary.

freeSlot(dataFile, blockNum, recNum)
// Makes record recNum in block blockNum of file
// dataFile available. The block is returned to the
// system if it becomes empty.
```

What data structure is appropriate to support these operations? You may assume that you can distinguish slots of a block that do not contain a record from those that do. You can make this distinction either by having a convention for *null* values within a record or by adding an empty/full flag.

3. Describe pseudocode algorithms for insertion into and deletion from a table implemented externally with a hashed index file.

4. Execute the following sequence of operations on an initially empty ADT table *t* that is implemented as a B-tree of degree 5. Note that insertion into an empty B-tree will create a single node that contains the inserted item.

   ```
   t.tableInsert(10)
   t.tableInsert(100)
   t.tableInsert(30)
   t.tableInsert(80)
   t.tableInsert(50)
   t.tableDelete(10)
   t.tableInsert(60)
   t.tableInsert(70)
   t.tableInsert(40)
   t.tableDelete(80)
   t.tableInsert(90)
   t.tableInsert(20)
   t.tableDelete(30)
   t.tableDelete(70)
   ```

5. Describe a pseudocode algorithm for finding an item's inorder successor in an external B-tree.

6. Describe pseudocode algorithms for insertion into and deletion from an ADT table implemented with an index file organized as a B-tree.

7. Write a *rangeQuery* method for a B-tree in pseudocode. (See Exercise 3 of Chapter 12.) Assume that only the key values are needed (as opposed to the entire data record).

8. Integrate calls to the appropriate memory-management methods (see Exercise 2) into the pseudocode for *tableInsert* and *tableDelete* under both the B-tree and hashing schemes. (See Exercises 3 and 6.)

9. The B-tree traversal algorithm presented in this chapter assumes that internal memory is large enough to accommodate the recursive stack that contains up to *h* blocks, where *h* is the height of the B-tree. If you are in an environment where this assumption is not true, modify the traversal algorithm so that the recursive stack contains block numbers rather than the actual blocks. How many block accesses does your algorithm have to perform?

10. a. Write pseudocode B-tree implementations of traversals and range queries that need to access entire data records, not simply the search keys. How many block accesses do your methods require?

b. To reduce the number of block accesses required by these operations, various modifications of the basic B-tree structure are frequently used. The central idea behind such structures is to keep the data file itself sorted. First, assume that you can keep the data file in sequential sorted order—that is, the records are sorted within each block and the records in B_{i-1} are less than the records in B_i for $i = 2, 3,$ and so on to the number of blocks in the file. Rewrite your implementations of the traversal and range-query operations to take advantage of this fact. How many block accesses do these operations now require?

c. Because it is too inefficient to maintain a sequentially sorted data file in the face of frequent insertions and deletions, a compromise scheme is often employed. One such possible compromise is as follows. If a data record belongs in block B and B is full, a new block is allocated and linked to B, allowing the new record to be inserted into its proper sorted location. The difficulty is that you must now view each index record in the B-tree as indicating the first of possibly several blocks in a chain of blocks that might contain the corresponding data record. Rewrite the `table-Insert`, `tableDelete`, `tableRetrieve`, `traverseTable`, and `rangeQuery` operations in terms of this implementation. What is the effect on their efficiency?

11. Write an iterative (nonrecursive) version of internal `mergesort`, as given in Chapter 9, that is based on the external version that this chapter describes. That is, merge sorted runs that double in size at each pass of the array.

PROGRAMMING PROBLEMS

1. a. Implement the `externalMergesort` algorithm in Java by using the class `RandomAccessFile`. Assume that the file to be sorted is a file of type *int* and that each block contains one integer. Further assume that the file contains 2^n integers for some integer n.

b. Now assume that each block contains many integers. Write Java methods that simulate `readBlock` and `writeBlock`. Implement `externalMergesort` by using these methods.

c. Extend your implementation of `externalMergesort` by removing the restriction that the file contains 2^n blocks.

2. Implement the ADT table by using a sorted index file, as described in the section "Indexing an External File."

3. Implement the ADT table by using a hashed index file, as described in the section "External Hashing."

4. Implement the ADT table by using a B-tree, as described in the section "B-Trees."

5. Repeat Programming Problem 5 of Chapter 10, using an external table to implement `PhoneBook`.

A

Review of Java Fundamentals

PREVIEW This book assumes that you already know how to write programs in a modern programming language. If that language is Java, you can probably skip this appendix, returning to it for reference as necessary. If instead you know a language such as C++, this appendix will introduce you to Java.

It isn't possible to cover all of Java in these pages. Instead this appendix focuses on the parts of the language used in this book. First we look at the basics of program structure, including packages, classes, and methods. Then we discuss variables, data types, expressions, operators, arrays, and strings. We continue with exceptions, input and output, decision constructs, looping constructs, and files. Java classes are covered in Chapters 3 and 8, and references are described in Chapter 4.

PROGRAM STRUCTURE

Let's begin with the simple Java application in Figure A-1 that computes the volume of a sphere. It consists of two classes, *SimpleSphere* and *TestClass*. Each of these classes is contained in a separate file that has the same name as the class, with `.java` appended to the end. A typical Java program consists of several classes, some of which you write and some of which you use from the Java Application Programming Interface (API). A Java application has one class that contains a method *main*, the starting point for program execution. Running the program in Figure A-1 produces the following output:

```
The volume of a sphere of radius 19.1 inches is 29186.95
```

This application includes all of the basic elements of Java program structure (packages, classes, data fields, and methods). The sections that follow discuss each of these elements.

Packages

Java packages provide a mechanism for grouping related classes. To indicate that a class is part of a package, you include a *package* statement as the first program line of your code. For example, lines 1 and 17 in Figure A-1 indicate that both of these classes, *SimpleSphere* and *TestClass*, are in the package *AppendixA*. The format of the *package* statement is

> **package** *package-name*;

*To include a class in a package, begin the class's source file with a **package** statement*

Place the files that contain a package's classes in the same directory

Java assumes that all of the classes in a particular package are contained in the same directory. Furthermore, this directory must have the same name the package.

The Java API actually consists of many predefined packages. Some of the more common of these packages are *java.lang*, *java.util*, and *java.io*. The dot notation in these package names directly relates to the directory structure containing these packages. In this case, all of the directories corresponding to these packages are contained in a parent directory called *java*.

	File `SimpleSphere.java`
1. Indicates `SimpleSphere` is part of a package --->	`package AppendixA;`
2. Indicates class `Math` is used by `SimpleSphere` -->	`import java.lang.Math;`
3. Begins class `SimpleSphere` ------------------------>	`public class SimpleSphere {`
4. Declares a private data field `radius` ----------------->	`  private double radius;`
5. Declares a constant ------------------------------------->	`  public static final double DEFAULT_RADIUS = 1.0;`
6. A default constructor ----------------------------------->	`  public SimpleSphere() {`
7. Assignment statement ----------------------------------->	`    radius = DEFAULT_RADIUS;`
	`  } // end default constructor`
8. A second constructor ------------------------------------>	`  public SimpleSphere(double r) {`
9. Assignment statement ----------------------------------->	`    radius = r;`
	`  } // end constructor`
10. Begins method `getRadius` -------------------------->	`  public double getRadius() {`
11. Returns data field `radius` --------------------------->	`    return radius;`
	`  } // end getRadius`
12. Begins method `getVolume` -------------------------->	`  public double getVolume() {`
13. A comment -->	`  // Computes the volume of the sphere.`
14. Declares and assigns a local variable----------------->	`    double radiusCubed = radius * radius * radius;`
15. Returns result of computation ------------------------>	`    return  4 * Math.PI * radiusCubed / 3;`
	`  } // end getVolume`
16. Ends class `SimpleSphere` -------------------------->	`} // end SimpleSphere`

	File `TestClass.java`
17. Indicates `TestClass` is part of a package -------->	`package AppendixA;`
18. Begins class `TestClass` ----------------------------->	`public class TestClass {`
19. Begins method `main` ---------------------------------->	`  static public void main(String[] args) {`
20. Declares reference `ball` ------------------------------>	`    SimpleSphere ball;`
21. Creates a `SimpleSphere` object ------------------>	`    ball = new SimpleSphere(19.1);`
22. Outputs results -->	`    System.out.println("The volume of a sphere of radius "`
23. Continuation of output string ------------------------->	`            + ball.getRadius() + " inches is "`
24. Continuation of output string ------------------------->	`            + (float)ball.getVolume()`
	`            + "cubic inches\n");`
	`  } //end main`
25. Ends class `TestClass` -------------------------------->	`} // end TestClass`

Figure A-1

A simple Java application

***import* statement.** The *import* statement allows you to use classes contained in other packages. The format of the *import* statement is as follows:

> `import ` *package-name.class-name;*

The `import` statement provides access to classes within a package

For example, line 2 in Figure A-1 imports the class *Math* from the package *java.lang*. The following line also could have been used:

> `import java.lang.*;`

In this case, the * indicates that all of the items from the package *java.lang* should be imported. Actually, this particular line can be omitted from the program, since *java.lang* is implicitly imported to all Java code.

Classes

An object is an instance of a class

A Java class defines a new data type

An object in Java is an instance of a class. You can think of a class as a data type that specifies the data and methods that are available for instances of the class. A class definition includes an optional subclassing modifier, an optional access modifier, the keyword *class*, an optional *extends* clause, an optional *implements* clause, and a class body. Figure A-2 describes each of the components of a class.

When a new class is created in Java, it is either specifically made a subclass of another class through the use of the *extends* clause or it is implicitly a subclass of the Java class *Object*. Creating a subclass is known as inheritance and is discussed briefly in Chapter 3 and in depth in Chapter 8 of this text.

Component	Syntax	Description
Subclassing modifier (use only one)	**abstract**	Class must be extended to be useful.
	final	Class cannot be extended.
Access modifiers	**public**	Class is available outside of package.
	no access modifier	Class is available only within package.
Keyword **class**	**class** *class-name*	Class should be contained in a file called *class-name.java*.
extends clause	**extends** *superclass-name*	Indicates that this class is a subclass of the class *superclass-name* in the *extends* clause.
implements clause	**implements** *interface-list*	Indicates the interfaces that this class implements. The *interface-list* is a comma-separated list of interface names.
Class body	Enclosed in braces	Contains data fields and methods for the class.

Figure A-2

Components of a class.

To create an **object** or **instance** of a class, you use the *new* operator. For example, the expression

```
new SimpleSphere()
```

creates an instance of the type *SimpleSphere*.

Now let's briefly examine the contents of the class body: data fields and methods.

Data Fields

Data fields are class members that are either variables or constants. Data field declarations can contain modifiers that control the availability of the data field (access modifiers) or that modify the way the data field can be used (use modifiers). The access modifiers are effective only if the class is declared *public*. Although this text uses only a subset of the modifiers, Figure A-3 shows them all for completeness.

Type of modifier	Keyword	Description
Access modifier (use only one)	**public**	Data field is available everywhere (when the class is also declared *public*).
	private	Data field is available only within the class.
	protected	Data field is available within the class, available in subclasses, and available to classes within the same package.
	No access modifier	Data field is available within the class and within the package.
Use modifiers (all can be used at once)	**static**	Indicates that only one such data field is available for all instances of this class. Without this modifier, each instance has its own copy of a data field.
	final	The value provided for the data field cannot be modified (a constant).
	transient	The data field is not part of the persistent state of the object.
	volatile	The value provided for the data field can be accessed by multiple threads of control. Java ensures that the freshest copy of the data field is always used.

Figure A-3

Modifiers used in data field declarations.

A class's data fields should be ***private*** *or* ***protected***

Data fields are typically declared *private* or *protected* within a class, with access provided by methods in the class. Hence, a method within a class has access to all of the data fields declared in the class. This allows the developer of the class to maintain control over how the data stored within the class is used.

Methods

Methods are used to implement operations. The syntax of a method declaration is as follows:

```
access-modifier use-modifiers return-type
                      method-name (formal-parameter-list) {
    method-body
}
```

Usually, each method should perform one well-defined task. For example, the following method returns the larger of two integers:

A method definition implements a method's task

```
public static int max(int x, int y) {
    if (x > y) {
        return x;
    }
    else {
        return y;
    } // end if
}   // end max
```

Method modifiers can be categorized as access modifiers and use modifiers, with the access modifier typically appearing first. In the example just given, the access modifier *public* appears first, followed by the use modifier *static*. Again, although this text uses only a subset of modifiers, Figure A-4 shows them all for completeness.

The return type of a **valued method**—one that returns a value—is the data type of the value that the method will return. The body of a valued method must contain a statement of the form

A valued method must use ***return*** *to return a value*

```
return expression;
```

where *expression* has the value to be returned. A method can also return a reference to an object. For the method *max*, the return type is *int*. The type of the value must be specified immediately before the method name. If the method does not have a value to return, the return type is specified as *void*.

After the method name, the formal parameter list appears in parentheses. You declare a formal parameter by writing a data type and a parameter name, separating it from other formal parameter declarations with a comma, as in

```
int x, int y
```

Type of modifier	Keyword	Description
Access modifier (use only one)	**public**	Method is available everywhere (when the class is also declared as *public*).
	private	Method is available only within the class (cannot be declared *abstract*)
	protected	Method is available within the class, available in subclasses, and available to classes within the same package
	No access modifier	Method is available within the class and to classes within the package.
Use modifiers (all can be used at once)	**static**	Indicates that only one such method is available for all instances of this class. Since a *static* method is shared by all instances, the method can refer only to data fields that are also declared *static* and shared by all instances.
	final	The method cannot be overridden in a subclass.
	abstract	The method must be overridden in a subclass.
	native	The body of the method is not written in Java but in some other programming language.
	synchronized	The method can be run by only one thread of control at a time.

Figure A-4

Modifiers used in a method declaration.

When you **call**, or **invoke**, the method *max*, you pass it **actual arguments** that correspond to the formal parameters with respect to number, order, and data type. For example, the following method contains two calls to *max*:

When you call a method, you pass it actual arguments that correspond to the formal parameters in number, order, and data type

```
public void printLargest(int a, int b, int c) {
    int largerAB = max(a, b);
    System.out.println("The largest of "+ a + ", " + b + ", "
                 + " and " + c + " is " + max(largerAB, c));
```

An actual argument passed by value is copied within the method

Arguments passed to Java methods are **passed by value.** That is, the method makes local copies of the values of the actual arguments—*a* and *b*, for example—and uses these copies wherever *x* and *y* appear in the method definition. Thus, the method cannot alter the actual arguments that you pass to it.

An argument that is a reference can be used to directly access the object or array

Note, however, that when the formal parameter is an object or an array, the actual argument is a reference value that is copied. This means that you can change the contents of the array or object, but not the value of the reference itself. For example, you cannot have a method that creates a new object for a reference in the parameter list. If it does, the new reference value will simply be discarded when the method terminates, and the original reference to the object will be left intact.

There is one special kind of method called a **constructor.** Constructor methods have the same name as the class and no return type. The constructor is executed only when a new instance of the class is created. A class can contain multiple constructors, differentiated by the number and types of the parameters. The actual arguments you provide when creating a new instance determine which constructor is executed.

How to Access Members of an Object

You can access data fields and methods that are declared `public` by naming the object, followed by a period, followed by the member name:

```
SimpleSphere ball = new SimpleSphere();
ball.getVolume(); // accesses the public method volume
```

You can access members of a class that are declared `static` (data fields or methods that are shared by all instances of the class) by using the class name followed by the name of the static member. For example, the `static` field `DEFAULT_RADIUS` declared in line 5 of Figure A-1 can be accessed outside of the class as follows:

```
SimpleSphere.DEFAULT_RADIUS;
```

LANGUAGE BASICS

Each Java application must contain at least one class that has a method `main`

Let's now examine the elements of the language that allow you to perform simple computations. For example, the Java application in Figure A-1 computes the volume of a sphere. As we mentioned earlier, a Java application is typically a collection of classes, with one of the classes containing the method `main`. Java applications always begin execution with this method. Running this application produces the following output:

```
The volume of a sphere of radius 19.1 inches is 29186.95
```

A typical Java program consists of several classes, some of which you write and some of which you use from packages. Java programs can also be written as applets, but they are not used in this text and hence are omitted here.

The sections that follow provide an overview of the basics of Java and refer to the simple program in Figure A-1 by line number. Note that this simple application contains two classes, *SimpleSphere* and *TestClass*.

Comments

Each comment line in Java begins with two slashes (//) and continues until the end of the line. You can also begin a multiple-line comment with the characters /* and end it with */. Although the programs in this book do not use /* and */, it is a good idea to use this notation during debugging. That is, to isolate an error, you can temporarily ignore a portion of a program by enclosing it within /* and */. However, a comment that begins with /* and ends with */ cannot contain another comment that begins with /* and ends with */. Java also has a third kind of comment that is used to generate documentation automatically using *javadoc*, a documentation utility available in the Software Development Kit (SDK) 1.2. This comment uses a /** to start and a */ to end.

A variety of commenting styles are available in Java

Identifiers and Keywords

A Java **identifier** is a sequence of letters, digits, underscores, and dollar signs that must begin with either a letter or an underscore. Java distinguishes between uppercase and lowercase letters, so be careful when typing identifiers.

Java is case sensitive

You use identifiers to name various parts of the program. Certain identifiers, however, are reserved by Java as **keywords**, and you should not use them for other purposes. A list of all Java keywords appears inside the front cover of this book. The keywords that occur within Java statements in this book are in boldface.

Variables

A variable, whose name is a Java identifier, represents a memory location that contains a value of a primitive data type or a reference. You **declare** a variable's data type by preceding the variable name with the data type, as in

A variable contains either the value of a primitive data type or a reference to an object

```
double radius;  // radius of a sphere
String name;    // reference to a String object
```

Note that the second declaration does not create a *String* object, only a variable that stores the location of a *String* object. You must use the *new* operator to create a new object.

Primitive Data Types

The primitive data types in Java are organized into four categories: boolean, character, integer, and floating point. In Figure A-1, lines 4 and 14 declare

Category	Data Type	Wrapper Class
Boolean	boolean	Boolean
Character	char	Character
Integer	byte	Byte
	short	Short
	int	Integer
	long	Long
Floating point	float	Float
	double	Double

Figure A-5

Primitive data types and corresponding wrapper classes

variables of the primitive type *double*. Some of the data types are available in two forms and sizes. Figure A-5 lists the available primitive data types.

A boolean value can be either *true* or *false*. You represent characters by enclosing them in single quotes or by providing their Unicode integer value (see Appendix B). Integer values are signed and allow numbers such as –5 and +98. The floating-point types provide for real numbers that have both an integer portion and a fractional portion. Character and integer types are called **integral types.** Integral and floating-point types are called **arithmetic types.**

A value of a primitive type is not considered to be an object and thus cannot be used in situations where an object type is expected. For this reason, the package *java.lang* provides corresponding **wrapper classes** for each of the primitive types. Figure A-5 also lists the wrapper class corresponding to each of the primitive types.

A wrapper class is available for each primitive data type

Each of these classes provides a constructor to convert a value of a primitive type to an object when necessary. Once such an object has been created, the value contained within the object cannot be modified. Here is a simple example involving integers:

You can represent the value of a primitive data type by using a wrapper class

```
int x = 9;
Integer intObject = new Integer(x);
System.out.println("The value stored in intObject = "
                        + intObject.intValue());
```

The class *Integer* has a method *intValue* that retrieves the value stored in an *Integer* object. Classes corresponding to the other primitive types provide methods with similar functionality.

References

A reference variable contains an object's location in memory

Java has one other type, called a reference, that is used to locate an object. Unlike other languages, such as C++, Java does not allow the programmer to perform any operations on the reference value. When an object is created using the *new* operator, the location of the object in memory is returned and can be assigned to a reference variable. For example, line 21 of Figure A-1 shows the reference variable *ball* being assigned the location of a new *SimpleSphere* object. A special reference value of *null* is provided to indicate that a reference variable has no object to reference.

Literal Constants

You use literal constants to indicate particular values within a program. The 4 and 3 in line 15 of Figure A-1 are examples of literal constants that are used within a computation. You can also use a literal constant to initialize the value of a variable. For example, you use *true* and *false* as the values of a boolean variable, as we mentioned previously.

Literal constants indicate particular values within a program

You write decimal integer constants without commas, decimal points, or leading zeros.[1] The default data type of such a constant is either *int*, if small enough, or *long*.

Do not begin a decimal integer constant with zero

You write floating constants, which have a default type of *double*, with a decimal point. You can specify an optional power-of-10 multiplier by writing *e* or *E* followed by the power of 10. For example, *1.2e-3* means 1.2×10^{-3}.

Character constants are enclosed in single quotes—for example, *'A'* and *'2'*—and have a default type of *char*. You write a **literal character string** as a sequence of characters enclosed in double quotes.

Several characters have names that use a backslash notation, as given in Figure A-6. This notation is useful when you want to embed one of these characters within a literal character string. For example, the program in Figure A-1 uses the **new-line character** \n in the string " *cubic inches.*\n" to end the line of output with a carriage return. You will learn about this use of \n in the discussion of output later in this appendix. You also use the backslash notation to specify either a single quote as a character constant (*'\'*) or a double quote within a character string.

Constant	Name
\n	New line
\t	Tab
\'	Single quote
\"	Double quote
\0	Zero

Figure A-6

Some special character constants

Named Constants

Unlike variables, whose values can change during program execution, named constants have values that do not change. The declaration of a named constant is like that of a variable, but the keyword *final* precedes the data type. For example, line 5 in Figure A-1 declares *DEFAULT_RADIUS* as a named floating-point constant. Once a named constant such as *DEFAULT_RADIUS* is declared, you can use it, but you cannot assign it another value. By using named constants, you make your program both easier to read and easier to modify.

The value of a named constant does not change

Named constants make a program easier to read and modify

---

[1]Octal and hexadecimal constants are also available, but they are not used in this book. An octal constant begins with *0*, a hex constant with *0x* or *0X*.

Assignments and Expressions

You form an expression by combining variables, constants, operators, and parentheses. The **assignment statement**

An assignment statement assigns the value of an expression to a variable

```
radius = r;
```

assigns to the previously declared variable *radius* the value of the **expression** on the right-hand side of the **assignment operator** =, assuming that *r* has a value. The assignment statement

double radiusCubed = radius * radius * radius;

which appears in line 14 of Figure A-1, also declares *radiusCubed*'s data type, since it was not declared previously.

Arithmetic expressions.   You can combine variables and constants with **arithmetic operators** and parentheses to form **arithmetic expressions.** The arithmetic operators are

*	Multiply	+	Binary add or unary plus
/	Divide	-	Binary subtract or unary minus
%	Remainder after division		

Operators have a set precedence

The operators *, /, and % have the same precedence,[2] which is higher than that of + and -; unary operators[3] have a higher precedence than binary operators. The following examples demonstrate operator precedence:

a - b / c	means a - (b / c)	(precedence of / over -)
-5 / a	means (-5) / a	(precedence of unary operator -)
a / -5	means a / (-5)	(precedence of unary operator -)

Arithmetic operators and most other operators are **left-associative.** That is, operators of the same precedence execute from left to right within an expression. Thus,

Operators are either left- or right-associative

```
a / b * c
```

means

```
(a / b) * c
```

The assignment operator and all unary operators are **right-associative**, as you will see later. You can use parentheses to override operator precedence and associativity.

---

[2]A list of all Java operators and their precedences appears inside the back cover of this book.
[3]A unary operator requires only one operand, for example, the - in -5. A binary operator requires two operands, for example, the + in 2 + 3.

Relational and logical expressions. You can combine variables and constants with parentheses; with the **relational**, or **comparison**, **operators** <, <=, >=, and >; and with the **equality operators** == (equal to) and != (not equal to) to form a **relational expression.** Such an expression evaluates to *false* if the specified relation is false and to *true* if it is true. For example, the expression 5 != 4 has a value of *true* because 5 is not equal to 4. Note that equality operators have a lower precedence than relational operators. Also note that the equality operators work correctly only with the primitive types and references. The == operator determines only whether two reference variables are referencing the same object, but not whether two objects are equal.

Equality operators work correctly only with primitive types and references

You can combine variables and constants of the arithmetic types, relational expressions, and the **logical operators** && (and) and || (or) to form **logical expressions**, which evaluate to *false* if false and to *true* if true. Java evaluates logical expressions from left to right and stops as soon as the value of the entire expression is apparent; that is, Java uses **short-circuit evaluation.** For example, Java determines the value of each of the following expressions without evaluating *(a < b)*:

Logical expressions are evaluated from left to right

Sometimes the value of a logical expression is apparent before it is completely examined

```
(5 == 4) && (a < b)   // false since (5 == 4) is false
(5 == 5) || (a < b)   // true since (5 == 5) is true
```

Implicit type conversions for the primitive numeric types. Automatic conversions from one numeric data type to another can occur during assignment and during expression evaluation. For assignments, the data type of the expression on the right-hand side of the assignment operator is converted to the data type of the item on the left-hand side just before the assignment occurs. Floating-point values are truncated—not rounded—when they are converted to integral values.

Conversions from one data type to another occur during both assignment and expression evaluation

During the evaluation of an expression, any values of type *byte*, *char*, or *short* are converted to *int*. These conversions are called **integral promotions.** After these conversions, if the operands of an operator differ in data type, the data type that is lower in the following hierarchy is converted to one that is higher (*int* is lowest):

$$int \rightarrow long \rightarrow float \rightarrow double$$

For example, if A is *long* and B is *float*, A + B is *float*. A copy of A's *long* value is converted to *float* prior to the addition; the value stored at A is unchanged.

Explicit type conversions for primitive numeric types. Numeric conversions from one type to another are possible by means of a **cast.** The cast operator is a unary operator formed by enclosing the desired data type within parentheses. Thus, the sequence

You convert from one numeric type to another by using a cast

```
double volume = 14.9;
System.out.print((int)volume);
```

displays 14.

Multiple assignment. If you omit the semicolon from an assignment statement, you get an **assignment expression.** You can embed assignment expressions within assignment expressions, as in

        a = 5 + (b = 4)

This expression first assigns 4 to *b* and then 9 to *a*. This notation contributes to the terseness of Java and is sometimes convenient, but it can be confusing. The assignment operator is right-associative. Thus, *a = b = c* means *a = (b = c)*.

Other assignment operators. In addition to the assignment operator =, Java provides several two-character assignment operators that perform another operation before assignment. For example,

        a += b means a = a + b

Other operators, such as -=, *=, /=, and %=, have analogous meanings.

The operators ++ and -- are useful for incrementing and decrementing a variable

        Two more operators, ++ and --, provide convenient incrementing and decrementing operations:

        ++a means a += 1, which means a = a + 1

Similarly,

        --a means a -= 1, which means a = a - 1

The operators ++ and -- can either precede their operands, as you just saw, or follow them. Although *a++*, for instance, has the same effect as *++a*, the results differ when the operations are combined with assignment. For example,

        b = ++a means a = a + 1; b = a

Here, the ++ operator acts on *a before* the assignment to *b* of *a*'s new value. In contrast,

        b = a++ means b = a; a = a + 1

The assignment operator assigns *a*'s old value to *b* before the ++ operator acts on *a*. That is, the ++ operator acts on *a after* the assignment. The operators ++ and -- are often used within loops and with array indexes, as you will see later in this appendix.

        In addition to the operators described here, Java provides several other operators. A summary of all Java operators and their precedences appears inside the back cover of this book.

Arrays

An array is a collection of data that has the same type

An array is a collection of **elements** or **items** or **values** that have the same data type. Array elements have an order: An array has a first element, a second element, and so on, as well as a last element. That is, an array contains a finite, limited number of elements. Like objects, an array does not come into existence until it is allocated using the *new* statement. At that

Figure A-7

A one-dimensional array of at most seven elements

time, you specify the desired size of the array. Because you can access the array elements directly and in any order, an array is a **direct access**, or **random access**, data structure.

You can access array elements directly and in any order

One-dimensional arrays. When you decide to use an array in your program, you must declare it and, in doing so, indicate the data type of its elements. The following statements declare a **one-dimensional array**, *maxTemps*, which contains the daily maximum temperatures for a given week:

```
final int DAYS_PER_WEEK = 7;
double [] maxTemps = new double[DAYS_PER_WEEK];
```

The bracket notation [] declares *maxTemps* as an array. The array is then allocated memory for seven floating-point elements.

The declared length of an array is accessible using the data field *length* associated with the array. For example, *maxTemps.length* is 7. You can refer to any of the floating-point elements in *maxTemps* directly by using an expression, which is called the **index**, or **subscript**, enclosed in square brackets. In Java, array indexes must have integer values in the range 0 to *length* – 1, where *length* is the data field just described. The indexes for *maxTemps* range from 0 to *DAYS_PER_WEEK* – 1. For example, *maxTemps[4]* is the fifth element in the array. If *k* is an integer variable whose value is 4, *maxTemps[k]* is the fifth element in the array, and *maxTemps[k+1]* is the sixth element. Also, *maxTemps[++k]* adds 1 to *k* and then uses the new value of *k* to index *maxTemps*, whereas *maxTemps[k++]* accesses *maxTemps[k]* before adding 1 to *k*. Note that you use one index to refer to an element in a one-dimensional array.

Use an index to specify a particular element in an array

An array index has an integer value greater than or equal to 0

Figure A-7 illustrates the array *maxTemps*, which at present contains only five temperatures. The last value in the array is *maxTemps[4]*; the values of *maxTemps[5]* and *maxTemps[6]* are 0.0, the default initial value for floating-point numbers.

You can initialize the elements of an array when you declare it by specifying an **initializer list**. The initializer list is a list of values separated by commas and enclosed in braces. For example,

You can initialize an array when you declare it

```
double [] weekDayTemps = {82.0, 71.5, 61.8, 75.0, 88.3};
```

initializes the array *weekDayTemps* to have five elements with the values listed. Thus, *weekDayTemps[0]* is 82.0, *weekDayTemps[1]* is 71.5, and so on.

You can also declare an array of object references. The declaration is similar to that of an array of primitive types. Here is a declaration of an array for 10 *SimpleSphere* references:

```
SimpleSphere[] myMarbles = new SimpleSphere[10];
```

Note that all of the references will have the initial value *null* until actual *SimpleSphere* objects are created for them to reference. The following statement creates a *SimpleSphere* object for the first element of the array:

```
myMarbles[0] = new SimpleSphere(0.25);
```

Multidimensional arrays. You can use a one-dimensional array, which has one index, for a simple collection of data. For example, you can organize 52 temperatures linearly, one after another. A one-dimensional array of these temperatures can represent this organization.

An array can have more than one dimension

You can also declare **multidimensional arrays.** You use more than one index to designate an element in a multidimensional array. Suppose that you wanted to represent the minimum temperature for each day during 52 weeks. The following statements declare a **two-dimensional array**, *minTemps*:

```
final int DAYS_PER_WEEK = 7;
final int WEEKS_PER_YEAR = 52;

double[][] minTemps = new
                       double[DAYS_PER_WEEK][WEEKS_PER_YEAR];
```

These statements specify the ranges for two indexes: The first index can range from 0 to 6, while the second index can range from 0 to 51. Most people picture a two-dimensional array as a rectangular arrangement, or **matrix,** of elements that form rows and columns, as Figure A-8 indicates. The first dimension given in the definition of *minTemps* is the number of rows. Thus, *minTemps* has 7 rows and 52 columns. Each column in this matrix represents the seven daily minimum temperatures for a particular week.

In a two-dimensional array, the first index represents the row, the second index represents the column

To reference an element in a two-dimensional array, you must indicate both the row and the column that contain the element. You make these indications of row and column by writing two indexes, each enclosed in brackets. For example, *minTemps[1][51]* is the element in the 2nd row and the 52nd column. In the context of the temperature example, this element is the minimum temperature recorded for the 2nd day (Monday) of the 52nd week. The rules for the indexes of a one-dimensional array also apply to the indexes of multidimensional arrays.

As an example of how to use a two-dimensional array in a program, consider the following program segment, which determines the smallest value in the previously described array *minTemps*:

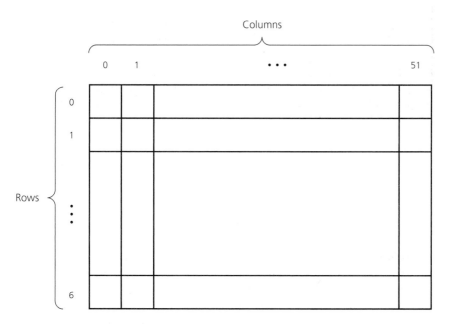

Figure A-8

A two-dimensional array

```
// minTemps is a two-dimensional array of daily minimum
// temperatures for 52 weeks, where each column of the
// array contains temperatures for one week.

// initially, assume the lowest temperature is
// first in the array
double lowestTemp = minTemps[0][0];
int dayOfWeek = 0;
int weekOfYear = 0;

// search array for lowest temperature
for (int weekIndex = 0; weekIndex < WEEKS_PER_YEAR;
                                    ++weekIndex) {
  for (int dayIndex = 0; dayIndex < DAYS_PER_WEEK;
                                    ++dayIndex) {
    if (lowestTemp > minTemps[dayIndex][weekIndex]) {
      lowestTemp = minTemps[dayIndex][weekIndex];
      dayOfWeek = dayIndex;
      weekOfYear = weekIndex;
    }  // end if
  } // end for
} // end for
// Assertion: lowestTemp is the smallest value in
// minTemps and occurs on the day and week given by
// dayOfWeek and weekOfYear; that is, lowestTemp ==
// minTemps[dayOfWeek][weekOfYear].
```

An example of using a two-dimensional array

It is entirely possible to declare *minTemps* as a one-dimensional array of 364 (7 * 52) elements, in which case you might use *minTemps[81]* instead of *minTemps[4][11]*. However, doing so will make your program harder to understand!

Although you can declare arrays with more than two dimensions, it is unusual to have an array with more than three dimensions. The techniques for working with such arrays, however, are analogous to those for two-dimensional arrays.

You can initialize the elements of a two-dimensional array just as you initialize a one-dimensional array. You list the initial values row by row. For example, the statement

```
int[][] x = {{1,2,3},{4,5,6}};
```

initializes a 2-by-3 array *x* so that it appears as

```
1       2       3
4       5       6
```

That is, the statement initializes the elements *x[0][0]*, *x[0][1]*, *x[0][2]*, *x[1][0]*, *x[1][1]*, and *x[1][2]* in that order. In general, when you assign initial values to a multidimensional array, it is the last, or rightmost, index that increases the fastest.

Passing an array to a method. If you want a method to compute the average of the first *n* elements of a one-dimensional array, you could declare the method as follows:

```
public double averageTemp(double[] temps, int n)
```

You can invoke the method by writing

```
double avg = averageTemp(maxTemps, 6);
```

where *maxTemps* is the previously defined array.

Arrays are always passed by reference to a method

The location of the array is passed to the method. You cannot return a new array through this value, but the method can modify the contents of the array. This restriction avoids the copying of perhaps many array elements. Thus, the method *averageTemp* could modify the elements of *maxTemps*.

USEFUL JAVA CLASSES

The Java Application Programming Interface provides a number of useful classes. The classes mentioned here are ones that are used within this text.

The *Object* Class

Every Java class inherits the methods of the class **Object**

Java supports a single class inheritance hierarchy, with the class *Object* as the root. Thus, the class *Object* provides a number of useful methods that are inherited by every Java class. In some cases, it is common for a class to redefine, or override, the version of the method inherited from *Object*. The paragraphs that follow summarize some of the more useful methods from the class *Object*.

public boolean equals(Object obj)

> Indicates whether some other object is "equal to" this one. As defined in the class *Object*, equality is based upon references— that is, upon whether both of the references are referencing the same object. This is referred to as shallow equality. It is common for a class to redefine this method for deep equality—in other words, to check the equality of the contents of the objects. Chapter 3 provides an example of overriding the *equals* method.

protected void finalize()

> Java has a garbage collection mechanism to destroy objects that a program no longer needs. When a program no longer references an object, the Java runtime environment marks it for garbage collection. Periodically, the Java runtime environment executes a method that returns the memory used by these marked objects to the system for future use. The garbage collector calls the *final-ize* method on an object when it determines that there are no more references to the object.

public int hashCode()

> Associated with each object is a unique identifying value called a hash code. This method returns the hash code for the object as an integer.

public String toString()

> Returns a string that "textually represents" this object. As defined in the class *Object*, this method returns a string that contains the name of the class of which the object is an instance, followed by the at sign character (@), and ending with the unsigned hexadecimal representation of the hash code of the object. For example, given the statement

> Sphere mySphere = **new** Sphere();

> the method call *mySphere.toString()* will return a string similar to *Sphere@733f42ab*.

String Classes

Java provides three classes that are useful when working with strings: *String*, *StringBuffer*, and *StringTokenizer*. The class *String* is a non-mutable string type; once the value of the string has been set, it cannot be modified. The class *StringBuffer* implements a mutable sequence of characters; it provides many of the same operations as the *String* class plus others for changing the characters stored in the string. Although at first glance it would seem reasonable for us to simply study *StringBuffer*, using *String* is more efficient. In fact, many methods within the Java API use the class *String*. The last class, *StringTokenizer*, provides methods for breaking strings into pieces.

The class *String*. Earlier, you saw that Java provides literal character strings, such as

```
"This is a string."
```

This section describes how you can create and use variables that contain such strings. Java provides a class *String* in the package *java.lang* to support nonmutable strings. A nonmutable string is one that cannot be changed once it has been created. Instances of the *String* class can be combined to form new strings, and numerous methods are provided for examining *String* objects. Our presentation includes only some of the possible operations on strings.

You can declare a string reference *title* by writing

```
String title;
```

When you initialize a string variable with a string literal, Java actually creates a *String* object to store the string literal and assigns the reference to the variable. Thus, you can assign a *String* reference by writing

```
String title = "Walls and Mirrors";
```

You can subsequently assign another string to *title* by using an assignment statement such as

```
title = "J Perfect's Diary";
```

Note that this actually creates a new *String* instance for *title* to reference.

*Use the method **length** to determine a string's length*

In each of the previous examples, *title* has a length of 17. You use the method *length* to determine the current length of a string. Thus, *title.length()* is equal to 17.

*Use **charAt** to reference any character within a string*

You can reference the individual characters in a string by using the method *charAt* with the same index that you would use for an array. Thus, in the previous example, *title.charAt(0)* contains the character *J*, and *title.charAt(16)* contains the character *y*.

You should not use the == operator to test whether two strings are equal. Using the == operator determines only whether the references to the strings are the same; it does not compare the contents of the *String* instances.

You can compare strings by using the *compareTo* method. Not only can you determine whether two strings are equal, but you can also determine which of two strings comes before the other according to the Unicode table. The *compareTo* method is used as follows:

*Use **compareTo** to compare two strings*

```
string1.compareto(string2)
```

The character sequence represented by the *String* object *string1* is compared to the character sequence represented by the argument *string2*. The result is a negative integer if *string1* precedes *string2*. The result is a positive integer if *string1* follows *string2*. The result is zero if the strings are equal. The ordering of two strings is analogous to alphabetic ordering, but you use the Unicode table instead of the alphabet. The following expressions demonstrate the behavior of *compareTo*:

```
"dig".compareTo("dog" )    //returns negative
"Star".compareTo("star")   //returns negative
"abc".compareTo("abc" )    //returns zero
"start".compareTo("star")  //returns positive
"d".compareTo("abc" )      //returns positive
```

You can concatenate two strings to form another string by using the + operator. That is, you place one string after another to form another string. For example, if

```
String s = "Com";
```

the statements

```
String t = s + "puter";
s += "puter";
```

Use the + operator to concatenate two strings

assign the string *"Computer"* to each of *t* and *s*. Similarly, you can append a single character to a string, as in

```
s += 's';
```

Besides adding two strings together, you can also concatenate a string and a value of a primitive type together by using the + operator. For example,

```
String monthName = "December";
int day = 31;
int year = 02;
String date = monthName + " " + day + ", 20" + year;
```

assigns the string *"December 31, 2002"* to *date*.

As we mentioned earlier, the class *Object* has a method called *toString* that returns a string that "textually represents" an object. The result of the *toString* method can be overridden in any class definition. This result is often combined with other strings by means of the + operator.

You can examine a portion of a string by using the method

```
public String substring(int beginIndex, int endIndex)
```

Use substring to access part of a string

The first parameter, *beginIndex*, specifies the position of the beginning of the substring. (Remember that 0 is the position of the first character in the string.) The end of the substring is at position *endIndex* - 1. For example, in

```
title = "J Perfect's Diary";
```

title.substring(2, 9) is the string *"Perfect"*.

Other useful *String* methods include the following:

public **int** indexOf(String str, **int** fromIndex)

> Returns the index of the first substring equal to *str*, starting from the index fromIndex.

public String replace(**char** oldChar, **char** newChar)

> Returns a string that is obtained by replacing all characters *oldChar* in the string with *newChar*.

public String trim()

> Returns a string that has all leading and trailing spaces in the original string removed.

The class *StringBuffer*.   In some situations, it is useful to be able to alter the sequence of characters stored in a string. But class *String* supports only nonmutable strings. To create mutable strings (strings that can be modified) use the class *StringBuffer* from the package *java.lang*. This class provides the same functionality as the class *String*, plus the following methods that actually modify the value stored in the *StringBuffer* object:

public StringBuffer append(String str)

> Appends the string *str* to this string buffer.

public StringBuffer insert(**int** offset, String str)

> The string *str* is inserted into this string buffer at the index indicated by *offset*. Any characters originally above that position are moved up and the length of this string buffer increased by the length of *str*. If *str* is *null*, the string "*null*" is inserted into this string buffer.

public StringBuffer delete(**int** start, **int** end)

> Removes the characters in a substring of this string buffer starting at index *start* and extending to the character at index *end* - *1* or to the end of the string buffer if no such character exists. If *start* is equal to *end*, no changes are made. May throw *StringIndex-OutOfBoundsException* if the value of *start* is negative, greater than the length of the string buffer, or greater than *end*.

public void setCharAt(**int** index, **char** ch)

> The character at index *index* of this string buffer is set to *ch*. May throw *IndexOutOfBoundsException* if the value of *index* is negative or is greater than or equal to the length of the string buffer.

public StringBuffer replace(**int** start, **int** end,
                        String str)

> Replaces the characters in a substring of this string buffer with characters in the specified string *str*. The substring to be replaced begins

at index *start* and extends to the character at index *end - 1* or to
the end of the string buffer if no such character exists. The substring
is removed from the string buffer, and then the string *str* is
inserted at index *start*. If necessary, the string buffer is lengthened
to accommodate the string *str*. May throw *StringIndexOutOf-
BoundsException* if the value of *start* is negative, greater than the
length of the string buffer, or greater than *end*.

The class *StringTokenizer*.   Another useful class when working with
strings is *StringTokenizer* in the package *java.util*. This class allows a
program to break a string into pieces or **tokens**. The tokens are separated
by characters known as delimiters. When you create a *StringTokenizer*
instance, you must specify the string to be tokenized. Other constructors
within *StringTokenizer* allow you to specify the delimiting characters
and whether the delimiting characters themselves should be returned as
tokens. Here is brief description of the three constructors for *String-
Tokenizer*:

Instances of the class ***String-
Tokenizer*** *are strings that
you can break into pieces called
tokens*

public StringTokenizer(String str)

> This constructor creates a string tokenizer for the specified string
> *str*. The tokenizer uses the default delimiter set, which is the
> space character, the tab character, the newline character, the car-
> riage-return character, and the form-feed character. Delimiter
> characters themselves are not treated as tokens.

public StringTokenizer(String str, String delim)

> This constructor creates a string tokenizer for the specified string
> *str*. All characters in the *delim* string are the delimiters for sepa-
> rating tokens. Delimiter characters themselves are not treated as
> tokens.

public StringTokenizer(String str, String delim,
>   **boolean** returnTokens)

> This constructor creates a string tokenizer for the specified string
> *str*. All characters in the *delim* string are the delimiters for sepa-
> rating tokens. If the *returnTokens* flag is true, the delimiter char-
> acters are also returned as tokens. Each delimiter is returned as a
> string of length 1. If the flag is false, the delimiter characters are
> skipped and serve only as separators between tokens.
>
> *StringTokenizer* also provides the following methods for
> retrieving tokens from the string:

public String nextToken()

> Returns the next token in the string. If there are no more tokens
> in the string, it throws the exception *NoSuchElementException*.
> Exceptions are discussed in the next section.

public boolean hasMoreTokens()

> Returns *true* if the string contains more tokens.

JAVA EXCEPTIONS

An exception is a mechanism for handling an error during execution

Many programming languages, including Java, support a mechanism for error handling called **exceptions**. Programs use exceptions in two ways: they indicate that an error has occurred by throwing an exception, and they "handle" the exception by catching the exception and executing code to deal with the error condition. You may already have seen exceptions when you used some of the methods from the Java API. For example, when an array subscript goes out of range, an exception `java.lang.ArrayIndexOutOfBoundsException` is thrown.

Catching Exceptions

To handle an exception, Java provides `try-catch` blocks. You place the statement that might throw an exception within a `try` block. The `try` block must be followed by one or more `catch` blocks. Each `catch` block indicates the type of exception you want to handle. A `try` block can have many `catch` blocks associated with it, since even a single statement may be capable of throwing more than one type of exception. Also, the `try` block can contain many statements, any of which might throw an exception. Here is the general syntax for a `try` block:

Use a `try` block for statements that can throw an exception

```
try {
    statement(s);
}
```

The syntax for a `catch` block is as follows:

Use a `catch` block for each type of exception that you handle

```
catch (exceptionClass identifier) {
    statement(s);
}
```

When a statement in the `try` block actually throws an exception, the remainder of the `try` block is abandoned, and control is passed to the `catch` block that corresponds to the type of exception thrown. The `catch` block is then executed. Upon completion of the `catch` block, execution resumes at the point following the last `catch` block.

The system decides which `catch` block to execute by considering the `catch` blocks in the order in which they appear, using the first one that produces a legal assignment of the thrown exception and the argument specified in the `catch` block. Thus, you must order the `catch` blocks so that with the most specific exception classes appear before the more general exception classes; otherwise, the code will not compile. For example,

The order of these two `catch` blocks in incorrect

```
try {
    int result = 99 / 0;
    // other statements appear here
} // end try
catch (Exception e) {
    System.out.println("Something else was caught");
```

```
} // end catch
catch (ArithmeticException e) {
  System.out.println("ArithmeticException caught");
} // end catch
```

compiles with the following error message:

```
TestExceptionExample.java:43: catch not reached.
    catch (ArithmeticException e) {
    ^
1 error
```

To get the code to compile successfully, you must switch the order of the *catch* blocks.

The following program demonstrates what happens when an exception is thrown and not caught. Figure A-9 illustrates these events.

```
class ExceptionExample {
  private int [] myArray;

  public ExceptionExample() {
    myArray = new int[10];
    // all initialized to zero
  }  // end default constructor

  public void addValue(int n, int value) {
    // add value to element n by calling addOne n times
    for (int i = 1; i <= value; i++) {
      addOne(n);
    } // end for
  } // end addValue

  public void addOne(int n) {
    // add 1 to the element n
      myArray[n] += 1;
  } // end addOne
} end ExceptionExample

public class TestExceptionExample {
  public static void main(String[] args) {
    ExceptionExample e1 = new ExceptionExample();
    e1.addValue(99, 3); // add 3 to element 99
  } // end main
} // end ExceptionExample
```

This program does not handle the exception that is thrown and, therefore, execution terminates

The method *addOne* causes *ArrayIndexOutOfBoundsException* from *java.lang* to be thrown when an attempt is made to access *myArray[99]*. Since *addOne* does not provide a handler for the exception (Point 1 in Figure A-9), the method terminates and the exception is propagated back to *addValue* to the point where *addOne* was called. The method *addValue* also does not provide an exception handler, so it also

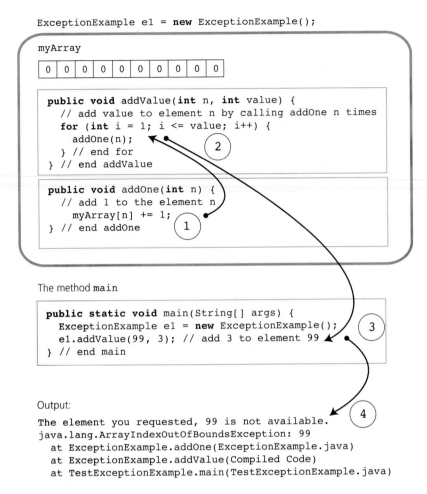

```
ExceptionExample e1 = new ExceptionExample();
```

```
myArray
```

| 0 | 0 | 0 | 0 | 0 | 0 | 0 | 0 | 0 | 0 |

```
public void addValue(int n, int value) {
  // add value to element n by calling addOne n times
  for (int i = 1; i <= value; i++) {
    addOne(n);
  } // end for
} // end addValue
```

```
public void addOne(int n) {
  // add 1 to the element n
    myArray[n] += 1;
} // end addOne
```

The method main

```
public static void main(String[] args) {
  ExceptionExample e1 = new ExceptionExample();
  e1.addValue(99, 3); // add 3 to element 99
} // end main
```

Output:

```
The element you requested, 99 is not available.
java.lang.ArrayIndexOutOfBoundsException: 99
  at ExceptionExample.addOne(ExceptionExample.java)
  at ExceptionExample.addValue(Compiled Code)
  at TestExceptionExample.main(TestExceptionExample.java)
```

Figure A-9

Flow of control in a simple Java application

terminates (Point 2 in Figure A-9) and the exception is propagated back to *main*. Since *main* is the main method of the program, and the exception is not handled in *main* (Point 3 in Figure A-9), the program terminates, and an error message similar to the following is displayed on the screen:

```
java.lang.ArrayIndexOutOfBoundsException: 99
  at ExceptionExample.addOne(ExceptionExample.java)
  at ExceptionExample.addValue(Compiled Code)
  at TestExceptionExample.main(TestExceptionExample.java)
```

Notice that the error message for the exception includes a **stack trace**, the sequence of method calls that led to the exception being thrown. This is the default behavior when no exception handler is provided. The message may also contain information specific to the exception at hand;

in this case, it contains the index value 99 that caused the exception to be thrown.

This code does not indicate that the method *addOne* might throw the exception *ArrayIndexOutOfBoundsException*. The method's documentation should indicate that this behavior is possible. Therefore, in addition to the documentation mentioned in Chapter 1, your methods should indicate the exceptions they might throw.

The exception *ArrayIndexOutOfBoundsException* could be caught at any point in the sequence of method calls. For example, *addOne* in the class *ExceptionExample* could be rewritten as follows to catch the exception:

```
public void addOne(int n) {
   try {
      myArray[n] += 1;
   } // end try
   catch (ArrayIndexOutOfBoundsException e) {
      System.out.println("The element you requested, " +
                         n + ", is not available.");
   } // end catch
} // end addOne
```

An example of handling an exception

This version of *addOne* produces the following output:

```
The element you requested, 99, is not available.
The element you requested, 99, is not available.
The element you requested, 99, is not available.
```

The method *addOne* is called three times by *addValue* when *e1.addValue(99,3)* executes, and hence the exception is thrown three times. When the exception was not handled, the program terminated the first time the exception occurred. By adding a *catch* block to handle the exception, we allow the code to continue execution.

Although the *addOne* method is where *ArrayIndexOutOfBounds-Exception* is thrown, it is not necessarily the best place to handle the exception. For example, if the call *e1.addValue(99, 10000)* executed, the message printed by *addOne* would have appeared 10,000 times! In this case it makes more sense for the handler to appear in the *addValue* method, and not in the *addOne* method. This assumes that *addOne* no longer handles the exception but propagates it back to *addValue*. Here is the code for *addValue* with the exception handler:

```
public void addValue(int n, int value) {
   try {
      for (int i = 1; i <= value; i++) {
         addOne(n);
      } // end for
   } // end try
   catch (ArrayIndexOutOfBoundsException e) {
      System.out.println("The element you requested, " +
                         n + " is not available.");
```

An improved way to handle an exception

```
        e.printStackTrace();
    } // end catch
} // end addValue
```

This method produces the following output:

```
The element you requested, 99 is not available.
java.lang.ArrayIndexOutOfBoundsException: 99
    at ExceptionExample.addOne(ExceptionExample.java)
    at ExceptionExample.addValue(Compiled Code)
    at TestExceptionExample.main(TestExceptionExample.java)
```

When *addOne* throws the exception *ArrayIndexOutOfBoundsException*, it is propagated back to *addValue*. The method *addValue* abandons execution of the statements in the *try* block, executes the statement in the *catch* block, and resumes execution after the last *catch* block. The message is printed only once, since the *for* loop is inside the *try* block, which is abandoned when the exception occurs. If the *try* block was placed inside the *for* loop (around the call to *addOne*), the exception would be thrown and handled at each iteration of the loop, causing the message to be printed multiple times.

The *catch* block also contains the method call *e.printStackTrace()*. Recall that the *catch* block specifies the type of exception handled and an identifier. This identifier provides a name for the caught exception that can be used within the *catch* block. In this case, the method *printStackTrace* is called for the exception object *e*. The *printStackTrace* method is one of many methods available to exception objects. Other uses of the exception name in the *catch* block are discussed in the next section on throwing exceptions.

Some exceptions must be handled

You may have noticed that some exceptions from the Java API cannot be totally ignored. You must provide a handler for these exceptions. For example, in the class *java.io.FileInputStream*, the constructor will throw *java.io.FileNotFoundException* if the file specified cannot be found. In this case, the compiler will complain if no exception handler is provided. For example, compiling the following code:

```
import java.io.*;
public class TestExceptionExample  {
  public static void getInput(String fileName) {
    FileInputStream fis;
    fis = new FileInputStream(fileName);
    // file processing code appears here
  } // end getInput

  static public void main(String[] args) {
    getInput("test.dat");
  } // end main
} // end TestExceptionExample
```

produces a compilation error message similar to the following:

```
TestExceptionExample.java:5: Exception
java.io.FileNotFoundException must be caught, or it
must be declared in the throws clause of this method.
    fis = new FileInputStream(fileName);
          ^

1 error
```

One way to resolve this error message is to provide an exception handler within the *getInput* method as follows:

```java
public void getInput(String fileName) {
  FileInputStream fis;
  try {
    fis = new FileInputStream(fileName);
    // file processing code appears here
  } // end try
  catch (FileNotFoundException e) {
    System.out.println("The file " + fileName +
                      " is not available");
    System.out.println(e);
  } // end catch
  System.out.println("After try-catch blocks");
} // end getInput
```

Here is the ouput when the file named *test.dat* does not exist:

```
The file test.dat is not available
java.io.FileNotFoundException: test.dat
  at java.io.FileInputStream.<init>(FileInputStream.java:56)
  at TestExceptionExample.getInput(TestExceptionExample.java)
  at TestExceptionExample.main(TestExceptionExample.java)
After try-catch blocks
```

Java has two types of exceptions: checked exceptions and runtime exceptions. The exception *java.io.FileNotFoundException* is an example of a checked exception. **Checked exceptions** are instances of classes that are subclasses of the *java.lang.Exception* class. They must be handled locally or explicitly thrown from the method (as discussed in the next section). They are typically used when the method encounters a serious problem. In some cases, the error may be considered serious enough that the program should be terminated.

Two types of exceptions: checked and runtime

Runtime exceptions occur when the error is not considered as serious. These types of exceptions can often be prevented by fail-safe programming. For example, it is fairly easy to avoid allowing an array index to go out of range, a situation that causes the runtime exception *ArrayIndexOutOfBoundsException* to be thrown. Runtime exceptions are instances of classes that are subclasses of the *java.lang.RuntimeException* class. *RuntimeException* is a subclass of *java.lang.Exception* that relaxes the requirement forcing the exception to be either handled locally or explicitly thrown by the method.

The *finally* block. As an option, you can follow the last *catch* block with a *finally* block that has the following form:

```
finally {
  statement(s);
}
```

This block is executed whether or not an exception is thrown within the *try* block. If an exception is thrown, the appropriate *catch* block executes and then the *finally* block executes. If no exception is thrown, the *finally* block executes upon completion of the *try* block. Note that you can have a *finally* block even if no *catch* block is present. Later in this appendix—in the section *File Input and Output*—you will see an example of a *finally* block that deals with a file when the program no longer needs it.

Throwing Exceptions

As we've mentioned, all exceptions in Java are instances of the class *java.lang.Exception* or one of its subclasses. When a method specification contains a *throws* clause, it also specifies the type of exception that the method can throw. If the method can throw more than one type of exception, each is listed after the *throws* clause, separated by commas. For example, here is the method header for one of the constructors for *FileInputStream*:

*A **throws** clause indicates that a method might throw an exception*

```
public FileInputStream(String name)
                       throws FileNotFoundException
```

The *throws* clause indicates that a method may throw an exception if an error occurs during its execution. In this case, the constructor will throw the exception *FileNotFoundException* if the file specified by *name* can't be opened.

An exception is thrown when the *throw* statement is executed. The syntax of this statement is

```
throw reference
```

where *reference* refers to an instance of a subclass of the class *java.lang.Exception*. When the *throw* statement executes, the remaining code in the *try* block or method is ignored. Typically, a *throw* statement will appear as follows:

*Use a **throw** statement to throw an exception*

```
throw new exceptionClass(stringArgument);
```

where *exceptionClass* is the type of exception you want to throw, and *stringArgument* is an argument to the *exceptionClass* constructor that specifies the detail message, a more detailed description of what may have caused the exception.

In certain situations, the Java API will have a predefined exception class that will suit the exception needs of your program. For example, the Java API has an exception *java.lang.IndexOutOfBoundsException* that could be used when an array's index is out of range.

You may also want to define your own exception class. Usually, you use *Exception* or *RuntimeException* as the base class for the exception. Base your decision as to which one to use upon how you want other parts of the program to treat the exception. If you don't want the exception to be ignored, extend *Exception*. If you don't care whether the exception is ignored, or if you have indicated in your precondition how the exception could be avoided, you might choose to extend *RuntimeException*. In either case, your class will inherit the same set of methods. Often, a constructor that includes a string parameter is provided. For example,

You can define your own exception class

```java
class MyRuntimeException extends RuntimeException {
  public MyRuntimeException(String s) {
    super(s);
  } // end constructor
  // All other methods are inherited.
}  // end MyRuntimeException

class MyException extends Exception {
  public MyException(String s) {
    super(s);
  } // end constructor
  // All other methods are inherited.
  // This exception must be handled in or
  // propagated from the method in which it occurs.
}  // end MyException
```

Once you've defined the new exception class, you can use it in the *throw* statement and *catch* blocks of your program. The constructor provides a way to identify the condition that caused the exception to occur. When constructing the new exception, you can include a string that describes the error condition. For example,

```java
throw new MyException("MyException: Provide reason");
```

A variety of methods available for exception objects provide access to this detailed message. For example, the methods *printStackTrace*, *getMessage*, and *toString* are just a few of the methods that include this detailed message in their output.

If you throw an exception that is not an instance of *RuntimeException* or one of its subclasses, you must either handle the exception within the method, using *try-catch* blocks, or throw the exception explicitly from the method. To indicate that the exception will be thrown by the method, you include a *throws* clause in the method's specification as follows:

```java
public void myMethod() throws MyException {
  // some code here...
  throw new MyException("MyException was thrown: reason");
} // end myMethod
```

Any method that calls *myMethod* must either provide a *catch* block for instances of *MyException* or contain a *throws* clause of its own for *MyException*.

TEXT INPUT AND OUTPUT

A typical Java application reads its input from a keyboard and writes its output to a monitor. Such input and output consist of **streams**, which are simply sequences of characters that either come from or go to an input or output (I/O) device.

The class of an input stream is *InputStream*, and the class of an output stream is *PrintStream*. The package *java.io* provides these classes and others related to input and output. The class *java.lang.System* provides three default stream variables: *System.in* for the **standard input stream**, *System.out* for the **standard output stream**, and *System.err* for the **standard error stream**, which also is an output stream. This section provides a brief introduction to simple input and output.

Input

As we just mentioned, the input stream *System.in* typically corresponds to keyboard input. But this source in its raw form—a sequence of bytes—cannot readily be used. Java provides a number of classes that facilitate getting the raw data into a form that is easily used within a program. In this case, two classes are required: *InputStreamReader* and *BufferedReader*.

InputStreamReader converts a stream of bytes to a sequence of characters

The class *InputStreamReader* transforms a given raw byte stream into a sequence of characters. But dealing with an input stream on a character-by-character basis is tedious. The class *BufferedReader* provides additional facilities that allow the character data to be read as a block or line of characters at a time. *BufferedReader* works with a given instance of *InputStreamReader*. The following code shows how to use these classes to read a line of input into the string *nextLine*:

```
BufferedReader stdin = new BufferedReader(
        new InputStreamReader(System.in));

String nextLine = stdin.readLine();
```

*Using **BufferedReader** with **InputStream** allows the **readLine** method to be used*

The *BufferedReader* method *readLine()* retrieves the next line of input as an instance of *String*.

But what if the program needs to view the characters in the string *nextLine* as a sequence of integers instead of as a sequence of characters? When the desired input value is not a string, it is usually a value of a primitive type. All of the primitive types provide a method for converting a string to the primitive type. For example, the class *Integer* provides the method *parseInt*. First, you extract the string containing the primitive type from *nextLine*, using the *StringTokenizer* class seen earlier.

*Use **StringTokenizer** to break the string into tokens, then convert each token to a value of the primitive type*

Then, you apply the method that converts the string to a primitive type value. The following code demonstrates this technique by extracting two integers *x* and *y* from *nextLine*:

```
BufferedReader stdin = new BufferedReader(
        new InputStreamReader(System.in));

String nextLine = stdin.readLine();

StringTokenizer input = new StringTokenizer(nextLine);
x = Integer.parseInt(input.nextToken());
y = Integer.parseInt(input.nextToken());
```

Output

Java provides the methods *print* and *println* to write character strings, primitive types, and objects to the standard output stream *System.out*. The method *println* differs from *print* in that it terminates a line of output so that subsequent output will start on the next line. When the argument is a string, it is simply placed in the output stream. For example, the following program segment uses *println* with a *String* argument:

*The methods **print** and **println** write to an output stream*

```
int count = 5;
double average = 20.3;
System.out.println("The average of the " + count
        + " distances read is " + average
        + " miles.");
```

produces the following output:

```
The average of the 5 distances read is 20.3 miles.
```

As we mentioned in the section on strings, the operator + can be used to concatenate strings with other strings, primitive types, and objects. Thus, the previous statements concatenate the string *"The average of the "* to the string that represents the value of *count*, and so on.

When *println*'s argument is a primitive type or an object, the *static* method *valueOf* from the *String* class is used to determine the corresponding string value that is placed on the output stream. For primitive types, this is a simple string representation of the value. For objects, this is ultimately the value returned by the object's *toString* method. Thus, for example, using the method *toString* as defined in the class *Object*, the statements

```
SimpleSphere mySphere = new SimpleSphere();
System.out.println(mySphere);
```

will produce output similar to

*The method **toString** is implicitly invoked when an object is an argument of **println***

```
SimpleSphere@733f42ab
```

You usually override *toString* with your own version. Here is an example that could be used in the class *SimpleSphere*:

```java
   public String toString() {
     return ("SimpleSphere: radius = " + radius);
   } // end toString
```

Now if you execute the statements

```java
   SimpleSphere mySphere = new SimpleSphere();
   System.out.println(mySphere);
```

the output appears as follows:

```
   SimpleSphere: radius = 1.0
```

SELECTION STATEMENTS

Selection statements allow you to choose among several courses of action according to the value of an expression. In this category of statements, Java provides the *if* statement and the *switch* statement.

The *if* Statement

You can write an *if* statement in one of two ways:

An if statement has two basic forms

```java
   if (expression)
       statement₁
```

or

```java
   if (expression)
       statement₁
   else
       statement₂
```

where *statement₁* and *statement₂* represent any Java statement. Such statements can be **compound**; a compound statement, or **block**, is a sequence of statements enclosed in braces. Though not a requirement of Java, this text will always use a compound statement in language constructs, even if only a single statement is required.

If the value of *expression* is *true*, *statement₁* is executed. Otherwise, the first form of the *if* statement does nothing, whereas the second form executes *statement₂*. Note that the parentheses around *expression* are required.

Parentheses around the expression in an if statement are required

For example, the following *if* statements each compare the values of two integer variables *a* and *b*:

```java
if (a > b) {
  System.out.println(a + " is larger than " + b + ".");
} // end if
System.out.println("This statement is always executed.");

if (a > b) {
  larger = a;
  System.out.println(a + " is larger than " + b + ".");
}
```

```
else {
  larger = b;
  System.out.println(b + " is larger than " + a + ".");
} // end if

System.out.println(larger + " is the larger value.");
```

You can nest *if* statements in several ways, since either *statement₁* or *statement₂* can itself be an *if* statement. The following example, which determines the largest of three integer variables *a*, *b*, and *c*, shows a common way to nest *if* statements:

```
if ((a >= b) && (a >= c)) {
  largest = a;
}
else if (b >= c) {    // a is not largest at this point
  largest = b;
}
else {
  largest = c;

} // end if
```

*You can nest **if** statements*

The **switch** Statement

When you must choose among more than two courses of action, the *if* statement can become unwieldy. If your choice is to be made according to the value of an integral expression, you can use a *switch* statement.

For example, the following statement determines the number of days in a month. The *int* variable *month* designates the month as an integer from 1 to 12.

*A **switch** statement provides a choice of several actions according to the value of an integral expression*

```
switch (month) {
  // 30 days hath Sept., Apr., June, and Nov.
  case 9: case 4: case 6: case 11:
    daysInMonth = 30;
    break;
  // all the rest have 31
  case 1: case 3: case 5: case 7:
  case 8: case 10: case 12:
    daysInMonth = 31;
    break;

  // except February
  case 2:  // assume leapYear is true if leap
           // year, else is false
    if (leapYear) {
      daysInMonth = 29;
    }
    else {
```

*Without a **break** statement, execution of a **case** will continue into the next **case***

```
                    daysInMonth = 28;
                } // end if
                break;

            default:
                System.out.println("Incorrect value for Month.");
        } // end switch
```

Parentheses must enclose the integral *switch* expression—*month*, in this example. The *case* labels have the form

    case *expression*:

where *expression* is a constant integral expression. After the *switch* expression is evaluated, execution continues at the *case* label whose expression has the same value as the *switch* expression. Subsequent statements execute until either a *break* or a *return* is encountered or the *switch* statement ends.

It bears repeating that unless you terminate a *case* with either a *break* or a *return*, execution of the *switch* statement continues. Although this action can be useful, omitting the *break* statements in the previous example would be incorrect.

If no *case* label matches the current value of the *switch* expression, the statements that follow the *default* label, if one exists, are executed. If no *default* exists, the *switch* statement exits.

ITERATION STATEMENTS

Java has three statements—the *while*, *for*, and *do* statements—that provide for repetition by iteration—that is, loops. Each statement controls the number of times that another Java statement—the **body**—is executed. The body can be a single statement, though this text will always use a compound statement.

The *while* Statement

The general form of the *while* statement is

    while (*expression*)
      statement

A while statement executes as long as the expression is true

As long as the value of *expression* is *true*, *statement* is executed. Because *expression* is evaluated before *statement* is executed, it is possible that *statement* will not execute at all. Note that the parentheses around *expression* are required.

Suppose that you wanted to compute the sum of positive integers that you enter at the keyboard on a single line. Since the integers are positive, you can use a negative or zero value to indicate the end of the list of integers. The following *while* statement accomplishes this task:

```java
int nextValue;
int sum = 0;
BufferedReader stdin;
StringTokenizer inputLine;

stdin = new BufferedReader(new InputStreamReader(System.in));
inputLine = new StringTokenizer(stdin.readLine());

nextValue = Integer.parseInt(inputLine.nextToken());

while (nextValue > 0) {
  sum += nextValue;
  nextValue = Integer.parseInt(inputLine.nextToken());
} // end while
System.out.println("The sum is " + sum);
```

If zero was the first value read, the body of the *while* statement would not execute.

Recall that the expression *inputLine.hasMoreTokens()* has the value *true* if the string has more tokens and *false* otherwise. This would be useful if you did not want to use the value zero to mark the end of the line. Thus, you could revise the previous statements as

```java
int nextValue;
int sum = 0;
BufferedReader stdin;
StringTokenizer inputLine;

stdin = new BufferedReader(new InputStreamReader(System.in));
inputLine = new StringTokenizer(stdin.readLine());

while (inputLine().hasMoreTokens()) {
  nextValue = Integer.parseInt(inputLine.nextToken());
  sum += nextValue;
} // end while
System.out.println("The sum is " + sum);
```

The *break* and *continue* statements. You can use the *break* statement—which you saw earlier within a *switch* statement—within any of the iteration statements. A *break* statement within the body of a loop causes the loop to exit immediately. Execution continues with the statement that follows the loop. This use of *break* within a *while*, *for*, or *do* statement is generally considered poor style.

Use of a break statement within a loop is generally poor style

The *continue* statement stops only the current iteration of the loop and begins the next iteration at the top of the loop. The *continue* statement is valid only within *while*, *for*, or *do* statements.

The for Statement

The *for* statement provides for counted loops and has the general form

A for statement lists the initial-ization, testing, and updating steps in one location

> **for** (*initialize*; *test*; *update*)
>   *statement*

where *initialize*, *test*, and *update* are expressions. Typically, *initialize* is an assignment expression that initializes a counter to control the loop. This initialization occurs only once. Then, if *test*, which is usually a logical expression, is *true*, *statement* executes. The expression *update* executes next, usually incrementing or decrementing the counter. This sequence of events repeats, beginning with the evaluation of *test*, until the value of *test* is *false*. As with the previous constructs, *statement* is usually a compound statement.

For example, the following *for* statement displays the integers from 1 to *n*:

```
for (int counter = 1; counter <= n; ++counter) {
   System.out.print(counter + " ");
} // end for

// this statement is always executed
System.out.println();
```

If *n* is less than 1, the *for* statement does not execute at all. Thus, the previous statements are equivalent to the following *while* loop:

```
int counter = 1;
while (counter <= n) {
   System.out.print(counter + " ");
   ++counter;
}  // end while

// this statement is always executed
System.out.println();
```

In general, the logic of a *for* statement is equivalent to

A for statement is equivalent to a while statement

```
initialize;
while (test) {
   statement;
   update;
} // end while
```

with the understanding that if *statement* contains a *continue*, *update* will execute before *test* is evaluated again.

The following two examples demonstrate the flexibility of the *for* statement:

```
for (byte ch = 'z'; ch >= 'a'; --ch) {
// ch ranges from 'z' to 'a'
   System.out.println(ch);
```

```
}   // end for

for (double x = 1.5; x < 10; x += 0.25) {
// x ranges from 1.5 to 9.75 at steps of 0.25
   System.out.println(x);
}   // end for
```

The *initialize* and *update* portions of a *for* statement each can contain several expressions separated by commas, thus performing more than one action. For example, the following loop raises a floating-point value to an integer power by using multiplication:

```
// floating-point power equals floating-point x
// raised to int n; assumes int expon
for (power = 1.0, expon = 1; expon <= n; ++expon){
   power *= x;
}   // end for
```

Both *power* and *expon* are assigned values before the body of the loop executes for the first time.

Because the *for* statement consolidates the initialization, testing, and updating steps of a loop into one statement, Java programmers tend to favor it over the *while* statement. For example, notice how the following *while* loop sums the values in an array *x*:

*A **for** statement is usually favored over the **while** statement*

```
sum = 0;
int i = 0;
while (i < x.length) {
   sum += x[i];
   i++;
} // end while
```

This loop is equivalent to the following *for* statement:

```
for (int i = 0, sum = 0; i < x.length; sum += x[i++]) {
}
```

In fact, this *for* statement has an empty body!

You can omit any of the expressions *initialize*, *test*, or *update* from a *for* statement, but you cannot omit the semicolons. For example, you can move the *update* step from the previous *for* statement to the body of the loop:

*You can omit any of the initialization, testing, and updating steps in a **for** statement, but you cannot omit the semicolons*

```
for (int i = 0, sum = 0; i < x.length; ) {
   sum += x[i++];
} // end for
```

You also could omit both the initialization and the update steps, as in the following loop, to read and process positive integers:

```
for ( ; inputLine.hasMoretokens(); ) {
   statements to process nextValue in inputLine
} // end for
```

This *for* statement offers no advantage over the equivalent *while* statement:

```
while (inputLine.hasMoretokens())
```

Although you can omit the *test* expression from *for*, you probably will not want to do so, because then the loop would be infinite.

The *do* Statement

Use the *do* statement when you want to execute a loop at least once. Its general form is

A do statement loops at least once

```
do {
    statement
} while (expression);
```

Here, *statement* executes until the value of *expression* is `false`.

For example, suppose that you execute a sequence of statements and then ask the user whether to execute them again. The *do* statement is appropriate, because you execute the statements before you decide whether to repeat them:

```
BufferedReader stdin = new BufferedReader(
        new InputStreamReader(System.in));
char response;
do {
    . . . (a sequence of statements)

    System.out.print("Do it again?");
    response = stdin.read(); // returns a single character
} while ( (response == 'Y') || (response == 'y') );
```

FILE INPUT AND OUTPUT

You have used **files** ever since you wrote your first program. In fact, your Java source program is in a file that you probably created by using a text editor. You can create and access such files outside of and independently of any particular program. Files can also contain data that is either read or written by your program. It is this type of file that concerns us here.

A file is a sequence of components of the same data type

A file is a sequence of components of the same data type that resides in auxiliary storage, often a disk. Files are useful because they can be large and can exist after program execution terminates. In contrast, variables of primitive data types and objects, for example, represent memory that is accessible only within the program that creates them. When program execution terminates, the operating system reuses this memory and changes its contents.

Since files can exist after program execution, they not only provide a permanent record for human users, they also allow communication between programs. Program *A* can write its output into a file that program *B* can use later for input. However, files that you discard after program execution are also not unusual. You use such a file as a scratch pad during program execution when you have too much data to retain conveniently in memory all at once.

It is useful to contrast files with their closest Java relatives, arrays. Files and arrays are similar in that they are both collections of components of the same type. For example, just as you can have an array of elements whose type is *char*, so also can you have a file of elements whose type is *char*. In both cases, the components are characters. However, in addition to the previous distinction between files and all other data types—files can exist after program execution and arrays cannot—files and arrays have two other differences:

- **Files grow in size as needed; arrays have a fixed size.** When you declare an array, you specify its maximum size. Thus, a fixed amount of memory represents the array. A well-written program always checks that an array can accommodate a new piece of data before attempting to insert it. If the array cannot accommodate the data, the program might have to terminate with a message of explanation. You can increase the array size—hopefully by changing the value of a named constant—and compile and run the program again.[4] On the other hand, if you declare the array's maximum size to be larger than you need, you waste memory. In contrast, the size of a file is not fixed. When the system first creates a file, the file requires almost no storage space. As a program adds data to the file, the file's size increases as necessary, up to the limit of the storage device. Thus, at any given time, the file occupies only as much space as it actually requires. This dynamic nature is a great advantage.

- **Files provide both sequential and random access; arrays provide random access.** If you want the 100th element in the one-dimensional array x, you can access it directly by writing x[99]; you do not need to look at the elements x[0] through x[98] first. You could choose, of course, to process an array's elements sequentially, but you would do so by accessing each successive element directly and independently of any other element.

  However, you can access elements in a file either directly or sequentially. If you want the 100th element in a file, you can access it directly by position without first reading past the 99 elements that precede it. On the other hand, you could also read all

---

[4]Chapter 4 describes resizable arrays. If you reach the end of such an array, you can increase its size during execution. However, this process requires copying the old array into the new array.

of the first 100 elements one at a time, in sequential order, without specifying any element's position.

Files are classified as follows. A **text file** is a file of characters that are organized into lines. The files that you create—by using an editor—to contain your Java programs are text files. Because text files consist of characters, and accessing characters by position number is usually not convenient, you typically process a text file sequentially. A file that is not a text file is called a **binary file** or sometimes a **general file** or a **nontext file**.

Text Files

Text files are designed for easy communication with people. As such, they are flexible and easy to use, but they are not as efficient with respect to computer time and storage as binary files.

One special aspect of text files is that they *appear* to be divided into lines. This illusion is often the source of much confusion. In reality, a text file—like any other file—is a sequence of components of the same type. That is, a text file is a sequence of characters. A special **end-of-line symbol** creates the illusion that a text file contains lines by making the file *behave* as if it were divided into lines. On some systems this end-of-line symbol is simply a carriage return, while on others it consists of a carriage return and line feed character. You need not worry about how your system actually views the end-of-line symbol; this is taken care of by the Java runtime system.

A text file contains lines of characters

When you create a text file by typing data at your keyboard, each time you press the Enter, or Return, key, you insert one end-of-line symbol into the file. When an output device, such as a printer or monitor, encounters an end-of-line symbol in a text file, the device moves to the beginning of the next line. In Java, you can specify this end-of-line symbol by using the character \n.

Files end with a special end-of-file symbol

In addition, you can think of a special **end-of-file symbol** that follows the last component in a file. Such a symbol may or may not actually exist in the file, but Java behaves as if one did. Figure A-10 depicts a text file with these special symbols.

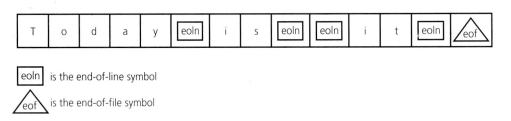

| T | o | d | a | y | eoln | i | s | eoln | eoln | i | t | eoln | eof |

eoln   is the end-of-line symbol

eof   is the end-of-file symbol

Figure A-10

A text file with end-of-line and end-of-file symbols

Any program that uses input or output files must import classes from the package *java.io*. Input files are supported by two main classes: *FileInputStream* and *FileReader*. Output files are also supported by two main classes: *FileOutputStream* and *PrintWriter*. The package also provides a class *File* that provides an abstraction for the file within a program. Instances of the class *File* are not used directly for input or output, but for getting or setting characteristics of a file, such as its access mode. Actual read or write access to the file is done through streams.

Use streams to access a file

Opening a stream to a file.   Before you can read from or write to a file, you need to **open** a stream to the file. That is, you need to create a stream instance. One way to open a stream to a file for reading is to use the class *FileReader* and provide the file's name when you declare the file stream. For example,

You must initialize, or open, a stream before you can use it

```
FileReader inStream = new FileReader("Ages.dat");
```

declares an input stream variable *inStream* and associates it with the file named *Ages.dat*. The file name can be either a literal constant, as it is here, or a string variable.

Alternatively, you can use an instance of *File* by writing

```
File inFile = new File("Ages.dat");
FileReader inStream = new FileReader(inFile);
```

Unfortunately, the methods available from the class *FileReader* do not lend themselves very well to text processing. Because of this, the stream instance is usually embedded within an instance of the class *BufferedReader*. (This is the same class that we used to read input from the keyboard.) *BufferedReader* provides the method *readLine* for obtaining a line of text as a *String* object. A line is considered to be terminated by an end-of-line character, as we mentioned earlier. Here is an example of opening a stream to a file and adding the functionality of the class *BufferedReader*:

The method **readLine** *reads a line of text as a string*

```
FileReader fr = new FileReader("Ages.dat");
BufferedReader input = new BufferedReader(fr);
```

Often, this is combined into a single statement:

```
BufferedReader input = new BufferedReader(
                        new FileReader("Ages.dat"));
```

Note that the *FileReader* constructor will throw the exception *FileNotFoundException* if the file is not found. Since this is a checked exception, the statement must be enclosed in a *try* block. Therefore, the actual code used to open a stream to a text file would be similar to the following:

If the file is not found, an exception is thrown

```
BufferedReader input;
try {
  input = new BufferedReader(new FileReader("Ages.dat"));
  // read data from file
} // end try
```

```
catch (FileNotFoundException e) {
  System.out.println(e);
  System.exit(1); // exit the program if the file is not
                  // found
} // end catch
```

Now, using the instance of *BufferedReader*, data can be read from the file. As with keyboard input, you can use a *StringTokenizer* to break up the string returned by *readLine* into tokens for easier processing. But how do you know when you have read all of the data in the file? *BufferedReader* provides a method *ready* that determines whether the underlying character stream is ready. This method returns a boolean value that can be used in a *while* loop to determine whether more data is available in the file, as follows:

*The method **ready** can be used to determine whether the file contains more data*

```
StringTokenizer line;
while (input.ready()) {
    line = new StringTokenizer(input.readLine());
    // process line of data
    ...

}   // end while
```

You can also detect when the end of the file is reached by checking whether the method *readLine* returns *null*. For example, the following loop will process all of the lines in the file:

```
StringTokenizer line;
String inputLine;
while ((inputLine = input.readLine()) != null) {
  line = new StringTokenizer(inputLine);
  // process line of data
  ...

} // end while
```

The method *readLine* can throw the exception *IOException*, another checked exception. Also, *readLine* must appear within the same *try* block that creates the *BufferedReader* instance; otherwise, the compiler won't be able to verify that the instance has been initialized properly. One way you can handle this is simply to add another *catch* block for the *IOException* to the *try* statement. Or, since *FileNotFoundException* is a subclass of *IOException*, you can use a single *catch* block as follows:

```
BufferedReader input;
StringTokenizer line;
String inputLine;
try {
  input = new BufferedReader(new FileReader("Ages.dat"));
  while ((inputLine = input.readLine()) != null) {
    line = new StringTokenizer(inputLine);
```

```
    // process line of data
    ...

  }
} // end try
catch (IOException e) {
  System.out.println(e);
  System.exit(1); // I/O error, exit the program
} // end catch
```

File output. To write text to a file, you need to open an output stream to the file. One way to open a file for writing is to use the class *FileWriter* and provide the file's name when you declare the file stream. For example,

```
FileWriter outStream = new FileWriter("Results.dat");
```

Open an output stream to a file before writing to it

declares an output stream variable *outStream* and associates it with the file named *Results.dat*. The file name can be a literal constant, as it is here, or a string variable. If the file *Results.dat* does not exist, a new empty file with this name is created. If the file *Results.dat* already exists, opening it erases[5] the data in the file.

Like *FileReader*, the *FileWriter* class itself does not provide useful methods for writing data to the file. Another class, *PrintWriter*, provides two methods: *print* and *println*. These methods are already familiar to you; they are the same methods used by *System.out*. Here is a simple example of writing data to a file:

```
try {
  PrintWriter output = new PrintWriter(
        new FileWriter("Results.dat"));
  output.println("Results of the survey");
  output.println("Number of males: " + numMales);
  output.println("Number of females: " + numFemales);

  // other code and output appears here...

} // end try
catch (IOException e) {
  System.out.println(e);
  System.exit(1); // I/O error, exit the program
} // end catch
```

Closing a file. When you have finished using a file, you should close the stream associated with that file. To close a stream (input or output), you use the method *close* as follows:

```
myStream.close();
```

*When you are finished using a file, call **close** to close the stream*

---

[5] The data might not actually be erased, but the file will behave as if it were empty.

The file associated with this stream is no longer available for input or output until you open it again.

Adding to a text file. When you open a stream to a file for writing, you can specify a second argument in addition to the file's name to indicate whether the file should be replaced or appended. If this second argument to the *FileOutputStream* constructor is *true*, the file is appended rather than replaced. For example,

You can append data to a file

```
PrintWriter ofStream = new PrintWriter(
            new FileOutputStream("Results.dat", true));
```

This retains the old contents of the file *Results.dat*, and you can write additional components.

Copying a text file. Suppose that you wanted to make a copy of the text file associated with the stream variable *original*. Copying a text file requires some work and provides a good example of the statements you have just studied. The approach taken by the following method copies the file one line at a time:

```java
public static void copyTextFile(String originalFileName,
                                String copyFileName) {
// ----------------------------------------------------------
// Makes a duplicate copy of a text file.
// Precondition: originalFileName is the name of an existing
// external text file, and copyFileName is the name of the
// text file to be created.
// Postcondition: The text file named copyFileName is a
// duplicate of the file named originalFileName.
// ----------------------------------------------------------
  try {
    BufferedReader ifStream = new BufferedReader(
            new FileReader(originalFileName));
    PrintWriter ofStream = new PrintWriter(
            new FileWriter(copyFileName));
    String line;

    // copy lines one at a time from given file
    // to new file
    while ((line = ifStream.readLine()) != null)
      ofStream.println(line);
    }  // end while

    ifStream.close();  // close the files
    ofStream.close();
  }  // end try
  catch (IOException e) {
    System.out.println("Error copying file");
  }  // end catch
```

```
  finally {
    ifStream.close();   // close the files
    ofStream.close();
  } // end finally
}   // end copyTextFile
```

The *finally* block allows the files to be closed regardless of whether an exception is thrown. It is executed after correct execution of the *try* block or after an exception is handled in a *catch* block.

Searching a text file sequentially. Suppose that you have a text file of data about a company's employees. For simplicity, assume that this file contains two consecutive lines for each employee. The first line contains the employee's name, and the next line contains data such as salary.

Given the name of an employee, you can search the file for that name and then determine other information about this person. A **sequential search** examines the names in the order in which they appear in the file until the desired name is located. The following method performs such a sequential search, given a class to represent a person:

```
public class Person {
  private String name;
  private double salary;

  public Person(String n, double s) {
    name = n;
    salary = s;
  }   // end constructor
  // other methods appear here
}   // end Person


public Person searchFileSequentially(String fileName,
                                     String desiredName) {
// -----------------------------------------------------------
// Searches a text file sequentially for a desired person.
// Precondition: fileName is the name of a text file of
// names and data about people. Each person is represented
// by two lines in the file: The first line contains the
// person's name, and the second line contains the person's
// salary. desiredName is the name of the person sought.
// Postcondition: If desiredName was found in the file,
// a Person object that contains the person's
// name and data is returned. Otherwise, the value null
// is returned to indicate that the desiredName was not
// found. The file is unchanged and closed.
// -----------------------------------------------------------
  try {
    BufferedReader ifStream = new BufferedReader(
                     new FileReader(fileName));
```

```
String nextName;
String nextSalary;

boolean found = false;
while (!found &&
        (nextName = ifStream.readLine()) != null) {
  nextSalary = ifStream.readLine();
  if (nextName.compareTo(desiredName) == 0) {
    found = true;
  } // end if
} // end while

if (found) {
  return new Person(nextName,
                    Double.parseDouble(nextSalary));
}
else {
  return null;
} // end if
} // end try
catch (IOException e) {
  System.out.println("Error processing file");
} // end catch
finally {
  ifStream.close(); // close the file
} // end finally
} // end searchFileSequentially
```

This method needs to look at all the names in the file before determining that a particular name does not occur. If the names were in alphabetical order, you could determine when the search had passed the place in the file that should have contained the desired name, if it existed. In this way, you could terminate the search before you needlessly searched the rest of the file.

Object Serialization

In the method *searchFileSequentially*, we assumed that all of the information about a person had been placed in a text file in a very specific format. In that example, the data fields were strings and primitive values, so it was simply a matter of writing the name data field on one line and the salary on the next line. But what about situations in which the data is more complex? For example, suppose that the *Person* class also kept track of the person's dependents by using an ADT list.[6] To save this information to a text file involves a more complicated scheme, since we may not know beforehand how many dependents an employee has.

---

[6] Chapter 3 introduces the ADT list.

When data is stored to a file for later use by the same program or another program, it is called **data persistence**. Normally, any information stored in the various variables and data structures in a program is lost when the program terminates execution. In many cases, however, it is desirable to save the data to a file for later retrieval before terminating the program. Java provides a mechanism for creating persistent objects, called **object serialization**. Serialization is the process of transforming an object into a sequence of bytes that represents the object. Deserialization is the process of transforming a sequence of bytes back into an object. Once an object is serialized, it can be stored in a file and read back at a later time using deserialization.

Object serialization transforms an object into a sequence of bytes

Any object that is to be saved using object serialization must implement the interface *java.io.Serializable*. This interface is somewhat unique in that it contains no methods. It is used to signal the compiler that the instances of this class may need to have their state serialized or deserialized.

One interesting aspect of object serialization is that when an object is serialized, all objects that it references are also serialized, as long as the referenced objects are instances of a class that implements the *Serializable* interface. For example, suppose that the following is the *Person* class described earlier:

```java
class Person {
  private String name;
  private double salary;
  private ListInterface dependents;

  public Person(String n, double s) {
    name = n;
    salary = s;
    // assume that ListArrayBased also implements the
    // Serializable interface
    dependents = new ListArrayBased();
  } // end constructor

  public void addDependent(Person p) {
    dependents.add(p);
  } // end addDependent

  public String getName() {
    return name;
  } // end getName

  // other methods for class appear here
} // end Person
```

When an instance of the *Person* class is serialized, all of the referenced objects are also serialized—the *String* object *name* and the list *dependents*. When the object is deserialized, both it and the objects it originally referenced will be restored to their original state. You accomplish the actual serialization of an object by using the *writeObject* method of the stream class *ObjectOutputStream*. You deserialize an object by using the *readObject* method of the stream class *ObjectInput-Stream*. Much like *PrintWriter* and *BufferedReader*, *ObjectOutput-Stream* and *ObjectInputStream* add functionality to *FileOutput-Stream* and *FileInputStream*, respectively. The following statements save a *Person* object *p* to a file *EmployeeDB.dat*:

```java
ObjectOutputStream ooStream = new ObjectOutputStream(
                new FileOutputStream("EmployeeDB.dat"));
ooStream.writeObject(p);
```

The following method demonstrates how the file could be searched sequentially for a particular person (this method parallels the method given for text files):

```java
public Person searchFileSequentially(String fileName,
                                     String desiredName) {
// ----------------------------------------------------------
// Searches a text file sequentially for a desired person.
// Precondition: fileName is the name of a binary file
// of Person objects. desiredName is the name of the person
// sought.
// Postcondition: If desiredName was found in the file,
// a Person object that contains the person's
// name and data is returned. Otherwise, the value null
// is returned to indicate that desiredName was not
// found. The file is unchanged and closed.
// ----------------------------------------------------------
  try {
    ObjectInputStream ioStream = new ObjectInputStream(
                              new FileReader(fileName));
    Person nextPerson;

    boolean found = false;
    while (!found &&
           (nextPerson = ioStream.readObject()) != null) {
      if (nextPerson.getName().compareTo(desiredName) == 0) {

        found = true;
      }  // end if
    }  // end while

    if (found) {
      return nextPerson;
    }
    else {
      return null;
    } // end if
  }  // end try
```

```
   catch (IOException e) {
      System.out.println("Error processing file");
   }  // end catch
   finally {
      ioStream.close();  // close the file
   } // end finally
}  // end searchFileSequentially
```

A COMPARISON TO C++

The following examples will help you compare a construct in C++ with the
equivalent construct in Java.

`// Java comment on a single line`
`/* Java comment`
`that crosses multiple lines */`
`/** Javadoc-style comments */`
	`// C++ comment on a single line`
	`/* C++ comment`
	`that crosses multiple lines */`

`// Java uses packages to group related` `// classes together`	`// C++ uses libraries to group related` `// functions and classes together`

`// Java class`
`// Each member has an access modifier`
`// (public, private, protected, or none for`
`//   package access)`
`class Person {`
`   private String name;`
`   private int age;`
`   private double gpa;`
`   public Person() {`
`   } // end default constructor`
`   ...`
`}  // end Person`
	`// C++ class - by default, all members are`
	`// private unless labeled otherwise`
	
	`class Person {`
	`   string name;`
	`   int    age;`
	`   double gpa;`
	`public:`
	`   Person();`
	`};  // end Person`

`// No equivalent in Java, a class`
`// containing only public data could be`
`// used`
	`// C++ structure - by default, all members`
	`// are public unless labeled otherwise`
	`struct person {`
	`   string name;`
	`   int    age;`
	`   double gpa;`
	`};  // end person`

`// Java supports single inheritance of`
`// classes. Interfaces can be used to`
`// specify additional behavior`
	`// C++ supports multiple inheritance`

```// Java does not support templates but does // have a single inheritance hierarchy // built upon the class Object class Stack { public void push(Object newItem) { ... } ... } // end Stack```	```// C++ supports templates as a // parameterized type template <class T> void Stack<T>::push(T newItem) { ... }```
```// Java does not rely on a preprocessor; // functionality is provided by the Java // language itself```	```// C++ uses a preprocessor for compiler // directives such as file inclusion```
```// Java methods must appear as part of a // class```	```// C++ can have stand-alone functions```
```// Java constant // Must be declared within a class or a // method final int SIZE = 50;```	```// C++ constant // Can be declared globally or within a // class or a function const int SIZE = 50;```
```// Java valued method public boolean isLeapYear(int year) { // Returns true if year is a leap year; // otherwise returns false. boolean leap = false; boolean yearEndsIn00 = (year % 100 == 0); if (yearEndsIn00 && (year % 400 == 0)) leap = true; else if (!yearEndsIn00 && (year % 4 == 0)) leap = true; return leap; } // end isLeapYear```	```// C++ valued function bool isLeapYear(int year) { // Returns true if year is a leap year; // otherwise returns false. bool leap = false; bool yearEndsIn00 = (year % 100 == 0); if (yearEndsIn00 && (year % 400 == 0)) Leap = true; else if (!yearEndsIn00 && (year % 4 == 0)) leap = true; return leap; } // end isLeapYear```

<table>
<tr><td>

```
// Java variable declarations
// Variables must be declared within a
// class or a method
int        day, month, year;
double     power, x;
char       response;
boolean    done;
// Simple reference declaration; no
// object is instantiated until the new
// operator is used. Java supports only
// dynamic allocation of objects
Sphere ball;
// Creating an object using a default
// constructor
Sphere ball = new Sphere();
// Using constructor with parameters
Sphere ball = new Sphere(1.0);
```

</td><td>

```
// C++ variable declarations
// Variables can be declared globally
// as well as within classes and methods
int    day, month, year;
double power, x;
char   response;
bool   done;
// Objects can be declared statically
// using the default constructor
Sphere ball;
// Also by using a constructor with
// parameters
Sphere ball(1.0);
// Dynamic allocation is supported using
// pointers and the new operator
Sphere *ball = new Sphere();
```

</td></tr>
<tr><td>

```
// Equality in Java
// == and != check for shallow equality
// For object equality, must override the
// equals method from class Object
```

</td><td>

```
// Equality in C++
// == and != check for shallow equality
// For object equality, must provide the
// functions operator == and operator !=,
// for example
```

</td></tr>
<tr><td>

```
// Java array, primitive types
double[] r = new double[SIZE];
double[] s = new double[SIZE];

for (int i = 0; i < SIZE; i++) {
  r[i] = 0.0;
} // end for

// Java array using references
Sphere[] marbles = new Sphere[SIZE];
for (int i=0; i < SIZE; i++) {
  marbles[i] = new Sphere(0.3);
} // end for
```

</td><td>

```
// C++ array
typedef double arrayType[SIZE];
arrayType r;
double    s[SIZE];

for (int i = 0; i < SIZE; ++i) {
   r[i] = 0.0;
} // end for
```

</td></tr>
<tr><td>

```
// Java Standard Output
System.out.println("Enter month and " +
     "day for year " + year +
     "as integers: ");
```

</td><td>

```
// C++ Standard Output
cout << "Enter month and day "
     << "for year" << year
     << " as integers: ";
```

</td></tr>
</table>

```
// Java Standard Input                    | // C++ Standard Input
BufferedReader stdin = new BufferedReader(| cin >> x >> y;
        new InputStreamReader(System.in));|
String nextLine = stdin.readLine();       |
StringTokenizer input =                   |
            new StringTokenizer(nextLine);|
x = Integer.parseInt(input.nextToken());  |
y = Integer.parseInt(input.nextToken());  |
```

SUMMARY

1. Java packages provide a mechanism for grouping related classes. To indicate that a class is part of a package, you include a *package* statement as the first program line of your code.

2. To use classes contained in other packages, you must include an *import* statement before the class definition. The format of the *import* statement is

   import *package-name.class-name*;

3. An object in Java is an instance of a class. A class can be thought of as a data type that specifies the data and methods that are available for instances of the class. A class definition includes an optional subclassing modifier, an optional access modifier, the keyword *class*, an optional *extends* clause, an optional *implements* clause, and a class body.

4. Data fields are class members that are either variables or constants. Data field declarations can contain modifiers that control the availability of the data field (access modifiers) or that modify the way the data field can be used (use modifiers).

5. Methods are used to implement object behaviors. The general form of a method definition is

   access-modifier use-modifier type name(formal-parameter-list) {
   *   body*
   }

   A valued method returns a value by using the *return* statement. A *void* method can use *return* to exit.

6. When you invoke a method, the actual arguments must correspond to the formal parameters in number, order, and type.

7. A method makes local copies of the values of any arguments that are passed. Thus, the arguments remain unchanged by the method. When the argument is a reference, a method can modify the object it references, but not the value of the reference variable itself.

8. You can access data fields and methods that are declared *public* by naming the object, followed by a period, followed by the member name.

9. Each comment line in Java begins with two slashes (//) and continues until the end of the line.

10. A Java identifier is a sequence of letters, digits, underscores, and dollar signs that must begin with either a letter or an underscore.

11. The primitive data types in Java are organized into four types: integer, character, floating point, and boolean.

12. A Java reference is used to locate an object. When an object is created using the *new* operator, the location of the object in memory is returned and can be assigned to a reference variable.

13. You define named constants by using a statement of the form

    final   *type-identifier = value;*

14. Java uses short-circuit evaluation for expressions that contain the logical operators && (and) and || (or). That is, evaluation proceeds from left to right and stops as soon as the value of the entire expression is apparent.

15. An array is a collection of references that have the same data type. You can refer to the elements of an array by using an index that begins with zero. First the array must be instantiated with the number of elements desired. Then you can assign the references of the array an object.

16. A string is a sequence of characters. The *String* class supports nonmutable strings, while the *StringBuffer* class supports mutable strings. In the *String* class, you can access the entire string, a substring, or the individual characters. In the *String-Buffer* class, you can access and actually manipulate the entire string, a substring, or the individual characters.

17. The method *System.out.println* places a value into an output stream. Reading a value from an input stream is more involved. You must first establish a stream for *System.in*. Then, for easier input, wrap the stream in an instance of *BufferedReader*.

18. The general form of the *if* statement is

    ```
    if (expression)
        statement₁
    else
        statement₂
    ```

    If *expression* is true, *statement₁* executes; otherwise, *statement₂* executes.

19. The general form of the *switch* statement is

    ```
    switch (expression) {
      case constant₁:
    ```

```
        statement₁
        break;
  . . .
        case constantₙ: case constantₙ₊₁:
            statementₙ
            break;
        default:
            statement
  }
```

The appropriate *statement* executes according to the value of *expression*. Typically, `break` (or sometimes `return`) follows the statement or statements after each `case`. Omitting `break` causes execution to continue to the statement(s) of the `case` that follows.

20. The general form of the `while` statement is

    ```
    while (expression)
        statement
    ```

    As long as *expression* is true, *statement* executes. Thus, it is possible that *statement* will never execute.

21. The general form of the `for` statement is

    ```
    for (initialize; test; update)
        statement
    ```

    where *initialize*, *test*, and *update* are expressions. Typically, *initialize* is an assignment expression that occurs only once. Then if *test*, which is usually a logical expression, is true, *statement* executes. The expression *update* executes next, usually incrementing or decrementing a counter. This sequence of events repeats, beginning with the evaluation of *test*, until *test* is false.

22. The general form of the `do` statement is

    ```
    do
        statement
    while (expression);
    ```

    Here, *statement* executes until the value of *expression* is false. Note that *statement* always executes at least once.

23. In Java, files are accessed using streams.

24. Data persistence is supported in Java through object serialization. You serialize an object by using the method `writeObject` from the stream class `ObjectOutputStream`, and you deserialize an object by using the method `readObject` from the stream class `ObjectInputStream`.

CAUTIONS

1. Remember that = is the assignment operator; == is the equality operator.

2. Do not begin a decimal integer constant with zero. A constant that begins with zero is either an octal constant or a hexadecimal constant.

3. Without a *break* statement, execution of a *case* within a *switch* statement will continue into the next *case*.

4. You must be careful that an array index does not exceed the size of the array. Java will throw the exception *ArrayIndexOutOf-Bounds* if an index value is less than zero or greater than or equal to the length of the array.

5. Opening an existing file for output erases the data in the file, unless you specify append mode.

B

Unicode Character Codes *(ASCII Subset)*

Dec	Char	Dec	Char	Dec	Char	Dec	Char
0	NUL	32	(blank)	64	@	96	` (reverse quote)
1	STX	33	!	65	A	97	a
2	SOT	34	"	66	B	98	b
3	ETX	35	#	67	C	99	c
4	EOT	36	$	68	D	100	d
5	ENQ	37	%	69	E	101	e
6	ACK	38	&	70	F	102	f
7	BEL	39	' (apostrophe)	71	G	103	g
8	BS	40	(	72	H	104	h
9	HT	41	)	73	I	105	i
10	LF	42	*	74	J	106	j
11	VT	43	+	75	K	107	k
12	FF	44	, (comma)	76	L	108	l
13	CR	45	–	77	M	109	m
14	SO	46	.	78	N	110	n
15	SI	47	/	79	O	111	o
16	DLE	48	0	80	P	112	p
17	DC1	49	1	81	Q	113	q
18	DC2	50	2	82	R	114	r
19	DC3	51	3	83	S	115	s
20	DC4	52	4	84	T	116	t
21	NAK	53	5	85	U	117	u
22	SYN	54	6	86	V	118	v
23	ETB	55	7	87	W	119	w
24	CAN	56	8	88	X	120	x
25	EM	57	9	89	Y	121	y
26	SUB	58	:	90	Z	122	z
27	ESC	59	;	91	[	123	{
28	FS	60	<	92	\	124		
29	GS	61	=	93	]	125	}
30	RS	62	>	94	^	126	~
31	US	63	?	95	_ (underscore)	127	DEL

Note: The codes 0 through 31 and 127 are for control characters that do not print.

C

Java Resources

Java Web Sites

Sun Microsystems, the creators of the Java programming language, maintain one of the best Web sites of information on Java at

```
http://java.sun.com
```

Of particular interest is the Java 2 Software Development Kit (SDK), Standard Edition, version 1.2.2. This is the version of the Java compiler used to compile all of the code contained in this text. You can download it from the following Web page:

```
http://java.sun.com/products/jdk/1.2
```

The next section describes how to use this package to compile and execute a Java program.

You can also browse the Java 2 documentation or download your own copy from the following Web page:

```
http://java.sun.com/products/jdk/1.2/download-docs.html
```

Other popular Java Web sites include

> **Gamelan:** `http://www.gamelan.com`
>
> **JavaWorld:** `http://www.javaworld.com`
>
> **JavaReport:** `http://www.javareport.com`

Using the Java 2 Software Development Kit

This section summarizes the commands used to compile and execute Java applications within an MS-DOS window on a PC running Windows 95/98/NT. These commands also work in a command window on most UNIX machines.

Follow the instructions provided by Sun Microsystems to unpack and install the Java 2 SDK on your system. This discussion assumes that you have created a simple Java program in the file *Hello.java* as follows:

```
public class Hello {
  public static void main(String[] args) {
    System.out.println("Hello Java!");
  } // end main
} // end Hello
```

Compiling a Java program. To compile the Java program *Hello.java*, use the command *javac* followed by the file name of the Java program, as follows:

```
javac Hello.java
```

Java expects that your file name will be consistent with the name of the class it contains, and that it will end with *.java*.

If your program contains errors, they will be listed on the screen. If the program compiles successfully, you will see no messages, and a new file called *Hello.class* will appear in your directory. This file contains the bytecode for your program.

Running a Java program. Java programs are executed using the Java Virtual Machine (JVM). To run your program using the JVM, use the command *java* followed by the name of the *.class* file created by the Java compiler:

```
java Hello
```

Note that you should not include the *.class* extension. At this point, the program is executed and produces the following output:

```
Hello Java!
```

The Web site for this textbook contains all of the code contained in this text, plus further instructions for compiling and using the code.

APPENDIX D

Mathematical Induction

Many proofs of theorems or invariants in computer science use a technique called **mathematical induction,** or simply **induction.** Induction is a principle of mathematics that is like a row of dominoes standing on end. If you push the first domino, all the dominoes will fall one after another. What is it about the dominoes that allows us to draw this conclusion? If you know that when one domino falls the next domino will fall, then pushing the first domino will cause them all to fall in succession. More formally, you can show that all the dominoes will fall if you can show that the following two facts are true:

- The first domino falls.
- For any $k \geq 1$, if the kth domino falls, the $(k + 1)^{\text{th}}$ domino will fall.

The principle of mathematical induction is an axiom that is stated as follows:

AXIOM D-1. **The principle of mathematical induction.** A property $P(n)$ that involves an integer n is true for all $n \geq 0$ if the following are true:

1. $P(0)$ is true.

2. If $P(k)$ is true for any $k \geq 0$, then $P(k + 1)$ is true.

A **proof by induction on n** is one that uses the principle of mathematical induction. Such a proof consists of the two steps given in Axiom D-1. The first step is called the **basis,** or **base case.** The second step is the **inductive step.** We usually break the inductive step into two parts: the **inductive hypothesis** ("if $P(k)$ is true for any $k \geq 0$") and the **inductive conclusion** ("then $P(k + 1)$ is true").

Example 1

The following recursive method, which is given here in pseudocode, computes x^n:

```
power2(x, n)

    if (n == 0)
        return 1
    else
        return  x * power2(x, n—1)
```

You can prove that *power2* returns x^n for all $n \geq 0$ by using the following proof by induction on *n*:

Basis. *Show that the property is true when n = 0.* That is, you must show that *power2(x, 0)* returns x^0, which is 1. However, as you can see from the definition of *power2*, *power2(x, 0)* is 1.

Now you must establish the inductive step. By assuming that the property is true when $n = k$ (the inductive hypothesis), you must show that the property is true when $n = k + 1$ (the inductive conclusion).

Inductive hypothesis. *Assume that the property is true when n = k.* That is, assume that

$$power2(x, k) = x^k$$

Inductive conclusion. *Show that the property is true when n = k + 1.* That is, you must show that *power2(x, k + 1)* returns the value x^{k+1}. By definition of the method *power2*,

$$power2(x, k + 1) = x * power2(x, k)$$

By the inductive hypothesis, *power2(x, k)* returns the value x^k, so

$$power2(x, k + 1) = x * x^k$$
$$= x^{k+1}$$

which is what you needed to show to establish the inductive step.

The inductive proof is thus complete. We demonstrated that the two steps in Axiom D-1 are true, so the principle of mathematical induction guarantees that *power2* returns x^n for all $n \geq 0$. (**End of proof.**)

Example 2

Prove that

$$1 + 2 + \cdots + n = \frac{n(n+1)}{2} \quad \text{when } n \geq 1$$

It will be helpful to let S_n represent the sum $1 + 2 + \cdots + n$.

Basis. Sometimes the property to be proven is trivial when $n = 0$, as is the case here. You can use $n = 1$ as the basis instead. (Actually, you can use any value of $n \geq 0$ as the basis, but a value of 0 or 1 is typical.)

You need to show that the sum S_1, which is simply 1, is equal to $1(1 + 1)/2$. This fact is obvious.

Inductive hypothesis. Assume that the formula is true when $n = k$; that is, assume that $S_k = k(k + 1)/2$.

Inductive conclusion. Show that the formula is true when $n = k + 1$. To do so, you can proceed as follows:

$$
\begin{aligned}
S_{k+1} &= (1 + 2 + \cdots + k) + (k + 1) && \text{(definition of } S_{k+1}) \\
&= S_k + (k + 1) && \text{(definition of } S_k) \\
&= k(k + 1)/2 + (k + 1) && \text{(inductive hypothesis)} \\
&= (k(k + 1) + 2(k + 1))/2 && \text{(common denominator)} \\
&= (k + 1)(k + 2)/2 && \text{(factorization)}
\end{aligned}
$$

The last expression is $n(n + 1)/2$ when n is $k + 1$. Thus, if the formula for S_k is true, the formula for $S_{k + 1}$ is true. Therefore, by the principle of mathematical induction, the formula is true when $n \geq 1$. (**End of proof.**)

Example 3

Prove that $2^n > n^2$ when $n \geq 5$.

Basis. Here is an example where the base case is not $n = 0$ or 1, but instead is $n = 5$. It is obvious that the relationship is true when $n = 5$ because

$$2^5 = 32 > 5^2 = 25$$

Inductive hypothesis. Assume that the relationship is true when $n = k \geq 5$; that is, assume that $2^k > k^2$ when $k \geq 5$.

Inductive conclusion. Show that the relationship is true when $n = k + 1$; that is, show that $2^{k + 1} > (k + 1)^2$ when $k \geq 5$. To do so, you can proceed as follows:

$$
\begin{aligned}
(k + 1)^2 &= k^2 + (2k + 1) && \text{(square } k + 1) \\
&< k^2 + k^2 \text{ when } k \geq 5 && (2k + 1 < k^2; \text{ see Exercise 3)} \\
&< 2^k + 2^k \text{ when } k \geq 5 && \text{(inductive hypothesis)} \\
&= 2^{k + 1}
\end{aligned}
$$

Therefore, by the principle of mathematical induction, $2^n > n^2$ when $n \geq 5$. (**End of proof.**)

Sometimes, the inductive hypothesis in Axiom D-1 is not sufficient. That is, you may need to assume more than $P(k)$. The following axiom is a stronger form of the principle of mathematical induction:

AXIOM D-2. The principle of mathematical induction (strong form). A property $P(n)$ that involves an integer n is true for all $n \geq 0$ if the following are true:

1. $P(0)$ is true.

2. If $P(0), P(1), \ldots, P(k)$ are true for any $k \geq 0$, then $P(k + 1)$ is true.

Notice that the inductive hypothesis of Axiom D-2 ("If $P(0), P(1), \ldots, P(k)$ are true for any $k \geq 0$") includes the inductive hypothesis of Axiom D-1 ("If $P(k)$ is true for any $k \geq 0$").

Example 4

Prove that every integer greater than 1 can be written as a product of prime integers.

Recall that a prime number is one that is divisible only by 1 and itself. The inductive proof is as follows:

Basis. The statement that you must prove involves integers greater than 1. Thus, the base case is $n = 2$. However, 2 is a prime number and, therefore, it trivially is a product of prime numbers.

Inductive hypothesis. Assume that the property is true for each of the integers $2, 3, \ldots, k$, where $k \geq 2$.

Inductive conclusion. Show that the property is true when $n = k + 1$; that is, show that $k + 1$ can be written as a product of prime numbers.

If $k + 1$ is a prime number, there is nothing more to show. However, if $k + 1$ is not a prime number, it must be divisible by an integer x such that $1 < x < k + 1$. Thus,

$$k + 1 = x * y$$

where $1 < y < k + 1$. Notice that x and y are each less than or equal to k, so the inductive hypothesis applies. That is, x and y can each be written as a product of prime numbers. Clearly $x * y$, which is equal to $k + 1$, must be a product of prime numbers. Because the formula holds for $n = k + 1$, it holds for all $n \geq 2$ by the principle of mathematical induction. (**End of proof.**)

Example 5

Chapter 2 discusses the following recursive definition:

$$rabbit(1) = 1$$
$$rabbit(2) = 1$$
$$rabbit(n) = rabbit(n - 1) + rabbit(n - 2) \text{ when } n > 2$$

Prove that

$$rabbit(n) = (a^n - b^n)/\sqrt{5}$$

where $a = (1 + \sqrt{5})/2$ and $b = (1 - \sqrt{5})/2 = 1 - a$.

Basis. Because $rabbit(0)$ is undefined, begin at $n = 1$. Some algebra shows that $rabbit(1) = (a^1 - b^1)/\sqrt{5} = 1$. However, notice that $rabbit(2)$ is also a special case. That is, you cannot compute *rabbit*(2) from *rabbit*(1) by using the recurrence relationship given here. Therefore, the basis in this inductive proof must include $n = 2$.

When $n = 2$, some more algebra will show that $rabbit(2) = (a^2 - b^2)/\sqrt{5} = 1$. Thus, the formula is true when n is either 1 or 2.

Inductive hypothesis. Assume that the formula is true for all n such that $1 \le n \le k$, where k is at least 2.

Inductive conclusion. Show that the formula is true for $n = k + 1$. To do so, you can proceed as follows:

$$
\begin{aligned}
rabbit(k + 1) &= rabbit(k) + rabbit(k - 1) && \text{(recurrence relation)} \\
&= [(a^k - b^k) + (a^{k-1} - b^{k-1})]/\sqrt{5} && \text{(inductive hypothesis)} \\
&= [a^{k-1}(a + 1) - b^{k-1}(b + 1)]/\sqrt{5} && \text{(factorization)} \\
&= [a^{k-1}(a^2) - b^{k-1}(b^2)]/\sqrt{5} && (a + 1 = a^2; b + 1 = b^2) \\
&= (a^{k+1} - b^{k+1})/\sqrt{5}
\end{aligned}
$$

Because the formula holds for $n = k + 1$, it holds for all $n > 2$ by the principle of mathematical induction. (**End of proof.**)

Note that the previous proof requires that you show that $a + 1 = a^2$ and $b + 1 = b^2$. Although simple algebra will demonstrate the validity of these equalities, exactly how did we discover them after the factorization step? Some experience with inductive proofs will give you the confidence to determine and verify the auxiliary relationships—such as $a + 1 = a^2$—that are necessary in a proof. Here, after we introduced the factors $(a + 1)$ and $(b + 1)$, we observed that if these factors were equal to a^2 and b^2, respectively, we could finish the proof. Thus, we tried to show that $a + 1 = a^2$ and $b + 1 = b^2$; indeed, we were successful. Inductive proofs often require adventurous algebraic manipulations!

SELF-TEST EXERCISES

1. Prove that $1 + 2^1 + 2^2 + \cdots + 2^m = 2^{m+1} - 1$ for all $m \ge 0$.
2. Prove that the sum of the first n odd positive integers is n^2.
3. Prove that $rabbit(n) \ge a^{n-2}$ when $n \ge 2$ and $a = (1 + \sqrt{5})/2$.

EXERCISES

1. Prove that the sum of the first n even positive integers is $n(n + 1)$.
2. Prove that $1^2 + 2^2 + \cdots + n^2 = n(n + 1)(2n + 1)/6$ for all $n \ge 1$.
3. Prove that $2n + 1 < n^2$ for all $n \ge 3$.
4. Prove that $n^3 - n$ is divisible by 6 for all $n \ge 0$.
5. Prove that $2^n > n^3$ when $n \ge 10$.

6. Prove that $n! > n^3$ when n is large enough.

7. Recall the following recursive definition from Chapter 2:

   $c(n, 0) = 1$
   $c(n, n) = 1$
   $c(n, k) = c(n - 1, k - 1) + c(n - 1, k)$ when $0 < k < n$
   $c(n, k) = 0$ when $k > n$

   a. Prove that $c(n, 0) + c(n, 1) + \cdots + c(n, n) = 2^n$.
      Hint: Use $c(n + 1, 0) = c(n, 0)$ and $c(n + 1, n) = c(n, n)$.

   b. Prove that $(x + y)^n = \displaystyle\sum_{k=0}^{n} c(n, k)\, x^k y^{n-k}$

8. Prove that $rabbit(n) \le a^{n-1}$ when $n \ge 1$ and $a = (1 + \sqrt{5})/2$.

9. Suppose that the rabbit population doubles every year. If you start with two rabbits, find and prove a formula that predicts the rabbit population after n years.

Glossary

abstract base class A class without instances that forms the basis of other classes that descend from it. An abstract base class contains zero or more abstract methods.

abstract method A method that must be overridden in the derived class. If the derived class does not override the abstract method from the abstract base class, the derived class must also be declared abstract.

abstract data type (ADT) A collection of data values together with a set of well-specified operations on that data.

abstraction See *data abstraction* and *procedural abstraction*.

access time The time required to access a particular item in a data structure such as an array, a linked list, or a file.

activation record A record that contains a method's local environment at the time of and as a result of the call to the method.

address A number that labels a location in a computer's memory.

adjacency list The n linked lists that implement a graph of n vertices numbered $0, 1, \ldots, n - 1$ such that there is a node in the ith linked list for vertex j if and only if there is an edge from vertex i to vertex j.

adjacency matrix An n-by-n array `graph` that implements a graph of n vertices numbered $0, 1, \ldots, n - 1$ such that `graph[i][j]` is 1 if there is an edge from vertex i to vertex j, and 0 otherwise.

adjacent vertices Two vertices of a graph that are joined by an edge. In a directed graph, vertex y is adjacent to vertex x if there is a directed edge from vertex x to vertex y.

ADT See *abstract data type*.

aggregate data type A data type composed of multiple elements. Some examples of aggregate data types are arrays and files.

algorithm A step-by-step specification of a method to solve a problem within a finite amount of time.

allocation See *dynamic allocation* and *static allocation*.

analysis of algorithms A branch of computer science that measures the efficiency of algorithms.

ancestor class See *superclass*.

ancestor of a node N A node on the path from the root of a tree to N.

argument A variable or expression that is passed to a method. An actual argument appears in a call to a method and corresponds to a formal parameter in the method's declaration. See also *parameter*.

array   A data structure that contains a fixed maximum number of elements of the same data type that are referenced directly by means of an index or subscript.

array-based implementation   An implementation of an ADT that uses an array to store the data values.

assertion   A statement that describes the state of an algorithm or program at a certain point in its execution.

average-case analysis   A determination of the average amount of time that a given algorithm requires to solve problems of size *n*. See also *best-case analysis* and *worst-case analysis*.

AVL tree   A balanced binary search tree in which rotations restore the tree's balance after each insertion or deletion of a node. (The AVL tree is named for its inventors Adel'son-Vel'skii and Landis.)

axiom   A mathematical rule or relationship. Axioms can be used to specify the behavior of an ADT operation.

back of a queue   The end of a queue at which items are inserted.

backtracking   A problem-solving strategy that, when it reaches an impasse, retraces its steps in reverse order before trying a new sequence of steps.

balanced binary tree   A binary tree in which the left and right subtrees of any node have heights that differ by at most 1. Also called a height-balanced tree.

base case   The known case in either a recursive definition or an inductive proof. Also called the basis or degenerate case.

base class   See *superclass*.

basis   See *base case*.

best-case analysis   A determination of the minimum amount of time that a given algorithm requires to solve problems of size *n*. See also *average-case analysis* and *worst-case analysis*.

BFS   See *breadth-first search*.

BFS spanning tree   A spanning tree formed by using a breadth-first search to traverse a graph's vertices.

Big O notation   A notation that uses the capital letter O to specify an algorithm's order. For example, "$O(f(n))$" means "order $f(n)$." See also *order of an algorithm*.

binary file   A file whose elements are in the computer's internal representation. A binary file is not organized into lines. Also called a general file or nontext file.

binary operator   An operator that requires two operands, for example, the + in 2 + 3. See also *unary operator*.

binary search   An algorithm that searches a sorted collection for a particular item by repeatedly halving the collection and determining which half could contain the item.

binary search tree   A binary tree in which the search key in any node *N* is greater than the search key in any node in *N*'s left subtree, but less than the search key in any node in *N*'s right subtree.

binary tree   A set of zero or more nodes, partitioned into a root node and two possibly empty sets that are binary trees. Thus, each node in a binary tree has at most two children, the left child and the right child.

binding   The association of a variable with both a memory address and the type of data the variable holds. See also *dynamic binding* and *static binding*.

block   A group of data records in a file.

block access time   The time required to read or write a block of data associated with a file.

box trace   A systematic way to trace the actions of a recursive method.

breadth-first search (BFS)   A graph-traversal strategy that visits every vertex adjacent to a vertex *v* that it can before it visits any other vertex. Thus, the traversal will not embark from any of the vertices adjacent to *v* until it has visited all possible vertices adjacent to *v*. See also *depth-first search*.

B-tree of degree *m*   A balanced search tree whose leaves are at the same level and whose nodes each contain between $m - 1$ and $\lceil m/2 \rceil$ records. Each nonleaf has one more child than it has records. The root of the tree can contain as few as one record and can have as few as two children. Typically, a B-tree is stored in an external file.

bubble sort   A sorting algorithm that compares adjacent elements and exchanges them if they are out of order. Comparing the first two elements, the second and third elements, and so on, will move the largest (or smallest) element to the end of the array. Repeating this process will eventually sort the array into ascending (or descending) order.

bucket   A structure associated with a hash address that can accommodate more than one item. An array of buckets can be used as a hash table to resolve collisions.

buffer   A location that temporarily stores data as it makes its way from one process or location to another. A buffer enables data to leave one process or location at a different rate than the rate at which it enters another process or location, thus compensating for the difference in these rates.

bytecode   The result from a Java compiler when it translates a Java program. Bytecode must then be executed by a Java Virtual Machine. See also *compiler* and *Java Virtual Machine*.

ceiling of *x*   Denoted by $\lceil x \rceil$, the value of *x* rounded up. For example, $\lceil 6.1 \rceil = 7$.

chain   A linked list used within separate chaining, which is a collision-resolution scheme associated with hashing.

chaining   See *separate chaining*.

child of a node *N*   A node directly below node *N* in a tree.

circuit   A special cycle that passes through every vertex (or edge) in a graph exactly once.

circular doubly linked list   A doubly linked list whose first node references the list's last node and whose last node references the list's first node.

circular linked list   A linked list whose last node references the first node in the list.

class   A Java construct that enables you to define a new data type.

client   The program, module, or ADT that uses a class.

closed-form formula   A nonrecursive algebraic expression.

clustering   The tendency of items to map into groups of locations in a hash table, rather than randomly scattered locations. This difficulty, typical of the linear-probing, collision-resolution scheme in hashing, can cause lengthy search times.

code   Statements in a programming language.

coding   Implementing an algorithm in a programming language.

cohesion   The degree to which the portions of a module are related. See also *highly cohesive module.*

collision   A condition that occurs when a hash function maps two or more distinct search keys into the same location.

collision-resolution scheme   The part of hashing that assigns locations in the hash table to items with different search keys when the items are involved in a collision. See also *bucket, chain, clustering, double hashing, folding, linear probing, open addressing, probe sequence, quadratic probing,* and *separate chaining.*

compiler   A program that translates a program written in a high-level language, such as Java, into a language that a computer can execute. To achieve platform independence, a Java compiler produces bytecode, which must be executed by a Java Virtual Machine on a given computer. See also *bytecode* and *Java Virtual Machine.*

compile time   The time during which a compiler translates a program from source form into a form that can be executed. See also *run time.*

complete binary tree   A binary tree of height *h* that is full to level $h - 1$ and has level *h* filled from left to right.

complete graph   A graph that has an edge between every pair of distinct vertices.

completely balanced binary tree   A binary tree in which the left and right subtrees of any node have the same height.

connected component   For a graph that is not connected, a subset of the graph's vertices that a traversal visits beginning at a given vertex.

connected graph   A graph that has a path between every pair of distinct vertices.

constructor   A method that initializes new instances of a class. See also *default constructor.*

containment   See *has-a.*

cost of a path   The sum of the weights of the edges of a path in a weighted graph. Also called the weight or length of a path.

cost of a program   Factors such as the computer resources (computing time and memory) that a program consumes, the difficulties encountered by those who use the program, and the consequences of a program that does not behave correctly.

cost of a spanning tree   The sum of the weights of the edges in a weighted graph's spanning tree.

coupling   The degree to which the methods in a program are interdependent. See also *loosely coupled modules.*

cycle   A path in a graph that begins and ends at the same vertex. See also *circuit* and *simple cycle.*

data abstraction   A design principle that separates the operations that can be performed on a collection of data from the implementation of the operations. See also *procedural abstraction.*

data field   A component of a Java class that stores data of a particular type. See also *member* and *method.*

data flow   The flow of data between modules.

data record   An element in a file. A data record can be anything from a simple value, such as an integer, to an object, such as an employee record. See also *block* and *record*.

data structure   A construct that is defined within a programming language to store a collection of data.

deep copy of an object   A copy that includes the data structures that the object's data field(s) reference. See also *shallow copy of an object*.

default constructor   A constructor that has no parameters.

degenerate case   See *base case*.

depth-first search (DFS)   A graph-traversal strategy that proceeds along a path from a given vertex as deeply into the graph as possible before backtracking. That is, after visiting a vertex, a DFS visits, if possible, an unvisited adjacent vertex. If the traversal reaches a vertex that has no unvisited adjacent vertices, it backs up and then visits, if possible, an unvisited adjacent vertex. See also *breadth-first search*.

derived class   See *subclass*.

descendant class   See *subclass*.

descendant of a node *N*   A node on a path from *N* to a leaf of a tree.

DFS   See *depth-first search*.

DFS spanning tree   A spanning tree formed by using a depth-first search to traverse a graph's vertices.

dictionary   See *table*.

digraph   See *directed graph*.

direct access   A process that provides access to any element in a data structure by position, without the need to first access other elements in the structure. Also called random access. See also *sequential access*.

directed edge   An edge in a directed graph; that is, an edge that has a direction.

directed graph   A graph whose edges indicate a direction. Also called a digraph. See also *undirected graph*.

directed path   A sequence of directed edges that begins at one vertex and ends at another vertex in a directed graph. See also *simple path*.

disconnected graph   A graph that is not connected; that is, a graph that has at least one pair of vertices without a path between them.

divide and conquer   A problem-solving strategy that divides a problem into smaller problems, each of which is solved separately.

double hashing   A collision-resolution scheme that uses two hash functions. The hash table is searched for an unoccupied location, starting from the location that one hash function determines and considering every n^{th} location, where n is determined from a second hash function.

doubly linked list   A linked list whose nodes each contain two references, one to the next node and one to the previous node.

dummy head node   In a linked list, a first node that is not used for data but is always present. The item at the first position of the list is thus actually in the second node. See also *head record*.

dynamic allocation   The assignment of memory to a variable during program execution, as opposed to during compilation. In Java, all objects are created using dynamic allocation. See also *static allocation*.

dynamic binding   Binding that occurs during program execution. Also called late binding. See also *static binding* and *static member*.

dynamic object   A dynamically allocated object. An object whose memory is allocated at execution time and remains allocated only as long as you want.

early binding   See *static binding*.

edge   The connection between two nodes of a graph.

empty string   A string of length zero.

empty tree   A tree with no nodes.

encapsulation   An information-hiding technique that combines data and operations to form an object.

event   An occurrence, such as an arrival or a departure, in an event-driven simulation. See also *external event* and *internal event*.

event-driven simulation   A simulation that uses events generated by a mathematical model that is based on statistics and probability. The times of events are either read as input or computed from other event times. Because only those times at which the events occur are of interest and because no action is required at times between events, the simulation can advance from the time of one event directly to the time of the next. See also *time-driven simulation*.

event list   An ADT within an event-driven simulation that keeps track of arrival and departure events that will occur but have not occurred yet.

exhaustive search   A search strategy that must examine every item in a collection of items before it can determine that the item sought does not exist.

exception   An unusual or exceptional event that occurs during execution of a program.

exception handler   Java code whose execution deals with an exception when one occurs.

extensible class   A class that enables you to add capabilities to its derived classes without having access to the base class's implementation. Extensible classes can be declared abstract.

external event   An event that is determined from the input data to an event-driven simulation. See also *internal event*.

external methods   Algorithms that require external files because the data will not fit entirely into the computer's main memory.

external sort   A sorting algorithm that is used when the collection of data will not fit in the computer's main memory all at once but must reside on secondary storage such as a disk. See also *internal sort*.

fail-safe programming   A technique whereby a programmer includes checks within a program for anticipated errors.

Fibonacci sequence   The sequence of integers 1, 1, 2, 3, 5, . . . defined by the recurrence relationship

$$a_1 = 1, a_2 = 1, a_n = a_{n-1} + a_{n-2} \text{ for } n > 2$$

field   A data element within a record.

FIFO See *first in, first out.*

file A data structure that contains a sequence of components of the same data type. See also *binary file, index file,* and *text file.*

file component An indivisible piece of data in a file.

file pointer An indicator, such as an integer, that points to an element within a file. For example, an index record, which points to a data record in an external data file, contains such an indicator, namely, the number of the block that contains the data record.

file window A marker of the current position in the file.

final class A class that cannot be a superclass. That is, you cannot derive another class from a final class.

final data field A data field whose value cannot change during program execution.

final method A method that cannot be overridden by another class.

first in, first out (FIFO) A property of a queue whereby the removal and retrieval operations access the item that was inserted first (earliest). See also *last in, first out.*

folding A hashing technique that breaks a search key into parts and combines some or all of those parts, by using an operation such as addition, to form a hash address.

4-node A tree node that contains three data items and has four children. See also *3-node* and *2-node.*

free list A list of available nodes used in an array-based implementation of an ADT.

front of a queue The end of a queue at which items are removed and retrieved.

full binary tree A binary tree of height h with no missing nodes. All leaves are at level h, and all other nodes each have two children.

garbage collection The return to the operating system of memory that was allocated to a program but is no longer being used.

general file See *binary file.*

general tree A set of one or more nodes, partitioned into a root node and subsets that are general subtrees of the root.

grammar The rules that define a language.

graph A set V of vertices, or nodes, and a set E of edges that connect the vertices.

graph traversal A process that starts at vertex v and visits all vertices w for which there is a path between v and w. A graph traversal visits every vertex in a graph if and only if the graph is connected, regardless of where the traversal starts.

growth-rate function A mathematical function used to specify an algorithm's order in terms of the size of the problem.

has-a A relationship between classes whereby one class contains an instance of another class. Also called containment. See also *is-a.*

hash function A mathematical function that maps the search key of a table item into a location that will contain the item.

hashing   A method that enables access to table items in time that is relatively constant and independent of the items by using a hash function and a scheme for resolving collisions.

hash table   An array that contains the table items, as assigned by a hash function.

head   See *head reference*.

header   See *head record*.

head reference   A reference to the first node in a linked list. Also called a head.

head record   A record that contains the external reference to the first node in a linked list, along with global information about the list, such as its length. Also called a header. See also *dummy head node*.

heap   A complete binary tree whose nodes each contain a priority value that is greater than or equal to the priority values in the node's children. Also called a maxheap. See also *minheap*.

heapsort   A sorting algorithm that first transforms an array into a heap, then removes the heap's root (the largest element) by exchanging it with the heap's last element, and finally transforms the resulting semiheap back into a heap.

height-balanced tree   See *balanced binary tree*.

height of a tree   The number of nodes on the longest path from the root of the tree to a leaf.

hierarchical relationship   The "parent-child" relationship between the nodes in a tree.

highly cohesive module   A module that performs one well-defined task. See also *cohesion*.

implement   (1) To create a program for an algorithm. (2) To use a data structure to realize an ADT.

import   To locate a program module in a library and include it in the current program.

index   (1) An integral value that references an element in an array. Also called a subscript. (2) Another name for an index file.

index file   A data structure whose entries—called index records—are used to locate items in an external file. Also called the index.

index record   An entry in an index file that points to a record in the corresponding external data file. This entry contains a search key and a file pointer.

induction   See *mathematical induction*.

inductive conclusion   See *inductive step*.

inductive hypothesis   See *inductive step*.

inductive proof   A proof that uses the principle of mathematical induction.

inductive step   The step in an inductive proof that begins with an inductive hypothesis ("if $P(k)$ is true for any $k \geq 0$") and demonstrates the inductive conclusion ("then $P(k + 1)$ is true").

infix expression   An algebraic expression in which every binary operator appears between its two operands. See also *postfix expression* and *prefix expression*.

information hiding   A process that hides certain implementation details within a module and makes them inaccessible from outside the module.

inheritance   A relationship among classes whereby a class derives properties from a previously defined class. See also *superclass* and *subclass*.

inorder successor of a node N   The inorder successor of N's search key. The inorder successor is in the leftmost node of N's right subtree.

inorder successor of x   The search key in a search tree that an inorder traversal visits immediately after x.

inorder traversal   A traversal of a binary tree that processes (visits) a node after it traverses the node's left subtree, but before it traverses the node's right subtree. See also *postorder traversal* and *preorder traversal*.

insertion sort   A sorting algorithm that considers items one at a time and inserts each item into its proper sorted position.

instance   An object that is the result of calling *new*. The operator *new* returns a reference to the instance.

interface   (1) In Java, a program component that declares methods required of a class. (2) The communication mechanisms between modules or systems.

internal event   An event that is determined by a computation within an event-driven simulation. See also *external event*.

internal node of a tree   A node that is not a leaf.

internal sort   A sorting algorithm that requires the collection of data to fit entirely in the computer's main memory. See also *external sort*.

invariant   An assertion that is always true at a particular point in an algorithm or program.

is-a   A relationship between classes whereby one class is a special case of another class. You implement an *is-a* relationship by using inheritance. See also *has-a*.

iteration   (1) A process that is repetitive. (2) A single pass through a loop.

iterative solution   A solution that involves loops.

iterator   A class that interacts with another class representing a collection of objects to provide access to either the next or previous item within the collection.

Java Virtual Machine   A program written for a particular computer that executes bytecode, which is the result of compiling a Java program. See also *bytecode* and *compiler*.

key   (1) The portion of an index record that corresponds to the search key in a record in an external data file. (2) Another name for search key.

language   A set of strings of symbols that adhere to the rules of a grammar.

last in, first out (LIFO)   A property of a stack whereby the deletion and retrieval operations access the most recently inserted item. See also *first in, first out*.

late binding   See *dynamic binding*.

leaf   A tree node with no children.

left child of a node N   A node directly below and to the left of node N in a tree.

left subtree of a node N   The left child of node N plus its descendants in a tree.

length of a path   See *cost of a path*.

level of a node   The root of a tree is at level 1. If a node is not the root, its level is 1 greater than the level of its parent.

life cycle of software   The phases of software development: specification, design, risk analysis, verification, coding, testing, refining, production, and maintenance.

LIFO   See *last in, first out*.

linear implementation   An implementation that uses either an array or a reference-based linked list.

linear linked list   A linked list that is not circular.

linear probing   A collision-resolution scheme that searches the hash table sequentially, starting from the original location specified by the hash function, for an unoccupied location.

linked list   A list of elements, or nodes, that are linked to one another such that each element references the next element.

list   An ADT whose elements are referenced by their position. See also *sorted list*.

load factor   A measure of the relative fullness of a hash table, defined as the ratio of a table's current number of items to its maximum size.

local environment of a method   A method's local variables, a copy of the actual value arguments, a return address in the calling routine, and the value of the method itself.

local identifier   An identifier whose scope is the block that contains its declaration.

local variable   A variable declared within a method and available only within that method.

loop invariant   An assertion that is true before and after each execution of a loop within an algorithm or program.

loosely coupled modules   Two or more modules that are not dependent on one another. See also *coupling*.

machine language   A language composed of the fundamental instructions that a computer can execute directly.

mathematical induction   A method for proving properties that involve nonnegative integers. Starting from a base case, you show that if a property is true for an arbitrary nonnegative integer k, then the property is true for the integer $k + 1$.

maxheap   Another name for a heap. See also *minheap*.

member   A component of a class that is either data or a method. See also *data field* and *method*.

mergesort   A sorting algorithm that divides an array into halves, sorts each half, and then merges the sorted halves into one sorted array. Mergesort can also be adapted for sorting an external file.

message   A request, in the form of a method call, that an object perform an operation.

method   A component of a class that implements a behavior of the class. See also *data field* and *member*.

minheap   A complete binary tree whose nodes each contain a priority value that is less than or equal to the priority values in the node's children. See also *maxheap*.

minimum spanning tree   A graph's spanning tree for which the sum of its edge weights is minimal among all spanning trees for the graph.

modular program   A program that is divided into isolated components, or modules, that have clearly defined purposes and interactions.

module   An individual component of a program, such as a method, a group of methods, or other block of code.

multigraph   A graphlike structure that allows duplicate edges between its vertices.

multiple indexing   A process that uses more than one index file to an external data file.

node   An element in a linked list, graph, or tree that usually contains both data and a reference to the next element in the data structure.

nontext file   See *binary file.*

object   An instance of a class.

object-oriented programming (OOP)   A software engineering technique that views a program as a collection of components called objects that interact. OOP embodies three fundamental principles: encapsulation, inheritance, and polymorphism.

object serialization   The process of transforming an object into a sequence of bytes that represent the object.

object type compatible   A characteristic of objects that enables you to use an instance of a subclass where an instance of the superclass is expected, but not the converse. The object type of an argument in a call to a method can be an instance of the subclass of the corresponding parameter's object type.

O($f(n)$)   Order $f(n)$. See *Big O notation* and *order of an algorithm.*

OOP   See *object-oriented programming.*

open   A process that prepares a stream to a file for either input or output. A state of readiness for I/O.

open addressing   A category of collision-resolution schemes in hashing that probe for an empty, or open, location in the hash table in which to place the item. See also *double hashing, linear probing,* and *quadratic probing.*

order of an algorithm   An algorithm's time requirement as a function of the problem size. An algorithm A is order $f(n)$ if constants k and n_0 exist such that A requires no more than $k * f(n)$ time units to solve a problem of size $n \geq n_0$. See also *Big O notation.*

order-of-magnitude analysis   An analysis of an algorithm's time requirement as a function of the problem size. See also *order of an algorithm.*

override   To redefine a method of a class within a subclass.

package   A collection of related classes.

package access member   A member of a class that is accessible only by the methods of the class and by other classes in the same package.

parameter   An identifier that appears in the declaration of a method and represents the value that the calling program will pass to the method. See also *argument.*

palindrome   A character string that reads the same from left to right as it does from right to left, for example, "deed."

parent of a node N   The node directly above node N in a tree.

partition   To divide a data structure such as an array into segments.

path   A sequence of edges in a graph that begins at one vertex and ends at another vertex. Because a tree is a special graph, you can have a path through a tree. See also *directed path* and *simple path.*

perfect hash function   An ideal hash function that maps each search key into a unique location in the hash table. Perfect hash functions exist when all possible search keys are known.

pivot element   An element that an algorithm uses to organize data by value. For example, the quicksort algorithm partitions an array about a particular element called the pivot.

planar graph   A graph that can be drawn in a plane in at least one way so that no two edges cross.

polymorphism   The ability of a variable name to represent, during program execution, instances of different but related classes that descend from a common superclass.

pop   To remove an item from a stack.

position-oriented ADT   An ADT whose operations involve the positions of its items. See also *value-oriented ADT*.

postcondition   A statement of the conditions that exist at the end of a module.

postfix expression   An algebraic expression in which every binary operator follows its two operands. See also *infix expression* and *prefix expression*.

postorder traversal   A traversal of a binary tree that processes (visits) a node after it traverses both of the node's subtrees. See also *inorder traversal* and *preorder traversal*.

precondition   A statement of the conditions that must exist at the beginning of a module in order for the module to work correctly.

predecessor   (1) In a linked list, the predecessor of node N is the node that references N. (2) In a directed graph, vertex x is a predecessor of vertex y if there is a directed edge from x to y, that is, if y is adjacent to x. See also *successor*.

prefix expression   An algebraic expression in which every binary operator precedes its two operands. See also *infix expression* and *postfix expression*.

preorder traversal   A traversal of a binary tree that processes (visits) a node before it traverses both of the node's subtrees. See also *inorder traversal* and *postorder traversal*.

primitive data type   One of the Java data types `boolean, byte, char, double, float, int, long,` or `short`.

priority queue   An ADT that orders its items by a priority value. The first item removed is the one having the highest priority value.

priority value   A value assigned to the items in a priority queue to indicate the item's priority.

private member   A member of a class that is accessible only by methods of the class.

probe sequence   The sequence of locations in the hash table that a collision-resolution scheme examines.

problem solving   The entire process of taking the statement of a problem and developing a computer program that solves that problem.

procedural abstraction   A design principle that separates the purpose and use of a module from its implementation. See also *data abstraction*.

protected member   A member of a class that is accessible by methods of the class, by derived classes, and by other classes in the same package.

public class   A class that is accessible by any other class.

public member   A member of a class that is accessible by any client of the class.

push   To add an item to a stack.

quadratic probing   A collision-resolution scheme that searches the hash table for an occupied location beginning with the original location that the hash function specifies and continuing at increments of 1^2, 2^2, 3^2, and so on.

queue An ADT whose first (earliest) inserted item is the first item removed or retrieved. This property is called first in, first out, or simply FIFO. Items enter a queue at its back and leave at its front.

quicksort A sorting algorithm that partitions an array's elements around a pivot p to generate two smaller sorting problems: Sort the array's left section, whose elements are less than p, and sort the array's right section, whose elements are greater than or equal to p.

radix sort A sorting algorithm that treats each data element as a character string and repeatedly organizes the data into groups according to the ith character in each element.

random access See *direct access*.

random access file A file whose elements are accessible by position without first accessing preceding elements within the file.

range query An operation that retrieves all table items whose search keys fall into a given range of values.

rear of a queue Another term for the back of a queue.

recognition algorithm An algorithm, based on a language's grammar, that determines whether a given string is in the language.

record A group of related items, called fields, that are not necessarily of the same data type. See also *data record*.

recurrence relation A mathematical formula that generates the terms in a sequence from previous terms.

recursion A process that solves a problem by solving smaller problems of exactly the same type as the original problem.

recursive call A call within a method to the method itself.

red-black tree A representation of a 2-3-4 tree as a binary tree whose nodes have red and black child references.

reference (1) A reference variable in Java. (2) Generically, an element that references an object.

reference-based implementation An implementation of an ADT or a data structure that uses references to organize its elements.

reference variable A Java variable that references an object.

right child of a node N A node directly below and to the right of node N in a tree.

right subtree of a node N The right child of node N plus its descendants in a tree.

rightward drift (1) In an array-based implementation of a queue, the problem of the front of the queue moving toward the end of the array. (2) In a Java program, the problem of nested blocks bumping against the right-hand margin of the page.

root The only node in a tree with no parent.

rotation An operation used to maintain the balance of a red-black or AVL tree.

run time The execution phase of a program. The time during which a program's instructions execute. See also *compile time*.

scope of an identifier The part of a program in which an identifier has meaning.

search A process that locates a certain item in a collection of items.

search key   The part of a record that identifies it within a collection of records. A search algorithm uses a search key to locate a record within a collection of records. Also called a key.

search tree   A tree whose organization facilitates the retrieval of its items. See also *AVL tree, binary search tree, B-tree of degree m, red-black tree, 2-3 tree,* and *2-3-4 tree.*

selection sort   A sorting algorithm that selects the largest item and puts it in its correct place, then selects the next largest item and puts it in its correct place, and so on.

semiheap   A complete binary tree in which the root's left and right subtrees are both heaps.

separate chaining   A collision-resolution scheme that uses an array of linked lists as a hash table. The ith linked list, or chain, contains all items that map into location i.

sequential access   A process that stores or retrieves elements in a data structure one after another, starting at the beginning. See also *direct access.*

sequential access file   A file whose elements must be processed sequentially. That is, to process the data stored at a given position, you must advance the file window beyond all the data that precedes it.

sequential search   An algorithm that locates an item in a collection by examining items in order, one at a time, beginning with the first item.

shallow copy of an object   A copy that does not include any data structures that the object's data fields might reference. See also *deep copy of an object.*

shortest path   Between two given vertices in a weighted graph, the path that has the smallest sum of its edge weights.

siblings   Tree nodes that have a common parent.

simple cycle   A cycle in a graph that does not pass through a vertex more than once.

simple path   A path in a graph that does not pass through a vertex more than once. See also *directed path.*

simulation   A technique for modeling the behavior of both natural and artificial systems. Generally, its goal is to generate statistics that summarize the performance of an existing system or to predict the performance of a proposed system. A simulation reflects long-term average behavior of a system rather than predicting occurrences of specific events.

software engineering   A branch of computer science that provides techniques to facilitate the development of computer programs.

solution   Algorithms and ways to store data that solve a problem.

sorted list   An ADT that maintains its elements in sorted order and retrieves them by their position number within the list. See also *list.*

sorted order   The order of a collection of data that is in either ascending or descending order.

sorted run   Sorted data that is part of an external sort.

sorting   A process that organizes a collection of data into either ascending or descending order. See also *external sort* and *internal sort.*

sort key   The part of a record that determines the sorted order of the entire record within a collection of records. A sorting algorithm uses a sort key to order records within a collection of records.

source program A program written in a programming language that needs to be compiled. For example, a Java program. Also called source code.

spanning tree A subgraph of a connected, undirected graph G that contains all of G's vertices and enough of its edges to form a tree. See also *BFS spanning tree* and *DFS spanning tree*.

stack An ADT whose most recently inserted item is the first item removed or retrieved. This property is called last in, first out, or simply LIFO. Items enter and leave a stack at its top.

static allocation The assignment of memory to a variable during compilation, as opposed to during program execution. In Java, only primitive types and references use static allocation. See also *dynamic allocation*.

static binding Binding that occurs at compilation time. Also called early binding. See also *dynamic binding* and *static member*.

static member A class member in which there is only one copy available for all instances of the class. Static members can be bound at compilation time. See also *static binding*.

stream An object that moves data into a program (an input stream) or out of a program (an output stream).

string A sequence of characters. A Java string is an object of type *String*.

structure chart An illustration of the hierarchy of modules that solve a problem.

stub A partially completed method that you use during the development and testing of other modules of a program.

subclass A class that inherits the members of another class called the superclass. Also called derived class. See also *inheritance*.

subgraph A subset of a graph's vertices and edges.

subscript See *index*.

subtree Any node in a tree, together with all of the node's descendants.

subtree of a node N A tree that consists of a child of N and the child's descendants.

successor (1) In a linked list, the successor of node N is the node that N references. (2) In a directed graph, vertex y is a successor of vertex x if there is a directed edge from x to y, that is, if y is adjacent to x. See also *predecessor*.

superclass A class from which another class—called a subclass—is derived. A subclass inherits ther superclass's members. Also called a base class. See also *inheritance* and *subclass*.

symmetric matrix An n-by-n matrix A whose elements satisfy the relationship $A_{ij} = A_{ji}$.

table An ADT whose data items are stored and retrieved according to their search-key values. Also called a dictionary.

tail reference A reference to the last node in a linked list. Also called a tail.

tail recursion A type of recursion in which the recursive call is the last action taken.

text file A file of characters that are organized into lines.

3-node A tree node that contains two data items and has three children. See also *4-node* and *2-node*.

time-driven simulation   A simulation in which the time of an event, such as an arrival or departure, is determined randomly and compared with a simulated clock. See also *event-driven simulation*.

top-down design   A process that addresses a task at successively lower levels of detail, producing independent modules.

top-down implementation   An implementation method in which you implement and test a module before implementing its submodules.

top of a stack   The end of a stack at which items are inserted, retrieved, and deleted.

topological order   A list of vertices in a directed graph without cycles such that vertex x precedes vertex y if there is a directed edge from x to y in the graph. A topological order is not unique, in general.

topological sorting   In a directed graph without cycles, the process of arranging the vertices into a topological order.

traversal   An operation that processes (visits) each element in an ADT or data structure. See also *inorder traversal, postorder traversal,* and *preorder traversal*.

tree   A connected, undirected graph without cycles. See also *binary tree* and *general tree*.

2-node   A tree node that contains one data item and has two children. See also *4-node* and *3-node*.

2-3 tree   A tree such that each internal node (nonleaf) has either two or three children, and all leaves are at the same level. A node can have a left subtree, a middle subtree, and a right subtree.

   If a node has two children and contains one data item, the value of the search key in the node must be greater than the value of the search key in the left child and smaller than the value of the search key in the right child. If a node has three children and contains two data items, the value of the smaller search key in the node must be greater than the value of the search key in the left child and smaller than the value of the search key in the middle child; the value of the larger search key in the node must be greater than the value of the search key in the middle child and smaller than the value of the search key in the right child.

2-3-4 tree   A tree such that each internal node (nonleaf) has either two, three, or four children, and all leaves are at the same level. A node can have a left subtree, a middle-left subtree, a middle-right subtree, and a right subtree.

   If a node has two or three children, it adheres to the specifications of a 2-3 tree. If a node has four children and three data items, the value of the smaller search key in the node must be greater than the value of the search key in the left child and smaller than the value of the search key in the middle-left child; the value of the middle search key in the node must be greater than the value of the search key in the middle-left child and smaller than the value of the search key in the middle-right child; the value of the larger search key in the node must be greater than the value of the search key in the middle-right child and smaller than the value of the search key in the right child.

type compatible   See *object type compatible*.

unary operator   An operator that requires only one operand, for example, the – in –5. See also *binary operator*.

undirected graph   A graph that has at most one edge between any two vertices and whose edges do not indicate a direction. See also *directed graph*.

user   The person who uses a program.

user interface   The portion of a program that provides for user input or control.

valued method   A method that returns a value. See also *void method*.

value-oriented ADT   An ADT whose operations involve the values of its data items. See also *position-oriented ADT*.

vertex   A node in a graph.

visit   The act of processing an item during a traversal of an ADT or a data structure.

void method   A method that does not return a value. See also *valued method*.

weighted graph   A graph whose edges are labeled with numeric values.

weight of an edge   The numeric label on an edge in a weighted graph.

weight of a path   See *cost of a path*.

worst-case analysis   A determination of the maximum amount of time that a given algorithm requires to solve problems of size *n*. See also *average-case analysis* and *best-case analysis*.

Answers to Self-Test Exercises

Chapter 1

1. $0 \leq index \leq n$ and $sum = item[0] +... + item[index]$.

2. **Purpose:** Computes the sum of the first five positive elements in an array.

   Given: $array$ is an array of n elements, $n \geq 5$, at least five elements in the array are positive.

   Results: The method returns the sum of the first five positive integers in the array; the array and n are unchanged.

   ### Another solution:

   Purpose: Computes the sum of the first five positive elements in an array.

   Given: $array$ is an array of n elements.

   Results: If the array contains at least five positive integers, then the method returns the sum of the first five positive integers; otherwise, returns 0; the array and n are unchanged.

Chapter 2

1. The product of n numbers is defined in terms of the product of $n - 1$ numbers, which is a smaller problem of the same type. When n is 1, the product is $anArray[0]$; this occurrence is the base case. Because $n \geq 1$ initially and n decreases by 1 at each recursive call, the base case will be reached.

2.
```java
public static void countDown(int n) {
// Precondition: n > 0.
// Postcondition: Writes n, n - 1, ... , 1.
   if (n > 0) {
      System.out.println(n);
      countDown(n-1);
   } // end if
}  // end countDown
```

3.
```java
public static double product(double anArray[], int first, int last) {
// Precondition: anArray[first..last] is an array of real numbers, where
// first <= last.
// Postcondition: Returns the product of the numbers in
// anArray[first..last].
   double result;
```

```
   if (first == last) {
      result = anArray[first];
   }
    else {
      result = anArray[last] * product(anArray, first, last-1);
   }
   return result;
} // end product
```

4. *writeBackward*, *binarySearch*, *kSmall*, and the method *countDown* in Self-Test Exercise 2.

5. 6.

6. The three recursive calls result in the following moves with poles *A*, *B*, and *C*: Move a disk from *A* to *C*, from *A* to *B*, and then from *C* to *B*.

Chapter 3

1. A wall is a visualization of abstraction and modularity. Modules should be as independent as possible: Walls prevent other parts of the program from seeing the details of modules. A contract is a specification of what the module, which is behind the wall, is to do. The contract governs the slit in the wall; it specifies what is to be passed to the module and what will be passed out. The contract does not specify how to implement the module.

   These concepts help during the problem-solving process by encouraging you to divide the problem into small parts and to focus first on what you want done rather than on how to do it.

2. By assuming that the list has items at positions *i* and *j*, we know that the list operations *get* and *remove* will be successful.

```
swap(aList, i, j)
// Swaps the iᵗʰ and jᵗʰ items in the list aList.

   // copy iᵗʰ and jᵗʰ items
   ithItem = aList.get(i)
   jthItem = aList.get(j)

   // replace iᵗʰ item with jᵗʰ
   aList.remove(i)
   aList.add(i, jthItem)

   // replace jᵗʰ item with iᵗʰ
   aList.remove(j)
   aList.add(j, ithItem)
```

   Notice that the order of operations is important because when you delete an item, *remove* renumbers the remaining items.

3. milk, eggs, butter

4. Specify *createList*, *isEmpty*, *size*, and *removeAll* as you would for the ADT list.

```
add(item)
// Adds item to the end of the list.


remove()
// Removes the item at the end of a list.
```

```
get()
// Returns the item at the end of a list.
// The list is left unchanged by this operation.
```

5. `createSortedList()`
   ```
   // Precondition: None.
   // Postcondition: An empty sorted list is created.
   ```

   `sortedIsEmpty()`
   ```
   // Precondition: None.
   // Postcondition: Returns true if the list is empty;
   // otherwise returns false.
   ```

   `sortedSize()`
   ```
   // Precondition: None.
   // Postcondition: Returns the number of items that are in
   // a sorted list.
   ```

   `sortedAdd(item)`
   ```
   // Precondition: item is the item to be inserted.
   // Postcondition: item is inserted into its proper sorted
   // position in the sorted list. If the insertion was not
   // successful, throws a ListIndexOutOfBoundsException.
   ```

   `sortedRemove(item)`
   ```
   // Precondition: item is the item to be deleted.
   // Postcondition: If item was in the list, it is deleted.
   // Otherwise, throws a ListIndexOutOfBoundsException.
   ```

   `sortedGet(index)`
   ```
   // Precondition: index is the number of the desired item
   // in the list.
   // Postcondition: If 1 <= index <= sortedSize(), returns
   // the item in the list whose position number is index.
   // Otherwise, throws a ListIndexOutOfBoundsException.
   ```

   `locateIndex(item)`
   ```
   // Precondition: item is the item to be located.
   // Postcondition: If item is in the list, returns its
   // position number. Otherwise, if item is not in the
   // list, returns the position where it belongs in the
   // list; item and the list are unchanged.
   ```

6. `convertToSortedList(aList)`
   ```
   // Creates a sorted list from the items in the list
   // aList.

       sortedList.createSortedList()
       for (index = 1 to aList.size()) {
         item = aList.get(index)
   ```

```
                sortedList.sortedAdd(item)
        } // end for
        return sortedList
```

7. Duplicate values in an ADT list are permissible and do not affect its specifications, because its operations are by position. For a sorted list, however, you need to revise the specifications to accommodate duplicates. You could either prevent the insertion of duplicate items or allow duplicates. If you do allow the insertion of duplicates, you need to decide where to insert them, whether to delete all occurrences of an item or only the first instance, and which of several duplicate items to retrieve.

Chapter 4

1. **a.** No. If *curr* references the last node and *prev* references the next-to-last node, *prev.set-Next(curr.getNext())* sets the *next* reference of the next-to-last node to *null*.
   b. This case is the same as deletion of the first node.
   c. Locating the last node requires a traversal of the list and so takes more effort than locating the first node. Once the last node is located, however, it is easier to delete than the first node because you do not change *head*.

2. Assume a class *CharNode* that is analogous to *IntegerNode* (see pages 159 and 160).

   a.
   ```
   head = new CharNode('J', null);
   CharNode newNode = new CharNode('E', head);
   head = newNode;
   newNode = new CharNode('B', head);
   head = newNode;
   ```
   b.
   ```
   head = new CharNode('B');
   CharNode secondNode = new CharNode('E');
   head.setNext(secondNode);
   CharNode thirdNode = new CharNode('J', null);
   secondNode.setNext(thirdNode);
   ```

3. **a.**
   ```
   prev.setNext(curr.getNext());
   curr.setNext(null);
   prev = null;
   curr = null;
   ```

   b.
   ```
   head = curr.getNext();
   curr.setNext(null);
   curr = null;
   ```

   c.
   ```
   CharNode newNode= new CharNode('A');
   newNode.setNext(head);
   head = newNode;
   ```

   d. The variable *head* references a node that contains '*A*'; this node references a node that contains '*J*'. The *next* portion of the last node is *null*.

4. ```
   public void displayNodeI(int i) {
       IntegerNode curr = head;
       for (int count = 1; count < i; ++count) {
   ```
   ```

```
      curr = curr.getNext();
    } // end for
    System.out.println(curr.getItem());
 }  // end displayNodeI
```

5. *i,* ignoring the assignments to *count* in the *for* statement.

6.
```
static int ithItem(IntegerNode nextNode, int i) {
   int result;
   if (i == 1) {
     result = nextNode.getItem();
   }
   else {
     result = ithItem(nextNode.getNext(), i-1);
   } // end if
   return result;
} // end ithItem
```

7. *writeListBackward2(reference to 'B') // original call*
   writeListBackward2(reference to 'E')
     writeListBackward2(reference to 'J')
       *writeListBackward2(**null**)*
     write J
   write E
 write B

Chapter 5

1. The positions of the queens are given as *(row, column)* pairs.

      Solution 1: (2, 1), (4, 2), (1, 3), (3, 4)

      Solution 2: (3, 1), (1, 2), (4, 3), (2, 4)

2. $- * / a\, b\, c * + d\, e\, f$

3. $a\, b * c - d / e\, f - +$

4. Infix: $(a - b / (c + d * e)) - f$; postfix: $a\, b\, c\, d\, e * + / - f -$

5. No.

6. $<T> = \$ \mid cc<T>d$

7. The proof that $f(n) = 2n + f(n - 1)$ has the closed-form solution $f(n) = n(n + 1)$ where $f(0) = 0$, is by induction on *n*.

    Basis. *Show that the property is true for n = 1.* Here, $1(1 + 1) = 2$, which is consistent with the recurrence relation's specification that $f(1) = 2(1) + 0$.
    You now must establish that

$$\text{property is true for an arbitrary } k \Rightarrow \text{property is true for } k + 1$$

    Inductive hypothesis. *Assume that the property is true for n = k.* That is, assume that

$$f(k) = k(k + 1)$$

Inductive conclusion.   *Show that the property is true for n = k + 1.* That is, you must show that $f(k + 1) = (k+1)(k+2)$. Now

$$f(k + 1) = 2(k + 1) + f(k) \qquad \text{from the recurrence relation}$$
$$= 2k + 2 + k(k + 1) \qquad \text{by the inductive hypothesis}$$
$$= k^2 + 3k + 2$$
$$= (k+1)(k+2)$$

which is what you needed to show to establish that

property is true for an arbitrary k ⇒ property is true for k + 1

The inductive proof is thus complete.

Chapter 6

1. D, C, B, A.
2. `stack1`: 1 4 5; `stack2`: 3 6   (elements listed bottom to top).
3. Use an array-based implementation if you know the maximum string length in advance and you know that the average string length is not much shorter than the maximum length. Clearly, you would use a reference-based implementation if you could not predict the maximum string length. In addition, if the maximum string length is 300, for example, but the average string length is 30, a reference-based implementation would use less storage on average than an array-based implementation.
4. Assuming that the specifications of the stack operations for both implementations are identical, the program itself should require no change. Both versions of the stack operations should perform identically on the client's side of the "wall." You must, of course, replace the array-based class definition for the stack with the reference-based one.
5. **a.** The stack is empty when the last close brace is encountered. When the loop ends, `balancedSoFar` is `false`.
    b. When the loop ends, the stack contains one open brace and `balancedSoFar` is `true`.
    c. When the loop ends, the stack is empty and `balancedSoFar` is `true`.
6. 2
7. *a b / c ∗*
8. The precedence tests control association. The ≥ test enables left-to-right association when operators have the same precedence.
9. **a.** Stack contains A, then A B.
    b. Stack contains A, then A B, then A B D.
    c. Stack contains C, then C B, then C B D, then C B D E, then C B D E I, then C B D E, then C B D, then C B D F, then C B D F G.

Chapter 7

1. A, B, C, D.
2. `queue1`: 2 3 5; `queue2`: 4 6   (elements listed front to back).
3. **a.** When the `for` loop ends, the stack and queue are as follows:
    Stack: a b c d a ← top
    Queue: a b c d a ← back

The *a* at the top of the stack matches the *a* at the front of the queue. After deleting the *a* from both ADTs, the *d* at the top of the stack does not match the *b* at the front of the queue, so the string is not a palindrome.

   b. The letters that you delete from the stack and the queue are the same, so the string is a palindrome.

4. **a.** 1;   **b.** 3;   **c.** 3;   **d.** 2;   **e.** 3;   **f.** 1;
   g. 2;   **h.** 2;   **i.** 1;   **j.** 1;   **k.** 1;   **l.** 2

5. You cannot generate a departure event for a given arrival event independently of other events. So to read the file of arrival events and generate departure events, you would need to perform the same computations that the simulation performs.

6.

Time	Action	bankQueue (front to rear)	eventList (front to rear)
29	Update *eventList* and *bankQueue*: Customer 2 enters bank	23 2	A 30 3
	Customer 3 begins transaction, create departure event	23 2	A 30 3 D 31
30	Update *eventList* and *bankQueue*: Customer 4 enters bank	23 2 30 3	D 31
31	Update *eventList* and *bankQueue*: Customer 3 departs	30 3	*empty*
	Customer 4 begins transaction, create departure event	30 3	D 34
34	Update *eventList* and *bankQueue*: Customer 4 departs	*empty*	*empty*

Chapter 8

1. **a.** `Sphere mySphere = `**`new`**` Sphere(2.0);`
   b. `Ball myBall = `**`new`**` Ball(6.0, "Beach ball");`
   c. `System.out.println(mySphere.diameter() + " " + myBall.diameter());`

2.
```
class Planet extends Ball {
   private double distance;

   public double distanceFromSun() {
      return distance;
   } // end distanceFromSun

   public void setDistanceFromSun(double newDistance)
      distance = newDistance;
   } // end setDistanceFromSun
} // end Planet
```

3. **a.** The method *resetBall* cannot access *theRadius* directly. The data field *theRadius* is private within the *Sphere* class, so a derived class cannot access it.

   b. The method *resetBall* can access *theRadius* directly. Instead of writing *setRadius(r)* in the implementation of *resetBall*, you can write *theRadius = r*. This change is unnecessary, however.

4. **a.** A reference can be declared as type *SortedListInterface* anywhere that a reference variable can be declared. Thus, it can be used in declaring a data field for a class, as a method parameter, or as a local variable to a method.

    b. A class that implements *SortedListInterface* must be used when an actual instance of a sorted list needs to be created.

5. **a.** Abstract classes and interfaces are similar in that neither can have objects directly instantiated from them.

    b. They differ in that abstract classes can contain data fields and methods with implementations, but interfaces can contain only constants and method specifications.

6. A derived class cannot access and therefore cannot override a private method in its base class.

Chapter 9

1. $(n - 1) + (n - 2) + \cdots + 1 = n * (n - 1)/2$

2. $n + (n - 1) + \cdots + 2 = n * (n + 1)/2 - 1$

3. **a.** $O(n^3)$;   **b.** $O(\log n)$;   **c.** $O(n)$

4. **a.** You can stop searching as soon as *searchValue* is less than a data item, because you will have passed the point where *searchValue* would have occurred if it was in the data collection.

    b. Sorted data, using the scheme just described in the answer to Part *a*: best case: $O(1)$; average case: $O(n)$; worst case: $O(n)$.

       Unsorted data: $O(n)$ in all cases.

    c. Regardless of whether the data is sorted, the best case is $O(1)$ (you find the item after one comparison) and both the average and worst cases are $O(n)$ (you find the item after $n/2$ or n comparisons, respectively).

5. At each pass, the selected element is underlined.

20	<u>80</u>	40	25	60	30
20	30	40	25	<u>60</u>	80
20	30	<u>40</u>	25	60	80
20	<u>30</u>	25	40	60	80
20	<u>25</u>	30	40	60	80
20	25	30	40	60	80

6. Find the smallest instead of the largest element at each pass.

<u>20</u>	80	40	25	60	30
30	80	40	<u>25</u>	60	20
<u>30</u>	80	40	60	25	20
60	80	<u>40</u>	30	25	20
<u>60</u>	80	40	30	25	20
80	60	40	30	25	20

7. **Pass 1**

<u>25</u>	<u>30</u>	20	80	40	60
25	<u>30</u>	<u>20</u>	80	40	60
25	20	<u>30</u>	<u>80</u>	40	60
25	20	30	<u>80</u>	<u>40</u>	60
25	20	30	40	<u>80</u>	<u>60</u>
25	20	30	40	60	80

  Pass 2

<u>25</u>	<u>20</u>	30	40	60	80
20	<u>25</u>	<u>30</u>	40	60	80
20	25	<u>30</u>	<u>40</u>	60	80
20	25	30	<u>40</u>	<u>60</u>	80
20	25	30	40	60	80

There are no exchanges during Pass 3, so the algorithm will terminate.

8. 25   <u>30</u>   20   80   40   60
    25   30   <u>20</u>   80   40   60
    20   25   30   <u>80</u>   40   60
    20   25   30   80   <u>40</u>   60
    20   25   30   40   80   <u>60</u>
    20   25   30   40   60   80

9. • `mergesort` sorts an array by using a mergesort to sort each half of the array.

    • Sorting half of an array is a smaller problem than sorting the entire array.

    • An array of one element is the base case.

    • By halving an array and repeatedly halving the halves, you must reach array segments of one element each—that is, the base case.

10. Vertical bars separate the array into regions, as the partition develops. The pivot is 38.

    38 | 16   40   39   12   27   pivot | unknown   Swap 16 with itself to move it to S_1.
    38 | 16 | 40   39   12   27   pivot | S_1 | unknown
    38 | 16 | 40 | 39   12   27   pivot | S_1 | S_2| unknown
    38 | 16 | 40   39 | 12   27   pivot | S_1 | S_2| unknown   Swap 12 and 40.
    38 | 16   12 | 39   40 | 27   pivot | S_1 | S_2| unknown   Swap 27 and 39.
    38 | 16   12   27 | 40   39   pivot | S_1 | S_2| unknown   Swap 38 and 27 to position pivot.
    27   16   12 | 38 | 40   39 S_1 | pivot | S_2

11. **a.** A binary search is $O(\log_2 n)$, and so is faster than a mergesort, which is $O(n \log_2 n)$.
    b. A binary search is $O(\log_2 n)$, and so is faster than displaying the array, which is $O(n)$.

Chapter 10

1. **a.** 60;   **b.** 60, 20, 40;   **c.** 20, 70; 10, 40; 30, 50;   **d.** 20 and 70, 10 and 40, 30 and 50;
    e. 40, 20, 60;   **f.** 10, 40, 30, 50;   **g.** 70, 10, 30, 50

2. **a.**   1: A; 2: B, C; 3: D, E; 4: F; 5: G
    b.   1: A; 2: B; 3: C; 4: D; 5: E; 6: F; 7: G

3. 4

4. Complete: b, c, d, e; Full: e; Balanced: b, c, d, e.

5. Preorder: A, B, D, E, C, F, G; Inorder: D, B, E, A, F, C, G;
    Postorder: D, E, B, F, G, C, A.

6.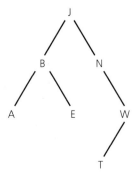

7. 60, 20, 10, 40, 30, 50, 70 is one of several possible orders. (This order results from a preorder traversal of the tree.)

8. The array is 30 20 50 10 25 40 60.

9.

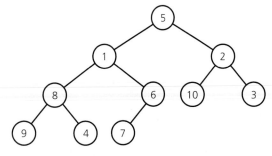

10. No. H should be in G's right subtree. U and V should be in T's right subtree.

11. The algorithm compares each given search key with the keys in the following nodes:
    a. 60, 20, 40, 30;   **b.** 60, 20, 10

12. Inserting the array elements into a binary search tree produces

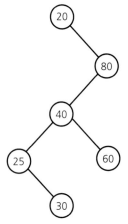

An inorder traversal of this tree results in the sorted array.

13. **a.**

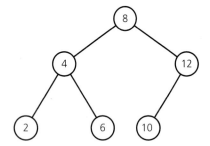

b. The tree has minimum height and is complete but not full.

Chapter 11

1. ```
tableReplace(x, replacementItem)
   // Precondition: replacementItem's search key is x.
   if (tableDelete(x))
      tableInsert(replacementItem)
```

2. No.

3. It is neither a semiheap nor a heap.

4. After inserting 12:                    After removing 12:

 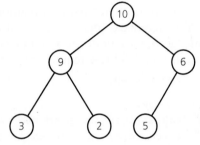

5. The array that represents the heap is 6 4 5 1 2 3.

6. The array that represents the heap is 7 5 6 4 3 2.

7. The array is 10 9 5 8 7 2 3 1 4 6.

# Chapter 12

1.

2. **a.**                                        **b.**

 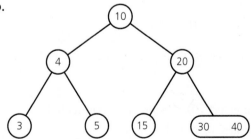

3. **a.** See the answer to Self-Test Exercise 1.
   **b.**
```

4.

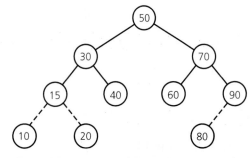

5. A balanced binary search tree.

6. Each node in a red-black tree requires memory for two references and two reference colors. These references and reference colors require no more memory than the four references in a node in a 2-3-4 tree. In addition, a node in a red-black tree requires a reference for only one data item, whereas a node in a 2-3-4 tree requires references for three data items.

7. `tableDelete(searchKey)`

```
i = h(searchKey)
while ( (table[i] is occupied and table[i].getKey() != searchKey)
        or (table[i] is deleted) ) {
    ++i
} // end if
if (table[i] is not empty) {
    // table[i].getKey() == searchKey
    Mark table[i] deleted
    return true
}
else {
    return false
} // end if
```

8. 8, 10, 1, 3, 5, 7, 9, 0, 2, 4, 6.

9. `table[1]` → 15 → 8

`table[2]` is *null*

`table[3]` → 17→ 24 → 10

`table[4]` → 32

Chapter 13

1. **a.** Directed, connected; **b.** Undirected, connected

2. DFS: 0, 1, 2, 4, 3; BFS: 0, 1, 2, 3, 4.

3.

	0	1	2	3	4
0	0	1	0	0	0
1	0	0	1	1	0
2	0	0	0	0	1
3	0	1	0	0	0
4	1	0	0	0	0

4. a g d b e c f

   g a d b e c f

   a g d b e f c

   g a d b e f c

5. No. See Observation 2 on page 628.

6.

7.

8. Path 0, 4, 2, 1 has weight 7.

   Path 0, 4, 2 has weight 5.

   Path 0, 4, 2, 3 has weight 8.

   Path 0, 4 has weight 4.

Chapter 14

1. Sequential access: Copy the original file *file1* into the file *file2*. Write a new block containing the desired record and 99 blank records. Copy *file2* to the original file *file1*.

   Direct access: Create a new block containing the desired record and 99 blank records. Write the new block to the file as the 17th block.

2. *externalMergesort(unsortedFileName, sortedFileName)*

```
Associate unsortedFileName with the file variable inFile
    and sortedFileName with the file variable outFile

blocksort(inFile, tempFile1, numBlocks)
// records in each block are now sorted; numBlocks == 16
mergeFile(tempFile1, tempFile2, 1, 16)
    mergeRuns(tempFile1, tempFile2, 1, 1)
    mergeRuns(tempFile1, tempFile2, 3, 1)
    mergeRuns(tempFile1, tempFile2, 5, 1)
    mergeRuns(tempFile1, tempFile2, 7, 1)
    mergeRuns(tempFile1, tempFile2, 9, 1)
    mergeRuns(tempFile1, tempFile2, 11, 1)
    mergeRuns(tempFile1, tempFile2, 13, 1)
    mergeRuns(tempFile1, tempFile2, 15, 1)
```

```
        mergeFile(tempFile2, tempFile1, 2, 16)
           mergeRuns(tempFile2, tempFile1, 1, 2)
           mergeRuns(tempFile2, tempFile1, 5, 2)
           mergeRuns(tempFile2, tempFile1, 9, 2)
           mergeRuns(tempFile2, tempFile1, 13, 2)
        mergeFile(tempFile1, tempFile2, 4, 16)
           mergeRuns(tempFile1, tempFile2, 1, 4)
           mergeRuns(tempFile1, tempFile2, 9, 4)
        mergeFile(tempFile2, tempFile1, 8, 16)
           mergeRuns(tempFile2, tempFile1, 1, 8)
        copyFile(tempFile1, outFile)
```

3.  ```
    tableRetrieve(tIndex[1..20], tData, searchKey)
       buf.readBlock(tIndex[1..20], 10)
       tableRetrieve(tIndex[1..9], tData, searchKey)
          buf.readBlock(tIndex[1..9], 5)
          tableRetrieve(tIndex[1..4], tData, searchKey)
             buf.readBlock(tIndex[1..4], 2)
             tableRetrieve(tIndex[1..1], tData, searchKey)
                buf.readBlock(tIndex[1..1], 1)
                return null
    ```

4.  ```
    tableRetrieve(tIndex[1..20], dataFile, searchKey)
       buf.readBlock(tIndex[1..20], 10)
       tableRetrieve(tIndex[11..20], dataFile, searchKey)
          buf.readBlock(tIndex[11..20], 15)
          tableRetrieve(tIndex[11..14], dataFile, searchKey)
             buf.readBlock(tIndex[11..14], 12)
             j = 26
             blockNum = 98
             dataBuf.readBlock(tData, 98)
             Find record dataBuf[k] whose search key equals searchKey
             tableItem = dataBuf[k]
             return tableItem
    ```

Appendix D

1. Proof by induction on m. When $m = 0$, $2^0 = 2^1 - 1$. Now assume that the statement is true for $m = k$; that is, assume that $1 + 2^1 + 2^2 + \cdots + 2^k = 2^{k+1} - 1$. Show that the statement is true for $m = k + 1$, as follows:

    $$(1 + 2^1 + 2^2 + \cdots + 2^k) + 2^{k+1} = (2^{k+1} - 1) + 2^{k+1}$$
    $$= 2^{k+2} - 1$$

2. Proof by induction on n. When $n = 1$, the first odd integer is 1 and the sum is trivially 1, which is equal to 1^2. Now assume that the statement is true for $n = k$; that is, assume that $1 + 3 + \cdots + (2k - 1) = k^2$. Show that the statement is true for $n = k + 1$, as follows:

    $$[1 + 3 + \cdots + (2k - 1)] + (2k + 1) = k^2 + (2k + 1)$$
    $$= (k + 1)^2$$

3. Proof by induction on n. When $n = 2$, $rabbit(2) = 1 = a^0$. Now assume that the statement is true for all $n \leq k$; that is, assume that $rabbit(n) \geq a^{n-2}$ for all $n \leq k$. Show that the statement is true for $n = k + 1$, as follows:

$$
\begin{aligned}
rabbit(k + 1) &= rabbit(k) + rabbit(k - 1) \\
&\geq a^{k-2} + a^{k-3} \\
&= a^{k-3}(a + 1) \\
&= a^{k-3}(a^2) \\
&= a^{k-1}
\end{aligned}
$$

Index

A

Abstract classes, 348–351, 435, 440, 435, 440
Abstract modifier, 346
Abstract data type
    17–18,106–110
    appointment book operations and, 119–121
    axioms and, 122–124
    basic description of, 17–18, 105–150
    binary search tree, 422–429, 452–482. *See also* Binary search tree
    binary tree, 422–452. *See also* Binary trees
    classes and, 126–136
    contract, 107
    data structures versus, 109–110
    designing, 22, 118–123, 248–250
    exceptions and, 135–137
    graphs, 612–643. *See also* Graphs
    heaps, 520–531. *See also* Heaps
    implementing, 124–144
    lists, 314–315. *See also* Lists
    position-oriented, 314–315, 422
    priority queues, 497–498, 517–534. *See also* Priority queues
    queues, 297–332. *See also* Queues

    in solution development, 248–254
    sorted lists, 117–118, 167, 183–186. *See also* Sorted lists
    specifying, 111–124
    stack, 247–296, 314–315. *See also* Stack
    table, 497–539. *See also* Table
    that suggests another 121–122
    value oriented, 422
Abstraction
    basic description of, 16–18, 108
    data, 17, 108–111
    procedural, 17, 106
Access modifiers, 341–342
Accessors, 34
Activation records, 55, 295, 447
add operation, 108, 114, 125, 137, 197, 315, 357–360, 362
Address calculators, 578
Addressing, open, 584–588, 593
ADT. *See* Abstract data type.
Adjacency lists, 617–619
Adjacency matrix, 616–619
Algebraic expressions, 218, 222–231, 266–271, 425, 434
    infix/infix expressions, 223–225, 231, 266, 268–271
    postfix expressions, 223–225, 229–231, 266–270

    prefix expressions, 223–231
Algorithm(s)
    analysis of, overview of, 372–384
    average-case analysis of, 380–381, 383, 410, 412–413, 594–595
    balanced braces and, 255–256
    basic description of, 4–5
    BFS algorithm, 622–623, 630–631
    big O notation and, 376–381
    bubble sort, 388–390, 412
    cubic, 379
    deletion, 461–462
    design guidelines for, 22
    DFS algorithms, 620–622, 626–627, 629–630
    Dijkstra's shortest-path algorithm, 635–636
    execution time of, 373, 374–375
    exponential, 379
    graph-traversal, 619–623
    growth rates, 375–376, 412–413
    heapsort, 412, 530–534
    information hiding and, 16–18
    inorder traversal, 429, 433–434, 470–471, 479
    insertion, 390–394, 409, 412, 458–461, 552–555
    invariants and, 9
    k^{th} smallest element, 399–408

respiratory

JAVA OPERATORS

Operators within the same box have the same precedence, which is higher than operators in lower boxes.

Operator	Meaning	Associativity	Usage
[ ]	array index	left	*array_name*[*expr*]
.	member selection	left	*object.member*
( )	method arguments	left	*method_name*(*expr_list*)
( )	instance construction	left	*class_name* (*expr_list*)
++	postfix increment	left	*lvalue* ++
--	postfix decrement	left	*lvalue* --
++	prefix increment	right	++ *lvalue*
--	prefix decrement	right	-- *lvalue*
~	bitwise complement	right	*~expr*
!	logical complement	right	!*expr*
+	unary plus	right	+*expr*
-	unary minus	right	–*expr*
( )	cast	right	(*type*) *expr*
new	object instantiation	right	new *type*()
			new *type* (*expr_list*)
			new *type* [*expr*]
*	mutiplication	left	*expr* * *expr*
/	division	left	*expr* / *expr*
%	remainder	left	*expr* % *expr*
+	addition	left	*expr* + *expr*
-	subtraction	left	*expr* - *expr*
+	string concatenation	left	*strExpr* + *strExpr*
<<	left shift	left	*expr* << *distance*
>>	signed right shift	left	*expr* >> *distance*
>>>	unsigned right shift	left	*expr* >>> *distance*
<	less than	left	*expr* < *expr*
<=	less than or equal to	left	*expr* <= *expr*
>	greater than	left	*expr* > *expr*
>=	greater than or equal to	left	*expr* >= *expr*
instanceof	type comparison	left	*ref* instanceof *refType*